CHRISTIAN TRADITION TODAY

LOUVAIN THEOLOGICAL & PASTORAL MONOGRAPHS
—————————— 28 ——————————

CHRISTIAN TRADITION TODAY

A Postliberal Vision
of Church and World

Jeffrey C.K. Goh

PEETERS PRESS
LOUVAIN

© 2000, Peeters, Bondgenotenlaan 153, 3000 Leuven, Belgium

ISBN 90-429-0937-4 (Peeters Leuven)
D. 2000/0602/142

ACKNOWLEDGMENTS

I am grateful above all to Professor Terrence Merrigan for directing this doctoral dissertation and for his sustained efforts in bringing to fruition his conviction that I ought to undertake this project. The Catholic University of Leuven has financed the entire research by an IRO scholarship. I am deeply grateful for the generosity of its educational system. Amongst the many professors of the Faculty of Theology who have been very supportive over the years, mention must be made of Johan Verstraeten, Jacques Haers, s.j., Lambert Leijssen, Reimund Bieringer and Joseph Selling. Dr. Emmanuel Katongole of Uganda remains a constant dialogue partner on the postliberal school of thought. Without the support of my wife Angie, this project would have been inconceivable. To her, I dedicate this study.

Jeffrey Goh
Leuven, Belgium.

To
Angie

TABLE OF CONTENTS

VIII

INTRODUCTION

As David Tracy once wrote, "Each of us contributes more to the common good when we dare to undertake a journey into our own particularity ... than when we attempt to homogenize all differences in favor of some lowest common denominator."[1] To George A. Lindbeck, retired Pitkin Professor of Historical Theology and Fellow of Silliman College at Yale University, elucidating one's own religious particularity is much more than an advisable journey. The primary task of Christian theologians, Lindbeck claims, is to dwell in the distinctive particularity of the Christian faith. This claim is legitimated not only by an ecclesio-theological necessity, he argues, but also on socio-cultural grounds. This latter point is predicated on a deep conviction of the Christian faith's capacity to contribute not only to the good of the Church, but also to the good of the modern world in which the Church is situated.

When Lindbeck published *The Nature of Doctrine*[2] in 1984, he made some proposals which churned up more theological dust than the slim volume at first appeared capable of doing. The growing

---

[1] David Tracy, "Defending the Public Character of Theology," *ChCent* 98 (1981) 353.

[2] George A. Lindbeck, *The Nature of Doctrine: Religion and Theology in a Postliberal Age* (Philadelphia: Westminster, 1984). Hereafter referred to as ND.

audience and chorus of response, both positive and otherwise, continue unabated. This is so, not only because he urges the espousal of Christian particularity and distinctiveness — something countless others have for ages been and are doing — but because the theological programme upon which his proposal rests is as rigorous as it is provocative. It is this very emphasis on Christian particularity which shapes Lindbeck's distinctive theology and generates some promising features as well as problematic issues.

While the "circular" rather than "linear nature of the case,"[3] coupled with "several interlocking plot-lines"[4] adopted in *The Nature of Doctrine*, do not render the book light literature, nevertheless, its general thesis is readily intelligible. Lindbeck advances three inter-related lenses: [1] a cultural-linguistic lens for viewing religion and [2] a corresponding rule-theory for assessing religious doctrine, he argues, are more useful in the ecumenical context than other models; furthermore, [3] an intratextual theology consistent with these views of religion and doctrine is necessary for the survival of the Church in modern liberal culture as well as being effective in contributing to the common good of the larger community.[5]

In regard to these three topics, two common pointers demand close attention: first, there is Lindbeck's stress on particularity; and, second, there is the question of the hermeneutics of tradition. On the particularistic element, it seems that some background factors that have motivated Lindbeck are especially noteworthy.[6]

---

[3] ND, 11.

[4] Gordon E. Michaelson, "The Response to Lindbeck," *ModTh* 4 (1988) 109.

[5] Lindbeck considers the more original theme of his work to be the rule theory of doctrine, and is surprised at the degree of debate centred on his articulation of the cultural-linguistic theory of religion.

[6] Lindbeck has described, in archeological and architectural terms, the process of change in his theological thinking, in "Confession and Community: An Israel-like View of the Church," *ChCent* 107 (1990) 492-96.

Firstly, as Lindbeck observes, contemporary Christianity is in "the awkwardly intermediate stage of having once been culturally established but... not yet clearly disestablished."[7] What is troubling him and many scholars is the perceived growing impotence on the part of Christians, in contemporary liberal culture, to assert an effective influence in line with Gospel values.[8] If we accept the observation that Alasdair MacIntyre made more than thirty years ago, religious indifference has increasingly marginalized the debate between theist and atheist, robbing it of any cultural relevancy. The problem, it seems, is not the direction in which secular knowledge is advancing, but the directions in which theism is retreating. "Theists are offering atheists less and less in which to disbelieve," MacIntyre diagnosed. "Theism thereby deprives active atheism of much of its significance and power and encourages the more passive theism of the indifferent."[9] Similarly, there is a pervasive observation by people both inside and outside the Church today, "that in fact the Christian conception of human nature and vocation seems to differ from the dominant cultural assumptions on the subject only by retaining a slight aura of piety; that there is no prophetic 'bite' in it; that it presents no real alternative

[7] ND, 134. See also Lindbeck, "The Church's Mission to a Postmodern Culture," in *Postmodern Theology: Christian Faith in a Pluralist World*, ed. Frederic B. Burnham (New York: Harper and Row, 1989), 44; "Barth and Textuality," *ThT* 43 (1986) 366; "Scripture, Consensus, and Community," in *Biblical Interpretation in Crisis: The Ratzinger Conference on Bible and Church*, ed. Richard John Neuhaus (Grand Rapids: Eerdmans, 1989), 74.

[8] Lindbeck recognizes the pluralist context within which Christian theology must be conducted, but his hostility towards liberalism is clear: "Liberal pluralism is anything but a utopian social order. It constitutes a fragile and messy environment within which wheat and tares both grow. Its advantage is that it is more open than any other kind of polity to criticism and correction from within." See his review of Jeffrey Stout's *After Babel* in *ThT* 46 (1989) 60.

[9] Alasdair MacIntyre, *The Religious Significance of Atheism* (New York: Columbia University Press, 1966), 24.

to the status quo."[10] Agreeing with Lindbeck, Stanley Hauerwas suggests that what is particularly "awkward" in this intermediate situation is "the very characterization of Christianity as a system of beliefs that is correlative of our cultural establishment in liberal societies."[11] For it is precisely when Christians themselves subscribe to this characterization that they culpably permit the faith community to be robbed of the transformative resources that mark believers as Christians.

Secondly, at century's end, a consuming plurality impinges itself upon our consciousness as a cultural phenomenon that permeates every facet of human society. This is manifest in the religious as much as in the secular domains of the contemporary world. The landscape of Christian theology, in particular, is marked by what seems like a horrendous cacophony and a sour lack of distinctiveness. It comes as no surprise when Jeffrey Stout, echoing the thoughts of many observers, notes that Christian theology seems unable "to command attention as a distinctive contributor to public discourse in our culture."[12] The academy, it seems, is ready for a forceful articulation of a theological agenda that speaks from and for the distinctive voice of the Christian faith, in the midst of a pluralistic surrounding.

Thirdly, the fragmentation that characterizes the transition from the modern to the postmodern era has heightened the distrust of meta-narratives and hackneyed traditions. In the process, the

---

[10] Douglas John Hall, *Professing the Faith* (Minneapolis: Fortress, 1993), 210. "Religious indifference" is high on the list of problems Pope John Paul II consistently identifies as needing urgent redress by the Church community. See, for example, the Apostolic Letter, *As the Third Millennium Draws Near*, in *Origins* 24:25 (1994) 404.

[11] See Stanley Hauerwas, *After Christendom* (Nashville: Abingdon, 1991), 23-25.

[12] Jeffrey Stout, *Ethics after Babel: The Language of Morals and Their Discontents* (Boston: Beacon, 1988), 163.

Christian message finds it increasingly more difficult to rely on convention and custom for its transmission.[13] New ways must be found to commend the Gospel to human experience and reflection. Again, the danger in this situation is that Christian profession will be adapted too uncritically to existing cultural presuppositions, trends, and values. On the positive side, the postmodern distrust of an overarching common foundation for human rationality, and a corresponding emphasis on particular social relations, historical, cultural and linguistic variability and so forth, constitute a unique opportunity for Christian theology to again make its particular claims heard. A surprisingly new avenue is now open for Christian theologians to engage in the general debates in issues brought forth by such postmodern philosophers as Rorty, Derrida, Lyotard, and Foucault. In sum, it is suggested that the passing of the modern era is creating "new opportunities for Christian affirmation as it is freed from the strictures imposed by characteristically modern presuppositions."[14]

[13] Lindbeck refers to the changing modes of thought and language as paradigm shifts and suggests that the Christian faith community needs new conceptualizations to help express ancient traditions in this time of revolutions and upheaval. See George Lindbeck, "Theological Revolutions and the Present Crisis," *ThEd* 19 (1983) 65-70.

[14] J. A. DiNoia, "American Catholic Thought at Century's End: Postconciliar, Postmodern, Post-Thomistic," *Thomist* 54 (1990) 513. Thus, although Jean-Francois Lyotard defines the postmodern as "incredulity toward metanarratives," in *The Postmodern Condition*, trs. Geoff Bennington and Brian Massumi (Minneapolis: University of Minnesota Press, 1984), xxiii, Diogenes Allen can boldly claim: "In a postmodern world Christianity is intellectually relevant." See idem, "Christian Value in a Post-Christian Context," in *Postmodern Theology: Christian Faith in a Pluralist World*, ed. Frederic B. Burnham (San Francisco: Harper & Row, 1989), 25. Lindbeck has also argued that the postmodern situation is again favourable for the retrieval of the biblical world as a "followable" world. See Lindbeck, "Scripture, Consensus, and Community," 94.

Fourthly, Lindbeck deems it a prophetic duty to expose the psycho-social crisis in which the Church and civilization find themselves.[15] He believes that by starting with experience and then adjusting the vision of the kingdom of God accordingly, the liberals' apparent successes are doomed on account of their unfaithfulness to God's future. The currently regnant approach, which assumes experience as the basis of faith, doctrine as symbolic of the meanings found in that experience, and the Scriptures as needing translations into categories acceptable to modern society, must be vigorously opposed for stifling the community-building power of the Bible and for the harm it is doing to the identity of Christianity.

If the four matters enumerated above — the loss of Christian influence in the larger society, the alarming plurality in Christian theology, the fragmentation of the Christian narrative, and the psycho-social crisis in which the Church and civilization stand — constitute a crisis for Christianity, then the point of the crisis, properly understood, should impel Christian thinkers to search for the roots of the problem and view the situation as a turning point of our history where both a deliberative assessment and an intelligible remedial proposal for communal adoption are called for. The pressing question for Christians is how, in the face of this crisis, it is possible to sustain genuine faithfulness to the Christian tradition, particularly with regards to the biblical traditions, while at the same time recognizing the necessity for new forms of apologetic in connection with the Christian profession regarding God and human destiny. Of particular relevance in this respect is the question of schooling Christians in this transitional stage: How are Christians made in a (post)modern liberal culture?

---

[15] See ND, 125.

The crisis, in Lindbeck's view, is best characterized as the loss of the once universal classic hermeneutical framework. Consistent with that characterization, the cure must lie in a concerted effort at retrieving the classic hermeneutic. Thus, in Lindbeck's assessment, nothing is more corrosive to the integrity of the Christian faith than a strategy of accommodation to the secular culture and thought-world characteristic of liberal theology. His proposal for the Christian community is therefore an invitation to become a postliberal tribe[16] whose task, clearly, is to fight the "acids of modernity"[17] through generating a genuine "desire to renew in a posttraditonal and postliberal mode the ancient practice of absorbing the universe into the biblical world."[18] Lindbeck thus eschews claims that transcend a culture or subculture, and presents a postliberal emphasis on intratextual theology based on a narrativist approach to the Bible as the most promising way forward. Describing his own theology as "postmodern," "postrevisionist," or "post-neo-orthodox," but most especially as "postliberal,"[19] Lindbeck's particularistic insistence supplies that much-welcomed voice in a sea of seemingly ambiguous, if not disturbing and confusing, plurality.

[16] ND, 135.

[17] ND, 127;

[18] ND, 135.

[19] ND, 135 n.1. Postliberal theology refers to the theological movement that began with Hans Frei's proposals for intratextual biblical hermeneutics and found its most forceful and systematic articulation in George Lindbeck. Lindbeck's postliberal theology is indebted, hermeneutically, to Frei rather than Ricoeur, theologically, to Barth rather than Schleiermacher, philosophically, to the later work of Wittgenstein and, culturally, Lindbeck's counterfashionable stance is closer to Alasdair MacIntyre (who is not mentioned) than to any form of the regnant 'liberal individualism' of the Western society. See Nicholas Lash, "Review of *The Nature of Doctrine*," *NewBf* (1985) 509. It is because Lindbeck draws heavily on the work of his Yale colleagues, Hans Frei and David Kelsey, that his book marks the emergence of what has come to be called a Yale school

Fifthly, Lindbeck had spent more than four decades teaching in both the Divinity School and the Department of Religious Studies at Yale, a career that also occasioned long years of reflection on theological education and ministry-formation. Some two and a half decades into that career, he undertook the writing of a report on ecclesiastically independent theological education in university divinity schools in America. That exercise convinced him that the institutional bridge was at best tenuous between the university and organized religions in the American society.[20] Three forces were discerned to be at work in causing this state of affairs: [1] The expansion of religious studies in university graduate schools has

---

of postliberal theology, the principal features of which are literary and narrative interpretations of the Bible, and "a moderately conservative Barthian and churchly theology." See Owen C. Thomas, "Review of *The Nature of Doctrine*," *ATR* 67 (1985) 108. In "Postliberal Theology," in *The Modern Theologians*, ed. David Ford, II:115-28, William Placher talks about the recent work of Frei, Lindbeck, Thiemann and Hauerwas that has come to be known as postliberal theology bearing a family resemblance to Barth's descriptive theology which emphasizes the "distinctive approach to religion in its particularity and communality." The "Yale School," which now represents this theology, includes Placher and William Willimon as well. This postliberal theological family has been influenced primarily by Kierkegaard, Barth, Kuhn, Wittgenstein, Ryle, Berger, Geertz and Auerbach. See also Sheila G. Davaney and Delwin Brown, "Postliberalism," in *The Blackwell Encyclopedia of Modern Christian Thought*, ed. A. E. McGrath (Oxford: Blackwell, 1993), 453-56. "Postliberalism," however, is met with a strong resistance. No where are the postliberals more rudely awakened to the vehemence of this resistance than in the virulent round of responses to Willimon's account of "postliberalism" in *The Christian Century*. One gets the impression that the unbending rhetoric of many of the postliberals has contributed to an entrenched opposition. See Willimon, "Answering Pilate: Truth and the Postliberal Church," *ChCent* 104 (1987) 82-85 and Monica Maxon et al., "A Challenge to Willimon's Postliberalism," *ChCent* 104 (1987) 306-10.

[20] See George Lindbeck, *University Divinity Schools: A Report on Ecclesiastically Independent Theological Education* (New York: The Rockefeller Foundation, 1976). For a positive reception of Lindbeck's report, see John W. Donohue, "Dreading to Leave an Illiterate Ministry," *Am* 134 (1976) 258-60.

infected theological education and made it less theological, characterized as these schools were by strictly academic interest in all
religions and a faith commitment to none. Broad programmes of
religions in general overshadowed the study of any religion in particular. [2] The ecumenical movements contributed towards diluting the curriculum of university divinity schools by homogenizing
it. [3] American society, caught in the malaise of postindustrial
civilization, was the third force adversely affecting divinity
schools, resulting in a generation of students no longer disposed to
the academic rigour of thinking in some coherently identifiable
idiom. This exercise helped crystallize Lindbeck's views on theological education which found expression in the recommendation,
despite endless criticisms that he anticipated might come from his
professional colleagues, that divinity schools must place greater
stress on scholarliness and, more importantly, must provide "self-
consciously particularistic" programmes that would train students
to become competent speakers of their specific religious heritage.
It was only in this way, he argued, that the main religions could be
institutionally represented and a worthwhile pluralism achieved.

Sixthly, Lindbeck's long involvement in ecumenism has had a
lasting effect on his scholarly work. A Lutheran-delegated
observer to the Second Vatican Council (1962-65), he has since
done most of his research and writing in the context of participation in ecumenical dialogues at different levels, mostly with
Roman Catholics.[21] He candidly admits that it is the ecumenical
movement even more than his teaching at Yale that has been the
context of his thinking.[22] In *The Nature of Doctrine*, Lindbeck's
theoretical strategies are explicitly articulated in furtherance of
his ecumenical goals. Avowedly instrumentalistic, his theoretical

[21] See, for example, George Lindbeck, *The Future of Roman Catholic Theology* (Philadelphia: Fortress, 1970).
[22] Lindbeck, "Confession and Community," 493.

project aims to be *ecumenically and religiously neutral*.[23] For
schematic coherence, Lindbeck attempts to ground this proposed
religious neutrality and ecumenical efficacy in a congenial
scheme of neutral grammatical rules.

Given these six background factors, Lindbeck has chosen to
make a clear response to the question "How should one do theology?" There is, in the view of many, an irreducible reality in the
pluralistic panorama of Christian theology: methodological
choices are doctrinally determined, and doctrines are affected by
methodological choices.[24] What principal methodological considerations, then, are most apposite to theology's task in serving the
Church and the larger community today? With an audacity
equaled only by his theological acumen, experience, literary skill,
and a faith commitment to boot, Lindbeck advocates the postliberal approach to theology as the way forward for the Church. A
proposal with a triple-attraction of fidelity, applicability and intelligibility, postliberal theology employs a cultural-linguistic understanding of religion, a regulative or rule theory of assessing doctrine, and an intratextual theology centered on the culture-forming
power of the Bible as the Christian communal text. The fecundity
of Lindbeck's proposal is aptly summed up by one commentator
thus: There is in Lindbeck's programmatic proposal "a new
framework for serious theological and Church discussion in a
society with many religions and widespread secularization. After

---

[23] ND, 9.

[24] See, for example, George P. Schner, "Postliberal Theology and Roman
Catholic Theology," *RSRev* 21 (1995) 306; Chester Gillis, *Pluralism: A New
Paradigm for Theology* (Louvain: Peeters, 1993), 165; Miroslav Volf, "Theol-
ogy, Meaning, and Power," in *The Future of Theology*, ed. Miroslav Volf et al.
(Grand Rapids: Eerdmans, 1996), 99. John E. Thiel has also noted that for
"Thiemann as for Lindbeck, method is not ancillary to the Christian faith that
theology expounds, but a locus among the claims that the church counts as cen-
tral to belief." See his *Nonfoundationalism* (Minneapolis: Fortress, 1994), 66.

reading it three times, I found it was still generating new perspectives, problems and projects in constructive theology, and even its most debatable points served to open up the deepest theological and philosophical issues afresh."[25]

Although the strictly theological part of *The Nature of Doctrine* is presented in its final chapter, and, even there, only as an "addendum" to the main argument of the book, there is every indication that Lindbeck's work is, in fact, driven by his postliberal, intratextual, theology — a theology which betrays the potency of a deep concern to defend and promote the Christian faith. "Prompted by convictions about the kind of theological thinking that is most likely to be religiously helpful to Christians and perhaps others in the present situation," Lindbeck declares, his motivations are "ultimately more substantively theological than purely theoretical."[26]

Whether one challenges Lindbeck's views or embraces them, there is no denying that the provocative programme that he presents in *The Nature of Doctrine* and other writings has had a significant impact on contemporary theology, with every indication that it will continue to be a potent force around which much literature will gravitate for years to come.

In choosing Lindbeck's work as the focus of this study, we bring to it a deep conviction that his work has a profound contribution to make to the theological fraternity, the Church community, and the larger society. Thus convinced of the positive value of Lindbeck's work, therefore, the point of departure of this study is proposed as a dialogue with Lindbeck, a dialogue which, to be sure, will encompass a critical analysis of both Lindbeck's work and the many scholarly responses to him, particularly since the publication of *The Nature of Doctrine*.

[25] See David F. Ford, "Review of *The Nature of Doctrine*," *JTS* 37 (1986) 282.
[26] ND, 10.

However, an assessment of Lindbeck is by no means an easy
task, not least because his work is, in the shared view of his commentators, a "very compact discussion"[27] and "dense distillation,"[28] "tightly argued,"[29] "powerful and provocative,"[30] that
"demands concentration and patience,"[31] "details of which are
difficult and obscure."[32] His thesis has been described as "deceptively simple,"[33] "highly compressed, programmatic, and even
runic,"[34] full of "rigour and subtlety,"[35] his strategy rendering
his work "nearly impervious to precise analysis,"[36] in part
because his work is more suggestive than definitive, thus opening it to different possible readings.[37] Moreover, as Lindbeck
acknowledges, the points he makes in the book are dependent on
each other and mutually illuminating. And he adds: "Its persua-
siveness, if any, does not depend on moving step by step in a
demonstrative sequence, but on the illuminating power of the
whole. It may be that if light dawns, it will be over the whole

[27] Charles Wood, "Review of *The Nature of Doctrine*," *RSRev* 11 (1985)
236, 237 & 240.

[28] David F. Ford, "Review of *The Nature of Doctrine*," *JTS* 37 (1986) 277.

[29] John Milbank, *Theology and Social Theory* (London: Blackwell, 1990),
382.

[30] Gerard Loughlin, *Telling God's Story: Bible, Church and Narrative Theology* (Cambridge: Cambridge University Press, 1996), 19.

[31] Mark L. Horst, "Engendering the Community of Faith in an Age of Individualism," *QR* 8 (1988) 90.

[32] Michael Kitchener, "Review of *The Nature of Doctrine*," *Th* 89 (1986) 51

[33] James Buckley, "Review of *The Nature of Doctrine*," *Am* 153 (1985) 105.

[34] Bruce Marshall, "Aquinas as Postliberal Theologian," *Thomist* 53 (1989)
363.

[35] David Fergusson, "Meaning, Truth, and Realism in Bultmann and Lindbeck," *RelSt* 26 (1990) 196.

[36] Jay Wesley Richards, "Truth and Meaning in George Lindbeck's *The
Nature of Doctrine*," *RelSt* 33 (1997) 41.

[37] Charles Hawkins, *Beyond Anarchy and Tyranny in Religious Epistemology*
(Lanham: University of America Press, 1997), 20.

landscape simultaneously."[38] His approach also raises a number of methodological and substantive controversies, the major ones of which we shall address in the present study.

At this stage, it should perhaps be mentioned that, in keeping with good theological enterprises, the philosophical underpinnings for his theoretical argument are well-clarified and articulated by Lindbeck at the outset. In this regard, we subscribe to the view that the hermeneutical presupposition is the key issue in any theology. To a large extent, the end-result is determined by the hermeneutical choice of each author, whether or not this is explicitly set out. Arguably, the crux in theological discussions is the hermeneutical question: "How is truth revealed?" Our thesis is that the *theological task is a hermeneutical task, and hermeneutical work is possible only because truth is revealed in a dialectical way*. It is in the way each theologian conceives of the dynamics of encounter in every context that s/he postulates and schematizes the dialectical relationship between theology and revelation, religion and experience, doctrine and truth, Church and culture and so on. We shall examine, in particular, how Lindbeck's hermeneutical approach impacts on his method of ecclesiological thinking.

We must now state clearly our own criteria for assessing, or better, dialoguing with, Lindbeck's work. A total of four, these criteria are chosen not as exclusive criteria by any means, but as convenient road-posts intended as guides for discussions. To be sure, in choosing these criteria, we are not in any way claiming neutrality, as if neutrality were possible in the first place. Nor are we setting out the text systematically in function of these criteria. Rather, these criteria are kept consciously in the background as constant guides, among other guides. These criteria are: faithfulness to tradition; intelligibility; coherence in argumentation; and

---

[38] ND, 11.

adequacy of the hermeneutical choice to the theological task. Theology, at the end of the day, is concerned basically with two questions — God and humans — the understanding of whose relationship is expressed in an all-encompassing rubric: "What does it mean to be human under God?" In light of this fundamental anthropological rubric, all kinds of questions could be addressed to Lindbeck's project. In particular, the question of ecclesial patterns bears inseparable affinity with specific models for doing theology, for viewing religions, and for assessing the nature and functions of doctrines. In all this, the question of the hermeneutics of tradition is profoundly relevant.

As we attempt an assessment of Lindbeck's work, substantially aided to be sure, by the many responses to his proposals, we shall begin with the necessary groundwork for a hermeneutics of tradition. We shall draw together various conceptual elements, those with which Lindbeck works as well as those which ought to be integrated, into a coherent matrix for a critical dialogue with Lindbeck's project. In keeping with what we said earlier, Chapter One will first clarify our own hermeneutical orientation. Proceeding in two steps, we begin with a pre-theological investigation into the anthropological reality of tradition, with Gadamer and MacIntyre as our principal interlocutors. This lays the foundation that legitimates the transition to a particular tradition, in this case, the Christian tradition. There, our investigation focuses on the basis upon which we may claim that, despite a diversity of Christian denominations each having its hermeneutical key for distinguishing what is and what is not authentic in relation to the tradition, there is a clear warrant for the title 'Christian tradition'. Our survey will support the claim of a common acceptance of the primacy of Scripture for the faith life of the Christian community. Beginning our study in this way, it is hoped, will provide an intelligible framework for the rest of our study.

With the starting point thus defined, Chapters Two and Three will examine Lindbeck's intratextual argument centred on a narrativist reading of Scripture. Chapters Four and Five will then turn to the implications of Lindbeck's theoretical arguments on religion and doctrine, respectively, culminating in a synthesis of their impact on what it means to be Church. Bitterly controversial issues include anti-foundationalism, relativism, fideism, sectarianism, apologetics, the admissibility of experience in theology, the so-called "deadly dilemma," and the hermeneutical impasse between the so-called "Yale school" and "Chicago school." In regard to the evident hermeneutical impasse which has been rendered more entrenched by the intransigence inherent in each position, our study will aim at a critical assessment of the operating presuppositions, strengths and weaknesses of opposing views. Serving to focus as well as delimit the boundary of discussion in each chapter, five primary analogues have been chosen, namely, *authority*, *de-Christianization*, *revelation*, *experience* and *truth*, in relation, respectively, to *tradition*, *Bible*, *hermeneutics*, *religion* and *doctrine*.

This schema will hopefully fulfil the aim of this study which, in the first place, is to clarify Lindbeck's work — which he characterizes as prolegomena thus far[39] – in relation to its lasting significance for constructive theology. Along the way, the survey of all the major scholarly responses will offer a useful resource-reference for future dialogues with this leading theoretician of the "Yale school" of thought. Substantively, we hope that our thesis on the dialectical nature of truth-revelation may complement Lindbeck's hermeneutical orientation, and that an outline for ecclesiology may emerge from this dialogue with Lindbeck's particular theology.

[39] Lindbeck, "Dulles on Method," *ProE* 1:1 (1995) 60, and "The Gospel's Uniqueness: Election and Untranslatability," *ModTh* 13 (1997) 423.

TRADITION AND AUTHORITY

On the threshold of the third millennium, the regnant frame of culture emphasizes themes of contestation and heterogeneity over those of harmony and continuity which were assumed in former years. In this climate, reliance on the past as an authority to support one's value-claims is often viewed with suspicion. What is demanded, at least implicitly, is an adequate justification of these claims free from privileged warrants in a public domain. This demand envisages criteria of judgment which are neutral, objective and non-partisan. There are various factors contributive to this view. Modern science with its methodological emphasis on verification through observable data displaces traditional beliefs and especially calls into question the traditional foundations of metaphysics. The rise of historical consciousness brings to awareness human temporality and conditionality and, in turn, challenges any notion of fossilized layers of truth bequeathed by the past. A liberal, egalitarian political philosophy advocating equality for all citizens undercuts particular cultural claims to superiority and privileged viewpoints. In the religious domain, a growing sensibility to religious pluralism inevitably calls into question the admissibility of a theological argument that appeals to the Scriptures, tradition and experiences specific to one particular community.

And yet, tradition constitutes an inescapable dimension of human life, even when one is not conscious of its pervasive influence. In line with postliberal theology in general, the

postliberal theology of George Lindbeck is a reaction against liberal theology. Ever since the Enlightenment in the seventeenth
century, liberal theology has assumed that one must subject all
beliefs to universally acceptable criteria. Diverse forces in contemporary culture, some of which we enumerated above, per-
suade people to think that "being rational" demands that we
question all inherited assumptions before accepting any belief as
standing up to the scrutiny of universally acceptable criteria. In
contrast to the liberal theological tradition, the postliberals advocate a return to "tradition" and "authority."[1]

   In this chapter, we seek to make some preliminary clarifications of our own hermeneutical orientation in regards to tradition
and authority. We shall do so in two steps. In Section I, we begin
with a pre-theological investigation into the anthropological reality of traditions in general and reflect on the ways in which tradition is tied to human freedom and constitutes a fundamental
structure of human social life. We choose two modern authors,
from among the many authors, whose contributions cannot be
ignored, as our principal interlocutors. These are Hans-Georg
Gadamer and Alasdair MacIntyre who represent two important

---

   [1] See William C. Placher, *Unapologetic Theology* (Louisville: Westminster,
1989), 11. Lindbeck notes that the "modern mode is antipathetic to the very
notion of communal norms.... The suggestion that communities have the right to
insist on standards of belief and practice as conditions of membership is experienced as an intolerable infringement of the liberty of the self. This reaction is
intensified by the growing contradiction between traditional standards and the
prevailing values of the wider society as communicated by education, the mass
media, and personal contacts" [ND, 77]. We shall see that the question of the
source and impulse for religious belief is implicit in Lindbeck's treatment of religions and doctrines. In "Scripture, Consensus, and Community," Lindbeck
underscores the fact that conflict of interpretation combines with a feeble sense
of faith to dissolve communal authority in times of change. He strenuously
argues that communal authority in the Christian sphere depends on consonance
with the Bible.

foci of intellectual attention in this field. We should mention at
the outset that our aim here is neither to suggest nor to collate all
the arguments that can legitimately be advanced against the
analyses of these two much-discussed authors. Rather, our intention is to critically extract a few elements of their arguments germane to our own discussion, namely, the normativity of tradition,
as a source of Christian theology, and some aspects of its
hermeneutics.

This first step will yield useful pointers for a reflection that,
hopefully, leads to a legitimate transition to a particular tradition,
in this case, the Christian tradition. The observations of Section I
on the reality of tradition in human life will then be carried over
to Section II where we examine the role of tradition in the living
faith of the Christian community and its openness to change. The
issue of authority will be the principal analogue. Our investigation will focus on the basis upon which we may claim that,
despite a diversity of Christian denominations, each having its
hermeneutical key for distinguishing what is and what is not
authentic in relation to the tradition, there is a clear warrant for
the title 'Christian tradition'. Our survey will support the claim
of a common acceptance of the primacy of Scripture for the
faith-life of the Christian community, allows for creativity within
the dynamics of a hermeneutic of tradition, and accepts the thesis
of a dialectical revelation of truth. Beginning our study in this
way, it is hoped, will provide an intelligible framework for the
rest of our investigation.

Section I: The Anthropological Dimension of Tradition

1.1 Tradition and Hermeneutics: Gadamer's Contribution

1.1.1 Tradition and Human Linguisticality

Gadamer[2] has been greatly influenced by his teacher, Martin Heidegger. One particular point of lasting influence is Heidegger's philosophy of time and becoming which focuses on the linguistic dimension of human life. The centrality of language in Gadamer's project means that language is not only an instrument for expression, but is in fact constitutive of the world.[3] This "linguisticality of being" becomes the central motif guiding Gadamer's account of the transmission and reformulation of human value systems inherited from the past. "Language," he says, "is the fundamental mode of operation of our being-in-the-world and the all embracing form of the constitution of the world."[4]

In the transmission and reformulation of past values, our language-horizon is essentially open-ended in its reference back to the past on the one hand, and its orientation to the future on the

---

[2] Hans-Georg Gadamer, *Truth and Method*, trs. Garret Barden and John Cumming (London: Sheed and Ward, 1975). We can only select a few elements in Gadamer's work that have special bearing on our topic. For a detailed exposition, see Joel C. Weinsheimer, *Gadamer's Hermeneutics: A Reading of Truth and Method* (New Haven: Yale University Press, 1985).

[3] "Man's relation to the world is absolutely and fundamentally linguistic in nature, and hence intelligible" [*Truth and Method*, 432-33].

[4] Gadamer, "On the Universality of the Hermeneutical Problem," in *Philosophical Hermeneutics*, trs. D. E. Linge (Berkeley: University of California Press, 1976), 4. In Gadamer's view, human life is largely constituted by the way we reformulate and transmit the value system we inherit from the past. Georges De Schrijver captures the crucial importance of this insight from Gadamer who is led "to define the essence of human beings in terms of an ongoing process of language formulation and interpretation. People are basically caught up in the

other, even while we use language as a tool to formulate and articulate our present understanding of things. Furthermore, we are
confronted by the facticity of our temporal existence which *a priori* [i] imposes on us the unavoidable encounter with an endless
mass of materials that inexorably stretches *beyond* our present perception and to which we need to give meaning, and [ii] forecloses
the possibility of our grasping meaning other than as a provisional
and perspectival truth-acquisition. Granted that this is the case, we
are at once confronted with the question of what *authority* does
tradition have. Before we look for a solution to that problem, we
need first to traverse Gadamer's analysis of the hermeneutical
experience as dialogue and as fusion of horizons. There, tradition
must be posited as the condition of possibility of human understanding, thought and life.

1.1.2 The Necessity of Tradition for Thought and Life

Gadamer attempts to show that all understanding takes place in
and through dialogue. Understanding is the product of the ques-
tion-and-answer dialectic which, he points out, is contingent, open
and ultimately beyond the inquirer's control. The value of discourse is that it paves the way to new knowledge. This can only
happen in a genuine discussion where parties come with "clean
hands," as it were, realising their ignorance of something and
desiring to learn more about it. Pertinent questions, and not rhetorical ones, must be raised in order to involve both the questioner
and the object of the question in a true dialogue. However, while
the question may be open, it is never boundless. It has to be lim-

'linguisticality of being' (*Sprachlichkeit des Seins*) in such a way that linguistic
self-interpretation and becoming prove correlative to each other." See Georges
De Schrijver, "Hermeneutics and Tradition," in *Authority in the Church*, ed. Piet
F. Fransen (Leuven: University Press, 1983), 33.

ited by the horizon of the questioner. In other words, in order to contribute to dialogue, the question needs a *sense of direction* which renders an answer possible. "Sense is always the direction of a possible question. The sense of what is correct must be in accordance with the direction taken by a question."[5]

In the case of a dialogue with a text, which is the principal focus of Gadamer's hermeneutics, questioning arises in a manner which is sudden and which connotes the spontaneity with which an idea springs forth. This notion of *suddenness* marks the gateway to Gadamer's emphasis on the spontaneity and the dialogic character of understanding.[6] The dialogic character of understanding is shown in the suddenness which motivates thought and calls for a response. As questions arise, the interpreter becomes aware of one's own limits and finitude. To be sure, this questioning activity is not altogether predetermined, save that it is thrust upon the interpreter by the subject-matter at hand. The *dialectical character* of thinking is illustrated by Gadamer when he equates the "art of questioning" with "the art of thinking."[7]

Hermeneutics is thus, for Gadamer, a *conversation* with a text. In the context of the historical-hermeneutical problem, Gadamer's

---

[5] *Truth and Method*, 327.

[6] See *Truth and Method*, 329. For an analysis of the notion of suddenness, see John P. Hogan, *Collingwood and Theological Hermeneutics* (Lanham: University Press of America, 1989), 52. On the dialogical character of interpretation, Sandra Schneiders writes: "The process of interpretation that gradually expanded the meaning of the text was the dialogical one described by Gadamer, in which the interpreter interrogates the text about its subject matter not by examining the surface affirmations of the text (the text as answer) but by trying to discern the question to which the text is an answer (the question behind the text)." See S. M. Schneiders, *The Revelatory Text* (San Francisco: Harper, 1991), 176.

[7] See *Truth and Method*, 330: "The art of questioning is that of being able to go on asking questions, i.e., the art of thinking. It is called 'dialectic,' for it is the art of conducting a real conversation."

solution is that interpretation becomes a possibility when the historical text presents a question to the interpreter. Understanding comes about when the right questions are asked of the text. In this regard, Gadamer posits a *Vorgriff der Volkommenheit* ("fore-conception of completion")[8] which refers to a presupposition involved in grasping the subject matter mediated through the text. This must obtain both *before* and *as* we read a text, and consists in the presupposition that the text makes sense.[9] The text would not be intelligible otherwise. How do we perceive the authority of tradition in Gadamer's concept of conversation?

1.1.3 The Authority of Tradition

Tradition plays an important role in all of this, for conversation is conducted, and understanding only happens, within a shared tradition. However strange or foreign the subject matter of a text is to us, there must be a degree of familiarity which makes the task of hermeneutics possible. Gadamer describes the position between strangeness and familiarity which the interpreter occupies as the "intermediate place" between the "historically intended separate object" and the belongingness of that object to a tradition. This "intermediate place" is the "true home," the locus, of hermeneutics where a fusion of horizons[10] between text and interpreter takes place.[11]

[8] See *Truth and Method*, 261.

[9] See Hogan, *Collingwood and Theological Hermeneutics*, 54.

[10] Gadamer views the process of understanding as an encounter between the text and reader, an encounter that he describes as a "fusion" of two horizons [*Truth and Method*, 269-74]. "Horizon is another way of describing context. It includes everything of which one is immediately aware and of which one must in fact remain unaware if there is to be a focus of attention; but one's horizon is also the context in terms of which the object of attention is understood. This horizon can be called life or world — but must always be conceived of as mobile, fluid, and temporal." See Weinsheimer, *Gadamer's Hermeneutics*, 157.

[11] See *Truth and Method*, 262-63. Some of the repeated criticisms of

The concept of a tradition is thus central to Gadamer's hermeneutics. Humanity's relationship with tradition is never an objectifying process where tradition is conceived of as something other, something alien. Instead, Gadamer insists that we are always standing *within tradition.* In this light, tradition "is always part of us, a model or exemplar, a recognition of ourselves which our later historical judgment would hardly see as a kind of knowledge, but as the simplest preservation of tradition."[12]

Gadamer's challenge to the Enlightenment's claim to objectivity is therefore understandably emphatic. He refers to the Enlightenment's "prejudice against prejudice itself, which deprives tradition of its power."[13] The word "prejudice" (*Vorurteil*) points to the role of pre-reflective knowledge of the whole, bequeathed to the interpreter by tradition. That knowledge functions as a condition for the possibility of understanding and acquiring further knowledge. "Prejudice" here in no way suggests that the outcome

Gadamer's scheme centre on the point of his having laid down an universal criterion which guarantees successful communication, by means of which Gadamer's theory, according to Clodovis Boff, "exempts itself a priori from analytical criticism." Charging Gadamer with having permitted "a teeming anarchy of every sort of reading," he remarks that "too much meaning is terribly strong light." See idem, *Theology and Praxis: Epistemological Foundations* (Maryknoll, NY: Orbis, 1987), 134. Werner G. Jeanrond, too, notes that Gadamer's theory is over-optimistic for tending to neglect the possibility of distorted communication and the problem of non-understanding of a text by a reader. See idem, *Theological Hermeneutics* (London: Macmillan, 1991), 68. Part, at least, of these objections are met by Frans Josef van Beeck's brief explanation cited in footnote 30, *infra.* In any case, criticisms of this sort are not principally directed at Gadamer's insights on the inevitability of tradition.

[12] *Truth and Method,* 250.

[13] See *Truth and Method,* 240. In his exposition, Josef Bleicher pictures the interpreter as being "always embedded in a context of tradition which can be regarded as the sharing of basic and supportive prejudices." See idem, *Contemporary Hermeneutics: Hermeneutics as Method, Philosophy and Critique,* (London: Routledge and Kegan Paul, 1980), 110.

of the investigation is pre-determined.[14] A prejudice, or pre-judgment, in Gadamer's sense, is not the same as an unwarranted or
unjustifiable bias. On the contrary, it is precisely our fundamental
or absolute presuppositions which make interpretation and understanding possible at all.[15] It is the questioning process which
exposes presuppositions and purges illegitimate prejudices. It is
the coincidence of the "fore-meaning" of the text and of the present horizon of understanding of the interpreter in a shared tradition that permits understanding to take place.

One of Gadamer's central concerns is thus to free us from the
Enlightenment's (and, of course, its contemporary progeny's)
"prejudice against prejudice." His project unmasks for us the fallacy of the Enlightenment's quest for radical autonomous reason
and ahistorical values. This quest is often accompanied by an
uncritical and blanket rejection of all authorities and tradition.
Gadamer's concern is to reclaim the past in a way which, on the
one hand, does not posit an abdication of our own critical reason
and, on the other hand, serves as a critical unmasking of our own
prejudices towards the normativity of the past. Our temporality
precludes pure objectivity, however much we may try to remove
prejudice and partiality. How, then, do we circumvent the slippery
slope of scepticism and relativism? And, further, where do human
beings derive that sense of reliability needed to trust life?

Gadamer brings his understanding of the linguisticality of being
to bear and stresses the need to reformulate everything which gives
the appearance of having been encapsulated in eternally-fossilized

[14] Openness, in Gadamer's view, "does not mean that we present ourselves as
a blank slate ready to be inscribed. Because we are concerned and interested, our
receptivity implies that we are willing to integrate the meaning of the text with
our previous preconceptions by making them conscious, bringing them into view,
and assimilating them to what the text reveals." See Weinsheimer, *Gadamer's
Hermeneutics*, 167.

[15] See *Truth and Method*, 245-46.

language forms. Through ongoing human reflection and activity, horizons continually change, so much so that "the historical life of a tradition depends on constantly new assimilation and interpretation."[16] In Gadamer's understanding of tradition as a process of ongoing interpretation, what should not be overlooked is that judgments of the past *question* us and "prejudice" the judgments we live by; they reveal us to ourselves, so to speak. They do so, however, only through our participating in a dialectical struggle with the meaning handed down by, and not our ready giving up on, the past.[17]

To begin with, Gadamer does not present language as merely a human instrument with no independent status. A text, once written, acquires a being of its own and thereby *exceeds* the subjective intention of its author. That explains why understanding is not merely a reproductive but a creative act as well. At the same time, however, it should be stressed that this creative act of interpretation is by no means merely subjective. Granted that we may make new discoveries in the process, and creative ones at that, and that we realise our knowledge is perspectival and inexhaustive, still, we find that in an authentic interpretation, we are being continually questioned, prompted and inspired by the past. Tradition, in other words, "coincides with the ongoing process of handing

---

[16] *Truth and Method*, 358.

[17] In the latest translation of *Truth and Method* (New York: Continuum, 1994), Joel Weinsheimer and Donald G. Marshall took pain to highlight the active sense of the German term for the ongoing conversation that characterises tradition – *Überlieferung*. In the Translators' Preface, they emphasize: "We are likely to think of 'tradition' as what lies merely behind us or as what we take over more or less automatically. On the contrary, for Gadamer 'tradition' or 'what is handed down from the past' confronts us as a *task*, as an effort of understanding we feel ourselves required to make because we recognize our limitations, even though no one compels us to do so. It precludes complacency, passivity, and self-satisfaction with what we securely possess; instead it requires active questioning and self-questioning" [p. xvi].

down certain ancient values to the present, in accordance with our present horizon of understanding."[18] Gadamer thus asserts that understanding is a historical process taking place in a "historically operative consciousness" in which the horizon of the past merges with the horizon of the present.[19]

1.1.4 Tradition in Historical Consciousness and Application

From Heidegger's philosophy of time and becoming, Gadamer develops his concept of "effective historical consciousness" (*wirkungsgeschichtliches Bewusstsein*).[20] By means of the notion of "effective history," Gadamer directs our attention to the "historical reality not only as initiating event but also as modified and amplified by all that the initiating event has produced."[21] The concept of effective history contrasts sharply with the posi-

---

[18] De Schrijver, "Hermeneutics and Tradition," 34.

[19] See Hogan, *Collingwood and Theological Hermeneutics*, 23. On Gadamer distancing himself from the truth-claims embodied in the traditionalist's concept of tradition, De Schrijver comments: "If one insists on the literal and petrified normativity of a tradition, the full acquisition of truth will necessarily be out of reach, for hermeneutics teaches us that truth is located half-way between stagnation and fluidity. The advance of truth seeks a clarification of meaning which will be adequate for the present, by detaching itself from the *prejudice* of stagnation involved in a mere regressive recollection of the past" ["Hermeneutics and Tradition," 35].

[20] See *Truth and Method*, 305-41. Elsewhere, Gadamer clarifies: "What I have called *wirkungsgeschichtliches Bewusstsein* is inescapably more being than consciousness, and being is never fully manifest." See his "On the Scope and Function of Hermeneutical Reflection," *Continuum* 8 (1970) 92. In their 1994 translation, Weinsheimer and Marshall chose to translate this key concept as "historically effected consciousness." They try to "capture Gadamer's delineation of a consciousness that is doubly related to tradition, at once 'affected' by history (Paul Ricoeur translated this term as 'consciousness open to the effects of history') and also itself brought into being – 'effected' – by history, and conscious that it is so" [p. xv].

[21] See Schneiders, *The Revelatory Text*, 159-60.

tivistic nineteenth-century understanding of history as comprising events and data at once available for research by historians.
History was regarded as "an independent, free-standing, once-
and-for-all-established collection of events presumed to have
happened in an enclosed sphere called the past." By contrast,
effective history is made up of events that are neither free-standing nor fixed, but are "generative of consequences which then
enter constitutively into the reality of those events and help to
determine their historical significance."[22] In this regard,
Gadamer highlights two important points: first, we are never outside tradition but are always participants in it; and, second, tradition thrives on a dynamism which is effective within our consciousness and influences all of our ongoing experience and our
knowing processes.[23]

To focus, as Gadamer has done, on the *intentio textus ipsius*, is
to accept the text itself (with its structure and meaning) as the
primary object of interpretation.[24] However, once a text is written
and published, it takes on a history of its own as people in different settings read and interpret it. In this sense, the text
becomes independent of its author as well as of the original
addressees, and renders itself free for new hermeneutical relationships.[25] To attempt to reconstruct the intention of the author

[22] Sandra Schneiders, "Living Word or Dead(ly) Letter," *CTSAP* 47 (1992)
51.

[23] This has fruitfully influenced the works of many authors. See, for example,
Schneiders, *The Revelatory Text*, esp. 42-43, 68 & 148-52; Ray L. Hart, *Unfinished Man and the Imagination* (New York: Seabury, 1979), esp. 256-64.

[24] See Gerald O'Collins, *Fundamental Theology* (London: Darton, Longman
and Todd, 1981), 254.

[25] "The horizon of understanding cannot be limited either by what the writer
originally had in mind, or by the horizon of the person to whom the text was
originally addressed. What is fixed in writing has detached itself from the contingency of its origin and its author and made itself free for new relationships."
Truth and Method, 356-57.

(*intentio auctoris*) is a legitimate, but limited undertaking.[26] Gadamer takes the matter a step further in referring to application (*Applikation* or *Anwengdung*) as being the essential term of the hermeneutic process: "We are forced to go, as it were, one stage beyond romantic hermeneutics, by regarding not only understanding and interpretation, but also application as comprising one unified process."[27] Theoretical interpretation of the text must ensue in a proper use, that is, in its application to the present.

1.1.5 Tradition and Human Freedom

In all this, Gadamer tries to hold in healthy balance the dual elements of past and present, of objectivity and subjectivity. If the past does not come to us in absolute chemical purity, neither can interpretation be thought of as an action of one's subjectivity alone. Rather, understanding ought to be seen as "the placing of oneself within a process of tradition, in which past and present are constantly fused."[28]

---

[26] *Truth and Method*, 336.

[27] *Truth and Method*, 274-75. Weinsheimer points out: "Among the deficiencies of romantic hermeneutics, as Gadamer describes them, is that it overlooked the historicity of the interpreter and the tension between past and present that this historicity necessitates. Thus, it also overlooked the problem of application where this tension is most manifest... It took no account at all of the historical nature of experience. It presupposed that the object of understanding is a text to be deciphered and in that sense understood." See idem, *Gadamer's Hermeneutics*, 154 & 185. So, Linell E. Cady comments: "Gadamer insists that application is not a secondary practical concern but an intrinsic component of the one hermeneutical act of understanding/interpreting/application." See idem, "Hermeneutics and Tradition: The Role of the Past in Jurisprudence and Theology," *HTR* 79 (1986) 442.

[28] *Truth and Method*, 258. This has been identified as Gadamer's major point in his view on the authority of tradition. See Francis Schüssler Fiorenza,

Also held in tensile balance in Gadamer's scheme are the pairs: history and preservation, tradition and human freedom. One must consciously allow oneself to be tradition-implicated, by embracing and cultivating it or, in a word, preserving it. And yet, preservation is a "reasoned" act in history. [29]

Gadamer's sensitivity to the authority of the past and the dynamics of the present, coupled with his caution against taking the past as coming to us in its pristine, unalloyed purity or understanding as a purely subjective exercise, has led van Beeck to suggest that "Gadamer's plea in favour of tradition is intended to *liberate* us (as well as the convictions we profess to live by), both from our subjective prejudices and from the objectivist authorities that claim dominion over us."[30]

On our part, and looking ahead, we might tentatively conclude that the disclosure of new truths is contingent upon human freedom in two respects: [i] freedom *from* a fixation on fossilized truths, *for* a possible new horizon of understanding; and [ii] freedom *from* our subjective prejudices, *for* possible reception of genuine wisdom from the past.

"Systematic Theology: Task and Methods," in *Systematic Theology: Roman Catholic Perspectives*, ed. Francis Schüssler Fiorenza and John Galvin (Minneapolis: Fortress, 1991), I:44.

[29] "The fact is that tradition is constantly an element of freedom and of history itself. Even the most genuine and solid tradition does not persist by nature because of the inertia of what once existed. It needs to be affirmed, embraced, cultivated. It is, essentially, preservation such as is active in all historical change. But preservation is an act of reason, though an inconspicuous one" [*Truth and Method*, 250].

[30] In this regard, van Beeck makes a scathing rebuttal of Stobbe's distortion of Gadamer and exposes the latter's failure to see Gadamer's basic intention concerning his plea in favour of tradition. See idem, *God Encountered: A Contemporary Catholic Systematic Theology* (Collegeville, MN: Liturgical, 1993), 2:14-16.

1.1.6 Tradition and the Classics, the Art and the Law

Gadamer refers to three different strands of hermeneutics, namely, the hermeneutics of the classics, aesthetic hermeneutics and legal hermeneutics. The notion of "the classic" is significant for his hermeneutics.[31] *Classics* are outstanding examples of human understanding. They influence our horizon and guide our self-understanding and, to that extent, command an "effective-history." They encounter us with a certain authority and claim. Arguing for a pre-judgment in favour of the classics, Gadamer registers, as we saw, a protest against the Enlightenment impoverishment brought about by its prejudice against tradition. He calls for a return to the Aristotelian ethics as a remedy for this impoverishment, stating categorically: "I am absolutely convinced, quite simply, that we have something to learn from the classics."[32] The lasting influence of the classics attests to their value and significance. The normative concept of the classical denotes a specific way of being historical, "the historical process of preservation that, through the constant proving of itself, sets before us something that is true."[33] This analysis holds two points in a tensile balance: the classic does not simply describe a historical phenomenon that was past and lost; nor does it refer to an old value now seen to be so perfect as to warrant its elevation to the realm of the suprahistorical.

Another element in Gadamer's view which has been very influential in religious thought concerns *aesthetic judgment*. He

---

[31] See, for example, *Truth and Method*, 253-58.

[32] *Truth and Method*, 490. The centrality of the classics in Gadamer's thought is stressed by Weinsheimer in these terms: "This, in brief, is the first and last principle of Gadamer's hermeneutics. It is the fundamental presupposition of *Truth and Method*, and towards its legitimation all Gadamer's arguments tend." See Weinsheimer, *Gadamer's Hermeneutics*, 133.

[33] *Truth and Method*, 255.

highlights the fact that truth flourishes in works of art in ways
that are unattainable in other human projects, and which challenge the usual rational discourse.[34] For instance, the claim that
empirical knowledge of facts is the norm of all knowledge, is
called into question. There are different ways of attaining truth,
and "hermeneutics, symbolism and the use of imagination are as
needful for the exploration of reality as are observation and
knowledge."[35] Art often captures, more than mere human observation can, the essential meaning of the original facts. But the *art
object* must be clearly distinguished from the *work of art*. The
former is a mere physical entity which becomes a work of art
only when it is being contemplated (such as a text, statue, paint-
ing), heard (such as a musical score) or played (such as the script
of a play).

However, it is the paradigmatic character of *legal hermeneutics*
which prompts Gadamer to adopt it for illustration when he
exposes the weaknesses inherent in the procedures of the human
sciences. It is in legal hermeneutics that Gadamer says that he
finds the model for the relationship between past and present he is
seeking. He first stresses the importance of recognizing that *application* forms an integral element of all understanding, that it is not
just some secondary practical concern. It was, he observes, the
detachment from this understanding in the eighteenth and nineteenth centuries that led to the rise of literary hermeneutics and
historical studies as the regnant methodology for research in the

---

[34] "That truth is experienced through a work of art that we cannot attain in
any other way constitutes the philosophic importance of art, which asserts itself
against all reasoning." *Truth and Method*, xii-xiii. He goes on to state that art
contains "a claim to truth which is certainly different from that of science, but,
equally certainly, not inferior to it" [p. 87].

[35] See John Macquarrie, *Twentieth Century Religious Thought* (London:
SCM, 1988⁴), 389.

human sciences. Using this methodology for research rendered the historical and cultural horizon highly visible, but it also concealed the interpreter's horizon, one's questions, operative presuppositions and interests. To illustrate the misconception of the hermeneutical process inherent in this view, Gadamer has recourse to legal interpretation. In legal hermeneutics, two poles are considered: one is the text of the law, and the other is the "sense" with which that law is applied in particular judgment. "A law is not there to be understood historically, but to be made concretely valid through being interpreted."[36] The only way to understand a law properly is to see how the claim it makes is understood and applied in every new, particular, situation. What is crucial is for the judge to discover the "legal idea" of a law and then apply it to the concrete facts of the present.[37]

1.1.7 Tradition and Praxis

A contribution towards a better understanding of hermeneutics and tradition is made by two of Gadamer's celebrated critics, Jürgen Habermas and Paul Ricoeur. A brief word on these two interlocutors will serve to round up this short overview.

Gadamer and Habermas represent two different schools of hermeneutics, namely, the humanistic and the social-critical, respectively.[38] Gadamer emphasizes *communication* as the heart

---

[36] *Truth and Method*, 275.

[37] "The judge who adopts the transmitted law to the needs of the present is undoubtedly seeking to perform a practical task, but his interpretation of the law is by no means on that account an arbitrary re-interpretation. Here again, to understand and to interpret means to discover the 'legal idea' of a law by linking it with the present." *Truth and Method*, 292-93. In the common law jurisdiction, where judicial decisions are based on a system of precedents, judges extract the *ratio decidendi* of a past case for application to the facts now before the court.

[38] See De Schrijver, "Hermeneutics and Tradition," 32.

and criterion of hermeneutics, which is attained by the objective criterion of the "fusion of horizons" where language plays the pivotal role. He assumes that understanding will always be successful as long as the understanding subjects willingly submit themselves to the claims of the text and enter into the tradition which the text represents. In so doing, he has underscored the authority of the past but somewhat eclipsed the role of reflection and critique in the appropriation of that past. Commentators have thus pointed out Gadamer's lack of emphasis on the need for mutual correction of the two participants — tradition and interpreter — in authentic conversation. A fusion of horizons not only broadens understanding but is an event that potentially involves correction and even rejection. Gadamer's scheme is inadequate to the extent that criticism is operative in one direction only: recovery of the past operates to change the present by altering the reading of historical texts and opening up more authentic possibilities of existence. When truth is thus implicitly portrayed as forgotten truths awaiting recovery, the possibility that tradition itself might stand in need of criticism is effectively sidelined.[39] In this context, two points raised by Habermas are incisive.

First of all, Gadamer's hermeneutical insight is sound insofar as understanding "simply cannot leap over the interpreter's relationships to tradition." This underscores the hermeneutical value of prejudgments. However, the very fact that "understanding is structurally a part of the traditions that it further develops through appropriation" does not necessarily imply that "the medium of tradition is not profoundly altered by scientific reflection." Gadamer, in Habermas' view, "fails to appreciate the power of reflection that is developed in understanding." This is deemed to

---

[39] Thomas B. Ommen, "Theology and the Fusion of Horizons," *Ph&Th* 3 (1988) 64.

be crucial especially because, in Habermas' opinion, reflection "proves itself being able to reject the claim of tradition."[40] Habermas' resistance against any suggestion of an essential passivity of conversation helps bring to the fore what is not lost to Gadamer, namely, the appreciation that, though it has a legitimate authority, tradition should not be accepted blindly.[41]

Secondly, nevertheless, it is Gadamer's insistence on the universality of his hermeneutics that provokes Habermas' sharpest criticism. The crux of that criticism consists in a rejection of Gadamer's universal claim by pointing to the *limits* of understanding. A hermeneutical consciousness, such as the one Gadamer proposes, is, in Habermas' view, "incomplete" insofar as it manifests a failure to incorporate "the limit of hermeneutical understanding."[42] Language, for Gadamer, is the very locus where past and present merge. This centrality accorded to language is where

[40] Jürgen Habermas, "A Review of Gadamer's *Truth and Method*," in *Understanding and Social Enquiry*, ed. Fred R. Dallmayr and Thomas McCarthy (Notre Dame: University of Notre Dame Press, 1977), 64.

[41] Richard Bernstein, for example, observes that Gadamer's hermeneutic does feature a movement toward argumentation and a justification of interpretation. That this is so is manifest in Gadamer's insistence that understanding does not simply repeat the past but "applies" it to the present. Gadamer, Bernstein acknowledges, appeals to "a concept of truth that (paradigmatically speaking) amounts to what can be argumentatively validated by the community of interpreters who open themselves to what tradition 'says to us'." See *Beyond Objectivism and Relativism* (Philadelphia: University of Pennsylvania Press, 1983), 153-54.

[42] Jürgen Habermas, "On Hermeneutic's Claim to Universality," in *The Hermeneutics Reader*, ed. Kurt Mueller-Vollmer (Oxford: Blackwell, 1986), 302. For Habermas' continued criticism of Gadamer, see idem, "The Universality of the Hermeneutical Problem," in *Hermeneutics, Questions and Prospects* (Amherst: University of Massachusetts Press, 1976); *The Theory of Communicative Action*, vol. 1, trs. Thomas McCarthy (Boston: Beacon, 1979), 134; "The Hermeneutic Approach," in *On the Logic of the Social Sciences* (Cambridge, MA: MIT Press, 1988).

Habermas finds fault with Gadamer's theory. Calling attention to the *material* conditions under which the "fusion of horizons" can take place, Habermas points out that language, too, is a medium of domination. Habermas' consideration represents the critical introduction of an ideological awareness into hermeneutics. In this context, De Schrijver's summation of the debate is apposite, viz.:

> While the humanistic strain represented by Gadamer was mainly concerned with the interpretation of ancient texts, so as to clothe them in a suitable language adequate to the present horizon of understanding, Habermas focuses on the critical *unmasking* of the ideological power-components contained in the language of tradition as well as in contemporary formulations.[43]

Gadamer, in response, pointedly contends that a critical social science that legitimately attempts to "go behind language in order to legitimate strategic action aimed at liberation finds itself necessarily trapped within the very constraints it sought to escape."[44]

---

[43] See De Schrijver, "Hermeneutics and Tradition," 41. As Thomas McCarthy clarifies in *The Critical Theory of Jürgen Habermas* (London: Hutchinson, 1978), 182-83: "Language is *also* a medium of domination and social power. It serves to legitimate relations of organized force. In so far as the legitimations do not articulate the relations of force that they make possible, in so far as these relations are merely expressed in the legitimations, language is also ideological." Gadamer, of course, denies having opposed all questioning of tradition. Criticising Habermas' ideals, Placher points out that while repressive tradition can inhibit open conversation, so can the suspicion of tradition. See *Unapologetic Theology*, 115.

[44] See David K. Krieger, *The New Universalism: Foundations for a Global Theology* (Maryknoll, NY: Orbis, 1991), 149. See also Gadamer, "On the Scope and Function of Hermeneutical Reflection," 84. The dispute between Gadamer and Habermas continues to engage both authors as well as generate ongoing debates between scholars. We cannot, however, take the discussion any further than we have done here. For a recent commentary, see Susan E. Shapiro, "Rhetoric as Ideology Critique: The Gadamer-Habermas Debate Reinvented," *JAAR* 62/1 (1994) 123-50.

While Gadamer draws upon the analogy of dialogue to unpack the dynamic relationship between the text and the reader in the process of interpretation, Ricoeur interjects with the shocking statement that "interpretation begins where dialogue ends."[45] What Ricoeur brings to focus is the essential difference between the oral conversation and the process of text-interpretation: there is an immediacy in oral discourse that is absent in text-interpretation, the latter being characterised by what Ricoeur calls the *distanciation* effected by writing.[46] What Ricoeur seeks to set aside is the erroneous assumption that "reading is to writing as hearing is to speaking," which in turn is based on the erroneous belief that writing is simply another form of speech. What must be pointed out here is that Ricoeur's insight is not directed to the object of discourse, that is, the truth-claims regarding the subject-matter. Nor does it purport to cast doubt on the dynamic, dialogic-structure (of question and answer) of the process of attaining that object.[47] What Ricoeur seeks to do is to draw from the Gadamer-Habermas debate elements that would throw light on "the status of historical heritages, transmission, and tradition, as the locus of the emergence of values in history."[48] He critically extracts

[45] See Paul Ricoeur, *Interpretation Theory: Discourse and the Surplus of Meaning* (Fortworth, TX: Texas Christian University, 1976), 32.

[46] See Ricoeur, *Interpretation Theory*, 43-44 and "The Hermeneutical Function of Distanciation," *PhT* 17 (1973) 129-41. Gadamer has often been accused of underplaying the distance between text and reader. This accusation, pertinent as far as it relates to *Truth and Method*, does not apply to his later work, particularly *Reason in the age of Science*, trs. Frederick G. Lawrence (Cambridge, MA: MIT, 1981). Gadamer is described as one of the most important defenders of *phronesis* (i.e., practical wisdom) of our time. See Charles W. Allen, "The Primacy of *Phronesis*: A Proposal for Avoiding Frustrating Tendencies in Our Conceptions of Rationality," *JR* 69 (1989) 359-74.

[47] See Schneiders, *The Revelatory Text*, 142.

[48] Paul Ricoeur, "Ethics and Culture: Habermas and Gadamer in Dialogue," *PhT* 17 (1973) 155.

selected arguments from both authors from which he then builds
his own solution. He seeks to demonstrate two things: [i] to succeed as a programme, a hermeneutic of traditions must incorporate
a critical distance as an integral part of the hermeneutical process;
[ii] to succeed as a critical contribution, a critique of ideologies
too must integrate a certain regeneration of the past and hence a
reinterpretation of tradition.[49] Ricoeur locates his solution in a
"practical mediation," his thesis being that philosophy conceived
of as *theoria* is incapable of solving the problem of the origin of
values, and that the promise of a solution lies in *praxis*. Thus, the
antinomy of values (of reason/freedom and tradition/authority)
that characterises the debate between a hermeneutic of traditions
and a critique of ideologies finds its echo "at the level of the cultural conditions of axiology." His remarks bear a cogent argument:

> None of us finds himself placed in the radical position of creating
> the ethical world *ex nihilo*. It is an inescapable aspect of our finite
> condition that we are born into a world already qualified in an ethi-
> cal manner by the decisions of our predecessors, by the living cul-
> ture which Hegel called the ethical substance, and by the reflection
> of wise and experienced men. In brief, we are always already pre-
> ceded by evaluations beginning from which even our doubt and our
> contestation become possible.[50]

He stresses, on the other hand, that it is not our nature to receive
and take on board every value as we find it. Stirred by an interest
in emancipation, we attain what Ricoeur calls an "ethical distance" in our relation to tradition. This is nothing short of the loss
of the "ethical naiveté" or the blemish of "Hegel's beautiful substance." But, Ricoeur insists, there are no alternative routes to

---

[49] See Ricoeur, "Ethics and Culture," 159-60.
[50] Ricoeur, "Ethics and Culture," 164-65.

emancipation other than "by incarnating it within cultural acquisitions."[51]

1.2 Tradition and Argumentation: MacIntyre's Contribution

If, according to Max Stackhouse, "nothing has marked twentieth-century intellectual and social life so much as the protest against liberalism,"[52] this 'protest' has taken on the proportions of an intellectual preoccupation in the case of our next major thinker, the moral philosopher Alasdair MacIntyre. Relentless in his criticism of ideologies that feed the fragmented and conflicting beliefs and practices that characterize contemporary ethical life, MacIntyre's defense of tradition against liberalism is currently one of the best known and most substantially articulated. Although his attempt is not new in the twentieth century, his contribution to the understanding of the epistemology of tradition is very significant. What we shall do here is extract a few key elements from his substantial works, which are germane to our task.

1.2.1 Tradition as a Socially-Embodied Reality

The leitmotif in *After Virtue*[53] is MacIntyre's definition of a "living tradition" as an "historically extended, socially embodied argument."[54] His reflection encompasses an attempt to envisage

[51] Ricoeur, "Ethics and Culture," 164-65.

[52] Max Stackhouse, "Alasdair MacIntyre: An Overview and Evaluation," *RSRev* 18 (1992) 203.

[53] Alasdair MacIntyre, *After Virtue: A Study in Moral Theory* (Notre Dame: University of Notre Dame Press, 1984²).

[54] *After Virtue*, 222. MacIntyre laments the absence of a "rational way of securing moral agreement in our culture" (p. 6). His basic position is that modern morality is in a state of chaos and confusion, so much so that we do not even recognize the seriousness of our plight, let alone have the resources to deal with

human life holistically, as a unity. Within that unity, his philosophy of ethics accords a pride of place to virtues which he characterizes as having an adequate *telos*. Two obstacles conspire to frustrate this teleological vision, one social, the other philosophical. Social obstacles include the tendency in modernity to partition human life into segments, to such an extent that the unity of human life is lost. Philosophically, obstacles originate from analytical philosophy and existentialism. There, complex human actions are thought of atomistically in terms of individual components, all of which are thought to be amenable to disconnected attention. When, therefore, human life and human actions are seen as nothing more than a "sequence of individual actions and episodes," an approach characteristic of the thought and practice of modernity, one can hardly conceive of the self as "a bearer of the Aristotelian virtues."[55]

What we have here is, in one sense, a battle between rationalism and historicism: what MacIntyre attempts to establish in *After Virtue* is that modernity's abandonment of the Aristotelian perspective in moral and political philosophy "was a mistake with disastrous consequences."[56] In what seems like an attempt

---

it. This bankruptcy of contemporary moral resources has prompted him to examine, in *After Virtue*, the natural impulses and linguistic practices of modern people. His strategy is to "turn to history;" his method is to resort to a "genetic account" of modern practices. For this description of MacIntyre's project in *After Virtue*, see Thomas S. Hibbs, "MacIntyre, Tradition and the Christian Philosopher," *ModSch* 68 (1991) 212. MacIntyre's aim is to retrieve and rehabilitate the Aristotelian tradition of virtue ethics. John A. Doody observes that it is MacIntyre's retrieval of this Aristotelian tradition which is seen by scholars as central to today's debate between communitarianism and liberalism. See his "MacIntyre and Habermas on Practical Reason," in *ACPhilQ* 65 (1991) 145.

[55] *After Virtue*, 204-05.

[56] For this description, see J. F. Gannon, "MacIntyre's Historicism," *CrCur* 39 (1989) 91. As a "moral philosopher, MacIntyre's primary concern is the dis-

to compromise between rationalism and historicism,[57] MacIntyre proceeds to bring forth a "core conception" of the virtues which "in some sense embodies the history of which it is the outcome." He wishes to describe the logical stages of development this conception takes. But, before doing so, he first sets down some basic convictions, namely: [a] his concept of selfhood is "a concept of a self whose unity resides in the unity of a narrative which links birth to life to death as narrative beginning to middle to end"; [b] human behaviour cannot be adequately characterized independently of intentionality; [c] human intentions, in order to be intelligible both to the agents themselves and to others, cannot be characterized independently of the settings in which the intentions are expressed; [d] it is central to the notion of a "setting" that it has a history.[58]

His description of the three stages[59] of this conception's logical development is instructive for the understanding of tradition and thus bears repeating here. In describing *stage one* of virtues' logical development, MacIntyre argues from "common experience"[60] to establish the point that virtues are quite integral to achievement in every conceivable particular human practice. Virtues are thus part of "any coherent and complex form of socially established co-operative activity through which goods internal to that form of activity are realised in the course of trying to achieve those standards of excellence [that] are appropriate to, and partly definitive of, that

array of our postmodern ethics," so writes Gerald McCool in "The Tradition of St. Thomas Since Vatican II," *TD* 40 (1993) 331.

[57] The attempt to compromise is diagnosed by Will Morrisby in "Two Critiques of Nihilism," *Int* 12 (1984) 132.

[58] *After Virtue*, 186, 205 & 206. Jeffrey Stout has argued that *After Virtue*'s historical narrative is inadequate. See his *Ethics after Babel* (Boston: Beacon, 1988), chs. 9-10 and "Virtue among the Ruins," *NZsTR* 26, no.3 (1984) 256-73.

[59] See *After Virtue*, 186, where the three-stage development is first mentioned.

[60] A description preferred by Gannon in "MacIntyre's Historicism," 92.

form of activity, with the result that human powers to achieve excellence, are systematically extended." However, participation in any of the particular human "practices" (games, arts, sciences, politics, and so on) constitutes but a segment of human life. Thus, MacIntyre goes on to *stage two*, where he attempts a definition of the *humanitas* so that human participation in particular practices will not be seen in isolation, but conceived in their totality within an integrated vision of human life. In this vision, the intelligibility of human actions must be ascertained in terms of their being "embedded" in a "narrative sequence" having a "certain teleological character." Designating a human person in this context as "a story-telling animal," MacIntyre intends to define a human person as one who becomes, "through history, a teller of stories that aspire to truth." To aspire to truth, for MacIntyre, is to seek "the good" which requires one to situate the virtues not only in relation to practices ("achieving goods internal to practices") but in relation to the good life for humanity. This leads him to conclude, rather tautologically, that "the good life for man is the life spent in seeking for the good life for man."[61] Still, this is insufficient, so that a *third* stage of development is posited. To exercise the virtues is a task one can achieve only *qua* individual,[62] that is to say, a subject living in particular social circumstances and as bearer of a particular social identity. To that social identity, one owes "a variety of debts" for what one inherits and for what constitutes the social "given" of one's life, one's "moral starting point."[63]

---

[61] *After Virtue*, 212, 214, 215, 216 & 219.

[62] On the question of an individual with personal identity, see *After Virtue*, 216-17. MacIntyre is here arguing against the individualism of modernity.

[63] MacIntyre summarizes in these terms: "What I am therefore, is in key part what I inherit, a specific past that is present to some degree in my present. I find myself part of a history and that is generally to say, whether I like it or not, whether I recognize it or not, one of the bearers of a tradition" [*After Virtue*, 222].

This tradition is characterized by MacIntyre as "vital" and not "dying or dead," as "constituted by argument about the goods," and, as embodying "continuities of conflict." He then offers an important definition for tradition: "A living tradition then is an historically extended, socially embodied argument, and an argument precisely in part about the goods which constitute that tradition."[64] In that vision, the character of all living traditions is marked and influenced by the past. But MacIntyre also holds in tensile balance faithfulness to the past and an *openness to the future*. For when he extols the virtue of having "an adequate sense of the traditions to which one belongs or which confront us," he does so not in pursuit of a "conservative antiquarianism," but to acknowledge the fact that it is through an adequate sense of tradition that one has "a grasp of those future possibilities which the past has made available to the present."[65]

In the successor volume, *Whose Justice? Which Rationality?*,[66] MacIntyre is again steadfast in his historicist-particularist vision, and

---

[64] *After Virtue*, 222.

[65] *After Virtue*, 223. MacIntyre continues, "Living traditions, just because they continue a not-yet-completed narrative, confront a future whose determinate and determinable character, so far as it possesses any, derives from the past." In response to his critics, MacIntyre acknowledges, in the postscript to the second edition of *After Virtue*, the apparently paradoxical quality of his own project: "An historicist defence of Aristotle is bound to strike some sceptical critics as a paradoxical as well as a Quixotic enterprise. For Aristotle himself, as I pointed out in my discussion of his own account of the virtues, was not any kind of historicist... To show that there is no paradox here is therefore one more necessary task; but it too can only be accomplished on the larger scale that the successor volume to *After Virtue* will afford me" [*After Virtue*, 277-78]. For a positive, though qualified, assessment of MacIntyre's defence, see Jeffrey Stout, "Homeward Bound: MacIntyre on Liberal Society and the History of Ethics," *JR* 69 (1989) 220-32.

[66] Alasdair MacIntyre, *Whose Justice? Which Rationality?* (Notre Dame: University of Notre Dame Press, 1988).

insists at the outset that "the concept of rational justification which is at home in that form of enquiry is essentially historical."[67] MacIntyre's emphasis on the historicity of all thinking raises a host of issues.

1.2.2 Rationality is Tradition-Bound

The *first* of these issues is the relationship between tradition and rationality.[68] What MacIntyre wants to stress is that there is no such thing as a rationality that is not the rationality of some tradition: rationality is always essentially tradition-bound. To support this claim, he begins with a scenario of "radical conflict" in theoretical conceptions of justice. Instead of consensus, our society is marked by "division and conflict."[69] His historicist-particularist lens enables him to categorically affirm, at the outset, the inescapable plurality of justices and rationalities in history.[70] How does one decide in the face of competing claims, all vying for allegiance? How ought we to proceed if we are to be rational?

[67] *Whose Justice?*, 7.

[68] This relationship has been identified by Thomas S. Hibbs as "a leitmotif of MacIntyre's writings," in "MacIntyre's Postmodern Thomism: Reflections on *Three Rival Versions of Moral Enquiry*," *Thomist* 57 (1993) 282; see also his "MacIntyre, Tradition, and the Christian Philosopher," 217 where he assesses the book in these terms: "The fundamental motif of the book is that justice and rationality are ineluctably tied to particular traditions of thought and social practice." That is the easier part. The more problematic issue, as we shall see, consists in understanding MacIntyre's particularist means to universalism without which objectivity would give way to relativism.

[69] MacIntyre notes a striking fact about modern political orders in that "they lack institutionalized forums within which these fundamental disagreements can be systematically explored and charted, let alone there being any attempt made to resolve them" [*Whose Justice?*, 2-3].

[70] He thus affirms, early in the first chapter, that: "Indeed, since there are a diversity of traditions of enquiry, with histories, there are, so it will turn out, rationalities rather than rationality, just as it will also turn out that there are justices rather than justice" [*Whose Justice?*, 9].

The difficulty associated with the need to choose certain procedures rather than others is evident in view of the rationality behind
every choice.[71] MacIntyre's own historicist-particularist approach
is a "recoverist" project,[72] articulated as a corrective to what the
Enlightenment thinkers and their progeny have obscured for us.[73]
This Enlightenment legacy has saddled us with a conception of
rationality which is impotent in solving contemporary moral disputes. For the Enlightenment thinkers, there is a universal rationality into which every living person can tap.[74] This is precisely
the error MacIntyre warns us against, that is, a conception of rationality that is not tradition-bound or is independent of distinctively

[71] MacIntyre deals with the problem in these terms: "Fundamental disagreements about the character of rationality are bound to be peculiarly difficult to
resolve. For already in initially proceeding in one way rather than another to
approach the disputed questions, those who so proceed will have had to assume
that these particular procedures are the ones which it is rational to follow. A certain degree of circularity is ineliminable" (*Whose Justice?*, 4). It would seem
that when John Hick, a pluralist who reasons from the philosophy of religions,
demands that intelligibility be furnished to support the Christian theory of the
Incarnation, he operates within the "circularity" of the rationality of his discipline. This clearly places him outside the particular tradition of the Christian
communal faith.
[72] This is the label ascribed to MacIntyre's project by Russel Hittingger in *A
Critique of the New Natural Law Theory* (Notre Dame: University of Notre
Dame Press, 1988), 1.
[73] He avers: "What the Enlightenment made us for the most part blind to and
what we now need to recover is... a conception of rational enquiry as embodied
in a tradition, a conception according to which the standards of rational justification themselves emerge from and are part of a history in which they are vindi-
cated by the way in which they transcend the limitations of and provide remedies
for the defects of their predecessors within the history of that same tradition"
[*Whose Justice*, 7].
[74] "Rational justification was to appeal to principles undeniable by any rational person and therefore independent of all those social and cultural particularities which the Enlightenment thinkers took to be the mere accidental clothing of
reason in particular times and places" [*Whose Justice?*, 6].

variable social and cultural underpinnings. This ideal of rational justification is a legacy of Enlightenment which it has proved impossible to attain. In justifying anything, we are in fact narrating how the argument has gone so far: rationality is a concept with a history. Again, stressing the phenomenon of 'embedding' as he did in the earlier volume, MacIntyre offers an alternative conception which is a *tradition-constituted and tradition-constitutive rational enquiry*, from which standpoint "what a particular doctrine claims is always a matter of how precisely it was advanced, of the linguistic particularities of its formulation, of what at that time and place had to be denied, if it was to be asserted, of what was at that time and place presupposed by its assertion, and so on. Doctrines, theses, and arguments all have to be understood in terms of historical context."[75]

MacIntyre then emphasizes, as crucial, "that the concept of tradition-constituted and tradition-constitutive rational enquiry cannot be elucidated apart from its exemplifications." Consonant with that, the bulk of *Whose Justice? Which Rationality?* consists of a detailed treatment of four particular traditions, together with brief references to others. The four are: [i] the Aristotelian tradition of moral and political thought that "emerges from the conflicts of the ancient *polis*, but is then developed by Aquinas in a way which escapes the limitations of the *polis*;" [ii] the Augustinian tradition that "entered in the medieval period into complex relationships of antagonism, later of synthesis, and then of continuing antagonism to Aristotelianism;" [iii] the Calvinist Augustinian tradition and its encounter with Aristotle in 17th-century Scotland that was then "subverted from within" by the Humean tradition; and [iv] modern liberal individualism[76] stemming from the Enlightenment tradition

[75] *Whose Justice?*, 7 & 9.

[76] *Whose Justice?*, 10. One might note that, by "liberalism," MacIntyre is not making a reference to any specific political doctrine, but rather to "a mentality

"born of antagonism to all tradition." By this lengthy analysis, MacIntyre evidently seeks to give his readers a sense of a "tradition" and the dynamics of its historical development.[77] "A tradition," he proposes, "is an argument extended through time." His explicit aim in telling these lengthy narratives is to arrive at a "true account of justice and practical rationality."[78] His shift from rationalities and justices (that is, in the plural) at the beginning of the book, to the singular, here noted at the end of the book, is an inherent tension in MacIntyre's work which we shall examine later. For MacIntyre, rationality can exist only within a tradition. This means that there can be no external, tradition-free standard for comparing traditions.

Philosophers of the Enlightenment, beginning with Descartes, have created the belief that human rationality is, like the Cartesian ego or Kantian reason, identical in all of us, and effectively transcendental and ahistorical.[79] This inevitably leads to liberalism. The liberals see themselves as having finally freed politics and theory of every "given."[80] But MacIntyre points out that liberalism, too, has its roots and its operative presuppositions. Liberalism's agenda of

that pervades and corrupts the ways in which we think, act, and feel." See Richard J. Bernstein, "Philosophy and Virtue for Society's Sake," *Com* 115 (1988) 306.

[77] *Whose Justice?*, 10 & 349. Bernstein reminds us that it would be to seriously misread MacIntyre if we failed to see this as his primary objective in relating the narratives of different traditions in the first place. See "Philosophy and Virtue," 306.

[78] *Whose Justice?*, 12 & 389.

[79] Effectively, the attitude is that: "In science and philosophy, in all manifestations of human culture, only those truths are acceptable as a foundation for human reasoning which are directly accessible to all sane humanity, without reference to any specific tradition or historical reality." See Benno van den Toren, "A New Direction in Christian Apologetics: An Exploration with reference to Postmodernism," *EuroJT* 2:1 (1993) 51-52.

[80] That much of the problem in society MacIntyre seeks to address in his works has to do with "authority," has not escaped his commentators. See Doody,

"unsituated discourse" is doomed to failure, for we are inevitably
the products of history and culture. We cannot but work in a tradition. We cannot but labour under the limitations that the particularity and positivity of our tradition imply and we cannot claim to use
our reason, or expect others to do so, free of such limitations.[81] At
the end of the enquiry, MacIntyre points out that the liberal search
for rational standards and methods, which are hailed by their adherents as something that transcend historical contingencies, has been
"a history of continuously unresolved disputes, so that there
emerges no uncontested and incontestable account of what tradition-independent morality consists in and consequently no neutral
set of criteria by means of which the claims of rival and contending
traditions could be adjudicated." Far from being able to rise above
traditions, liberalism has grown into yet another tradition.[82]

The failure of the liberal search for tradition-independent rational standards and methods is very instructive, so it bears pointing
out that, after tracing the historical development of the four
selected rational traditions, MacIntyre reiterates his verdict in
these terms:

"MacIntyre and Habermas," 146-49; Hibbs, "MacIntyre's Postmodern
Thomism," 291-93.

[81] On the other hand, we are in no way suggesting that human beings are
totally conditioned or determined by tradition. As Barbara Ward writes in *Faith
and Freedom* (New York: Norton, 1954), 12: "When we, today, try to assess the
balance between forces — the conditioning forces of environment and of man's
blind reaction to them on the one hand and his free acts of insight, reason, creation and control on the other — we are insensibly biased toward a belief in
determinism."

[82] *Whose Justice?*, 334, 326-48. As van den Toren remarked, "the choice for
liberalism is as much a matter of historical background as is the choice for other
traditions." See his "A New Direction," 53. Stout, however, thinks MacIntyre
has dismissed "liberalism" too easily. If every tradition is a particular history of
argument, then MacIntyre has so far only remotely begun to attend to the history
and the particularity of *that* tradition. See Stout, "Homeward Bound," 228-29.

[T]he project of founding a form of social order in which individuals could emancipate themselves from the contingency and particularity of tradition by appealing to genuinely universal, tradition-independent norms was and is not only, and not principally, a project of philosophers. It was and is the project of modern liberal, individualist society, and the most cogent reasons that we have for believing that the hope of a tradition-independent rational universality is an illusion derived from the history of that project. For in the course of that history liberalism, which began as an appeal to alleged principles of shared rationality against what was felt to be the tyranny of tradition, has itself been transformed into a tradition.[83]

1.2.3 Tradition and Incommensurability

The *second* issue generated by MacIntyre's historicism concerns the problem of incommensurability, which is closely related to the way he places great weight on the self-sufficiency and truth-relatedness of traditions. To be sure, he is acutely aware of what appears to follow from the claim that rationality is only internal to particular traditions. Given that each tradition will frame its own standpoint without any reference to external ideas, the conclusion to which such arguments so far lead us is twofold: *first*, rational debates can proceed, at the fundamental level, only *within*, never *between*, traditions; *second*, translation from one tradition to another is precluded.[84] To MacIntyre, these conclusions seem too

---

[83] *Whose Justice?*, 10 & 335. Doody insists that the principal task of *Whose Justice? Which Rationality?* is to argue for this hermeneutical conception of reason and argumentation. See his "MacIntyre and Harbermas," 149.

[84] "A social universe composed exclusively of rival traditions," MacIntyre visualizes, "will be one in which there are a number of contending, incompatible but only partially and inadequately communicating, overall views of that universe, each tradition within which is unable to justify its claims over against those of its rivals except to those who already accept them. Is this indeed what

dire, for he wants to retain the possibility of communication between traditions on the basis of certain beliefs, images and texts that might be shared. This entails no less than trying to keep the best of both worlds, namely, to acknowledge the role of context in traditions, and to avoid being relativistic. But he at once faces two challenges. The *relativist* challenge taxes him as to how, since even these shared resources might be interpreted very differently and achieve very different status within different traditions, might there be a rationally determinable outcome? An appeal to a particular tradition cannot be other, it would seem, than an appeal to authority. Given that to be the case, in the face of the plurality of traditions, have we any defence at all against the relativist contention that no issue between conflicting traditions can be rationally adjudicated?[85] The *perspectivist* challenge taxes him on how, with only an arbitrary and perspectival viewpoint, one can offer good reason for adopting one tradition rather than another, except that one *already* stands within that tradition. 'Truth,' after all, is nothing but the contingent perspectives we happen to have on things, so that we cannot speak of the truth or falsity of rival traditions, or adjudicate between them. These challenges, MacIntyre suggests, can be met by recognising the special kind of rationality proper to traditions.

In developing his response, MacIntyre refutes a false dichotomy between [a] the Enlightenment conception of truth and rationality in which truth is guaranteed by rational methods

follows?" [*Whose Justice?*, 348.] Hauerwas, who explicitly depends on MacIntyre to a substantial degree as we shall see in later chapters, and Lindbeck, who does not mention him, would say yes. MacIntyre himself, however, is unwilling to accept these conclusions.

[85] The relativist would say: "There can be no rationality as such. Every set of standards, has as much and as little claim to our allegiance as any other" [*Whose Justice?*, 352].

commonly available to any reflective, rational person, and [b] a post-Enlightenment relativism that sees no possibility of an alternative conception of rationality now that the Enlightenment concept no longer holds. He presents an alternative account of rationality, the *tradition-constituted and tradition-constitutive enquiry*, that avoids the Enlightenment path and that portrays rationality as consisting in an openness to development. To do so, he turns to Newman's ideas on the development of Christian doctrine.[86] Traditions, he argues, move through three commonly identifiable stages and communication between them is more likely at some stages than at others. Stage *one* features the emergence of a tradition under a pure historical contingency. In this stage, beliefs, institutions and practices constitute the authoritative sources of the tradition, and to which adherence is unquestioningly and uncritically accorded. In stage *two*, encounters with other situations raise questions and doubts that are not adequately answered by traditional resources. Stage *three* witnesses to responses being made to those inadequacies which precipitate "a set of reformulations, reevaluations, and new formulations and evaluations, designed to remedy inadequacies and overcome limitations."[87] The final outcome can take either of two directions. One, a tradition is maintained where the proposed modification in belief and outlook is demonstrated to stand in a continuity with the rest of the tradition. However, the crisis may precipitate a realisation that the new tradition is more appropriate than the

[86] John Henry Newman, *University Sermons: Fifteen Sermons Preached before the University of Oxford 1826-1843* (London: SPCK, 1970), 312ff.

[87] *Whose Justice?*, 355. For suggestions to complement MacIntyre's attempt by theories of human nature and general standards of rationality, see Peter J. Mehl, "In the Twilight of Modernity," *JRE* 19 (1991) 21-54. For a critique that suggests that MacIntyre's notion of rational superiority is purely formal and, therefore, empty, see Franklin I. Gamwell, *The Divine Good* (New York: Southern Methodist University Press, 1996), 74-84.

old, and that the new tradition has better conceptual tools to understand human life and activity. Thus, despite the absence of a neutral rationality, a tradition can flounder when engaging another whose rationality it finds more plausible.

Among others, two things are postulated as both possible and necessary in MacIntyre's account. *First*, even though there is no neutral rationality, some kind of standard is obviously necessary to enable traditions in encounter to perform comparisons. MacIntyre thus outlines a variation on the correspondence theory of truth. In sharp contrast to the Enlightenment conception of 'facts,' he recognizes no neutral realm of facts to which appeal can be made for adjudicating conflicts among rival traditions. When 'the facts' are themselves regarded as ordered and structured by a culturally-transmitted theoretical framework of tradition, any simplistic conceptions of truth-as-correspondence become untenable. Such conceptions would give traditions a rote character and portray their progress as essentially a passive process. In essence, all traditions are trying to explain reality in as comprehensive a way as possible. Truth is ultimately determined when beliefs are perceived as corresponding with reality.[88] *Second*, different traditions operate within different languages in which different rationalities reside. The engagement between traditions is never easy, and requires a common language. This calls for bilinguality which entails the learning of a "second first-language,"[89] not in a facile manner, but through living and thinking with the concepts of the second language.

Thus, while traditions may have contingent foundations, in a process of challenge and response, initial positions may become revised and strengthened. Clearly, particular traditions may

---

[88] *Whose Justice?*, 375ff.

[89] *Whose Justice?*, ch. 19, passim; *Three Rival Versions*, 114.

develop a form of enquiry that requires the recognition of certain intellectual virtues, including the need to acknowledge inadequacies and the willingness to create critical reformulations. Further, these traditions may be able to recognize that similar issues are being addressed within other traditions. In sum, even as he upholds the distinctive nature of traditions, MacIntyre is able to leave intact an element of rational enquiry at work in a process of growth.[90] Truth, according to MacIntyre, is the goal of every enquiry. Our temporality inevitably means we are unable to claim an exhaustive or final account of reality. That, however, does not entail skepticism. MacIntyre offers the notion of *warranted assertibility* as a rational alternative to skepticism. Claims to truth are always made at a certain time and place. At some particular stage in a tradition's development, a certain claim may be regarded as "warrantedly assertible." Yet, the concept of truth, MacIntyre says, is *timeless*. He therefore finds it possible to combine the notion of *warranted assertibility* with the traditional notion of truth as *timeless*.[91]

In all this, MacIntyre is developing a thesis which has been present in his work at least since 1977.[92] It is a thesis which holds that a tradition is most open to rational comparison with rival traditions, and most amenable to radical change, when it falls into what he calls an "epistemological crisis." An epistemological crisis

[90] In fact, MacIntyre avers that, "to some degree, insofar as a tradition of rational enquiry is such, it will tend to recognize what it shares as such with other traditions, and in the development of such traditions common characteristics, if not universal patterns will appear" [*Whose Justice?*, 359].

[91] See *Whose Justice?*, 363ff. P. Mark Achtemeier maintains that, on account of his critiques of relativism and perspectivism, and his description of the rational resolution of conflicts between rival traditions, MacIntyre operates with a stronger notion of truth than mere warranted assertibility that is time and space-bound. See idem, "The Truth of Tradition," *SJT* 47 (1994) 365.

[92] See Alasdair MacIntyre, "Epistemological Crises, Dramatic Narrative and the Philosophy of Science," *The Monist* 60 (1977) 453-72.

arises when internal contradictions and inconsistencies within a
tradition become so huge that the tradition in crisis can no longer
make progress. He begins his explanation of an epistemological
crisis by noting the crucial relationship between what "seems" to
be so and what actually "is" so. An epistemological crisis occurs
when an accustomed way of relating *seems* and *is* breaks down. In
other words, what people "took to be evidence pointing unam-
biguously in some one direction now turns out to have been
equally susceptible of rival interpretations."[93] To share a culture is
to share schemata that are simultaneously constitutive of, and normative for, intelligible action by oneself and are also means for
interpreting the actions of others.[94] In an epistemological crisis, an
individual experiences a dissonance as one comes to "recognise
the possibility of systematically different possibilities of interpretation, of the existence of alternative and rival schemata which
yield mutually incompatible accounts of what is going on around
him."[95] Such an epistemological crisis occurs as easily at the level
of ordinary agents as it does at the levels of science or philosophy.
Typically for MacIntyre, he links epistemology to a narrative, for
"narrative requires an evaluative framework."[96] In addition, he
goes on to argue that a dramatic narrative "is the crucial form for
the understanding of human action,"[97] for, in a real sense, a crisis
is resolved by the construction of a new narrative which "enables
the agent to understand *both* how he or she could intelligibly have
held his or her original beliefs *and* how he or she could have been
so drastically misled by them."[98] In the field of science, the new

[93] "Epistemological Crises," 453.
[94] "Epistemological Crises," 453.
[95] "Epistemological Crises," 454.
[96] "Epistemological Crises," 456.
[97] "Epistemological Crises," 464.
[98] "Epistemological Crises," 455. Thus Charles Davis remarks: "The tradition avoids repudiation and remains worthy of rational assent as long as it can

narrative reconstructs the scientific tradition after its confrontation with a new theory.[99] For MacIntyre, the primacy of history requires him to subordinate social and scientific reasoning to historical reasoning. Scientific reason, he discovers, is intelligible only in terms of historical reason. *A fortiori*, this applies to social sciences.[100] Indeed, it is because of the possibility of constructing an intelligible narrative, i.e., relating theories as successive episodes in the history of science, that we are able to compare theories with one another and give an account of why one theory is superior to another.[101]

Early in *Whose Justice? Which Rationality?*, MacIntyre had already laid down his insight on the developmental nature of tradition.[102] Thus, the concept of tradition that emerges from MacIntyre's argument is one which, far from excluding conflict,

find within itself resources to meet new situations and questions with sufficient inventiveness for the reformulation and re-evaluation of its authoritative texts and beliefs." See idem, *Religion and the Making of Society* (Cambridge: Cambridge University Press, 1994), 109.

[99] "The criterion of a successful theory is that it enables us to understand its predecessors in a newly intelligible way. It, at one and the same time, enables us to understand precisely why its predecessors have to be rejected or modified and also why, without and before its illumination, past theory could have remained credible. It introduces new standards for evaluating the past. It recasts the narrative which constitutes the continuous reconstruction of the scientific tradition" ["Epistemological Crises," 460].

[100] "Epistemological Crises," 464.

[101] So MacIntyre can hold: "It is more rational to accept one theory or paradigm and to reject its predecessor when the later theory or paradigm provides a stand-point from which the acceptance, the life-story, and the rejection of the previous theory or paradigm can be recounted in more intelligible historical narrative than previously. An understanding of the concept of the superiority of one physical theory to another requires a prior understanding of the concept of the superiority of one historical narrative to another. The theory of scientific rationality has to be embedded in a philosophy of history" ["Epistemological Crises," 467].

[102] "A tradition is an argument extended through time in which certain fundamental agreements are defined and redefined in terms of two kinds of conflict:

posits the continued presence of conflict, both within each tradition and between traditions. For, in his view, to have negotiated an epistemological crisis successfully, empowers the adherents of a tradition "to rewrite its history in a more insightful way." He argues that traditions can supply rational resources sufficient for their adherents to recognize their own failures or inadequacies.[103] When the adherents of a crisis-ridden tradition admit the shortcomings of their own conceptual scheme, they may look to a rival tradition for new resources. How would they be able to judge the superiority of rival standards? They would use the self-same standards by which they have found their own tradition wanting in the face of epistemological crisis, to judge whether a rival tradition is cogent and illuminating. Significantly, MacIntyre postulates that their effort, in this regard, "is augmented by the fact that a tradition is capable, in principle, of recognizing

those with critics and enemies external to the tradition who reject all or at least key parts of those fundamental agreements, and those internal, interpretative debates through which the meaning and rationale of the fundamental agreements come to be expressed and by progress a tradition is constituted" [*Whose Justice?*, 12]. Based on norms of evaluation it possesses, a tradition structures and interprets the data to which it attends. MacIntyre offers four criteria by which progress in a tradition-based inquiry may be demonstrated. See *Whose Justice?*, 79-80.

[103] *Whose Justice?*, 363, 361-64. It is interesting to note that Robert P. George, who does not favourably assess MacIntyre's effort at resolving the paradox in his reliance on Aristotle for a particularist perspective, nevertheless thinks that MacIntyre has made an important point about the ways "traditions may fail, and be seen by their adherents to fail, to meet their own standards." See idem, "Moral Particularism, Thomism, and Traditions," *RevMeta* 42 (1989) 602. This remark resonates with Doody, who credits MacIntyre's discussion of the conflicts between traditions, and traditions in crisis, as evincing "a critical edge which Gadamer's philosophy lacks, as Habermas has continuously reminded us." See Doody, "MacIntyre and Habermas," 158. For other recent studies comparing Habermas to MacIntyre, see Kenneth Baynes, "Rational Reconstruction and Social Criticism: Habermas's Model of Interpretive Social Science," *PhFor* 21 (1989-90) 122-45; and Michael Kelly, "MacIntyre, Habermas, and Philosophical Ethics," *PhFor* 21 (1989-90) 70-93.

external challenges to its authority, by being able to translate those challenges into its own terms."[104]

MacIntyre suggests that, when two rival traditions confront each other, there is often no neutral way of characterizing their subject matters or the standards for judging them. He posits a two-stage progress in a genuine controversy. At the start, each tradition would characterize, on its own terms, the contentions of its rival, rejecting what it considers to be incompatible with its central tenet, and sometimes accepting the possibility of profiting from the rival on "marginal and subordinate questions." Next, when a tradition is developing, and certain insoluble antinomies appear, or the tradition encounters difficulties in developing the enquiry beyond a certain point, the rival tradition may provide resources to help explain the failings and defects. But MacIntyre very wisely stresses a practical difficulty. The latter stage is attainable only by those protagonists who possess "a rare gift of empathy as well as intellectual insight." It is important to stress that, in MacIntyre's scheme, the development of tradition, that is, a "rational tradition's modes of continuity," is distinguished from "abrupt general changes in belief," which constitute a rupture. He insists that "some *core of shared belief*, constitutive of allegiance to the tradition, has to survive every rupture" (emphasis added).[105]

1.2.4 Tradition and the Movement from Particularism to Universalism

The *third* issue generated by MacIntyre's historicism has to do with the tension between particularism and universalism, and, relatedly, the problem of objectivity in particular traditions. This tension

[104] *Whose Justice?*, 364, 370-88.
[105] *Whose Justice?*, 166, 166-67, 167, 356.

is, in fact, very much alive in *Whose Justice? Which Rationality?*
itself. Recall, for example, MacIntyre's statement in the first chapter:
"Since there are a diversity of traditions of enquiry, with histories,
there are, so it will turn out, rationalities, rather than rationality, just
as it will also turn out that there are justices rather than justice."
However, in the final chapter, after he has conducted a detailed study
into selected traditions, the particularist "plural" descriptions of justices and rationalities have culminated in a singular, objective, and
universal concept. The reason he gives is that the goal of the discussion of the nature of a tradition-constituted and tradition-constitutive
enquiry is "a true account of justice and of practical rationality." It
is not a discussion undertaken for its own sake.[106] The lengthy analysis of selected traditions serves as the necessary foundation for the
main thrust of MacIntyre's project, which is to deny that there are
such things as pure or abstract rationality and justice, as the Enlightenment thinkers would have us believe. It is quite simply not available to us to choose a tradition from a neutral standpoint with a view
to an impartial evaluation of traditions.[107]

---

[106] *Whose Justice?*, 389. An outline of his strategy was already offered in the
first chapter, in these terms: "[A]cknowledgment of the diversity of traditions of
enquiry, each with its own specific mode of rational justification, does not entail
that the differences between rival and incompatible traditions cannot be rationally resolved. How and under what conditions they can be resolved is something
only to be understood after a prior understanding of the nature of such traditions
has been achieved. From the standpoint of traditions of rational enquiry the problem of diversity is not abolished, but it is transformed in a way that renders it
amenable of solution" [pp. 9-10].

[107] MacIntyre diagnoses as follows: "[T]here is no place for appeals to a
practical-rationality-as-such or a justice-as-such to which all rational persons
would by their very rationality be compelled to give their allegiance. There is
instead only the practical-rationality-of-this-or-that-tradition and the justice-of-
this-or-that-tradition" [*Whose Justice?*, 346]. In "The Truth of Tradition,"
Achtemeier's main burden is to demonstrate the parallels between MacIntyre's
vigorous antifoundationalist critique of modern forms of epistemological objectivism and T. F. Torrance's critical realism.

Given that to be the case, MacIntyre understandably declares it an illusion to suppose that there is a neutral locus for rationality that harbours rational resources sufficient for enquiry independent of all traditions. The question, then, is whether such a strong particularism is not inescapably relativistic? But, MacIntyre preempts such criticism, arguing that a person outside all traditions, if such is possible in the first place, lacks sufficient rational resources for enquiry at all and, *a fortiori*, for enquiry into what constitutes a rationally preferable tradition. Lacking any relevant means of rational evaluation, such a person can come to no reasoned conclusion on any given tradition regarding the possibility of its vindication against any other. "To be outside all traditions is to be a stranger to enquiry; it is to be in a state of intellectual and moral destitution, a condition from which it is impossible to issue the relativist's challenge."[108]

Still, MacIntyre does not seem to have solved the problem of objective truth. But it is not his explicit aim to solve that problem entirely. Truth may arguably be the goal of every enquiry, but we need to go through the different stages of the development of a tradition to appreciate how that tradition struggles with the search for truth. Certainly, the test for truth in the present, MacIntyre explains, "is always to summon up as many objections of the greatest strength possible; what can be justifiably claimed as true is what has sufficiently withstood such dialectical questioning and framing of objections."[109] At the end, confronted by the rival traditions' claims to our rational allegiance, numerous questions need to be asked and answered. But of this much MacIntyre is utterly convinced: that we cannot ask and answer those questions from a standpoint external to all traditions, for the resources of adequate

[108] *Whose Justice?*, 367.
[109] *Whose Justice?*, 358. For his analysis of the three stages in the initial development of a tradition, see p. 355.

rationality are made available to us only in and through traditions. All this, to be sure, is eminently consonant with MacIntyre's insistence on what a commentator calls "the particularist means to universality."[110]

In *Three Rival Versions of Moral Enquiry*,[111] MacIntyre's attention turns to two particular traditions radically opposed to each other. The *encyclopaedist*[112] espouses the Cartesian autonomy of reason, which is "impersonal, impartial, disinterested, uniting, and universal," and free from all ties to any particular community.[113] The *genealogist*,[114] on the other hand, rejects the encyclopaedist conception of reason as "universal and disinterested," for it masks the interests of an underlying will to power. MacIntyre finds both conceptions objectionable, especially in reference to their formulation in terms of exclusive and exhaustive alternatives: "*Either* reason is thus impersonal, universal, and distinterested *or* it is the unwitting representative of particular interests, masking their drive to power by its false pretensions

[110] *Whose Justice?*, 358 & 369. See Hibbs, "MacIntyre's Postmodern Thomism," 278 n.4. [111] Alasdair MacIntyre, *Three Rival Versions of Moral Enquiry* (Notre Dame: University of Notre Dame Press, 1990).

[112] The encyclopaedist represents that epoch when the ninth edition of the *Encyclopedia Britannica* was published in Edinburgh, commencing 1875. It became the classic text, divorced from Revelation and tradition, that epitomised the rationalist confidence in the power of scientific reason to unify human knowledge. See Gerald McCool, "The Tradition of St. Thomas," 325-26.

[113] *Three Rival Versions*, 59.

[114] *The Genealogy of Morals* is seen by MacIntyre as Nietzsche's classic text, published in 1887, that provided "not only an argument in favor of, but a paradigm for, the construction of a type of subversive narrative designed to undermine the central assumptions of Encyclopaedia, both in content and in genre. Where the encyclopaedist aspired to displace the Bible as a canonical book, the genealogist intended to discredit the whole notion of a canon" (*Three Rival Versions*, 25). In that classic text itself, "Nietzsche set out to subvert both history and reason by dissolving the knower's perduring identity which both of them require." See McCool, "Tradition of St. Thomas," 332.

to neutrality and disinterestedness." This alternative formulation conceals "a third possibility, the possibility that reason can only move towards being genuinely universal and impersonal insofar as it is neither neutral nor disinterested, that membership in a particular type of moral community, one from which fundamental dissent has to be excluded, is a condition for genuinely rational inquiry."[115]

1.2.5 The Community Dimension of Tradition

By now, it is clear that, for MacIntyre, tradition as a rational enquiry is never located in an ahistorical "nowhere." Rather, rationality ensues from, resides in, and is only sustained within, a particular historically and culturally conditioned tradition. The rationality of every tradition is adequately grasped only through a close study of the historical *narrative* that saw the birth of the tradition, its struggles with epistemological crises, its growth and metamorphosis, and hence its continued life. Tradition is, then, much like a craft, practised in a community that understands and appreciates the heritage that cradles the craft and ensures its continued existence. The members of that community share a common vision on the most crucial issues that concern their identity and survival as a community; they share a common *telos*. Tradition is, in a positive sense, authoritative, for it safeguards the good and well-being of the community. True communities are "historically extended, socially embodied arguments" – arguments precisely about the aims and goods the community should seek.

In sum, a key feature of MacIntyre's account of traditions, implied as a corollary to the social-embodiment of traditions, is that they are community-based. He underscores the organic

[115] *Three Rival Versions*, 58-60.

connection between a tradition and the way of life of a particular community. In *After Virtue*, the practice of the "good life" within the community enjoys a priviledged position in MacIntyre's moral scheme. Relatedly, the notion of justice within a community is characterized by a common allegiance to, and a common pursuit of, the good. In *Whose Justice? Which Rationality?*, MacIntyre takes as his point of departure a central Aristotelian insight, namely, that we reason not as disembodied minds but as members of a particular community which in part defines how we reason and judge: Aristotle's tradition of justice and practical rationality presupposes citizenship in the Greek *polis*.[116] It makes no sense to speak of a tradition in abstraction from those community structures which legitimate the tradition, nurture it, function as the locus for its on-going argument,[117] and actualize a telos over time.[118] Thought and philosophical enquiry would be unintelligible apart from the community that thinks and enquires. As MacIntyre puts it, "philosophical theories give organised expression to concepts and theories already embodied in forms of practice and types of communities." In

---

[116] *Whose Justice?*, 133.

[117] See B. V. Johnstone, "Faithful Action: The Catholic Moral Tradition and *Veritatis Splendor*," *StuMor* 31 (1993) 299; Stackhouse, "Alasdair MacIntyre," 206.

[118] See Hibbs, "MacIntyre's Postmodern Thomism," 293. In this respect, Stackhouse makes an important observation on MacIntyre which bears repeating: "It is not that he is opposed to principles *per se*; it is that principles, in his view, are more instrumental than regulative. They are less to be heeded because they have some universal validity than they are to be heeded if and when they conduce to some fulfillment of desire or moral possibility of community otherwise not at hand. In other words, they have to be linked to and justified by their relation to some specific end that can be actualized in concrete practice." See Stackhouse, "Alasdair MacIntyre," 205. As we shall see in chapter 5, the argument that doctrines do not function solely in regulative terms provides a critical edge over George Lindbeck's restrictive consignment of doctrines to a purely regulative role.

Three Rival Versions, MacIntyre continues in the same vein and argues that we can only come to know our good as humans by participating in "a community in which we may discover what further specifications our good has to be given."[119]

More significantly, perhaps, is the point that, in view of its social embodiment, a tradition cannot be understood in abstraction from those community structures which support the ongoing argument. In referring to the institutionalization of the process of verification of tradition, MacIntyre affirms that moral tradition must have some *structures of authority*.[120] The significance of the relationship between tradition and these social structures is revealed in the fact that the community depends on its institutions and practices for the discerning of what belongs or does not belong in the tradition. This element of tradition is, of course, internal to its reality and not something external and added. Nevertheless, institutions exist to serve the tradition, not the other way around.

---

[119] See *Whose Justice?*, 390; *Three Rival Versions*, 136-37. For an argument that MacIntyre is not a communitarian as he has often been portrayed, see Doody, "MacIntyre and Habermas," 157-158. See also Hauerwas, "Communitarians and Medical Ethicists: or 'Why I Am None of the Above'," *CSR* 23 (1994) 293-99. It is never a simple case of "communitarianism" versus "liberalism." See Gregory Jones, "Why There Is No One Debate between 'Communitarians' and 'Liberals'," *PRS* 17 (1990) 53-70. Exposing a necessary revision to communitarian theories, Christopher Lasch writes: "By overemphasizing the importance of shared values, defenders of a communitarian politics expose themselves to the familiar charge that community is simply a euphemism for conformity. The answer to this charge is that tradition, and tradition alone, is precisely what makes it possible for men and women to disagree without trying to resolve their disagreements by the sword." See idem, "The Communitarian Critique of Liberalism," *Soundings* 69 (1986) 67. Vital traditions, as MacIntyre points out, embody continuities of conflicts and consensus.

[120] See *Whose Justice?*, 358.

1.2.6 Truth and Dialectical Questioning

How then is truth established in a historical process? Central to a tradition-constituted enquiry, and at each stage in its progress, is always its *current problematic*. For it is the resolution or other-wise of that agenda of unresolved problems and issues which will largely decide the rational progress of a given tradition. The test for truth in the present, MacIntyre explains, "is always to summon up as many objections of the greatest strength possible; what can be justifiably claimed as true is what has sufficiently withstood such dialectical questioning and framing of objections."[121] Even to ascertain what "sufficiency" consists in would require a dialec-tical testing of the competing answers that may be offered. In the process, some standard forms of argument are bound to emerge, and some ground rules for proper dialectical questioning will get established. When incoherence on a certain belief is identified, that will impel further enquiry without at once becoming a con-clusive reason for rejecting established belief. To be sure, at every stage, "beliefs and judgments will be justified by reference to the beliefs and judgments of the previous stage." This will continue until something "more adequate" emerges, that is, something that is "less incoherent" and "in some specifiable way less vulnera-ble" to dialectical questioning and objection than their historical predecessors.

In this way of conceiving truth and rationality, every tradition is portrayed as starting from "the contingency and positivity of some set of established beliefs." Truth, seen as embodied in a tradition-constituted enquiry, at once clashes with the standard Cartesian understanding of truth as clear and distinct — and thus immediately accessible — idea. At the same time, if the correct

---

[121] *Whose Justice?*, 358.

understanding of the starting point of a tradition-constituted enquiry is essentially anti-Cartesian, a correct perception of its end-point is necessarily anti-Hegelian. To be sure, there is an implicit conception of a final truth in a tradition-constituted enquiry – "that is to say, a relationship of the mind to its objects which would be wholly adequate in respect of the capacities of that mind." But, the mind cannot possibly be conceived as capable, on its own, of knowing itself as thus adequately informed. MacIntyre thus regards "the Absolute Knowledge of the Hegelian system" as a chimaera.[122] In the course of systematizing and ordering the truths they regard themselves as having discovered, the adherents of a tradition may accord certain truths the status of *first principles* (metaphysical or practical). But these principles will then have to vindicate themselves, so to speak, in the historical process of dialectical justification. They will survive or get dethroned in a process of rational justification which is both dialectical and historical. They may in due time be regarded as both necessary and evident, but even if they do become so regarded, "such first principles are not self-sufficient, self-justifying epistemological first principles."[123] In sum, the test for truth and the criteria for adequacy of the test are historical, and develop within the particular tradition.

Section II: Tradition in Christian Theology

1.3 Transition from an Anthropological to a Theological Perspective

We are now in a position to draw some provisional, largely inter-related, conclusions to make a transition to Christian tradition and to help clarify our own hermeneutical orientation. We

---

[122] *Whose Justice?*, 360-61.
[123] *Whose Justice?*, 360.

recall that our aim in this chapter is first of all to establish that tradition is a necessary component or source of Christian theology. Once that is established, attention may then be rendered to related hermeneutical issues. The preliminary groundwork in the previous section offers some pre-theological insights into the anthropological reality of tradition, useful for a theological interpretation of the Christian tradition. These insights may now be integrated with more explicitly Christian thoughts and conveniently organized under four headings.

1.3.1 Particularity and Rationality

Our survey yields a resounding affirmation of *particularity*. The question for us is how, theologically, the particularity of the Christian tradition ought to be appreciated in relation to the world.

In the case of Gadamer, his concept of theological hermeneutics acknowledges some, albeit minimal, legitimacy in the distinction drawn by Bultmann between [i] an *existentiell* reality, i.e., that an experience of the act of God as a personal event in one's own life is mediated by faith, and [ii] an *existential* reality, i.e., that a reflective interpretation of the basic terms of the Christian faith does not depend on explicit faith. In other words, Bultmann claims that while an 'authentic' human understanding on an *existentiell* level is properly Christian and an interpreter of Holy Scriptures knows that one is forgiven only through faith in Jesus Christ, an appreciation of the claim of the Christian kerygma can be had, and its basic categories of faith *can* be examined as possibilities of human existence, by nonbelievers.[124] Bultmann's distinction critically points

---

[124] See, especially, Rudolf Bultmann, "Is Exegesis Without Presuppositions Possible?" in *Existence and Faith*, ed. Schubert Ogden (Cleveland: World Publishing, 1960), 289-306; idem, "The Problem of Hermeneutics," in *Essays Philosophical and Theological* (London: SCM, 1955), 234-69.

up the difference between *being religious* and *conducting reflection upon religion*. But, while Gadamer accepts that there are "general conditions" that govern all forms of interpretation, he is insistent that particular requirements apply to specific kinds of understanding. Hence, he is critical of Bultmann's attempt to move biblical interpretation out of the circle of Christian faith. In this respect, two points are particularly germane.

In the first place, faith, in Gadamer's view, is not a human person's own achievement "but a gracious act of God that happens *to* the [person]."[125] Authentic human existence is closely linked, he argues, to the impact of divine grace as a necessary aid to overcome the failure of human understanding. In the last analysis, an admission of a transcendent intervention must call into question any scientific methodology's claim to universality. Theologically, we cannot ignore a crucial factor that lies *beyond* merely human self-understanding: an adequate understanding is mediated not by philosophy but by the Christian gospel which proclaims an event that, ultimately, transcends human understanding. Gadamer thus dismisses as inadequate an interpreter's *preunderstanding* in biblical hermeneutics which is defined exclusively in terms of a philosophical analysis of the question of the meaning of life. Ultimately, his argument hinges on the claim that revelation carries with it an authority which gives theological hermeneutics its particular character. This authority is best understood in light of the recognition, in a properly *theological* hermeneutics, that the Christian message has absolute authority over those who proclaim it. The ongoing *application* of scriptural meaning cannot be regarded as adding anything to the texts which are interpreted: indeed, a

---

[125] Gadamer, *Philosophical Hermeneutics*, 53-54. He affirms the Christian conviction that "man cannot reach an understanding of himself by his own means" [p. 206].

unique experience mediated by grace and by the interpreter's participation in Christian tradition is posited by Gadamer as the condition for the possibility of authentic understanding.[126] He thus portrays the Christian interpreter's *preunderstanding* as one shaped by her/his experience of the power and authority of the gospel in the life of the Christian community. Bultmann's insistence on the existential foreunderstanding can only be, Gadamer concludes, *Christian*-specific.[127]

In the second place, since Christian preunderstanding comes not only from common existential experience, but from the shared experience of a believing community, Gadamer emphasizes the tradition in which an interpreter is located and to which one belongs. This at once ties the problem of theological hermeneutics with his concept of effective-history. The horizon of past Christian communities and the texts they produced now come before the interpreter of today. The linkage is maintained by a continuity in language and experience. There is, as it were, a fabric of meanings afforded by tradition that constitutes the faith community and moulds the interpreter. In the light of Gadamer's "effective-historical" interpretation which involves a moment of application, an interpretation of the Christian tradition may be regarded as authentic only if it is properly grounded in a Christian tradition of experience.[128] This bonding to tradition is operative, Gadamer claims, on the prereflective, rather than the reflective, level.

---

[126] In this respect, even the paradigmatic legal hermeneutics falls short, for "the gospel of salvation does not acquire any new content from its proclamation in preaching such as could be compared with the power of the judge's verdict to supplement the law" [*Truth and Method*, 295ff].

[127] *Truth and Method*, 296. "The hermeneutical significance of fore-understanding in theology seems itself theological."

[128] Thomas B. Ommen locates the "central risk" of Gadamer's approach in its inadvertent undermining of "the claim of the Christian gospel itself to provide a decisive illumination of the meaning of human existence." See idem,

With MacIntyre, one could justifiably argue that just as it is only from within the confines of a particular tradition that the criteria for moral judgments are best appreciated, it is only from within the parish walls, so to speak, of the Christian faith community that one can best grasp the meaning of its beliefs and practices. Just as rationality is best understood in light of where it is embedded within a local tradition or narrative, the Christian tradition is best approached from a tradition-specific, intra-ecclesial perspective. On this score, Ratzinger's articulation is incisive. "Tradition," he points out, "always presumes a bearer of tradition, that is, a community that preserves and communicates it, that is the vessel of a comprehensive common tradition and that becomes, by the oneness of the historical context in which it exists, the bearer of concrete memory." His thesis is understandably emphatic: "The Church is tradition, the concrete situs of the *traditio* of Jesus."[129] This, as we shall see, will have a significant impact on theological authorship.

In our response to the contemporary cultural and intellectual situation, in which a concern with the past appears suspect, Gadamer and MacIntyre uncover for us certain aspects of the anthropological reality of tradition at the level of society in general. They supplement the works of Christian theologians[130] who are keenly aware of the human phenomenon of tradition, its connection with history, its cohesive function between successive generations, and

"Bultmann and Gadamer: The Role of Faith in Theological Hermeneutics," *Thought* 59 (1984) 356. For a more detailed critique of the model of faith-determined hermeneutics, see Ommen, "The Preunderstanding of the Theologian," in *Theology and Discovery: Essays in Honor of Karl Rahner*, ed. W. Kelly (Milwaukee: Marquette University Press, 1980), 231-61.

[129] Joseph Cardinal Ratzinger, *Principles of Catholic Theology* (San Francisco: Ignatius, 1987), 100.

[130] Thoughtful summaries of major authors' understanding of tradition may be found in Johnstone, "Faithful Action;" Avery Dulles, "Tradition and Cre-

its role in securing "a society's continuity, identity and unity."[131]
The social reality of the past comes to us not as a disinterested
object of study from afar, but as something with which we are
constantly and inevitably engaged in every facet of thought,
understanding and life, not least the ethical and religious life. The
self is always already placed by and within a tradition not of one's
making, but which offers possibilities as well as limitations to
what the self can do and be. A Christian's individual identity does
not begin *de novo*, but is always, as MacIntyre and Ratzinger
would have it, shaped by a Christian communal tradition.

And yet, both Gadamer and MacIntyre avoid a radical relativism which would have us uncritically sunk in the particularity
of our own tradition. In relation to the age-old debate on "faith
and reason," for instance, they suggest that these are not mutually
exclusive. The traditional Catholic understanding regards faith as
neither above nor beyond reason, even though it depends for its
origin and existence upon the grace of God.[132] A key to MacIntyre's project is his characterisation of the basic error of modern
liberal conviction as the view that rationality requires detachment.

ativity in Theology," *First Things* 27 (Nov. 1992) 20-27; idem, "Tradition as a
Theological Source," in *The Craft of Theology: From Symbol to System* (New
York: Crossroad, 1992), 87-104.

[131] See O'Collins, *Fundamental Theology*, 192-94; J. Fichtner, "Tradition (In
Theology)," in *New Catholic Encyclopedia* (New York: McGraw Hill, 1989),
18:668; Josef Rupert Geiselmann, *The Meaning of Tradition*, trs. W. J. O'Hara
(London: Burns & Oates, 1966), 81.

[132] In his encyclical, *Fides et Ratio*, Pope John Paul II teaches that the content
of revelation ought "never debase the discoveries and legitimate autonomy of
reason." And yet, while the capacity on the part of reason to question must never
be curtailed, reasons must also be questioned by tradition. The relationship
between faith and reason "is best construed as a circle," by which he means that
"theology's source and starting point must always be the word of God revealed
in history, while its final goal will be an understanding of that word which
increases with each passing generation." *Origins* 28 (1998) 337.

Gadamer, too, calls into question modernity's prejudice against tradition and its presumption that commitment is incompatible with objectivity. Faith, it is suggested, implies total commitment, whilst reason requires a certain detachment. In this line of reasoning, total commitment and rational detachment are regarded as contradictions in terms. Our survey thus far yields a different vision, one which combines rationality with commitment in what MacIntyre calls a "tradition-constituted and tradition-constitutive enquiry."[133]

A religious tradition rooted in a particular history and a particular set of events *can* justify itself as rational. For, critical thinking depends for its condition of possibility on a background of assumptions and presuppositions that inhere in tradition, without suggesting that these assumptions and presuppositions are beyond questioning altogether. This conclusion is counterpoised against the dominant negative conception of reason in Enlightenment, as well as in the modern quest for emancipatory autonomy in various spheres of life, not least the religious life, that authority is diametrically opposed to reason.[134] While the role and authority of tradition feature prominently in the works of both Gadamer and MacIntyre, it is in the latter that the conception of rationality being tradition-bound finds special focus and extensive treatment. This will be useful when we study the question of Christian truth-claims.

---

[133] On relating MacIntyre to the faith-and-reason debate, see Ian Markham, "World Perspectives and Arguments: Disagreements about Disagreements," *HeyJ* 30 (1989) 1-12; idem, "Faith and Reason: Reflections on MacIntyre's 'Tradition-Constituted Enquiry,'" in *Critical Perspectives on Christian Education*, ed. J. Astley and L. J. Francis (Leomister: Gracewing, 1994), 484-93.

[134] Thus Gadamer notes, authority "is ultimately based not on the subjection and abdication of reason, but on an act of acknowledgement and knowledge – the knowledge namely, that the other is superior to oneself in judgement and insight and that for this reason his judgement takes precedence – i.e., priority over one's own" [*Truth and Method*, 297].

Of special concern to us is whether the universality of Christian truth-claims can ever be brought together with the particularity of the Christian tradition. If "particularity is all we have," as MacIntyre and the postmodernists, in opposition to the post-Enlightenment suspicion of particularity, are said to suggest, does it not turn every universal into an idolisation of particularity?[135] Does not an affirmative response to the question suggest, to borrow an image from Richard Neuhaus,[136] that the public square is empty, in the sense that there is no standpoint which is not, after all, silenced by its own limitations of tradition and context? And yet, MacIntyre does not in the least suggest a radical absence of "privileged or universal discourse which pertains in the interstices between distinct contexts."[137] This is clear from his extensive exposition of critical dialogue *between* traditions. In sum, the rationality inherent in a particular tradition offers a gateway to public conversations. In the case of Christian theology, there is the added element of the universality of the christological message that characterizes the Christian tradition, which makes it publicly relevant.

This analysis helps prepare the stage for our dialogue with Lindbeck and postliberal religious epistemology. Lindbeck's commitment to particularity is the defining feature of his theological project. Modernity is interpreted by Lindbeck as insisting that in order to say something is true, one must first obtain a non-partisan, universal, ahistorical standpoint from which to speak. Postliberal theology defines itself squarely against this liberal

---

[135] This way of presenting the issue is made by Alister McFadyen, "Truth as Mission: The Christian Claim to Universal Truth in a Pluralist Public World," *SJT* 46 (1993) 440.

[136] Richard J. Neuhaus, *The Naked Public Square* (Grand Rapids: Eerdmans, 1984).

[137] For a suggestion that it does, see McFadyen, "Truth as Mission," 441. On this score, our survey suggests that McFadyen may have overstated MacIntyre's position.

understanding. Lindbeck calls us to plumb the particularity of our own religious tradition and look at the world through the "lens" of our received tradition. His attention is trained on the integrity of the faith rather than the universality of its transmission and intelligibility. Faith, for him, has culture-forming power precisely on account of its distinctive particularity.[138] His treatment of certain regnant theological models at variance with his own will constitute the bulk of this study from the next chapter on.

1.3.2 The Dialectical Revelation of Truth

Christian tradition is in a 'dialectical situation' in modern culture. The term 'dialectical' denotes a situation of tension: on one hand, Christian tradition needs to be 'relevant' without becoming 'trivial' or being reduced to a rubber stamp for liberalism; on the other hand, it needs to be challenging and demanding of commitment without becoming 'isolationist?'[139] It is 'dialectical' in that each position Christianity adopts involves apparent contradictions, a situation she tries to get out of only to face a new set of contradictions. Concretely, if the Church decides to insist on the purity of her message, she risks becoming isolated. But if she decides to overcome this tension by adopting the position of rendering her message in terms and ways understandable to moderns, she risks

---

[138] Thus assessed by Walter Kasper, "Postmodern Dogmatics: Toward a Renewed Discussion of Foundations in North America," *Communio* 17 (1990) 185.

[139] Paul Lauritzen, "Is Narrative Really a Panacea?" JR 67 (1987) 322-39 underscores this dialectical challenge as he reviews the work of Hauerwas and Metz, particularly their attention to 'narrative' as a way out. This might also explain Lindbeck's option for the cultural-linguistic model of religion. Jeffrey Stout, *Flight from Authority* (Notre Dame: University of Notre Dame Press, 1981), esp. Part II, addresses this dialectical situation.

losing the distinctiveness of her message. She is, as it were, always caught on the two horns of a dilemma: whatever side she takes, she meets a seeming dialectical impasse.

Truth, in this dialectical situation in which Christian tradition finds itself, is not static, but is dialectically revealed. The term *dialectic*, in its common philosophical usage, is often associated with Plato and Hegel. In Plato, dialectic simply means conversation or dialogues by which he sought to lead his listeners to the true essence of things through the gradual clarification of concepts. Central to this process is the conviction that the truth of a statement is only revealed in the encounter of the statement and its contradiction. Hegel developed this idea further and applied it to the whole of reality. Reality, according to him, is essentially becoming, and moves from stage to stage in the triple pace of thesis-antithesis-synthesis. Our thinking proceeds the same way. It is not a static 'plucking' of the truth. It is a struggle to overcome a contradiction (antithesis), which gives rise to a richer understanding (synthesis). And because this process does not stop, but is continuously reconstituted into a thesis-antithesis-synthesis dialectic, it denies any static conception of truth. It is, in fact, in this sense that one can refer to the entire spectrum of logic as dialectics (as Plato did) — to mean the rules and forms of human thinking as such. Dialectics, then, is identical with formal logic.[140] What must be borne in mind, however, is that this dialectical process is founded on oppositions – oppositions which may surface both *within* and *between* traditions. Here, Gadamer and MacIntyre's analyses yield useful pointers.

Granted that we are embedded in a particular tradition whose communal text we accept as authoritative, still, Gadamer insists,

---

[140] The art of dialectics, Gadamer writes, "requires that one does not try to out-argue the other person, but that one really considers the weight of the other's opinion" [*Truth and Method*, 330].

truth is found through a merging of horizons in the dialectical conversation with the past. His fusion of horizons challenges all static
visions of Christian tradition and truth.[141] In this respect, he offers
an understanding that carries two essential elements. On the one
hand, the present fusion of horizons shows that we are not ensnared
in our own Christian linguistic tradition for, behind the differences
of traditions and cultures, there lies the basic fact of linguisticality
that provides the condition of possibility for translation, conversation and communication. On the other hand, we never leave behind
our own Christian linguistic starting point in our "hermeneutic travels." In sum, while conversation cannot depend on an absolute
viewpoint in which contingency is dissolved, the fact that we stand
within a stream of effective history nevertheless suggests that there
is always the possibility to understand, and to be understood from,
other contexts. Precisely at this juncture, commentators have
pressed home a pertinent point crucial for theological reflections.
They hold that Gadamer places undue weight on the presumption of
an existing consensus supplied by effective history. In doing so, he
has not adequately accounted for the often tortuous ways of forging
consensus or even carrying on a conversation. This criticism
applies not only where a shared tradition does not exist, but even

[141] Thomas B. Ommen, "Theology and the Fusion of Horizons," *Ph&Th* 3
(1988) 62. Our words never completely "manifest the incalculable vastness of
the reality they attempt to express," Paul Crowley notes, thus leaving a surplus
of meaning in each new expression of understanding. There is an inescapable
tension between every finite historical interpretation and the infinitude of truth
towards which the language of interpretation aspires. Hence, "hermeneutical
experience is 'dialectical' because the event of understanding itself involves a
back-and-forth relationship between the horizon of the hermeneutical subject
who questions and the horizon of the tradition that is questioned in and through
a traditionary object of understanding, for example, the Bible or the Nicene
Creed." See Crowley, *In Ten Thousand Places: Dogma in a Pluralistic Church*
(New York: Crossroad, 1997), 108-09.

within a tradition where an element of ideology is factious and con-tentious. When horizons amongst different interest-groups within the Christian tradition differ, more than Gadamer's conversation and understanding are required to settle disagreements. A dialecti-cal struggle must be posited through which we can come to a deeper understanding of our own form of life as well as uncover our own prejudices. Commentators thus surface the point that hermeneutics must include an element of *reflection* and *critique* in order to secure an adequate fusion of horizons.[142] Tracy, for instance, employs Ricoeur's understanding of hermeneutics as a corrective to Gadamer.[143] Tradition is not merely appropriated as a result of conversation or understanding, but by means of a dialectic of understanding, explanation and new understanding. The use of diverse explanatory methods may produce a pluralism of readings of the sources from the past; but, pluralism is not necessarily a bar-rier to truth and may in fact generate corrective interpretations of tradition.

In theology, the idea of Christians being "authorised," on account of revelation, to speak of God, is often fraught with risk, if only because historically, this "authority" has been put to deeply corrupt use. "Theology," Rowan Williams reminds us, "is perennially liable to be seduced by the prospect of bypassing the question of how it *learns* its own language." He alerts us to the tendency in theologies of different shades to operate with "a model of truth as something ultimately separable in our minds from the dialectical process of its historical reflection and appropriation." Where this happens in any theology, whether east or west, Catholic or Protestant, conservative or liberal, what it manifests is "an impatience with debate, conflict,

---

[142] Ommen, "Theology and Foundationalism," *SR* 16 (1987) 169-70; idem, "Theology and the Fusion of Horizons," 66.
[143] David Tracy, *The Analogical Imagination* (New York: Crossroad, 1981).

ambivalence, polysemy, paradox. And this is at heart an impatience with learning, and with learning about learning."[144]

MacIntyre leads our discussion a step further. For him, the presence of other traditions in turn enables the members of a particular tradition to understand themselves as being part of a living tradition. That a tradition is particular and community-based, does not imply that it is closed to the rest of the world, and, in that sense, does not render it incommensurable. This will be of relevance when we deal with the incommensurability thesis and charges of relativism and fideism in any theological outlook. For the moment, we note that the survival of a tradition, or its conversion to a new tradition, through epistemological crises, testifies to its potential to learn from a tradition alien to itself. There, dialogue with other traditions is posited as a genuine possibility, and the 'translatability' of concepts is an operative supposition. With Gadamer, Christian theologians should not seek to free themselves from the past, but rather begin where they are and seek, in dialogue, to expand their horizons.[145] With MacIntyre, fidelity to its own essence, coupled with a readiness to reconstitute its particular narrative, is the key to the survival of every historical heritage, the Christian heritage included, as it negotiates its way through pluralistic surroundings.

An added attraction in MacIntyre's commitment to a particular tradition is its implicit advocacy of tolerance. A crucial twofold observation may be made at this point which touches our entire study. In its *prescriptive* task, Christian theology may legitimately commend commitment to the particularity of the Christian tradition and yet be open to intra-tradition, ecumenical and inter-religious dialogues. The basic error, as MacIntyre points out, is the

---

[144] Rowan Williams, "Trinity and Revelation," *ModTh* 2 (1986) 197-98.

[145] William C. Placher, "Revisionist and Postliberal Theologies and the Public Character of Theology," *Thomist* 49 (1985) 410 n.40.

modern liberal conviction that rationality requires detachment or
that commitment is incompatible with objectivity. In its *descriptive* task, Christian theology would correctly attend to the function
of its tradition within its tradition-specific historical and cultural
framework. To be sure, the Christian tradition, like any other tradition, avoids repudiation and remains worthy of rational assent as
long as it can find within itself resources to meet questions arising
from new situations with sufficient inventiveness to allow the
reformulation and re-reading of its authoritative texts and beliefs.
On MacIntyre's terms, however, a description would be inadequate if it omits the reality of encounter and change inherent in the
'enquiry' that goes on *within* the Christian tradition, and if the
description denies the legitimacy of engagement and dialogue. In
relation to other religions, rationality requires that Christians dialogue with different traditions; it demands and legitimates the
learning of a 'second first language'. While commitment to a tradition is largely justified by *internal explanations* for disagreement, one must concede the possibility that one's tradition could
be confronted by epistemological crisis and that a different tradition might have resources that could contribute to our making better sense of the world. This is a point of crucial directional import
for, as we shall see, the postliberal theology advocated by Lindbeck tends to espouse the descriptive task as the only task proper
to an authentic Christian theological enterprise. What must not be
lost sight of is the fact that what the Christian tradition embodies
is the narrative of an argument. It is through an eventful narrative
that its unity and continuity is preserved in the context of an
unavoidable conflict of interpretations.

Among other things, this discussion points to the fact that
Christian theology cannot do away with the notion of revelation (a
notion to which we shall return). Theology will always involve a
systematic reflection on revelation and different conceptions of

revelation necessarily issue in different methods of theological reflection. The biblical world of revelation no doubt has normative claims on all Christians. But the Christian challenge consists precisely in risking a true encounter with God — who is revealed in the biblical narrative — if one dare embark on a dialectical truth-hunt. To be sure, what is 'revealed' is never a pure 'truth' as such. For that reason, one may even advance the argument better if one chooses, in place of the notion of truth as "dialectically revealed," the expressions "dialectically constituted" or "dialectically constructed." For what takes place in the dialectic is the coming together of two privileged dialogue-partners — the Christian tradition and an interpreter — both laden with already extant views of truth. Whatever the choice, one may accept the point that insofar as it is a committed dialectical search for truth, a moment of dialectical construction is never final. The process continues. Hence, one speaks of a hermeneutical spiral.[146]

1.3.3 Tradition and Creativity

Christian tradition, like any other living tradition, envisages growth and creativity. Christianity claims truth although its tradition undergoes continual reappropriation as a condition for its continued life. As a living tradition, the Christian tradition balances permanence with change in ever-new expressions. New expressions entail the notions of development of, and creativity within, tradition. A study of Christian tradition will profit from an integration of the two notions of growth and creativity.

First, our temporality suggests a developmental grasp of truths, rather than a once-and-for-all fixed perception. Our doctrinal tradition

---

[146] Jacques Haers, "A Risk Observed." *LS* 21 (1996) 60. We shall not enter into a discussion of Protestant dialectical theology. For a brief survey, see Henri Bouillard, "Dialectical Theology," in *Sacramentum Mundi*, II:75-78.

represents but "a narrow strip of infinity."[147] Rahner upholds Chalcedon as a good first word but not the last word; it is not the end but the beginning.[148] In theology, with Newman, the idea of development became an inner dimension of the tradition. The question is, what is the appropriate horizon of understanding against which a criticism of tradition, or a suggestion for development, may be judged admissible? Gadamer engenders a vision of the tradition itself functioning as the horizon guiding authentic development. There is growth and development only on satisfying the proviso that these are linked to the source that is transmitted to us, much like "a loan" which we would do well to distinguish from "learning." Learning involves an initial reception of an existing 'wisdom' which the diligent learner may in turn seek to prove, correct, and enrich. Valid though one's procedures may be, the eventual learning must not be confused with the tradition which was received in the first place.[149]

Christian tradition has been established on the basis of the Christ-event, a historical event that has been accorded a permanent significance in the faith community. It does not seem unreasonable to insist that the norm of a possible criticism, or development, of Christian tradition must be a 'return to the source', for, it is *this* source which contains the "expression of what was originally experienced, done and meant," and constitutes the touchstone of the Christian faith.[150] Accordingly, a position is manifestly

---

[147] Frederick E. Crowe, "Dogma Versus the Self-Correcting Process of Learning," in *Foundations of Theology*, ed. Philip McShane (Dublin: Gill & Macmillan, 1971), 29.

[148] Karl Rahner, "Current Problems in Christology," in *Theological Investigations*, I:149-200. John Morris, "Chalcedon and Contemporary Christology," *Angelicum* 74 (1998) 42-43 urges the recognition of doctrinal statements as not only normative, but also non-exhaustive.

[149] See Johnstone, "Faithful Action," 293.

[150] Karl-Heinz Weger, "Tradition," in *Sacramentum Mundi*, ed. K. Rahner et al. (New York: Herder & Herder, 1968), 269.

unsound which espouses that everything traditional can be revised at will and recast in an entirely new mould. Clearly, it is one thing to develop a better formulation of the Christian faith; it is quite another to discard the core of the Christian faith as handed down in its tradition, and still claim the work to be authentically Christian. The latter case may be regarded as unacceptable in the fashion of a defaulting loanee who seeks to wipe the slate clean through insisting unilaterally that the loan does not exist.[151]

Next, there is the question of creativity within tradition. Christian tradition, in this understanding, is not static. A static view evokes the idea of something 'fixed' so that, even with qualification, it seems there is something of the Christian tradition understood as 'deposit' that may not be redeemed. Christian tradition is certainly not the sole depository of truth. But where the language of 'deposit' is used, it must be wedded to and supplemented by an image of dynamism. This latter image is more in keeping with the idea of a dialectical search for truth. The historical progress of the Christian tradition suggests that it works itself out in the vicissitudes of history. And this is consistent with creativity. The very condition of a tradition as a living tradition, MacIntyre reminds us, is its ability to sustain a 'creative' tension. Christian theology is not wrong to ask whether the Church is able to form a people willing to combine fidelity to its tradition with the questioning of that tradition. MacIntyre underscores the point that it is only by participation in the dialectical discipline – examining, testing, refining and developing over time – of a particular tradition that adherents are able to advance their understanding of a given subject matter.[152] Gadamer's hermeneutics also offers an interesting reflection

---

[151] As Dulles suggests, "to be in a position to criticize, a person must first of all have appropriated the tradition of the Church." See idem, "Handing on the Faith Through Witness and Symbol," *LL* 27 (1991) 299.

[152] See Achtemeir, "The Truth of Tradition," 357.

on this point. There is, for Gadamer, a creative interplay between the interpreter and the text, which allows for both the 'subjective' and 'objective' element in the constitution of meaning.

At the theological level, the issue is, according to Avery Dulles, "whether faithful mediation of the past redemptive act leaves room for, requires, or even perhaps enhances human activity, and, conversely, whether human creativity contributes to the mediation of the past event."[153] Dulles' views may be summarised in six points. [1] There is a growing consensus among theologians that, "to let the past live, one must grasp its spirit and adapt its forms." [2] Tradition expresses itself primarily in life and action (the "tacit") and only secondarily in explicit statements.[154] [3] Authentic expressions of the life of faith communicate a community-faith. [4] Expressions can be creative because the revelation borne by the tradition is transcendent and open to an infinite variety of possible linguistic and cultural embodiments. [5] But the crucial proviso to any creative extension to the tradition, is its dependence on the same tradition as the "matrix" within which the extension is proposed. [6] The novelty of Christianity subsists in the dimension of its aspiration beyond all time to the eschatological future.[155]

[153] Dulles, "Tradition and Creativity," 20.

[154] Dulles is deeply influenced by Maurice Blondel for whom tradition may be transmitted orally, in writing and by praxis. The stability of tradition hinges not on verbal or conceptual conformity with past statements, but in "a *living synthesis*," so that the most important vehicle for its transmission is *faithful action*. Blondel's action-oriented notion of tradition precludes any exclusive consideration of tradition as discursive thought. His argument is that the essence of what is being transmitted is not just a doctrine or a received teaching, else "it would be only a poor substitute for written texts." As a lived reality, tradition is beyond any exhaustive rational analysis. See Maurice Blondel, *History and Dogma*, trs. Illtyd Trethowan (London: Harville, 1964), 215, 267 & 367.

[155] Dulles, "Tradition and Creativity," 21-24. Dulles draws from the works of a number of authors, amongst which is Jürgen Moltmann's *The Theology of Hope*, trs. James W. Leitch (London: SCM, 1967), esp. 302.

1.3.4 Two Hermeneutical Consequences

In relation to the Christian tradition, a few consequences follow from our acknowledging [i] a compatibility between particularity and rationality, [ii] a dialectical revelation of truth, and [iii] creativity as part of the dynamics of the living tradition. Two of these consequences may be noted in anticipation of discussions in later chapters.

1.3.4.1 Authority and Authorship

First, underlying both Gadamer and MacIntyre's analyses is a resounding recognition of the *authority* of tradition. The past has cognitive value for us, and exerts a degree of authority on us, only insofar as we freely, or at least tacitly, accept that it bears wisdom useful for application in the situation of today. Furthermore, both Gadamer and MacIntyre point to the fact that accepting the authority of tradition is a necessary condition for a genuine realisation of human freedom. Our dialogue with the past would then manifest a twofold human freedom: [a] freedom from a subjective bias against the past, as a condition of possibility for reception of genuine wisdom from the past; [b] freedom from a static understanding of the past, as a condition of possibility for new horizon of understanding.[156] In both instances, a healthy respect for the past[157] is the gateway to the future, for the horizon of understanding resident in a tra-

---

[156] For theological discussions on human freedom and human social life in relation to the anthropological reality of tradition, see, for example, Weger, "Tradition," 269-74; Louis Janssens, "Personalist Morals," *LS* 3 (1970) 5-16; idem, "Artificial Insemination: Ethical Considerations," *LS* 8 (1980) 3-29; O'Collins, *Fundamental Theology*, 192-95.

[157] "Tradition is only democracy extended through time," G. K. Chesterton once wrote. "Tradition may be defined as an extension of the franchise. Tradition means giving votes to the most obscure of all classes, our ancestors. It is the

dition is dependent for its continued life on a constant recalling of that tradition, as well as an on-going process of interpretation.[158] The relevance of both Gadamer and MacIntyre for theological discourse is at once apparent, for a characteristic proper to all religions lies in its special need to maintain continuity with the formulations and practices of its past.[159] There is, then, to a large degree, a continuity between the nature and function of the human reality of tradition and the nature and function of the reality of the Christian tradition. At the same time, we are enjoined not to commit the error of falsely assuming that the Christian tradition "simply conformed to the clear and typical trajectory of tradition in 'ordinary' human affairs."[160]

A work that exhibits sensitivity to all this, is James Gustafson's *Treasure in Earthen Vessels*,[161] in which he makes a study of the Church understood as a *community* of followers of Jesus Christ. Examining, first of all, the social and historical consistency (or

democracy of the dead." See idem, *Orthodoxy: The Romance of Faith* (New York: Doubleday, 1959), 47-48.

[158] For a description of such an interpretation as "authentic encounter," see Frans Josef van Beeck, "Tradition and Interpretation," *Bijdragen* 51 (1990) 259, 271. But it is an encounter only if the interpreter is open to the risk of being changed thereby. See Jacques Haers, "A Risk Observed," *LS* 21 (1996) 46-60. It is recognized in theology that a "complete hermeneutic, calls for a 'mediation' or 'fusion' of the past into a living tradition [, and] not simply a recourse to the past of a text and its meaning." See J. Fichtner, "Tradition (In Theology)," 18:668. The significance of the interpreter's horizon will be relevant when we discuss George Lindbeck's intratextual theology.

[159] Robert Bellah, in *Habits of the Heart* (New York: Harper & Row, 1985), notes that communities, in a sense, are constituted by their past. In order not to forget that past, a community must be involved in retelling its story, its constitutive narrative. In so doing, it holds up examples of the men and women who have embodied and exemplified the meaning of the community. These stories of collective history and exemplary individuals are an important part of the tradition which is central to any community.

[160] O'Collins, *Fundamental Theology*, 192-94.

[161] J. M. Gustafson, *Treasure in Earthen Vessels: The Church as a Human Community* (New York: Harper & Row, 1961).

"unity" and "continuity") of life in the Church within a nondoc-
trinal framework, he establishes that, common with other human
communities, the Church has its "natural" processes and its
"political" dimension as well. Relying solely on social science
and philosophy, he is able to account for the unity and consistency
of the Church, without recourse to doctrinal categories such as
"the presence of Christ," or "the work of the Holy Spirit."[162] This
socio-philosophical approach serves as a critique of every theological reduction of complex human affairs, and urges the incorporation of non-doctrinal categories into theological discourse.
However, social science and philosophy alone do not fully explain
the *meaning* of Christian life,[163] so that "a sociological oversimplification is as inadequate as a theological one." Relating social
interpretation to theological interpretation of the Church is
absolutely essential if we are to engage in a fruitful study of the
Church as a *community of language* that continuously interprets its
memory of the Christ-event, and provides understanding for its
beliefs, as well as engenders its appropriate praxis. In the course
of Gustafson's arguments, one thesis stands out: *The Church, or
any of its denominations, would put its distinctive social identity in
jeopardy, if it became callous about its continuity with its past.*[164]
The implication is that Christians must value their tradition, and,

---

[162] *Treasure in Earthen Vessels*, ix-x.

[163] The principal aspect of human living, Bernard Lonergan diagnoses, is constituted by meaning. See Bernard Lonergan, *Method in Theology* (London: Darton, Longman & Todd, 1971), 138-40. But, unlike in other domains of human
living, Christians locate meaning in their faith in a historical narrative that essentially reverts back "through their history and tradition to a definitive and *absolute
point of reference*, an unsurpassable climax in the first century of our era." See
O'Collins, *Fundamental Theology*, 97.

[164] See Gustafson, *Treasure in Earthen Vessels*, esp. 42-85. The thesis stated
here is our reformulation, with indebtedness to De Schrijver, who adds: "An
organised religion cannot survive if it fails to keep alive its 'common memory' by
means of rituals, religious customs, catechetics, liturgical and moral preaching,

additionally, that they must regard it as something distinct from ordinary human traditions and, by extension, other religious traditions as well. This difference will be investigated in Section II.

Having first recognized the authority of Christian tradition, we must move one step further in our hermeneutical endeavour and ask about Christian authorship – the legitimacy of individual creativity within theology.[165] The very nature of active interpretation and appropriation suggests that mere repetition of the past is impossible. Just as there is no construction of worldviews *de novo*, so also there can be no seamless interpretation or translation of them into a new idiom that somehow encodes the same essence. A hermeneutics of tradition must espouse a historicist principle that integrates both givenness and agency. This may be done in a manner that does not set authority and authorship against one another but posits them in their intimate interconnection. Of relevance in this regard is Lindbeck's claim, which we shall examine, that Christian faithfulness entails adhering to "the same directives" that were involved in the creation of a tradition's founding narratives.[166]

prayers, etc." See his "Hermeneutics and Tradition," 42. This is a basic truth internal to every religion, and not just a phenomenon which a sociologist might describe.

[165] Careful not to allow the usurpation of tradition's authority by theological authorship, Lindbeck, as we shall see, regards narrative intratextuality, and not authorial talent, as the proper medium of historicity and change for speaking the language of faith in the present. Particularly useful for our discussions are the works of John E. Thiel, such as "Theological Authorship: Postmodern Alternatives?," *HeyJ* 30 (1989) 32-50; *Imagination and Authority: Theological Authorship in the Modern Tradition* (Minneapolis: Fortress, 1991).

[166] ND, 81. In chapter 5, we shall examine Lindbeck's attempt to reconceptualize ecclesiastical doctrines and their claim to authority. Van Beeck maintains that *ad extra*, the Church is duty-bound to "foster an empathetic, questioning interest in the modern world and its concerns" and that, *ad intra*, the Church requires "the constant and creative exercise of *a hermeneutic of doctrine*" in order to disengage the "deepest intentions" of past authoritative formulas from "dated judgments"

Informed by Gadamer and MacIntyre, our hermeneutical approach posits that the same dialectic that characterizes the dialectical revelation of truth prevails in the reading of the Christian communal text, primarily the Scriptures.[167] It is only by accepting and respecting the text as being vested with an independent authority, that one enters into genuine dialogue. But the interpreter also approaches the text as oneself an 'authority,' understood in the sense of an independent reader who has a history and a set of presuppositions or prejudices. It is in this encounter that reading-as-real-dialogue takes place between reader and text. The emergence of truth is dependent on the holding of two poles in tensile balance, the objective pole of tradition in which one is embedded and the subjective pole of the hermeneutical adventure. In this understanding, the principle of agency may be highlighted in a double sense: the *divine* agency and the *human* agency.[168]

and to convey the essence of Christian faith to every new age. See idem, *Catholic Identity after Vatican II* (Chicago: Loyola University Press, 1985), 87. Bearing these and other considerations in mind, Mark Heim offers interesting reflections on how Lindbeck's insights on doctrine might relate to the development of Asian theology. See "The Nature of Doctrine and the Development of Asian Theology," *Bangalore Theological Forum* 19 (1987) 14-31.

[167] Biblical study, ultimately, is interpretation, a process involving a dialectic between explanation and understanding, and culminating in bridging a distance that enriches rather than imprisons the text. See Paul Ricoeur, "Explanation and Understanding," in *The Philosophy of Paul Ricoeur: An Anthology of His Work*, ed. C. E. Reagan and D. Stewart (Boston: Beacon, 1978), 149-66. On dialectic, see further, Gadamer, *Reason in the Age of Science* (Cambridge: MIT, 1981), 45-50; Paul Ricoeur, "What Is Dialectical?" in *Freedom and Morality*, ed. John Bricke (Lawrence: University Press of Kansas, 1976), 173-89. David J. Bryant, "Christian Identity and Historical Change: Postliberals and Historicity," *JR* 73 (1993) 33 suggests that there ought to be a "dialectical interplay between framework and experience," a recognition which will be crucial when we critique Lindbeck's basic structure of religion as grammar in chapter four.

[168] In *Boundaries of Human Habitation* (Albany: State University of New York Press, 1994), Delwin Brown identifies a few principles in the widespread historicism which shapes the present age. The first of these is the *principle of his-*

Without denigrating the normativity of the past, attention to the dynamics of tradition may thus entail our speaking of truth-emergence in the future tense, by which we seek to capture the inevitable presence of the past in the present that is dialectically struggling *towards* a disclosure.[169] The dynamics of this process is partly captured by Gadamer's theory of linguisticality and effective history. This dialectical revelation of truth is crucial for understanding the dynamic reality of tradition. Just as a 'pure' tradition is a chimera, so too is a 'pure intratextuality' when it comes to the Christian Bible.[170] A unilateral intratextual reading would not adequately describe the dynamics in truth-disclosure and the complementarity between authority and authorship.

When theologians affirm Scripture as normative for theology, David Kelsey observes, they are declaring their commitment to the Christian faith while at the same time affirming that Scripture has certain properties, especially as "authority" for the common

torical particularity: we live within particular cultural processes that determine both the limitations and potentialities of specific historicized existence. There is also the *principle of agency*: though created, we are also agents who impact on our surroundings and bring into being new forms of human and natural existence. We are hence *both* constituted and creative, conditioned by the past and our environments and dynamically interacting with them as constructive agents of the present and the future. Brown defines tradition as "a continuously reformed and formative milieu, a dynamic stream of forces in which we live (or die), move (or stagnate), gain (or lose) our being" [p. 4].

[169] David Linge explains that, for Gadamer, "like Heidegger's notion of being, tradition is not a thing existing somehow behind its disclosure….[T]radition is precisely its happening, its continuing self-manifestations, much as Heidegger defines being as eventful, i.e., as disclosive rather than substantive." See "Editor's Introduction," in *Philosophical Hermeneutics*, liv.

[170] Werner Jeanrond thus locates a major problem in Lindbeck's work, which we shall examine, to lie in its "ecclesiological proposals which are developed on the basis of 'pure narrativity' while risking the neglect of the truth question." See idem, "Community and Authority," in *On Being the Church*, ed. Colin Gunton and Daniel Hardy (Edinburgh: T & T Clark, 1989), 101.

life of the Christian community.[171] The expression "Scripture is authoritative for theology" is thus a self-involving statement that says something about the religious faith and experience of the speaker. Contemporary understanding and the experience of theologians do not themselves generate Christian faith wholly dissociated from retrieval of the Christian narrative from Scripture and Tradition. But, as Kelsey observes, shaping one's life by this particular narrative also depends on being able to give reasons why this narrative offers plausible answers to life's ultimate questions. This narrative is amenable to rational enquiry and assessment, as distinct, of course, from rationalistic proof. In particular, it affords the believers a "seriously imaginable" vision of the right way to live within the context of the wider culture.[172] Thus, an important element to be included in theological hermeneutics is the experience which every theologian brings to the hermeneutical task. Our dialogue with Lindbeck will assume a point of departure that upholds the validity of a "continuous dialectical exchange" between the world of the Bible and our contemporary world.[173] Also, given our affirmation of an active role on the part of the human agent in the dialectics of truth-revelation, we shall avoid an essentialist understanding of culture which assumes that culture is one, given and constant and, like an Aristotelian essence, does not change.

[171] Communal authority is a key issue in the work of Lindbeck who characteristically places the interpretation of Scripture at the centre of the current crisis in shaping ecclesial thought and practice. For him, communal authority can only depend on consonance with the Bible. See his "Scripture, Consensus, and Community."

[172] See David H. Kelsey, *The Uses of Scripture in Recent Theology* (Philadelphia: Fortress, 1975), 89, 109, 170-75.

[173] B. A. Gerrish, "The Nature of Doctrine," *JR* 68 (1988) 92. In assessing the claims of a distinctive Christian ethics, which traditionally focuses on the four classical sources of Scripture, tradition, reason and experience, David

A further consequence of admitting authorship as complementary to authority is that theologians who forge out of the diverse
elements of the past new possibilities for the present, will naturally offer a plurality of theologies. In this connection, Wolfhart
Pannenberg addresses two hermeneutical questions raised by historical consciousness: [a] the strangeness of the scriptural worldviews to modern believers, and [b] the plurality of frequently competing interpretations of Scripture and doctrine which characterise
the Christian history. On the first problem, Pannenberg turns to
Gadamer and underscores the difference between the historical
horizon of the text and that of the interpreter. The interpretive act
exhibits the radically historical nature of human existence and
understanding.[174] On the second problem, recourse is made to
Gadamer's insight that the act of interpretation *applies* the claim
of the text from the past to the new historical context of the interpreter. This bringing to language, which effectively modifies both
the horizons of the text and that of the interpreter, is a creative act
on the part of each interpreter. This, for Pannenberg, essentially
accounts for the reality in which, hermeneutically, there necessarily exists a plurality in the interpretations of Christianity's Scripture-in-Tradition.[175] Hence, while some theologians, like Lindbeck
and the postliberals, are content to focus singularly on the inner

Hollenbach reverts to fundamental theology. He finds that these sources, far from
being independent variables in the theological equation, mutually, if partially,
condition and critique each other. In view of this interplay between the sources
that come from the past (Scripture and tradition) and those that we exercise in the
present (reason and experience), the proper approach to them is one of critical
correlation rather than an "either-or" choice. See David Hollenbach, "Fundamental Theology and the Christian Moral Life," in *Faithful Witness*, ed. Leo J.
O'Donovan and T. Howland Sanks (New York: Crossroad, 1989), 167-84.

[174] Wolfhart Pannenberg, *Basic Questions in Theology*, trs. G. H. Kehm (London: SCM, 1970), 1:115-17.

[175] Pannenberg, *Basic Questions in Theology*, 1:117.

dynamics of Scripture-in-Tradition, others may be attracted to the possibility and the potential for dialogue with other traditions. These latter theologians may acknowledge that no single thought or value system is fully adequate on its own, but that all can benefit from the experience and insight of others both as correctives and resources.[176] The Christian task cannot be simply to recover the biblical narrative within the Church. Besides the problematic nature of much of the biblical message, the salvific nature of this message cannot be communicated apart from engagement with the concrete issues of the day. We shall thus be asking whether we do not forfeit the authority of the Christian message if we fail to take the message to the public arena or if we trivialize or evade aspects of the human.

1.3.4.2 Extra-Textual Intrusions

Second, Christian tradition, conceived of in MacIntyre's term as a narrative of an argument, must not be regarded as so authoritative that it is untouchable. In this respect, Gadamer and MacIntyre offer two particularly useful pointers for addressing materials that seem extraneous to a supposedly 'pure' tradition.

---

[176] See, e.g., Sheila G. Davaney, "Between the One and the Many: A Response to Delwin Brown's Theory of Tradition," *AJTP* 18 (1997) 145. Arguing that faith is not a closed system, Frans Josef van Beeck emphasizes "the freedom afforded by the faith's open structures." He thus regards a diversity of "theological traditions, schools, and systems, interpreting the great Tradition in various perspectival fashions" as being healthy and "integral to systematic theology's catholicity." If Lindbeck's *The Nature of Doctrine* "suggests that complete doctrinal consensus is a practical impossibility, this reinforces that positive need for pluriformity as integral to true ecumenical catholicity in doctrine and, *a fortiori*, in theology." See van Beeck, *God Encountered* (San Francisco: Harper & Row, 1989), I:76-77. David Tracy sees diverse situational causes as inevitably giving rise to a conflict of interpretations. Each theologian is bound to find "some elective affinity between some questions and responses in the situation

We begin with MacIntyre's refusal to hunker down to a narrow parochialism even though he insists on the rationality of starting with a particular tradition. This yields a point of significance in that, since MacIntyre retains a notion of rationality operative not only within but also *between* the boundaries of traditions, one can legitimately question those theologies that attack all Enlightenment-inspired liberal approaches, on how they can justify a total rejection of external or 'secular' reason.[177] In aid of the interpretation of the Christian message, Roman Catholic theology has a long tradition of appreciating the role of philosophy in providing foundations for the theological task. In this context, according to some interesting metaphors adopted by authors, theologians may rightly debate the validity of theology using the "spoils from Egypt," or whether "Jerusalem" *can* learn from "Athens."[178]

and some interpretation of the questions and responses of the Christian tradition and hence to the Christ event." See idem, *The Analogical Imagination: Christian Theology and the Culture of Pluralism* (New York: Crossroad, 1981), 372. Reflections on the "pluralistic and ambiguous nature of tradition" has also led Werner Jeanrond to suggest that the Church needs to undertake a continuous assessment of its doctrinal symbols and criteria of ecclesial authenticity. See idem, *Theological Hermeneutics*, 180. Karl Rahner finds a place for a legitimate pluralism in theology. See "Pluralism in Theology and the Unity of the Creed in the Church," in *Theological Investigations*, trs. David Bourke (London: Darton, Longman & Todd, 1974), 11:3-23. He argues against a closed system of Catholic theology proposed by defenders who limit the task of theologians to the mere defense and explicitation of fixed, absolutized propositions. See "Reflections on Methodology in Theology," in ibid., 68-114.

[177] John Reader, *Beyond All Reason* (Cardiff: Aureus, 1997), 85 & 88.

[178] See, e.g., Dan R. Stiver, "Much Ado about Athens and Jerusalem: The Implications of Postmodernism for Faith," *Rev&Exp* 91 (1994) 83-102; Thomas Guarino, "'Spoils from Egypt': Contemporary Theology and Nonfoundationalist Thought," *LTP* 51 (1995) 573-87; Gordon D. Kaufman, "Is There Any Way from Athens to Jerusalem?," *JR* 59 (1979) 340-46; Fred Lawrence, "Athens and Jerusalem: The Contemporary Problematic of Faith and Reason," *Gregorianum* 80 (1999) 223-44; Andrew F. Walls, "Old Athens and New Jerusalem: Some

Next, when theological hermeneutics moves away from insisting upon an inviolable intratextual "purity" and attends to the *role of the reader* in the interpretive task, this hermeneutics will also accord attention to the context and the experience the reader brings to bear.

In exposing the reality of conflicts in interpretations, and the need for the continuous reinterpretation of tradition in every new situation, Gadamer and MacIntyre offer an initial framework for approaching the Christian tradition. We can see the fecundity of this framework operating in two respects. *At the level of individuals*, the past is always part of the present and opens to the future in the form of stories which one appropriates through socialisation into the believing community that is shaped by that story. The continuity of the Christian tradition is thus largely achieved by narrative, in the common practice of constantly reinterpreting and retelling its story. If that is the case, the four major authors whom we have identified – Gadamer, Habermas, Ricoeur and MacIntyre – alert us to the need to be attentive to the active contribution of the individual members of the faith community who interpret the Christian beliefs and symbols, including the Creeds and the Scriptures. Since a Christian finds herself placed in an existing tradition, she finds that tradition as having already been interpreted by others. And since traditions by their very nature undergo change and metamorphosis, she cannot assume the posture of an "ideal spectator" who enjoys, in a detached fashion, a free sample of an unencumbered "original position" or "founding story." Rather, she is reminded of, among other things, a distance separating a text and its reader, a hegemony of ideologies inherent in every story, and a dialectical reader-response before a fusion of horizons

Signposts for Christian Scholarship in the Early History of Mission Studies," *IBMR* 21 (1997) 146-53.

obtains in any interpretation. Of relevance to our later discussions is whether the scriptural canon can be reduced to a singular, unchanging depth grammar that Christians need to be faithful to in every new historical moment and setting. Furthermore, a Christian tradition, like any living tradition posited as a "historically extended, socially embodied argument," suggests rival interpretations and creative tensions as its permanent features. It is a false dichotomy to insist on respect *either* for the authority of tradition *or* for the liberal creativity of the individual; creativity is a necessary component of a living Christian Tradition.[179]

At the communal level, interpretation may be seen as the constant adjustment that is necessarily undertaken by a community in order to stay in continuity with tradition. If a "pure" tradition is a chimera, any claims of a self-sufficient "deposit of faith" or a pure intratextual self-validation may be challenged. Further, we see that the history of the Christian tradition is indubitably characterised by bitter internal conflicts of interpretations over beliefs and practices. The Christian Tradition truly embodies MacIntyre's sense of a "narrative of an argument." Constantly threatened with the prospect of being put asunder, the Christian tradition tells a story of

---

[179] In this connection, it is interesting to note that MacIntyre has enumerated "four sources of systematic unpredictability in human affairs" [*After Virtue*, 89]. *First*, we cannot predict radical conceptual innovations, for we cannot invent the innovation. Thus, we cannot predict the future of science, social, moral or religious innovations. *Second*, an observer, hamstrung by his inability to predict his future action before he has made up his mind, can no more predict the impact of his future action on others than he can predict the reaction of those others. *Third*, in relation to game-theory approaches, there is an "indefinite reflexivity of game-theoretic situations" [*After Virtue*, 92], an imperfect knowledge of the situations because players tend to maximize other players' lack of information, the fact that several games are played simultaneously, and we seldom begin with fixed sets of players and well-defined areas for playing the game. *Fourth*, human life is subject to the vagaries and vicissitudes of contingency. See generally, *After Virtue*, 71-102.

growth through changes and incorporation of new insights, some of which may even seem revolutionary.[180] On the other hand, with all these changes through time, the question may legitimately be posed: What, if any, is the constant element that gives the Christian tradition its specific identity? What is it that has authority for, and commands the respect of, all Christians? What is that element, constitutive of the corner-stone of the Christian tradition, that ultimately guides every theological project in its free use of that tradition as a source? This is the issue we must address.

Given the fact of diverse denominations, the aim of this Section II is first to establish the normativity of tradition, and of its text, at the institutional level, for Christian theology. The fact of diversity demands, as a priority, that the degree of ecumenical convergence on this issue be first addressed. After that, we can seek to identify the essential "difference" in Christian tradition which distinguishes it from others. We shall examine the question of truth in tradition, and, relatedly, how that truth is dialectically revealed and lived in the life of the Church, and reconciled with growth and creativity.

1.4 The Normative Significance of Tradition and Scripture in Christian Theology

1.4.1 The Primary Theological Sense of the Term Tradition

The word *tradition* comes from the Latin *traditio* which corresponds to the Greek *paradosis*. In the first place, it admits of two possible meanings: the *process* of transmission, that is to say, "the transmission in the church, of beliefs, doctrines, rituals, and entities such as the scriptures;"[181] or, the *object* of transmisson, "that

---

[180] See Charles Davis, *Religion and the Making of Society* (Cambridge: University Press, 1994), 109-10.

which has been 'handed over' or 'passed on'."[182] In the second place, when we turn to the New Testament, we observe that although the noun *paradosis* and the verb *paradidomi* are both used in different senses, it is very evident that, from the outset, the Christian churches were concerned with the faithful transmission of tradition. Thus, while Paul rejects merely human traditions (Gal. 1:14; Col. 2:8), he also speaks of divine or apostolic tradition to which Christians are exhorted to hold fast. For example, he refers to his instructions to the community at Thessalonica by word of mouth or by letter (2 Thes. 2:15), to the rules of conduct meant for all the members of the community to live by (2 Thes. 3:6), to the eucharistic institution narrative (1 Cor. 11:23-26) and to the tradition of the appearances of the risen Christ which represents an early summary of the entire Gospel in the form of primitive credal formulae (1 Cor. 15:3-4). What epitomises Paul's sentiment is the crucial allusion to tradition as something he treasures as of "first importance" (1 Cor.15:3) — "I received (*parelabon*)... I delivered (*paredoka*)" (1 Cor. 11:23; 15:3).[183] From

---

[181] See George H. Tavard, "Tradition," in *The New Dictionary of Theology*, ed. Joseph A. Komonchak et al. (Dublin: Gill and Macmillan, 1987), 1037.

[182] See Thomas P. Raush, *The Roots of the Catholic Tradition* (Wilmington: Michael Glazier, 1988), 14.

[183] See Raymond F. Collins, *Introduction to the New Testament* (London: SCM, 1987), 11-12, where he says: "Paul's use of the technical rabbinic language shows that both he and the churches to which he addressed himself were concerned with the faithful transmission of the traditions about Jesus." That which the Church preaches and believes, from the Apostolic Age to the present time, is that "Jesus Christ is Lord" (see Rom. 10:9; Ph. 2:11; 1 Cor. 12:3; Acts 17:7). This profession of faith which manifests both a fundamental ascription of lordship to Jesus and a radical allegiance to him, carries with it a transcendental guarantee: the origin is God himself; it is embodied in Christ; and it is communicated by the Holy Spirit. Thus, Yves Congar writes in "Norms of Allegiance and Identity in the History of the Church," *Concilium* 3/9 (1973) 12: "The principle or norm of allegiance, or faithfulness, is the 'rule of truth' or 'rule of faith'. This is not a formal norm in regard to faith itself, but the very substance of that

there, what emerges is a primary theological sense of tradition which fundamentally refers to *the community's shared experience of their Lord through faith*.[184] The history of the early inception of the Christian tradition demands a "strong" reading of the prerequisites for community. It cannot be over-emphasized that a particularistic christology decisively affects the very structure, the content and the process of transmission of this tradition. It was an explicitly Christian community that had to struggle with the Jewish tradition which it inherited and which eventually broke with Judaism. Similarly, explicitly Christian communities were necessary to form a kind of contrast-society to the patterns which existed in the larger social context. In all this, the *memory* of the Crucified and Risen One was crucial for holding the faith community together and for ensuring the integrity of its tradition.

  The theological key to a communal perception of Christian tradition is inseparably linked with revelation, and may be succinctly postulated as follows: "In the history of Israel and then definitively in the life, death and resurrection of Jesus Christ, the saving revelation of God took place."[185] That is the very substance of the norm which the first apostles handed down. It began with the *foundational encounter* which the initial small group of disciples had with Jesus whom they experienced as the Christ,[186] and whom

faith: *that which* the apostles handed down, having received it from Jesus Christ, and the Church has handed down after them, in so far as it is normative for belief."

[184] Raush, *The Roots of the Catholic Tradition*, 14-15.

[185] O'Collins, *Fundamental Theology*, 195. The *Catechism of the Catholic Church*, 638 states: "The Resurrection of Jesus is the crowning truth of our faith in Christ, a faith believed and lived as the central truth by the first Christian community; handed on as fundamental by Tradition, established by the documents of the New Testament; and preached as an essential part of the Paschal mystery along with the cross." See also Acts 13:32-33.

[186] Geiselmann examines the nature of paradosis in light of Jude 3 and 2 Peter 2:20, both of which indicate that the knowledge of our salvation in Jesus Christ

successive generations of Christians continue to encounter in Scripture and in the learning, the practice and the living of their faith.

However, this primary theological sense does not prevent ascription of different contents to the term *tradition*. In fact, in theological discourse, the word *tradition* is "notoriously fluid."[187] This fluidity has attracted concerted attention from Protestants and Catholics alike. A brief examination of their respective positions, to see if there is theological convergence, and, if so, to what degree and in which respects, is imperative.

1.4.2 The Ecumenical Convergence on the Term Tradition

In 1963, the World Council of Churches (of which the Roman Catholic Church has never been a member) held its Faith and Order Conference in Montreal. The Conference later released a report entitled "Scripture, Tradition and Traditions"[188] which would go on to have profound influence on ecumenical discussions of tradition and Scripture.[189] The Montreal Conference noted

---

is conveyed to us by paradosis. "It has its source in the testimony of the Twelve, and the content of their paradosis is their witness to Jesus' sufferings, death and resurrection as saving events." See idem, *The Meaning of Tradition*, 9.

[187] See Schneiders, *The Revelatory Text*, 71. For a thorough study of the historical and theological development of tradition up to the eve of Vatican II, see Yves Congar, *Tradition and Traditions: An Historical and A Theological Essay*, trs. M. Naseby and T. Rainborough (New York: Macmillan, 1967). For a contemporary treatment of the implications of various positions on tradition, see *Perspectives on Scripture and Tradition*, ed. Joseph E. Kelly (Notre Dame, IN: Fides, 1976).

[188] The report is reproduced in *Documentary History of Faith and Order, 1963-1993*, ed. Günther Gassmann, (Geneva: WCC, 1993), 10-18.

[189] For two excellent studies in this area, see George H. Tavard, "The Ecumenical Search for Tradition: Thirty Years After the Montreal Statement," *JES* 30 (1993) 315-30; Avery Dulles, *The Craft of Theology*, 87-104.

the significance of tradition as follows: "The very fact that Tradition precedes the Scriptures points to the significance of tradition."[190] The best-known recommendations of its report pertain to the different meanings of the word *tradition*: " We speak of the *Tradition* (with a capital T), *tradition* (with a small t) and *traditions*. By the *Tradition* is meant the Gospel itself, transmitted from generation to generation in and by the Church, Christ himself present in the life of the Church. By *tradition* is meant the traditionary process. The term *traditions* is used in two senses, to indicate both the diversity of forms of expression and also what we call confessional traditions."[191]

In the same year, 1963, in the context of the Consultation on Church Union (COCU) at Oberlin, Ohio, a report was adopted on "Scripture, Tradition, and the Guardians of Tradition," which affirmed the existence of a "historic Christian Tradition," to which "each of our churches inevitably appeals... in matters of faith and doctrine," though it still lacks "clearer delineation and characterization."[192]

In the Roman Catholic Church, the emphasis on tradition is well known. In his opening address at the first session of Vatican II, Pope John XXIII implicitly posited a twofold distinction of

---

[190] See Montreal Report, No.42, in Gassmann, *Documentary History of Faith and Order*, 11. In Dulles' view, Montreal has shown "a disposition on the part of Protestants as well as Orthodox to assert the primacy and indispensability of tradition as against a '*sola scriptura*' principle." See idem, "Scripture: Recent Protestant and Catholic Views," *ThT* 37 (1980) 16. See also Joseph Ratzinger, "Dogmatic Constitution on Divine Revelation, Chapters I-II," in *Commentary on the Documents of Vatican II*, ed. Herbert Vorgrimler (New York: Herder & Herder, 1969), III:170-98.

[191] Montreal Report, No.39. For a brief commentary on the distinctions sharpened by Montreal, see Yves Congar, *Diversity and Communion* (London: SCM, 1988), 134-36.

[192] *COCU: The Reports of the Four Meetings* (Cincinnati, OH: Forward Movement Publications, 1965), 24.

tradition when he stated the following: "The substance of the doctrine of the Deposit of faith is one thing, and the way in which it is presented is another."[193] Vatican II's *Dogmatic Constitution on Divine Revelation (Dei Verbum)*, refers to divine revelation itself as the singular source, which the Church transmits orally and in written form. The aim in couching "tradition" in the singular was to capture a generic notion as an integral factor of the Church's life.[194] Locating its starting point for reflection in the event of divine revelation, *Dei Verbum* introduces the understanding of tradition as the "transmission of divine revelation," through preaching the Gospel, practising an exemplary way of life, establishing institutions, and committing the message of salvation to writing.[195] *Dei Verbum* is primarily concerned with tradition "as an organ of apprehension and transmission rather than as a set of precepts."[196] This is manifest in a passage which, while it describes tradition functionally, also stresses the importance of its content: "Tradition transmits in its entirety the Word of God which has been entrusted to the apostles by Christ the Lord and the Holy Spirit."[197] Hence, while Avery Dulles is certainly correct in seeing tradition (primarily) designated in *Dei Verbum* as "the mode in which the Church perpetuates its faith and its very existence,"[198] it is equally clear that the term tradition is used in the text to represent content as well. This is clear when the importance of tradition in the life of the Church is stressed: "What was handed on by the apostles comprises everything that serves to make the People of God live their lives in

---

[193] See "Pope John's Opening Speech to the Council," in *The Documents of Vatican II*, ed. Walter M. Abbot (New York: America, 1966), 715.

[194] See *Dei Verbum*, 8 and Tarvard, "Ecumenical Search for Tradition," 317.

[195] See *Dei Verbum*, 7.

[196] See Dulles, *The Craft of Theology*, 94.

[197] *Dei Verbum*, 9.

[198] See Dulles, *The Craft of Theology*, 94.

holiness and increase their faith. In this way the Church, in her doctrine, life and worship, perpetuates and transmits to every generation all that she herself is, all that she believes."[199]

Finally, in the Anglican-Roman Catholic dialogue, the 1975 ARC-USA Statement on the Ordination of Women made reference to "what may be called an essential Tradition which, as witnessed in the Scriptures, the ecumenical creeds, the church's liturgical tradition, and its proclamation and teaching, constitutes the basic identity of the Christian community." This essential Tradition (with a capital T) is described as having been "variously elaborated and interpreted in dogma and doctrinal tradition."

While, in view of the foregoing, we can clearly conclude to an ecumenical convergence on Christian Tradition as an essential category, we have yet to clarify the *content* of that convergence. To begin with, both the Montreal Report and *Dei Verbum* revert to the divine self-revelation of God as their basic theological underpinning. In the former, the testimony of prophets and apostles is described as having inaugurated "the Tradition of his revelation." In the latter, it is only after the teaching on God's self-revelation has been clearly stated that the theme of tradition is taken up.[200] By means of its three-fold typology of tradition, the Montreal Report seeks to present a holistic coverage of the *entire living Christian heritage*, so that *the Tradition* (with a capital T) refers to "the Gospel itself" as the "object" of the traditionary process, "transmitted from generation to generation in and by the Church."

---

[199] See *Dei Verbum*, 8.

[200] See the Montreal Report, 42, in Gassmann, *Documentary History*, 10-11 and *Dei Verbum*, 2-6. With revelation understood as "primarily a personal dialogue or encounter rather than the communication of truths," this common anchorage in revelation has the advantage of circumventing polemical debates on how much revealed truths does Scripture or tradition contain. See O'Collins, *Fundamental Theology*, 204-05.

Dei Verbum, too, as we saw, speaks of *that* which was handed down by the apostles as comprising *everything* "that serves to make the people of God live their lives in holiness and increase their faith."[201] But, viewed holistically, this content of a living faith discloses a trinitarian[202] structure as well. In sum: "What is transmitted in the process of tradition is the Christian faith, not only as a sum of tenets, but as a living reality transmitted through the operation of the *Holy Spirit*. We can speak of the Christian Tradition (with a capital T), whose content is *God's* revelation and self-giving in *Christ*, present in the life of the Church."[203]

Such an understanding of tradition is incomplete, however, if it posits a radical distinction between content and process. The term *paradosis,* as we saw earlier, connotes both data and mode. A definition that neglects to clarify their mutual integration is flawed. George Tavard makes apposite observations on the impracticality of the Montreal typology. He notes that far from being a "gimmick," the Montreal typology reflected a theological conception. The reason why that typology is not widely used, he suggests, is to be found in its "doctrinal content." In his view, the doctrinal principle regarding the connection between the first term *Tradition* (i.e., the transmitted gospel, which is ultimately "Christ himself in the life of the Church") and the second term *tradition* (i.e., the process of its transmission), "parallels the familiar distinction

---

[201] See the Montreal Report, No.39, in Gassmann, *Documentary History,* 10; *Dei Verbum*, 8.

[202] One specific element in Christian Tradition is its emphasis on worshipping a God "who has chosen to make himself known in and through Christ." When, therefore, Christians refer to the Holy Trinity, they speak about a specific God, with Jesus Christ as an indispensable referent. See Alister E. McGrath, "The Christian Church's Response to Pluralism," *JETS* 35 (1992) 488.

[203] The Montreal Report, No.46, in Gassmann, *Documentary History*, 11.

in nineteenth-century Roman Catholic theology between passive and active tradition. The former is identical with the data that are transmitted; the latter is the process of their transmission." To support his claim that a clear distinction between data and process is flawed, Tavard argues with the aid of the Great Commission in Mt. 28:19. There, Scripture suggests that the transmission of the gospel is integral to the gospel itself, for the heart of the gospel implies transmission. Tavard is emphatic in claiming that: "A church that would preach the gospel and one that would preserve it as a datum or deposit but would not preach it would not only be different churches; they would not, in fact, profess the same gospel."[204] From here onwards, we shall use the term *Tradition* (with a capital T) in its holistic and integrative sense.[205]

We can justifiably conclude that Tradition is an essential category for Christian theology. This Tradition, in its holistic sense, integrates both content and transmission, and encompasses the life and the text of the Christian community in which Christ is rendered present. The preeminent *text* of the Christian community is the Scripture. In many ways, the problem of the relationship between Tradition and Scripture has remained the most obstinate throughout Christian history. It was at its most acute during the Protestant Reformation of the sixteenth century. In our holistic and integrative understanding of Tradition, the issue at stake is, primarily, the role to be credited to Scripture and Tradition in

[204] Tavard, "The Ecumenical Search for Tradition," esp. 322-25. There is support from the exegetes that, in the New Testament, the terms *gospel* and *word of God* are not confined to designating a message. "Rather, it is a process in which the messenger and his activity, as well as the result of his proclamation — viz., the faith of the believers — are integral parts." See O. A. Piper, "Gospel (Message)," in *IDB* 2:446.

[205] Other denotations will be qualified by adjectives or explanatory remarks, or otherwise evident in the context in which they are used, especially in quotations.

"transmitting and actualizing" the foundational experience of the divine self-communication.[206] A related issue is, of course, the question of the hermeneutical principle to be employed for discerning what is genuine in Tradition.

The diversity of confessions that characterize Christianity also yields, as the Montreal Report explicitly acknowledges, a diversity of hermeneutical keys for disclosing the truths in Scripture, of disciplinary and doctrinal commitments, and of forms of ecclesial authority. As we shall see, Lindbeck and his postliberal colleagues who champion the nonfoundational approach to theology, though ecumenical in their outlook, have developed their arguments from very visibly Protestant confessional perspectives.

1.4.3 The Relationship between Scripture and Tradition

Ever since the Reformation, the Protestant position has insisted on Holy Scripture alone as "the infallible and sufficient authority in all matters pertaining to salvation, to which all human traditions should be subjected." Historical study and ecumenical encounter

---

[206] See O'Collins, *Fundamental Theology*, 195. We shall not rehearse the historical background and development of this problem. One of the best studies remains the work by the French Dominican Yves Congar, namely, *Tradition and Traditions* (London: Burns and Oates, 1966). Gabriel Moran has also surveyed the controversy in *Scripture and Tradition: A Survey of the Controversy* (New York: Herder and Herder, 1963). For a more recent study, see O'Collins, *Fundamental Theology*, 208-24. For remarks from Catholic authors who stress the importance of *traditio*, see David Tracy, *Blessed Rage for Order* (New York: Seabury, 1975), 84 n.30; Schneiders, *The Revelatory Text*, 78; Fichtner, "Tradition (In Theology)," 14:228; Juan Luis Segundo, *The Liberation of Dogma*, trs. P. Berryman (Maryknoll, NY: Orbis, 1992), 203. For a Protestant response to the Catholic understanding of tradition, see Thomas N. Finger, *Christian Theology: An Eschatological Approach* (Scottdale, PA: Herald, 1985), I:236-43. See also Wolfhart Pannenberg, *Systematic Theology*, trs. G. W. Bromiley (Grand Rapids, MN: Eerdmans, 1991), I:28-29.

have contributed to the growth of an awareness that "the proclamation of the Gospel is always inevitably historically conditioned." This is evidenced in an important declaration in the Montreal Report: "The very fact that Tradition precedes Scriptures
points to the significance of tradition."[207] We might say that the
Reformation principle of *sola scriptura* is qualified by the awareness that Scripture is part of Tradition and, to use a recurring
theme in MacIntyre's writings, *embedded* in Tradition. Theologically, David Tracy formulates the principle as "Scripture in tradition." In that formulation, the emphasis is neither on the old
Roman Catholic "Two-Source Theory" of 'Scripture and tradition', nor the Reformation's *sola scriptura*.[208] Scripture becomes a
part of the living Tradition insofar as it is rightly interpreted in
every new setting. Still, the significance of Scripture is stressed in
the Montreal Report, as in the statement that "the Tradition of the
Gospel [is] testified in Scripture." Conversely, there has been a
clear renewal of biblical authority on the Roman Catholic side
since Vatican II.[209] Thus, *Dei Verbum* refers to "the Gospel," "the
message of salvation" of "Christ the Lord, in whom the entire
Revelation of the most high God is summed up," having, "under
the inspiration of the Holy Spirit," been committed to writing.[210]

---

[207] Montreal Report, No.42, in Gassmann, *Documentary History of Faith and Order*, 11.

[208] Tracy believes this notion of 'Scripture in tradition' to be "the most fruitful theological one for assessing the central role of Scripture for Christian theology as the plain *ecclesial* sense." Tracy proposes possible plural readings of the
plain sense. See idem, "On Reading the Scriptures Theologically," in *Theology
and Dialogue: Essays in Conversation with George Lindbeck*, ed. Bruce D. Marshall (Notre Dame, IN: University of Notre Dame Press, 1990), 37-38.

[209] See John R. Donahue, "Scripture: A Roman Catholic Perspective,"
Rev&Exp 79 (1982), 231-33, where he gives a sketch of the eclipse of authority
and prestige of the Bible within Catholicism during the period between the Council of Trent and Vatican Council II.

[210] See *Dei Verbum*, 7.

In this formulation, Scripture objectifies or expresses revelation, but always upon the understanding that behind Scripture stands an earlier expression in the apostolic preaching and, prior to that, in the message of Jesus himself. Tradition, then, was prior in time. At the same time, *Dei Verbum* also presents Scripture as more than a mere witness to, or objectification of, Tradition, when it states: "In the sacred books the Father who is in heaven comes lovingly to meet his children, and talks with them." As the Word of God, Scripture is the locus "where God continues to speak to those whom he summons to answer in faith." Tradition is never described as the Word of God. In this sense, Scripture takes precedence over Tradition, for the Church is always summoned to hear the Word of God in faith.[211] In this sense, the Church is the creature of the Word. Yet in the order of human experience, the Church was prior. It might be said that, in the order of being (*ordo essendi*), the Gospel comes before the Church, but in the order of knowledge (*ordo cognoscendi*), the Church is prior.[212]

Admittedly, while affirming the special position of the written Word of God, Vatican II also insists on the indispensability of Tradition. This tension in *Dei Verbum* is accentuated in the Council's insistence that "the Church does not draw her certainty about all revealed truths from the holy Scriptures alone." In this sense,

---

[211] See Donahue, "Scripture: A Roman Catholic Perspective," 235-36. This view resonates with Karl Rahner's assertions: "Nonetheless, everything in the later utterances of faith must be measured by Scripture (*sola scriptura*) since it is in Scripture that the one whole apostolic faith has been objectivated and has given itself, and laid down for all future times, its *norma non normata*." See Karl Rahner, "Scripture and Tradition," in *Sacramentum Mundi*, ed. Karl Rahner et al. (New York: Herder & Herder, 1970), VI:56. See also Gregory Baum, "The Bible as Norm," *Ecumenist* 9 (1971) 71-77.

[212] Carl E. Braaten, "The Problem of Authority in the Church," in *The Catholicity of the Reformation*, ed. C. E. Braaten and Robert W. Jensen (Grand Rapids: Eerdmans, 1996), 55.

Tradition is not an independent source[213] of revelation, but a *crite-rion* by means of which the authenticity of an interpretation of revelation is tested. Tradition and Scripture are likened to a mir-ror, bound closely together, and constituting a *single* sacred deposit.[214] Dulles captures the dynamic at work in Vatican II when he observes that *Dei Verbum*: [1] insists that it is not from Scrip-ture alone that the Church draws its certitude about everything that has been revealed; [2] in asserting the "formal insufficiency" of Scripture, leaves open the question of its "material sufficiency;" [3] no where explicitly describes Scripture as a norm for validat-ing Tradition, although implicitly it does suggest that nothing con-trary to the Word of God in Scripture could claim to be an authen-tic part of the Tradition.[215] That, however, does not represent the entire dynamic at work in Vatican II, where an ecumenical open-ness was evident. Thus, when it deals with "Sacred Scripture in the Life of the Church" in chapter VI, *Dei Verbum* presents the Church as standing *under* Scripture, venerating it and nourished by it. It insists that Scriptures should "firmly strengthen" and "constantly rejuvenate" theology and the life of the Church.[216]

---

[213] The issue at Vatican II was no longer the question of Tradition as an inde-pendent source. In fact, the Council altogether avoided using the word source (*fons* in Latin) for either Scripture or Tradition. See Donahue, "Scripture," 236.

[214] See *Dei Verbum*, 7, 9 & 10.

[215] See Dulles, *The Craft of Theology*, 97.

[216] See *Dei Verbum*, 21 & 24. The *Catechism of the Catholic Church* often teaches that the Bible provides the most important message which Catholic faith hears. The leadership or magisterium of the Church 'is not superior to the Word of God, but is its servant" [*CCC*, 86]. Thus Lindbeck, a Lutheran observer at Vatican II, argues that Christian communal authority depends on consonance with the Bible. "There is agreement on this among all the major traditions despite their differences on the interrelations of Bible, tradition, and magisterium. The primacy of Scripture is fundamental for the patristic tradition the Orthodox follow, the *sola scriptura* for the Reformers, and, on the Roman Catholic side, servant role of the magisterium in reference to Scripture was clearly asserted in

The crux of the problem, at one level, has to do with the currently diverse hermeneutical principles for ascertaining what is
genuine within the Tradition. Significantly, the Montreal Report
finds that, whatever the key, none of the diverse denominational
principles of interpretation relies on an authority which is
"thought to be alien to the central concept of Holy Scripture."[217]
If we accept a holistic and integrative perception of Tradition,
Scripture and the tradition of Scriptural interpretation would only
form a part of a larger whole. It would seem that it is "neither fea-
sible nor possible" to rely on Scriptures as the sole criterion for
sorting out what the Montreal Report calls the "distorted" or
"impoverished" traditions from the genuine Tradition.[218]

This brief discussion on the relationship between Tradition and
Scripture discloses three points. *First*, there is the ecumenical convergence regarding Scripture as the indispensable text-source for
any Christian theology. *Second*, Scripture is not co-extensive with
Tradition as a source for theology. *Third*, diverse claims of authority behind different hermeneutical keys may be relativised by
grounding them all in the *common reference to the central concept
of the Scripture-in-Tradition*.

Various issues, though they are only ancillary to our main
theme in this chapter, often impinge upon discussions of the
Christian Tradition. Some of these issues will recur in the rest of
this study. Three of these may be briefly examined.

Dei Verbum at Vatican II. Although less explicitly, Vatican II because although
it did not explicitly reject a two-source interpretation of Trent's statements on
Scripture and tradition, it nevertheless favours a one-source construal — so that,
here too, primacy is accorded to the interpretive rather than independent authority of tradition." See idem, "Scripture, Consensus, and Community," 90-91.

[217] See the Montreal Report, No.53, in Gassmann, *Documentary History*, 12-13.

[218] See O'Collins, *Fundamental Theology*, 207; the Montreal Report, No.48,
in Gassmann, *Documentary History*, 12.

1.4.4 Three Ancillary Hermeneutical Issues

1.4.4.1 The Authority of the Foundational Stage of the Tradition

That Christianity invests its ancient foundation with authority is commonplace. Christians accord due weight to what Tracy rightly affirms, namely, that the "original and normative responses to the Christ event are those expressions of the earliest communities codified in the texts named the New Testament." This means that there is scriptural warrant for the most fundamental truth in the Christian faith, the Christ-event-person. The original testimonies have become, in Tracy's words, "not just more texts, more expressions, but *Scripture*" (emphasis added).[219] What is less obvious, however, is how that authority is conceived and what weight it carries in relation to the foundational stage of Christianity.

Hannah Arendt's analysis of the ancient inception of authority throws light on our understanding of what constitutes authority. Noting that "authority has vanished from the modern world" because "we can no longer fall back upon authentic and undisputable experience common to all," she takes us back to what authority *was* rather than what it *is*.[220] The very word and concept of 'authority' are Roman in origin. The Romans understand the "sacredness of foundation" as the proper key to authority: once something has been *founded*, it remains binding for future generations. This is reflected in the central feature of Roman politics

[219] See Tracy, *The Analogical Imagination* (New York: Crossroad, 1981), 248-49. Kelsey has explained that to call a text or set of texts "scripture" is to make a "self-involving" statement, and to ascribe to it a "wholeness," an "authority" for the common life of the Christian community, and an essential role in establishing and preserving the community's identity. See Kelsey, *The Uses of Scripture in Contemporary Theology* (Philadelphia: Fortress, 1975), 89.

[220] Hannah Arendt, "What Is Authority?," in *Between Past and Future* (New York: Penguin, 1956, 1987 reprint), 91.

which is the preservation of the city of Rome. Unlike the Greeks, there is no question of founding another polis: "The founding of a new body politic – to the Greeks an almost commonplace experience – became to the Romans the central, decisive, unrepeatable beginning of their whole history, a unique event." The contrast is equally revealing in the religious domain. Instead of the Greek propensity to depend on the "immediately revealed presence of the gods," Roman religion was a *re-ligare* which means "to be tied back, obligated, to the enormous, almost superhuman and hence always legendary effort to lay the foundations, to build the cornerstone, to found for eternity." In their common and permanent rootedness in, and being tied to, the past, religious and political activities were considered to be identical.

That was the original context from which authority appeared. The word *auctoritas* is derived from *augere* (to augment), so that those in authority were understood as constantly augmenting the foundation. Interestingly, authority is not viewed in terms of power. The authoritative character of any augmentation needed "neither the form of command nor external coercion to make itself heard." In a primarily political context, the past was sanctified through tradition. This tradition is preeminently a tradition of witness: "Tradition preserved the past by handing down from one generation to the next the testimony of the ancestors, who first had witnessed and created the sacred founding and then augmented it by their authority throughout the centuries."

The Church, Arendt suggests, adapted so well to the Roman political and spiritual heritage passed to it upon the decline of the Roman Empire that "it made the death and resurrection of Christ the cornerstone of a new foundation, erecting on it a new human institution of tremendous durability." The Constantinian era inaugurated the intimate Church-state relationship and overcame the anti-political and anti-institutional tendencies of the Christian faith. But this "politicization of the Church," Arendt argues, changed the Christian religion, resulting in the following outcome:

> The basis of the Church as a community of believers and a public institution was no longer the Christian faith in resurrection (though this faith remained its content) or the Hebrew obedience to the commands of God, but rather the testimony of the life, of the birth, death, and resurrection, of Jesus of Nazareth as a historically recorded event. As witnesses to this event the Apostles could become the 'founding fathers' of the Church, from whom she would derive her own authority as long as she handed down their testimony by way of tradition from generation to generation.[221]

Authority, as Arendt describes it, was not only chronologically referred to the past. Old age was regarded by the Romans as containing the very climax of human life, not for the accumulated wisdom and experience, but because the old man had grown closer to the ancestors and the past. Unlike today, where growth is pictured towards the future, the Romans pictured growth as archeologically-directed.

This ancient understanding of authority differs in one significant sense from the one developed by Sandra Schneiders. Evincing a preference to detach the element of chronological significance from her analysis, Schneiders presents Tradition in three senses, namely, as *foundation*, *content* and *mode*, all of which are said to be necessary if we are to do justice to the fluidity of the term in theological discourse.[222] In its *foundational* sense,[223] Tradition (with capital T) has been equated with the Holy Spirit that

---

[221] Arendt, "What Is Authority?," 121-26.

[222] Schneiders, *The Revelatory Text*, 71-81.

[223] Studying the Tradition beginning with its foundational sense, resonates with O'Collins' approach which distinguishes a "period of *foundational* revelation which ended with the apostolic age and gave way to the era of *dependent* revelation in which Christian believers now live." See his *Fundamental Theology*, 195.

Jesus *handed over* (from the Latin *tradere*) to his disciples upon completion of the salvific work the Father sent him to do. The Spirit that is handed over, indwells each of the baptized. This presentation of the Tradition in foundational terms clarifies two points: [i] it explicitates the centrality of the Holy Spirit in the Church's life, and [ii] it locates and highlights the authority proper to the foundational phase of the Tradition.[224] Further, as *content*, Tradition is "the sum total of appropriated and transmitted Christian experience, out of which Christians throughout history select the material for renewed syntheses of the faith."[225] This explains the historical interaction between the "Spirit-animated Church" and the whole of history, and accounts for two qualitatively different movements of the living Tradition: the *apostolic tradition* and the *ongoing tradition*. Third, as *mode*, Tradition renders its content available to successive generations, most eminently in Christian life, in liturgy, preaching of the Gospel, spiritualities, doctrinal teachings, theological works, catechetics, sacraments, family life, and ministries.[226]

It is in reference to the different movements of the living Tradition that Schneiders' analysis contributes to our discussion on authority. We think fallaciously, she argues, if we ascribe signal and normative importance to apostolic tradition simply on account of its proximity in time to Jesus, for such an assumption can only assign a diminishing credit to later generations. Her departure

---

[224] A pneumatological emphasis is reminiscent of Congar's vision. For Congar, it is the Spirit that maintains the integrity of the Tradition and guarantees the fidelity of the Christian community to the original experience of God's encounter with humanity through Christ. See *Tradition and Traditions*, 338-46. Congar's work preceded Vatican II, and influenced the formulation of *Dei Verbum*, 8. For a pneumatic reading that is closely bound to the ecclesial dimension, see Ratzinger, "Dogmatic Constitution on Divine Revelation, Chapter II," 189.

[225] Schneiders, *The Revelatory Text*, 72.

[226] *The Revelatory Text*, 72 & 79.

from the original understanding of authority described by Arendt is evident as she explains:

> The importance of apostolic tradition arises from the fact *that* it happened and because of the nature of *what* happened. In other words, its importance lies in its foundational and mediational character, not in its chronological priority or qualitative superiority to subsequent experiences of revelation.[227]

It is the foundational character of the apostolic tradition that constitutes the criterion of validity of the ongoing tradition. From Schneiders, we could draw three preliminary points for later reflections: [i] The foundational stage of the Christian faith which gave rise to the apostolic tradition is invested with authority. [ii] But this authority is not exclusive, for the Spirit inspires an ongoing, living Tradition. [iii] Qualitatively, contemporary experience is graced with the capacity to serve as a medium for revelation.[228]

Clearly, varied though the proposals for an adequate classification of Tradition may be, the touchstone of this Tradition is always a reference back to the foundational encounter of the early Christian community with its Lord. That foundation is preeminently christological and, at least implicitly, trinitarian in structure. The Spirit continues the work accomplished by the Son, sent by the Father.

---

[227] *The Revelatory Text*, 76 & 80.

[228] Revelation, Rowan Williams argues, concerns "what is *generative* in our experience – events or transactions in our language that break existing frames of reference and initiate new possibilities of life.... And to recognize a text, a tradition or an event as revelatory is to witness to its generative power. It is to speak from the standpoint of a new form of life and understanding whose roots can be traced to the initiating phenomenon" ["Trinity and Revelation," 199].

1.4.4.2 The Sensus Fidei and the Interpretation of the Christian Tradition

The second ancillary issue is the role of the *sense of faith* in the interpretation of the Christian Tradition. Avery Dulles has discussed what he calls the 'loci' of Tradition, that is, the places where, or the vehicles by which, the faithful interact with the Tradition. For him, the process of "traditioning" the faith includes practically all of the Church's activities. He identified one of these loci as "the sense of the faithful." Yves Congar has stressed that the term *sensus fidelium* "covers two things that are related but different." According to him, the *sensus fidei* (sense of faith) "is a quality inherent in a *subject*, on whom the grace of faith, charity, the gifts of the Spirit confer *a faculty of perceiving the truth of the faith and of discerning anything opposed to it*." It is what Michael Fahey calls a "religious 'sixth sense'," or what *Lumen Gentium*, 12 refers to as a "supernatural instinct" of the whole people of God that allows them "to recognize what is authentic or inauthentic as well as what is central or what peripheral to the Christian faith." It is, in the words of Francis Sullivan, "a subjective quality of the one who believes." The *sensus fidelium* (sense or mind of the faithful), on the other hand, pertains to an *objective* meaning, referring *not* to the believer but to what is believed. It is, according to Congar, "what can be grasped from outside, objectively, about *what the faithful, and especially layfolk, believe and profess*." The term *consensus fidelium* will then apply to the universal agreement of the whole people of God on a particular issue of faith, with regard to which Vatican II speaks of infallibility.[229]

---

[229] See Yves Congar, "Towards a Catholic Synthesis," *Concilium* 148 (1981) 74; Avery Dulles, "Faith and Revelation," in *Systematic Theology*, ed. Fiorenza and Galvin, I:121-23; Michael A. Fahey, "Church," in ibid., II:44; Francis A. Sullivan, *Magisterium: Teaching Authority in the Catholic Church* (New York:

A church that stresses the role of its Magisterium[230] needs to be mindful that the *sensus fidei* is not sidelined. The Roman Catholic Church, for example, stresses the deposit of faith, of which the Church's Magisterium is the guardian. This is the theory and practice of the Counter-Reformation and of the prevailing Vatican orientation.[231] But this orientation is rather inadequate "for theological research today and in the future."[232] The question is, what role does the subjective sense of faith have?

Karl Rahner's distinction of "divine-apostolic tradition" and "human tradition" and the problem it generates offers a good starting point. He explains this distinction as follows:

> Tradition, *historically* speaking, is simply the concrete sum of the theological propositions to be found in the Church, along with their transmission, in so far as the ordinary or extraordinary magisterium has not discounted such propositions as not permissible in the

Paulist, 1983), 21-23, 187; Luigi Sartori, "What is the Criterion for the *Sensus Fidelium*?" *Concilium* 148 (1981) 56-60; William M. Thompson, "Sensus Fidelium and Infallibility," *AEccR* 167 (1973) 450-86; John J. Burkhard, "*Sensus Fidei*: Theological Reflection Since Vatican II: 1965-1984, 1985-1989," *HeyJ* 34 (1993) 41-59, 123-36.

[230] On Catholic thinking about the nature and function of the Magisterium, see Francis A. Sullivan, *Magisterium: Teaching Authority in the Catholic Church* (New York: Paulist, 1983).

[231] See Tavard, "Ecumenical Search for Tradition," 327. This understanding is reproduced by Tavard who was requested to write paragraph 53 of the Montreal Report. The Content thereof is consonant with *Dei Verbum*, 10.

[232] See Tavard, "Ecumenical Search for Tradition," 327. It has also been observed by Nancy C. Ring that, in Vatican II, the term 'deposit of faith' departed from the New Testament concept that in Jesus Christ, God's revelation to humanity has been completed, and assumed a narrower application related solely to the dogmatic statements as enunciated by the magisterium. See her "Deposit of Faith," in *The New Dictionary of Theology*, ed. Joseph A. Komonchak et al. (Dublin: Gill and Macmillan, 1987), 278. See also *Lumen Gentium*, 25, and *Dei Verbum*, 10.

[233] Karl Rahner, "Virginitas In Partu," *Theological Investigations*, trs. Kevin Smyth (Baltimore: Pelican, 1966), 4:141 n.2.

Church. This tradition contains, without precise, conscious and official distinction both the *traditio divina-apostolica* and *traditio
humana* (theological views and efforts and opinions, of profane,
human origin), which are propagated together.[233]

The last phrase, "propagated together," points to a possible
problem, namely, an inflated claim by the Magisterium to be the
sole interpretive authority vis-à-vis a fixed "deposit of faith."[234]
The problem is not the essential ecclesial teaching office as such,
for, as a prominent feature of the Catholic perception of how
authentic interpretations of the Tradition may be safeguarded,
there is much to be said in its defence.[235] Rather, the problem concerns two points: the risk of over-emphasis on fixed layers of truth
that Gadamer warned against; and the diminution of the *sensus
fidei*.[236]

To find a legitimate place for the *sensus fidei* with respect to
Tradition, the angle of the *reception* of Tradition may be pursued.[237] Tradition is linked to the Christian community as a
whole. This community not only transmits its patrimony, but also

[234] See Segundo, *The Liberation of Dogma*, 177-79 & 283 n.22.

[235] This is essentially linked to an ecclesial interpretation of the Christian Tradition. For an excellent study, see Joseph Ratzinger, "Dogmatic Constitution on
Divine Revelation, Chapter II," 181-98. For a critical study of the historical
development of the teaching authority in the Church, see Joseph Moingt,
"Authority and Ministry," in *Authority in the Church and the Schillebeeckx
Case*, ed. Leonard Swidler and Piet F. Fransen (New York: Crossroad, 1982),
202-25.

[236] For a recent study in this area, see Richard R. Gaillardetz, *Witnesses to
Faith: Community, Infallibility and the Ordinary Magisterium of Bishops* (New
York: Paulist, 1992).

[237] The category of "reception" has been receiving growing attention. For
examples, see Yves Congar, "Reception as an Ecclesiological Reality," *Concilium* 77 (1972) 43-86; Ormond Rush, "Reception Hermeneutics and the 'Development' of Doctrine: An Alternative Model," *Pacifica* 6 (1993) 125-40; Edward
J. Kilmartin, "Reception in History: An Ecclesiological Phenomenon and Its
Significance," *JES* 21 (1984) 34-54; A. Grillmeier, "The Reception of Chal-

returns to it "periodically for self-criticism and self-reform."
This communitarian dimension of Tradition involves the *principle of reception* in two respects: a dimension of the Church's life
(i.e., a teaching plays no role in the life of the People of God if it
is not received); and the aspect of the exercise of Christian
authority (i.e., despite its formal title, a teaching has no persuasive authority if it is not received by the People of God). Implicit
in this principle, then, are the concepts of *sensus fidei* and *gratia
verbi*.[238] Accordingly, Tradition may be said to comprise [a]
divine gift, which includes the Word of God, Jesus Christ, divine
grace and the gospel, and [b] human response to that gift,
reflected in language, in witness, and in life.[239]

The relation of Tradition to the *sensus fidei* has also been examined in terms of the external and the internal dimensions of Tradition. The *external* dimension of Tradition relates to *martyria*,
whereas its *interior* dimension is linked to the *sensus fidei*.[240] In
the external dimension, *paradosis* of the redemptive history inaugurated by Jesus is attained in the form of a proclamation by bearing witness (*martyria*) to that history. That testimony of "faith in
Salvation in Jesus Christ"[241] is undertaken by all members of the

cedon in the Roman Catholic Church," *EcuRev* 22 (1970) 383-411; Michael J.
Himes, "The Ecclesiological Significance of the Reception of Doctrine," *HeyJ*
33 (1992) 146-60.

[238] Tavard explains the former as "the faith received from tradition, both from
the documentary tradition that is in the Scriptures, in the great councils, and in the
monuments of the past, and from the living tradition of those who have been given
a responsibility of teaching, preaching, and leading," and the latter as "both the
God given capacity to speak and bear witness by virtue of and for the sake of faith,
and the presence of the eternal Word, the Father's gift, dwelling in the heart
through the Holy Spirit." See Tavard, "Ecumenical Search for Tradition," 328-29.

[239] Tavard, "Ecumenical Search for Tradition," 327.

[240] As Josef Rupert Geiselmann has done in *The Meaning of Tradition*, 15-23.

[241] For Rudolf Bultmann, in the centre of the "word of faith" (or *evangelium*)
stands Christ and the saving event, the "word of the cross" (1Cor. 1:19), the

faith-community, and not by the Magisterium alone. In carrying
out their task of *martyria*, the faithful are assisted by various gifts
of the Holy Spirit.[242] In its interior dimension, Tradition is most
closely linked with the *sensus fidei* which has both ecclesial and
subjective aspects. The *sensus fidei*, Geiselmann argues, is always
anchored in the apostolic ministry. The apostolic ministry, on the
other hand, is an "integral organ of the Church." This apostolic
ministry endures in the Church, not as a disembodied entity but as
an element of the Church's faith and praxis. The *sensus fidei* is
thus the *sensus ecclesiasticus* which, in turn, does not exist independently of the Tradition as "the word perpetually living in the
hearts of the faithful." Hence, the subjective meaning of the
term.[243]

1.4.4.3 The Character of Truth in Tradition and Theology

The third ancillary issue is the much-discussed character of
truth in Christian Tradition and theology. We are not concerned
here with a comprehensive treatment of the Christian truth-claims.
Nevertheless, within a short compass, it is useful to briefly look at
a few elements that provide the broad contours of a specifically
Christian claim to truth.

[a] *The Christocentric Character of the Christian Truth*. With
MacIntyre, we begin not with some universal structures of truth,
but with a Christian view which establishes the structure of rationality within the narrative of the Christian community's Tradition.

"message of reconciliation" (2 Cor. 5:20). The New Testament makes it abun-
dantly clear that, however rich a form it may take, that "word of faith" is a definitive word, conveyed by tradition. He insists that there never was a 'gospel'
(*evangelium*) without tradition (*paradosis*). See his *Theology of the New Testament*, trs. Kendrick Grobel (London: SCM, 1955), II:98.

[242] Geiselmann, *Meaning of Tradition*, 15,16,17.

[243] *Meaning of Tradition*, 20, 21.

That truth cannot be appreciated by those who ignore the pains and struggles generated by the epistemological and other crises in the unfolding of that narrative. Despite all its historical crises, Christian Tradition has never lost sight of its basic and singular kernel, the unicity of Jesus Christ.[244] That Tradition, and its truth claims, are fundamentally christocentric. Christianity claims that God has utilised a "scandalous particularity" to "definitively" reveal himself. That claim, according to the Tradition, is borne out by the Incarnation. Philosophically, one may argue that *if* God has a message, that message *has* to be *incarnated* in a particular culture, and not ahistorically. There is no substitute for that. Yet, it is a message that must, in turn, be incarnated in every culture, with the proviso that every later "inculturation" must refer to the original, or foundational, experience.[245]

[b] The Eschatological Nature of the Christian Truth. Christian Tradition not only looks backward to its origin in the past, but also forward to the community's *telos* which, ultimately, is the fullness of Christ at the eschaton.[246] Tradition, in this backward and forward movement, is most profoundly understood as a *verb*. While the basic core of the Tradition is always presumed, the primary focus now is not so much on a fixed content that is passively received and blindly transmitted. Rather, Tradition is regarded more in terms of "a human act" by which wisdom bequeathed by

---

[244] For a study that acknowledges the uniqueness and universality of Jesus Christ as representing the key question in every Christian theology of religions, see Jacques Dupuis, *Jesus Christ at the Encounter of World Religions* (Maryknoll, NY: 1991), ch. 9.

[245] For a fuller articulation of this line of argument, see Stanley Harakas, "Must God Remain Greek?" *EcuRev* 43 (1991) 194-99.

[246] See the Montreal Report, No.56, in Gassmann, *Documentary History*, 13; *Lumen Gentium*, 48-51, and *Gaudium et Spes*, 38-39. Christian truth, according to Alister McFadyen, "is a universal horizon of hope which may only be verified eschatologically." See idem, "Truth as Mission," 449.

our forebears is "insightfully embraced and creatively reimag-
ined" in anticipation of a genuinely new future.[247] Christian truth-
claims, as they are presented in Scriptures, are thus fundamentally
of the nature of promises. Here, the justification of MacIntyre's
notion of *warranted assertibility* that we saw in Section I, has, in
the Christian category, an eschatological import.[248] The truth of
Christianity, in light of eschatology, must remain a matter of faith
and hope, rather than 'knowledge' in any strict sense. In our temporal existence, we are not, and never can be, in possession of
complete truth. However, eschatology, in Christian theology,
involves a tension between 'realized' (present) and 'future' (antic-
ipatory) eschatology. While it is only in the future that the full
truth is disclosed, that future horizon has also decisively broken
into the present, through the person and action, or, in a word, the
mission, of Jesus.[249] At one level, the incomplete truth within
Christian temporal existence opens the possibility for discovery of
greater truth in dialogue. In any event, from now till the eschaton,
truth, for Christians, must be *lived*. Christian truth is least comprehended as abstract principles for life. For Christians, truth consists
most profoundly in the *doing* of the faith, inspired by Christ's

[247] See Timothy E. O'Connell, "Vatican II and Moral Theology: Legacy and
Agenda," *Chicago Studies* 35 (1996) 108.

[248] Ronald Thiemann suggests, with reference to the truth-claims of the Scriptural narrative, that, "investigation into warranted assertibility must examine the
identity of the promiser, the nature and content of the promises, and the demands
made of those who await their fulfillment. It is only in the context of that relationship that Christian claims to truth can be justified." See idem, *Revelation and
Theology* (Notre Dame: University of Notre Dame Press, 1985), 94.

[249] Christian theology threads together the Christian understanding of creation, redemption and consummation. Christians affirm the person of Christ as
the norm and foundation of eschatology. "The future is an exploration of what
has already been given in Christ and the Spirit." See Dermot A. Lane, "Eschatology," in *The New Dictionary of Theology*, ed. Joseph A. Komonchak et al.
(Dublin: Gill and Macmillan, 1987), 341.

gospel of love. In the words of Kilmartin, "practice illuminates; practice tells the truth."[250] Truth, somehow, coincides with our *mission* in this present world. That mission would necessarily comprise, amongst other things, bearing faithful witness to Christ, notably in service. It might even be argued that while Christianity would lose its self-identity if it ceased to assert Jesus' uniqueness, it would also lose its self-identity if it ignored its service "in and for the world."[251]

[c] The Universality of the Christian Truth. A 'recognizable' Christian account of the Christ event cannot but contain some claim to universality, although the schemes proposed for conceptualizing this universality may be diverse. This claim finds theological expression in the doctrine of God's universal salvific will (1 Tim. 2:4), achieved in Jesus, through whom redemption is no longer restricted by the particularity of membership of the tribe of Israel.[252] Christian monotheism parallels its universal truth-claims. God's singularity and universality account for the fundamental fact of the world; that while pluralism is the order of the day in the present, the plurality of the world will be dissolved in God's unity, even if that universal oneness is postponed as an eschatological reality.

[250] Kilmartin, "Reception in History," 54. Michael Himes resonates the same insight with these words: "Any claim... to grasp the truth of revelation apart from living the life of Christian communion is false. One cannot truly know what the Gospel means without living in accord with it, which requires living in loving communion with one's brothers and sisters." See idem, "Ecclesiological Significance of Reception of Doctrine," 152-53.

[251] This argument has been advanced by Michael L. Cook in "Revelation as Metaphoric Process," *TS* 47 (1986) 406.

[252] The great commission at the end of Matthew's Gospel summarises one of the most important themes of the entire Gospel, namely, "the disciples are to share their discipleship not only with their fellow Jews but also with the non-Jews." See Daniel Harrington, *The Gospel of Matthew* (Collegeville: Liturgical, 1991), 416-17.

And yet, combining the particularity of the Christian perception
of truth with its tenuous claim to universal Truth is arguably the
most difficult task in theology. We cannot wait till the eschaton to
face the challenges of the liberal disdain for the intolerance of particularity or the postmodernist suspicion of overarching universality. How, if at all, is Christian Truth rationally universal? Is it universal in modernity's sense as being accessible or defensible
through public-universal forms of rationality? Or does the fact
that it is so hide-bound to the particular communal-tradition of
faith rob it of any external public form? And, does the universal-
ity-claim of Christian Truth assume a public form that remains
constant in the face of the vicissitudes of history? It is inevitable
that diverse strategies are proposed by different theological
schemes, with charges and counter-charges of 'foundationalism'
and 'fideism' being levelled against each other. We shall see in
later chapters if some of the sharp edges of the debates between
the postliberals and their perceived opponents might not be
remoulded somewhat. For the moment, a reflection on MacIntyre's critique of modernity yields the understanding that the universality of Christian Truth, insofar as it pertains to the public
framework of meaning, lies in *communication*. When we move
away from the agenda of an enforcement of our own particular
and single frame of thought on the public, then the nature of "public" in public meaning gravitates towards dialogue and communication between different frames of thought. Truth then emerges in
communication.[253]

[d] Christian Truth and Theology. Given his emphatic thesis
that the Church is "the concrete situs of the *traditio* of Jesus,"
Ratzinger's systematic presentation of what it means to be a

---

[253] This analysis is indebted to McFadyen whose main burden in "Truth as
Mission" is to unpack the intelligibility of the universality of Christian Truth.

church theologian features the basic argument that the integrity of theological teaching cannot exist without church teaching. "For a church without theology is impoverished and blind. A theology without a church, however, soon dissolves into arbitrary theory... a limping academic theology."[254] What our study has so far shown is the need of a critical openness, the determination of truth being closely dependent on the creation of conditions for *undistorted* communication. Critical openness also demands the search for criteria for assessing truth, which always leads to the discussion of the authority attributed to historical sources traditionally recognized by the churches as normative — Scripture and Tradition. In addition, the Roman Catholic Church traditionally appeals to the Magisterium as the particular teaching office that exercises authoritative interpretation of both these sources.

Critical openness in theology may require a readiness to regard theological claims as hypotheses which are, in principle, criticizable and revisable, and thus ought to be tested against alternative opinions in ongoing discussions.[255] The diversity of methods with which theologians operate betray the "preoccupations, fundamental convictions, biases or dispositions" they have towards

---

[254] Ratzinger's arguments are presented in a 1986 lecture in Toronto entitled "The Church and the Theologian," as quoted in Richard J. Neuhaus, *The Catholic Moment* (San Francisco: Harper & Row, 1987), 138-40. Although a Christian theologian may properly belong both to Church and academy, Lindbeck prioritises the former. Frei avers that: "Both vocations are best served when theology is seen in service to the church first, to the academy second. Academic theology is that second-order reflection which is appropriate, albeit very modest instrument in aid of the critical description and self-description of specific, religious-cultural communities, in our case the Christian church." See his "Epilogue: George Lindbeck and *The Nature of Doctrine*," in *Theology and Dialogue*, ed. Bruce D. Marshall (Notre Dame: University of Notre Dame Press, 1990), 278. See further, Congregation for the Doctrine of the Faith, "Instruction on the Ecclesial Vocation of the Theologian," *Origins* 20 (1990) 117-26.

[255] Thomas B. Ommen, "Theology and Foundationalism," *SR* 16 (1987) 170.

the subject matter they investigate.[256] The history of theology features repeated examples of a tendency on the part of theologians to absolutize their own conceptual schemes so as to treat them as self-sufficient ends of inquiry, rather than as vehicles for the disclosure of truth about God.[257] And yet, because the theologian stands within history, the verification of theological claims can never be conclusive in negative or positive terms. Religious statements can never attain absolute certainty. The theologian, at best, can form judgments and articulate a case for the alleged substantiation or non-substantiation of any given religious assertion.[258] In this context, we shall further argue for a creative interplay between Tradition and experience in theological discourse. When an inordinate emphasis is placed on either Tradition or experience, the result is a loss of the dialectic between the two poles. An over-emphasis on the pole of Tradition makes it difficult to relate experience critically and constructively to Scripture-in-Tradition. Conversely, an undue emphasis on experience eclipses the biblical message.

Christian Tradition embodies a received Truth about reality clothed in individual and corporate experience. In its constant struggle to discern accurately the places of continuity and discontinuity with this Truth in a given time, three risks confront the Church. First, there is the risk of over-accommodation to the surrounding culture, which eclipses the Church's "unique capacity to guide out of its own culturally transcendent resources," and turns it into "an indiscriminate tool of cultural affirmation." Second,

---

[256] Roger Haight, "Critical Witness: The Question of Method," in *Faithful Witness: Foundations of Theology for Today's Church*, ed. L. J. O'Donovan and T. H. Sanks (New York: Crossroad, 1989), 201.

[257] T. F. Torrance, *Reality and Scientific Theology* (Edinburgh: Scottish Academic, 1985), 150-53.

[258] Wolfhart Pannenberg, *Theology and the Philosophy of Science* (Philadelphia, PA: Westminster, 1976), 343-44.

there is the risk of sectarian irrelevance, which preserves the Church's unique sense of self as guide at the expense of "containing the uncontainable truth in rigidly and narrowly interpreted words and forms."[259] Third, there is the risk of an utter refusal to look at what lies 'behind' the Scriptural text. For ideological reasons, we ought to be interested in whether there are any serious misrepresentations of the events to which the biblical canon bears witness. The historical detail of what lies behind the text may be a matter of pressing theological relevance.[260]

1.5 Concluding Remarks

The Church emphasizes the normative significance of Tradition and its Scriptures in theology. However much the various denominations may differ in their interpretation of the Tradition, there is an irreducible constancy that underscores their common reference to the core of the Christian faith enshrined in Scripture, the good news of redemption inaugurated by Christ who pitched tent amongst us, who suffered, died and was raised, and who is now present in the life of the Church through the Spirit. Uniquely christocentric and trinitarian, Christian Tradition transmits a community-faith which has as its touchstone the foundational encounter of the first believers with their Lord, Jesus Christ. However, the narrative character of the Tradition, combined with its eschatological orientation, necessarily entails those dialectical conversations which characterize fusions of horizons, growth and creativity. Christian truth, in this light, is best conceived of as being dialectically revealed, rather than as fossilized layers of

---

[259] Tilden H. Edwards, *Spiritual Friend: Reclaiming the Gift of Spiritual Direction* (New York: Paulist, 1980), 93-94.

[260] Mark G. Brett, *Biblical Criticism in Crisis?* (Cambridge: Cambridge University Press, 1991), 10.

truth. The historical appropriation and application of the Tradition bespeaks an inevitable internal pluralism in the interpretation of the Tradition and a diversity of hermeneutical approaches where, amongst other things, experience, context and the role of the interpreter are relevant factors. Living and dynamic, the Tradition manifests an effective history that does not regard its function as one of preserving a "pure" Christianity from extra-traditional sources. Unlike some strands of Wittgensteinian thought, Christian Tradition is not such an isolated, autonomous and particular language-game as to suggest a radical incommensurability which entirely discounts dialogue with other traditions.

This brief survey helps prepare the way for our critical dialogue with Lindbeck whose acute awareness of a Christian history that is characterized by a plurality of frequently competing interpretations of Scripture and doctrine has led him to some tightly-argued ecumenical proposals for accommodating historically divisive differences. The diverse issues generated by his proposals can be gathered into three clusters. First, Lindbeck's hermeneutical approach stresses intratextual-particularity, with special reference to Scripture-in-Tradition and the task of Christian theology. His postliberal agenda then inspires the next cluster of issues which centres around his views on religions. Finally, his theory on the nature and function of Church doctrines within a normative framework culminates in a postliberal vision of what it means to be Church – the *situs* of the Tradition. To the first of these clusters of issues — the Bible and its hermeneutical problems – we must now turn.

CHAPTER II

BIBLE AND DE-CHRISTIANIZATION

2.1 Preliminary Clarifications

When Lindbeck declares: "It is the text, so to speak, which absorbs the world rather than the world the text,"[1] he provides the key to his rather complex postliberal, intratextual theology, a theology that sets a radical agenda for the relation of the Church's ancient scriptural text to the modern world. This is Lindbeck's proposal for resolving the prevailing pluralistic, liberal, cacophony. It is also a "community-building hermeneutic" which Lindbeck proposes as a possible resolution of the current crisis in biblical interpretation.[2]

Starting at once with Lindbeck's intratextual theology, our order of topics may seem to run counter to the order set out in *The Nature of Doctrine*. It is true that, in the book, Lindbeck begins with a social-science approach to religion and, from there, seeks to address theological issues and to propose a form of theology congruent with it. In the process, he develops a number of variations that speak directly to the Church. Nevertheless, three factors, in particular, may support and help clarify our choice of a different starting point. *Firstly*, Lindbeck has made it clear in the book that the order of topics he treats is optional in some respects, so that it

---

[1] ND, 118.

[2] See the various contributions, including Lindbeck's, in *Biblical Interpretation in Crisis: The Ratzinger Conference on Bible and Church*, ed. Richard J. Neuhaus (Grand Rapids: Eerdmans, 1989).

is possible to begin with the comments on theological method in the last chapter, rather than with the possibility of doctrinal reconciliation in the ecumenical enterprise in the first.[3] To be sure, Lindbeck's cultural-linguistic model of religion is constructed from the now familiar socio-cultural theories which suggest that a community's perception of reality is decisively shaped by its language, cultural tradition and symbolic framework. Granted, too, that the notion of intratextuality begins from there. However, as we shall argue, what marks the originality of, and the hermeneutical controversy surrounding, Lindbeck's work, lies precisely in his proposal that the canonical Scripture constitutes the basic material for this cultural-linguistic framework. *Secondly*, Lindbeck is first and foremost a theologian, so that even in this book, while the pot is cooking a dish amenable to different denominational palates, the hearth is in fact fired from a different stove; the theoretical argument may be in function of ecumenical efficacy, the underlying motivation is no less inspired by a desire to conceive the task and method of Christian theology at the end of the second millennium. *Thirdly*, of the various matters that detain Lindbeck and direct his scholarly work, he is, as the preponderance of his writings for the past fifteen years show, most deeply disturbed by the state of degenerating biblical literacy within the Church and the cultural debiblicisation resulting therefrom. His intratextual theology, with its focus on the culture-forming and community-building power of the Bible, becomes the centre-piece of his theological enterprise, "prompted," as he admits, "by convictions about the kind of theological thinking that is most likely to be religiously helpful to Christians and perhaps others in the present situation."[4] If necessary, he suggests, the Christian community must return to

---

[3] See ND, 11.
[4] ND, 10.

communal enclaves to socialize members into the highly particular biblical vision of authentic Christian life. Such strong convictions cannot but deeply affect his theological vision, and Lindbeck himself positively confesses to the overriding significance of his theological project above other issues he raises in the text.[5] Indeed, in the final pages of *The Nature of Doctrine*, Lindbeck again summarizes prophetically the psychosocial crisis in which the Church and civilization stand, a crisis he feels compelled by a sense of urgency to address through intratextual theological fidelity. Arguably, then, the final chapter of *The Nature of Doctrine* is the most important, for the articulation of the postliberal theology announced in the sub-title of that book seems clearly to be his overriding concern.[6] Other arguments, engaging though they are, not only play a subordinate role to this theological priority, but may in fact be fruitfully read as a necessary consequence of his particular theology. Hence, we begin with Lindbeck's theology rather than his other theoretical studies.

A fundamental question in contemporary theology, characterized as it is by a multitude of divergent opinions on every conceivable issue, is the task of theology. Is Christian theology largely a task of rendering the Christian faith intelligible and credible? If it is not, what ought that task be? If it is, what is the best methodological approach to that task? Further, in regard to the lively debate over the public character of theology, is this unpacking of the intelligibility and credibility of faith directed to the inner community of the faithful, or to the community at large? What does it mean to be Church in modern, plural, and liberal

---

[5] See ND, 120.

[6] See James Buckley, "Doctrine in the Diaspora," *Thomist* 49 (1985) 446; Gordon Michaelson, "The Response to Lindbeck," *ModTh* 4 (1988) 110-11. Michaelson maintains the thesis that accurately analyzing Lindbeck entails clarifying his postliberal theological stance.

society? What do contemporary theologians have to say about these and related issues?

Contemporary society is marked by rich plurality as a cultural phenomenon. The term "pluralism" signifies a heightened consciousness of the reality of plurality around us – a consciousness which is acutely reflected in Christian theology. Sensitized by this phenomenon, theologians themselves add to this plurality by a rich diversity of understanding as to what the task of theology is, as well as by, at times acrimonious, proposals regarding what a properly "Christian" approach to address this phenomenon ought to be. Theologians anxious to get into the current "mainstream" may be sailing with the tide of pluralism, and producing theologies that are ambiguously thin on the distinctive claims of the Christian faith. In their positive attempt to accommodate others, they have unwittingly relativised the Christian faith to a point quite beyond recognition.[7] By contrast, Lindbeck chooses to systematically argue the case for promoting biblical literacy, for retrieving the distinctively pre-modern, "narrativist" reading of the Bible, and for a method of doing theology called "intratextual" theology. All these are consistent with the distinctive, particular, cultural-linguistic tradition of the Christian faith. And Lindbeck claims that, ultimately, this particular way of doing theology is the only way to save the Church and to ensure Christianity's positive contributions to the world. We keep the faith by keeping the Church's ancient story enshrined in the Bible, and the Church witnesses best to Christ in the modern world when she christianizes the surrounding culture with the biblical meaning-system.

---

[7] In this regard, see Joseph Cardinal Ratzinger, "Relativism: The Central Problem for Faith Today," *Origins* 26 (1996) 310-16; Paul Griffiths and Delmas Lewis, "On Grading Religions, Seeking Truth, and Being Nice to People – A Reply to Professor Hick," *RelSt* 19 (1983) 75-80.

A number of issues arising from this deceptively familiar and simple proposal require clarification. A set of issues pertains to the reasons that prompted Lindbeck's biblical-narrativist choice. These reasons, once clarified, will hopefully contribute to a greater intelligibility of Lindbeck's hermeneutical slant, so that, in the next chapter, we shall then be better able to attend to the theological issues and problems generated by Lindbeck's scheme and critically examine various responses his proposal has attracted.

In this chapter, we are concerned with exploring why Lindbeck is calling the Church community to return to the literary content — the narrative — of the Bible, and to the pre-modern mode of reading that narrative, as well as the theological issues concomitant with that call. Two factors, one socio-cultural, and the other theological, seem to have been decisive in influencing Lindbeck's narrative option. Divided into three sections, this chapter begins with Lindbeck's socio-cultural observations on the historic role of the Bible, the weakening of that role in today's society, and the consequences of that weakening. Next, we take a brief look at the profound influence some biblically-grounded scholars have had on Lindbeck. The first two sections will help inform our analysis of Lindbeck's intratextual and narrativist proposal for ecclesial and theological adoption in the third section.

Section I:
The Bible's Historic Role and the Consequences of a De-Christianization of Culture

We need to begin with the past, Lindbeck suggests, because only with a better understanding of the historic role of the once universal classic hermeneutical framework – a powerful way of interpreting and using Scripture – can we present a cogent argument for present need and possibility.[8]

In a string of essays on biblical interpretation,[9] as well as in *The Nature of Doctrine*, Lindbeck writes from a deep concern for what he calls a "de-Christianization of culture." It is useful, at the outset, to note that Lindbeck is not talking about a de-Christianization of society, at any rate, not just yet. Rather, Lindbeck draws our attention to the "awkwardly intermediate stage" in which contemporary Christianity finds itself. In this intermediate stage, Christianity is in jeopardy of being culturally disestablished,[10] and society, in his view, suffers as a result. On what bases does Lindbeck make this dire observation?

2.2 The Biblical World, a Cultural Phenomenon

Repeatedly, Lindbeck draws attention to the fact that, until recently, *the* text above all texts for most people in traditionally Christian countries was the Bible; and that *the* world above all other worlds – fairy-tale, superstitious, pagan Greek and Roman classic, Newtonian scientific, and so forth – was the linguistic and imaginative world of the Bible. The whole culture was impregnated with the stories, images, conceptual patterns and particular turns of phrase of the Holy Scripture of Christendom. If anyone

[8] See Lindbeck, "Scripture, Consensus, and Community," in *Biblical Interpretation in Crisis*, 75-76.

[9] See Lindbeck, "The Bible as Realistic Narrative," *JES* 17 (1980) 81-85; "Barth and Textuality," *ThT* 43 (1986) 361-76; "The Story-Shaped Church," in *Scriptural Authority and Narrative Interpretation*, ed. Garret Green (Philadelphia: Fortress, 1987), 161-78; "Scripture, Consensus, and Community," *This World* 23 (1988) 5-24; "The Church's Mission to a Postmodern Culture," 37-55; "The Gospel's Uniqueness," *ModTh* 13 (1997) 423-50.

[10] ND, 134. On cultural de-Christianization, see "The Church's Mission," 44; "Barth and Textuality," 366; "Scripture, Consensus, and Community," 87.

should doubt that this was a culture to which even the illiterates and non-Churchgoers belonged, Lindbeck would remind them that "knowledge of the Bible was transmitted not only directly by its reading, hearing, and ritual enactment, but also indirectly by an interwoven net of intellectual, literary, artistic, folkloric, and proverbial traditions." As the knowledge of the Bible percolated down the different strata of society through these multifarious and pervasive modes of transmission, the result that obtained was a scripturally literate culture. Within such a culture, not only did people speak colloquially of a Samson, a Solomon, a Judas, a Martha or a Mary, but even professed non-believers or secularists, if educated, would actually know the scriptural texts so well as to put many contemporary pastors and theologians to shame.[11]

In this context, Lindbeck stresses the lasting power of a familiar text – of any category, for that matter – for a "familiar text can remain imaginatively and conceptually powerful long after its claims to truth are denied." For example, the deists and atheists of the eighteenth-century Enlightenment, who turned the European high culture of the time non-Christian, were completely absorbed in the linguistic and imaginative world of the Bible, even if they did not realise it, or explicitly denied it.

Similarly, major figures in the nineteenth and early twentieth centuries are illustrative of this point. Nietzsche, who with singular zeal attempted to repudiate the biblical beliefs, and to dislodge the linguistic and imaginative universe of the Bible, was nevertheless well-schooled in Scriptures. The powerful appeal in Marx's theory, too, rested substantially on its departure from the all-too-distant biblical eschaton and an incisive inversion of that eschatology to a secularized or this-worldly version. In the case of Freud,

---

[11] See Lindbeck, "The Church's Mission," 38; and "Barth and Textuality," 370-71.

recent scholarship indicates the close interaction of the structures
of his thought with his Jewish heritage. Huxley, too, in his nineteenth-century campaign to replace religion by science, rode on
the slogan "justification by verification" – a slogan he evidently
posed as a critical counterpoint to the Pauline and Reformation
"justification by faith." But Huxley's campaign should not be
read as all-harmful; in fact, it actually contributed much to society
for, through his "ennobling and ethnically strenuous view of science," flowed the right conviction for responsible conduct in a
genuine love for humanity.[12]

But why do texts — any texts — exert such powerful influence
on human imagination? Lindbeck suggests this has to do with the
human *psyche*. Herein lies a crucial building block for Lindbeck's
central theological thesis. Texts, in his view, have the capacity to
influence human hearts and minds, *whether or not they are
believed*. "Once they penetrate deeply into the psyche," he claims,
"especially the collective psyche, they cease to be primary objects
of study and rather come to supply the conceptual and imaginative
vocabulary, as well as the grammar and syntax, with which we construe and construct reality."[13] Non-biblical examples abound that
corroborate this discovery. In world classics, Homer's *Odyssey*, for
instance, has inspired untold numbers of adventures into unknown
times and places, including even the hidden recesses of the human
mind. In the field of science, the Ptolemaic cycles and epicycles,
the regularity of Newtonian physics, and the relativity of Einstein's
universe, have all been put to countless uses and misuses. And novels, too, leave their indelible mark in the way Tolstoy's novel, *War
and Peace*, irreversibly alters every careful reader's view on

[12] See Lindbeck, "The Church's Mission," 39; and "Barth and Textuality,"
371.
[13] Lindbeck, "The Church's Mission," 39-40.

humanity. From observations such as these, Lindbeck draws a conclusion that bears a critical significance to the intelligibility of his intratextual theology: "Thus, texts of many kinds in many media, from unwritten myths to television projections, can become, as Calvin said of the Bible, the spectacles through which we see nature, human beings, and God."[14]

All the more, because of the Bible's preeminence in traditionally Christian lands, the biblical lenses have functioned as the most powerful, penetrating, and comprehensive ones. To be sure, these lenses have been used for wholly different, and at times bitterly opposed, construals of reality. So Lindbeck highlights the fact that in each of these varied construals, the biblical influence is evident, even when God is removed. Indeed, the extent to which this scriptural idiom has penetrated Western culture is seen in the many enduring literary classics which are veritable subtexts of the biblical texts. Examples would include not only Dante's *Divine Comedy* and Milton's *Paradise Lost*, but also works of little overt theological content like the Shakespearean plays. Akin, in a way, to the Jewish rabbinic midrash, Shakespeare's stories are told with biblical meanings and often epitomise the kind of astute insights into what human life looks like when viewed biblically. In sum, Lindbeck agrees with the claim by literary critics that "the basic substructure of the literary imagination of the West is biblical."[15]

---

[14] Lindbeck, "The Church's Mission," 40. Lindbeck's acceptance of Calvin's understanding in this respect is repeatedly affirmed and the metaphor of the "biblical lens" is established as a lasting trajectory. See, for example, "Scripture, Consensus and Community," 86; "The Gospel's Uniqueness," 429. To learn a language, in the philosophical sense of learning its 'grammar', is to learn a worldview, Nancey Murphy points out. This confirms Lindbeck's claim that *texts create a world*. "To understand biblical language is to enter sympathetically into that world, just as one becomes *absorbed* in a good novel." See Nancey Murphy, *Anglo-American Postmodernity* (Boulder: Westview, 1997), 148.

[15] Lindbeck, "The Church's Mission," 41. See also "Barth and Textuality," 371.

This biblical imagination filtered down to the ordinary spheres, far removed from the literary world. Thus, in articulating their ordinary experiences, the general populace was most adept in the proverbial uses of Scripture. As a result, all of experience, even the revered classics of Greece and Rome, was "absorbed" into the scriptural world and permeated, as it were, by the biblical meaning-system. To say that Christendom, up to recent times, dwelt in the biblical world, was neither an exaggeration nor a mere metaphor. *It was a cultural phenomenon.*[16]

2.3 The Fading of the Biblical World, a Cultural De-Christianization

This *cultural phenomenon* in which the Bible carried linguistic and imaginative influence, was of great religious import, not least because it provided the condition for the communal shaping of convictions and conduct. Scripture was a dwelling place for the imagination because the Bible was a language with many senses. But after the Reformation, the Bible became increasingly an object of study that generated fixed and univocal meanings. Concurrently, there came the sudden fading of the biblical component in Western culture.

Hans Frei, Lindbeck's late colleague at Yale, has added an important note to this historical sketch. Frei suggests that a profound "reversal" took place, beginning in the seventeenth century, with regard to the way people read the Bible. Prior to the seventeenth century, the Bible was used to give shape to the "real world" — the form of life — in which people lived. In other words, people quite simply fitted their lives and experiences into

---

[16] For an argument that the Bible has shaped the imagination of the West, see Northrop Frye, *The Great Code* (New York: Harcourt Brace Jovanovich, 1982).

the reality rendered in and through the biblical narrative, and not the other way around. Then came the great reversal. Speaking typically of the lamentable "eclipse" of the biblical narrative, Frei suggests that it was "philosophical" rather than properly "theological" hermeneutics which started the trend of distinguishing the literal sense of the biblical narrative from questions of historical reference or religious truth. Frei estimates that, from the late eighteenth century on, the narrative of the Bible no longer functioned for the people as the world into which their lives must be fitted. Instead, through various techniques of abstraction and interpretation, the biblical stories were rendered amenable to the "real world" of people's lives. This loss of the narrative interpretation was in great part attributed by Frei to mediating theology and the rapid rise of German "general (nontheological) biblical hermeneutics," with its principles of exegesis pivoted between historical criticism and religious apologetics. Instead of letting the biblical story provide the framework within which the rest of the world made sense, these mediating and hermeneutical theologians of England and Germany made sense of the biblical story by first putting it in a general philosophical framework. Typically, reliance was placed on an antecedent conceptual framework within which to read and render the biblical narrative meaningful to modern readers. This was for Frei "the great reversal": "interpretation was a matter of fitting the biblical story into another world with another story rather than incorporating that world into the biblical story."[17] The point of reference had now all but shifted, so that, in Frei's summation of this new approach, "the explicative meaning of the narrative texts came to be their ostensive or ideal reference," whereas "their applicative meaning or

[17] Hans Frei, *The Eclipse of Biblical Narrative* (New Haven: Yale University Press, 1974) [hereafter cited as *Eclipse*], 130.

religious meaningfulness was either a truth of revelation embodied in an indispensable historical event or a universal spiritual truth known independently of the texts but exemplified by them, or, finally, a compromise between two positions amounting to the claim that while the historical fact is indispensable to revelation, the meaningfulness of revelation depends on its being set in some broader religious or moral context."[18]

This eclipse of the biblical narrative was, in Frei's estimation, part and parcel of the Enlightenment's turn to the subject which finally wrought a thorough change in hermeneutics. In the precritical mode, biblical narrative was simply accepted as a normative subject matter and "the understanding process itself had no contribution to make to the object to be interpreted or to the interpretive results." But now, the focus of hermeneutics had dramatically shifted to an acute attention on the context and spirit of the individual author, grammatical interpretation, subjective consciousness, and the process of the interpreter's understanding.[19]

As this trend continued into the nineteenth century, the most significant change in hermeneutics was, according to Frei, the preoccupation with meaningfulness rather than with the rules and principles for interpreting texts. Schleiermacher, with his predilection for the "consciousness" expressed in texts, was, for Frei, the key representative of this new hermeneutics of understanding.

In Lindbeck's view, there are two, unidentical, elements to the biblical eclipse: [1] the loss of biblical literacy, and [2] the loss of biblical imagination. Lindbeck accepts that while biblical literacy is always a precondition for any imaginative use, intimate knowledge of the text as an object does not necessarily result in its use

[18] Frei, *Eclipse*, 124.
[19] Frei, *Eclipse*, 306. This reversal might also be harshly diagnosed as the essence of the myth of modernity, the story that kills all stories. See Terrence Tilley, *Story Theology* (Wilmington, Del.: Michael Glazier, 1985), 30-36.

as a language with which to construe the universe. The latter observation holds true particularly with regard to pietists, fundamentalists, social activists, and historical critics. Moreover, the decline of biblical literacy does not correspond to the rise of a secularised culture, as can be seen in the period of the Enlightenment whose champions sprang from within a biblically cultured society. Indeed, as an ironical addition to this argument, the Bible-believing fundamentalists of today may know precious little of the meaning and content of Scripture.

The abrupt decline in biblical literacy is a *de-Christianization of culture*.[20] Language and imagination, which had been previously impregnated with the biblical meaning-system, have been debiblicized at an alarming rate. This debiblicization affects the whole society — intellectuals and nonintellectuals, the religious and non-religious, those inside and outside the Church, clergy and laity, professedly Bible-loving conservatives and allegedly less biblical liberals. The influence of the biblical world, for long the mainstay of Western culture, has suddenly crumbled. And yet, this de-Christianization of culture is not necessarily a de-Christianization of society: statistical surveys continue to give a growing number of people throughout the world who profess Christian faith and there is no lack of success-reports posted by Christian renewal movements. Nevertheless, the fact remains that ignorance of the Bible, especially in the younger generation, is a commonplace. Biblical allusions in non-Christian authors, such as Hobbes and Machiavelli, for example, escape the younger readers of today in tertiary education. To be sure, the Bible is not the only "classic" that has fallen prey to the "contemporary amnesia." All the major western classics and histories are "fading from the collective

---

[20] See Lindbeck, "Scripture, Consensus, and Community," 87; "The Church's Mission," 48; "Barth and Textuality," 366; "Habitable Texts," 156; ND, 134.

memory." In fact, all strata of society are being debiblicized, sparing not even the professedly biblical sectors. Robert Bellah and his associates,[21] for instance, proffer evidence to support the argument that, beginning in the 'sixties and culminating in the 'seventies, the older and more biblical idioms in books were replaced by a kind of "therapeutic expressive individualism." A most telling piece of evidence is that this actually took place within conservative evangelical publishing houses. Where Christ still featured as the personal saviour, He was no longer presented as the forgiver and redeemer from sin, but typically as the friendly guide to personal happiness and fulfillment.[22]

At the climax of Lindbeck's story on the rise and decline of the biblical culture is the bad news, that within this dismal scenery, the greatest casualty is the Bible. "It was an integral part of the whole heritage, and as the heritage fades, so also does scriptural knowledge."[23]

2.4 Contemporary Society and the Consequences of Biblical Weakening

The loss of familiarity with the Bible, which for Lindbeck only started in the relatively recent past, has gathered alarming momentum in the last generation. During Barth's time, it was apparently not a problem with which he had to contend. This perhaps explains his presupposition of an audience well-informed about the Bible, however disastrously they might misread it. He operated on the basis that people knew the Bible well enough to be able to

---

[21] See Robert Bellah et al., *Habits of the Heart* (New York: Harper & Row, 1985).

[22] See Lindbeck, "Barth and Textuality," 369-70.

[23] Lindbeck, "The Church's Mission," 46. See also Lindbeck, "Barth and Textuality," 370.

access the self-interpreting text, once they had learned to stop imposing extraneous systems of thought on Scripture. But today, whatever the merit of Barth's optimism, there is no doubt, in Lindbeck's assessment, of a serious state of biblical illiteracy, not only in society at large, but even within the Church.

In this postmodern age, the imaginations of literary writers are no longer impregnated with Scripture or at least with a scripturally-influenced heritage. As authors steeped in the Bible diminish in number, this augurs ill for the future of the western literary tradition. But the consequences filter down deeper than the level of the literary world. This is disconcerting, because the success of the Church's cultural mission, Lindbeck suggests, is closely dependent on society's traditional cultural heritage. Lindbeck's analysis leads him to extend the dire prognosis to other matters of import.

First, because "imagination is basic to thought," Lindbeck argues, "the weakening of the biblical substructure of our culture's communal imagination may dry up the wellsprings of western humanistic creativity in general."[24] Imaginative living within the Bible becomes difficult as the skill to imaginatively inscribe extra-textual realities into the world of the text has weakened. We no longer encounter the world in biblical terms. Second, this loss of biblical knowledge precipitates an impoverishment of public discourse once the common "ethnic" language is no longer available in which the meaning, purpose, and destiny of such fundamental issues as national goals can be articulated. This collapse in public discourse is described by Lindbeck as "intercommunicative or linguistic." When believers and nonbelievers shared a common scriptural language, they could communicate, even if they disagreed, on a whole range of issues. But, the loss of the linguistic

[24] Lindbeck, "The Church's Mission," 47.

and conceptual means that came in the wake of the loss of the biblical narrative renders society mute on these same issues. Abraham Lincoln, for instance, had at his disposal a biblical idiom of judgment, sin, hope, and mercy with which he could address the whole country in a powerful manner. It has since become increasingly harder for nations or Christian communities or even individuals to live within the linguistic world of the Bible.[25] Third, and relatedly, as the culture of Christians and non-Christians become de-Christianized, there is, as it were, a confusion of tongues: "Genuine argument is impossible, and neither agreements nor disagreements can be probed at any depth." Even a moderating voice in times of conflict may lack a common language in which to express itself. Is this a problem in civil society? Lindbeck answers in the affirmative. "Without a shared imaginative and conceptual vocabulary and syntax," Lindbeck speculates, "society cannot be held together by communication, but only by brute force." In light of these observations, because Lindbeck situates the biblical cultural contribution at the very heart of the literary heritage of the West, a biblical culture can only be described as indispensable to the welfare of western society; its current eclipse can only spell gloom.[26]

When we take the current phenomenon of globalization into view, as well as the key role the West plays in matters that affect the world, Lindbeck's extension of the dire consequences under discussion to the world is readily intelligible: the loss of the biblical culture is injurious to the entire world; a renewal of that

---

[25] Lindbeck, "Barth and Textuality," 370.

[26] Lindbeck thinks that "traditionally Christian lands when stripped of their historic faith are worse than others. They become unworkable or demonic... From this point of view, the Christianization of culture can be in some situations the churches' major contribution to feeding the poor, clothing the hungry and liberating the imprisoned." See "Confession and Community: An Israel-like View of the Church," *ChCent* 107 (1990) 495.

biblical culture has to be the prime contribution of Christianity to the modern world. Arguably, the most important aspect of Lindbeck's proposal is his conviction that "the viability of a unified world of the future may well depend on counteracting the acids of modernity."[27] He thus urges a return of the pre-modern mode of Scripture reading. Impressed by the significance of Lindbeck's conclusion, Stanley Hauerwas and Gregory Jones reiterate the message that "for those who call themselves Christian, the best hope for providing a unified world of the future is to be found in a recovery of the distinctive particularity of the Christian tradition."[28]

But what are the prospects of such a recovery in the terms proposed by Lindbeck? This assessment, which is intimately bound up with Lindbeck's theological agenda, must be delayed until Section III, after we have taken a look at Lindbeck's theological background.

Section II: Theological Influences on Lindbeck

In a culture that is in the process of being de-Chrstianized, that is experiencing a heightened awareness of pluralism, and that faces the challenge of fragmentation in this postmodern age, the question, "How do we do theology" takes center stage for methodologically conscious theologians such as Lindbeck. Closely related to this basic methodological question are issues like "How ought we to read the Bible?" and "How do we tell the Christian story?" We have just seen in the previous section that Lindbeck urges a retrieval of an earlier mode of thought, namely,

[27] ND, 127.
[28] Stanley Hauerwas and Gregory Jones, "Seeking a Clear Alternative to Liberalism," *B&R* 13 (1985) 9.

the premodern mode. In formulating his response, Lindbeck has been deeply influenced by Karl Barth, Eric Auerbach, Hans Frei and his colleagues at Yale, an influence he repeatedly acknowledges. Ultimately, however, the theological base is derived from Barth. In fact, Barth is virtually the only author whom Hans Frei, Paul Holmer, David Kelsey and Lindbeck, all Yale-related, openly mention with agreement.[29] They have all, with their own particular emphases, adopted Barth's understanding of theology as sustained commentary on the biblical stories, as a legitimate paradigm for their own postliberal narrative theology. In David Tracy's assessment, "Lindbeck's substantive theological position is a methodologically sophisticated Barthian confessionalism. The hands may be the hands of Wittgenstein and Geertz but the voice is the voice of Karl Barth."[30]

In citing authors as particular influences, we stress that it is not so much what they said as what Lindbeck does with what they said, which makes them significant. When this is kept in mind, an appreciation on two points follows. *Firstly*, we can see the originality of Lindbeck's thought and, as some commentators have already remarked, the seminal and ground-breaking character of his work, despite the manifest influence of his precursors. *Secondly*, we can appreciate Lindbeck's departure from his sources of influence on particular points, something which perhaps is inevitable, given the brilliance of his own unique sensibility and the novelty of his contribution. A brief sketch of the pertinent

[29] See Mark I. Wallace, "The New Yale Theology," *CSR* 17 (1987) 169. For a full list of these authors' major works, see p. 155 n.2 of the same article.

[30] David Tracy, "Lindbeck's New Program for Theology," *Thomist* 49 (1985) 465. For an assessment of Lindbeck's reliance upon St. Thomas, see Bruce D. Marshall, "Aquinas as Postliberal Theologian," *Thomist* 53 (1989) 353-402, and Lindbeck's response, "Response to Bruce Marshall," *Thomist* 53 (1989) 403-06.

thoughts of Lindbeck's precursors from whom he openly draws much inspiration will assist us both in situating and assessing Lindbeck's own visions and in drawing out the differences his proposal exhibits from their thoughts.

On Lindbeck's part, we get an explicit acknowledgement in these terms: "Karl Barth's exegetical emphasis on narrative has been at second hand a chief source of my notion of intratextuality as an appropriate way of doing theology in a fashion consistent with a cultural-linguistic understanding of religion and a regulative view of doctrine."[31] This acknowledgement discloses two points of great significance: *first*, there is a direct linkage between the exegetical emphasis on narrative and the intratextual methodology in theology which Lindbeck advances as indispensable for the life of the Church; and, *second*, Barth's influence on Lindbeck, though paramount, has been "second hand."[32] We will begin with the second point, the influence of Barth.

2.5 *Barth's Influence*

Much of Barth's huge literary legacy does not have immediate bearing on Lindbeck's project. For our purposes, we shall briefly note five related points in Barth's vision which are germane to our discussion.

2.5.1 A Positivistic View of Revelation as the "Impossible Possibility"

First, we begin with Barth's argument for the possibility of a starting point for theology. The pathway of the possible is crucial to Barth in view of his early understanding of God as the "wholly

---

[31] ND, 135.

[32] Lindbeck again indicated his second-hand knowledge of Barth in "Barth and Textuality," *ThT* 43 (1986) 361.

other" who cannot be posited as being reachable by human creatures on human terms or through inherent human capacity. God is
conceived as totally beyond the finite realm. While human beings
are caught up in sin, God is by his very nature Goodness and
Truth; sinful humanity can never encounter this God as an object
at our disposal. Instead, God is always subject – the One who acts
rather than is acted upon. Given this emphasis on God's radical
transcendence, Barth is understandably passionate about the
"impossible possibility"[33] of human speech about God. *How* can
we come to know anything about God at all? *How* do we bridge
the gap that must exist between the radically transcendent being of
God and the poor cognitive equipment of us wretched human
creatures? Before anything else, a necessary precondition for theological discourse must be in place, that is, the antecedent entry of
the divine into the human sphere. How does Barth account for that
entry? Barth's answer to th*e how* question always boils down to
the concept of revelation. Typically, Barth posits that this "impossible possibility" is brought about by *a prior action* — a self-revelation — by God. On its own, the human mind is impotent when
it comes to knowing the divine. But, thanks to his wholly gratuitous grace, God has decided to reveal himself to humanity
through Christ, his Word. An essential part of this revelation
depends on a wholly free God. It is a mistake, in Barth's opinion,
to suggest that God is available to humanity in a general way,
either in nature or in human experience. God makes Himself
known only when He breaks into the realm of the human.

In relation to the Bible, which for Barth is the only true locus of
human confrontation with God, Barth's thesis runs thus: "The
reality of the Word of God in all its three forms ... is grounded

---

[33] An expression of Eberhard Jüngel's in *Karl Barth: A Theological Legacy*
(Philadelphia: Westminster, 1986), ch. 2.

only in itself. So, too, the knowledge of it by humanity can consist only in its acknowledgement, and this acknowledgement can become real only through itself and can become intelligible only in terms of itself."[34] Barth is keen to put an end to all forms of what he calls "Christian Cartesianism," or the notion of an immanent possibility of experience of God's Word.[35] This has led commentators to call Barth's theology of revelation positivistic. He is said to have failed to attend to the contextual element of the human subjective pole in the God-human relationship.[36] Obviously, Barth's understanding of what constitutes human experience becomes an important issue for theology.

2.5.2 A Holistic and Bipolar Conception of Experience

Barth maintains a *holistic and bipolar* conception of experience. Because he takes a *holistic* approach to experience, Barth avoids emphasizing any one anthropological locus of experience of God. However, Christian experience of God ought also to be examined

---

[34] Karl Barth, *Church Dogmatics*, trs. G. T. Thomson (Edinburgh: T & T Clark, 1978), I/1:187. Barth had already treated the "three forms" of God's Word referred to under the section entitled, "The Word of God in Its Threefold Form," where his analysis proceeded under the captions: "The Word of God as Preached" (Proclamation); "The Written Word of God" (Bible); "The Revealed Word of God" (Revelation).

[35] See Barth, *Church Dogmatics*, I/1: 205-08.

[36] On the charge of positivism, see, for example, Dietrich Bonhoeffer, *Letters and Papers from Prison*, ed. Eberhard Bethge (London: SCM, 1971), 280. On Barth's neglect of the human context, see Alan Torrance, "Christian Experience and Divine Revelation in the Theologies of Friedrich Schleiermacher and Karl Barth," in *Christian Experience in Theology and Life*, ed I. Howard Marshall (Edinburgh: Rutherford, 1988), 112. Frei, who adopts Barth, suggests that the crucial issue is whether or not a theologian affirms that salvation depends not only on what Jesus said and did, but that he existed as God incarnate. He calls this belief that God in Jesus Christ directly intervened in the finite realm the "positivity" of Christian faith. See Frei, *Eclipse*, 58.

by a model of bipolarity that characterizes all human experience
of God, the two poles being the objective and subjective poles of
human relationship with God. The objective pole, which features
prominently in Barth's exposition, typically focuses on humanity's total determination by God in his self-revelation. *Knowledge*
is thus defined by Barth as "the confirmation of human acquain-
tance with an object whereby its truth becomes a determination of
the existence of the man who has the knowledge." Religious experience is the "unitary determination" of the whole human person
through one's being confronted by the transcending Truth embodied in the Word of God.[37] So unique is the Bible in Barth's hands
that, effectively, he has all but reduced every claim of authentic
human experience to a confrontation with, and a judgment by, the
Word of God. Clearly, what has been eclipsed in this analysis is
the subjective pole which consists in personal experiences of the
Christian in one's relationship with God, the context within which
one is addressed by God, and the personal response one makes to
this address. One may properly conclude that Barth's exposition
suffers from a lack of attention on the latter pole.[38]

It is typical of Barth to stress the priority of God's Word in the
determination of human existence over any claim of an inherent
ability in the human person in the decisions one makes or the
actions one takes in life. In particular, it is a fundamental Barthian
feature to insist that there is no question of mutual involvement or
interrelation or cooperation between divine determination and
human self-determination. That this is so, Barth explains, is
because "if a man lets himself be told by the Word of God that he
has a Lord, that he is the creature of this Lord, that he is a lost sinner blessed by Him, that he awaits eternal redemption and is thus

---

[37] See Barth, *Church Dogmatics*, I/1:198; Torrance, "Schleiermacher and
Barth," 103.

[38] Torrance, "Schleiermacher and Barth," 111-12.

a stranger in this sphere of time, this specific content of the Word experienced by him will flatly prohibit him from ascribing the possibility actualised in this experience with a possibility of his own."[39]

2.5.3 A Polemic Against the Protestant Liberal Tradition

Thirdly, in the first edition of *The Epistle to the Romans*,[40] Barth's polemical objectives are clearly aimed at the liberal Protestant tradition of the nineteenth century, starting with Schleiermacher, and the Protestant modernist theology that it spawned. This theology, which held sway for the one hundred years previous to Barth, is judged by him as a culpable betrayal of the Christian gospel in the name of Christianity. Theologians since Schleiermacher have, in Barth's view, been guilty of accommodating the notion of revelation to modernity's expectations of intelligible scientific knowledge, and, in their misdirected zeal to dialogue with their secular audience, have watered down the gospel message and compromised the task and integrity of proper Christian theological interpretation.

In Barth's judgement, the most serious offence committed by the ranks of the liberal theologians is, firstly, to be oblivious to the abyss of human sinfulness that separates God and humanity, an

---

[39] Barth, *Church Dogmatics*, I/1: 199. In this, as in other direct quotations, we do not propose to make any changes that would be suitably more sensitive to the gender-conscious climate of contemporary theology. Alterations would only render the original cumbersome to read.

[40] Since then, Barth has in many ways and in various publications, including the second edition of his commentary on *The Epistle to the Romans*, modified his views. For instance, without intending any diminution of God's transcendence, freedom and initiative, Barth later toned down somewhat his insistence on the radical otherness of God. For a brief account of these modifications, see John Macquarrie, *Twentieth-Century Religious Thought* (London: SCM, 1988[4]), 318-24.

abyss only the gratuitous revelation of God can bridge, and, secondly, to fail to recognize the qualitative distinction between the Word of God and the words of humanity. The liberal tradition from Schleiermacher on identified piety or religiosity as a universal condition of human experience from which was derived a mediating principle capable of justifying Christianity's intelligibility to modern culture. The typical error generated by this mediating theology is disclosed in its subordination of the Word of God to human words, revelation to experience, and the infinite to the finite – even though, clouded by sin, it remained strangely unaware of what it was doing.

Barth's dialectical theology[41] thus assumes a combative stance against the liberal tradition's subjectivist point of departure which he diagnoses as a theological expression of human self-sufficiency riding on the rising tide of individualism in Western culture. His polemical objectives are clearly oriented against modern[42] theology's sinful human pretensions. In this Cartesian style of theologising, human self-certainty provides the mediating principle or foundation upon which the knowledge of God rests. Barth insists that the theological task, properly undertaken, must be in obedience to grace, and to faithfulness to theology's singular content, namely, the Word of God in all of its three forms as preached,

---

[41] "The term 'dialectical theology'," Macquarrie explains, "points to the belief that one cannot characterize God in some simple formula, but may have to speak of him paradoxically, balancing each affirmation with a corresponding negation in order to do justice to a god who so infinitely transcends our finite creaturely being." See Macquarrie, *Twentieth-Century Religious Thought*, 320 and 323.

[42] John E. Thiel has discerned Barth's powerful influence on twentieth-century theology where the rubric of "modern theology" not only defines a historical period but also pejoratively designates a misguided theological task viewed from a nonfoundational perspective. This negative characterization of modern theology is also found in Lindbeck, amongst others. See *Nonfoundationalism* (Minneapolis: Fortress, 1994), 51.

written, and revealed. But Protestant modernism, in Barth's view, brings about an inversion of that understanding: instead of acknowledging that, in relation to God, humanity has constantly to listen to His word as something which he does not know and does not have the inherent possibility to anticipate and acknowledge, now even the very act of acknowledging the veracity of God's Word "becomes man's own, a predicate of his existence, a content of his consciousness, his possession."[43]

Put in contemporary terms, three related issues flow from this. First, Christian theology must properly remain non-foundational. There can be, Barth maintains, "no foundation, support, or justification" for theology in any philosophy, theory, or epistemology.[44] It is patently wrong to presuppose, as modern foundationalist theologians do, an *a priori* "theory of knowledge as a hinterland."[45] The modern preoccupation with methodological first principles is, for Barth, a formal way of making exaggerated claims for human capacities to know and comes under a corrupt epistemic tradition that must be rejected. Second, any attempt to translate the Christian message is but an illusion of mediating theology which does nothing but subverts God's revelation. Revelation constitutes the "absolute ground," with no recourse to any appellate court. And since the privileged ground of the reality and truth of revelation is located "wholly and in every respect" within itself, the theological task of expounding its promise in faith, and for the Church, lies not in translation, but in respecting the integrity of its proclamation.[46] Third, any apologetical theology which is concerned with justifying and translating the Gospel to render it intelligible to modern culture at large must be dismissed as spurious.

---

[43] Barth, *Church Dogmatics*, I/1: 61-62 and 214.
[44] Barth, *Church Dogmatics*, I/1: xiii.
[45] Barth, *Church Dogmatic*, II/1, trs T. Parker et al. (Edinburgh: T & T Clark, 1985), 5.
[46] Barth, *Church Dogmatic*, I/1: 305.

2.5.4 Intratextualilty as a Theological Necessity

Fourthly, following from what has been said so far, there can be no doubt that Barth's theology is thoroughly intratextual. For him, the loci of Christian theology, both with respect to conceptuality as well as language, cannot but reside in the Bible. The liberal enterprise, in his view, seeks to translate Christian discourse into a philosophical vocabulary alien to the plain language of God's self-revelation in Christ. In contrast, he insists that the task of theology is to dialogue not with the external world, but with the self-vindicating message of the biblical texts. He states categorically: "Theology can have no more urgent concern than always remaining true to itself... as scriptural theology."[47] But why did Barth take that route, seemingly brushing aside any claim of normativity for experience? Is human experience of no theological import in Barth's theology?

Experience was obviously important in the works of Schleiermacher. If this is less obvious in the case of Barth, it is only because it was less explicitly articulated, which does not diminish the underlying significance of experience for Barth. Nevertheless, the disparity between these two theological giants' respective understandings of

[47] Barth, *Church Dogmatics*, I/1: 285. M. Wyschogrod, a Jewish theologian, argues that the desire to make theology pass philosophic muster is an essentially gentile aspiration, whereas concern to preserve theology's autonomy from philosophy reflects sensibilities essentially Jewish. He sees the difference between the two disciplines as revolving around the Bible: "philosophy looks to reason for its foundation, whereas theology is rooted in the biblical text, to which alone it is responsible." See *The Body of Faith* (New York: Seabury, 1983), 75. He singles out Barth as displaying an eminently Jewish sense of textual responsibility. "Reading a page of Barth," he writes, "is something like shock therapy because it introduces the reader or listener to a frame of reference that attempts only to be true to itself and its sources and not to external demands that can be satisfied only by fitting the church's message into their mold, a mold foreign to it and therefore necessarily distorting" [p.79].

the role human experience plays in theology is huge and is destined
to lead to disputes. Schleiermacher is known for the conception of
piety and religious feeling which lies at the heart of his theology;
Barth is famous for his theology of revelation which, while it
accords a central significance to human experience, does so within a
"profoundly holistic conception of human experience as it is
addressed by God,"[48] as we saw earlier. This and other fundamental
differences between Barth and Schleiermacher remain differences of
foundational import which, as we shall see from the critical
responses to Lindbeck, show no sign of any quick dissolution.

In any attempt to understand the radical differences between Barth
and Schleiermacher, their profoundly different *contexts* and specific
concerns must not be overlooked. For it is there that we uncover some
clues as to why Barth took his trenchant biblical route earlier in the
century, a route which Lindbeck would himself take at the close of the
century. In this respect, Alan Torrance supplies a useful summary:

> Schleiermacher was writing as the Christian apologist seeking to
> offer more than simply a defence of the faith, but rather, positive
> apologetics — the advocacy of the Christian faith construed in terms
> congenial to the intellectual living in a period characterised by the
> decaying Enlightenment, the flood-tide of Romanticism and Kant-
> ian-Fichtian idealism — a time of surging cross-currents of thought
> and the radical questioning of traditional approaches to all spheres
> of life. Barth on the other hand was writing as the theologian
> churchman who had witnessed (and continued to witness in the rise
> of the Third Reich) the detrimental compromise of theology by the
> demands of German culture and the vacillating fashions of nine-
> teenth-century philosophy. His concern was to allow the methods
> and categories operative in his theology to be moulded radically and
> rigorously by the Word of God, by God's unique and full self-reve-
> lation in Christ as the eternal Word made flesh.[49]

---

[48] Torrance, "Schleiermacher and Barth," 83.
[49] Torrance, "Schleiermacher and Barth," 83-84.

For Barth, then, it serves no useful purpose to try and argue from the presumed vantage point of an external onlooker. The onlooker would only overlook the fact that, as we know it in the biblical promise, human self-knowledge, precisely as self-determination, is subject to determination by God. Our very self-determination needs this determination by God in order to be an experience of His Word.[50] So Barth can write: "We may quietly regard the will and conscience and feeling and all other possible anthropological centres as possibilities of human self-determination and then understand them in their totality as determined by the Word of God which affects the whole man."[51]

Barth's loyalty to the world of the text would take obstinate precedence over other considerations. He is, consequently, ready to tolerate discrepancies in logic and perception, bracketing even the law of noncontradiction and the results of rational observation. Evidently, adequacy to the world of the biblical text is a greater virtue than consistency.[52] In terms of theological import, this meant accepting truths which are neither supported by logic nor authenticated by experience. The Bible's claim to truth excludes all other claims. By this fervid espousal of the truth of the Bible, Barth has virtually ascribed to Scripture an autocratic status.[53]

[50] See Barth, *Church Dogmatics*, I/1:199-200.

[51] Barth, *Church Dogmatics*, I/1:202; see also 204. According to R. W. Jenson, Barth's theology is characterised by a clear antagonism to each of the three motifs of Enlightenment, viz.: (i) the emergence of the sort of autonomous, even absolutist 'Mensch'; (ii) the aspiration to 'critique', as an intellectual policy of suspicion over against all "appearances" of truth; (iii) a mechanistic world-view. See idem, "Karl Barth," in *The Modern Theologians*, ed. David Ford (Oxford: Blackwell, 1989), I:23-49. See also Barth, *Protestant Theology in the Nineteenth Century*, trs. B. Cozens and J. Bowden (London: SCM, 1972), 19.

[52] For this assessment of Barth, see George Hunsinger, "A Response to William Werpehowski," *ThT* 3 (1986) 359.

[53] See this description in Erich Auerbach, *Mimesis* (Princeton, NJ: Princeton University Press, 1963), 12.

This overriding textual loyalty is sponsored by Barth's narrative reading of Scripture. For Barth, embedded in scriptural narratives are truths so novel that they defy our logic and escape containment by present experience. But, far from explaining away the incomprehensible newness in the world carved by the texts, Barth insists that what is beyond comprehension may not be beyond imagination. It is, in Barth's view, the primary function of biblical narratives to enlighten our imagination with regard to the truths embedded in this "strange new world" of the text in which people speak and hear, think and understand, act and react in ways which might be described as distinctively Christian.

In this understanding, Barth moves from the particular to the general, never the other way around. It is only in this direction that we can begin to explain the powerful and shocking encounters with the truth-claims of the Bible. Here, again, is Barth's insight on what constitutes the authentic conditions of experience. For Barth, as we saw earlier, the very conditions for experience need to be transfigured and made new, in accordance with God's gratuitous promise, namely, the promise to renew the world through the death and resurrection of Jesus Christ.

2.5.5 An Acceptance of Objective Realism

Fifthly, Barth takes a specific point of departure in his theological work that should not be lost sight of. His theology always presupposes a very definite *order of being*, the authenticity of which is grounded in Scripture. In witnessing to God's revelation, Scripture confronts and relates God and humanity, divine facts and human attitudes, and enforces an order of knowing in correspondence to the Divine will.[54] In the words of a commentator,

---

[54] See Barth, *Church Dogmatics*, I/2:5.

"Barth's position clearly involves assuming that theological assertions, if true, are true because there is some sort of objective order
that they conform to, independently of our ability to recognize
them as true; this sort of position is known as *realism*."[55]

Reality, for Barth, has been disclosed in the Christ event. Theology is not confined to interpreting Jesus' narrated identity or
arranging the communal language in a coherent manner. In
essence, theology seeks to unfold the original revealed fact, which
is God's self-disclosure in Christ. In Barth's understanding, therefore, religious language, be it of the first or the second order, *does*
make ontological assertions and not merely intrasystematic utterances *about* reality. Barth's thought has been described thus:
"Christian beliefs and doctrines are true to the extent that they
correspond to the objective order revealed by God."[56]

2.6 Frei's Influence

Lindbeck owes much of his theological inspiration to Hans Frei,
not only for the latter's thought, but also for his felicitous reading
of Barth and Auerbach. This has prompted a commentator to suggest that Lindbeck could not have developed the distinctive
account in *The Nature of Doctrine* without the work of Frei. This
direct and profound indebtedness to Frei has been repeatedly
acknowledged by Lindbeck himself,[57] and spotted by others.[58]

[55] Graham White," Karl Barth's Theological Realism," *NZsTR* 26 (1984) 57.
[56] Wallace, "The New Yale Theology," 169.
[57] See ND, 12 & 138 n.35; and "The Gospel's Uniqueness," 449.
[58] Placher has identified Frei as "the chief exemplar and inspiration of the
theological method his friend and colleague George Lindbeck has called postliberal theology." Referring to Lindbeck's own forward to *ND*, Placher adds: "Frei
was a much more important influence in its development than the relatively
sparse references to him might suggest." See Placher's "Introduction" to *Theol-*

Again, our aim here is not to summarise Frei's substantial legacy within a short compass, but to selectively mention five elements that are most germane to our discussion.

2.6.1 The Argument for Realistic Biblical Narratives

In his magnum opus, *The Eclipse of Biblical Narrative*, Frei uses the term "history-like," as against "historical," to describe the biblical narrative from creation to consummation. Like a realistic narrative, the characters and intention of the Bible are given in the story itself. The meaning of the story is not located "behind" the text (in history) or somewhere "above" the text (in universal principles). Rather, the meaning is nestled in the very form and substance of the story, "constituted," Frei maintains, "through the mutual, specific, social context, and circumstances that form the indispensable narrative web."[59] For Frei, then, it makes scant theological sense to prospect behind the scenes, as it were, and to mine the historicity or intentionality outside of the linguistic world of the narrative. The story provides the meaning; it *is* the meaning. Going beyond the story to quarry the past either for historical referents or pre-compositional stages would do violence to the meaning that is given narratively.

While it is certainly true that it was Barth who helped shape Frei's thinking from the start, it was in fact Auerbach and Ryle who provided Frei with the sort of categories for appropriating Barth's hermeneutics and christology.[60] In this respect, we briefly underline two related elements.

ogy and Narrative, ed. G. Hunsinger and W. C. Placher (New York: Oxford University Press, 1993), 3 & 20-21 n.1.

[59] Frei, *Eclipse*, 280.

[60] Frei acknowledges three authors as being particularly influential: Karl Barth, Erich Auerbach, and Gilbert Ryle. See the Preface in *Eclipse*, vii.

First, Erich Auerbach argues that the vivid concreteness of the narrative constitutes a kind of realism. Realistic narratives, in their overarching stories, assume their own linguistic rules and integrity. Beginning with Homer, Auerbach suggests, this realistic tradition focuses on a reality within the story which operates independently from any external reference at all. The real world a story creates is the world to which we are lured. It contains nothing but itself. What is on offer by Homer, however, is purely a world for us to enter and enjoy, for it serves no other purpose. "The Homeric poems conceal nothing," Auerbach suggests, because "they contain no teaching and no secret second meaning." In other words, Homer can be analyzed, but he cannot be interpreted.[61]

By contrast, Auerbach sees the Bible as being unlike any other ancient book. The biblical narratives demand interpretation, and the hidden secrets embedded in them beckon interpretive efforts that constantly find something new to feed upon and some new insights to uncover. Furthermore, the need for interpretation reaches out beyond the original Jewish world of meaning, to the Assyrian, Babylonian, Persian and Greco-Roman categories, and now engulfs the entire human world and relates everything to Jesus Christ.[62]

But most crucially, the biblical narratives disclose a world that makes an absolute, tyrannical claim upon us: "it insists that it is the only real world, is destined for autocracy." The demand of the Holy Scripture is that of an all-consuming communal text that engulfs the whole of extra-biblical history. The rationale is a straightforward assertion: "All other scenes, issues, and ordinances have no right to appear independently of it, and it is

---

[61] Auerbach, *Mimesis*, 13.
[62] *Mimesis*, 16.

promised that all of them, the history of all mankind, will be given their due place within its frame, will be subordinated to it." Thus, beginning with the creation of the universe, and ending with its final consummation, everything known and knowable about the world must be incorporated as an ingredient of the divine plan into the world of the Bible. In other words, the origin and the destiny of the world are written into its sacred pages.[63]

A distinction needs to be drawn between a "primary world" and a "secondary world." Modern novels may create realistic narratives, but their fictional world is only a secondary world, without actual claim to refer to our primary world. By contrast, the realistic narratives of the biblical texts claim themselves to narrate the primary world – a world into whose framework all other events must be inscribed. Auerbach's point is clearly on the *claim* that these different texts make, not whether they render the "only" real world. Frei suggests that this mode of understanding parallels that of Barth, and he concludes that narratives define, in a way that non-narratives do not, "the one common world in which we move and have our being."[64] This is also for Frei the dominant way the Bible had been read for the first seventeen centuries of Christian tradition.

Second, in addition to Auerbach, another important influence comes from Gilbert Ryle[65] who furnished Frei with a way of thinking about personal identity. Ryle was critical of the Cartesian "myth" which drew a distinction between the inner and the outer person: the public life of the person consisted of matter and physical existence, with its bodily history; and the private life of the

[63] *Mimesis*, 15.

[64] Hans Frei, "Eberhard Busch's Biography of Karl Barth," in *Types of Christian Theology*, ed. G. Hunsinger and W. C. Placher (New Haven: Yale University Press, 1992) [hereafter cited as *Types*], 161.

[65] See Gilbert Ryle, *The Concept of Mind* (New York: Barnes and Noble, 1962).

person consisted of consciousness and mental existence, with its collateral history of the mind. On this mythical construction, every human act is seen as comprising two separate components, namely, an inner, mental act of the mind, and an external, physical act of the body. Ryle dissolved the two into one, that is, a single action carried out in a particular way and context. Reasoning in this manner, and using many illustrations, Ryle concluded that the identity of a person was not made up of some nebulous inner essence mysteriously related to, or revealed by, external words and bodily actions. Rather, a person's identity is constituted by his or her pattern of speech and actions. Frei therefore writes: "For descriptive purposes, a person's uniqueness is not attributable to a super-added factor, an invisible agent residing inside and from there directing the body." Instead of trying to pin down an inner intention from which to trace a transition, be it hypothetical or real, to an outer action, thereby according to human interiority a priority status as the true self, Frei pinpoints the development from intention to action as constituting the person. His conclusion is that one is the person one has become through one's enacted intentions.[66]

This analysis provides Frei with the tools to counter the dominant theological agenda of the time, the agenda set by Bultmann and the old and new quests for the historical Jesus. Contrary to any suggestion that Jesus' inner certainty was the very nature of his person, Frei argues that Jesus' identity is gleaned from the Gospels which narrate "what he did and underwent, and not simply his understanding or self-understanding."[67] The Gospels could and did narrate Jesus' identity, their many episodes vividly showing us the sort of person he was, regardless of whether any particular incident

---

[66] Hans W. Frei, *The Identity of Jesus Christ: The Hermeneutical Bases of Dogmatic Theology* (Philadelphia: Fortress, 1975) [hereafter cited as *Identity*], 42-43.

[67] Frei, *Types*, 184.

actually took place in the way it was narrated. Particularly important are the passion narratives where the narrative flow yields the unitary character of Jesus most powerfully. The particular nature of the biblical narratives fosters another striking pointer: the Gospels reveal that Jesus is who he is above all in his resurrection. This in turn becomes the central message within the coherent unity of the Old and New Testaments. Jesus as the Resurrected One identified in the text determines the tone, the content and the frame within which Christians could intelligibly read the narratives as Scriptures, find meaning for the whole of their existence, and making sense of "the one common world in which we all live and move and have our being."[68]

In sum, Frei wants to show that "the story, as story – not necessarily as history – should be taken in its own right and not symbolically and that, if it is read for its own sake, it suggests that Jesus' identity is self-focused and unsubstitutably his own."[69]

2.6.2 Fitting Our Life into the Bible

The urgency of the Bible's claim to truth converts us to "either its subjects or its rebels."[70] "Far from seeking, like Homer, merely to make us forget our own reality for a few hours," Auerbach discovers, the world of the Scripture stories "seeks to overcome our reality: we are to fit our life into its world, feel ourselves to be elements in its structure of universal history."[71] This understanding of the Bible as seeking to 'overcome our reality' has been influential in the development of narrative theology and has been instrumental in persuading Frei to employ the idea of the Bible as a

---

[68] Frei, *Types*, 161.
[69] Frei, *Identity*, 102.
[70] This phrase comes from Gerard Loughlin, *Telling God's Story*, 36.
[71] Auerbach, *Mimesis*, 15.

consuming text in order to articulate the primacy of the biblical story for theology. The Bible, from Genesis to the Apocalypse, sets forth a complete story of the world, from its beginning to its ending, and constitutes the only true story of the world. All other stories must be inscribed into the biblical story and, from within the world disclosed in the Bible, find their place and meaning. It is not for the biblical story to find its place and meaning in other stories. Rather, the biblical story provides the lens with which we view God, the world and ourselves. When we allow the biblical story to become our story, it overcomes our reality. Our perspectives change; we now see the world differently and we act differently, very much as a character in the Bible's story.

This fruitful mode of reading the Bible, Frei argues, is consistent with the greater part of the Christian tradition, from Augustine to the Reformation and even into the modern era, except for those rebellious biblical interpretive quests.[72] In this regnant form of scriptural reading, the Bible's "narrated, narratable world is at the same time the ordinary world in which we are responsible for our actions."[73] For Frei, Barth uses exegesis, ethics, and *ad hoc* apologetics, in order to show how the biblical world is our world. Barth is likened to a theological poet who carefully crafted together a dogmatic imagination through combining second-order talk and imaginative restatements of parts of the original biblical narrative. Throughout all this, however, the controlling subject matter for Barth always resides in the Holy Scripture.[74]

As we noted earlier, Frei suggests that it was between the sixteenth and the eighteenth centuries that the idea of the human person as "a subject" and an individual self with inalienable rights emerged. People began to read the Bible in a new way. They no

[72] Frei, *Eclipse*, 1.
[73] Frei, *Types*, 161.
[74] Frei, *Types*, 162.

longer saw themselves as characters in the world structured by the text, but as individuals to whom the text had to speak. Reading the Bible this way entailed defining our real world in terms of our daily experience, so that the Bible is consciously placed in this "real" world for its meaning to be explicated. Frei is acutely aware that his narrative approach to reading the Bible runs counter to the dominant culture, engulfed as the latter currently is in the modern liberal spirit, and ruled as it is by external stories constituting its ostensive or ideal reference. In a liberal, individualistic cultural milieu, biblical narratives take a back seat to individual concerns. Inspired by Barth, however, Frei makes it practically his theological project to recall the Church to the pre-critical but formerly regnant and fruitful mode of reading the Bible. One senses that this project has much to do with his battle against "subjectivism, individualism and psychologism" – charges which he lays, albeit with "large qualifications," as he admits, at the door of Schleiermacher.[75]

2.6.3 The Argument Against Apologetics

In broad outlines, Frei traces a dichotomy of major biblical interpretations running from the eighteenth century down to contemporary time. On one side, the biblical narratives are regarded as disclosing eternal truths about God and human nature. The text is seen as generating a complex of symbolic structures that reveal universal pictures through abstract means without specific reference to the human world. On the other side, the biblical narratives are regarded as the records of historical events reachable by historical-critical methods. Both approaches, in Frei's assessment, are unsatisfactory, for they distort the meaning of the text: the

[75] Frei, *Eclipse*, 318.

first, for its "liberal" universalizing approach and, the second, for its "proto-fundamentalist" sourcebook approach. Failing to take seriously both the narrative character of the text and, especially, the way in which the passion narratives identify Christ and should identify Christians, these approaches have lost sight of the way these texts were read throughout most of the Christian tradition. The particular characters and episodes of the biblical narratives are neither simply the illustrations for some general moral lessons, nor primarily concerned with the question of historical accuracy.[76] This sets the stage for Frei's argument against apologetics.

When a theology begins with apologetics, Frei argues, the result is the kind of misreading of the Bible that we have witnessed during the past two centuries. A Christian theologian who takes contemporary human experience as the point of departure, and seeks to uncover the truth of the biblical narratives by relating them to that experience, will finish up with some moral lessons or critically established historical titbits. No longer treated for what they are, biblical narratives end up being distorted – their narrative structures are ignored, and their meaning eclipsed. A theology that begins with the human world is clearly erroneous in Frei's view.[77] To be faithful to its mission, Christian theology should stick to its *descriptive* task of unraveling the internal logic of the Christian faith, to give an account of the faith. Theologians ought not to attempt to systematically ground that account by an appeal to universal, ahistorical criteria. To do theology properly, Frei proposes,

[76] See, generally, Placher, "Introduction," 7-8.

[77] Placher, "Introduction," 8. See also Hunsinger's "Afterword" to *Theology and Narrative*, where he writes: "The key move behind this apologetic aim and correlationalist method, as Frei sees it, is allowing the criteria of meaningfulness to be determined on rational grounds independently of biblical narrative. This move ensures that an independently validated anthropology, whatever it may be, will set the terms for the significance of Jesus Christ" [p.238].

"we raise the question in a drastically non-apologetic, non-perspectivalist fashion: 'What does this narrative say or mean, never mind whether it can become a meaningful possibility of life perspective for us or not.' Its meaning on the one hand, and its possible as well as actual truth for us on the other, are two totally different questions."[78] A theological preoccupation with the apologetical task is a waste of energy because it is "self-defeating – except as an *ad hoc*" exercise.[79]

To be sure, Christians who have understood the meaning and the truth of the scriptural world do desire to connect that world with different aspects of the world of their daily struggles, and both Frei and Barth would accept the need for theology to make connections with the wider culture. Indeed, theologians ought to feel free to make use of philosophy, literary theories, or anthropology where these contribute towards explaining the encompassing world of the Christian Scriptures. What Frei brings to attention is the particular features of the biblical narrative-world. Acknowledging the advantages and, at the same time, mindful of the dangers, Frei points out that a theological approach may be classified as "disastrous" only if: (1) it completely rules out any legitimate use of philosophy whatsoever, either as an issue or a means for reflection; or (2) with "a pathetic obeisance," it relies on philosophy as the "master key" for comprehending the very possibility, shape and rational certainty for Christian theology.[80] Following Barth, paramount in Frei's consideration is that none of the other linguistic worlds, or their descriptions, or arguments with them, should be permitted to take precedence over, or to serve as a "pre-description" for, the world of the Christian discourse. In Frei's scheme, a proper understanding of the Christian faith begins from

[78] Frei, *Eclipse*, 40.
[79] Frei, *Identity*, xii.
[80] Frei, *Types*, 197.

within its own faith perspective, and never the other way around where the Christian faith looks outward for general theories to understand and describe itself. It is patently wrong to attempt to step outside the encompassing world of the Christian communal text.[81]

Does not this insistence on making sense of the world from a Christian perspective sound obstinately "dogmatic"? Frei argues that a strict reliance on the structure of Christian faith yields its own kind of persuasive power, without, at the same time, suggesting that it constitutes a convincing case for the unbeliever. He rests content with Barth's suggestion that a good dogmatics is the best apologetics. A full-scale apologetics, on the other hand, distorts both the logic of faith and the meaning of the biblical texts. The proper approach is to take the coherent biblical narrative as the story to be dwelt in, and not as a text to be interpreted for those who live outside its narrated world.

2.6.4 Focus on the Particular, Contra Universal – A Communal Route

Intratextuality is, for Frei, the safeguard for Christian particularity. His approach sidesteps any claim regarding universal symbolism or historical referents harboured by the biblical text. Concerned with a pervasive lack of enthusiasm amongst theologians to take the biblical narratives seriously as narratives, Frei presses his criticisms against any general hermeneutical theory.[82] A general

---

[81] See Frei, *Types*, 161.

[82] Frei criticizes the hermeneutical theory represented by Ricoeur and Tracy in "The 'Literal Reading' of Biblical Narrative in the Christian Tradition," in *Theology and Narrative*, ed. G. Hunsinger and W. C. Placher (New York: Oxford University Press, 1993), 117-52. Ricoeur and Tracy's work are, in Frei's view, illustrative of the deep flaws in the whole tradition of hermeneutics. In the

theory limits our interpretation of the particular Christian text *ab initio*. This robs our particular communal text of its characteristic power of shaping our understanding of God's Word.

Frei's abhorrence of general hermeneutical theories finds acute expression in his zeal to prevent even his own narrative theory from becoming a prioritising theory, thereby forcing the text to fit into the theory. To better preserve the particularity of the text, he calls for a return of the key insights of precritical exegesis. In other words, he takes a communal route, relying on the long tradition of the Christian Church in its reading of sacred Scriptures. That long tradition consistently features a literal reading of the text — a consistency Frei now relies on as a kind of informal priority, underpinned, to be sure, by communal consensus for seventeen centuries.[83] As it is not just some particular literary theory, literal reading does not "break" in the face of changes in literary fashion or the discrepancy between practice and theory. And yet, as a set of rules characterizing a long-standing traditional practice of Christian reading of biblical texts, literal reading will "stretch" to fit any number of theories about the human person, and historical as well as textual referents. Regarding the future of the "literal reading," Frei thus suggests: "The less entangled in theory and the more firmly rooted not in a narrative (literary) tradition but in its primary and original context, a religious community's 'rule' for faithful reading, the more clearly it is likely to come into view, and the stronger as well as more flexible and supple it is likely to look."[84]

last analysis, these scholars seriously erred on two counts: [1] in treating the Gospel narratives about Jesus as presentations of a certain mode-of-being-in-the-world rather than primarily as narratives about the singular person of Jesus; and [2] in hinging Jesus' identity primarily on his alleged self-consciousness somehow expressed in words and deeds, rather than as constituted by his enacted intentions particularized in the narratives.

[83] See Placher, "Introduction," 17.
[84] Frei, "Literal Reading," 139.

In reverting to the communal practice, Frei consciously aligns his definition of the Church to a culture. He draws insights from Clifford Geertz[85] in making his proposal: "Culture consists of socially established structures of meaning. I'm suggesting that the Church is like that – a culture, not only of course for the observer but also for the agent, the adherent, who would understand it. There is a sacred text — a typical element in a religious system – and there are informal rules and conventions governing how the sign system works in regard to sacred scripture. The kind of theology that I like best is the kind that is closer to this outlook rather than to philosophy, or to historiography."[86]

Clearly, then, Frei is passionate in rejecting the universal rules of hermeneutics and embracing the particularities of the communal text. In making this strategy the bedrock of his theology, Frei, like Barth before him, demonstrates his affinities with postmodern thinkers – affinities shared by others in the so-called Yale school. On one specific point, however, Frei goes further than his colleagues in the postliberal camp and clearly marks a significant difference from Lindbeck. This is the christological focus. Although it is his emphasis on narrative reading of the Bible that propels Frei to prominence, the central element of his theology in fact lies in its christology.

2.6.5 Focus on Christology – Another Communal Route

A proper analysis of Frei's method for theology cannot fail to note his intense christological focus.[87] It is perhaps this focus on

---

[85] Clifford Geertz, *The Interpretation of Cultures* (New York: Basic Books, 1973).

[86] Frei, *Types*, 13.

[87] We are indebted to Mike Higton for the analysis in this section. See his "Frei's Christology and Lindbeck's Cultural-Linguistic Theory," *SJT* 50 (1997) 83-95.

christology, on which Frei grounds the central element of his theology, that will prove most durable as compared with other orientations within the so-called Yale school, particularly those that are
more dependent on socio-cultural or even literary theories. Frei's
approach involves two steps, both of which depart from the practice of the Church.

First, in *The Identity of Jesus*, Frei's basic datum is the Christian communal conviction that Jesus of Nazareth, the man who
lived and died some two thousand years ago, is present to us
today.[88] As the Church understands it, Jesus' *presence* is not physical, save symbolically through the sacrament, nor communicative, save in the communal reading and preaching of the Word.
But this presence is nevertheless taken to be personal and is determinate of the unsubstitutable historical personage called Jesus of
Nazareth. Moreover, this "presence" is no longer thought of or
practised as being confined by space and time. Turning to *identity*,
Frei argues that Jesus Christ has always been held, in Christian
conviction, to be the unsubstitutable person portrayed by the
Gospel texts, whatever is decided about their historicity. The
Gospels are, for Frei, largely history-like, realistic narratives.[89]
Relying on a complex mix of five points, Frei unpacks his christological argument for the presence of Christ. These are: [1] an
appeal to the Gospel narratives which point to the identity of Jesus
through a coalescence of temporal change and continuity, and
which display an overall shape, reaching a climax where the central character, Jesus Christ, is revealed through his cross and resurrection; [2] an Anselmian sort of ontological argument which
suggests that the Jesus of Nazareth who lived two thousand years
ago, who suffered, died, and rose again, cannot be thought of as

---

[88] See Frei, *Identity*, 1-10. Part One of the book covers the subject of "presence," while Part Two deals with "identity."

[89] Frei, *Identity*, xiv-vi.

not present, because then one would not be thinking of Jesus Christ;[90] [3] a pneumatological explication of Christ's current presence in the Spirit; [4] an eschatological explanation of Christ's direct presence in the eschaton; and [5] an exposition of the Church as Christ's presence.[91] This whole complex of argumentation serves to develop a formal rule for Christian communal speech and practice, through a strategy of placing the word "presence" against the norm designated by the communal text, in which the particular identity of Jesus Christ is paradigmatically depicted.

Thus, in a fully christological way, the Christian community points to the Bible as its source and starting point for christology. Furthermore, Jesus' identity is *re-presented* in the Church in such a way that the Church can be thought of as "the indirect, localised presence of Jesus Christ in and for the world."[92]

Secondly, Frei goes further in his later work,[93] conscious now that his proposal might also be classified as yet another literary theory. The Church, Frei points out, does more than point to the Bible; it used the Bible in a particular way — the narrative way — for the first seventeen centuries. It is narrative reading that most prominently allowed the Church to be spoken to by the Bible, and that accorded the Bible an independent normative status. This is not a contingent fact of history; it is the result of the Christian community's traditional acceptance of Jesus of Nazareth as their Lord and Saviour who provided them with the source and norm for authentic human living – an acceptance that impels believers to read the Bible as Holy Scriptures in which lies encoded the life, words and

[90] Frei, *Identity*, 145-46.

[91] Frei, Identity, 157-64.

[92] Frei, *Identity*, 158. For further discussions, see M. A. Higton, "'A Carefully Circumscribed Progressive Politics': Hans Frei's Political Theology," *ModTh* 15 (1999) 55-83.

[93] See especially "Literal Reading" referred to in n.82 above.

actions of that specifically historical true God and true Man.

In sum, then, by turning to christological and ecclesiological emphases, Frei makes a claim that goes beyond any secular socio-cultural or literary theories. Identity and presence are entirely one in Christ. Establishing the priority of the identity of Christ – the "who" question — has, for Frei, the advantage of shifting atten-tion away from any ascription of a foundational role to experience in imaginative speculations on "how" Christ's presence may be accounted for. Further, prioritising the identity question impels the believer to turn to the four Gospels where Jesus' character is most clearly portrayed. There, the narrative requires no external assis-tance for unravelling its meaning. Biblical narrative realism offers the only context a theologian could possibly need for scriptural explication.

Brief though it may be, Section II has provided some indicators of potent theological claims. We now turn in the next section to see how far Lindbeck has utilised these insights in developing his own theological agenda, and where he has departed from these insights as he developed his own particular and comprehensive programme.

Section III: Lindbeck's Postliberal Theological Agenda

Lindbeck's chief practical concern lies in proposing the useful-ness of the distinctive Christian faith-tradition in contemporary pluralistic settings, both for the Church and for the larger society. Translated into a theological agenda, this concern is paradigmati-cally encapsulated in the complex notion of intratextuality as the central theme in his postliberal theology. Featured prominently in this theology is a passionate plea for a return of the premodern mode of Bible-reading and for the Church to be shaped by that reading.[94] And, relative to that plea, a host of issues, none of which may be treated as peripheral, cohere in Lindbeck's theological outlook where two elements are particularly outstanding – elements which thread together a complex of argumentations into a rich fabric. These are [1] the conception of the task of theology and theological method, and [2] an understanding of what it means to be Church. We shall address the first of these two elements in this chapter and leave the second for the final chapter where ecclesiological implications that surface throughout the present study will be collated for a critical synthesis.

2.7 The Task of Theology and Theological Method

Three preliminary observations are in order. First, in a general sense (and this recalls what we have seen in our first chapter), Lindbeck insists there are no neutral criteria for evaluating the Christian faith or, indeed, the viability of his comprehensive scheme. Second, Lindbeck's proposal has a specific character of its own, based as it is on a set of three criteria: faithfulness as intratextuality; applicability as futurology; and intelligibility as skill. It is with regard to these criteriological priorities that Lindbeck knows he faces some of his toughest critics.[95] Third, Lindbeck's polemic is clearly ranged against the liberal theological task and its reliance on universal foundations for apologetic strategies. Before anything else, it is useful to turn at once to his argumentation for the postliberal, nonfoundationalist alternative to apologetics.

[94] In searching for a particular "well-integrated" moral tradition to affiliate himself with, MacIntyre locates himself at the point at which premodern moral tradition begins to be displaced by liberal modernity. See Stout, "Homeward Bound," 222.
[95] See Buckley, "Doctrine in the Diaspora," 446.

2.7.1 A Nonfoundational Approach to Theology

The task of theology, Lindbeck maintains, is to render "a normative explication of the meaning a religion has only for its adherents."[96] A seemingly innocuous declaration, but for the word "only," it has far-reaching implications. To start with, the search for universal foundations for legitimising religious beliefs is at once outlawed, and even attempts at uncovering common human structures for describing human religious inclinations are frowned upon. Examples may be multiplied, but they all point to a controlling polemical interest ranged squarely against the liberal, subjectivistic reasoning which spawns an individualistic modern culture.

In order to be "theologically faithful," Lindbeck shuns the liberal project of translating traditional Christian categories into terms comprehensible to the modern world. A postliberal theology resists the temptation to accommodate itself to contemporary human experience, in part because that carries with it the risk of theology becoming irrelevant. The task of theology, in keeping with the cultural-linguistic approach that Lindbeck has fostered, is to be carried out intrasemiotically or intratextually.[97] Put differently, the postliberal agenda aims at transformation, not conformation.

Even though Lindbeck is steadfast in his opposition to the liberal programme, he positively acknowledges its missionary zeal. The

[96] ND, 113.
[97] See ND, 116. Various other authors hold similar views. See William Werpehowski, "Ad Hoc Apologetics," *JR* 66 (1986) 282-301. To avoid becoming irrelevant, Harvey Cox focuses on a revival of traditional religion that is at the same time critical of modernity and a theological alliance with modernity, in *Religion in the Secular City* (New York: Simon & Schuster, 1984). Stanley Hauerwas, in *A Community of Character* (Notre Dame: University of Notre Dame Press, 1981), inspired by the work of Alasdair MacIntyre, holds that liberal theology and politics combine to produce a climate vacuous of moral consensus, and render the crisis increasingly intractable.

contemporary situation, after all, is so engulfed by pluralism that
communal traditions no longer remain unbroken, nor is faith automatically transmitted down successive generations. Religiousness
now often involves choosing from competing alternatives. In such
settings, a liberal apologetic approach is attractive on account of its
universal foundations from which religions can be evaluated and traditional meanings translated into currently intelligible terms. From
this angle, theological liberalism is admirably committed to making
religion experientially intelligible to both its despisers and apprecia-
tors alike in the modern culture. The Gospel that has become opaque
to today's world may now be clarified systematically and it is tempting to assess the faithfulness of this endeavour on the basis of its successes in communicating to the modern mind.[98]

Larger problems come to the fore, however, when a foundationalist approach is adopted, and Lindbeck judges that the liberal approach is, on that score, seriously flawed. Precisely in
attempting to relieve the modern predicament, the liberals are
contributing to the unhappy fate that besets Christianity in this
modern age. The issue, ultimately, turns on the validity of the
foundational enterprise to which the liberals are committed. It is
an enterprise that rests squarely on uncovering universal principles or structures, be they metaphysical, existential, phenomenological, or hermeneutical.[99] Postliberals are skeptical about the
liberal search for foundations and propose an alternative that is
marked by a critical position from which to stamp the identity of
the Church against the modern world. In a language that gives a
clear stamp to Lindbeck's polemical objectives, the postliberal
task, he suggests, is to counteract the "acids of modernity."[100]

[98] See ND, 128-29.

[99] See ND, 129.

[100] ND, 127. Here, we recall the potency of Barth's strenuous attack against
modernist thoughts.

The moderns no longer understand the traditional Christian words, the truth and transforming power of the Christian message having been subsumed under modernity's own ethos, values and directions. There is nothing more corrosive of the tradition-specific Christian culture and identity than the liberal search for universal foundations for an apologetical enterprise.

The advent of a postliberal age provides the Church with an opportunity to strengthen its identity amid a culture of alarming pluralism. But the Church can only begin to tackle the problem, if it stays faithful to its own traditional cultural-linguistic particularities. This entails a nonfoundational or anti-foundational stance in theology.[101] Christian theology, to be faithful, must be configured in terms that closely adhere to the normativity of the biblical world as it has been read and interpreted in the ecclesial community through the ages. In that mode of reading and interpreting the Bible, faithfulness is assessed in terms of its adequacy to the scriptural text alone, that is, to intratextuality, and not in terms of a correlated adequacy of text and contemporary experience. Lindbeck thus eschews a correlational approach to theology as foundationalist, as losing the specificity of the ecclesial dimension of the theological enterprise, and as privileging contemporary experience too excessively. Postliberals understand their theological responsibility as faithfulness, and faithfulness is adjudicated upon the criterion of intratextuality, or adequacy to the inherent message of the communal text.

Lindbeck's nonfoundationalist arguments are closely bound up with his anti-apologetical orientation, so that this analysis continues as we turn to his description of a proper apologetic exercise as *ad hoc*.

---

[101] Lindbeck's antifoundationalist approach, which is operative throughout *The Nature of Doctrine*, finds its most explicit expression on pp.130-32. See also his article, "Theologische Methode und Wissenschaftstheorie," *Theologische Revue* 74 (1978) 267-80.

2.7.2 The Case for Ad Hoc Apologetics

An important criterion for theology is intelligibility.[102] But when Lindbeck's intratextual hermeneutics is carried over to his understanding of apologetics and dialogue, it is predictable that only a restricted scope is ascribed to both. He repudiates any extrabiblical foundations, or ontological grounding, for proving or disproving either the truth or falsity of the Christian witness. His aim here is neither to sever all links between theology and philosophy, nor to suggest that the Church's classic apologetic task of offering warrants for Christianity's truth claims has been thoroughly misguided. All too clearly, he is addressing the "errant" liberal theological enterprise which grounds the Christian witness in common structures of experience and rationality.

Consonant with this vision, and drawing an analogy from the rules of "depth grammar," Lindbeck maintains that intelligibility is adequately grasped only by *skill* rather than in theory. The significance of Lindbeck's compact argument bears repeating: He is making the forceful claim that one can only *properly* speak the language of a given faith as an insider, having the right skills, living the faith, practising what it teaches, and demonstrating the truth of its teaching in performance and not in doctrinal argumentation. The right skills refer to the skill in performing the theological task of unpacking the meaning of the biblical narratives according to the inner logic of the texts; the skill in showing the capacity of the biblical world to provide a holistic meaning system for comprehending the whole of human life; and the skill, ultimately, in concretely living out the Gospel values to the full in every conceivable setting in life.[103] In sharp contrast, however,

---

[102] On criteria for constructive theology, see Roger Haight, *Dynamics of Theology* (New York: Paulist, 1990), 210-12.

[103] For Lindbeck's analysis on "intelligibility as skill," see ND, 128-34.

modern liberal theology has especially been committed to the apologetic enterprise as validating the intelligibility of Christian claims before the court of epistemic scrutiny that characterises post-Enlightenment culture. But postliberals, Lindbeck declares, are bound to be skeptical about apologetics and foundationalist logic. This skepticism, it seems, has been spawned by several factors, some of which we shall now sketch.

First, the apologetical enterprise hopes for dialogue with the modern world. This, above all else, shapes the liberal concern for the intellectual credibility of the Christian faith. In appealing to purported neutral grounds as the entry point for conversation with modernity, the apologists rely on universal theories as foundations for theological knowledge, and as first principles both acceptable to the conversation partners of modernity and capable of rendering Christian claims intelligible. And yet, philosophers articulating a nonfoundational critique of knowledge have demonstrated the inherent deficiencies of foundationalism,[104] especially in the latter's indefensible reliance on the impugned "universals."

Second, in their desire to dialogue with the modern world, the apologetically-oriented theologians are wont to adopt some form of "critical correlation" of traditional Christian sources with contemporary experience.[105] The inherent risk with the correlational approach is that theologians, differing in their analyses of what human beings need ("i.e., in their anthropologies and/or in their analyses of the requirements of the contemporary situation and experiences"), tend to look for different things in the Bible and in Jesus. In the process, they approach the Bible with some

---

[104] For a brief discussion of selected authors who adopt an approach to philosophical criticism called nonfoundationalism, see Thiel, *Nonfoundationalism*, chapter 1; Placher, *Unapologetic Theology*, ch. 2.

[105] See Lindbeck, "The Bible as Realistic Narrative," 84.

hermeneutical framework — be they phenomenological, existentialist, transcendental Thomist, Marxist, or evolutionary — which are extra-biblical in nature. In their attempt to make the Gospel relevant to contemporary human experience, both the questions raised and the answers received are at least partly pre-determined by the interpretive frameworks that they choose. The end result of this multiplicity of correlational apologetical approaches, Lindbeck judges, is "a pluralism that threatens to become chaos."[106]

Third, perhaps a more important factor in Lindbeck's nonfoundationalist orientation, stems from sociological concerns.[107] Lindbeck, as we saw, is deeply concerned with the decline in biblical literacy. He places Western culture in an intermediate stage "where socialization is ineffective, catechesis impossible, and translation a tempting alternative."[108] The present age appears to him woefully as the passing of Christendom, and Christians are becoming a diaspora.[109] In these circumstances, Lindbeck's chief practical concern, as we observed earlier, is to cultivate the distinctive Christian culture, language and practice. He is therefore not so much concerned with making validity-judgment on the philosophical rationality of apologetics, as he is with articulating the usefulness of an intratextual approach to the Christian Gospel to preserve Christian identity. What Lindbeck finds objectionable in the foundationalist approach to theology is that this approach contributes to the erosion of Christian identity: as it measures the

---

[106] Lindbeck, "The Bible as Realistic Narrative," 83.

[107] This observation is made by Thiel in *Nonfoundationalism*, 61.

[108] ND, 133.

[109] Lindbeck, "The Story-Shaped Church," 174; "The Church," in *Keeping the Faith*, ed. Geoffrey Wainwright (Philadelphia: Fortress, 1988), 190. For Lindbeck's reliance on Rahner's description of "diaspora," see "Ecumenism and the Future of Belief," *Una Sancta* 25:3 (1968) 4; and "The Sectarian Future of the Church," in *The God Experience*, ed. Joseph Whelan (New York: Newman, 1971), 227.

intelligibility of the Gospel message by bringing the criteria of the larger culture to bear, the natural outcome is a loss of Christian particularity.

Fourth, in line with Barth's theology, Lindbeck eschews all apologetic strategies which are aimed at justifying Christian beliefs in the public realm. These strategies are thought either to amount to an impossible exercise, or are unsuccessful in securing public agreement. The public realm is far too fragmented for such strategies to be successful. In this respect, Lindbeck resembles a postmodern as he indeed describes himself to be,[110] for giving up the Enlightenment optimism that all rational agents can come to the same conclusions.

Fifth, deeply persuaded as he is that religions are like languages and cultures (or "community-forming semiotic systems"[111]), Lindbeck claims that "they can no more be taught by means of translation than can Chinese and French." Like languages, "religions can best be understood in their own terms, rather than by transposing them into an alien speech." Further, like linguistic grammar, the grammar of religion is best learned by practice, not by theory, nor by analysing experience.[112]

We shall return to the question of translation shortly. For the moment, we note that Lindbeck is quick to clarify that antifoundationalism "is not to be equated with irrationalism."[113] Preempting criticisms precisely at this point, Lindbeck argues that intratextuality implies neither relativism (that is, turning religions into self-enclosed and incommensurable intellectual ghettoes) nor fideism (that is, seeing religions as blind faiths).[114] As we shall see in the

---

[110] ND, 135 n.1
[111] Lindbeck, "The Gospel's Uniqueness," 423.
[112] ND, 129.
[113] ND, 130.
[114] ND, 128.

next chapter, the charges of relativism and fideism continue to plague the postliberals to this day, with no sign of any let up from its detractors or any concerted effort at formulating a spirited reply from its proponents.

On the question of relativism, Lindbeck turns to other disciplines and observes that the cultural-linguistic orientation, with its intratextual focus, is common in history, anthropology, sociology, and philosophy. Practitioners in these fields are interested in descriptive rather than apologetic intelligibility. There is a case for saying, in Lindbeck's view, that the postliberal commitment to intratextual description, far from being relativistic, actually enjoys interdisciplinary advantages. On the other hand, the liberal attempt to explain religions by translating them into extraneous conceptualities may well appeal, paradoxically, only to theologians and some other religious people.[115]

Still, what about rationality? Lindbeck insists that his outlook does not entail a fideistic retreat from reason. The issue, as he formulates it, is not one of reasonableness. Rather, the case turns, in his view, on the undeniable logic of a context-dependent rationality in theology as against the possibility, which he denies, of formulating any neutral, framework-independent language. For, he insists, rationality, as it actually functions, has to be context-specific, an argument that clearly resonates with MacIntyre's claim that rationality is always tradition-specific. Clearly, then, the bottom line for Lindbeck is a trenchant denial of the liberal theologian's reliance on allegedly neutral, universal criteria to underpin theology's intellectual discourse. The liberal commitment to the foundational enterprise of uncovering universal principles or structures may carry, as Lindbeck concedes, great strength in rendering religion experientially intelligible to a culture which has

[115] ND, 129-30.

otherwise "become opaque" to the world of the Gospel. But, even though this is motivated by commendable missionary zeal, Lindbeck's charge against the liberal agenda is that it smacks of an "accommodation to culture."[116]

That said, the question remains of how the intelligibility and possible truth of the Christian message could be presented to secular moderns or people of other faiths. In a formulation that finds wide acceptance, Lindbeck suggests that resistance to translation does not entail a whole-scale ban on apologetics. Again, in an argument that recalls Barth, Lindbeck reiterates that while revelation ought to dominate all aspects of the theological enterprise, this does not exclude — and he tacitly discloses through his work that he in fact practises — "a subsidiary use of philosophical and experiential considerations in the explication and defense of the faith."

As a community of faith, the Christian community's claims are not necessarily made apart from giving reasons. Lindbeck suggests that the reasonableness of Christianity, like any religion, "is largely a function of its assimilative powers, of its ability to provide an intelligible interpretation in its own terms of the varied situations and realities adherents encounter."[117]

Following from this, the sort of apologetics appropriate to postliberals is only *ad hoc* in nature. Ad hoc apologetics eschews any systematically prior or controlling theories, and proceeds contingently with the sole aim of describing the intratextual significance of the faith.[118]

[116] See ND, 130, 131, 129 and 132. Important questions involved here include dialogue with secular modern thought and the public character of theology which we need to address in the next chapter.

[117] ND, 131.

[118] See ND, 129 & 131. For detailed discussions on postliberal ad hoc apologetics, see William Weperhowski, "Ad Hoc Apologetics," *JR* 66 (1986) 282-

Intratextuality remains the overarching theme, acting as it does as the rallying point around which a host of issues cohere. We now turn to see more closely the particular features of Lindbeck's intratextual proposal.

2.7.3 An Intra-Textual Theology: Scriptural Absorption of the Universe

That Lindbeck's intratextual insistence is heavily influenced by Barth and Frei is well documented by Lindbeck himself as well as his commentators. What have not been sufficiently highlighted, if at all, are the novelties he introduces to intratextual theology, quite apart from the fact that it is his work that gives this particular theology a name and propels it to its current prominence.

2.7.3.1 "Text" and the Question of Communal Priority

To begin with, text, as Lindbeck uses the term, is not confined to the written form. Texts can be transmitted orally, enacted ritually, and represented pictorially. In other words, Lindbeck is speaking about semiotic systems in relation to which he is able to include unwritten religions of nonliterate societies.[119] But he clarifies:

> What is characteristic of them is that, unlike utterances or speech acts, they are fixed communicative patterns which are used in many different contexts for many purposes and with many meanings. In their written form, texts can have a comprehensiveness, complexity, and stability which is unattainable in any other medium. This is one

301; David Ford, "The Best Apologetics Is Good Systematics," *ATR* 67 (1985) 232-54; David Kamitsuka, "The Justification of Religious Belief in Pluralistic Public Realm: Another Look at Postliberal Apologetics," *JR* 76 (1996) 588-606.

[119] See ND, 116 and "Barth and Textuality," 361.

reason why textualized religions – religions with sacred scriptures – have an enormous competitive advantage over pre-literate ones. It is also a reason why it is not altogether absurd to talk, as some literary critics do, about the priority of the written over the spoken word.[120]

If literate cultures prioritise the written over the spoken word, Lindbeck argues, then pre-literate cultures treat their communal ritual and oral tradition as "cognitively and linguistically basic." In both cases, however, basal priority determines the framework within which individual utterances are meaningful. Thus understood, it is erroneous to grant priority to the spoken words and to treat texts simply as their written form. For to do so is to restrict texts to a singular "intended" meaning, rather than to allow their fecundity to range over varied cultural terrain.

Two things are at once apparent. First, although Lindbeck claims that the Bible is the central document in the Christian traditions, he does not limit his discussion to narratives or to readings of the Bible. Second, and here Lindbeck eminently comes into his own, he develops his intratextal approach in a systematic direction, offering a methodology for the study of religious traditions as a whole, and, within that study, paying specific attention to doctrines that define a particular religion. Further, he seeks to offer participants in the ecumenical enterprise a way out of their impasses on doctrine which entails neither confessional compromise nor cause for future confusion. Towards this end, as we shall study in later chapters, Lindbeck expands on Barth's and Frei's intratextualist approach by taking a detour through Wittgenstein's linguistic analysis and Geertz's cultural anthropology to accommodate the study of religions and religious doctrines. At this point, we only examine his theological proposal.

[120] Lindbeck, "Barth and Textuality," 361.

2.7.3.2 *The Case for the Possibility of Intratextual Theological Reading*

Cultural-linguists locate religious meaning within the text or semiotic system. Meaning, then, is immanent, derived from the way a specific language is used in a particular tradition, literate or otherwise. The proper way to understand what the term "God " signifies, for example, is to examine how the word operates within the particular culture and language of a religion to shape reality and experience. This is to properly comprehend a particular religious tradition intrasemiotically, an approach that is cultural-linguistically sensitive and thus tradition-specific. It is in this sense that theological description in the postliberal mode is intratextual.[121] But how is intratextual theology possible?

"Meaning is more fully intratextual in semiotic systems," Lindbeck announces. These systems contrast with other forms of ruled human behaviour such as carpentry. Even among semiotic systems, intratextuality is greatest in natural languages, cultures, and religions which are "potentially all-embracing and possess the property of reflexivity." It is on these properties that theology hinges its intratextual possibility: not only can religion itself be interpreted from within, but, in a strong sense, practically *everything* may conceivably be described and interpreted from *within* religion by means of religiously shaped second-order concepts. Adopting Geertz,[122] Lindbeck argues that because of their "comprehensiveness, reflexivity, and complexity," religions can only be adequately described by what Ryle called a "thick description." A 'thick description' refuses to treat a religion as a

---

[121] See ND, 114.

[122] Lindbeck is influenced in his cultural view of religion by the Yale cultural-anthropologist, Clifford Geertz. See, especially, the latter's "Religion as a Cultural System," in *The Interpretation of Cultures*, 87-125.

formalizable symbolic system. Instead, the proper object of
analysis is the *informal* logic of the actual living out of a life in
that religious culture. Only by a detailed familiarity with the
"imaginative universe" in which "acts are signs," can one comprehend and describe the meaning of these acts for the adherents
of a religion. "As interlocked systems of construable signs," a
culture or a religion, according to Geertz, "is not a power, something to which social events, behaviors, institutions, or processes
can be causally attributed; it is a context, something within which
they can be intelligibly — that is, thickly — described."[123] To
describe the basic meaning of a text is thus an intratextual task,
which involves explicating its content and the perspectives it
offers for interpreting extra-textual reality.

   In the case of religions, more than any other type of semiotic system, the descriptive task is only properly executed in a
manner "literally intratextual" – a term that will be explained
as we now turn to see *how* this intratextual reading is carried
out.

2.7.3.3 Rules for Intratextual Reading of Scripture

   As we move on to this "how" question, we again note that all
the "rules" proposed in response thereto are congruent with a theology that seeks to enhance the distinctive Christian identity. The
major world-faiths all feature relatively fixed canons of writings
which their adherents accept as normative codifications of their
religiously important insights. If one of the criteria for assessing
the adequacy of a theological proposal is faithfulness, then a test
of that faithfulness is "the degree to which descriptions correspond to the semiotic universe paradigmatically encoded in holy

---

[123] See ND, 114 -15; Geertz, *The Interpretation of Cultures*, 3-30.

writ."[124] This is pre-eminently true of Judaism, Christianity, and Islam, the three so-called "religions of the book." The task of theology consists in interpreting a religious text so as to uncover its immanent meanings in the very religious language used. Upon this understanding, a theological enterprise is, for Lindbeck, faulty when the "classics"[125] of a religion are interpreted in ways other than what seem natural within a given culture or society. Consonant with this understanding, a few rules of interpretation are intrinsic.

Before turning to these rules, or responses to the "how" question, a few preliminary remarks are in order. *Firstly*, the responses will, in part, contribute towards further clarifying the case for the possibility of intratextual theological reading, except that now the discussion is more directly oriented towards the Bible. For although Lindbeck speaks in terms of semiotic systems in his general analysis of religions, when it comes to unpacking the dynamics of the Christian category, his attention turns exclusively to its holy writ — the Bible — which encodes its semiotic system. *Secondly*, these so-called rules are not explicitly enumerated as such by Lindbeck, but are here collated, or reconfigured, as it were, in service of the flow of our discussion. *Thirdly*, four of these rules are in fact drawn from Lindbeck's presentation of the principal formal characteristics of the classic hermeneutics[126] he calls the

---

[124] ND, 116.

[125] Lindbeck explicitly states that his usage of the term "classic" denotes those texts which are culturally established for whatever reason. This naturally differs from David Tracy's denotation. For Tracy, "certain expressions of the human spirit so disclose a compelling truth about our lives that we cannot deny them some kind of normative status." See David Tracy, *The Analogical Imagination*, 108. Both Lindbeck and Frei have been critical of Tracy's broader view of religious classic – a point we shall address in the next chapter.

[126] See Lindbeck, "The Gospel's Uniqueness," 431-32.

Church to return to. *Finally*, though the point is minor, it is the *substantive* conceptual or categorial translation that forms the subject matter of Lindbeck's discussion, and not translation from the original Greek or Hebrew into other natural languages.

[a] Rule One: Respect Biblical Uniqueness as Untranslatability, Eschatologically Understood

At the heart of Lindbeck's postliberal thesis, as Williamson has noted, is a sustained critique of theological liberalism for its attempt to "translate" the language of the Bible into the speech and thought forms of modern culture. To Lindbeck and the postliberals, "translation" necessarily leads to a dissolution of the biblical witness, whereas the first responsibility of the Christian community is to remain faithful to the original culture and language of faith as recorded in the Bible.[127]

To underline Lindbeck's polemic against the liberal theological project, the first rule of intratextual reading therefore strictly prohibits translation. Consistency seems a key strength in Lindbeck's analysis in this respect.

The interpretive strategies characteristic of different religions are text-specific and contingent, Lindbeck observes. In each case, the considerations are internal in nature rather than external. Turning to the historic Christian mainstream, Lindbeck finds that the strongest of these considerations pertain to the Bible. Since the Bible itself makes no mention of the appropriateness, or otherwise, of translating its message, Lindbeck essentially commits himself to making a rational choice in this respect. Following Frei's lead, he takes what we have termed a "communal route."

[127] See Joseph C. Williamson, "Challenging Lindbeck," *Ch&Cr* 50 (1990) 299.

That is to say, he chooses the classic interpretive practice of the faith community, one which contains an implicit denial of the possibility of translation.

Consistent with the classic biblical hermeneutic, a double claim of comprehensiveness is advanced, which constitutes the general form of untranslatability. The classical premise affirms that:

[1] *every humanly conceivable reality can be translated (or redescribed) in the biblical universe with a gain rather than a loss of truth or significance;* and

[2] *nothing can be translated out of this idiom into some supposedly independent communicative system without perversion, diminution or incoherence of meaning.*

Various metaphors furnished by thinkers down the ages all assert that the Bible offers "a totally comprehensive framework, a universal perspective, within which everything can be properly construed and outside of which nothing can be equally well understood."[128] These include Calvin's Scripture as "spectacles" without which the world cannot be fully and clearly seen; Aquinas' "*revelabilia*" which denotes all entities and truths of whatever nature that are capable of revealing God as known in and through the Bible; and Barth's "strange new world" as descriptive of the all-inclusive or all-absorbing character of the Bible.

What benefits might there be in resisting the temptation to translate the faith into contemporary thought patterns? The present pluralistic cacophony, in Lindbeck's view, is very much a product of theology itself, with an influence on the sense of the faithful which cannot but be disintegrating. The difficulty is not resolved by exhortation to read the Bible, nor by enlarging or correcting our awareness of the biblical witness (in response, for example, to the liberationist and feminist emphases). The crux of

[128] Lindbeck, "The Gospel's Uniqueness," 429.

the matter is one of conceptual structure. A refusal to translate the scriptural message into an alien idiom saves us from the illusion that we have captured the essence of the gospel and can contribute to a biblically informed *sensus fidelium*. Further, granted that we are in an age of transition where the "expanded horizons" and "vastly accelerated change" seem to demand a pluralized theology to be able to relate the faith to new situations and non-Western cultures, the lack of a unifying framework that characterizes the translation strategy will only intensify the multiplicity and compound the present "mutual unintelligibility." By contrast, if the classic hermeneutic admonition against translation is heeded, and "the Bible is read as a unified whole telling the story of the dealings of the Triune God with his people and world," even a plurality of theologies will be mutually intelligible for sharing the same conceptual language.[129]

But difficulties abound which seek to derail any claim to biblical untranslatability, thus necessitating a couple of remarks to clear the path, so to speak, to legitimate this negatively-phrased rule.

First, in philosophy, Donald Davidson's argument against the notion of incommensurability or untranslatable conceptual frameworks or languages holds sway. Such a notion is said to be incoherent because the very absence of some common measure or some common ability to translate would render the recognition of instances of untranslatability or incommensurability impossible.[130] Lindbeck needs to get round Davidson, which he does, by insisting that he is referring not to the strong sense of untranslatability that he attempts to rebut but, instead, to Charles Pierce's concept of a "vague" sign determinable only by its "context and use."

---

[129] See Lindbeck, "Scripture, Consensus, and Community," 88-89.
[130] Donald Davidson, "The Very Idea of a Conceptual Scheme," republished in his *Inquiries into Truth and Interpretation* (Oxford: Clarendon, 1985), 37-54.

Further, as we saw earlier in Alasdair MacIntyre, even without a
common communicative system, interpreters who have acquired
proficiency in an alien tongue can recognize what is untranslatable
in that "second first language," without for a moment suggesting
that they have provided a translation.

Second, Lindbeck is here addressing not an empirical but a dogmatic question. In a real sense, no amount of research can conclu-
sively determine whether the Bible is capable of accommodating
all that can be said in non-biblical languages, or vice versa. Claims
of this kind are embedded in the practices of religious communities and articulated in their formal doctrines. On the other hand,
while they are not exhaustively verifiable, these claims operate as
working hypotheses for research purposes, whose plausibility may
be empirically measured. A decisive confirmation or refutation
must, however, await the eschaton.[131]

Meanwhile, on this side of the eschaton, Christians accept the
untranslatable biblical sign of "the Holy Trinity" as signifying the
God whose identity is otherwise unknown but for his dealings
with the world testified by Scripture. The "Holy Trinity" of the
Biblical witness is, to draw an analogy from basic education, like
the notion of zero which is fundamental to the Arabic system but
absent from Roman numerals. The powerful zero, indispensable in
modern day mathematics, cannot be translated into Latin. Similarly, it is to commit a category error, Lindbeck claims, to translate biblical categories, such as the Holy Trinity, into alien conceptuality. With the biblical lenses, everything is clarified;
without them, everything is distorted. It is on this double claim of
comprehensiveness that the general form of biblical untranslatability ultimately rests.[132]

---

[131] See Lindbeck, "The Gospel's Uniqueness," 428-29.
[132] "The Gospel's Uniqueness," 430.

The Bible, Lindbeck concedes, says nothing explicitly about whether its message or that of any other religion can be translated. Like Frei, he falls back on long-established communal practices, namely, the classic interpretive hermeneutics. Embedded in that heritage, he discovers, is the claim that the Gospel, when rightly used, "constitutes a discourse disclosing the meaning of every-thing humanly conceivable with unique and thus necessarily untranslatable depth and fullness."[133]

[b] Rule Two: Observe the Unifying Canonical Framework

Continuing from the previous rule, the second rule draws atten-tion to the canonical interpretive framework of the various texts. The collection of highly diverse writings as they are handed down in the single collection called the Bible, were classically read and interpreted as a coherent, canonical unity.[134]

A canonical interpretive framework accords due theological weight to the Old Testament which provides the readers with a fundamental identity description of God in Creation, in the accounts of Exodus and in God's dealings with Israel. This iden-tity description is, for Christians, only completed and fulfilled by the stories of Jesus' life, death and resurrection. But again, it is only when these chronologically later stories are read in the con-text of what went before, that the *kronos* (the element of horizon-tal time) finds its true transition to *kairos* (the element of the right time, the proper season).

---

[133] "The Gospel's Uniqueness," 428.

[134] Lindbeck has acknowledged his indebtedness to B. S. Childs in this regard. See, for example, "Confession and Community: An Israel-like View of the Church," 493; "The Gospel's Uniqueness," 449 n.13. Childs has single-handedly started a mode of reading Scriptures which later scholars named for him as the canonical-critical approach. His initial principal works are *Introduc-tion to the Old Testament as Scripture* (London: SCM, 1979) and *The New Tes-*

In this canonical-critical approach, the gospels will not be quarried for information disclosive of its historical past – particularly with regard to the historical Jesus – but rather will be read in the light of its primary purpose of proclaiming "the risen, ascended, and ever-present Christ whose identity as the divine-human agent is unsubstitutably enacted in the stories of Jesus of Nazareth."[135]

[c] Rule Three: Practise the Communal Linguistic Rule

As a textualist who accepts the ubiquity of language,[136] Lindbeck suggests that our perception of the world is moulded by the socially constructed discourses that govern the life of the community of which we are a part. We contribute to these discourses, tell stories about others, and find stories told about ourselves. We tell the community-story — by which we are told — in the same way the community has always been telling and re-telling it. Consciously or otherwise, we are embedded in a community-language which squarely locates us in a reciprocal relationship of community and members, story and story-tellers, and many inter-related narratives.

Communal practice as a whole is always the touchstone of the postliberal intratextual proposal. The third rule governing Scripture interpretation is to stick closely to the communal linguistic rules for reading and interpreting the Bible. These are "internal" rules, that is, rules that are embedded in the speech and practices of the community of believers. These rules, likened to the rules of

tament as Canon: An Introduction (London: SCM, 1979). For an interesting exploration of the parallels between Gadamer's hermeneutics and Childs's work, see S. Fowl, "The Canonical Approach of Brevard Childs," *ExpT* 96 (1985) 173-76.

[135] ND, 121; "The Bible as Realistic Narrative," 85.
[136] See Loughlin, *Telling God's Story*, 18.

grammar, may be tacitly practised, or expressly articulated in Church doctrine and theological reflection.

In any event, these rules accept the continuity from Genesis to Apocalypse, or creation to final consummation, within a unified canon in which: [1] the diverse writings were attributed to a singular, divine, source; [2] the central subject matter is Jesus Christ as the Word of God; and [3] the dominant purpose is the formation or transformation of sinful human creatures towards covenantal faithfulness to the Creator-God.

[d] Rule Four: Construe the Biblical Accounts as Realistic Narratives

The intratextual way of reading Scripture, Lindbeck announces, depends heavily on literary considerations.[137] The fourth rule respects the specific literary features of the overarching biblical story and urges that we construe the biblical accounts as realistic narratives. Classical hermeneutics respected an overarching framework of transhistorical meta-narrative that provides a comprehensive meaning system, stretching as it does from the first thing (the creation), to the last thing (the eschaton). Within that all-encompassing frame, events and realities far removed from ordinary everyday experience are woven into a cosmic fabric onto which the kind of events and realities fundamental to the life of the believing community are realistically embroidered.

As "a student of religion,"[138] Lindbeck does not expend all his energies on literary-critical study of the Bible which, in the last quarter of a century, has seen an upsurge of interest. Literary-critical study involves employing various techniques, including the

[137] See ND, 120.
[138] For this modest self-description, see Lindbeck, "The Search for Habitable Texts," *Daedalus* 117 (1988) 153.

technique of deconstruction, to conduct close readings of the biblical text in the fashion of scholars in departments of literature.
However, the focus of Lindbeck's interest in this regard is on *pre-
modern exegesis* — a category of study which is convergent with
the literary-critical approach. In particular, Lindbeck is attracted to
the Christian "narrative," "typological," and "allegorical" reading of the sacred texts, in view of which he has been included in
the many commentaries on narrative theology where Hans Frei
features prominently as a prime motivator. In terms of religious
conviction, Lindbeck subscribes to the claim that "powerful interpretation and religious power" are "virtually coterminous."[139]
Clearly, then, while he is not opposed to the historical-critical
approach, Lindbeck's search is for "habitable texts" or, in agreement with Ronald Thiemann, a "followable world"[140] that constituted the once universal classic hermeneutical framework.

As a professed narrativist, Lindbeck's narrative-preference
issues in a theological agenda with far-reaching consequences.
Stories are human constructions, socially inspired and enacted.
They constitute our deepest convictions about ourselves and the
social world in which we find ourselves. We change that social
world, once we change the stories that we tell about it: a community changes when the stories that community tells, and lives by,
are changed.

Unlike the textualist, on the other hand, Lindbeck places significance not so much on the act of story-telling (i.e., narrativity or
textuality), but the actual, particular stories told. He is most concerned with the *particular* world narrated. This renders Lindbeck
an orthodox theologian who in his theological works argues for

[139] Lindbeck, "Habitable Texts," 153.
[140] Ronald Thiemann, "Radiance and Obscurity in Biblical Narrative," in
Scripture, Authority and Narrative Interpretation, ed. G. Green (Philadelphia:
Fortress, 1987), 21-41.

the superiority of the Christian story of Christ over all others and proffers it as the story to live by.[141]

But what does the term "realistic narrative" mean? First of all, it specifies a particular literary genre, namely, the non-fictional. There is common agreement that a correct textual interpretation calls for the ascertaining of the literary genre of the text to be interpreted. In the case of the Bible, its canonical unity holds together materials of diverse forms – poetic, prophetic, legal, liturgical, sapiential, mythical, legendary, and historical. Much like "a vast, loosely-structured, non-fictional novel,"[142] the Bible embraces all these forms under an overarching story. That story may be exemplified in diverse modes of accounts, including the parabolic, the novel and the historical, but they all fit into a realistic narrative frame. Secondly, the narrative realisticality of the Bible is primarily in function of disclosing the identity of God as the active agent.[143] Articulating thoughts that are influential within the postliberal camp, Kelsey writes:

> Narrative is taken to be the authoritative aspect of scripture; it is authoritative in so far as it functions as the occasion for encounter with an agent in history, viz., the Risen Lord. Hence we may say that scripture is taken to have the logical force of stories that render a character, that offer an identity description of an agent.[144]

Does Lindbeck see his narrative approach as diametrically opposed to historical-critical scholarship? In a positive remark on the works of Hans Küng and Edward Schillebeeckx,[145] Lindbeck

---

[141] For this judgment on Lindbeck's orthodoxy, see Loughlin, *Telling God's Story*, 19; Donald G. Bloesch, *Holy Scripture: Revelation, Inspiration and Interpretation* (Carlisle: Paternoster, 1994), 216.

[142] Kelsey, *The Uses of Scripture in Recent Theology*, 48.

[143] See Lindbeck, "The Bible as Realistic Narrative," 84; ND, 120-21.

[144] Kelsey, *The Uses of Scripture in Recent Theology*, 48.

[145] See Lindbeck, "The Bible as Realistic Narrative," 85.

agrees that the "historical-critical enterprise is absolutely indispensable in keeping theologians and the church honest." In point of fact, Lindbeck often highlights non-opposition between his chosen method of studying the sacred texts and historical-critical exegesis,[146] and has even confirmed that, without the use of historical-critical tools, there could be no retrieval of the classic hermeneutics in which he is particularly interested.[147]

And yet, for Lindbeck, as for his colleagues at Yale, the hallmark of his postliberal theological proposal is a decisively measured break with the historical-critical approach to biblical studies. Prescinding from any claim that diachronical studies of Scriptures are primary, Lindbeck concentrates instead on the Bible as a literary document. In adopting what has now come to be known as a central element of the Yale school – namely, "narrative theology" — Lindbeck proposes that the key for understanding the Bible lies not in the linguistic roots of the text, nor its historical setting or process of redaction, but in the story preserved by the text. The truth of the text does not depend on the status of its overall historicity, or the historicity of any of its parts, as historical-critical exegetes may suggest. Its truth rests on its *assimilative power* or its capacity to draw us into a *particular* framework of meaning. It is through this particular framework that we construe the whole universe. And it is by this particular meaning system that we are equipped with the religious power to live a certain way of life – as sons and daughters of God.

And how does the historical-critical enterprise fail in this task? Perhaps the most serious drawback of historical criticism is located in its failure to read Scripture in view of its principal canonical purpose — as the faith community has always read it – namely, of disclosing the agent-identity of Jesus Christ. Putting

[146] See Lindbeck, "Habitable Texts," 153.
[147] See Lindbeck, "The Gospel's Uniqueness," 439.

aside the question of accuracy, one could ask whether critical-his-torical information is constructively helpful. Because critical his-tory "possesses no means of its own to move from what texts meant in the past to what they can and should mean now for believers," Lindbeck argues, "it is thus incapable of providing communally persuasive guidance in the present for Christian faith and life." He goes further, stating that even "the hermeneutical supplements devised to repair its failures (most brilliantly, per-haps, by Bultmann) are also unsuccessful."[148]

[e] Rule Five: Attend to Figural Interpretation

The fifth rule is to attend to "figural interpretation." The narra-tive structure of the Bible, Lindbeck claims, is filled with figura-tion or typology.[149] Typological or figural devices in Scripture serve to unify the canon as well as to encompass the cosmos. It is by the use of typology that the Hebrew Scriptures were incorpo-rated into the existing canon whose primary focus is on Jesus Christ, and, through his cosmic reference, whose area of compe-tence extends to the whole of extrabiblical reality.

For example, not only did the figure of King David serve to typo-logically foreshadow Jesus in sacred Scriptures, but he even acted as a type for Charlemagne in the Carolingian period, particularly as a stimulus for organising "the educational and parish systems that stand at the institutional origin of Western civilization."[150] It would seem, from examples such as these, that typological interpretation has an obvious edge over the allegorical approach in that the former does not rob the Old Testament or the postbiblical personalities and events of their own reality. From this, Lindbeck concludes that typol-

---

[148] "The Gospel's Uniqueness," 439.
[149] "The Gospel's Uniqueness," 432.
[150] ND, 117.

ogy can actually be a powerful means for imaginatively inscribing
the whole of reality into a Christ-centred world.[151]

Secondly, Israel as type features prominently among Lindbeck's ecclesiological insights. "That Christians thought of the
church as in some sense Israel is a commonplace," he declares.
Israel, as example, was compelling not least because Christians
had, from the start, identified themselves as the same people of
God which the Old Testament described so literally.[152] Israel's
story was, in many ways, used as the "template" for the existence
of the first Christians. Indeed, in classic hermeneutics, the Hebrew
scriptures were the basic ecclesiological texts: Christians saw
themselves within those texts, read in the light of Christ, as chosen
people, bound together by an ever-faithful and forgiving God.
However, two trends threatened to displace the typological significance of Israel. One of these, espoused by the *supersessionists*,
claimed to have replaced Israel, thereby displacing the Jews as the
chosen people and turning the Church into the antitype of Israel.
The other trend, represented by strident *triumphalists*, believed
that the Church could not be unfaithful as Israel had been, thereby
reducing the Jews to a rejected race. Such beliefs, which resulted
from "self-serving gentile Christian misappropriations of intra-
Jewish polemics," ran counter to much of the New Testament witness, especially Paul's, and contributed towards perverting the
fundamental belief in Jesus as the crucified Messiah. What is
needed today, in continuity with the historic classic tradition, is to
discern what is good about the Israel of old, not what is bad, and
to reject the supersessionist and triumphalist errors. Israel can then
be prototypical of the Church, so that the "stories of unfaithfulness and the thunderings of the prophets" can be read as directed

---

[151] ND, 118.
[152] "The Gospel's Uniqueness," 435.

"first against the Jews, second against heretics, and third against unrighteousness in professedly Christian societies."[153]

Furthermore, Lindbeck, as we noted earlier, suggests that the postliberal descriptive task is not simply metaphorical but "literally intratextual."[154] In interpreting biblical typology, the categories of analogy and metaphor come into play to enhance a literal reading of the communal text according to its "plain sense." The plain sense is, according to a widely accepted definition supplied by Kathryn Tanner, "what a participant in the community automatically or naturally takes a text to be saying on its face insofar as he or she has been socialized in a community's conventions for reading the text as Scripture."[155] But Lindbeck also enters a caveat: "Typology does not make scriptural contents into metaphors for extrascriptural realities, but the other way around." Intratextualists therefore resist the modern believers' impulse to "find their stories in the Bible," and seek instead to "make the story of the Bible their story." With specific reference to suffering and the Cross, he maintains: "The cross is not to be viewed as a figurative representation of suffering nor the messianic kingdom as a symbol for hope in the future; rather, suffering should be cruciform, and hopes for the future messianic."[156]

---

[153] "The Gospel's Uniqueness," 436-37. See also "Confession and Community," 495.

[154] ND, 116.

[155] See Kathryn E. Tanner, "Theology and the Plain Sense," in *Scriptural Authority and Narrative Interpretation*, ed. Garrett Green (Philadelphia: Fortress, 1987), 63. In adopting Tanner's analysis, Lindbeck also concedes that "the sense which is obvious to a given community of readers ... is therefore itself historically variable rather than unchanging 'literal' meaning ingredient in the text" ["The Gospel's Uniqueness," 432]. This, however, begs the question of continuity which we shall address in the next chapter.

[156] ND, 118.

In Lindbeck's estimation, "typological interpretation has collapsed under the combined onslaughts of rationalistic, pietistic, and historical-critical developments." Instead of functioning as the lens with which to view the world, Scripture is now held captive by scholars who treat it as "an object of study and whose religiously significant or literal meaning [is] located outside itself." Instead of reading the texts in their own terms, and making the intratextual meanings primary, there is now a preoccupation with "facticity and experience." In sum: "Whether it will be possible to regain a specifically biblical understanding of providence depends in part on the possibility of theologically reading scripture once again in literary rather than nonliterary ways."[157]

Recalling Barth's attention to the unsurpassed wholeness and rich details of the Bible, Lindbeck again sounds the clarion call: "In order to fully hear the Word of God in Scripture, theologians and the Christian community at large are called upon to engage in close reading of the entire canon in its entire typological and christological narrative unity in ways which are imaginatively rich, conceptually exact, argumentatively rigorous, and forever open to the freedom of the Word, to new understanding."[158]

[f] Rule Six: Follow the Mechanics of the Absorbent Text

Finally, the sixth rule requires an intratextualist to be attentive to the all-important direction of interpretation. Lindbeck stresses that the *proper* direction of interpretation is *from Scriptures to extra-scriptural realities*, never the other way around: "it is the religion instantiated in Scripture which defines being, truth, goodness, and beauty," so that the external exemplifications of these

---

[157] ND, 119.
[158] "Barth and Textuality," 362.

realities are to be moulded in the light of the scriptural typolo-gies.[159]

To describe the basic meaning of Scriptures is to perform an intratextual task of "explicating their contents and perspectives on external reality that they generate." To those steeped in the authoritative canonical writings of their religious community, Lndbeck claims, the world of these writings is the most real. In this light, a scriptural world is able to absorb the universe: "It sup-plies the interpretive framework within which believers seek to live their lives and understand reality."[160] "When the text thus controls communal reading," Lindbeck claims, "Scripture can speak for itself and become the self-interpreting guide for believ-ing communities amid the ever-changing vicissitudes of his-tory."[161]

Lindbeck's proposal actually carries two components. *First*, his interpretive method is the text-immanent approach which assumes that "Scripture creates its own domain of meaning." Scripture supplies its own interpretive framework; the Bible is its own inter-preter.[162] *Second* - and here he makes a big jump — he insists that "the task of interpretation is to extend this over the whole of real-ity." In a notable definition which encapsulates his theological programme, Lindbeck claims: "Intratextual theology redescribes reality within the scriptural framework rather than translating Scripture into extrascriptural categories. *It is the text, so to speak, which absorbs the world, rather than the world the text*"[163] [emphasis added]. Intratextual theology seeks to transform and define the entire universe according to the biblical world, while

[159] "Barth and Textuality," 362.
[160] ND, 117.
[161] "Barth and Textuality," 362.
[162] See Lindbeck, "The Bible as Realistic Narrative," 84; "The Gospel's Uniqueness," 433.

extratextual theology, be it propositional or symbolic, seeks to reinterpret the biblical world in the light of nonbiblical thought systems with the avowed aim of rendering Scripture more meaningful and relevant to the contemporary setting.[164] Explicitly following Barth, Lindbeck insists that the believer is not someone who seeks conformity with extratextual realities. Rather, it is for the believer to conform to the Jesus Christ depicted in the narrative. "An intratextual reading tries to derive the interpretive framework that designates the theologically controlling sense from the literary structure of the text itself."[165]

Faithfulness, then, so far as Lindbeck is concerned, must be faithfulness to the Scriptural paradigm. The notion of *faithfulness as intratextuality* is therefore tested by "the degree to which descriptions correspond to the semiotic universe paradigmatically encoded in holy writ." Applied specifically to Christianity, theology's faithfulness is judged by its adequacy in critically describing "how life is to be lived and reality construed in light of God's character as an agent as this is depicted in the stories of Israel and Jesus."[166]

In sum, Scripture, at once unique and untranslatable, is endowed, according to the close-knit fabric of Lindbeck's theology, with the capacity to absorb the entire universe on account of the narrative unity and self-interpreting qualities of its texts. The comprehensiveness of the Bible bespeaks its universality, a quality that entails uniqueness and untranslatability, eschatologically considered. In this eschatological consideration, the all-interpreting is at the same time the uninterpretable.

---

[163] See ND, 117-18. The inspiration behind all this has, of course, come mainly from Hans Frei and David Kelsey.

[164] See ND, 114, 129, 132.

[165] ND, 120.

[166] See ND, 116, 121.

2.7.4 The Need for Creativity and Self-Criticism

At this point, especially in view of Lindbeck's assertion of literal intratextuality, one may wonder, in view of our finding in this regard in the first chapter, if there is any space for creativity in a theologian's craft. In response, Lindbeck points to the fact that the descriptive task of the theologian extends to the entire range of the interpretive medium. And because this range, in relation to a religion, is potentially all-encompassing, the descriptive enterprise will necessarily entail a creative aspect. "There is, indeed," Lindbeck suggests, "no more demanding exercise of the inventive and imaginative powers than to explore how a language, culture, or religion may be employed to give meaning to new domains of thought, reality, and action." "Theology," he comments, "can be a highly constructive enterprise."[167]

Then again, when a case is so strenuously made for the self-referential character of the self-interpreting Scripture, as Lindbeck has done, one wonders, too, whether the postliberals have not all but retrenched the element of self-criticism. Sensitive to this issue, Lindbeck points to *sola gratia* for explanation. Understood as the unconditionality of grace, "grace alone" most aptly describes God's choice or "election" of Israel where two aspects are ingredient: there is, on the one hand, an unconditionality of election (Deut. 7:6-8) in relation to which the lack of reason cannot be replaced by human action or righteousness (cf. Gen. 26:5 and Neh. 9:7-8). God's decree stands prior to human actions; secondly, because God is ever-faithful, this election is irrevocable. However desperately unfaithful Israel (and now, the Church) may be, God shows sinful humanity that He is supremely faithful as Covenant-Keeper (see Rom. 11:29 ff.). Having denied, by

[167] ND, 115.

supersessionism, that Israel remains God's beloved despite its
unfaithfulness, the Church, too, with all its infidelity, denies
itself any rightful claim to an irrevocable promise from God.
What the Church needs today is, Lindbeck proposes, to embrace
a two-fold recognition of self-criticism: [a] to recognize a need
for communal self-criticism embedded in election – this "Israel-
like self-critical recognition of the possibilities of corruption and
unfaithfulness of the community" can be of great intrareligious
and interreligious implications; and [b] to undergird this self-
criticism by the *sola gratia* – this produces the cash-benefit of
Jews and Christians being maximally critical of their own communities without disloyalty.[168]

2.7.5 A Critical Retrieval of Premodern Hermeneutics

Lindbeck's project has been self-designated as "the search for
habitable texts."[169] In two different senses, this search may be
described as rational. *Firstly*, a habitable text is one which acts
eminently as a "followable" guide for our thoughts, words and
actions as we encounter changing circumstances. It must, in other
words, "supply followable directions for coherent patterns of life
in new situations." And if it does so, Lindbeck announces, it can
be considered "rational" to dwell within it.[170]
Secondly, the retrieval of premodern hermeneutics that Lindbeck
speaks about is critical rather than uncritical. This makes a whole
lot of difference, strategy-wise: on the one hand, primacy is
accorded to classic interpretation (with the [i] non-translational, [ii]
canonical, [iii] grammatical, [iv] narrational, [v] figural, and [vi]
universally absorbing strategies that we saw earlier) as the source of

---

[168] "The Gospel's Uniqueness," 443.
[169] See "The Search for Habitable Texts," *Daedalus* 117 (1988) 153-56.
[170] "Habitable Texts," 155.

the constructive proposals for what the text means now in our time and place; and, on the other hand, the bases of these proposals must now undergo the corrective scrutiny of historical criticism. The one cannot do without the other. However, we make a valid move in combining the premodern with the modern techniques only if we proceed from the side of the premodern, and never the other way around. Although they must now undergo historical-critical scrutiny, the base-sources from classic interpretation cannot be removed without irreparably damaging scriptural authority. Modern biblical scholarship is reality-limiting; by contrast, classic hermeneutics audaciously captures the whole of reality under the Bible's embrace. There again, historical criticism, though insufficient, is essential: firstly, to free classic hermeneutics of the supersessionism that we saw earlier, and to again render available Israel as type to the Church; and, secondly, as damage-control with regard to fundamentalistic and individualistic reading tendencies. Lindbeck's summary regarding this strategy thus bears repeating:

> [I]t seems that contemporary Christian communities are likely to remain adrift apart from the retrieval of premodern scriptural interpretation including the prototypical role that this gives to Israel, and it also seems that historical criticism is a necessary (though not sufficient) condition for this retrieval providing its focus is corrective and it is not made into a launching pad for tradition-independent speculations.[171]

2.8 A Prognosis

We have seen that, for Lindbeck, a heavily textualized religion such as Christianity, can be expected to survive as long as its Scriptures are not ignored. Today, however, the biblical heritage is no longer a major force shaping the mainstream of our culture.

---

[171] "The Gospel's Uniqueness," 438-39.

Lindbeck sees no future for Christianity — and, by extension, a unified world — except in its own intratextual world.[172] Underlying all his complex and intricate argumentations, we hear a passionate plea to the Church community to work on re-building its particular, distinctive, biblical culture, not only for the preservation of Christian identity, but for the sake of the world's future as well.

A conference was called in response to Lindbeck's controversial book, *The Nature of Doctrine*. "Certainly," Frederic Burnham, who edited the collection of essays presented at the conference, suggests, "we must restore the language of the Bible to its former currency in the culture, if possible."[173] These words, as Williamson points out, capture both the challenge and the problematic character of Lindbeck's whole project.[174] How does Lindbeck assess the prospect?

2.8.1 Applicability as Futurology

Faithfulness and applicability are paired in Lindbeck's conceptual scheme. Theologies, he says, are assessed by their applicability as well as their faithfulness.[175] Theologies ought to be judged on the basis of "how relevant or practical they are in concrete situations."[176] He draws an analogy from prophecy. Noting

---

[172] See Lindbeck, "Barth and Textuality," 374.

[173] *Postmodern Theology*, ed. Frederic B. Burnham (San Francisco: Harper and Row, 1989).

[174] Williamson, "Challenging Lindbeck," 299.

[175] Just as MacIntyre contends that a tradition will evince its rationality by demonstrating an ability to cope with new situations and problems, so Lindbeck claims applicability as futurology. "A theological proposal is adjudged both faithful and applicable to the degree that it appears practical in terms of an eschatologically and empirically defensible scenario of what is to come" [ND, 125].

[176] ND, 124.

that concern for the future is linked with prophecy in Christian tradition, he points out: "Prophets proclaim what is both faithful and applicable in a given situation, and they oppose proposals that, whatever their apparent practicality, are doomed because of their unfaithfulness to God's future." The coming kingdom being the hoped-for future in our theological proposal, the faithfulness and applicability of this proposal are measured against its practicality in light of "an eschatologically and empirically defensible scenario of what is to come." Like biblical prophetic work, the purpose of our exercise, Lindbeck declares, "is not to foretell what is to come, but to shape present action to fit the anticipated and hoped-for future." Unlike biblical prophetic work, however, the theological form of this activity is not a "first order intuition," but only a second order endeavour that avails itself of all that the empirical studies have to offer in an attempt to discern "the signs of the times."[177] To be sure, this effort to discern the signs of the times in no wise follows the liberal procedure of starting with present experience and then adjusting the vision of the kingdom of God to fit that experience. Postliberalism is committed to the reverse methodology, even when the present cultural climate militates against it.[178]

As part of *The Christian Century*'s "How My Mind Has Changed" series, Lindbeck reflected on how his view of what has to be done to re-Christianize culture has developed, in a more structured way, in three interrelated directions: hermeneutical, organizational and ecclesiological. "Renewal depends, I have come to think, on the spread of proficiency in premodern yet postcritical Bible reading, on restructuring the churches into something like pre-Constantinian organizational patterns, and on the

---

[177] ND, 125.
[178] ND, 125-26.

development of an Israel-like understanding of the church."[179]
Precisely in view of the *interrelatedness* of these three elements,
we have indicated in the Introduction that a sketch of the ecclesiology that emerges from this study will be included at the end.
The present chapter addresses his intratextual proposal for theology, thus requiring our attention to stay with the singular issue of
the viability of a retrieval of the premodern hermeneutics on
which his theological proposal is, in performative terms, dependent.

Two steps towards retrieval need to be traversed, it would seem.
The *first* step is to reject the biblical scholars' demand for uncontroverted evidence (described by Lindbeck as equivalent to the
category mistake of "evidentialism" in philosophy). In practice,
this demand requires traditional readings to pass muster before the
scrutiny of historical-critical techniques in order to be accepted.
Against this demand, Lindbeck falls back on the communal *sensus
fidelium* down through the ages. The issue then turns on an appropriate attitude towards tradition, particularly the tradition within
which one purports to work. Consonant with what we said in the
first chapter regarding the liberal prejudice against tradition, it is
patently wrong, Lindbeck suggests, "for those seeking to work
within a tradition to reject its beliefs and interpretations simply
because there is no critically acceptable evidence for them." For
to pursue the demand for strict evidence to its logical conclusion
would only paralyse the system, considering the fact that "everything we do, say, and think is dependent on inherited background
convictions of unknown or unknowable evidential grounding." To
be sure, where there is evidence against a traditional interpretation, as in the case of supersessionism which has been shown to

[179] "Confession and Community: An Israel-like View of the Church,"
ChCent 107 (1990) 492-96.

contradict other centrally important strands within the tradition, a veto power on the part of historical criticism can be respected. In no case, however, are we granting the historical critical enterprise a central role in grounding and developing the faith.[180]

The *second* step consists in combining the literary techniques of premodern interpretation with their contemporary literary counterparts. The kind of constructive work this will engender is aimed at unpacking the meaning of the ancient texts for present-day communities which want to take them as authoritative.[181]

Evidently, what is proposed here is in line with the Anselmian theological approach of faith seeking understanding which, in the hands of Lindbeck, is counterpoised against a hermeneutical mind-set aligned to the philosophical warrants of evidentialism. The assumption is still largely operative, it seems, even in contemporary postmodern climate, that it is intellectually immoral to believe without what modernity has defined as evidence. To the extent that this is true, Lindbeck accepts that the postcritical retrieval of premodern hermeneutics is likely to result in cognitive dissonance. But what are the prospects of a successful retrieval?

What Lindbeck has given us across the range of writings is a mixture of factors in the contemporary situation which either facilitate or obstruct the retrieval of the pre-modern hermeneutics.

On the positive side, Lindbeck includes the following: [i] The old rational foundations and legitimating structures having crumbled, even their defenders cannot ask of a text that features "richness, comprehensiveness, and stability" anything more than that it be followable. "There are fewer and fewer intellectual objections to the legitimacy or possibility of treating a classic, whether religious or non-religious, as a perspicuous guide to life and

---

[180] "The Gospel's Uniqueness," 439-40.
[181] "The Gospel's Uniqueness," 440.

thought," Lindbeck claims.[182] [ii] There are glimpses of hope, for instance, in the movement of "canonical criticism" launched by Lindbeck's Yale colleague, Brevard Childs, whose interpretation of the Bible takes the unity and canonical shape of its diverse books as an indispensable point of departure. There are also parallel intratextual trends in nontheological disciplines which lend interdisciplinary support for an intratextual proposal for theology. [iii] Despite the damage done by theology, the *sensus fidelium* endures, in part because of its relative independence of professional theologians. The message of Scripture, after all, is in the main transmitted through liturgy, preaching, catechesis, personal reading, and the general culture. The message is further kept alive, not by critical theological scholarship — or better, despite it — but through ecclesial communion.[183] Promising signs may thus be seen in those movements in the churches which feature engaged Bible reading in combination with a vital liturgical life.[184]

On the debit side, the following are included: [i] The sources of nourishment and support for a biblical culture have grown weaker. Vatican II's scriptural renewal has nothing to show for it at the popular level. The Bible has become an increasingly closed book for the educated laity, both on Protestant and Catholic sides, and the crisis deepens so long as instructions are guided by historical criticism, the technical training for which is prolonged and arduous. The historical-critical method was originally devised and welcomed for its great potential for emancipating the Bible from ecclesiastical dogma as well as blind faith. Even the Vatican-appointed Pontifical

---

[182] "Habitable Text," 156.

[183] "Scripture, Consensus, and Community," 89.

[184] In his McCarthy lecture at the Gregorian University, Lindbeck treated this latter, communitarian, aspects of the contemporary Church under the rubric of "unitive ecumenism." See "Two Kinds of Ecumenism: Unitive and Interdenominational," *Gregorianum* 70 (1989) 647-60.

Biblical Commission acknowledges it as a valid method that implies no *a priori*, so long as it is objectively used. But, where its use is accompanied by extraneous *a priori* principles, the hermeneutical choices which govern the interpretation can be, in the word of the Commission, "tendentious."[185] Lindbeck's own assessment is that, now, it is "the scholarly rather than the hierarchical clerical elite which holds the Bible captive and makes it inaccessible to ordinary folk."[186] In this circumstance, God is prevented from speaking the Word through the Bible to the Church and the world.[187] [ii] Even more fundamental an obstacle than scholarly or intellectual considerations is the present psychosocial situation which is more favourable to liberalism than postliberatism. We see this in at least two areas: [a] Modern life is disruptive of the bonds of tradition and tends to displace communal values. The natural fall out is a crop of highly rational, pluralistic modern individuals who zealously guard their right to personal choices and individual fancies. The liberal programme of indulgence is immensely more attractive than the postliberal insistence on communal particularity. [b] Theology as a course is being increasingly replaced in various theological faculties by religious studies. As the institutional settings favourable to intratextual interpretation of religion dwindle, so also will the conditions for intratextual practice steadily weaken. The whole cultural climate, it would seem, is antithetical to postliberalism.[188]

---

[185] See Joseph A. Fitzmyer, *The Biblical Commission's Document "The Interpretation of the Bible in the Church" : Text and Commentary* (Roma: Editrice Pontificio Istitutio Biblico, 1995), 44. Fitzmyer thinks that the method is particularly apt for analysis of ancient literature because of its "historical" concern. See p.45.

[186] "Scripture, Consensus, and Community," 90.

[187] Thus prompting the numerous calls like Stanley Hauerwas, *Unleashing the Scriptures* (Nashville: Abingdon, 1993); *Reclaiming the Bible for the Church*, ed. C. E. Braaten and R. W. Jensen (Grand Rapids: Eerdmans, 1995).

[188] See ND, 124 and 126-27.

Under such a climate, the ancient form of catechesis is practically impossible. In classical catechesis, potential adherents of the faith put themselves through a prolonged catechetical instruction by which they are taught, not just some "tag ends" of the Christian religious language, but the stories of Israel and their fulfilment in Christ, and the proper way of leading their lives in response to those stories.[189] And yet, we must learn those stories well, and be good performers of the messages encoded in those stories. In the face of a hostile de-Christianized culture, the Christian community may well be compelled to face up to the "sectarian future" of the Church, a topic to which we turn in the next paragraph.

2.8.2 Social Sectarianism and Communal Enclaves

Much of Lindbeck's provocative writing stems from a conviction that we need to arrest the gradual erosion of the distinctive Christian identity caused by liberalism. His repudiation of the liberal agenda is explicit throughout the book and is only thinly veiled as he speculates about the future. It is in conjunction with his speculation about the future, about having to counteract "the acids of modernity," that Lindbeck brings up the topic of communal enclaves. The "viability of a unified world," he says, "may well depend on communal enclaves that socialize their members into highly particular outlooks supportive of concern for others rather than for individual rights and entitlements, and of a sense of responsibility for the wider society rather than for personal fulfilment." Provided that the Church stresses service rather than domination, "it is likely to contribute more to the future of humanity if it preserves its own distinctiveness and

---

[189] See ND, 132-33.

integrity rather than yields to the homogenizing tendencies associated with liberal experiential-expressivism."[190]

A short sketch of Lindbeck's theological arguments and their background motivations, such as we have just provided, may clarify the potency of his proposal. And yet, nothing we have said could reduce the provocative impact of these words from Lindbeck – words, to be sure, which seem to so naturally follow from his arguments. It seems that Lindbeck, since the 1960's, has been persuaded by the view that the future of the Church and, indeed, the world, will require some kind of "sociological sectarianism."[191] Today, his position cannot be more explicitly stated. *Enclaves of mutual support* form a part of his formula against the tide of advancing debiblicization. He suggests that such "networks of socially deviant groups of the deeply committed are often the seed-beds of new life."[192] And, again, on the question of practical

---

[190] ND, 127-28. Clearly, it is not in the interest of withdrawal from society, but for better witness within the world and for better provision of skills and practices to the members, that Lindbeck advocates a Church which differentiates itself sharply from the host culture. See David Fergussen, *Community, Liberalism and Christian Ethics* (Cambridge: Cambridge University Press, 1998), 42.

[191] Lindbeck, "Ecumenism and the Future of Belief," 6 and "The Sectarian Future of the Church," 231.

[192] See ND, 127 and "Barth and Textuality," 372. This formulation is reminiscent of Dietrich Bonhoeffer's notion of the "secret (or arcane) discipline." In a world come of age, we see the disappearance of God and the religious *a priori*. Twice referred to in his prison letters (dated 30 April 1944 and 5 May 1944, both to Eberhard Bethge), the secret discipline was proposed by Bonhoeffer as a safeguard for the Christian faith. In essence, the discipline refutes attempts to translate the faith into non-religious terms. Commentators have identified several salient features of the discipline: (a) it sees worship in a world come of age only for a small group of Christians intensely loyal to Christ, who are linked as members of the one Body in worship, and who keep a low-profile; (b) it aims to protect the traditional content of the Bible and the faith of the Church against profanation by inappropriate secular elements; (c) it refuses to expose the Christian secrets cheaply to a world that does not understand; and (d) it is a penitential, purgative secrecy with a primary ecclesiological reference. See Dietrich Bonho-

relevance, he is convinced that "religious communities are likely to be practically relevant in the long run to the degree that they do not first ask what is either practical or relevant, but instead concentrate on their own intratextual outlooks and forms of life."[193] Relevance, insofar as it is pegged on current trends, would only risk "increased balkanization."[194]

All told, Lindbeck's tradition-specific hermeneutic is underpinned by a deep conviction of the positive contribution that Christianity, in all its authentic particularity, is able to make towards creating a world better than it now is. Even though, as we said earlier, we will defer analysing the ecclesiological implications of Lindbeck's writing to the end of our study, we can mention in passing a few major elements that are apparent. The Church is story-shaped and Israel-like, called, as servant, to signify the eschatological kingdom, practically relevant only in espousing its own particular intratextual outlooks and forms of life. This basic orientation requires a rethinking of the character and marks of the Church, its mission to the modern world, the nature of ministry, the process of initiating new members into its fold, its catechetical pedagogy, and so forth.

How might Lindbeck's theological outlook be assessed? What are some of Lindbeck's operative presuppositions? How do these

effer, *Letters and Papers from Prison*, ed. E. Bethge (London: SCM, 1971); J. A. Phillips, *Christ for Us in the Theology of Dietrich Bonhoeffer* (New York: Harper & Row, 1967); E. Bethge, "The Challenge of Dietrich Bonhoeffer's Life and Theology," *The Chicago Theological Seminary Register*, Feb., 1961; L. Rasmussen, "Worship in a World-Come-of-Age," in *A Bonhoeffer Legacy*, ed. A. J. Klassen (Grand Rapids: Eerdmans, 1981), 268-80.

[193] ND, 128. In "Barth and Textuality," 374 Lindbeck again asserts: "A religion, especially a heavily textualized religion such as Christianity, can be expected to survive as long as its Scriptures are not ignored. It has no future except in its own intratextual world. One may hope that more and more Christian theologians, whether Protestant or Catholic, will soon get the message."

[194] "The Gospel's Uniqueness," 427.

presuppositions sit with other approaches to theology? An assessment of Lindbeck is by no means an easy task, not least because of the compact nature of his writings and both the methodological and substantive controversies he provokes. Is his rejection of the liberal alliance with modernity an abandonment of all dialogue with secular modern thought? Is it a denial of the public assertion of the truth of the Gospel we proclaim? Is the exclusion of experience justified? Has his nonfoundationalist approach circumvented relativism and fideism? Is intratextuality not unduly restrictive? Is narrative a panacea? These, and many others, are persistent questions which interpreters raise, questions to which we need to turn in the following chapter.

CHAPTER III:

HERMENEUTICS AND REVELATION

3.1 Preliminary Remarks

Lindbeck's postliberal theology is a critical orthodoxy. His key concern is to reclaim the authority of Scripture for the Church[1] where the liberal theological agenda has failed. He attempts to exposit the claims and theological perspectives of the Christian communal text – primarily the Bible – in all its scandalous particularity and narrative self-sufficiency, and steadfastly resists the modern liberal temptation to accommodate to a universal rationality. Proffering a community-building-hermeneutics, Lindbeck issues an urgent reminder to the theological fraternity of its responsibility to reflect on the subject matter of theology and the proper mode of its explication in the face of a culture that is fast becoming de-Christianized.[2] While it clearly bears close family resemblances with the approaches of his Yale confreres, Lindbeck's programme also takes on its own characteristics. How do interpreters respond to his proposal?

[1] Albert C. Outler writes: "The aim of a postliberal hermeneutics is to reposition Holy Scripture as a unique linguistic medium of God's self-communication to the human family. Its primary task is to represent the Bible as the human medium of a divine revelation that has endured and will endure in and through the cultural metamorphoses that succeed each other as history unfolds." See idem, "Toward a Postliberal Hermeneutics," *ThT* 42 (1985-86) 286.

[2] The thesis that underpins Lindbeck's project has been summarised by John Neuhaus as follows: "The Bible can be profitably read in our day as a canonically and narrationally unified and internally glossed (that is, self-referentially

3.1.1 Some Remarks on Positive Reception

Lindbeck's proposal has attracted a great deal of debate. We begin with a brief remark on positive reception before turning to the critical remarks.

Lindbeck's theological programme discloses the diagnostic and visionary character of his writings, and a propensity for constructive responses to the new theological situation of our day. With Lindbeck, authors across a wide spectrum of the Christian theological enterprise who find that his approach resonates with their basic convictions now have a name – postliberalism – with which to describe their thoughts. A new set of postliberal, tradition-specific, and intratextually coherent vocabulary has quickly eased into much of their writings since the second half of the 1980's. The result is an increased conceptualization in cultural-linguistic terms specific to the Christian faith. That we now speak of a postliberal approach as a major theological alternative is testimony to the recognition Lindbeck has galvanized. His new programme is commended for calling the Church and academic theology to return to its primary communal source, the Scripture.[3] He brings to awareness, once again, the important message that "the Christian vision of reality is most effectively communicated to a dechristianized culture by a combination of righteous action and explicit witness to the God who has reconciled the world in Christ Jesus."[4] Undeniably, Lindbeck's project seeks to promote the specificity of the Christian Tradition

and self-interpreting) whole centred on Jesus Christ, and telling the story of the dealings of the Triune God with his people and his world in ways which are typologically applicable to the present." See Paul Stallsworth, "The Story of an Encounter," in *Biblical Interpretation in Crisis*, ed. J. Neuhaus (Grand Rapids: Eerdmans, 1989), 182.

[3] See Mark I. Wallace, *The Second Naiveté* (Macon: Mercer University Press, 1990), 110; John Milbank, "An Essay Against Secular Order," *JRE* 15 (1987) 201-02.

[4] Ronald F. Thiemann, "Response to George Lindbeck," 382.

and is true to its task of "transmitting the texts and traditions on which all Christian faith depends for its own identity and future."[5] It takes "a great deal of courage," in the face of a de-Christianized, pluralistic, and fast-changing culture, to insist that a "strategy of liberal conformation" is "socially ineffective in the short run and self-destructive in the long run."[6] There is little doubt about the validity of his postliberal concern that an untrammelled liberalism can only be maintained at a heavy cost to Christian identity. In a way which is "enormously powerful, personally moving, and community gathering,"[7] Lindbeck's programme stresses Christianity's particular approach to God's universal saving action. Francis Clooney rightly points out a particular form of the Christian paradox highlighted by Lindbeck's textual perspective: "The *whole* of the world is the locus of the story of God's universal saving action, *and yet* the canon of texts known as the Bible is the *privileged, particular language* of this salvation and understanding." Christian theology would do well to carefully maintain the paradox that, although our faith refers to a reality that is not 'merely' a product of language, it is nevertheless, for Christians, constitutively shaped by the experience narrated in the Bible.[8] Adopting the Scripture narrative as the central referent is also consonant with the philosophical claim that any great tradition rests on a canon which is, in its origin and at its core, narrative in form. "What a tradition of enquiry has to say, both to those within and to those without," writes MacIntyre, "cannot be disclosed in any other way."[9]

[5] Carl E. Braaten, *No Other Gospel!* (Minneapolis: Fortress, 1992), 19-20.

[6] Miroslav Volf, "Theology, Meaning, and Power," in *The Future of Theology* (Grand Rapids: Eerdmans, 1996), 100.

[7] See remark by George Weigel in Stallsworth, "The Story of an Encounter," 176.

[8] See Francis X. Clooney, "Reading the World in Christ," in *Christian Uniqueness Reconsidered*, ed. Gavin D'Costa (Maryknoll, NY: Orbis, 1992), 67.

[9] Alasdair MacIntyre, *Whose Justice? Which Rationality?*, 11.

However, not everyone accepts the cultural analysis on the basis of which Lindbeck proposes his pragmatic solution. Lindbeck, some observe, gives the impression that modernity is equated with secularization in its most radical form. That is disputed. Instead, it is argued that what is going on sociologically is that there are only small groups of radicals in different ecclesial communities giving the false impression of a de-Christianized culture.[10] Others contest the claim that the New Testament situation was different from ours in that the early Christians relied on scriptural interpretive categories, while modern liberals use extrabiblical ones. Lindbeck's attributing the present crisis over the lack of consensus about the meaning of the Jesus story to the liberal proclivity to read Scripture from an external standpoint meets with the rebuttal that the biblical writers themselves were not committed to theologizing exclusively from within the canon.[11] The success of his proposal for the re-Christianization of culture is also doubted.[12] Even if Lindbeck is right in his dire prognosis that the Christian Church is in a liminal era in which faithful catechesis is impossible, a typical pastoral voice would not let that stop the quest for such catechesis.[13] Also

[10] See Weigel's and Neuhaus's interventions in Stallsworth, "The Story of an Encounter," 176-77. Lindbeck's cultural analysis, "which resembles Alasdair MacIntyre's picture of communities of virtue escaping the barbarians by hunkering down behind thick walls and following a new St Benedict, was simply too dire." John Thiel, however, believes that Lindbeck's diagnosis and prognosis are corroborated by evidence. See idem, *Imagination and Authority* (Minneapolis: Fortress, 1991), 161.

[11] See Dan O. Via, *The Revelation of God and/as Human Reception in the New Testament* (Harrisburgh: Trinity, 1997), 210-1. That the biblical authors were creatively different was the thesis of Timothy Radcliffe in "Tradition and Creativity," *NewBf* 70 (1989) 57-66.

[12] See Miroslav Volf, "Theology, Meaning, and Power," 110.

[13] See John H. Westerhoff III, "Will Our Children Have Faith?" in *The Echo Within*, ed. C. Dooley (Allen: T Moore, 1997), 190.

doubted is the suggestion that only in the modern period have interpreters within the Christian community sought to escape from the
pressures of canonicity. People in the ancient Church, with a firm
view on the nature of God as a-pathetic perfect Being, tended to
include occurrences of wonders in the literal sense and to exclude
from it all scriptural ascriptions of emotions to God. Ironically,
interpreters today are more ready to concede that God "suffers"
than that God works "wonders."[14] Nevertheless, critical comments
are almost invariably made alongside positive appreciation, so that
at issue is primarily whether the major problems raised by critics
dislodge Lindbeck's principal intentions.

3.1.2 The Aim and Burden of this Chapter

Truth, we believe, is revealed dialectically, and theology is possible precisely on account of this and not on account of the radical
positivity of revelation on which the young Barth of the *Römer-
brief* insisted.[15] From the outset, it might seem, we will be diametrically opposed to Lindbeck's arguments. Nothing could be
more mistaken. Difficulties are inherent in any serious dialogue
with different theological options facing the theological enterprise.
At root, however, there are, in all properly *Christian* theological
undertakings, some basic commonalities which, when uncovered,
will call for a revision of the criticisms advanced by one group
against another. Some of these commonalities will be uncovered
in this and subsequent chapters, but the larger picture will hopefully emerge more clearly towards the end of this study. In this

---

[14] See Nicholas Wolterstorff, "Will Narrativity Work as Linchpin?" in *Relativism and Religion*, ed. C. Lewis (London: MacMillan, 1995), 104.

[15] For a Bonhoefferian interpretation of Barth's project, see Heinz Zahrnt,
The Question of God, trs. R. A. Wilson (New York: Harcourt Brace Jovanovich,
1969).

chapter, we shall use the notion of revelation as the prime analogue for assessing Lindbeck's proposal. We shall lay out the
problem thematically under three major difficulties which critics
raise — and which recur in later chapters — namely, the adequacy
of narrative hermeneutics, nonfoundationalism, and textual revelation. In doing so, we assume a three-fold burden: we shall argue
the thesis that [i] narrative intratextuality in Lindbeck's programme is necessary but insufficient for biblical interpretation and
theology; and so, [ii] despite criticisms, many of which appear to
us to be valid, Lindbeck's principal intentions remain sound; but
[iii] a foundational alethiology is a necessary supplement to Lindbeck's project.

There are operative presuppositions that underline Lindbeck's
approach to scriptural authority. Uncovering these presuppositions
is our first task in a critical dialogue with Lindbeck.

3.2 The Sufficiency of Narrative-Reading for Reclaiming
   Scriptural Authority

3.2.1 Uncovering Operative Presuppositions

That *Scripture is authoritative for Christians* constitutes the
first operative presupposition on the part of Lindbeck. A seemingly benign claim, this presupposition raises no qualm among his
detractors, save to reserve for debate the extent of the term
"authority." For, it seems, there is common acceptance of the
notion of "authority" as being analytic to the concept of "Scripture": to designate a set of texts as Christian Scripture is to affirm
its authoritative status for the common life of the Christian community.[16]

---

[16] See Kelsey, *The Uses of Scripture in Recent Theology*, 89 & 97.

A common agreement is also at hand to support a "regional" hermeneutics proper to each category of written texts. At issue is whether particular hermeneutical considerations demand a sort of "sacred hermeneutics" privileging the interpretation of sacred Scriptures. In general terms, two opposing answers are prevalent. A typically "liberal" approach denies that an authoritative textual status suggests any rigid rules of interpretation, arguing that the texts must be free to speak for themselves rather than to repeat a predetermined understanding. A typically "conservative" view, on the other hand, one which Lindbeck shares, suggests that a proper understanding of the scriptural text cannot be had without a prior commitment to its authority. The rationale in this position rests on the peculiar character of Scriptures whose message is not readily accessible to those not predisposed to receive it. "If we approach it as we would other materials, subjecting it to scrutiny and testing it by our ordinary reason and experience, we will only miss its message, because that message transcends our ordinary reason and experience."[17] The second operative presupposition on the part of Lindbeck is thus the insistence on some sort of "*sacred hermeneutics*" for the proper interpretation of Scriptures.

The Bible, as we saw, has been held captive by different forces at work in the history of the Church. Distributed over a wide spectrum, these forces include liberal critical scholarship as well as conservative Church expectations. Over and over again, every generation is confronted with the task of rendering it possible for the Bible to fulfil its authoritative role for the life of the community. Recent movements contrarily named "radical" and "conservative," such as Bultmann's programme of demythologization and

---

[17] Charles M. Wood, "Hermeneutics and the Authority of Scripture," in *Scriptural Authority and Narrative Interpretation*, ed. Garrett Green (Philadelphia: Fortress, 1987), 4.

the "biblical theology" movement, shared the common goal of making the core of the Scripture message readily accessible for contemporary faith life. These and other attempts having failed, is there a suitable alternative that is methodologically sound, doctrinally faithful, and sensitive to communal tradition as well? Lindbeck's response is a resounding "yes" and he turns exclusively to *"narrative interpretation"* to play that role. This constitutes his third, and explicit, operative presupposition. The question that at once arises is: Has not the narrative reading of the Bible thereby been pressed into services beyond its inherent capacity?

Fourthly, and most seriously under the rubric of this chapter, *textual revelation* is implicitly assumed to be constitutive of the whole of revelation. The questions we raise are: Is this kind of theology "theological" enough? Is it a sufficient speech about God? Would not a more adequate alethiology be needed for interpreting the Christian Tradition in a modern world?[18]

And finally, Lindbeck's scheme is known for the supposition that he makes regarding the absorbent quality of the text. Is absorption an inherent textual quality? Is it a one-way traffic as Lindbeck presupposes?

3.2.2 Is the Narrative "Linchpin" Adequate to the Task?

The Bible is a collection of texts written over a period of a few thousand years, by people of vastly different social, cultural, political and linguistic backgrounds. In very broad terms, the differences amongst the texts may be highlighted thus: [i] rootedness

---

[18] "In responding to Lindbeck," Timothy Jackson suggests, "the theological realist will appeal to the classical distinction between epistemology (theory of knowledge) and alethiology (theory of truth) [from the term *aletheia* in John 14:6]. Epistemology describes *how we test* for the truth, while alethiology describes *what we test for*, that is, the *nature* of truth." See Jackson, "Against

and conditionality in various socio-cultural climates; [ii] different theological perspectives; [iii] different degrees of historicity;[19] and [iv] a diversity of materials that include such features as the poetic, prophetic, legal, liturgical, sapiential, mythical, legendary, and historical.[20] And yet, these vastly different writings belong to a single canon, a fact that bears profound implications. Lindbeck's claims for scriptural authority rest on the literary genre of the Bible "as a whole" in its "canonical unity." What holds these diverse materials together, Lindbeck claims, is an "overarching story which has the specific literary features of realistic narrative."[21] It is on the twin qualities of canonicity[22] and narrativity that Lindbeck claims the Bible can be profitably read in our day.[23]

Narrative interpretation, by no means a monolithic movement, enjoys an ascendancy in the current theological scene.[24] Apart

Grammar," 241. He has warned against conflating the two concepts in "The Theory and Practice of Discomfort: Richard Rorty and Pragmatism," *Thomist* 51 (1987) 279.

[19] See Maurice Wiles, "The Limitations of Narrative Interpretation," 43-44.

[20] As Lindbeck suggests in "The Bible as Realistic Narrative," 84.

[21] Lindbeck, "The Bible as Realistic Narrative," 84; ND, 120.

[22] In a cultural-linguistic analysis, a book or a formal list of documents does not make a canon, unless there is a community that takes it as authoritative. Thus, the "canonization of Christian scripture is more adequately understood as the bestowal upon these texts of a specific function, rather than simply as their churchly recognition or their exaltation to a higher status." Consequently, "a canon is a canon only in use; and it must be construed in a certain way before it can be used." See Charles M. Wood, *The Formation of Christian Understanding* (Philadelphia: Westminster, 1981), 90 & 93.

[23] See Lindbeck," Scripture, Consensus, and Community," 75.

[24] See Bloesch, *Holy Scripture*, 209. For a brief survey, see Garrett Jones, "Narrative Theology," in *The Blackwell Encyclopedia of Modern Christian Thought*, ed. A. E. McGrath (Oxford: Blackwell, 1993), 395-98. There is an enormous literature on biblical narrative. For an indication of the irreducible variety of approaches to, and understanding of, narrative theology, see "A Symposium on Story and Narrative Theology," *ThT* 32 (1975) 133-73, and *Why Nar-*

from Frei, whose work is credited for inspiring the present interest
in narrative theology, there is no lack of theologians of note who
now positively construct theologies on narrative insights. Thiemann, for instance, claims that narrative "highlights both a predominant literary category within the Bible and an appropriate
theological category for interpreting the canon as a whole."[25]
Wood, too, is persuaded by the "overall narrative character of the
canon," and suggests that the entire canon may thereby be construed as "a story which has God as its 'author'."[26] All these
claims, however, are not without some attendant difficulties.

3.2.2.1 Is the Hermeneutical Use of the Canon Arbitrary?

Maurice Wiles, like many others, suggests that a few problems assail the narrativist claim. He contends, firstly, that there
is a two-fold arbitrariness to their insistence on a controlling
canon. Wood, for instance, refers to the hermeneutical use of
the canon as a conscious decision "to read scripture *as if it
were a whole*," and *as if* God is the author.[27] This contention
need not detain us for long. For all it takes is to go a small step
further than Wood has done here, and ground that decision on
the uncontroverted evidence of communal tradition. In the third
century, precisely to arbitrate between the competing concerns
of the time, the early Church sought to and did close the canon,

rative?, ed. S. Hauerwas and L. G. Jones (Grand Rapids: Eerdmans, 1989). The
Introduction by the editors is instructive. For critical comments, see George
Stroup, "Theology of Narrative or Narrative of Theology?" *ThT* 47 (1991) 424-
32. See also Michael L. Cook, *Christology as Narrative Quest* (Collegeville:
Liturgical, 1997).

[25] Ronald F. Thiemann, *Revelation and Theology* (Notre Dame: University of
Notre Dame Press, 1985), 83.

[26] Wood, *Formation of Christian Understanding*, 100.

[27] See Wood, *Formation of Christian Understanding*, 70.

and thereby solidified a unified collection of religious texts accepted down the ages as Scripture.[28] In line with our discoveries in the first chapter, a return to tradition in this regard is rationally defensible.

But Wiles takes the matter further. Narrative is one out of several possible categories around which the canon can be organised. Lindbeck may still seem unreasonable if, in insisting upon the canon as a whole as bearing "the specific literary features of realistic narrative," he ignores two attendant difficulties: [i] the many elements in the canon which do not fall within the narrative category, such as the prophetic and wisdom literature and much of the epistolary writings;[29] and [ii] an "irreducible diversity" that attends even the admittedly rich bulk of explicitly narrative material, as even Thiemann acknowledges.[30] Narrative is no panacea, to be sure, for there is more than one story to be told and Christian authors like Metz and Hauerwas appear to be telling and listening to radically divergent tales. Given the glaring divergence in the practical consequences by which the truthfulness of the Christian story is judged, the legitimate question is: "How does an appeal to narrative establish the truthfulness of Christian convictions, even on the pragmatic grounds" which Lindbeck espouses?[31] In this light, Wiles' contention shows greater promise.

---

[28] For an instructive historical-critical analysis of the events leading to the formation of the canon, see Raymond F. Collins, *Introduction to the New Testament* (New York: Doubleday, 1983), 1-40.

[29] Biblical scholars commonly hold that taking the communicating of God's Word through his deeds enacted in narrative accounts, though useful as an approach, is not universally applicable. Representative of this view is Joseph A. Fitzmyer, *Scripture, the Soul of Theology* (New York: Paulist, 1994), 44.

[30] Thiemann, *Revelation and Theology*, 86.

[31] See Paul Lauritzen, "Is 'Narrative' Really a Panacea?" *JR* 67 (1987) 322-39.

3.2.2.2 *Does the Canon Yield a Coherent Singular Description of an Agent?*

Relying, as we saw, on Kelsey, Lindbeck claims that "the primary function of the canonical narrative" is to render an "identity description" of God as an active Agent, centred on Jesus Christ.[32] Against this central tenet of the narrativist focus, two distinct but related issues arise. The first issue, paraphrasing Wiles, is whether the canon yields a coherent, singular, identity description. Testing the text where the postliberals may arguably have the strongest case on this point, namely, the Gospels, which are clearly more narrative than Scripture as a whole, the question is whether they do not in fact yield "identity descriptions" of Jesus? This contention is not without merit. After all, the four canonical Gospels do render four significantly different portraits of Jesus as, for instance, the Righteous (Matthew), Suffering (Mark), Forgiving (Luke) Messiah, and as Divine Visitor (John).[33] Having said that, the difficulty posed by these, and other, differences, may plausibly be resolved, at least in part, by the Church's traditional understanding that the different Gospel perspectives on God are complementary to, rather than contradictory of, each other and are, together, contributory to a larger and richer tapestry of God's relationship with humanity. In regard to the four seemingly different

[32] Thiemann is in basic agreement with Frei and Lindbeck on this score in *Revelation and Theology*, 83. He explains more fully how God's identity is conveyed by the biblical stories in "Radiance and Obscurity in Biblical Narrative," 21-41. Note that our discussion does not concern the issue of double agency (Israel and Christ) current in the debate over God's actions in the world. On this latter debate, see *Divine Action*, ed. B. Hebblethwaite (Edinburgh: T & T Clark, 1990).

[33] These metaphors are our own formulations. For a recent study on christological portraits in the New Testament, see Raymond E. Brown, *An Introduction to New Testament Christology* (Mahwah, NJ: Paulist, 1994).

Gospel-portraits of Jesus, therefore, Frei points to the understanding in the ancient Church: "He was the Messiah, and the four-fold storied depiction in the gospels, especially of his passion and resurrection, was the enacted form of his identity as Messiah."[34]

Be that as it may, it is a theological impoverishment, Tracy reminds us, if we fail to notice that, *without abandoning the plain sense of the passion narrative*, which he finds insightful, there have always been legitimately different Christian readings of the common confession and the common narrative. And these differences are not just manifest in contemporary biblical interpretations, but were clearly current among the original Christian communities as well as among the redactors who crystallised their oral traditions. Thus, much is overlooked if we fail to take into consideration the following, among other, variations overlooked in the Frei-Lindbeck narrative reading: the "Anglo-Saxon penchant" for reading Luke as moral realism; the uncertainty of the "nonclosure" in Mark (original ending in 16:8) which is attractive to modernists and postmodernists alike; the forceful "community-forming manual-like" character of Matthew; and the "oratorio," "rhythmic" character of John. [35]

Vigorous challenges are also posed by Jewish scholars who argue that the Christian account of the unity of biblical narrative and the identifiability of the God of Jesus Christ is achieved only through a misunderstanding of the Jewish account of God in the Hebrew Scripture. Their work strengthens our context-awareness that Scripture readings are inextricably community- and tradition-relative.[36]

[34] Frei, "The 'Literal Reading' of Biblical Narrative in the Christian Tradition," 121.

[35] See David Tracy, "On Reading the Scriptures Theologically," in *Theology and Dialogue*, esp. 43-51.

[36] See Michael Goldberg, "God, Action, and Narrative: *Which* Narrative? *Which* Action? *Which* God?" *JR* 68 (1988) 39-56; idem, *Jews and Christians, Getting Our Stories Straight* (Nashville: Abingdon, 1985).

3.2.2.3 The Hegemony of an Exclusive and Comprehensive Narrative-Genre[37]

The second issue is related to specific categories of texts which do not, without some apparent difficulties, fit into Lindbeck's claim of a "canonical narrative" description of God's agency. The apocalyptic emphasis in the New Testament is illustrative of this point. Since a natural reading of the narrative account of the agency of God leads up to "an imminent denouement," Wiles insists,[38] and since nothing of the sort actually took place, does that not affect the story? Or should the apocalyptic portion be excised from the identity description of God? Either way, a challenge to narrative accuracy and comprehensivity has been posed. Lindbeck, in short-circuiting the complex variety of expressions in the Bible with a predetermined focus on one particular genre (the category of narrative) and one particular character (Jesus), that purports to shape Christian identity across the centuries in a single paradigm,[39] violates the text's built-in plurality of discourse.[40]

From two angles, Wiles' objection alerts us to some potential dangers in the postliberal project. First, the postliberals are inspired, as we saw, by a positive desire to reclaim the authority of the Bible from the alleged tyranny of critical scholars. When the entire scriptural canon, despite its rich diversity of texts, is forced to fit into one category – the narrative category — are we not now

[37] Note that Auerbach and Frei did not develop a literary genre. Realistic narrative is not, for them, a "genre" in the sense it is used by literary critics. That, however, is no bar to literary criticisms in view of which "genre" is here used.

[38] See M. Wiles, "Scriptural Authority and Theological Construction: The Limitations of Narrative Interpretation," in *Scriptural Authority and Narrative Interpretation*, ed. G. Green (Philadelphia: Fortress, 1987), 48.

[39] See David J. Bryant, "Christian Identity and Historical Change," *JR* 73 (1993) 34.

[40] See Wallace, *The Second Naiveté*, 44.

prejudiced by the tyranny of postliberal scholars as well? Second, the postliberal project is attractive for tackling the urgent need to rehabilitate scriptural authority in the Church, convinced of the failure on the part of liberal theologians to effectively discharge this task.[41] In this light, Wiles' objection is sound insofar as he suggests that it is incumbent on the postliberals to ensure that their critical stance against the liberals does not result in something that is "dangerously misleading."[42]

In this regard, one senses an unconscious hegemony in the exclusivity of claims made for narrative. Ironically, there is what Paul Nelson calls the "liberal-universalistic" tradition that adopts narrative as a theological resource because we are, in essence, narrative creatures. But Lindbeck and the postliberals espouse narrative on account of the advantages it gives theology and not because humans are narrative beings. The advantages, however, come with a price: the voices in *other* basic genres of the diverse scriptural texts are stifled, and the richness of a pluralistic enjoyment of the texts seems not to be tolerated. Consequently, a call for caution in the exclusive use of narrative may not be out of place.[43]

The narrative approach is enormously useful for bringing out the *communicative power* of biblical stories as a means of transmitting the Word of God. From Genesis to Apocalypse, the Bible confronts the reader with very odd messages in a story-form,

[41] Thiemann, for instance, suggests that the turn to narrative is a suitable alternative to the primacy of anthropology predominant in modern theology. See *Revelation and Theology*, 85.

[42] See, generally, Wiles, "The Limitations of Narrative Interpretation," 46-50. On the canonical approach initiated by B. Childs bearing a "totalitarian tendency," see Mark Brett, *Biblical Criticism in Crisis* (Cambridge: Cambridge University Press, 1991), 11ff.

[43] See Frederick J. Ruf, "The Consequences of Genre: Narrative, Lyric and Dramatic Intelligibility," *JAAR* 62 (1994) II: 799-817.

whether symbolic or "history-like." And yet, narrative is not syn-onymous with story:[44] a story is a mixed form, and may contain much that is not narrative, such as a poem, a wisdom saying and a legal code. What the narrativists are particularly interested in, are three aspects that define a narrative: [i] the interaction of charac-ter and action; [ii] sequential time; [iii] coherence and intelligibil-ity.[45] What is missing, it seems, is an adequate, if any, attention to the crucial role of the *voice*, or the narrator, who *re*-presents the narrative. Frederick Ruf, for example, stresses the aspect of "rep-resentation" by turning to a contemporary narratologist, Gerard Genette, who defines narrative as "the representation of an event or sequence of events, real or fictitious, by means of language."[46] That language betrays the *relation* between the narrating voice and the narrated persons, events, objects, and words. It is an *external*

---

[44] Exegetical expositions of the Gospels as stories abound, e.g., D. Rhoads and D. Michie, *Mark as Story* (Philadelphia: Fortress, 1982); J. D. Kingsbury, *Matthew as Story* (Philadelphia: Fortress, 1986); Robert C. Tannehill, *The Nar-rative Unity of Luke-Acts* (Philadelphia: Fortress, 1986 [I] and 1990 [II]). For a theological exposition of biblical narrative, see Johann B. Metz, *Faith in History and Society* (New York: Seabury, 1980), 205-18.

[45] Thiemann, for instance, holds the view that "Narrative as a literary cate-gory emphasizes the interaction of circumstance and character, incident and iden-tity, in an ordered chronological consequence." Narrative's "ordered temporal-ity" means that "events must be configured into a coherent whole which recognizes the events without destroying their temporal succession." See *Revela-tion and Theology*, 86. See further, S. Crites, "The Spatial Dimensions of Narra-tive Truthtelling," in *Scriptural Authority and Narrative Interpretation*, ed. G. Green, 97-117.

[46] Gerard Gennette, *Figures of Literary Discourse*, trs. A. Sheridan (New York: Columbia University Press, 1982), 127. Save for their use of the term "story," which needs to be clearly distinguished from "narrative," R. Scholes and R. Kellogg's definition is also useful: "By narrative we mean all those liter-ary works which are distinguished by two characteristics: the presence of a story and a story-teller." See their *The Nature of Narrative* (New York: Oxford Uni-versity Press, 1966), 4.

relationship, one in which the narrator stands apart from the goings on, *seeing* actions, events, and objects from *without*, *surveying* them, *understanding* them and *encompassing* them.[47] By means of this focused description of the relationship between the voice and the narrative event, persons, objects and words, which no doubt suggests a more restrictive category of narrative, Ruf draws the important conclusion that "the narrator is *magisterial*," that is to say, "*master* of the events, persons, objects and their meaning."[48] Two implications may be drawn from this.

On the one hand, with Thiemann, Ruf admits that a principal benefit of narrative is coherence (in that it provides "configural unity" to Scripture) and intelligibility (in that God's agency becomes internally intelligible within Scriptures without recourse to foundationalist theology). Indeed, the cohesion of narrative intelligibility is enhanced by the fact that a *singular* voice has comprehended the characters and events. If that voice is authoritative, even authoritarian, it is precisely because it has seen and understood and, "now, it tells." Where "aporia" and "peripeteia" – discontinuities and surprises in a narrative – exist, they do not seriously undercut the authority, for the narrative is able to "move toward a discernible conclusion" regardless.[49] Intelligibility remains intact.

On the other hand, Ruf draws the shocking conclusion that this particular intelligibility is *possessed* by the narrator and *promised* to the reader as well. The reader, then, will tend to see himself or herself as similarly "magisterial",[50] a sort of "master" of people and events. "Denying the possibility of a lack of control," narrative

---

[47] Ruf, "Consequences of Genre," 803.

[48] Ruf, "Consequences of Genre," 804.

[49] See Thiemann, *Revelation and Theology*, 82-89.

[50] Ruf, "Consequences of Genre," 810. For a critique of Ruf's views, see Daniel Beaumont, "The Modality of Narrative," *JAAR* 65 (1997) 125-39.

understood in terms of such comprehensiveness may well be quite unable to present innocent suffering adequately.[51] Further, literary critics find the whole idea of a clear, coherent narrative dissonant with the chaos of experience. In light of all this, a different, and more adequate, characterization of narrative from the one Lindbeck and the postliberals have suggested, may be needed. We turn to Paul Ricoeur. As "concordant discordance," narrative, for Ricoeur, includes "pitiable and fearful incidents, sudden reversals, recognition, and violent effects within the complex plot."[52] Ricoeur stresses that the *form* of the Gospel narrative is often "qualified" by a structural trait intrinsic to the narrated action. Particularly evident in the parables, this qualifier is the narrative's tendency to highlight the extravagant, the paradoxical, the hyperbolic. Stressing a point overlooked by Lindbeck and his confreres, Ricoeur reminds us that the Gospel narratives "intensify ordinary experience to the point of the extraordinary, not to distract from the ordinary but to illumine from within."[53] As a case in point, the parable of the Good Samaritan (or the Prodigal Son) not only illustrates a virtuous lifestyle, but extravagantly portrays a "compassion without limit."[54] This extravagance within the narrative form results in a "dislocation" for the readers in our "project of making a whole of our lives." Even though the whole narrated story of Jesus may bring us to a "re-orientation," our experience is nevertheless marked by a "jarring, disorientating encounter" with a heightened and shockingly different vision of the ordinary. This dislocation is so radical, Ricoeur claims, that even the later re-orientation cannot help us "to remake a whole."[55]

[51] Tiina Allik, "Narrative Approaches to Human Personhood," *Ph&Th* 1 (1987) 311.

[52] Paul Ricoeur, *Time and Narrative*, trs. K. McLaughlin and D. Pellauer (Chicago: Chicago University Press, 1984), I:65-66.

[53] Summary by Mark K. Taylor, "In Praise of Shaky Ground," *ThT* 43 (1986) 44.

[54] See Paul Ricoeur, "Biblical Hermeneutics," *Semeia* 4 (1975) 37-73.

[55] "Biblical Hermeneutics," 125-26.

Tiina Allik thus finds in Ricoeur's characterization of narrative a denial of the "magisterial" quality which a comprehensive characterization would, as the postliberals claim, otherwise have. An adequate understanding, in Allik's view, must acknowledge "the creatureliness and materiality of human agency."[56] Pointing out the "detachment" and "hubris" that accompany a broad comprehensiveness in narrative – to which, in our view, Lindbeck and the postliberals are prone — Ruf calls for a "clear-headed" view before giving in to the human need for a unified cohesion.[57] Tracy, too, notes the "disharmonious," "centrifugal," diverse readings of the common narrative and confession, and urges that theologians honour that diversity. The plain sense of the passion narrative should then define the possible range of Christian construals and should not confine its diversity.[58]

It is a 'confining' trait in narrative that prompts Ronald Grimes to bemoan the fact that "'narrative' and 'story' are exercising an almost incantatory sway over the field of religious studies."[59] But narratives must be situated in a real world where there is interaction "in complex ways with other symbolic forms and genres that continue to shape and determine our world."[60] Edward Oakes rightly warns of an acute danger where the invocation of the term 'narrative' brings in its tow an abandonment of the notion that narratives are truly located in real life. Instead of using narrative as a refuge from difficult issues, it is useful to follow Ricoeur's lead

[56] Allik, "Narrative Approaches," 326. For a view that positively assesses Ricoeur's hermeneutical theory as eliminating the subjective bias in the hermeneutical tradition, see Mary Gerhart, "Paul Ricoeur's Hermeneutical Theory as Resource for Theological Reflection," *Thomist* 39 (1975) 496-527.

[57] Ruf, "Consequences of Genre," 815.

[58] Tracy, "On Reading the Scriptures Theologically," 46.

[59] R. Grimes, "Of Words the Speaker, of Deeds the Doer," *JR* 66 (1986) 1-17.

[60] E. Oakes, "Apologetics and the Pathos of Narrative Theology," *JR* 72 (1992) 52.

and see narrative as providing a genuine access to the world. This is workable only if we accept that narratives are "necessarily incipient actions." Narratives alone would be a deficient form if they are used as "substitutes for action." For, as Grimes remarks, "Most of our utterances lack sufficient body and drama to arc all the way across the gap between text and event."[61] He relates this to a deep-seated Protestant aversion to any argument grounded in good works. A performatively grounded hermeneutic ought to set aside the Protestant suspicion that deeds and actions can lead to a self-appropriated righteousness: "We are still afraid that if enactment were to take its place alongside narration, we would have to perform, that is do good works or do something other than write and speak in order to be religious."[62] This is sufficient to prompt Oakes to hypothesize on the true locale for Protestantism's "real neuralgia to apologetics." From their inherited suspicion of the claims that reason renders faith intelligible, Protestant authors may tend to offer various permutations of the view that faith is so utterly the work of God that no defence against wider challenges is either necessary or legitimate.[63]

The fact, therefore, that Christian discourse is essentially narrational, does not mean that one can assume an objective posture, standing apart from the story and refusing to engage as participants. Nicholas Lash understandably rejects the deconstructionist dictum that nothing exists but the text. He pursues the argument that the process of "reading" is an active endeavour, which always entails "interpreting."[64] The question of a faithful reading, or a 'truthful' one, depends on the type of text read and the way it is meant to be interpreted. Lash contributes significantly to our

---

[61] Grimes, "Of Words the Speaker, of Deeds the Doer," 7-8.
[62] Grimes, "Of Words the Speaker, of Deeds the Doer," 6.
[63] Oakes, "Apologetics and the Pathos of Narrative Theology," 53.
[64] N. Lash, *Theology on the Way to Emmaus* (London: SCM, 1986), 29.

discussion with his affirmation of the *incipient character* of some texts which "only begin to deliver their meaning in so far as they are 'brought into play' through interpretive performance."[65]

3.2.2.4 The Fallacy of Absorbing the World

Lindbeck's project has a critical edge worthy of adoption. The target of his criticism is a liberal theological programme that "translates" the biblical message to render easier "the continued commitment to the faith of the would-be believers." But this, Lindbeck maintains, tends to "replace Scripture rather than lead to it" as well as to encourage Christians to "accommodate to the prevailing culture rather than shape it."[66] A radical change is called for: instead of conforming to contemporary logic, the Christian story should transform it; instead of the world absorbing the text, the text ought to absorb the world. There is thus "no deeper guiding metaphor" in Lindbeck's thought than "reversing the direction of conformation."[67] But three difficulties in this traffic control must be noted.

First, the sharp contours that Lindbeck sketches in the two poles of text and world are blurred on closer scrutiny, on account of an inherent ambiguity in the metaphor of absorption. Extratextual realities had shaped the textual world from the outset. It would be "hermeneutically naïve" to speak of inhabiting the biblical world as a pure space because we are "never outside the wider culture," and can never be completely dislodged from this wider dwelling place even if we try. The wider culture, in any case, "is not a monolithic whole but a differentiated network of beliefs and practices."[68]

---

[65] Lash, *Theology on the Way to Emmaus*, 42.

[66] See Lindbeck, "Scripture, Consensus, and Community," 87 and ND, 130.

[67] N. Wolterstorff, *What New Haven and Grand Rapids Can Learn from Each Other*, (Grand Rapids: Calvin College, 1993), 2.

[68] Volf, "Theology, Meaning, and Power," 101-3; Tilley, "Intratextual Theology in a Postmodern World," 102.

Second, the claim that the Bible "embraces" our experience or "absorbs" our world is perplexing, because it is "anthropomorphizing" the text – speaking as if it does things. Scripture texts record the acts, practices and performances of others with reference to times past, pointing us to the present and the future. They bring forth patterns of relationship between Jesus Christ and text and context, rather than actively "render Christ, identify God, shape our identities." The appropriate understanding is that these texts "metaphorically create" the relationship between Jesus Christ and text and context. "They are not things which act (perform or function) but examples of how our identities are formed only in relation to what others have done in these texts."[69]

Third, Christ as the total 'context' of our lives is both already and not yet, so that *pace* Lindbeck, "a 'world inside the text' implies also an imploded and suspended, albeit repeated text."[70]

How might Lindbeck respond to these objections? Would a recourse to a more expansive reading of the "literal sense" help?

3.2.3 On the "Literal," the "Plain," and the "Fuller" Senses

The "literal sense" of Scripture is that "sense whose discernment has become second nature to members of the community."[71] In the hands of Thiemann, this becomes a useful tool for rebutting the allegation of arbitrary decision against the narrativist approach to Scripture. In the hands of Frei, the tradition of the *sensus literalis* becomes the best possible method with which one can approach a consensus reading of the Bible as the sacred text in the fragmented Christian Church. In defending that thesis, Frei stresses a "modest" view of what counts as

---

[69] Buckley, *Seeking the Humanity of God*, 77-78.

[70] J. Milbank, *The World Made Strange* (Oxford: Blackwell, 1997), 156-57.

[71] Thiemann, *Revelation and Theology*, 65-66.

valid interpretation, and of *the scope of material* amenable to this kind of reading.[72] It is not an assertion that all scriptural texts are to be read as narratives, far less an assertion that they are all narratives, as Wiles' objection would seem to suggest.[73] In fact, Frei concedes that apart from some aspects of the Synoptics and John's Gospel, "obviously the Psalms, Proverbs, Job and the Pauline epistles are not realistic narratives."[74] Rather, Frei's thesis is that "the narrative meaning of the stories about Jesus was the uniquely privileged *sensus literalis* of the whole of scripture for the groups by and for whom those stories were composed."[75] Two features in Frei's understanding are especially germane to our discussion.

First, there is faithfulness to tradition. Acknowledging his indebtedness to Lindbeck, Frei, in his later writings, affirms the literal sense as the paradigmatic form of what Lindbeck suggests regarding the mechanics of the absorbent text traditionally understood in the Christian community. In that traditional communal usage, the "literal ascription to Jesus of Nazareth of the stories connected with him is of such far-reaching import" that it functions to reshape extratextual realities. Frei then makes a key connection between intratextuality and narrative reading that bears repeating:

> The reason why the intratextual universe of this Christian symbol system is a narrative one is that a specific set of texts, which happen to be narrative, has become primary, even within scripture, and has been assigned a literal reading as their primary or "plain" sense. They have become the paradigm for the construal not only of what

[72] Frei, "The Literal Reading of Biblical Narrative," 119.

[73] Wolterstorff emphatically suggests that Frei is by no means contending that the narrative of the literal sense of the Gospels is realistic throughout. See "Will Narrativity Work as Linchpin?," 85.

[74] Frei, *Eclipse*, 15-16.

[75] See Lindbeck, "The Story-Shaped Church," 164.

is inside that system but for all that is outside. They provide the interpretive pattern in terms of which *all* of reality is experienced and read in this religion.[76]

In his turn, supporting Frei's argument, Lindbeck further suggests that when the literal sense is appreciated as that which a community of faithful readers takes to be "the plain, primary and controlling significance of a text," then it offers a way round the sort of problems typically associated with appeals to authorial intentions or to historical data ingredient in the text. The point is not that the Christian Bible is exclusively narrational. But, on historical-critical grounds, the postliberals can rationally argue that if one wants to know what the Bible originally meant in the Christian community, one must read the texts in "chiefly narrational terms" because that was the dominant view even after the New Testament canon was added to the Old, and continued through to the post-Reformation era, before interpretive methods began to shift.[77]

Second, Frei, in his later writings, makes an effort to steer his proposed narrative reading of Scriptures away from general theories.[78] His proposal for narrative reading is not to be treated as a member of a general class of narrative theology, far less as "a foundational warrant" for the Gospels to provide "existential and ontological meaningfulness."[79] Frei argues for literal readings on the ground that these are "warranted by their agreement with a

---

[76] Frei, "The 'Literal Reading' of Biblical Narrative," 147-48.

[77] See Lindbeck, "The Story-Shaped Church," 164.

[78] Wolterstorff correctly notes that Frei's project has too often been wrongly described as that of developing a narrative mode of biblical interpretation whereas, in fact, his project was one of *intervention* in the ongoing scripture-reading practice of the Christian community. See his "Will Narrative Work as Linchpin?," 72.

[79] In "Biblical Narrative and Theological Anthropology," 121-43, Kelsey assumes the burden of proving the thesis that while "the importance of narrative

religious community's rules for reading its sacred text."[80] He perceives within Christian tradition a broad consensus over some practical rules for scriptural reading, including: [i] that the Gospels irreducibly narrate the identity of Jesus Christ, and should not be forced to produce other references; and [ii] that all the texts in the canon are to be read as a unity.[81] In this regard, attention has not been sufficiently given, if at all, by critics to the greater susceptibility of Lindbeck, as compared to Frei, to the criticism of an arbitrary dependence on literary theories. This is a point for which the groundwork has been laid in the previous chapter. There, while presenting theological influences on Lindbeck, we labelled as "communal routes" two conscious moves made by Frei as he became increasingly apprehensive of the risk of his narrative interpretation being viewed as a general hermeneutical theory. The flip side of the Barthian stress on biblical particularity, as we saw, is a deep abhorrence of general theories that threaten in any way to rob that particularity of its overriding voice. A general theory becomes a prioritising theory, leading interpretive efforts to move in predetermined directions, and *ab initio* constraining the meaning of the particular Christian text. Strategically, Frei first prioritises the Christian community's rule for a faithful reading of Scripture. Next, he focuses on Christology and prioritises the identity of Christ. There, again, he pivots his theological exercise on the traditional communal practice of narrative-reading that requires no external assistance for unravelling the internal meaning of the Gospels. That meaning is most intimately related to how and why Jesus Christ is experienced as present to the Christian community then and now. To be sure, Lindbeck, operatively, also takes the

rests on claims about human personhood," the narrativity of Scriptures "*cannot* serve to authorize a theological anthropology."

[80] Frei, "The 'Literal Reading' of Biblical Narrative," 144.

[81] "The 'Literal Reading' of Biblical Narrative," 144-45.

communal route. But he lacks the essential Christological focus that defines Frei's theological legacy. In this comparison, Lindbeck renders himself more vulnerable to criticisms for prioritising a literary theory and for narrative hegemony.[82]

In any event, both Frei and Lindbeck have implicitly affirmed that the "literal sense" and the "plain sense" are, in the context of Christian reading of Scripture, coterminous. This takes us to a second feature, namely, the heuristic function of the literal or plain sense of a text. In a much-quoted passage, Kathryn Tanner defines the plain sense of a Scriptural text as "what a participant in the community automatically or naturally takes a text to be saying on its face insofar as he or she has been socialized in a community's conventions for reading that text as scripture."[83] In so defining, Tanner has effectively ascribed a *functional role* to the "plain sense" that is comparable with "Scripture" and "canon." A functional approach is not property-ascriptive: it does not, in the first place, give information about text-content; it is not "factualistic or reportorial" but transforming.[84] It points out the way the text functions in a religious community. Communal practice in appealing to a text being the touchstone, the functional reality of the plain sense effectively governs all of the community's interpretive conventions. It is, as it were, *a heuristic tool*[85] in the hands of the

---

[82] M. Higton only alludes to this problem. He has, however, taken on the important burden of demonstrating that, on account of Frei's focus on Christology, there is something evidently lasting about the theology of the Yale-school that goes beyond a dependence on a simplistic secular social theory. See idem, "Frei's Christology," 86.

[83] Tanner, "Theology and the Plain Sense," 63. For a rather different suggestion of the literal sense of the biblical text as comprising verbal meaning, illocutionary and perlocutionary force, and the relation to the centre, see chapter 3 of Francis Watson, *Text and Truth* (Edinburgh: T & T Clark, 1997).

[84] Lindbeck, in Stallsworth, "The Story of an Encounter," 152-53.

[85] We believe that this expression, which is ours, correctly characterizes the plain sense.

community which uses Scripture "to shape, nurture, and reform the continuing self-identity of the church."[86] The plain sense is thus a purely formal definition that: [i] does not prejudge the material character of the plain sense of a text, thereby respecting the freedom different communities have to formulate their own understanding; and [ii] does not prejudge each community's understanding of the text as it passes through different times and encounters different circumstances, thereby preserving the flexibility the community requires in dealing with new problems.[87] It is not certain if Lindbeck subscribes to this 'relaxed' view of the plain sense; his reliance on Aquinas may suggest otherwise.[88] And yet, elsewhere and later, he adopts Tanner's description and concedes that the sense which is obvious to a given community of readers has to be "historically variable rather than unchanging 'literal' meaning ingredient in the text."[89] But then, this surfaces an underlying tension in Lindbeck's arguments. On the one hand, Lindbeck posits an unchanging paradigmatic structure in the Bible, that shapes the imagination of believers across the centuries. This is a singular paradigm, seemingly unaffected by history, that is capable of generating a constant identity. On the other hand, he reverts to the changing historical contexts, and the rootedness in cultures, to allow for different understandings of the literal sense. Consistency demands a choice of the one or the other.[90]

In any event, to allow for flexibility is to simultaneously relax the demand for unchanging constancy — a point we shall discuss later. This, however, does not in the least perturb Tanner, who

---

[86] Tanner, "Theology and the Plain Sense," 62.

[87] "Theology and the Plain Sense," 65.

[88] See his remarks in Stallsworth, "The Story of an Encounter," 152.

[89] Lindbeck, "The Gospel's Uniqueness," 432.

[90] See David Bryant, "Christian Identity and Historical Change," *JR* 73 (1993) 35.

244   J.C.K. GOH

finds in this flexibility the building block for her thesis that the
plain sense of the Christian Scripture helps mould "a tradition that
is self-critical, pluralistic, and viable across a wide range of geographical differences and historical changes of circumstances."[91]

How would Catholics react to all this talk about the literal and
plain senses of the biblical texts? For a start, the problem of the
Protestant insistence on *sola scriptura* looms large. In the highly
polemical situation of the sixteenth century, partisan considerations required of the Council of Trent to regard Scripture and Tradition as "two sources" of revelation, which in turn prompted the
Reformers' polemical insistence that the *sola scriptura* not be
compromised. In the process, the fact was overlooked that, in
every interpretive community, there always existed a tradition of
text-interpretation, no doubt with its operative presuppositions and
understandings as well, to which outsiders were not privy. Even
within the broad interpretive community, a contemporary interpreter may hold the view that because the literal sense can mean
so many different things, it is hardly a useful notion at all. In any
event, a few questions may demand prior sorting out before asking
about the *sensus literalis* of the text. These prior questions could
include the problems of relating [i] the *subject matter* (e.g., God,
events, ideals, and their ranking and relationship), [ii] *context*
(e.g., author, authorial intention, community, community usage of
the text, and their ranking and relationship), [iii] the Scriptural *text*
itself, and [iv] the question of *truth* (e.g., definition and test).[92]
They point to a larger vision in which textuality, correctly stressed
by Lindbeck, is a necessary, but insufficient element in biblical

[91] Tanner, "Theology and the Plain Sense," 60.
[92] See James J. Buckley, *Seeking the Humanity of God* (Collegeville: Liturgical, 1992), 70-72, 194 n.21; idem, "The Hermeneutical Deadlock between Rev-
elationalists, Textualists, and Functionalists," *ModTh* 6 (1990) 325-39.

interpretation and theology. Catholics (and many Protestants as well) are also likely to agree with Tracy who distinguishes between two senses of the plain sense: the principal sense as Tanner has it (the "obvious or direct sense of the text for the Christian community"), and the secondary sense which makes at least a modest use of literary-critical methods for clarification of meaning.[93]

The plain or literal sense must indeed remain the foundational one on which others depend. But exactly what is the literal sense may not always be an easy matter, for even the words of the prophets harbour meanings richer than they themselves knew about. Scripture is traditionally used in the life of the Church for prayer, devotion and proclamation. But medieval and patristic exegesis often related these three spiritual senses to the three theological virtues of faith, charity and hope which, in substance, correspond to Christology, moral life, and eschatology. Underlying all this is the indispensable dimension of factum, that is, the facticity of the Christian event. Typically, therefore, according to Cardinal Ratzinger, a Catholic interpretation would open the facticity of the text to "the Christological fact and presence, to the application and realization of the grace of Christ in our charitable life, and to the eschatological tension in the hope of the complete reign of God."[94]

Next, within the Catholic tradition, Scripture reading often goes beyond the "plain sense" to the "fuller sense" of a text. Not only do the fuller, or deeper, meanings of a text go beyond authorial intentions, whatever these might be, but to respect the *sensus plenior* of a text is to accept that, under the guidance of the Holy Spirit, the texts continue to be revelatory and authoritative as

---

[93] Tracy, "On Reading the Scriptures Theologically," 38.

[94] See Ratzinger's and Dulles' interventions in Stallsworth, "The Story of an Encounter," 153-55.

novel circumstances unfold. The meanings of the texts grow
fuller, as the reader allows its deeper meanings to emerge. To be
sure, this method of reading Scripture also enjoys a venerable tradition.

In the twelfth century, Aquinas clarified an ancient division,
and distinguished between the 'literal' meaning of the words of
the text and the 'spiritual' meaning of the 'things' described in
Scripture (*Quodlibet* VII.q.6.a.14). For Aquinas, it is with the
meaning of the *res* or 'things' that the *sensus plenior* is concerned.
Recent decades have witnessed a revival of this patristic and
medieval perspective, particularly in Roman Catholic circles. Raymond Brown has, perhaps more than any other, contributed the
most to this contemporary discussion.[95] New Testament exegesis
of the Old Testament, he points out, is "more-than-literal" exegesis. *Sensus plenior* is thus "the deeper meaning, intended by God
but not clearly intended by the human author, that is seen to exist
in the words of scripture when they are studied in the light of further revelation or of development in the understanding of revelation."[96] Two related issues deserve brief mention.

First, just as fuller senses may be acknowledged within each
Testament (and not just confined to the Old Testament-New Testament relationship), these are also ingredient in the development
of *post*-biblical perception of what revelation is about.[97] Second,
Tracy has suggested that a "classic" is a text to which the community returns again and again. Perhaps here lies an opening for
the postliberals and Tracy to find some common ground. For, is it

[95] The point of reference in contemporary literature is Raymond E. Brown,
The Sensus Plenior of Sacred Scripture: A Dissertation (Baltimore: Pontifical
Theological Faculty of St. Mary's University, 1955).

[96] Raymond E. Brown, "Hermeneutics," in *The Jerome Biblical Commentary*, ed. R. E. Brown et al. (Englewood Cliffs, NJ: Prentice-Hall, 1968), 616.

[97] See W. Harrington, "Senses of Scripture," in *The New Dictionary of Theology* (Dublin: Gill & Macmillan, 1987), 946.

not the case that *rereading* classics in any community of interpretation tends to follow the guiding principles (the "rules of grammar") practised by that community? Might we not also see in the Protestant core practice of unleashing the vitality of the text in the moment of preaching (a regular feature of *rereading* Scriptures), an interpretive act in aid of revelation? All this would seem to point to a fecundity in the notion of revelation – i.e., revelation as something which is not fixed for all times, but somehow in process.[98] Tracy's notion of "classic" has attracted much criticism on account of its alleged foundational leanings. The so-called Lindbeck-Tracy (or Yale-Chicago) debate features some rather intractable problems which we shall examine in the next chapter. A critical analysis of Lindbeck's anti-foundational orientation will help provide some background to this debate.

3.3 Is Lindbeck's Postliberal Ban on Foundationalism Justified?

The term "foundationalism" is almost invariably used in a pejorative sense, as a term of accusation, by those who label themselves as nonfoundationalists. Defined from the latter's perspective, "foundationalism" is "the view that mediately justified beliefs require epistemic support for their validity in immediately justified beliefs, or from a disciplinary perspective as the view that systems of knowledge, in content and method, require first principles."[99] Essentially a theory about knowl-

---

[98] On rereading classics and repeated preaching, themes which prompted our tentative conclusion on the processorial nature of revelation, see W. Brueggemann, *Theology of the Old Testament* (Minneapolis: Fortress, 1997), 596.

[99] Thiel, *Nonfoundationalism*, 2. See also J. Stout, *The Flight from Authority* (Notre Dame: University of Notre Dame Press, 1981), 3-5; Thiemann, *Revelation and Theology*, 44-46; R. Rorty, *Philosophy and the Mirror of Nature* (Oxford: Blackwell, 1979), 157-63.

edge, foundationalism is also said to insist that to ground or support a belief, one cannot demand a chain of justifications that is either circular or that constitutes an infinite regress; the regress must end in a "foundation" of beliefs that are beyond question.[100] In insisting on some "ultimately sufficient reason," the foundationalist's epistemic expectations entail the actual discovery of a "self-evident, noninferential belief"[101] as the theoretical starting point for justifying belief. Nonfoundationalism, positioned in contradistinction to the foundationalism it has thus defined, maintains that one cannot speak of ontological or epistemological foundations for knowledge that serve to ground other claims.

At the *philosophical level*, nonfoundationalism ultimately rests its case on the proof that foundationalism promises "an epistemic security, completeness and stability that knowledge does not possess."[102] At the *practical level*, the foundational mode of theological reasoning is said to founder on the mistaken assumption that rational justification needs more than pragmatic consensus to establish its validity.[103] At the *confessional level*, foundationalism is frowned upon for selling the particularity of the Christian message short. The nonfoundationalists suggest that their position is more intelligible by contrast, but not before clouding a few issues in the process, with "interesting implications for virtually all of the *loci* or areas that theology might address."[104]

---

[100] See N. Murphy, "Introduction" to *Theology Without Foundations*, ed. S. Hauerwas et al. (Nashville: Abingdon, 1994), 9.

[101] Thiemann, *Revelation and Theology*, 44-45.

[102] See this formulation in Thiel, *Nonfoundationalism*, 12.

[103] See Thiemann, *Revelation and Theology*, 43-45.

[104] Thiel, *Nonfoundationalism*, 92.

3.3.1 Ignoring a Core Missionary Zeal in the Foundationalist Enterprise

Firstly, as a term ascribed to Roman Catholic discourse, foundationalism describes an attempt which, at its core, seeks to conduct theological discourse in a way that speaks to people outside the Christian fold and seeks to make faith credible to them. Under a strong, if not overriding, interest in "making sense," such an attempt features a willingness to operate from the epistemological assumptions of conventional intellectual discourse. In many ways resembling the work of Schleiermacher, who sought to render Christian faith claims intelligible to "the cultured despisers of religion," and thus often referred to as continuing his project,[105] these apologetic overtures – now equated by the postliberals with the foundationalist perspective – may seem to betray a tendency to gloss over the radicality of Christianity that the Barthian school stresses. But even if that tendency is real, something which is by no means conceded by the apologetical school without demur,[106] it is part of a strategy for mission *ad extra*, rather than a theological reduction for intra-communal profession of faith. The strength of this foundationalist perspective, then, quite naturally coincides with its alleged reductionist deficiency. If the nonfoundationalists grudgingly credit this perspective with gaining a measure of credibility for the Christian faith by rendering it more reasonable in public discourse, they are far more audible in expressing their

[105] With attention to the rhetorical dimension, one may find Lindbeck accusing, albeit indirectly, Catholics of subordinating the Word to some other canon of intelligibility. In this, Lindbeck follows Bretschneider, Brunner and Barth in placing the blame squarely on Schleiermacher. See J. Thiel, "Schleiermacher as Catholic," *HeyJ* 37 (1996) 61-82.

[106] At the end of the day, it may well be just a matter of explicitness in specific Christian references, depending on the target-audience. See Tracy, "On Reading the Scriptures Theologically," 59.

concern that the scandalous particularity of the faith has been compromised. After all, at its core, they insist, the Christian faith is peculiarly *unreasonable*.[107]

In this light, foundationalism is not particularly attractive to biblical scholarship. The work of biblical interpretation is to respect the voice of the Bible – a voice that is peculiarly its own. Making truth claims in its own categories, the Bible itself is repeatedly odd and unaccommodating in the face of the dominant reason of culture. When, therefore, much of what appears like historical-critical work in biblical interpretation attempts to gloss over "the oddity of the tradition, the inscrutable and the miraculous," this is judged to be in alliance with modern rationality, and thus in service of something like foundationalism. Precisely because compatibility with modern reason is achieved, through translating the message into the canon of modernity, the result has become "the least challenging, least interesting, and least important" in the theological claims of sacred Scriptures. Scripture scholars themselves are now wondering whether it is not the case that "the very criticism that set out to make the text available on its own terms has now made the text unavailable on its own terms."[108]

3.3.2 Discomfort with Mediating Theology as the Real Concern

Having said that, one must inquire whether nonfoundationalism does not have its own problems, though the reticence on this score by its proponents would seem to suggest otherwise. For instance,

---

[107] Some ideas in this paragraph may resonate with Brueggemann, *Theology of the Old Testament*, 84. It has also been argued that Rahner's "indirect method" qualifies him as a practitioner of ad hoc apologetics. See Nicholas M. Healy, "Indirect Method in Theology: Karl Rahner as an Ad Hoc Apologist," *Thomist* 56 (1992) 613-33.

[108] See Bruggemann, *Theology of the Old Testament*, 84-85.

postliberal theology appears committed to the latest philosophical developments, yet it combines this with a forceful call for a return of the *pre-modern* mode of intratextual theology.[109] The principal concern of this theology is that extrabiblical theories or universal experience not be prioritised for a normative reading of Scripture, lest the revelational authority of the Christian tradition be put in jeopardy. The peculiar logic of the Christian message — something that makes perfect sense within the faith community – cannot depend on extrinsic philosophical speculations for its validation, lest it be invalidated by the very same persuasions. Thus, Lindbeck stresses the particularities of the Christian faith, arguing that it must be the norms in Scripture which define being, truth, and beauty. All non-scriptural exemplifications of these need to be transformed by the Gospel. Thiemann's focus on the prevenience of God's grace then takes on a great significance, in light of which mediating or apologetic theologies are said to be too concerned with epistemological justifications. In their polemics against foundationalist approaches, Lindbeck and Thiemann conclude that modernity, in its philosophical and anthropological dimensions, cannot be taken as normative without compromising the truth of the Gospel. Much of modern theology, in their view, has become dangerous precisely because it has committed itself to the apologetic enterprise — undertaken as fundamental or foundational theology – "as a way of validating the intelligibility of Christian claims before the epistemic demands of post-Enlightenment culture."[110]

There is, to be sure, a pre-history to all this. At its root, the nonfoundationalist discomfort is a continuation of a past debate, betraying Barth's discomfort with Schleiermacher's attempts at reconciling Christianity and post-Enlightenment culture, resulting

[109] This point is observed by Thiel in *Nonfoundationalism*, 79.
[110] Thiel, *Nonfoundationalism*, 60-61.

in "mediating" theologies that seek common grounds between theology and secular culture through the use of such concepts like "general human experience," a transcendental anthropology or an epistemological or communicative theory. With their tendency to compromise the absolute truth of the Gospel, mediating or apologetical theories, so it is alleged, would justify revelation before the bar of modern philosophy and culture, subordinate the Word of God to finite, sinful human experience, abandon theology's properly ecclesial context and, ultimately, reduce theology to anthropology.

And yet, the nonfoundationalist reliance on philosophical nonfoundationalism in its current ascendancy in the academic world is not without some negative implications. One should not forget that the epistemological quest for certitude is not confined to any particular age, and Western philosophy can easily trace this to Plato and Aristotle. In modern times, the Cartesian search for self-justifying first principles was continued by the British empiricists, Locke and Hume, who privileged sense experience as a valid ground for philosophical argumentation, and by the German idealists, Kant, Fichte, and Schelling, who favoured, instead, the *a priori* first principles provided by human cognition. But it is precisely this idea of a *prima philosophia* that is now called into question by nonfoundationalist thought. In view of their own heavy reliance on contemporary philosophical insights, nonfoundationalist theologians do not outlaw recourse to philosophy for support on particular issues. They do, however, import this philosophical nonfoundationalism into theology to outlaw "metaphysically inclined reasoning" for substituting "its own claims for those of divine revelation."[111] But this move, as we shall shortly see, is creating some problems of its own.

---

[111] Thiel, *Nonfoundationalism*, 98.

3.3.3 The Exclusive, Fideistic and Relativistic Tendencies in Nonfoundational Theology

A uniform, singular, Christian theological discipline is a chimera. "What we call Christian theology," Thiel observes, is "actually the history of many interpretive approaches seeking the intelligibility of a religious tradition that is itself denominationally, culturally, and, of course, personally diverse."[112] In this pluralistic history, nonfoundationalism has recently appeared. However, its entry into modernity marks it as an ambivalent project that covers a wide field of critical enterprise. For our purposes, we shall first confine our discussion to the problem of the exclusive character of the nonfoundational theology proffered by Lindbeck and his confreres. Dismissing a particular notion of foundationalism as demanding that knowledge requires some foundational presupposition or certitude, they point out the dismissal of this demand by rigorous philosophy where Richard Bernstein's charge of "Cartesian anxiety" has found its mark.[113] Imported into the theological discipline, nonfoundationalism takes on an exclusive character.[114] To get to the core of this nonfoundational position, it is useful to attend to three indicators: [a] At the rhetorical level, how does Lindbeck use the metaphor "foundation" in his discourse? [b] At the anthropological level, what are his theological assumptions about human nature? [c] At the vocational level, how does he conceive of the theologian's responsibility?[115]

---

[112] *Nonfoundationalism*, 79. For a historical study of the Catholic foundational approach, see Monica Hellwig, "Foundation for Theology: A Historical Sketch," in *Faithful Witness*, ed. L. O'Donovan et al. (New York: Crossroad, 1989), 1-13.

[113] See especially Richard Bernstein, *Beyond Objectivism and Relativism* (Philadelphia: Pennsylvania University Press, 1983).

[114] Leading the way in the application of philosophical nonfoundationalist arguments to theology is Jeffrey Stout in *The Flight from Authority*.

[115] For a slightly different formulation of these indicators, see Thiel, *Imagination and Authority* (Minneapolis: Fortress, 1991), 169.

In the rhetorical use of the metaphor, Lindbeck and the postliberals tend to describe 'foundationalism' as a form of authority that
involves two features: [i] the presumption that the process of
belief-justification can logically culminate in a universally available truth; and [ii] the presumption that this logical conclusion is
rationally necessary to support the authoritative claims of a body
of knowledge. But the metaphorical character of this particular
epistemic rhetoric has failed to take into account the distinction
some philosophers make between "strong" and "weak" forms of
foundationalism.[116] William Alston, for example, is uncomfortable
with a wholescale ban on foundations. He distinguishes between
what he calls "iterative" and "simple" foundationalism. While
Alston concedes that an iterative, self-certain, demonstrable foundation for knowledge lies beyond the power of reasoning, he
insists there must be a "stock of directly justified beliefs."[117] One
cannot sacrifice the metaphor of "foundations" completely without calling into question our basic capacity to know anything, or
risk losing the basic warrantability of human judgements. If this
"stock" of "simple" ("weak" or "soft") foundations cannot be
proved, neither can they be disproved. Further, those privileged
assumptions which are basic to non-foundationalist thought are
themselves essentially 'foundational'.[118] This is particularly true
of the nonfoundationalist claim of divine revelation in Scriptures.

Value-judgements come into play in Lindbeck and the postliberals' use of the terms "foundations" and "foundationlessness,"

---

[116] F. S. Fiorenza distinguishes between "hard" and "soft" foundationalism
in *Foundational Theology* (New York: Crossroad, 1984), 285.

[117] W. P. Alston, "Two Types of Foundationalism," *JPhil* 73 (1976) 166.
Though a professed nonfoundationalist, N. Wolterstorff, too, accepts that there is
a stock of beliefs without which theorising would be impossible. See his *Reason
within the Bounds of Religion* (Grand Rapids: Eerdmans, 1976), 63.

[118] See Thiel, *Nonfoundationalism*, 83-84.

particularly in light of what they consider to be theologically problematic and theologically appropriate under a communal intratextual lens. "Foundations," in this light, designates "extrabiblical theories" or "universal human experiences," the appeal to which, in the shared view of the postliberals, represents a post-Enlightenment mentality that continues to portray the biblical text as needing external substantiation because any meaning that it possesses lies outside the scope of its own narrative content. What the postliberals insist on is a *contextual* reference, in this case, the Christian communal context, within which its Bible, doctrines, liturgy, and communal behaviour find their place and meaning. Hence, theology is the "precipitate," as conceived by Tanner, of the "Christian community's turn on itself in moments of self-reflection."[119] Faithfulness in theological reflections, Lindbeck is thus able to claim, is measured by intratextuality. In according interpretive primacy to systems other than what is native to the Christian communal context, the apologetical enterprise errs in assuming a superior contextual intelligibility residing outside of the Christian community, that is allegedly appropriate for judging its inner communal logic. "Foundationlessness," according to Lindbeck, is specifically understood in reference to Christian faith normatively expressed, practised and experienced in its rich history. Within that normativity, Lindbeck singles out the scriptural writings as the privileged locus which the Christian Tradition, despite its checkered career, has unwaveringly affirmed as God's revelation. Christian belief finds meaningfulness no where else other than in its own particularity.

And yet, it is precisely this clarification of the *contextual emphasis* of nonfoundational metaphors that betrays a serious limitation in nonfoundationalist rhetoric at the level of human rationality. For,

---

[119] Tanner, "Theology and the Plain Sense," 60-61.

philosophical nonfoundationalism, from which theological nonfoundationalism takes its cue, would hardly accept as "foundation-
less" any appeal to the revelational authority of a religious tradition
as Lindbeck has done. Instead, philosophical nonfoundationalism
would label any claim of revelational authority as foundationalism
and dismiss the same for lack of a warranted rational legitimation.
Lindbeck's abandonment of all metaphysical foundations involves
dire consequences for the doctrine of revelation which we shall
explore in some detail later. The point here, however, impinges on
the question of rationality. Indeed, at issue between the foundational and nonfoundational theologies, though so far remaining
largely implicit, is the age-old problem of "faith and reason." Nonfoundationalists reflect on faith, offer explanations of Christian
meaning, and criticise foundational claims in the network of belief.
However, since the authoritative Christian claims are so contextually particular, as the nonfoundationalists insist they are, the reasoning that attempts to investigate these claims cannot be free from
the influence of the very same network of belief. In other words,
this investigating-reasoning cannot stand apart from the very context in which its own background beliefs are situated. Reasoning,
according to the nonfoundationalist analysis, cannot be neutral.
Once contextuality extends to the activity of reasoning itself, as the
nonfoundationalists have done, it is difficult to see how "the powers of reflection, analysis, construction, and criticism" can be conceived of as anything more than a "circular reiteration of reasoning's background beliefs."[120] This is why Lindbeck is accused of
holding a fideistic position: the Christian message can only be
understood by its specific believers, its language making no sense
to outsiders because, in the words of Kai Nielsen, it is *sui generis*
and can be understood only in its own terms.[121]

[120] Thiel, *Nonfoundationalism*, 92-93.
[121] Barth and Wittgenstein, as Lindbeck's precursors, have both been accused

In this regard, too, nonfoundationalism attracts the criticism that it is relativistic. In philosophy, critics of nonfoundationalism suggest that nihilism may be the necessary consequence of epistemic relativism, and would argue that it is, on that count, self-defeating. In theology, the exclusivity suggested by a contextual approach to meaning collides headlong with one of its most basic epistemic commitments, namely, the primary, and *universal* value of theological understanding. After all, when the Gospel message is affirmed in faith to be universally true, how can we justify its theological explication to have only contextual validity? The nonfoundational approach suggests a *prima facie* inconsistency with a fundamental Christian belief as it threatens to relativize the truth that Christians profess as their own. Perhaps, however, the answer lies with a paradox inherent in the Christian claim: the story that belongs to our particular Christian community nonetheless has universal scope or applicability. The valid procedure is to *start from the particular* (which, translated into theological method, is *a return to the source*) before we can get to the universal. The Christian Scriptures, while the Scriptures of a particular community, purport to give a true account of the origin, character, and final end of the whole of creation, and thus intend to speak to all peoples in all contexts or, as the Old Testament theology would say, "to the nations."[122] While the nonfoundationalists cannot be fairly accused of overlooking this universal dimension in their theological outlook, it is nevertheless important to bear in mind that

of fideism. See K. Nielson, *Ethics Without God* (New York: Prometheus, 1973). For two recent authors who exonerate them from this charge, see S. G. Smith, "Karl Barth and Fideism: A Reconsideration," *ATR* 66 (1984) 64-78 and Y. Huang, "Foundation of Religious Belief After Foundationalism: Wittgenstein between Nielsen and Phillips," *RelSt* 31 (1995) 251-67.

[122] See E. Barnes, "Community, Narrative, and an Ecological Doctrine of Creation: Creation and Ecology Beyond Modern Atheism," in *Theology Without Foundations*, ed. S. Hauerwas et al. (Nashville: Abingdon, 1994).

when theology is strictly context-bound, as Lindbeck's is, it does suggest a crass relativism: our stories are true for us, theirs for them.[123]

More seriously for theologians, Lindbeck's contextual insistence impinges on the issue of theological freedom. When authority is located entirely in the context of Scripture, where the narrative framework determines the right meaning, then the legitimacy of theological creativity is seriously curtailed: narrative intratextuality, not authorial talent, is decisive. At the practical level, Lindbeck's anti-speculative strategy somehow parallels a concern characteristic of the Roman Catholic magisterium that individual authority be not elevated over the integrity of the Tradition.[124] In Lindbeck's estimation, however edifying a theological discussion may be, it is worse than profane if it does not promote familiarity with the narrated text.[125]

In sum, and rather paradoxically as it turns out, in abandoning any validity claims for universal theories, and in turning inward to the Christian communal contextuality of knowledge, in order to forcefully bring forth the particularity of the Christian message, Lindbeck's retrenchment of all foundations actually negates the very background beliefs his programme seeks to validate, and calls into question the particularity of the Christian revelation to

---

[123] It is thus not without merit that Tracy believes Lindbeck may have difficulties avoiding the charges of relativism, confessionalism and fideism. See idem, "Lindbeck's New Program for Theology," *Thomist* 49 (1985) 461. Philip D. Kenneson, however, assumes the burden of arguing against the charge that Lindbeck's postliberalism postulates the Christian faith as being incorrigible, i.e., as being exempt from external critique and correction. See idem, "The Alleged Incorrigibility of Postliberal Theology," in *The Nature of Confession*, ed. T. R. Phillips and D. L. Okholm (Downers Grove, IL: InterVarsity, 1996), 93-106.

[124] See Thiel, "Theological Authorship," *HeyJ* 30 (1989) 44; idem, *Imagination and Authority*, ch. 5.

[125] See Lindbeck, "Barth and Textuality," 373.

which he wishes us to return.[126] His "ambiguous" criticism of liberal foundationalism and his failure to embrace some form of theological realism like Barth's, is seen by some as a weakening factor in his call for the Bible to absorb the universe, making such a call "seem platitudinous at best and impossible at worst."[127]

In his acute critique of Lindbeck's Anselmian scripturalism, Carl Braaten commends the Yale school for keeping to "the task of transmitting the texts and traditions on which all Christian faith depends for its own identity and future." On the other hand, the strength of this programme is achieved by surrendering the "enterprise of fundamental theology, [and its task of] uncovering universal principles and structures." And all this, Braaten charges, is only "to secure a license to operate as one voice alongside others in a pluralistic setting." What does fidelity amount to when truth is the sacrifice in a neopragmatic programme? Braaten thus pointedly holds: "It is difficult to sustain the truth-claim of the gospel and the universal mission of the church on the basis of this program for theology. Fideism is linked to relativism as theology modestly restricts itself to its own data base and leaves all other disciplines to their own voices."[128]

While an over-dependence on a strong nonfoundationalist strand in philosophy in part explains the limitations in Lindbeck's nonfoundational claims, a different sort of contextual limitation, this time from a particular confessional heritage, carries further implications.

3.3.4 The Subtle Problem of Fiduciary Interests

"All theological and interpretive scholarship is in one way or another fiduciary."[129] In making this assertion, Brueggemann

---

[126] For the materials in this section, see Thiel, *Nonfoundationalism*, 87-88.
[127] See Wallace, *The Second Naiveté*, 110.
[128] Carl E. Braaten, *No Other Gospel!* (Minneapolis: Fortress, 1992), 19-20.
[129] Brueggemann, *Theology of the Old Testament*, 18. We all take sides,

surfaces the recognition that there is no innocent or neutral scholarship. Within systematic theology, for instance, in exposing
objective scholarship as theory-laden, Barth's own theological
premise could hardly be described as theory-free. In the field of
biblical exegesis, the proliferation of interpretive methods that
spring from "a wide range of socio-ecclesial-political-economic
contexts," that are "driven by different hopes, fears, and hurts"
only confirms the view that every interpretation is to some con-
siderable extent context- and interest-driven.[130] The question we
here raise against Lindbeck is whether, in staying clear of "the
lust for Cartesian autonomy," his is a mode of interpretation that
has succeeded in avoiding being authoritarian as well. Has he not,
while insisting upon the narrative category to the exclusion of others, unwittingly crafted a "canon within a canon" which is itself a
function of hegemonic interpretation?

A variety of implications emerge when confessional styles of
interpretation are brought into consideration. The diversity of confessions that characterize Christianity also yields, as we saw in the
first chapter, a diversity of hermeneutical keys for disclosing the
truths in Scripture, of disciplinary and doctrinal commitments, and
of forms of ecclesial authority. Lindbeck and his postliberal

Jacque Haers points out in "A Risk Observed," *LS* 21 (1996) 47. And "no interpretation can be free of interest," W. Jeanrond declares in *Theological
Hermeneutics* (London: Macmillan, 1991), 165. On the fiduciary element in
knowledge, see Michael Polanyi, *Personal Knowledge: Toward a Post-Critical
Philosophy* (London: Routledge & Kegan Paul, 1969). The methods adopted by
theologians, Roger Haight pointedly notes, "betray their own preoccupation in
dealing with the subject matter and the fundamental convictions they have in
relation to it." See Haight, "Critical Witness: The Question of Method," in
Faithful Witness: Foundations of Theology for Today's Church (New York:
Crossroad, 1989), 201.

[130] See Brueggemann, *Theology of the Old Testament*, 711. The postmodern
"rage and resentment against theological authoritarianism," as also a lust for
Cartesian autonomy, is as costly as an uncritical embrace of authoritarianism.

colleagues who champion the nonfoundational approach to theology, though ecumenical in their outlooks, have developed their arguments from very visibly Protestant confessional perspectives.[131] Far from intending to diminish the intellectual integrity of any of these authors in any way, we make this point only to surface a degree of inevitability in every theological work that is shaped contextually, particularly by confessional heritage. In the present case, far from being a weakness, it is the very Protestant emphasis on the Word that gives Lindbeck's work such appeal. The sore point that accompanies the package, though, is that Lindbeck's *undifferentiated and unmitigated* retrenchment of foundationalism and its related apologetical enterprise, on the one hand, and his espousal of a nonfoundational Christian identity, on the other, are purportedly offered as a *Christian* vision when, in fact, they are configured from classical Protestantism. For instance, Lindbeck's insistence on the biblical narrative, his antipathy to speculative theology and the apologetical enterprise, his banishment of all metaphysically-inclined reasoning, his strict denial of any normative significance to experience, his emphasis on *sola gratia*, and his commitment to the descriptive task of theology, centred on Scripture, and so forth, all bespeak the deep-seated influence that classical Protestantism has on his conceptual schemes.[132] This is not without significance as we consider how Lindbeck's work impacts on Catholic sensibilities.

---

[131] Lindbeck himself believes that modern criticism and its parasitic formations are no longer viable on account of actions and reactions arising from blindness to "the enabling role in all behavior, belief, and knowledge (including critical knowledge) of the tacit dimension, fiduciary frameworks, and of cultural-linguistic communicative contexts (or, in Dulles' preferred theological terminology, 'ecclesial transformative' ones)." See "Dulles on Method," *ProE* 1 (1992) 56.

[132] In Thomas Guarino's view, the nonfoundationalism of the non-correlational, Barthian-inspired postliberal school has definitive reservations about phi-

How does the nonfoundationalist unease with philosophy sit
with Catholic theology? Thiel uncovers a point of confessional
connection pertinent to our discussion.[133] The Protestant reformers
conceived of a proper theological work to be one of explicating
the plain sense of Scripture. In view of this conception of the theological task, speculative approaches to theology are frowned
upon. The unified stance of the postliberals is to post a radical
admonition to all practitioners of theological apologetics, that the
latter customarily allow extrabiblical theories to usurp narrative
authority. Lindbeck's inherited Protestant sensibilities are brought
to bear in formulating a forceful articulation aimed at promoting
Christian intratextual particularity. Foundationalism, in his view,
is part and parcel of the speculative armoury.

At issue, is not the use of philosophy, for theological nonfoundationalism relies heavily on philosophy as well. The issue, rather,
is the *proper* use of philosophy. In the Catholic tradition, speculative theologies have long found a home. If Protestant theologians
are increasingly embracing this position, particularly since the
modern period, it is because speculative strategies have been
found to be particularly congenial in the analysis of the human
condition. But the strategies are not put to service purely in function of anthropological studies. Instead, the analysis of the human
condition by speculative theologians is explicitly carried out in aid
of appreciating "the contemporary purport of the gospel message."[134] Philosophical insights are put to use as "timely elucidations

losophy in theology that springs from deep-seated *sola gratia, sola fide* convic-
tions. See his "Philosophy within Theology in Light of the Foundationalism
Debate," *Ph&Th* 9 (1995) 62-63. This is confirmed by Bruce Marshall who sees
Lindbeck's theology displaying Lutheran provenance. See his "George Lind-
beck," in *A New Handbook of Christian Theologians*, ed. Musser and Pierce
(Nashville: Abingdon, 1996), 276.

[133] Thiel, *Nonfoundationalism*, 98ff.
[134] Thiel, *Nonfoundationalism*, 99.

of the claims of faith expressed in scripture and tradition." All told, what is actually taking place is laborious work (in anthropology, hermeneutics, cosmology, process thought and so on) conducted by theologians inclined to do so, in a positive effort at offering theological interpretations that embrace a two-fold aim: [i] of presenting a genuinely Christian picture of faith in God whose revelation to humanity is definitive in Christ; and [ii] of rendering the presentation relevant and intelligible to contemporary experience. Our point in highlighting the *Christian* inspiration that undergirds the work of speculative and apologetical theologians, is to surface two errors that attach to Lindbeck's nonfoundational move.

First, Lindbeck is ecumenically sensitive and he maintains a strict policy of contextual-fidelity in theological work. Consistency on both counts would, ironically, militate against Lindbeck in the present discussion: he is, by reason of the rhetoric of nonfoundationalism, called to heed the diverse and nuanced expressions of the Christian tradition specific to different confessional contexts.[135] Just as his own negative characterization of the foundationalist and apologetical enterprise is inspired by classical Protestantism, so, a contextually faithful Roman Catholic understanding in this respect is funded by the more positive and less exclusivist vision engendered by Vatican II. If Catholic teaching seems to excessively privilege the Magisterium, this alone is no warrant for suggesting that Catholics have abandoned the centrality of Scriptures in their faith-life; in fact, Catholicism insists on the contrary since nothing is deemed authentic except what is authorised by Tradition where Scripture is primary. In terms of the contextuality of belief, therefore, the Catholic perception of "foundations" and "foundationlessness" is bound to differ from

---

[135] Thiel, *Nonfoundationalism*, 91.

what is typically Protestant, characterized, as the latter is, by exclusivist tendencies.

   Secondly, and in light of the above, when Lindbeck argues that what is *practically relevant* in the long run is for the Christian community to concentrate on its own intratextual outlooks and forms of life,[136] what in essence he is offering, as against the Christian apologetics we just saw, is a different strategy with regards to the Church's relationship with the modern world, not a different *Christian* content. Since the "Christian" element is common to both the apologetical and anti-apologetical approaches, what sets them apart is, arguably, a matter principally of strategies and emphases. That said, however, it must be conceded that Lindbeck's concern that modern apologetics, in its bridge-building effort to reach secular moderns, might run the risk of exposing Christian explanation to the "acids of modernity," is not without merit. His contention that the correlational approach to theology is symptomatic of the foundationalist error, deserves attention. We shall visit the debate on correlational methodology in the next chapter. At this point, our question is whether some form of nonfoundationalist theology is acceptable to Catholic thought, and, if so, what would it look like?

3.3.5 A Catholic Nonfoundationalism?

   In light of what we saw, two specific concerns, among others, raised by nonfounationalism are pertinent to the Catholic discourse.

   The first point featured in Lindbeck and other Barthian thinkers' report on the error of foundationalism is their common concern that philosophy not be established as the procrustean bed

---

[136] See ND, 128 and "The Gospel's Uniqueness," 427.

into which all biblical interpretations are forced. In view of what we saw earlier in relation to authentic Christian apologetical work, this issue need not detain us. Christian theology, even of the type that is carried out within the Roman Catholic fold, is highly pluralistic and diverse. And Catholic theology, even when it is foundational in kind, traditionally assumes, as its point of departure, that philosophy is but an *ancilla theologia*, rather than the other way around. If one fact is needed to dim the issue (we will never bury it, given the disputatious nature of theologians), it must be stated that Catholic theology wholly subscribes to the hegemony of revealed Christian truth over culture or philosophy. Lindbeck's now-famous dictum, "It is the text, so to speak, which absorbs the world, rather than the world the text," resonates with Catholic theology within the context of our description of the principal theological intent, viewed in relation to philosophy. Borrowing an expression from Thiel, we might conclude that Christian theologians, be they Catholics or Protestants, will rightly hold that "Athens will have something to do with Jerusalem, though always on Jerusalem's terms."[137] And, even within "Jerusalem," there is "crisis" in what narrative criticism amounts to,[138] so that the narrative category is hardly a "panacea."[139] Continuing with a play on metaphors, Vatican II having encouraged a plurality of philosophies, conceptual systems, and notional schemas, and fostered a new dialogue with contemporary thinkers and cultures, Catholics cannot but be persuaded to embrace what Guarino describes as the idea of "spoils from Egypt."[140] The epistemology of Vatican II

---

[137] Thiel, *Nonfoundationalism*, 108.

[138] Pherme Perkins, "Crisis in Jerusalem? Narrative Criticism in New Testament Studies," *TS* 50 (1989) 296-313.

[139] Paul Lauritzen, "Is 'Narrative' Really a Panacea? The Use of 'Narrative' in the Work of Metz and Hauerwas," *JR* 67 (1987) 322-39.

[140] See Thomas Guarino, "Spoils from Egypt," *LTP* 51 (1995) 573-87.

supports the view that the material identity of Christianity does not depend on a Christianized Aristotelianism or any particular philosophical system. In keeping with Aquinas' vision of reality, a plurality of philosophies and theologies may be critically appropriated. Catholicism has traditionally acknowledged that both faith and reason come from God, and that a proper interplay between theology and philosophy can be fruitfully illuminative and non-contradictory. An image originating from Origen, taking the "spoils from Egypt" is a critical two-fold procedure that: [i] encourages the taking of what is useful *for the service of God*, and [ii] cautions against appropriating wrong notions that would end up in heresies like the golden calf of Bethel.[141]

The second point may be more intractable. It concerns the seeming retrenchment by nonfoundationalists of any theological ontology and epistemology, and particularly any form of metaphysics. To Catholics, the nonfoundationalist hesitancy about metaphysics and epistemology reminds them of the traditional Protestant distrust of nature – no doubt born of the doctrine of *sola gratia*. Reflections in this direction run the risk of re-enacting past disputes, which is not the focus of this study. Perhaps more germane to our discussion is whether Lindbeck and the nonfoundationalists' argument has not, in fact, been mired in a false either/or dichotomy. In other words, are they not, in effect, suggesting that one must affirm either [i] the truth of the Gospel, or [ii] the foundationalist mediating theologies? If this suggestion is anywhere near the mark, then, according to Guarino, traditional Catholic rejoinders will come into play, namely: "Must nature be jettisoned in order for the truth of the gospel to appear? Should a radical divide be introduced between the orders of creation and

---

[141] Origen, "Letter to Gregory," in *The Ante-Nicene Fathers* (Grand Rapids: Eerdmans, 1956), 4:393-94.

salvation? Cannot one defend both the prevenience of grace, the hegemony of revelation, and foundational and mediating approaches, properly understood?"[142]

Tanner has suggested that to privilege human creatures with positive capacities in the context of the God-human relationship is symptomatic of a sort of pelagianism characteristic of modern theology.[143] Borrowing Przywara's term, Guarino's rejoinder is to inquire whether the nonfoundationalists are not guilty of "epistemological concupiscence" — i.e., sinning against God by denying that reason forms part of the human nature. And so, the old debate returns. The Protestant pessimistic view of fallen human nature is once more pitted against the more positive view of creation traditionally held by Catholics. Perhaps the jury is still out on this issue, just as it is out on a host of other issues that traditionally divide the Church. Our point, put somewhat simply, is this: scholars are more driven by an underlying fiduciary interest than they realize or care to admit.[144] Both "context" and "pre-text" are at play even as they read the Scriptures.

In sum, Catholic theology is a blend of foundational and nonfoundational (of the "weak" or "soft" variety) features. Compared to the beliefs of classical Protestantism, which inspire Lindbeck's theological programme, Catholic particularity represented in a nonfoundational theology would be far more tolerant of speculative insights which are considered helpful, in the Catholic conversation, in expressing Christian doctrinal contextuality. To the extent that an adequate response to all these issues will entail

[142] Arguments solicited for this section come from Thomas Guarino's review of Thiel's *Nonfoundationalism* in *Thomist* 60 (1996) 141-45.

[143] See Kathryn Tanner, *God and Creation in Christian Theology* (Oxford: Blackwell, 1988), 123.

[144] Mark L. Horst suggests in "Engendering the Community of Faith in an Age of Individualism," *QR* 8 (1988) 90 that one of the reasons for the slow reception of Lindbeck's book was because "it was greeted by the academy as the

rehearsing at length the old "grace and nature" dispute, we must pass over such a rehearsal, save to note that the question of revelation, which we judge to be a crucial over-arching issue in a dialogue with Lindbeck, will need to be properly addressed. Indeed, a primary weakness in his theological defence of the faith, despite its singular concern for the priority of the biblical framework, is located in his failure to offer a coherent structure for the revelational reference of biblical language.

3.4 The Contentions from Revelation

Retrieving the idea of revelation in any hermeneutics of Tradition is inevitable.[145] Revelation is the very basis upon which theology is possible at all.[146] It is a fundamental category in response to which theology is, consciously or otherwise, articulated. For Lindbeck, the Bible is the prime locus where God is revealed. Further, consistency for Lindbeck demands that we

manifesto of a group of theologians associated with Yale University." Our analysis here shows a more deep-seated difficulty which arises from fiduciary interests and denominational differences in doctrines. Michael Polanyi, who conducts a critical analysis of the fiduciary element in knowledge, suggests that "the attribution of truth to any stable alternative is a fiduciary act" involving personal commitment to beliefs which appear subjective to others. See idem, *Personal Knowledge: Towards a Post-Critical Philosophy* (London: Routledge & Kegan Paul, 1969), 294 and ch. 10.

[145] See Wallace, *The Second Naiveté*, 112; idem, "Can God be Named Without Being Known?" *JAAR* 59 (1991) 281-308; Mark Brett, *Biblical Criticism in Crisis* (Cambridge: Cambridge University Press, 1991), 160.

[146] Roger Haight underscores the theological significance of revelation thus: "Since the content of faith and hence the content of theological assertion, has its source in revelation, the whole discipline of theology tacitly assumes or explicitly rests on some view of this phenomenon." See idem, *Dynamics of Theology* (New York: Paulist, 1990), 52. Similarly, Van Beeck defines revelation as the "formal, generative element ('the soul')" of Tradition. See his *God Encountered*, II/1: 13.

understand the Bible as "Scripture" in the faith community *and* that we gather as a community in response to the claim that, *here in the sacred text*, God is decisively disclosed. Allowing for all this, to accept the Bible as a revelatory text is one thing, but to specify *what* is referenced by the term *revelation*, and *how* that reference is achieved, is quite another. Indeed, in theology, revelation has become quite a *crux interpretum*, and one's perception of how truth is revealed, and how God relates to the world, are decisive of the theology one produces. A great deal, therefore, turns on the notion of revelation with which Lindbeck implicitly operates. A few points, in particular, stand out under close scrutiny.

3.4.1 The Debate over Referentiality

In our presentation of the rules for narrative reading of Scriptures, a point that stands out in Lindbeck's exhortation is to *keep sharply in mind that meaning is not reference.*[147] In his adoption of intratextuality as a normative characteristic of Christian theology, Lindbeck is extending Frei's argument against all forms of 'referential hermeneutics.'[148] Critics see this as highly problematic, and their comments, even when initially targeted to Frei, would, *mutatis mutandis*, apply to Lindbeck as well. And yet, both Lindbeck and Frei do also state that they accept some implicit reference at work. This creates ambiguity and calls for clarifications. What significance does this ambiguity bear? How do we understand this apparent inconsistency?

---

[147] See also, on this point, Wolterstorff, "Will Narrativity Work as Linchpin?" 93.

[148] Wayne A. Meeks, "A Hermeneutics of Social Embodiment," *HTR* 79 (1986) 180-81.

3.4.1.1 The Consequences of Choosing a Narrative Hermeneutics

It is crucial for a proper understanding of Lindbeck to again see him in light of his principal intentions and thus the hermeneutical orientation he chooses. Recall Auerbach's view that the Bible exerts a tyrannical claim to truth that excludes all rival claims, so that the whole history of humanity is placed in the context of biblical destiny. Scripture unfolds a particular worldview. When readers allow themselves to be drawn into that enthralling worldview, they are lifted above mere spectatorship to a Word-obedient servanthood. As personal beliefs emerge within a captivating life-orientation, the readers rise above questions of historical factuality. This *orientation-approach*, grounded in a vision of the Bible as principally offering a destiny-laden truth-claim, has much in common with Kelsey's emphasis on the *life-transforming function* of Scripture in the believing community. When Lindbeck chooses Frei's narrative hermeneutics, he takes on board Auerbach's orientation-approach and Kelsey's life-transforming functional understanding of Scripture. In this rather pragmatic approach, Lindbeck is understandably indifferent to the question of truth. In an important sense, Lindbeck has gone far beyond superficial arguments on truth and falsehood,[149] so engrossed is he in Christian communal discipleship. Lindbeck's preference is for a *community-building hermeneutic*. Given Lindbeck's choice, it is in a sense inevitable that, as he insists on intratextual meaning, he tends to eclipse the objective cognitive authority of the Bible and its external referents. That, however, does not necessarily entail an outright denial of all referents.

---

[149] For this important assessment by John Neuhaus, see Paul Stallsworth, "The Story of an Encounter," 172.

Although attention to the literal sense of the Gospels is clearly regarded by Lindbeck and Frei as beneficial to the Christian community for a number of reasons, their argumentations have brought both of them to focus on just one particular point: they both assume the signal importance to the faith community of access to the identity of Jesus Christ.[150] Frei's argumentation is oriented in defence of the profound conviction that "it is precisely the fiction-like quality of the whole narrative, from upper room to resurrection appearances, that serves to bring the identity of Jesus sharply before us and to make him accessible to us."[151] Frei, as we saw, identifies the root cause of the eclipse of the Gospel message over the last three hundred years with a flawed practice of Gospel interpretation: the interpreters sought for truth and meaningfulness (or that which is edifying), with the result that the *"thereness"* of the realistic narrative given in the literal sense of the Gospel texts finally vanished from view. Against an alarming pluralism of interpretations that threatens to eclipse the literal sense, Frei stresses a distinction between interpretation and appropriation: issues of truth and utility must not play a controlling role in one's interpretation. Frei's clarification is germane: "We start from the text: that is the language pattern, the meaning-and-reference to which we are bound, and which is sufficient for us. We cannot and do not need to 'transcend' it into 'limit' language and 'limit' experience. The truth to which we refer we cannot state apart from the biblical language which we employ to do so. And belief in the divine authority of Scripture is for me simply that we do not need more."[152]

---

[150] That identity reveals a vulnerable God. See William C. Placher, *Narratives of a Vulnerable God* (Louisville: Westminster, 1994).

[151] Frei, *Eclipse*, 145.

[152] Frei, "Response to 'Narrative Theology: An Evangelical Appraisal'," *TriJ* 8 NS (1987) 22-23.

The immediate 'cash return', as it were, for Frei's investment in narrative hermeneutics is obvious: access to the identity of Jesus Christ. Nothing is more important. The reader follows two steps, in the right order: first, *interpret* according to the literal sense of the Gospels; and then, *appropriate* the transition from story to history at its pivotal point, where the identity of Jesus is most sharply disclosed, namely, in the passion-resurrection sequence. Against those who doubt the legitimacy of this transition, Frei pronounces that such doubts issue from an epistemology that mistakenly insists on evidence extraneous to the texts,[153] as symptomatic of an Enlightenment mentality. However, the criticism cannot be dismissed so lightly without hurting Frei's own case. The point is, that the proposition the narrative expresses is true if and only if Jesus exists and has the property predicated of him. In other words, in the process of interpreting the realistic narrative, the interpreter must *first appropriate* the historical truth of Jesus' existence *before* attending to the sense of the text. The consequence of this insight is to reverse Frei's order of things: first, conclude regarding the extra-biblical fact; then, conclude regarding the sense of the text. Extraneous data necessarily contribute to determining sense.[154]

Truth and utility, then, far from being peripheral issues as they first appear, are located right at the centre of Frei's narrative hermeneutics – a project grounded on the conviction that an epistemologically responsible access to the truth about the identity of Jesus Christ can be had *only* by following the two steps of interpretation and appropriation. Similarly, the issue of historicity of the Gospel narrative is, arguably, of prime importance in Frei's

[153] We are greatly assisted here by Wolterstorff, "Will Narrativity Work as Linchpin?," 100-01. See also David F. Ford, "On Being Theologically Hospitable to Jesus Christ: Hans Frei's Achievement," *JTS* 46 (1995) 532-46.

[154] See Wolterstorff, "Will Narrativity Work as Linchpin?," 102-04.

vision. The Gospels, in his view, clearly yield access to historical truth. To recap, Frei's central thesis is that a realistic or history-like biblical narrative accounts for the making of the Christian faith. The central claims of Frei's Christology are that we know Christ's identity through reading the Gospel narratives, and, fur-ther, that it is impossible to know who Christ is without knowing that he is present. The focus on the Risen Jesus as the promised Saviour precludes an identification of Jesus as mythical and thus logically entails belief that Jesus is risen and present. Two critical comments in this regard are worth examining. Firstly, as Wolter-storff points out, what Frei's effort ultimately yields, in terms of an epistemologically responsible access, is only a small slice of history, namely, the identity of Jesus of Nazareth, who is the risen Christ, present as the Lord of the community that professes him so. Frei, in Wolterstorff's opinion, tacitly contends that the com-munity would do well not only to be content with this narrow slice, but to treasure it.[155] But why? The answer is intimately related to the context in which Frei theologises. He perceives him-self to be in a dreadful situation where the biblical narrative is in a sorry state of eclipse brought about by members of the believing community who spend time interpreting Scriptures in ways that are fundamentally wrong. He thus speaks, with prophetic urgency, that "Christian reading of Christian Scriptures must not deny the literal ascription to Jesus ... of those occurrences, teachings,

---

[155] E. P. Sanders, in his substantial impact on the contemporary study of the historical Jesus, has been very keen to secure a proper starting point from which an inquiry into Jesus might proceed. Favouring the narrative tradition, he begins with a set of eight "indisputable facts" about Jesus, all drawn from the narrative tradition, from which conclusions might be extrapolated. See his *Jesus and Judaism* (London, SCM: 1985), 10-11. For a scrutiny of some of the alleged solid pillars of the narrative tradition, see William Arnal, "Major Episodes in the Biography of Jesus," *TJT* 13 (1997) 201-26. Inquiries of this sort tend to expose many assumptions in the so-called narrative tradition.

personal qualities and religious attributes associated with him in the stories in which he plays a part."[156] Secondly, however, Carl Henry questions the adequacy of such a move from the narrative directly to the logical and factual implications of Jesus' role. In the absence of direct arguments for the historical factuality of the resurrection, Henry fears that Frei offends against the New Testament's own claim that "historical disaffirmation of the resurrection would undermine the Christian faith."[157] Then, again, to Frei, Henry's insistence that the text must refer to some historical events other than itself, constitutes Henry as one who espouses an Enlightenment epistemology where the meaning of the narrative lies not in the text, but in events "behind" the text, thereby contributing to the eclipse.[158]

Lindbeck, too, adopts literary considerations for the purpose of stressing the identity description of Jesus as Agent. He looks for the "determinative," or "theologically controlling meaning of the tale," which he locates in the identity of Jesus literally rendered, and "not his historicity, existential significance, or metaphysical status." His intratextual reading therefore works within "the interpretive framework that designates the theologically controlling sense from the literary structure of the text itself."[159] It is the portrait of Jesus generated by this narrative to which the readers are required to conform, and not to other portraits such as Küng's reconstructed Jesus of history, Schillebeeckx's "metaphysical Christ of faith," or Tracy's "agapeic way of being in the world."

[156] Frei, "Literal Reading," 144-45.

[157] Carl F. H. Henry, "Narrative Theology: An Evangelical Appraisal," *TrinJ* 8 NS (1987) 7.

[158] See the attempt to fit Henry into Frei's typology by C. Hawkins, *Beyond Anarchy and Tyranny in Religious Epistemology* (Lanham: University Press of America, 1997), 10-11.

[159] ND, 120.

To be sure, both Lindbeck's and Frei's positions are more nuanced than critics make them out to be, for, in both authors, an element of external reference is at least implicit, even if this is not sufficiently articulated. Frei, for instance, in response to critics, argues that, by means of the biblical story, there is reference in the "double sense" of [i] historical reference and [ii] textual reference. *First*, there is historical reference in that the biblical story means what it says: the gospel story *literally identifies* the historical personage called Jesus of Nazareth. The gospel story is not about something else, nor about somebody else, nor about no body in particular, nor an allegory about a mode-of-being in the world. The story specifically renders Jesus' identity. Paradoxically, Frei at once brings that historical reference back to the text, for, *secondly*, in what he terms a "textual reference," his position is that "the text is witness to the Word of God, whether it is historical or not." And, in a fashion which encourages critics to characterize him as confining himself to *internal reference*, despite his claims to the contrary, he goes on to say that he is unable "to make the distinction between 'witness' to the Word of God, and Word of God written." The text, he states categorically, is sufficient for reference. In his view, we cannot but start from the text. There, we are bound by the pattern of the language or "the meaning-and-reference" that is textually inherent. This pattern, he adamantly insists, is sufficient for us; it is quite wrong, in his opinion, to seek to "transcend" it into "limit language" and "limit experience."[160] This has prompted Wolterstorff to pronounce that "the traditional view that proper reading of the scriptures is a mode of revelation in the present," is remarkably absent in Frei's scheme. Because of this absence, the full sense of "the Word of God" does not, in Wolterstorff's searching

---

[160] Frei, "Response to 'Narrative Theology," 22.

analysis, function in Frei's argument.[161] This indictment of Frei by Wolterstorff resonates with Henry who points out that for Frei, to read the biblical accounts narratively is "to set aside the ultimacy of narrated occurrence as historical revelation."[162] Indeed, in *The Identity of Jesus Christ*, Frei forecasts a decline of interest in divine revelation as the central technical concept in theology.

In a 1986 article, Lindbeck seems to acknowledge that Scripture points beyond itself. Not without some ambiguity, though, he writes: "Scripture textualizes everything, including theologians and the work they do. When this is expressly realised, the God unsubstitutably identified and characterized in the text, supremely in the story of Jesus, becomes, as Barth says, 'the basic text'."[163] Ambiguity is fuelled as he lays claim for a self-interpreting Bible that eclipses all references in metaphysical, epistemological and hermeneutical dynamics. Lindbeck concedes that "the implications of the story for determining the metaphysical status, or existential significance, or historical career of Jesus Christ may have varying degrees of theological importance." The crucial caveat which he enters, in this regard, is that these claims should never be taken as either primary or determinative.[164] Indeed, as Dulles points out, Lindbeck's reliance on the biblical narrative as realistic is founded on the conviction that it discloses the identity and character of God as the primary Agent. That, for Dulles, *ipso facto* suggests that the biblical narrative "has a reference beyond itself to the reality of the living God. It puts us in relationship to him."[165] This point is important, in our view, because, *unless the*

---

[161] Wolterstorff, "Will Narrativity Work as Linchpin?" 101.

[162] Henry, "Narrative Theology," 6.

[163] Lindbeck, "Barth and Textuality," 374.

[164] ND, 120-21.

[165] See Dulles' comments in Paul Stallsworth, "The Story of an Encounter," 174.

basic validity of Lindbeck's proposal is called into question, even when critics find Lindbeck's proposal too restrictive, that in itself does not displace the legitimacy of his primary intention or diminish its fecundity. What seems permissible in a dialogue with Lindbeck, though, is to see that an entry point to that dialogue is at hand when critics see all this talk about texts and textuality, and ask, as Thiemann has done, whether it has not eclipsed genuine talk about God.[166]

In this light, perhaps the more legitimate task of a critic is to examine Lindbeck's argument on referentiality, and see what impact this has on his intratextual theology, rather than seeking to displace its validity. This would seem to resonate with the appreciative and yet cautionary remark made by Joseph Cardinal Ratzinger precisely against Lindbeck's insistence on Scriptures being "self-referential" and "self-interpreting."[167] Criticisms on referentiality come from different quarters. For a clearer view of the various responses, it is helpful to examine how the Frei-Lindbeck exclusion of external references works in three directions: [a] against historical referents; [b] against metaphysical referents; and [c] against hermeneutical referents.

3.4.1.2 Against Historical Referents

Adopting a text-immanent interpretation[168] that manifests a concern for the *literal* meaning of the text, Lindbeck portrays the

---

[166] See Thiemann, "Response to George Lindbeck," 378; S. L. Stell, "Hermeneutics in Theology and the Theology of Hermeneutics: Beyond Lindbeck and Tracy," *JAAR* 61 (1993) 694. Thiemann's own theology of revelation has been critically assessed in John Sykes, "Narrative Accounts of Biblical Authority," *ModTh* 5 (1989) 327-42.

[167] See Joseph Cardinal Ratzinger's remark in Stallsworth, "The Story of an Encounter," 188.

[168] In contrast to "intertextuality" (the production of meaning by a text displacing another text and yet receiving from the other an extension of its own

believer as one who reads the biblical text for the purpose of learning how to follow Jesus as he is depicted in the biblical narratives. Most scholars could presumably agree with this general position. This means Lindbeck is not pre-occupied with "extraneous metaphysical, historical or experiential interests" on the side of the interpreter.[169] The Church has handed down the Bible in its present canonical form, to be valued by all Christians as authoritative text. Our task is not to seek clues to the essential meaning of Scripture in extraneous sources, or in our internal experience or the meaning system of modern secular culture. Scripture has its own integrity that cannot be tested against the demonstration of the historical factuality of the event to which it refers. Let the Bible speak on its own terms. In this narrow sense, Lindbeck is close to Barth. As regards the specific point of objective realism, however, Lindbeck's position represents a serious departure from his precursor.

Barth's struggle against historicism is well known. But his indifference to historical questions developed in the context of an adamant denial of the according of a priority status to historical criticism in biblical interpretation. It was *historicism* he was opposed to on principle, not historical investigation. Barth, commentators agree, located the real *locus* of the meaning of biblical texts *not within* the texts themselves, but rather in a point which lies beyond them. In other words, the self-revelation of God in Jesus Christ is understood as a real event in concrete, temporal

meaning) stressed in other literary theories, the term "intratextuality" is coined by Lindbeck to signify the immanent location of meaning, or the production of meaning that is internal to the signifying process of Scripture-in-Tradition, as a kind of rule to ensure that the biblical world will have primary force in the shaping of communities. See Meeks, "Social Embodiment," 179.

[169] See ND, 120; and comments by Werner Jeanrond in "The Problem of the Starting Point of Theological Thinking," in *The Possibilities of Theology*, ed., J. Webster (Edinburgh: T & T Clark, 1994), 74.

terms.[170] Not only would Barth have disapproved of a hermeneutic that "would completely localize meaning in the biblical narrative," he would have regarded such a move as a "serious anthropological reduction" similar to the historicism in hermeneutics which he was combating. For Barth, biblical narratives and Church language, if they are true, "correspond to an objective reality that does more than witness to a particular intra-systematic viewpoint."[171] Thiemann, evincing a major difference from Lindbeck on this matter, points out that Barth talks of "revelation" as God's self-interpretation. "Barth is interested in Scripture as self-interpreting text, because he sees Scripture as the vehicle of the self-interpreting triune God... It is Barth's view of revelation that warrants his intratextual view of theology. Without that doctrine of revelation, or its functional equivalent, textuality, intratextuality, and self-interpreting texts have no theological force."[172] Given this picture of Barth's objective realism, how Barthian is Yale's intratextual school?

Intratextuality, in the Frei-Lindbeck mould, does not regard biblical texts as functioning to disclose a more fundamental reality within history. The only legitimate referents are those which appear *under the descriptions* yielded by the biblical texts.[173] This is the natural corollary of a theology founded on the "realistic" or "history-like" scriptural narratives advocated by Frei and

[170] See Bruce L. McCormack, "Revelation and History in Transfoundationalist Perspective," *JR* 78 (1998) 35.

[171] M. I. Wallace, "The New Yale Theology," 170. For comments on Barth's realism, see also Paul Nelson, *Narrative and Morality* (Chicago: Pennsylvania State University Press, 1987), 75; Wallace, "Karl Barth's Hermeneutic," *JR* 68 (1988) 396-410; George Hunsinger, "Beyond Literalism and Expressivism," *ModTh* 3 (1987) 209-23.

[172] See Thiemann, "Response to George Lindbeck," 378.

[173] See Mark Brett, *Biblical Criticism in Crisis?* (Cambridge: Cambridge University Press, 1991), 156.

embraced by Lindbeck. But it is also an understanding of the biblical revelatory claims which is fundamentally at variance with
Barth's. Lindbeck's intratextual project has thus been described as
a "conflicted Barthian apology for construing all reality through
the template of the Bible without Barth's robust confidence in the
prevenient reality of God's speaking and acting in the world as the
guarantor of Christian truth-claims."[174] This has serious implications. First, Lindbeck's constructive scheme is in fact at odds with
Barth's understanding of theology in that Lindbeck assigns to theology a position from which only "utterances" and not "assertions" about God and the world are made. For Barth, the Christian
message embodies an eminent truth claim; Lindbeck, as we shall
see in a later chapter, is only interested in discussing the *function*
of Christian doctrines within the Christian community. The use to
which Barth's exegetical practices are put by Lindbeck has been
judged to be illegitimate for failing to entail agreement with their
dogmatic underpinnings. A nonfoundationalist reading of Barth is
achieved only through a radical surgery where his doctrine of revelation is cut out of his theology. Consequently, the claim that
Lindbeck's postliberal theology rests on Barth is a doubtful enterprise.[175] Tracy's assessment of Lindbeck's programme as Barthian
confessionalism will therefore have to be qualified.[176] Finally,
without a realist epistemology to undergird his claims, Lindbeck's
postliberal call for the biblical absorption of the universe stands in
real danger of being perceived as vacuous and unpersuasive.[177]

[174] Mark I. Wallace, "Can God Be Named Without Being Known?" *JAAR* 59 (1991) 282.
[175] See B. L. McCormack, "Beyond Nonfoundationalism and Postmodern Reading of Barth," *ZdT* 13 (1997) 94-95; see also idem, "Revelation and History in Transfoundationalist Perspective," *JR* 78 (1998) 18-37.
[176] Tracy, "Lindbeck's New Program for Theology," 465.
[177] See Wallace, "The New Yale Theology," 170.

James Barr, one of the foremost advocates of a shift in biblical theology from "history" to "story," is, like Lindbeck, supportive of Frei's thesis that the biblical narrative which moves from creation to consummation is "story" or "history-like," rather than history.[178] But this preference for "story" over "history" for depicting the true character of biblical narratives is, in Wolfhart Pannenberg's view, inadequate for theology. By deciding for "story," the interest in the reality of what is narrated becomes secondary, something which runs counter to the realism of the Old and New Testaments. Making a point germane to our discussion, Pannenberg suggests: "If theology seeks God's historical action in the sequence of events which the Bible records, and as they appear to modern historical judgment and according to their reconstruction on the basis of historical-critical research, it will be closer to the spirit of the biblical tradition than if it treats the texts simply as literature in which the facticity of what is recorded is a secondary matter."[179] Brevard Childs, too, asks whether, as a comprehensive categorial referent, the term "story" is an adequate substitute for history. In the book of Kings in the Old Testament, for example, the claim that its narrative is "history-like" must be challenged by the chronological elements of Israel's experience. To maintain the special features essential to Israel's witness to the divine intervention of God, the element of historical particularity must substantially qualify the term "story."[180]

---

[178] See James Barr, "Story and History in Biblical Theology," *JR* 56 (1976) 1-17. Barr speaks of the Israelite recital of God's deeds as story. Tracy, however, approaches the narrative as one of the many classic expressions of the New Testament, and views Frei's narrative-recovery as *one of the tasks* for theological interpretation of scriptural texts informed by literary-critical analyses. See Tracy, *The Analogical Imagination* (New York: Crossroad, 1981), 259-81.

[179] Wolfhart Pannenberg, *Systematic Theology,* trs. G. Bromiley (Grand Rapids: Eerdmans, 1991), 1:231.

[180] Brevard S. Childs, *Introduction to the Old Testament as Scripture* (Philadelphia: Fortress, 1979), 298-99.

In the Frei-Lindbeck emphasis on the world of the narrative, the narrative form does not merely illustrate meaning, but constitutes it. But this runs counter to much of modern biblical criticism which locates meaning outside the text. Because Scripture describes a world essentially different from the secular world we live in, Lindbeck insists that it depicts the only real world and harbours an enduring spiritual significance. If the Bible is to challenge us to assess our experience in terms of the biblical world, then we must let our world be absorbed into the narrative world of the text, instead of trying to fit the biblical narrative into the reality we have constructed. This narrative-intratextual emphasis is, for Childs, both helpful and disconcerting. It is helpful for "checking the abuses of a crude theory of historical referentiality which has dominated biblical studies since the Enlightenment." But he finds it "far too limiting" when the function of the Bible is unduly restricted to "that of rendering an agent or an identity." The prophets and the apostles, Childs points out, bore witness to "things which they saw and events which they experienced as testimonies to what God was doing in the world." Precisely because he agrees that the biblical referent must be determined by the text itself, Childs insists that "Scripture points referringly both to the Creator and the creation in a wide variety of different ways." Making a point which is crucial to our discussion, Childs exposes a false dilemma when we pit faith-construals starkly against external referents. "To recognise that the Bible offers a faith-construal," he insists, "is not to deny that it bears witness to realities outside the text. Christians have always understood that we are saved, not by the biblical text, but by the life, death, and resurrection of Jesus Christ who entered into the world of time and space."[181] Critics are therefore understandably critical of the Frei-

---

[181] See Childs, *The New Testament as Canon* (London: SCM, 1984) 545; *idem, Old Testament as Scripture*, 545.

Lindbeck view of "the self-sufficiency and autonomy of literary meaning," and their tendency to provide a mere "literary cloak" (i.e., a narrative construct which aims to 'render an agent') for an essential Barthian emphasis on the transcendent Word, namely Jesus Christ, addressing us through the biblical words.[182]

As he is principally concerned that the Bible be treated as normative and regulative for the identity, faith, and practice of the Church community, Lindbeck insists that the realistic character of the narrative does not depend on the historical or scientific facticity of the story in the text.[183] The focus on the *meaning* of the divine acts has the obvious advantage that Scripture does give the appearance of affording an independent testimony to the factuality of the redemptive acts for faith. However, the matter can hardly be left there; and the common impression of commentators is that Frei and Lindbeck stop too soon. It is commonplace that biblical history bulks large in redemptive acts. Unless the biblical data are assimilated to this history, we risk ending up with a narrative that exerts no claim to historical factuality. The resultant narrative, billed as adequate to nurture faith, and yet posited as independent of objective historical concerns, can only sponsor "a split in the relationships of faith to reason and to history." This may promote skepticism; it will certainly cloud historical referents and put the very tradition of historical revelation in jeopardy. On literary and hermeneutical grounds, Lindbeck insists that historical actualities are unnecessary for the interpretation of scriptural narratives. This

---

[182] For bibliographical references, see Henry, "Narrative Theology," 6-7. However, in view of the "ecclesiologically figural way" [more on this in chapter five] Lindbeck thinks the scriptural referents function, it has been argued that he does take the historical factuality of those referents in fundamental seriousness. See Ephraim Radner, *The End of the Church: A PneumatologicalChristian Division in the West* (Grand Rapids: Eerdmans, 1998), 33-34 n.57.

[183] See S. Holland, "How Do Stories Save Us? Two Contemporary Theological Responses," *LS* 22 (1997) 335.

total disinterest in the text's original reference to a particular
socio-historical context ends up promoting the theory that final
authority rests with the written text.[184]

Authors who think that "it is the concreteness of the text that
holds transformative power" may naturally tilt toward Lindbeck
and his Yale confreres. However, they could still find that this
"Yale argument" is neither sufficiently text-specific, nor as attentive to the social embodiment of the real world as the texts themselves are.[185] Facticity, therefore, is of deep concern to social historians of the New Testament such as Wayne Meeks (of Yale) and
Gerd Theissen (of Germany).[186] They seek to "describe the first
Christian group in ways that a sociologist or an anthropologist
might," seeking "in social history an antidote to the abstractions
of the history of ideas and to the subjective individualism of existentialist hermeneutics."[187] Precisely because these New Testament scholars are, like Lindbeck, concerned with the cultural-linguistic particularities of Christianity, their work has entailed
"trying to achieve what Geertz, after Ryle, calls a 'thick description' of ways in which the early Christian groups worked as religious communities, within the cultural and subcultural contexts
peculiar to themselves."[188] Their studies contribute substantially

---

[184] See Henry, "Narrative Theology," 10-12.

[185] See W. Bruggemann, *Texts Under Negotiation* (Minneapolis: Fortress, 1993), ix.

[186] See, for example, Gerd Theissen, *The Social Setting of Pauline Christian-
ity: Essays on Corinth* (Philadelphia: Fortress, 1982); Wayne A. Meeks, *The
First Urban Christians: The Social World of the Apostle Paul* (New Haven: Yale
University Press, 1983).

[187] Meeks, *The First Urban Christians*, 2.

[188] Meeks, "Social Embodiment," 179. When Lindbeck deals with social
embodiment, this is characteristically done in relation to his intratextual
hermeneutics. See Lindbeck, "Atonement and the Hermeneutics of Intratextual
Social Embodiment," in *The Nature of Confession: Evangelicals and Postliberals in Conversation*, ed. T. R. Phillips and D. L. Okholm (Downers Grove, IL:
InterVarsity, 1996), 221-40.

to an improved understanding of what a given text meant, through serious work in uncovering "the web of meaningful signs, actions, and relationships within which that text did its work." This is in keeping with Krister Stendahl's call to all biblical scholars, in execution of their primary intellectual task, to make clear distinctions between what the text meant in its original setting and what it means to present-day readers.[189]

Rapprochement between the socio-historical exegete and Lindbeck is unlikely, however. For the socio-historical concerns seem rather at odds with Lindbeck's primary focus which is [i] not on "text" as a metaphor for the entire semiotic system of the religious community, but [ii] is restricted to the "semiotic universe paradigmatically encoded in Holy Writ" (ND116), so that [iii] meaning is derived strictly from *within* the scriptural framework (ND 118) that [iv] "designates the *theologically controlling sense* from the literary structure of the text itself" (ND 120). Given this obvious difference, even when socio-historical scholars of the New Testament acknowledge Lindbeck's synchronic analysis of the texts as useful, their own textual sources will not be strictly canon-dependent, nor will they regard the dismissal of the social and historical background of the texts as sound, either exegetically or theologically.

Stephen Stell suggests a crucial distinction in the God-human relational framework. When Lindbeck speaks of "God" in Christian cultural-linguistic categories, "is he speaking of the intratextually identified God, or the identification of God in the text?" The question is crucial for clarifying the object of theological understanding: Is one seeking the reality of God as identified by the text but not confined therein, or is the textual identification of God accepted as final? Is that all there is to know about God? The distinction focuses on the right relationship between "this emerging

---

[189] See Krister Stendahl, "Biblical Theology, Contemporary," *IDB* 1:418-32.

God and the framework from which God emerges." Lindbeck's case rests on an interpretive framework that is strictly identified with the scriptural narrative. But Scripture clearly points *beyond* itself, to the reality of the *risen* Christ, as well as to his *living* presence amongst humanity. Furthermore, Scripture points to the unfolding future which its historical narrative does not and, indeed, cannot encompass. One may concur with Frei-Lindbeck that the identity of Jesus is unknown apart from the narrative framework. But that Jesus is now the Christ, the *living* Lord who is present in human community in Spirit, whose story continues to unfold existentially in every age, and whose final revelation lies beyond the pale of human history and everything in it, including the Holy Scripture that points to the eschaton. And so Stell can rhetorically ask: "From this perspective of Christ's unfolding identity and the triune reality of God, does not the context for Christian understanding necessarily consist in the mutual interplay of the traditioned experience of the living God and the experienced tradition of the narrative framework?" Stell's thesis integrates two components, the narrative framework of Scripture and particular present-day experiences. Both components are constitutive of one's interpretive framework and therefore for the very unfolding of Christ's presence.[190] The question of the normative status of experience is an important area to which we need to return when we look at Lindbeck's cultural-linguistic lens for viewing religion.

In sum, ironically, what seems on the face of it to be a high doctrine of Scripture turns out to be quite the contrary. Intratextuality, arguably, is introspection. It reflects timidity, the fear that an outward-looking vision might mean the loss of the very narrative around which the community has gathered. This retrenchment of

---

[190] See Stell, "Hermeneutics in Theology and the Theology of Hermeneutics," 694-95.

the text's sphere of influence to "the gathered, self-contained, introspective community" reduces the import of the text. What *kind* of a world would the text have absorbed? For Christians, might this not be seen as a negation of a world which is *already* God's creation? In a world that arises out of communal self-absorption through the expedient of its written text, have not the real possibilities for interaction with the wider human community been systematically all but erased? Where then might one possibly conceive of a genuine dialogue in and with this world?[191] An intratextual theological outlook that promotes the cultural-linguistic particularities of the faith community would still have to deal with the claims of the *divine presence* in human existence, were it to do justice to the Christian religion. This is noticeably absent in Lindbeck's proposal.

3.4.1.3 Against Metaphysical Referents

In Lindbeck's argument against foundationalism that we saw earlier, the horizons of radical historicity and temporality that saturate and condition human life and thought are stressed. Theology, we are told, must give due weight to the cultural and linguistic determinacy of forms of life. Attention, it seems, is directed to the all-encompassing reality of human finitude. Not only have these insights been pulsating through the works of Wittgenstein and Geertz, from whom Lindbeck openly draws inspiration, much of this absolutising of the flux in contemporary thought has been spurred by Heidegger, on whom Lindbeck does not explicitly rely. From Heidegger, we learn that the truth of Being is not an objective "out-there," but only resides in the horizon of history in different modes as, for instance, Form (Plato), Substance (Aristotle),

---

[191] See, substantively, Francis Watson, *Text, Church and World*, 135.

Esse (Aquinas), and History (Hegel). When historicity is thus assumed to be the overarching horizon of truth, no appearance of being can ever be equated with Being itself. In this framework of understanding, to argue that the truth of Being is ever disclosed in a final and definitive fashion is to remain trapped in the "onto-theo-logical tradition" of Western philosophy.[192] For theology, one immediate implication of this new horizon of temporality and socio-cultural determination is a deconstructed notion of truth that renders all universal and referential notions untenable. But what would theology look like if such an argument is pursued to its logical end?

"Revelation," in the Christian understanding, comes with certain particular implications. Lindbeck's nonfoundationalist point of departure would argue that contextual elements completely govern content. Aimed, no doubt, at stressing religious particularities, Lindbeck's theological formulation in this regard, however, unwittingly risks running counter to the understanding fostered by Tradition. Take Vatican II, for example. The Council recognized and affirmed history as a major factor in theological knowledge and formulation. A major achievement of the Council was its recognition of historical consciousness, pluralism, development of doctrine and openness to the world. But, in keeping with Tradition, the Council combined this perspective with two indispensable elements: [1] a referential notion of truth and a presumed ontology that must always undergird a contextual perspective; and [2] the fundamental Anselmian starting point of *faith seeking*

---

[192] In rejecting Western onto-theology, Louis-Marie Chauvet has charted a way for utilizing Heidegger's philosophy for theologizing in contemporary postmodern setting. Especially fecund, it seems, is his attempt to balance presence with the encompassing nature of absence. See idem, *Symbol and Sacrament: A Sacramental Reinterpretation of Christian Existence*, trs. P. Madigan and M. Beaumont (Collegeville: Liturgical, 1995).

understanding which recognizes that, though we never begin with an *a priori* ontology or epistemology, we do, and must, employ certain philosophies insofar as they are congruent with, and facilitate the explication of, Christian truth claims. In this light, a case can be made against Lindbeck's philosophical orientation towards deconstructing foundationalism and realism, for the end result of such an orientation is the risk of putting aside the traditional Church teaching at its most fundamental level, namely, the notion of revelation. When the whole of reality is reduced to the reality in the text, has not revelation been banished to a corner which is "entirely symbolic and non-referential"? Would this still be recognizable from the standpoint of the Christian Tradition?[193] From the angle of Lindbeck's text-immanent narrative hermeneutics, once all the text-transcendent referents have been removed from the interpretive process, what is left is a dubious relationship between narrative and the divine reality to which it points. The Christian vision would be greatly impoverished if we claimed, as Lindbeck and Frei do, that the divine reality was exhausted by literary presence. It amounts to a tragic lack of "an Archimedian lever" to lift us above the narrative and its dramatic literary depiction. Ironically, as it turns out, the Frei-Lindbeck concentration on the Risen Jesus and the drama surrounding the tomb does not *logically* entail belief that he is historically risen and alive, nor does it preclude an identification of the Risen Lord as mythical – a misidentification they set out to avoid.[194] Voices from the postliberal camp itself are concerned that in collapsing the revealed Word into the written Word, the Frei-Lindbeck account of revelation features a written Word that "witnesses to nothing beyond

[193] The argument in this section largely reflects Thomas Guarino, "Philosophy within Theology in Light of the Foundationalism Debate," 66-68.

[194] See Henry, "Narrative Theology," 13.

itself,"[195] thereby scuttling the assertion that Christian speaking and acting all respond to a prior initiative from God. In light of a God who precedes our speech and action, a project denying external biblical reference is wanting in theological intelligibility.[196]

To be sure, there is a danger inherent in any attempt at articulating an *ultimate human authority* for Christian faith. The Christian vision, adopting as early an image as the wanderings in the desert, in Exodus, where the people fashioned a god they could feel, touch, see and pray to, in place of the invisible God, has always been wary of putting excessive weight on our own formulas and schemas. When, therefore, the formulations in the Bible (or any interpretation of these formulations) are treated as normative in some *a priori* way without a metaphysical reference, they begin to take on an authority that is absolute. When an eternal and unchangeable status is thus accorded to Scriptures, the question that presents itself is "whether the penultimate has come to be regarded as ultimate?"[197]

In Lindbeck's futurology, the desired goal is the formation of a community whose forms of life correspond to the symbolic universe engendered by the text. Problems arise when one seeks to identify the location of that symbolic universe. Lindbeck locates it squarely in the text, so that his confessional theology amounts to, in his words, "absorbing the universe into the biblical world."[198] In the process, the one element that is implicitly assumed to remain constant in a world of flux is the "story" and the identity it shapes. This move is seen by commentators as

---

[195] William C. Placher, "Paul Ricoeur and Postliberal Theology: A Conflict of Interpretations?" *ModTh* 4 (1987) 48.

[196] See Thiemann, *Revelation and Theology*, 171-72.

[197] D. Bryant, "Christian Identity and Historical Change: Postliberals and Historicity," *JR* 47 (1991) 41.

[198] ND, 135.

being seriously flawed, for it falsely imputes a *constancy* to the text, its meaning, and its interpretive traditions which they never have, and turns them into insulated entities which they never are.[199]

John Milbank, for example, commends Lindbeck and Frei for calling the community back to narrative as being that alone which can 'identify' God for us; a speculative idea is mere 'extrinsic' knowledge that cannot save. If Jesus is the Word of God, the community that professes him so must carefully attend to his words and deeds. A speculative idea may reveal that God is love, but only the narrative can instruct us on what that love is. However, Lindbeck errs in overlooking the complexity of the narrative structure: he, in effect, seeks to make the biblical narrative itself assume a fixed, socially categorical role which "allows one to stress the socially and linguistically 'given' character of religious meaning for individuals."[200] But the setting the narrative structure is made to represent, and which social historians of the New Testament are keenly interested in, is never fully representable synchronically. Interpreting the narrative is thus never altogether an easy task; there is always a role for speculative theology. Lindbeck himself attempts some difficult abstractions when he proposes a few rules for narrative-interpretation. It is a mistake to assume that these rules stay invariant throughout Christian history, or that they are in any way more basic than past doctrines formulated under the intellectual circumstances of given time and

---

[199] See L. E. Cady, "Resisting the Postmodern Turn," in *Theology at the End of Modernity*, ed. S. G. Davaney (Philadelphia: Trinity, 1991), 89. N. Murphy sees the issue of relativism with regard to textual interpretation as being increasingly more explosive. Arguments will rage on whether it is possible or desirable to attribute stable meanings to texts. See her "Textual Relativism, Philosophy of Language, and the Baptist Vision," in *Theology Without Foundations*, 250.

[200] See John Milbank, "An Essay Against Secular Order," *JRE* 15 (1987) 201-02.

place.[201] That explains Milbank's suggestion that while Lindbeck aims to be anti-foundationalist, he ends up erecting a new "narratological foundationalism," albeit one based on the notion that "the biblical texts plus a few regulative principles for reading and performing it, constitute a finite and unchanging set of rules that can be *methodically* applied in a determinate and 'objective' manner to any given *external* context." The "context" that Lindbeck works on is said to have been wrongly conceived as "external and autonomous" to a textual dynamics which funds a developing tradition. A suitable revision to his strict category may lend greater credibility to a Christian tradition that claims to enjoy a self-critical process.[202] The consequence of all this is that, what we have from Lindbeck, finally, is a "metanarrative realism" that is "dangerously ahistorical." It is a metanarrative realism that has been converted into "a new narratological foundationalism" which is not postmodern. When an assumed "paradigmatic setting" is illegitimately grafted onto the narrative structures, Lindbeck portrays Christians as living within certain fixed narratives which, like *schemas*, regulate endlessly different cultural contents.[203]

Further, Lindbeck may appear to concede that the story undergoes some kind of transformation over and over again as it fuses "with the new worlds within which it is told and retold." But, even as fusion occurs, he insists on a "self-identical story" that bears "constancy" and an "abiding identity."[204] In any event, scholars like Meeks, who are mindful of the social contexts, would then suggest that Lindbeck is quite mistaken in confusing

---

[201] See John Milbank, *Theology and Social Theory: Beyond Secular Reason* (London: Blackwell, 1990), 385.

[202] Milbank," Against Secular Order," 221-22 n.2; idem, *Theology and Social Theory*, 385-86.

[203] Milbank, *Theology and Social Theory*, 386.

[204] ND, 83.

the *communicating structure* with "the whole cultural system comprising ethos, world-view, and sacred symbols [using Geertz's famous trilogy], of which the text is only one element." Perhaps the task of identifying the literary structure of the text is merely *descriptive*, so that Lindbeck is clearly mistaken when he seeks to elevate it to a *normative* status. To be sure, the history of the Christian communities, let alone the Jewish ones, has always treated "story" as one among many construals. The Frei-Lindbeck case in favour of "narrative" as the controlling pattern is supported neither by actual uses, nor by the different genres found within the canon.[205]

It is understandable that commentators see Lindbeck's postliberal concept of the nature and task of theology as being inherently antirealist. Donald Bloesch, for example, assesses this concept as being "primarily descriptive rather than ontologically normative" in part because it focuses on "the analysis [of Scripture] as narrative rather than on the text as the bearer of intrinsic, quasi-metaphysical meaning."[206] Scripture, in the hands of Lindbeck, turns into a "*mosaic* that redesigns reality," but it also "conjures up a vision of the world that does not necessarily comport with objective or historical reality." If it "creates a picture of a followable world," this does not refer to the actual, objective world. From a metaphysical realist perspective, Bloesch suggests that the task of theology goes beyond interpreting Scripture intratextually, for "church language 'is adequate to a revealed reality that does more than witness to a particular intrasystematic viewpoint.'"[207] The rise of postliberal theology, in Bloesch's view, has brought about

---

[205] Meeks, "Social Embodiment," 185.

[206] Donald G. Bloesch, *A Theology of Word and Spirit: Authority and Method in Theology* (Downers Grove, IL: InterVarsity, 1992), 17, 30.

[207] Donald G. Bloesch, *Holy Scripture: Revelation, Inspiration and Interpretation* (Downers Grove, IL: InterVarsity, 1994), 211-12, 215.

a shift in emphasis "from exploring the metaphysical implications of the faith to investigating the story of a people on pilgrimage. While reflecting certain biblical concerns, this development is nonetheless fraught with peril. Theology can ill afford to ignore the issue of truth, for it is truth that gives narrative its significance.... The divine incursion sets the stage for an excursus in ontology. Theology is certainly more a generalized description of the faith of the community: it entails a metaphysical probing of how this community is grounded in reality."[208]

In sum, Lindbeck, in attempting to develop a consistent focus on the intratextual disclosure of truth, is liable to be found wanting as regards the dialectic which obtains between [i] the reader and the text; [ii] framework and experience; [iii] church and canon; [iv] continuity and variation. At this point, it is evident that Lindbeck's theological proposal is open to criticism on account of his refusal to accept the usefulness of a general hermeneutics and, in relation thereto, the need to give credit to the reader in the act of reading.

3.4.1.4 Against Hermeneutical Referents

In opting for a literary reading of the Bible as the most adequate approach, Lindbeck espouses the use of explicitly biblical imagination as the only appropriate theological strategy for shaping contemporary religious praxis. This entails, within the logic of his proposal, a stern opposition to the foundationalist reliance on a formal and independent use of hermeneutics. A general or

---

[208] Bloesch, *Theology of Word and Spirit*, 133. Jeffrey Hensley, however, has assumed the burden of defending an interpretation of Lindbeck's project as compatible with metaphysical realism in "Are Postliberals Necessarily Antirealists?," in *The Nature of Confession*, ed. T. R. Phillips and D. L. Okholm (Downers Grove, IL: InterVarsity, 1996), 70-80.

philosophical hermeneutics is dismissed as inappropriate for theology and what is proper for Christian theology is confined to a specifically theological hermeneutics. And yet, at least in an *ad hoc* manner, Lindbeck makes good use of general hermeneutical insights for developing his tradition-specific mode of interpreting theological statements, only to dispose of general hermeneutics in favour of his specifically intratextual interpretation.[209]

Hermeneutics, however, has invalidated any total-objectivity claim (such as historical-critical research tends to make), as well as a purely-subjectivist approach (such as a reader-response-criticism is wont to do) to any human enquiry. In biblical interpretation and theology, hermeneutics has shattered all claims of innocently objectivist or purely subjectivist approaches. There is now a wide recognition that any interpretation of a text is the result of an interplay between text and reader, neither of which may be treated as a static entity. The extent to which, on the one hand, the text determines the act of reading, or, conversely, the reader determines the meaning of the text, remains an issue. But there is wide support for the view that, because "the semantic unity of any given text can unfold itself only in the act of reading," the active involvement of a reader or a group of readers is presupposed. To be adequate, therefore, any mode of reading must feature an emphasis on the dynamic and interactive nature both of the text and of the act of reading.[210]

Part of the price that attaches to hallowing the constitutive role of the text in Lindbeck's scheme is that the crucial role of *the reader as actor* is silenced. The suggestion of an unencumbered and direct reading of the Bible offends against the inevitable contribution to

[209] See Jeanrond, *Theological Hermeneutics*, 162.

[210] See Werner G. Jeanrond, "After Hermeneutics: The Relationship between Theology and Biblical Studies," in *The Open Text*, ed. F. Watson (London: SCM, 1993), 94.

the text's meaning that the active reader always makes.[211] Lindbeck's narrative understanding must be supplemented by an inclusion of the constitutive role of the reader. Allowing no critical conversation with the biblical text, Lindbeck in effect takes Scripture as an a-historical text, which is a contradiction in terms. What is needed, Richard Lints argues, is to embrace both the historical limitations of the text and its historical possibilities. To show a willingness to learn from the text, a reader needs to enter into a two-way movement: to submit to and be challenged by the text, and to be critical of it.[212] In this context, the fact that Gadamer gets no mention at all by Lindbeck is indicative of his deeply entrenched conviction that it is necessary to lock out, as it were, the present experience or the personal perspective of the reader as a necessary component in the interpretation of Scriptures. In doing so, he has seriously omitted valuable insights from contemporary hermeneutics, including ideological critiques such as Habermas and the feminist theologians are at pains to introduce.

Much of this can be attenuated if we turn to Ricoeur's ideas on revelation, where referentiality is ingredient. Reference to God is a form of testimony, bearing two dimensions: first, a meaningful testimony refers to an event in the past, the truth-claim of which is closely tied with its manifestation to a witness; second, this event, which cannot be repeated, is re-presented by an act of witnessing. The role of testimony, as Jean Ladriere sees it, is *mediatory*, forming the crucial link between the faith in its present state and the primary or originary event.[213] With regard to scriptural narrative

---

[211] See the equivalent criticisms of Frei by L. Poland, *Literary Criticism and Biblical Hermeneutics* (Missoula, MO: Scholars, 1985), 120-56; Gary Comstock, "Truth or Meaning," *JR* 66 (1986) 117-40.

[212] See R. Lints, "The Positivist Choice: Tracy or Lindbeck," *JAAR* 61 (1993) 668.

[213] See Jean Ladriere, "Meaning and Truth in Theology," *CTSAP* 42 (1987) 11.

figuration as the locus of revelation, the plausibility of the act of witnessing is dependent on two factors: [i] a configurative testimony, in the written text, of the initial revelatory, but prefigurative, event; and [ii] a subsequent revelatory interpretive experience which is a refigurative realization of the configuration.[214] In this understanding, Lindbeck's intuition of the irreplaceable value of the text is preserved. In addition, in two indispensable senses, *imagination* is posited as a fundamental component of the revelatory process: [i] there is, first, the act of figurative imagination which constructs a revelatory meaning out of the initial manifestation event; and [ii] there is, secondly, the imagination of the reader which constructs a revelatory meaning as testimony of divine revelation. The common objection that underscores all criticisms against Frei and Lindbeck in this regard is that they stop too soon. A configurative view of revelation is no doubt very important for preserving the primacy of Scriptures in the life of the Church, but it is inadequate for hermeneutics and theology. A significant factor plaguing Frei and Lindbeck in this respect has to do with their inadvertently positing revelation as a fixed datum within their narrative approach. In the process, they neglect that configuration and refiguration are two symbiotic poles in any Bible reading: *the reader has to lean on the primacy of the configuration as much as the configuration depends on the reader for its realisation.* In their polemic against liberal hermeneutics, which tends to focus too much on the signified idea at the expense of the textual particularities, Frei and Lindbeck are perceived by critics as positing a too radical corrective: in over-stressing the first pole (configuration), they neglect the second (refiguration).

---

[214] See Paul Ricoeur, "The Hermeneutics of Testimony," *ATR* 61 (1979) 435-61. See Further, "Toward a Hermeneutic of the Idea of Revelation," *HTR* 70 (1977) 1-37.

"Revelation," Leo Hettema correctly observes, "is the referent of the biblical and Christian imagination."[215]

The question that arises is how the relation between the text and the convictions of the reader may be conceived. In the words of MacAfee Brown, the issue is one of relating 'my story' and 'The Story'.[216] Thiemann, whose thought substantially echoes that of the others in the Yale school on this point, stresses the prevenience of God in Christian doctrine of revelation. Still, in connecting God's prevenience with the human response, his reflections introduce a key difference to what Lindbeck has evinced so far. Thiemann accepts that the biblical narrative eminently structures the text as a revelatory identification of God and Christ as agent, and that it invites the reader to enter into the world of the text. But Thiemann also allows a dynamic interplay between the biblical text and the reader, stressing the dynamics of this relationship as one of *address* and *affirmative response*. In performative terms, the affirmation from the reader is, first and foremost, a recognition of the narrated promise of God in sacred Scriptures, which must then ensue in a life of faithful obedience to the Word, translated concretely into a life of faith and discipleship.[217] In this scheme of understanding, only in the reader's act of refiguring

[215] Theo L. Hettema, *Reading for Good* (Kampen: Kok Pharos, 1996), 328. "Imagination" has been the focus of much theological attention in recent years. See Julian Hartt, *Theological Method and Imagination* (New York: Seabury, 1974); D. Tracy, *The Analogical Imagination* (New York: Crossroad, 1981); John Coulson, *Religion and Imagination* (Oxford: Clarendon, 1981); Gordon Kaufman, "Theology as Imaginative Construction," *JAAR* 50 (1982) 81-85; David J. Bryant, *Faith and the Play of Imagination* (Georgia: Mercer University Press, 1989); Garrett Green, *Imagining God* (San Francisco: Harper & Row, 1989); John E. Thiel, *Imagination and Authority*; Paul Ricoeur, *Figuring the Sacred: Religion, Narrative and Imagination*, ed. M. I. Wallace (Minneapolis: Fortress, 1995).

[216] See R. MacAfee Brown, "My Story and 'The Story'," *ThT* 32 (1975) 166-73.

[217] See Thiemann, *Revelation and Theology*, 143-45.

does the biblical message come to realisation. And yet, within this scheme of correlation, what remains normative in forming and transforming the life of the reader and the reading community is the Christian tradition encoded in the scriptural narrative. Only now, it is clear that the Tradition is posited as living and dynamic.[218]

3.4.2 Revelation as a Dynamic Process, Not a Fixed Datum

Even though 'The Story' is not conceived of as a fixed datum, it nevertheless has, in line with our findings in the first chapter, an indispensable foundational import. With a view to developing a more adequate understanding of the revelatory role the Story plays, we will now examine several related themes.

3.4.2.1 The Emphasis on Encounter

Apart from Ricoeur, another author whose work must be enlisted to attenuate the inadequacy of Lindbeck's hermeneutics is Gadamer. As we saw, truth for Gadamer is found through a "merging of horizons." The implication for our discussion is a conversational approach to truth where the reader of Scripture converses with the past, that is, the tradition encoded in the text. In this historical understanding, the meaning of tradition is not

---

[218] Hauerwas, following MacIntyre, perceptively reflects on the narrative character of moral communities and moral reasoning in *Character and Christian Life* (San Antonio: Trinity University Press, 1975); *A Community of Character* (Notre Dame: Notre Dame University Press, 1981); *The Peaceable Kingdom* (Notre Dame: University of Notre Dame Press, 1983); *Resident Aliens* (Nashville: Abingdon, 1989); *Unleashing the Scriptures* (Nashville: Abingdon, 1993). For an instructive analysis, see E. Katongole, *Beyond Universal Reason* (forthcoming in February, 2000, University of Notre Dame Press).

posited as a static past. Instead, its richness and inherent possibilities are seen as emerging through an encounter which reflects
both the tradition of the past and the particular needs and concerns
of the present. In this respect, "revelation" may aptly express two
related elements: first, it expresses the specificity of a givenness;
second, it accounts for "the process by which the project of God
concerning humanity finds its effectivity, in a religious history
prepared by the Old Testament and receiving its accomplishment
in the life and the teachings of Jesus Christ. The central scheme of
this process is the scheme of the encounter, in which a human
being is concretely placed before the word of God and its power
of salvation and in which he has to make a decision with respect
to what is thus proposed to him."[219]

Gadamer's understanding of linguisticality opens the way for
our understanding of a possible fusion of horizons in this
encounter: behind the basic differences separating the culture in
which the tradition of the Christian past was formulated and
handed down, and the immensely different cultural setting of contemporary society, stands a basic fact of linguisticality which
accounts for the possibility of translation, conversation, and communication. Gadamer does not suggest either that the tradition
loses its linguistic starting point, or that the reader dissolves her
contingency. Rather, in all hermeneutical travels, there is an effective history where every world, "as linguistically constituted, is
always open, of itself, to every possible insight and hence for
expansion of its own world picture, and accordingly available to
others."[220] There is, then, the possibility to account for "transformation" arising from the encounter between text and reader even
"into a communion in which we do not remain what we were."[221]

---

[219] Ladriere, "Meaning and Truth in Theology," 13-14.
[220] Gadamer, *Truth and Method*, 405.
[221] Gadamer, *Truth and Method*, 341.

However, as has been pointed out earlier, critics see Gadamer's account of fusion or transformation through conversation as rather incomplete. Amongst other things, his heavy reliance on an existing consensus supplied by effective history, and his neglect of ideological critiques, have been highlighted. However, the combination of Gadamer's and Ricoeur's insights offers a very fecund hermeneutical approach to Scripture as a revelatory text.

One must therefore regret that, for all its brilliance, Lindbeck's framework for biblical interpretation has no room for some *fundamental* insights from contemporary exegetes with a keen eye on hermeneutics. We take one illustration. Even before embarking on a critical exegesis, human temporality alerts the reader to heed the fact that, as regards the biblical text, there is a historical horizon behind the text, a semantic horizon within the text itself, and the present horizon of the reader. These triple-horizons can and must be integrated. The central motif in Sandra Schneiders' work is, like that of the postliberals, the biblical text as revelatory, that is, as the locus and mediation of God's *revelatory encounter* with us. And yet, she perceptively sketches a triple-world in relation to the text: first, the world behind the text; second, the world of the text; and third, the world before the text. To the first belongs history and imagination; to the second, witness and language; and to the third, the meaning of the text, which is something to be appropriated by readers of every age, the issue being one of conversion and transformation. In her exposition, it is clear that too much of the inevitable dynamics in every biblical interpretation – an encounter aimed at facilitating revelation — gets omitted where one chooses to ignore the hermeneutical insights of Gadamer and Ricoeur.[222]

[222] See Schneiders, *The Revelatory Text*. Anthony C. Thiselton has also argued that the work of the systematic theologian is to bring about a 'fusion' of the horizon of the New Testament writers and the horizon of today, so that what

3.4.2.2 The Emphasis on the Revelatory Process

That the Bible is revelatory is thus not in dispute. At issue is how Scripture study, as an attempt to receive, understand, and explicate this revelation, may be achieved without reductionism or domestication. The difficulty is that to understand revelation as the inscrutable disclosure of the mystery of God involves balancing the two elements: that revelation is not content-less and that the substance should not be hardened into a convenient package. To ignore the first, is to displace the foundational import of Tradition; to ignore the second, is to "disregard the character of the text that portrays God with remarkable, intentional artistic elusiveness."[223] There is, therefore, an irreducible *process* that cannot be ignored, for God and humanity encounter each other dialectically in a dialogue that never ends. Bruggemann thus writes: "There is in Israel's God-talk a remarkable restlessness and openness, as if each new voice in each new circumstance must undertake the entire process anew. Remarkably, the God of Israel, perhaps so characteristically Jewish, is willing to participate yet again in such an exchange that must be inordinately demanding. For Israel and for Israel's God, there is no deeper joy, no more serious requirement, no more inescapable burden, than to be reengaged in the process of exchange that never arrives but is always on the way."[224]

found expression within the horizon of the first-century writers can be re-expressed within our contemporary horizon. See his *The Two Horizons* (Grand Rapids: Eerdmans, 1980).

[223] Brueggemann, *Theology of the Old Testament*, 3. See also Ricoeur, "The Bible and the Imagination," in *Figuring the Scared*, ed. M. I. Wallace (Minneapolis: Fortress, 1995), 144-49.

[224] Brueggemann, *Theology of the Old Testament*, 84. See, further, Michael L. Cook, "Revelation as Metaphoric Process," *TS* 47 (1986) 388-411.

3.4.2.3 Dabar as Word-Event

This notion of revelation as a process rather than as a fixed datum is further augmented by reference to what the term *dabar* signifies in Old Testament theology. *Dabar* in Hebrew is word-event. That concept has carried through to the New Testament which, obviously, is rooted in Judaism despite its hellenistic overtones. The people of Israel first experienced the mighty acts of God as events of God's intervention before they committed them to words (spoken or written). Words (spoken or written) were aimed primarily at recording and explaining these events in the light of faith. Again, the people of Israel did not come into existence as a people and as the people of God except in a gradual process. The whole growth was first a series of events before a verbal articulation of them took place. Thus, for example, the exodus from Egypt was a liberation from Egyptian slavery and a flight from the land that different groups of Semites experienced. It was this common experience that bound these groups together. They became the "tribes of Israel" when they began to articulate their experience in words. The event, coupled with the word that records and explains the event, constitute the *dabar*. Revelation is thus through events explained by words.[225]

Part of the price that attaches to Lindbeck's intratextual strategy, which places all its stakes on the written Word, is that it overlooks the "event" component ingredient in the original Hebrew understanding of revelation which the early Christians inherited. Furthermore, it overlooks the continual unfolding of events as people the world over encounter God anew down through the ages with their vastly different cultural settings, experiences and questions.

---

[225] See L. A. Schokel, *The Inspired Word*, trs. F. Martin (New York: Herder & Herder, 1972); R. de Vaux, *The Early History of Israel*, trs. D. Smith (London: Darton, Longman and Todd, 1978).

3.4.2.4 The Polyphonic, Mediatory and Supplementary Characters of Textual Revelation

Even when attention is focused on the written text, critics are concerned that the postliberals are inattentive to a number of problems which their position suggests. Let us examine five of these.

(1) In the first place, Lindbeck and Frei assume that the Scriptures address one, homogeneous, community that speaks and listens in the cadences of the grammar encoded in the texts. This assumption is problematic on two counts. Firstly, Old Testament scholars surface the point that even if it is correct to suggest that the primary inclination of the text itself is targeted towards the Jewish race, Israel in the Old Testament is not speaking only to itself. Beyond their coherent community of grammar, there is a *second* hearing community – one that speaks many different grammars and dialects — that is also addressed, in times past as in the present, in potentially transformative ways, by this text. "Israel's rhetoric," in other words, "is endlessly an appeal to the nations." Secondly, to the extent that the Old Testament now receives a second hearing that reaches beyond the limits of Jewishness, Scripture exposition must perforce concern itself with more than the internal coherence of grammar. The task of the expositor, Brueggemann suggests, must encompass both audiences. "Whereas Israel is the primary addressee in the text," he says, "in the end it is the nations who are the beneficiaries, as they are invited into the Torah-based peace and justice that are rooted in Yahweh's governance."[226] Flowing from this, the Frei-Lindbeck implicit assumption that the rules of grammar remain constant and unchanging may again appear highly questionable. Further, their narrative intratextuality also posits *a revelatory immediacy* in the text that needs to be qualified. By

---

[226] This argument comes from Brueggemann, *Theology of the Old Testament*, 87-88.

contrast, the presence and reality of the second listening community enhances the credibility of Tracy's insistence that the claims of the text are not only revelational in a close and direct way, but also classic in the sense that all manner of people repeatedly refer to what is given in this text. "Classics," according to Tracy, are "certain expressions of the human spirit [which] so disclose a compelling truth about our lives that we cannot deny them some kind of normative status."[227] It would seem that Tracy invests his definition of a classic with a certain compelling force, not because of "manipulative management," but on account of the power intrinsic in the text – a power that draws not only the immediate listening community, but a second listening community as well.[228]

(2) In the second place, Lindbeck's narrativist assumption of a revelatory immediacy may be questioned on yet another count. Yahweh, as depicted in the Old Testament, is an irascible God, a meeting with whom was neither easy nor predictable. Biblical data narrating the manner of those meetings are regularly described as "stylized and routinized." According to exegetes, this suggests *the ongoing relatedness* of Yahweh to the community. While there are data on immediate relatedness, these are found to be few and far between. What is evidently more important for Old Testament scholarship in this respect is to examine the ways in which Yahweh is *mediated* in relation to Israel. On this score, a few summary points are at once germane. To begin with, scholars are clearly on the mark who speak about "mediated immediacy"[229] and about the tension between "mediateness" and "immediateness."[230] And yet, just as the meetings

---

[227] Tracy, *The Analogical Imagination*, 108.

[228] See comment by Brueggemann, *Theology of the Old Testament*, 88 n.73.

[229] As does Tracy in *The Analogical Imagination*, 377, 385.

[230] As does M. Noth in "The Re-presentation of the Old Testament in Proclamation," in *Essays on Old Testament Hermeneutics*, ed. C. Westermann (Richmond: John Knox, 1963), 85.

with an irascible God were unpredictable, so also the ongoing mediation is endlessly inexplicable and inscrutable, which behoves scholars to be cautious in their descriptions, lest they fall into the trap of thinking they have "captured" God. This is important, on account of the elusiveness of the rhetoric of the text which, as mediation of Yahweh, both conceals and discloses Yahweh at the same time.[231] Theology is impoverished wherever and whenever the reading community imagines that it entirely possesses or has imprisoned the God of the Bible, be it in radical biblicism (a dangerous Protestant inclination) or dogmatism (a dangerous Catholic tendency). Had Lindbeck's theological proposal stopped short entirely within narrative intratextuality, he might find himself a perfect target for criticism here. To his credit, however, Lindbeck tempers his exposition with a constant return to communal practice as a key to his proposal. The question of communal practice being a recurring category in Lindbeck's thoughts, we shall, of course, need to return to it in greater detail in subsequent chapters. Under the present discussion, however, two elements of tension in Lindbeck's project need to be clearly stressed. On the one hand, Lindbeck places a high premium on the performative dimension of religious life. Informed by Geertz's notion of "thick description," Lindbeck proposes that religious ideas are embedded in communal practice. This opens up the possibilities for expositing how religious reality is constituted and generated by concrete communal practice.[232] When Yahweh is thus perceived as being mediated in communal practice, there is a positive indicator that Lindbeck can fence off the indictment that rhetorical mediation of Yahweh

[231] See Samuel Terrien, *The Elusive Presence: Toward a New Biblical Theology* (New York: Harper & Row, 1978).

[232] On this theme, see G. A. Anderson, *A Time to Mourn, a Time to Dance* (University Park: Pennsylvania State University Press, 1991).

in the Bible is a sort of *"disembodied, ideational operation."*[233] On the other hand, critics are right in pointing out that, insofar as Lindbeck's narrative intratextual analysis goes, mediation with external references is pretty much denied, thereby giving the impression that the Bible "hands God over" to the reading community as possession or as prisoner. This tension in Lindbeck's presentation weakens his project. This weakness can be redressed by giving a more explicit mediatory role to the community which is now nurtured by the Bible, as Lindbeck so correctly argues, but which also produced the Bible in the first place, and which now needs to relate to Yahweh in an ongoing relationship.

(3) In the third place, some authors have highlighted a characteristic peculiar to the Bible which they call its "pluralistic and polysemic"[234] or "polyphonic" character.[235] Their combined view features the Christian Bible as weaving together many stories, and 'compressing' a diversity of voices, into a single narrative the connectedness of which is perceived by readers only by way of struggle. The Bible, it is admitted, is no easy read. What is needed is to avoid the temptation to "totalize" the text; instead, effort should be made to render this polyphonic character in a way that is "centered enough for its first listening community, which trusts its coherent grammar and its reliable cadences," and "open enough to be compelling for its second listening community, which may be drawn to its truthfulness but is fearful of any authoritarian closure or reductionism."[236]

(4) In the fourth place, Lindbeck is, to be sure, mindful of the danger that extrabiblical materials, inserted into the biblical world,

---

[233] The phrase comes from Bruggemann, *Theology of the Old Testament*, 574.

[234] P. Ricoeur, "Toward a Hermeneutic of the Idea of Revelation," *HTR* 70 (1977) 3.

[235] M. Coleridge, "Life in the Crypt or Why Bother with Biblical Studies." *BibInt* 2 (1994) 139-51.

[236] Brueggemann, *Theology of the Old Testament*, 88-89.

can take over as the basic framework of interpretation.[237] The
early Church had to deal with such "aberrations" when it fought
gnosticism. In his adherence to the principle of the autonomy of
the text, Lindbeck is saying that we cannot speak of extratextuality because there is nothing outside the text. But this is only a way
of describing a religious culture where the general theory of meaning permits the strong sense of interpreting everything (hence
absorption of the universe) by the world of the text. This does not
mean that there are no non-textual realities but, that, insofar as
they are meaningful, they are somehow already encoded within
the text. It is here that Lindbeck's distinction between intra- and
extratextual meaning is destabilised: the meaning of 'God' can
only be theologically determined by reference to a reality that is
external to the religious system constructed by humanity. That
reality is extra or supplemental to the system, including what is
textually encoded. Lindbeck and Frei suggest that no supplementation is needed, that the narrative description of God in Scripture
is all we need for knowing, obeying and trusting God. And yet, the
history of the making of Scriptures is replete with endless
instances of supplementation.[238] Is there any particular reason why

---

[237] ND, 118.

[238] A creative supplementation was the key uncovered by Timothy Radcliffe
as present among the first Christians as they sought to preserve the Tradition, and
as the key he proposes for contemporary hermeneutics of Tradition. See his
"Tradition and Creativity," NewBf 70 (1989) 57-66. In Paul's letter to the Galatians, for example, he adopts the language of a lawsuit, a language which
appealed to the experience of the people in a community where networks of
friendship and alliances, patronage and allegiances that structured the life of the
city were established. Paul's rhetoric was thereby aimed at conveying what it
meant to belong to the community called the Body of Christ. See H. D. Betz,
Galatians (Philadelphia: Fortress, 1979), 24. In 1 Corinthians, Paul again
adopted the language of the Greek city to analyse the factions that were splitting
the Church in Corinth. See L. L. Welborn, "On Discord in Corinth: 1 Corinthians 1-4 and Ancient Politics," JBL 106 (1987) 85-111. We can add the fact that

the diverse peoples of the late twentieth century should be bound entirely by the largely Hebrew world views integrated into the Old Testament or the Greek ones in the New Testament?[239]

(5) In the fifth place, extratextuality is also important in another fundamental theological sense, namely, with respect to the reality and the workings of the Holy Spirit. Meaning must reside in the dialectic between the text and the reading community. In this respect, an element clearly lacking in Lindeck's proposal is the Trinitarian dimension of revelation. By confining himself entirely to the text, Lindbeck has virtually restricted revelation to the Jesus of Nazareth, ignoring entirely the work of the Third Person in the Holy Trinity, the Holy Spirit, who ensures the communication of revelation till the eschaton.[240] Contemporary theology is replete with works suggesting that an adequate proposal for understanding many of the issues arising from the complex realities of today cannot fail to enlist assistance from a Trinitarian theology. A

when Mark used the title "messiah" of Jesus, he was using an image that he inherited from the Hebrews. As the first Christians began to add the Greek-speaking gentiles to their ranks, Matthew found it necessary to use the title "kurios" or "Lord" on Jesus, lordship rather than messiahship being a concept to which they were accustomed. See W. Foerster, "κύριος" in *Theological Dictionary of the NewTestament*, ed. G. Kittel (Grand Rapids, MI: Eerdmans, 1965), III: 1039-58. Raymond Brown refers to Thomas' profession of Jesus as "my Lord and my God" in John 20:28 as a formula which was "catalyzed by the Roman Emperor Domitian's claim to the title 'Lord and God' (*dominus et noster*)." See his *An Introduction to New Testament Christology* (Mahwah, NJ: Paulist, 1994), 189.

[239] Insofar as the discussion relates to the New Testament, see S. Harakas, "Must God Remain Greek?" *The EcuRev* 43 (1991) 194-99.

[240] Furthermore, the "'reality' of the Second Person of the Trinity," Kenneth Surin points out, "is not exhausted by the 'reality' of Jesus of Nazareth." There is the divine Logos who is the "essentially unrepresentable and non-narrative 'absent cause,'" and thus "inherently subtextual." The Logos is thus "able to resist all human formulations and eludes the grasp of all our discourses." See idem, *The Turnings of Darkness and Light* (Cambridge: Cambridge University Press, 1989), 220.

recent work closely associated with this discussion is Stell's dissertation in which he suggests that the relational nature of God demands that theological hermeneutics attend to the interrelatedness of Tradition and experience. We neglect to our theological impoverishment the "traditioned experience" and the "experienced tradition" of the Holy Spirit in Christian understanding.[241]

3.4.2.5 The Communicative Medium of Revelation: Symbolic or Narrational?

A selective discussion of issues, like we have offered up to now, by no means exhausts the debate. What is clear is that a great deal turns on one's judgment on the scope of theology and on what amounts to an adequate medium for the communication of revelation. In a dialogue with Dulles, Lindbeck again extols the virtues of the narrational, as opposed to Dulles' symbolic, communicative medium of revelation. Their dialogue is instructive regarding both striking commonalities and a deep theological divide.

In *Models of Revelation*,[242] Dulles accepts that revelation takes many forms. Consequent upon this fact, revelation allows for a variety of partial, yet possibly convergent, theological depictions including: [i] doctrine (propositional teaching); [ii] historical event (deed of God); [iii] mystical experience (loving union); [iv] dynamic word (event of proclamation); and [v] new awareness (shift of horizon).[243] While he suggests an organic interconnectedness in all models, Dulles' own constructive proposal posits

---

[241] See Stephen L. Stell, *Hermeneutics and the Holy Spirit* (dissertation, Princeton Theological Seminary, 1988).

[242] Avery Dulles, *Models of Revelation* (New York: Doubleday, 1983).

[243] See Dulles's own summary in *The Craft of Theology* (New York: Crossroad, 1996), 49.

revelation as the presence of God in Self-disclosure mediated symbolically.[244]

Lindbeck is in agreement with Dulles on the latter's use of the "method of models." The approach befits common sense. In the face of a pluralistic cacophony, dialogue on any given theme can proceed only if theologians get down to the first task of methodically identifying "options and issues" and developing them in terms of a typology of current theological treatments. To be sure, this first task can only be successfully discharged through a combination of a charitable heart and a critical eye in scrutinizing any model.[245] Dulles himself believes that criteria for evaluation are system-dependent. Significantly, he finds only a "limited utility" in criteria such as "conformity with Scripture, rootedness in tradition, inner coherence, plausibility, illuminative power, practical and theoretical fruitfulness, and suitability for dialogue with outsiders." Disclosing a clear preference for "the concept of symbolic mediation as a dialectical tool," he advances what he calls a "dialectical retrieval" by means of which he draws the best out of each model for a critical synthesis. Dulles assigns a specific connotation to "revelatory symbols" which cannot be ignored: these are not projections of the believer's subjectivity but are means by which "God chooses to bring people into living relationship with himself, as especially through the incarnate Word." While Dulles argues the case for "symbolic realism," Lindbeck's preferred course is the "realistic narrative." Their assessment of each other's approach underscores the differences in two major interpretive traditions.

---

[244] On the subject of symbolism and the usefulness of "dialogue" as a model of revelation, see D. Brown, "God and Symbolic Action," in *Divine Action*, ed. B. Hebblethwaite and E. Henderson (Edinburgh: T & T Clark, 1990), 103-29. The dialogue model is also defended in D. Brown, *The Divine Trinity* (London: Duckworth, 1985).

[245] See Lindbeck, "Dulles on Method," *ProE* 1 (1992) 54.

First, Dulles' method presupposes a strong sense of ecclesial commitment and aims to achieve a "greater consensus and more effectively serve the entire people of God as it builds itself up in unity and love."[246] Lindbeck, however, is persuaded by what he perceives as a lack of the right conditions in the present age for theologians to "seek methodically to do justice to all the embattled contestants by dispassionate typological analysis and dialectical retrieval."[247] The fact that such an exercise seems utopian to him is consistent with his own methodological approach which tends to obstinately pursue one (even radical) line of argumentation, even when an allowance for some integration from others' views may enhance his own. This will become increasingly evident as we examine his theories of religion and doctrine in later chapters.

Secondly, Lindbeck's reliance on the Protestant *sola scriptura* is most telling in his objection to the primacy accorded by Dulles to "real symbol" (or the equivalent of "word event"). He judges Rahner's transcendental metaphysics, which Dulles receives favourably, as being over-laden with "impersonalism." In his view, "the logic of symbols, unlike that of realistic narratives, is transitive," reliance on which means that Roman Catholics are one step removed from Scriptures, needing a recourse to ancient creeds and dogmatic affirmations of the Church by which to predicate Jesus' universal saviourhood. In contrast, narrativists of the Frei-Lindbeck type, who go straight to Scriptures as the primary source for teaching who Christ is in his unsubstitutable uniqueness, claim an advantage in obviating the "[theological], ecclesial and doctrinal detour." Because "the Bible is followable in its own right for the narrativist," Lindbeck argues, "dependence on community and tradition for the details of interpretation is lessened."[248]

---

[246] Dulles, *The Craft of Theology*, x.
[247] Lindbeck, "Dulles on Method," 55.
[248] Lindbeck, "Dulles on Method," 57-59.

Apart from the potentially disastrous consequences for both Protestantism and Catholicism which the proposal to lessen dependence on Tradition would bring (and has brought), Dulles' rejoinder raises four points worthy of note.[249] First, on the relative priority between symbolic realism and biblical realistic narrative as communicative media, an either/or dilemma is false; "symbolic communication" is never intended to stress particular symbols in isolation. To be sure, today, the principal Christian symbols of the cross, the empty tomb and others, are most powerfully derived from the Bible. But a broad symbolic-communicative understanding of revelation includes not just realistic narratives, but also ritual actions,[250] metaphors, parables and so forth. Second, therefore, in a typically Catholic fashion, Dulles offers a wider and richer notion of revelation than Lindbeck's Protestant focus on Scripture alone.[251] Symbolic realism certainly encompasses Barth's type of biblical realism, but revelation does not have to be equated exclusively with written accounts, to the exclusion not only of "the persons, things, and events through which God initially revealed himself to his people," but even, as we have argued, to the persons, things and events encompassed in a revelatory process of continuous, dialectical, encounter with God now, and forever more, assisted by the Holy Spirit. Third, Lindbeck's dismissal of Rahner's transcendental analysis is fatally flawed for overlooking the two poles of human knowl-

---

[249] See Dulles, "Rejoinder to George Lindbeck," *ProE* 1 (1992) 61-62.

[250] That the *lex orandi* is primary in the first-order level of piety and practice is admitted by Lindbeck, often explicitly. At the Ratzinger Conference, the primacy of worship was unanimously acknowledged. The most forceful intervention in this regard came from Tom Hopko. See Stallsworth, "The Story of an Encounter." Once that is recognized, one must perforce concede the gap between the world of the ancient biblical text and the world of modern worshippers. See T. F. Tracy, "Narrative Theology and the Acts of God," in *Divine Action*, ed. B. Hebblethwaite, 173-96, esp. 173-74.

[251] See J. Haught, "Revelation," in *The New Dictionary of Theology*, 884.

edge with which the latter operates and, in our view, for contradict-
ing an earlier appreciation he had for Rahner.[252] Rahner's scheme,
which includes both the transcendental and the categorical poles of
human knowledge, reflects a personalist view of God, and converges
with Polanyi's distinctions between "focal and subsidiary awareness," or "explicit and latent knowledge." It has been a leitmotif of
Dulles' theology to surface the fecundity of the "tacit" and the
"latent" dimensions precisely because they elude capture by discursive thought. Fourth, creeds and dogmas are not an ecclesial and doctrinal detour from biblical faith as Lindbeck suggests. Catholicism
has always understood the Church's dogma to be the fruit of a symbolic hermeneutical process consistent with Scripture-in-Tradition,
gathering up the explicit and latent meanings of the biblical texts,
and playing a key role in protecting them against distortion. Rhetorically, but with burning relevance, Dulles asks: "How close must
theology remain to the biblical narrative categories? Can it address
questions that would be incomprehensible to ancient Semites? Can it
content itself with 'redescription,' or must it engage in reflective and
critical analysis?"[253]

Lindbeck places too heavy a burden on Scripture to adjudicate all
the crucial questions that arise in all the churches, ignoring the fact
that, even in their final forms, the texts were only at their undeveloped beginnings. Scripture ends before the constitution of the
Church was complete. We cannot bypass the narrative, for, as Hopko
points out, we have no liturgy of the faithful without the liturgy of
the Word, but the narrative is not the whole thing. Communion with
Christ is at once liturgical, eucharistic, as well as mystical.[254]

---

[252] See Lindbeck, "Unbelievers and the 'Sola Christi'," *Dialog* 12 (1973)
184.

[253] Dulles, "Rejoinder to George Lindbeck," 62.

[254] See the interventions of Dulles (p.174) and Hopko (p. 181) in Stallsworth,
"The Story of an Encounter."

3.5 Concluding Remarks

A few conclusions are now clearly in order. Lindbeck attempts to be tradition-faithful, with reference to scriptural particularity. His community-building hermeneutics concerns itself only with the text's "inspiringness",[255] that is, its capacity to stimulate a faith-commitment in the reader, not in any arguments on "inspiredness," "inerrancy," or any referents "behind" or "above" the written text. With Lindbeck, we can insist on the scriptural disclosure of God in Jesus Christ as the active Agent, whose identity is most fully revealed in the passion narrative, read realistically and in a history-like manner. The communal significance of Lindbeck's insistence on authority residing precisely in the particularity of the Christian grammar, rather than in any other external locale, thus upholding the biblical narratives as Scripture, cannot be overexaggerated.[256]

One does not have to agree entirely with Lindbeck's historical overview, to accept the seriousness of his diagnosis that hermeneutics has lost sight of the realistic aspect of the biblical narrative. His call to the believing community to return to the uncompromising and untranslatable oddity of the Gospel as a message whose meaning is determined by the inner logic of the Tradition, is ignored only to the peril of the community that accepts the Bible as Scripture: the Church could end up with having nothing worth offering to the larger society. The Christian community is in the debt of people like Lindbeck who, with prophetic obstinacy, assume the "caretaker"[257] role of defending the intrinsic power of the biblical texts to communicate a world of meaning that the

---

[255] Henry, "Narrative Theology," 14.

[256] See Tracy, "On Reading the Scriptures Theologically," 38.

[257] See this description of Lindbeck in L. Cady, "Resisting the Postmodern Turn," 90.

reader is asked to inhabit. Biblical texts open up an imaginative
space and beckon every reader to be a faithful subject, not rebel.[258]
There is an irreducible truth in what Lindbeck says, that ought to
be decisive for all Christians: particular accounts were selected for
inclusion in the canon because they were intended to function
within the believing community in a transforming way; the Christian story is habitable. His insistence on "the interplay between
the communal reading of texts and their community-shaping
power"[259] deserves every support. The reliance on narrative intratextuality in Lindbeck's programme is clearly necessary, even
though it is inadequate for exhaustive biblical interpretation, for
theology and for solving crucial questions that arise in all the
churches. One could therefore agree with a great deal of what
Lindbeck says about narrative reading and still disagree with his
treatment of Scriptures. Faithfulness is a visible value in his project, but intelligibility remains an issue. Particularity seems to
have been purchased at the price of catholicity.

The inadequacy of Lindbeck's proposal for a "full Christian
theology"[260] surfaces from a closer scrutiny of three questions,
namely: [a] the adequacy of narrative alone to both the exclusive
and comprehensive tasks to which it is put by Lindbeck; [b] the
validity of nonfoundationalism as a background principle for his
intratextual arguments; and [c] the adequacy of confining revelation to the written Scripture texts. Our study yields useful pointers. First, narrative seems workable as the linchpin in Lindbeck's

[258] Loughlin, *Telling God's Story*, 36.

[259] See remark on Frei, which is equally applicable to Lindbeck, by J. A.
DiNoia, "American Catholic Theology at Century's End," *Thomist* 54 (1990)
515.

[260] See Tracy, "On Reading the Scriptures Theologically," 51. For criteria of
appropriateness to theological proposals, see Schubert M. Ogden, "Problems in
the Case for a Pluralistic Theology of Religions," *JR* 68 (1988) 493-508.

project, but not without riding roughshod over other genres and ignoring or harmonizing the rich diversity of biblical texts that stubbornly refuse to be dissolved in a peaceful synthesis. Drawing his first principles from biblical narrative may be legitimate, but problems arise when the ontological claims of the narrative itself are ignored. At issue also is the hegemonic tendency in an exclusive focus on narrative that overlooks its incipient nature. While the plain sense of the narrative is central to the life of the believing community, the risk is to stop short at "the obvious and direct sense of the text for the community," and be completely oblivious to the critiques (especially of the ideological sort) that critical scholarship, crucial in the contemporary scene, may have to offer. Other elements may also need to be supplemented.

Second, Lindbeck's ban on foundationalism ignores the basic claim that Christianity and Christian theology are foundational in nature on account of the notion of revelation. His nonfoundational stance, inspired by hidden fiduciary interests, ignores the *Christian* dimension in the foundational, apologetic enterprise both in terms of its motivation and its content. In the process, he overlooks the distinction between strong and weak forms of foundationalism and the difficulties in which his own arguments, relying on a strong strand from philosophy, are entrapped. Moreover, to be ecumenically consistent in his contextual emphasis, Lindbeck ought to be more sensitive to the Catholic context where, traditionally, speculative theologies are tolerated insofar as they assist in clarifying the Christian message.

Third, a study on the implications of the notion of revelation surfaces a string of problems for Lindbeck. His argumentation is at best ambiguous and at worst contradictory as regards the element of referentiality, in historical, metaphysical as well as hermeneutical terms. The Christian story is habitable because it is true; and it is true not only in a pragmatic functional sense, but also in the historical and metaphysical sense.[261] Here, his non-referential and self-interpreting claims for Scriptures is contradictory of Barth's objective realism. His insistence on Christian identity presupposes a constancy that critics deny. By bracketing off questions of facticity, his narratives lose their necessary social embodiment that defines a real world. Instead of offering the high doctrine of Scripture that many presume him to unfold, Lindbeck may be perceived as escaping from social engagement and concern for the suffering. The results are, paradoxically, a-historical, anti-apologetical, non-public and non-dialogical. In his zeal to protect the text from external influences, a clear weakness in Lindbeck's scheme is the loss of the constitutive role of the reader and, by extension, the creative contributions of theologians. There must be allowance for the reader's construction as she/he responds to both text and context. In aid of a description of the world created by the text that seeks to engage the reader in its meaning system, the hermeneutics of understanding developed by Gadamer and Ricoeur can be profitably enlisted.[262] Much is stifled in Lindbeck's implicit understanding of revelation as a fixed datum encoded in Holy Writ. Missing are the understanding of revelation as a process and an encounter, even extra-biblically. In part, this is explained by an understanding of *dabar* as word only, instead of word-event, and an oversight of the polyphonic nature of the text, and its mediatory role. Timidity prevents any allowance for an ongoing relatedness of God with His people in different cultures and contexts whose novel experiences and problems are brought to bear on a set of texts historically written to address different

---

[261] See Clark Pinnock's intervention in Stallsworth, "The Story of an Encounter," 175. To be sure, Lindbeck himself is aware of the way a cultural-linguistic approach can be judged "methodically atheistic" [ND, 20].

[262] See P. Perkins, "Crisis in Jerusalem? Narrative Criticism in New Testament Studies," *TS* 50 (1989) 299 n.10.

contexts and problems. A Trinitarian supplement will clearly be helpful to unpack this relatedness not only in Jesus of Nazareth, identified in the written text, but also in the workings of the Holy Spirit ingredient in the semiotic system of the Tradition.

Catholic theological "method" is, to a point, traditionally more pluralistic and wider in scope than its Protestant counterpart, as Dulles' dialogue with Lindbeck shows. The Anselmian dictum for theology – *fides quaerens intellectum* – is operatively dominant in both Protestant and Catholic traditions. For Catholics, to accept the Bible as primary source does not entail treating it as exclusive resource. There can be immediacy in God's presence in various ways, including the Scriptures. But, more often, mediation is effected symbolically and not only by way of realistic biblical narrative. And, even in the latter form, there is often a distanciation between the reader and the text, although interpretation aims at a fusion of horizons. Truth, we suggest, is revealed dialectically in different contexts of encounter. This dialectical dimension is lacking in Lindbeck: the constitutive role of the reader is silenced and her situation omitted; the role is assumed by the text itself. With Loughlin, we can emphatically state that "theology cannot begin with the Bible without at the same time beginning with its readers: the Church. Those who read and that which is read are mutually related in the event of reading."[263]

Lindbeck, at the end of the day, would want everything, the entire universe and all the theologians in it, to be absorbed into the text. It seems clear that his community-building hermeneutics operates on a sort of dogmatic conception of revelation which precedes the actual hermeneutic exercise. The weak point in his scheme is that, in adopting Frei's hermeneutical conception of revelation, Lindbeck introduces into his systematic theological

[263] Loughlin, *Telling God's Story*, 36.

reflection a dogmatic point of departure in which the *identity of Jesus Christ* is the basis for defining [i] the focus of interpretation; [ii] the choice of the locale (in this case, the written text, especially the synoptic Gospels); and [iii] the kind of structure to be discovered. Lindbeck's plea to take seriously the structure of the biblical narrative as expressing revelation is well worth retaining. However, configuration in the text is stressed at the expense of refiguration. A corrective is needed.

The theological divide seems entrenched. George Schner's background observation is apt: "If Catholic particularity is thought to be essentially committed to forms of mediation, optimistic anthropology, and correlation, it would seem to be irreducibly in opposition to Protestant confessional particularity committed to the primacy of Scripture, the appropriateness of a pessimistic anthropology, and a critical attitude toward culture."[264] More specifically, the way in which a Catholic theologian views Lindbeck's theological effort will reflect her own position in relation to his Protestant theological orientation and her evaluation of modernity and liberalism.[265]

In the face of the present pluralistic cacophony, Lindbeck's project, despite its limitations, has much to commend it, for the Church and for theology. But, to be more useful, it is in serious need of supplementation by ideas which he either ignores, or explicitly retrenches. In this regard, Tracy suggests[266] that the discussions in Neuhaus' *Biblical Interpretation in Crisis* bespeak the need for a historical material principle for interpreting Scripture. In particular, we note Ratzinger's foundation of a 'Christus

[264] George Schner, "Postliberal Theology and Roman Catholic Theology," *RSRev* 21 (1995) 306.

[265] As claimed by B. E. Hinze, "Postliberal Theology and Roman Catholic Theology," *RSRev* 21 (1995) 299.

[266] Tracy, "On Reading the Scriptures Theologically," 62 n.31.

totus' principle where at least three dimensions are pressingly pertinent: [a] an inclusiveness which means the Risen Christ will never be isolated from the Church; [b] a Trinitarian dynamism by which Christ is present through his Spirit; and [c] an obedience to the Christonomy.[267] The 'Christus totus' principle is highly germane to our discussion for two other reasons. First, Lindbeck, unlike Frei, manages to present the whole of his community-building hermeneutics with Christology appearing as nothing more than illustration. Frei's methodology, by contrast, is itself properly and substantially theological, and thus less vulnerable to charges of dependency on literary techniques. Second, an explicit reliance on Christology would link up better with insights from the Second Vatican Council. The Council explicitly encourages an active accommodation to the world, but *without sacrificing our distinctive Christian identity*. Accommodation is envisaged in the thesis of the *Pastoral Constitution on the Church in the Modern World* that the joys and sorrows of the people of our time, especially those of the poor, must be the joys and sorrows of the followers of Christ, so that nothing that is genuinely human should fail "to find an echo" in their hearts.[268] The assurance for the preservation of Christian identity lies in the Christological rule which structures the text, and which is described by Ratzinger as a remarkable "Christocentric theology" which appears for the first time in official documents.[269] Accommodation is warranted only on account of the cosmos-relatedness of Jesus Christ as the One who "perfects" human

[267] See Ratzinger's intervention in Stallsworth, "The Story of an Encounter," 166-67.

[268] See *Gaudium et Spes*, 1.

[269] See Joseph Ratzinger, "Pastoral Constitution on the Church in the Modern World, Chapter I, Part I," in *Commentary on the Documents of Vatican II*, ed. Herbert Vorgrimler (New York: Herder & Herder, 1969), 5:159.

activity. The Constitution's thesis ultimately relies for its validity on a set of teachings on who Jesus Christ is. [270]

This openness to the world makes a good transition to the next chapter which treats Lindbeck's view on religion. There, the debate intensifies with regard to the role of experience, fideism and sectarianism as against public discourse and dialogue. All this takes place in the midst of the consternation he causes by his famous typology. To that discussion we now turn.

---

[270] See James J. Buckley, *Seeking the Humanity of God* (Collegeville: Liturgical, 1992), 66-68.

CHAPTER IV

RELIGION AND EXPERIENCE

4.1 Preliminary Remarks

Lindbeck aligns himself with a postmodernity characterised by its search for meaning and truth in particular cultures and contexts. "Particularity," in his scheme, defines a search that features a marked reaction against a rationalism premised on pure objectivity inherited from the Enlightenment, and an individualism attributed to transcendental thought's turn to the subject. In this light, Lindbeck's postliberal dismissal of foundationalism confronts speculative thought as an unwelcome intrusion of Hellenic views into Christian revelation.[1] Understanding theology as a grammar aids his nonfoundational understanding of intelligibility, faithfulness, and applicability. Philosophers like Rorty and Stout have convinced him that meaning in general cannot be justified foundationally. Lindbeck thus chooses language over experience as a medium for meaning. The former regnant interest in the turn to the subject is now shifted to a linguistic turn where theology is neither concerned with the classical tradition of the science of God, nor the modern hermeneutics of Christian experience. Theology is now authenticated as a critical reflection on language as its prime analogue, where the admission of modern-day 'novel' experiences is resisted and the question of ontological referent is simply disre-

---

[1] As Thiel rightly points out, "Lindbeck's attempt to reconceive theology cultural-linguistically is a function of what he considers the actual tasks of a postliberal theology to be." Thiel, *Imagination and Authority*, 182.

garded. In all this, Lindbeck is clearly responding to what he judges to be problematic of modern, liberal theology.

This chapter takes a close look at Lindbeck's *linguistic turn* in emphasising religious particularity. Lindbeck distinguishes between three theories of religion and doctrine which enlighten the function of theology. In its technical argumentation, his study focuses on the relationship between religious language and religious experience. In his overall plan, Lindbeck ranges his offensive strategy in two main directions: [1] *a cultural-linguistic model of religion against an experiential-expressivist model*; and [2] *a rule-theory of doctrine against both the "propositionalist" and the "symbolist" theories*. In doing so, Lindbeck situates his project right at the cutting edge of the intellectual climate of the day, especially in regards to the postmodern abhorrence for universal rationality and the corresponding frenzied respect for cultural particularities. Serious questions have been raised against his typology of views on religion, however.

Our main objective here is to show that Lindbeck's exclusion of contemporary experience, consistent with his postliberal intratextual theology, is not sensitive to the experiences, insights and aspirations that arise from different contexts. This renders his programme inadequate to the task of theology since the advent of the postmodern era. In the process, we shall also argue that Lindbeck's typology, particularly in his characterization of certain authors, is deeply flawed in several respects. Initial observations will also be made – conclusions upon which will be delayed until after we have studied Lindbeck's theory on doctrine in the next chapter — that his cultural-linguistic lens cannot stand on its own without being parasitic on opponent models; and that a way beyond the hermeneutical impasse between the so-called Yale and Chicago schools is desirable. *Experience* is the principal analogue throughout this chapter.

4.2 Theories of Religion: A Pre-Theological Conceptual and Empirical Efficacy

Lindbeck launches his project by seeking at once to establish a critical edge for his fostered cultural-linguistic approach, in terms of *conceptual and empirical adequacy*, over the cognitivist and expressivist approaches to religion. Keeping his theological agenda in the background, he first situates his discussion within a *non-theological* assessment of the relations between religion and experience. Within such an assessment, *historical and psychosocial causes* are investigated, to explain why certain approaches have lost their appeal in contemporary culture and, conversely, why "situational pressures" are mounting in favour of adopting certain other approaches. But, while they aid our understanding of the world in which we live, causal considerations alone do not decide the question of truth-claims; nor do situational pressures alone settle the issue of empirical or conceptual adequacy. A *non-theological* investigation is, therefore, undertaken as a necessary, and yet only preparatory, step towards theological clarification.[2] But his theological convictions are necessarily prior to his writing project and thus inspire it at every turn.

4.2.1 A Typology of Approaches to Religion: A Triumvirate

First, as its name implies, the *cognitive-propositionalist* model of religion emphasizes the cognitive aspects of religion and stresses the propositional truth claims of Church doctrines. Experience here is predicated on epistemology, namely, what can be known in revelation and encapsulated in linguistic renderings that

[2] See ND, 11 & 30; 19-20.

are propositional, through intellectual judgment.[3] This approach to
religion cannot be a serious contender for adequacy in that, in
modern times, "propositional understandings of religion have long
been on the defensive and experiential-expressive ones in the
ascendancy."[4] There are historical and psychosocial causes contributive to this state of affairs. Historically, Kant may be seen as
a trail-blazer who "demolish[ed] the metaphysical and epistemological foundations of the earlier regnant cognitive-propositional
views." This cleared the ground for a greater acceptance of: (a)
scientific developments, and the corresponding retrenchment of
literal-propositional explanations of biblical doctrines, such as the
doctrine of creation; and (b) historical studies, and the corresponding awareness of the temporal-relativity of all doctrines.[5]
Psychosocially, the Kantian "turn to the subject" contributes to a
growing individualism. Together with rapid social changes and an
increasing awareness of religious pluralism in contemporary societies, these causes inexorably lead to what Peter Berger calls the
"deobjectification" of religion and doctrine.[6] In Lindbeck's estimation, the fact that increasingly fewer people are steeped in particular religious traditions or deeply immersed in particular religious communities, renders it difficult for people of today to
"perceive or experience religion in cognitivist fashion as the

[3] Gerard Loughlin identifies this with the Enlightenment view of religion as
'see-saying': "First, you see the world and sense the presence of God, and then
you say it, in word and deed, praise and service." See idem, "See-Saying/Say-
Seeing," *Th* 91 (1988) 202.

[4] See ND, 19. K. Surin explains that: "Proponents of the 'cognitive-propositionalist' model take religions to be essentially, but not necessarily exclusively,
forms of speech and action focused on a mind-independent sacred or divine reality." See his "'Many Religions and the One True Faith'," *ModTh* 4 (1988) 187.

[5] See ND, 20-21.

[6] P. Berger, *The Heretical Imperative* (New York: Doubleday, 1980);
Rumour of Angels (New York: Doubleday, 1969).

acceptance of sets of objectively and immutably true propositions."[7]

Adding to these observations are three criticisms Lindbeck makes against this view of religion. [a] In abstracting assertions from their background systemic context, cognitive-propositionalism falsely presumes there is a neutral, objective meta-language that allows isolated references to isolated reality. [b] In abstracting assertions from their social context, this approach falsely presumes that meaning and truthfulness can attach to a statement without a social-contextual anchorage. [c] In placing an obvious limit on the possible uses and meanings of religious language, this theory of religion presents only a truncated vision.[8]

The second model, which Lindbeck calls *experiential-expressivist*, is said to find favour with liberal theologians descended from Schleiermacher. This approach equates experience with "inner feelings, attitudes, or existential orientations," and religious language with "noninformative and nondiscursive symbols" of these vague inner feelings.[9] In this understanding of the relationship between religion and experience, the most apparent experiences of God are "revelations" in the sense of being the type of

---

[7] ND, 21. Authors commonly note that a propositional understanding of the creeds, for instance, poses a great stumbling block for many modern Christians. See, for example, A. Walker and A. Davison, "Belief and Faith in a Religiously Plural Society," *ModB* 35 (1994) 24. Be that as it may, we must point out that even as they argue against the recitation of propositional creeds as the best approach to nurture spirituality, authors are implicitly affirming the underlying conviction that it is the propositional dimension of doctrines which gives a religious community its identity.

[8] For the three criticisms, see ND, 106-08, 65, and 63-9, respectively. A useful summary is provided by C. Hawkins, *Beyond Anarchy and Tyranny in Religious Epistemology* (Lanham: University Press of America, 1997), 14-15.

[9] ND, 16. In Loughlin's term, this is "say-seeing," in that "we only recognize the world as *world* because we can say 'world'." See idem, "See-Saying/Say-Seeing," 204.

experience which grounds religious doctrines and behaviour as "expressive" of that experience.[10] Kant, in his famous reduction of God to a necessary transcendental condition of the ethical life, had undermined the traditional view of religion. In doing so, he created a lacuna which he failed to fill, a situation which appeared intolerably impoverished to the religiously sensitive. Schleiermacher helped fill the breach with his brand of experiential-expressivism, the key to which consists in the notion that "the source of all religions is in the 'feeling of absolute dependence'."[11] Although there are variations of theories within the experiential-expressive mould, proponents of this approach "all locate ultimately significant contact with whatever is finally important to religion in the prereflective experiential depths of the self and regard the public or outer features of religion as expressive or evocative (i.e., nondiscursive symbols) of internal experience."[12] Since this way of seeing religion has dominated the intellectual and empirical scene for more than two centuries, Lindbeck accepts that it should not be abandoned, save for good reasons. And, even with good reasons, he concedes that it would be difficult to dislodge the habits of thought engendered by this tradition, so deeply ingrained has it become in Western culture.

For his analysis of the experiential-expressive model of religion, Lindbeck relies on Bernard Lonergan who identified in different religions a common core experience at the pre-reflexive level. It is this core that forms the source, norm and possibility of

[10] For a concept of revelation that does not involve specific propositional content, see Keith Ward, *Religion and Revelation* (Oxford: Clarendon, 1994). For some philosophical senses of revelation, see J. J. Gellman, *Experience of God and the Rationality of Theistic Belief* (Ithaca: Cornell University Press, 1997).

[11] See F. Schleiermacher, *The Christian Faith*, trs. H. R. Mackintosh and J. S. Stewart (Edinburgh: T & T Clark, 1928), 16-18; ND, 21.

[12] ND, 21.

human objectification. Essentially "God's gift of love," this primordial experience may be variously designated as "an experience of the holy" in the sense of Rudolf Otto's *mysterium fasci-
nans et tremendum*, or Paul Tillich's "being grasped by ultimate
concern," or Ignatius Loyola's "consolation that has no cause."[13]
Lonergan himself is said to have singularly favoured the experience of love above all "inner, non-sensory experiences" as "prior
to all conceptualization or cognition." For David Tracy, the equivalent category is a "common human experience" of basic trust
which grounds "human commitments to the ultimate meaningfulness or worth of inquiring, deciding, and doing."[14] In the case of
Karl Rahner, this primordial experience is described as the experience "in which what is meant and the experience of what is meant
are still one."[15] All these characterizations appear to Lindbeck to
be highly problematic. Most crucially, his critique of this model
finds its mark in Lonergan's assumption, an assumption Lindbeck
ascribes to most other expressivists as well, that the "scholarly
study of religious phenomena on the whole supports the crucial
affirmation of the basic unity of religious experience." However,
it is precisely the distinctive features of this common core experience which cannot be specified.[16] And yet, Lindbeck insists,
unless the expressivists come up with definite specifications, their
assertion of commonality becomes logically meaningless and

[13] See B. Lonergan, *Method in Theology* (New York: Herder & Herder,
1972), 106.

[14] See ND, 32; Tracy, *Blessed Rage for Order* (New York: Seabury, 1975),
97-103. Lindbeck thinks experiential-expressivism and foundationalism are kin-
dred spirits, but the former is not a species of the latter, unless its theory of religious experience is linked to Rahner's transcendental epistemology. See R.
Steele in *Theology Without Foundations*, 179 n.35.

[15] See K. Rahner, *Foundations of Christian Faith*, trs. W. V. Dych (New
York: Seabury, 1978), 17.

[16] See Lindbeck, "Ebeling: Climax of a Great Tradition," *JR* 61 (1981) 309-14.

empirically vacuous.[17] In sum, the claim of the expressivist paradigm is [a] that religious experience can happen in a vacuum, [b]
that an account can be given of a religious experience apart from
the religious language in which it is couched and the religious
practice by which it is inspired, and [c] that a common inner experience can be expressed in various ways in different religions.
Lindbeck's key objection to this paradigm is grounded in the conviction that the liberal position is fundamentally incoherent,
unverifiable, and thus untenable.[18]

The alternative to these two models is the *cultural-linguistic*
model which draws heavily on the anthropological, sociological
and philosophical disciplines. There, Lindbeck suggests, the
emphasis lies not on the cognitive or the experiential aspects of
religion, but rather on "those respects in which religions resemble
languages together with their correlative forms of life" such as rituals, liturgies and modes of action, language and doctrines, beliefs
and practices, and so forth. Hence, through this lens, religions
resemble cultures.[19] Drawing from Wittgenstein and Geertz,[20]
Lindbeck suggests that religions, like cultures, are best
approached by "thick description" so that no single experience
can adequately account for what religions are all about. Rather,
the ordering of religion as a culture must proceed from language,
not experience. His proposal adamantly rests on understanding
religions as "comprehensive interpretive schemes ... which

[17] See ND, 32.

[18] See also Hawkins, *Beyond Anarchy*, 16-17. Thiel notes that Lindbeck's
theological programme seeks to counter the widespread commitment to a theological version of Cartesianism that he finds common among experiential-expressivists. See Thiel, *Imagination and Authority*, 182.

[19] ND, 17-18.

[20] The principal sources are L. Wittgenstein, *Philosophical Investigations*
(London: Macmillan, 1973), and C. Geertz, *The Interpretation of Cultures* (New
York: Basic Books, 1973).

structure human experience and understanding of self and world."[21] In doing so, he does not perceive religions as attempts to map reality by means of truth-formulations corresponding to ultimate reality, or as external expressions of primordial inner experiences potentially shared by all of humanity. Instead, religions are regarded as a linguistic and socio-cultural phenomenon, having "a kind of cultural and/or linguistic framework or medium" that shapes, moulds and constitutes the entirety of human life and thought.[22] Religions are, under this lens, comprehensive interpretive schemes whose functions may be likened to a Kantian *a priori*. Language is an *a priori* condition of experience, not its subsequent articulation or expression; religious conceptual categories are logically prior to religious experience, and serve to inform the latter. Lindbeck is aware that drawing an affinity between religion and Kant's philosophical idiom may well mislead, unless the huge differences are noted. Unlike Kant's categories, the *a priori* conditions Lindbeck refers to may be negatively described as: [1] *not transcendentally deduced*, for the religious framework, which structures human experience and understanding of self and world, is, in the first place, "a set of acquired skills"; and [2] *not universally necessary*, for they could be different in different religions. Their commonality stops at their *rootedness* in the "foundational certainties of a form of life."[23] Indeed, Lindbeck's position is so radically at odds with that major part of the theological tradition represented by Rahner and the transcendental Thomists that it deserves a closer examination, which we shall do shortly.

For the moment, to appreciate the close parallels between religions and cultural-linguistic systems, we note the following elements which Lindbeck sketches: [1] Like an idiom, a religious

---

[21] ND, 32.

[22] ND, 17-18, & 33.

[23] See L. C. Barrett, "Theology as Grammar," *ModTh* 4 (1988) 160; ND, 33.

framework provides its adherents with the linguistic tools to describe realities, formulate beliefs, and experience "inner attitudes, feelings, and sentiments." [2] Like a culture or language, a religion is a communal phenomenon. It shapes "the subjectivities of individuals rather than being primarily a manifestation of those subjectivities." [3] Like a culture or language, it has a distinctive vocabulary that comprises both discursive and nondiscursive symbols, along with a concomitant logic or grammar that regulates their meaningful applications. [4] Like a Wittgensteinian language-game, a religion is "correlated with a form of life." [5] Like every culture, a religion has both cognitive and behavioural dimensions to it, and, of course, a religious tradition as well. Religion is an embodiment of myths and narratives which are heavily ritualized. Integral to these rituals, are doctrines and ethical norms. A religious framework thus engenders sentiments or experiences, recommends actions, and develops institutions.[24]

Linguistic and cultural systems being the *preconditions* for any experience at all, the possibility of any unschematized or uninterpreted experiences is ruled out. An appeal to primordial experience must run foul of Wittgenstein's insight that there can be no experience which is not underpinned by language, and therefore no primordial experience antecedent to, and independent of, language.[25] The cultural-linguistic model thus advocates a movement

[24] ND, 32-33.

[25] Taking his cue from Wittgenstein's discussion of seeing-as in the *Philosophical Investigations* (Part II, Section XI), John Hick expands the notion to that of experiencing-as, some features of which resonate with Lindbeck's analysis. For Wittgenstein, we see something as we interpret it so that in seeing-as, an element of mental activity is mixed with the pure passivity of receiving lights, lines and colours and so on (or what may be called 'pure seeing'). Hick takes it further, arguing that whereas the concept of seeing-as is based only on sight, the finding of meaning (of significance) occurs through a multi-dimensional awareness of the world. In this awareness, interpretation is employed through the use of systems of concepts embodied in what Wittgenstein called language-games.

from religion to experience, and rejects an underlying unity to religious experience that expresses itself in different forms. Adherents of different religions, quite simply, have different experiences.[26] This view so dominates Lindbeck's presentation that it overshadows, and seemingly neutralizes, his occasional admissions of factors that could, if given adequate attention, substantially vary his assessment of the other models. He realizes that there are dialectical relations between experience and religion, and that it is simplistic simply to present a one-way movement from religion to experience. He admits that the causality is, in reality, reciprocal. We shall revisit this point later. For the moment, it bears noting that Lindbeck's unilateral and linear description of the relationship between religion and experience is inspired by his intratextual theology even as he ostensibly seeks to legitimize the latter by the former.

From his nonfoundational analysis of understanding with its denial of any generally recognized and neutral ways of perceiving ultimate reality, or any universal principles or structures that can provide objective foundations for judgments about rational credibility, Lindbeck now maintains that there is no way of assessing a religion by appealing to a "higher neutral standpoint."[27] Ultimate reality does not reside in objective, intelligible structure against

These language games are current, and community and tradition-bound. "Interpreting in this sense is normally an unconscious and habitual process resulting from negotiations with our environment in terms of the set of concepts constituting our operative world of meaning." See idem, *Disputed Questions in Theology and Philosophy of Religion* (New Haven: Yale University Press, 1993), 25; *Problems of Religious Pluralism* (London: Macmillan, 1985), 24.

[26] See ND, 40. Ronald Burke describes Lindbeck's scheme as follows: "In such a perspective, 'language' and 'doctrine' are the *source*, and *not the result*, of distinctively human experience... Doctrine shapes Christian perception and nurtures Christian identity." See his "Newman, Lindbeck and Models of Doctrine," in *John Henry Newman*, 33.

[27] ND, 11.

which the credibility of faith's understanding of it is to be tested. Instead, the intelligibility of reality is derived only from using the comprehensive interpretive scheme of a particular faith. When meaning found in a religious semiotic system is judged to be 'intratextual' to its particular language system, it follows that, through the media of stories, precepts and practices, a religion sets up an idiom "for construing reality, expressing experience, and ordering life."[28]

4.2.2 Arguments for the Superior Efficacy of the Cultural-Linguistic Model

Psychosocially, Lindbeck realizes that the cultural-linguistic outlook is hamstrung by the same factors that inhibit the ready acceptance of the propositionalist orientation. Modern individuals do not readily interiorize an outlook based on a cultural and linguistic framework that others have created. It is repugnant and an affront to personal integrity to suggest to a person in contemporary Western culture that to become religious entails a mandatory course in a particular set of grammatical and lexical rules. In contrast, it sits well with contemporary culture to visualize religious interests in a way that is consonant with the individual quest for personal meaning. The structures of modernity are such that they "press individuals to meet God first in the depths of their souls and then, perhaps, if they find something personally congenial, to become part of a tradition or join a church." Such a conviction is in accord with the highly *private* and individualistic outlook of religion bequeathed by Schleiermacher. Another cause for the attraction of the experiential model is its marketability in a world characterized by religious pluralism: it suggests that, as diverse

---

[28] ND, 47-48.

symbolizations of a common core experience of the Ultimate, different world religions are destined to mutually enrich each other, and should act accordingly.[29]

Conceptually, Lindbeck is aware that two problems ingredient in languages and cultures challenge a cultural-linguist's argument for superiority: [1] languages and cultures shy of making truth-claims, are time and space bound, to all appearances have no transcendent but only this-worldly origins, and thus seem "ill fitted to serve as analogues for religions such as Christianity, which, as traditionally interpreted, claim to be true, universally valid, and supernaturally revealed;"[30] [2] they appear to lack the sort of depth experiences one readily associates with the inner self. It is certainly more palatable to speak of one's inner-depth, rather than some grammatical and lexical rules, as the source and centre of authentic religiosity.[31] Even though he claims an ascendancy of the cultural-linguistic approach within the ranks of scholars across different disciplines, Lindbeck concedes that his fostered model is not likely to attract popular acceptance. This, however, does not stop him from arguing the case for the superior efficacy of the cultural-linguistic approach to religion at the pre-theological level. His argument may be examined in six points.

First, countervailing tendencies notwithstanding, Lindbeck is convinced that he is on the right track because of a growing gap between theological and non-theological approaches which he identifies as the most significant development in theories of religion. There, his confidence is bolstered by, he tells us, the fact that academics from various different disciplines have increasingly found the cultural-linguistic approaches congenial. They include

[29] See ND, 22-23.

[30] ND, 23. We note, ahead of the next chapter, that Lindbeck does not deny that Church doctrines make truth claims.

[31] ND, 24.

historians, anthropologists, sociologists, philosophers, psychologists and criminologists. At the same time, "experiential-expressivism has lost ground everywhere except in most theological schools and departments of religious studies where, if anything, the trend is the reverse."[32]

Next, this model places a high premium on the extent to which human experience is shaped, moulded and even constituted by cultural and linguistic categories. Cases like Helen Keller and the alleged "wolf children" persuasively illustrate that, unless we learn the appropriate cultural and linguistic symbols, we are unable to have certain feelings, or perceive certain realities, or actualize certain thoughts and actions. In particular, the kind of experience or worldview specific to religious traditions are beyond the reach of those who lack their particular linguistic frameworks. A religion is, in the first place, an external word. As *verbum externum*, it shapes the individuals and the world in which they live and operate. A religion is not, in the first place, a thematization of a pre-linguistic or pre-conceptual experience. To be sure, Lindbeck is well aware that Christians do not deny the crucial significance of the *verbum internum*, traditionally ascribed to the action of the Holy Spirit. But here, too, the cultural-linguist and the experiential-expressivist differ: the former sees the *verbum internum* as a capacity for hearing the true external word, whereas the latter views it as a common experience that finds diverse religious manifestations.[33]

---

[32] ND, 25. Paul Crowley suggests that the ascendancy of the experiential-expressive paradigm in theological schools and departments of religious studies has to do with the fact that "a rather complacent religiosity thrives in those locales." See his *In Ten Thousand Places: Dogma in a Pluralistic Church* (New York: Crossroad, 1997), 103.

[33] ND, 34.

Third, the efficacy of the cultural-linguistic model is argued for in terms of its capacity to integrate the distinctive elements of the other two models. Lindbeck again draws upon a philosophical idiom for his discussion. This time, affinity is drawn between his view and Aristotelian *hylomorphism*, namely, "the theory that form is not only distinguishable from matter but also logically prior to it because matter cannot exist without being informed."[34] Thus, although form cannot be separated from the experiential matter, the hylomorphic model prioritises the form over the experiential matter which it informs. Lindbeck's account may be summarised as follows:

(a)   The cultural-linguist's emphasis on the inversion of the relation between the internal and external dimensions parallels the cognitivist theories where priority is accorded to the external belief systems. Lindbeck suggests that the superiority of the cultural-linguistic model, in this respect, lies in its down-playing of the cognitive and the intellectualist dimensions. Instead, what is primary is "the conceptual vocabulary and syntax or inner logic which determine the kinds of truth claims the religion can make."[35]

(b)   The cultural-linguist also emphasizes the experiential or existential dimensions of religion, although in a different way from the expressivist. To start with, Lindbeck claims that because he stresses the "code" (i.e., the inner logic or rules of faith that govern proper Christian thought, speech and action) rather than "the encoded" (i.e., the propositional assertions), he is better able than a cognitivist to accommodate the expressivist concern for the unreflective dimensions of human existence. But his point is argued here on a very narrow turf. The cognitivist, he says, has

[34] Barret, "Theology as Grammar," 160; ND, 34-35.
[35] ND, 35.

denigrated the affective dimension of piety. Even though he does not agree with the expressivist paradigm, Lindbeck wants to transpose the category of the "ultimate concern" (important for the expressivists), so that religion is described as "that ultimate dimension of culture... which gives shape and intensity to the experiential matrix from which the significant cultural achievements flow."[36] Religion is not, as the cognitivists prefer, a deliberate choice to follow fixed propositions. Rather, to become religious "is to interiorize a set of skills by practice and training." Religion is not to be regarded as teaching "such and such, but rather *how* to be religious in such and such ways."[37] What is primary in matters religious is to learn how to feel, act, and think in conformity with the inner structure of a religious tradition whose richness and subtlety refuse to be domesticated by verbal articulation.

Lindbeck may claim that, in a sense, "experience and expression are no less important in a cultural-linguistic model than in an experiential-expressive one." But, as it turns out, it is difficult to find a real place for inner experience in Lindbeck's scheme, except what has been made possible by external conditions of possibility. This is evidently the case when Lindbeck stresses that what is central is the *means of communication and expression* as constituting the precondition, or "a kind of quasi-transcendental (i.e., culturally formed) *a priori* for the possibility," of those experiences and expressions. Indeed, we are quite unable to "identify, describe, or recognize experience qua experience without the use of signs and symbols." Hence, "the richer our expressive or linguistic system, the more subtle, varied and differentiated can be our experience."[38] Lindbeck probes deeper, posing questions even as to the very possibility of

[36] ND, 34.
[37] ND, 35.
[38] ND, 36 & 37.

sensory physiological processes in human subjects. In effect, he searches not simply the linguistic influences in the public domains of human reality, but the antecedent prelinguistic and pre-experiential structures of human physiology. There, his assertions are bold. Even the "presensory or preperceptual selection and organization of stimuli," he claims, "is not entirely prelinguistic." Embedded in a language are "classification and categorial patterns" that form a grid that enables a language-competent person to "organize the inexperienceably chaotic confusion that bombards our senses." He goes so far as to suggest that "human beings are so thoroughly programmed genetically for language use that apart from acquiring a language they cannot properly develop physiologically as other animals do, but remain peculiarly immature in their sensory and physical competence."[39]

Fourth, it is not plausible to speak of a common experiential core when the "experiences that religions evoke and mold are as varied as the interpretive schemes they embody." Far from thematizing the same experience, adherents of different religions, quite simply, have different experiences. What the experiential-expressivist identifies as the sense of the Holy, is not a common quality, but a "set of family resemblances." The cultural-linguist includes all the diverse feelings as elements of different *perceptual categories and forms of practice* in the world, both secular and religious. In the case of religion, it is *not necessary* to posit a universal experience in the depths of individuals that gets objectified in diverse forms. Instead, religions may plausibly be construed as diverse cultural-linguistic systems capable of evoking profound feelings, and engendering actions accordingly.[40] The experiential-expressivist is thus presented by Lindbeck as lacking the conceptual framework to preserve the integrity and

[39] ND, 37.
[40] ND, 40.

distinctiveness of religions, on account of what he terms the
"homogenizing tendencies associated with liberal experiential-
expressivism."[41] Again, using Lonergan as the foil, Lindbeck
refers to Friedrich Heiler whom Lonergan cites extensively.
Heiler defends a list of elements, drawn up from the Christian
particular perspective, which the major world religions [Chris-
tianity, Judaism, Islam, Zoroastrianism, Hinduism, Buddhism
and Taoism] may be said to all hold in common: "that there is a
transcendent reality; that he is immanent in human hearts; that
he is supreme beauty, truth, righteousness, goodness; that he is
love, mercy, compassion; that the way to him is repentance, self-
denial, prayer; that the way is love of one's neighbour, even of
one's enemies; that the way is love of God, union with him, or
dissolution into him."[42] Lindbeck denies the usefulness of this
characterization which exposes Christianity to being viewed as
Taoism or Buddhism by an adherent of an Eastern religion. Cultural-linguists are unimpressed by the superficial similarities of
two languages in terms of "overlapping sets of sounds" or "common objects of reference": that all religions preach "love" and
"ultimate importance" is an "uninteresting banality." More to
the point, the decisive factors for them are "the grammatical patterns, the ways of referring, the semantic and syntactic structures." They look for the "distinctive patterns of story, belief, ritual, and behaviour" specific to each religion which may well
disclose contradictory meanings in such common terms as
"love" and "God."[43]

---

[41] ND, 128.

[42] Summary by Lonergan in *Method in Theology*, 109. See F. Heiler, "The
History of Religion as a Preparation for the Cooperation of Religions," in *The
History of Religions*, ed. M. Eliade and J. Katigawa (Chicago: University of
Chicago Press, 1959), 142-53.

[43] ND, 41-42.

Fifth, Lindbeck presses the argument that there is no experience (pre-reflective or reflective) without some form of symbolization taking place. But, the crunch is, it is a conceptual confusion to refer to purely *private* symbolizations or experiences, for there cannot be a symbol system which does not originate from interpersonal or social interactions. Two arguments are proffered in support of this claim. Beginning with Wittgenstein, Lindbeck contends that "private languages are logically impossible." Wittgenstein is counterpoised as authority for challenging the view (which he ascribes to Lonergan, Rahner and Tracy) that, while "experience cannot be expressed except in public and intersubjective forms," it is, nevertheless, acceptable to espouse a "privacy in the origins of experience and language." Next, by what he calls a "more modest approach than a demonstration of [the] impossibility of unthematized but conscious experience," he asserts that, intellectually complicated a hypothesis though it may be, experiential-expressivism is quite unnecessary and should be removed by Ockham's razor. To argue this point, Lindbeck reverts to the medieval distinction between first and second intentions. First intentional use of a term like "animal," for example, in respect of the objects of the intention (*intentio objectiva*), refers to *this* or *that* particular creature, whereas, in the case of second intentional use, the term is a generic concept that embraces the different species of the animal kingdom. When the medieval distinction is applied to formal mental categories (*intentio formalis*), "the first intention is the act whereby we grasp objects, while the second intention is the act of grasping or reflecting on first formal intentions." Succinctly put, his thesis is that: "We are only unthematically aware of first intentional activities while we are engaged in them." In other words, it is only at the level of the second intention, that experience is actually focussed. Lindbeck thus suggests that our attention is focussed on objects, and not on the subjective experience involved in knowing them. The expressivist's focus on experience is quite unnecessary, he claims.[44]

Finally, and most importantly for the orientation of this chapter, Lindbeck claims that changes in religious traditions are the products of "interactions between a cultural-linguistic system and changing situations." In no way would he conceive of change and innovations in religious categories as "proceeding from new experiences." "Luther," he suggests, "did not invent his doctrine of justification by faith because he had a tower experience, but rather the tower experience was made possible by his discovering the doctrine in the Bible."[45] Contrary to the experiential-expressivist view, changes are not attributable to inspirations from some inner feelings; rather, they are due to a religious interpretive scheme being confronted with anomalous applications in new settings. In sum, the very meaningfulness of the notion of an inner experience of God posited as common to all human beings and all religions is discredited by Lindbeck.

4.2.3 An Assessment of Lindbeck's Typology

A critical assessment of Lindbeck's typology must take its lead from his presentation of the experiential-expressivism that he seeks to dethrone. Lindbeck seems concerned to introduce a healthy corrective to an undesirable egotistic trend in modern society. He seems to lament the loss, in the Christian community, of social cohesion where members over-emphasize liberal autonomy and individual experiences. In that light, Lindbeck's critique against the notion of "ubiquitous prereflective private experience common to all religions" may deservedly be hailed as "timely and

[44] For the materials in this paragraph, see ND, 37-38.
[45] ND, 39.

persuasive."[46] But, can the details of his typology stand close scrutiny?

Firstly, a label as general as experiential-expressivism, particularly when it is pinned on adherents of the liberal tradition, tends to oversimplify the richness of that long tradition without attending to its many nuances. In terms of specific elements, Lindbeck is concerned to refute a liberal turn to the subject, an inner-pre-reflective experience as foundational, all language and culture as merely expressive of the inner non-discursive experience, and a 'unilateral' perception of the relationship between experience and language. Lindbeck gives no indication that these are the very same questions which the liberals have been concerned with for some time. Tracy straightens the record: "Indeed, the turn to an explicitly hermeneutical position by many theologians in this 'dominant' tradition as well as the turn to a radical 'de-privatizing' of the same tradition by political, liberational, and feminist theologians are the major attempts within the general 'liberal' paradigm to address both the 'linguistic' (hermeneutical theologies) and the cultural (de-privatizing social-political theologies) issues which Lindbeck announces as news."[47] Contemporary thinkers have, particularly through the inspiration of Gadamer (whom Lindbeck does not mention) and Ricoeur, moved beyond the Romantic or 'unilateral' expressivist perception of experience, to rethink its dialectical implications. Still, these thinkers continue to adhere to a *correlational* view of understanding familiar to the liberal theological tradition. Furthermore, there is evidence of the "discovery of a non-empiricist notion of experience."[48] In sum,

---

[46] See McGrath, *The Genesis of Doctrine*, 22. McGrath even adds to the barrage of criticisms against this model.

[47] D. Tracy, "Lindbeck's New Program for Theology," *Thomist* 49 (1985) 463.

[48] Tracy, "Lindbeck's New Program," 463.

Tracy accuses Lindbeck of offering a caricature of liberalism by omitting to indicate much of the theological terrain with which the 'liberals' are concerned. Vanhoozer concurs with Tracy that, for Ricoeur, the relation between language and experience is dialectical. Placher also points out that Tracy acknowledges no single core experience which different religions simply express in different languages.[49] As a result, Lindbeck may well be populating the so-called experiential-expressivist paradigm with straw men.

A *second* comment on Lindbeck's presentation of experiential-expressivism exposes his erroneous characterization of the theologies of Schleiermacher, Rahner and Lonergan. In the case of Schleiermacher, we shall postpone some of the arguments against Lindbeck to the next chapter when we deal with Church doctrines. For the moment, the point must at once be made that Schleiermacher, contrary to Lindbeck's indictment, *does not* claim a "universally identical religious experience which different religions simply express in different languages."[50] It is true that Schleiermacher does designate the "experience of absolute dependence" as the core experience of religion in his *inductive* theological method. It is also true that this particular kind of experience is described by him as "an immediate self-consciousness." However, as Peter Berger emphatically asserts: "At no point does Schleiermacher maintain that religious experience is *nothing but* human self-consciousness." A critic misses too much who fails to note that, for Schleiermacher, Christianity is not only the superior,

---

[49] See Vanhoozer, *Biblical Narrative in the Philosophy of Paul Ricoeur*, 182 n.10; Placher, "Revisionist and Postliberal Theologies and the Public Character of Theology," *Thomist* 49 (1985) 397.

[50] Placher, "Revisionist and Postliberal Theologies," 397. For an analysis which corrects the erroneous ascription of an expressivist label to Schleiermacher, see G. Behrens, "Schleiermacher *contra* Lindbeck on the Status of Doctrinal Sentences," *RelSt* 30 (1994) 399-417.

but even the perfect, religion. A presentation does grave disservice
to the life and thought of this theological giant, if it harbours the
following two features: (1) a failure to include "Schleiermacher's
peculiar combination of christocentrism and consciousness-analy-
sis [which] produced a strongly dualistic organization for most of
his work;" and (2) the suggestion that Schleiermacher's method
"leads into a night in which all cats are gray, in which Christianity is dissolved into a general and inevitably pallid notion of religion."[51] Lindbeck's account suffers from an inclusion of both
these elements.

His identification of Rahner with experiential-expressivism
fares no better. To be sure, much of Rahner's conceptuality and
language does resonate with this model. In particular, by his transcendental method, Rahner postulates a central epistemological
category called "*Vorgriff*," variously translated as "pre-apprehen-
sion," "pre-grasp," "pre-concept," "anticipating grasp." This
epistemological starting point leads him to posit a prethematic
knowledge of God and a "supernatural existential" available to all
of humanity as a condition of possibility for grace and revelation.
This undergirds his notion of an implicit faith that awaits thematization in every new cultural situation. From there, his celebrated
theory of anonymous Christianity takes shape.[52] However, a commentator who isolates a particular element for critique fallaciously
truncates Rahner's theology. One common error in this direction
is the presupposition on the part of many critics that the whole
locus of Rahner's theology is the turn to the subject. As Walter

[51] See Berger, *The Heretical Imperative*, 121-23.
[52] Some relevant basic literature by Rahner are *Spirit in the World*, trs. W.
Dych (New York: Herder and Herder, 1976); *Hearers of the Word*, trs. M.
Richards (New York: Herder and Herder, 1969); "Christianity and the Non-
Christian Religions," in *Theological Investigations*, trs. K-H Kruger (London:
Darton, Longman & Todd, 1966), 5:115-34; *Foundations of Christian Faith*, trs.
W. V. Dych (New York: Seabury, 1978).

Kasper points out, Rahner's transcendental Christology does not "derive the content of Christology *a priori* from human thought and from human existence as it is lived."[53] So, also, Rahner's "categorial revelation" is never intended to represent a mere "explicit expression" of the "transcendental revelation." Indeed, after positing human beings as having the existential structures to seek God, and thus calling them "spirits in the world," Rahner portrays humans as free beings capable of understanding a communication from God if God freely speaks to him/her in history. But philosophy can go no further; it must elevate itself to theology. The philosopher must "turn to history in order to examine the various claims of a divine self-manifestation and to see if God has, in fact, freely and personally communicated Himself to [humanity] in a definite place at a definite time."[54] Clearly, the Rahnerian category does not separate God's offer of grace from Christ. Christian revelation is not merely an interpretation of experience, "but is 'already and always' its transformation. Wherever human experience is authentic, it is already anonymously Christian."[55] In this regard, it is a *cardinal principle* in Rahnerian studies to be ever mindful of the Incarnation as constituting the constant element underlying Rahner's theology. It is only in the light of the Incarnation that such Rahnerian notions as "supernatural existential," "implicit faith," and "anonymous Christianity" find their proper meaning.[56] J. A. Colombo's observation appears accurate

[53] Walter Kasper, *Jesus the Christ*, trs. V. Green (New York: Paulist, 1976), 49.

[54] See Kenneth Baker, "Rahner: The Transcendental Method," *Continuum* 2 (1964) 59.

[55] Anne Carr, "Theology and Experience in the Thought of Karl Rahner," *JR* 53 (1973) 376.

[56] Rahner synthesized his thought thus: "Christianity assumes that these presuppositions which it makes are inescapably and necessarily present in the ultimate depths of human existence, even when this existence is interpreted differently in its reflexive self-interpretation, and that at the same time the Christian

when he judges that "Lindbeck has ignored the specifically Christian theological context of the transcendental turn in Rahner's theology... In positing a real, prethematic knowledge of God, Rahner's transcendental anthropology is a *theological* anthropology, always already marked by the witness of categorial revelation, i.e., that grace as the supernatural existential is given to human beings in view of the Incarnation."[57] A critique is fatally flawed if it ignores that, in the Rahnerian scheme, both the categorial and the transcendental exist as two indispensable dimensions, which stand in relation to one another.[58]

That Bernard Lonergan is pigeon-holed by Lindbeck into the experiential-expressivist slot also comes under much criticism. There is no doubt that Lindbeck has engaged in serious dialogue with the work of Lonergan, and presented a paper at an international Lonergan congress fifteen years earlier,[59] but here, he

message itself creates these presuppositions by its call... The presuppositions which are to be considered here refer to man's essential being. They refer to his essential being as something which is always historically constituted, and thus as existing in confrontation with Christianity as grace and as historical message." Rahner, *Foundations of Christian Faith*, 24-25.

[57] J. A. Colombo, "Rahner and His Critics: Lindbeck and Metz," *Thomist* 56 (1992) 72 & 88-89. In view of this crucial understanding, attempts, such as that of Albert Liberatore in "Symbols in Rahner," *LS* 18 (1993) 145-58, which seek to explain Rahner's theology of symbols, are inadequate to the extent that the significance of the Incarnation in the Rahnerian system is omitted. See also an important article by Rahner, "Theology and Anthropology," in *Theological Investigations*, trs. G. Harrison (London: Darton, Longman and Todd, 1972), 9:28-45.

[58] Tracy continues to believe in the aim of transcendental reflection, but counsels the urgent need for "more careful attention to the linguistic-historical character of all such claims. See "Uneasy Alliance," 558-59 n.40, 566. He suggests that unless one takes a more qualified approach to transcendental arguments, one risks being unintelligible in today's "historically and hermeneutically informed philosophical milieu." See *Plurality and Ambiguity*, 30.

[59] See Lindbeck, "Protestant Problems with Lonergan on Development of Dogma," In *Foundations of Theology*, ed. P. McShane (Dublin: Gill & Macmillan, 1971), 115-23, 243-44.

presents Lonergan's theory of religion only as a foil to his own
cultural-linguistic alternative.[60] In giving a reading which is "wide
of the mark," Lindbeck commits the error of treating as the whole
of Lonergan's theory of religion what is really only a part.[61] Lindbeck's inability to categorize Lonergan clearly in a typological
presentation whose validity depends substantially on clear categorization, is indicative of the weakness of the typology itself. Lonergan's position is initially depicted as a valuable attempt to combine what is best in the first two categories. Later, Lonergan's
position is presented as a "two-dimensional experiential expressivism," which incorporates many of the advantages of the propositional approach. Finally, Lonergan's position is portrayed as a
"contemporary propositionalism." Dennis Doyle perceptively
concludes that Lonergan always manages to "loom larger than the
labels" Lindbeck pins on him.[62] Much of Lindbeck's proposal has,
in fact, already been long preempted by Lonergan in the latter's
works. To take one example, Lindbeck makes affinity-claims with
theories currently reigning in academic circles, on the basis of
which he asserts that the greater efficacy of the cultural-linguistic
approach lies in its capacity to bridge the gap between the non-
theological and the theological studies of religion. But, critics
point out, one of Lonergan's eminent achievements has been the
incorporation of the "social science perspective" into the theological enterprise. Far from proposing that religion is exclusively an
expression of human experience, with nothing more than a brief
mention of God, and without a social dimension, Lonergan
emphasizes belief as an inherently social process taking place
within the context of "the collaboration of mankind in the

[60] C. C. Hefling, "Turning Liberalism Inside Out," *Method* 3:2 (1985) 54.
[61] Hefling, "Turning Liberalism Inside Out," 56.
[62] See ND, 16-17, 104-05; D. M. Doyle, "Lindbeck's Appropriation of Lonergan," *Method* 4:1 (1986) 18-19.

advancement and dissemination of knowledge."[63] It is erroneous to impute to Lonergan a neglect of the external dimension in favour of the internal; what Lonergan does is to maintain "a fine balance between human experience and the social mediation of the communication of God."[64] Hence, in what would have been an essentially healthy corrective to Lindbeck's view, Lonergan's scheme acknowledges the role of new experiences in religious change *and* yet identifies the most important "impetus for change in the contemporary world as the emergence of cultural pluralism."[65]

To the extent that a theoretical model depends, for its adequacy, upon arguments based on the alleged inadequacies of the opponent models, that model must, when its criticisms of the opponent models are found wanting, itself be cast in some doubt. This observation applies to Lindbeck's typology. In this respect, dissenting voices on the accuracy of Lindbeck's typology come even from the postliberal camp itself. Placher, for instance, finds that Lindbeck's account of experiential-expressivism oversimplifies "an actually more nuanced position. For thoughtful revisionists, the relations between experience and language are more dialectical than Lindbeck sometimes admits." While he recognizes that any label oversimplifies, Placher nevertheless maintains the view that "'experiential-expressivism' does seem a convenient first approximation of these admittedly diverse theologians."[66] Hauerwas and Jones, too, express their "discomfort" at Lindbeck's narrow typology by which an impression is given that there are only two fundamental options, such as the

---

[63] Lonergan, *Insight* (New York: Herder & Herder, 1957), 703.

[64] Doyle, "Lindbeck's Appropriation of Lonergan," 23.

[65] Ibid.

[66] Placher, "Revisionist and Postliberal Theologies and the Public Character of Theology," *Thomist* 49 (1985) 397.

options of Frei and Ricoeur in discussions of narrative, when in fact there are many.[67]

Thirdly, Lindbeck's case is weakened by his reluctance to forthrightly support the propositional character of religions and the dialectics between religion and experience. Every religion, insofar as it is theistic, is concerned with words of or from God, so that religions must maintain some informative propositions as well as non-informative symbols of inner feelings. In choosing to argue the possession of some language as an indispensable precondition for the possibility of experience, Lindbeck reverses the experiential-expressivist vision and now posits a causality which works from religion to experience, and not the other way around. However, he later concedes that his initial suggestion was an oversimplification of a very complex situation, for the relation between religion and experience is "not unilateral but dialectical. It is simplistic to say (as I earlier did) merely that religions produce experiences, for the causality is reciprocal."[68] But this concession is too little, too late; the operative theorem has already been set, as is confirmed by his persistence in saying that, while there is an *interplay* between 'inner experience' and 'external' religious and cultural factors, it is the latter which take precedence over the former: "Instead of deriving [the] external features of a religion from inner experience, it is the inner experiences which are viewed as derivative."[69] This finds further confirmation as he explicitly inverses the model of the human becoming which is said to be operative in experiential-expressivism, insisting that the "humanly real is not constructed from below upward or from the inner to the outer, but from the outer to the inner, and from above downward."

[67] See S. Hauerwas and L. G. Jones, "Introduction: Why Narrative?" in *Why Narrative?*, ed. Hauerwas and Jones (Grand Rapids: Eerdmans, 1989), 7.

[68] ND, 33.

[69] ND, 34.

To tie in with his theory of language, Lindbeck adopts Wilfrid Sellars to assert that the learning of a language must come from the outside and hence is a "jump which was the coming into being of man."[70] He drives the point home as he insists: "All the heights and depths of human knowledge, faith and love are the *effects and not the causes* of the skill ... with which men and women learn to use their cultural and linguistic resources." And this is clearly consistent with the one-directional traffic of the "text absorbing the world," a metaphor by which his theory of religion is inspired. Applied to Christian theology, he finds a perfect fit for his theory in that "just as an individual becomes human by learning a language, so he or she begins to become a new creature through hearing and interiorizing the language that speaks of Christ." We belabour this issue to highlight two points central to this chapter: [1] In terms of textual evidence, it is clear that Lindbeck's concession to a dialectical dynamics between religious language and experience is mere rhetoric that plays no part whatever in his scheme. [2] Lindbeck makes a big jump – unwarranted, in our view – when he equates 'becoming a new creature in Christ' with abandoning any emerging experience that is at variance with the "official" *status quo*. We are to allow the world of the text to swallow up our world. But reading, as we saw, is a complicated business. Every reading is an interpretation. Appropriation and application are further steps down the road. Whose ideology controls the world of the text? To whose interpretation of the *status quo* are we asked to submit?

Relatedly, a *fourth* comment focuses on Lindbeck's schematic error in treating the different models as *options*, and making the cultural-linguistic model his choice.[71] For, clearly, it is a contradiction

---

[70] ND, 62; W. Sellars, *Science, Perception, and Reality* (London: Routledge and Kegan Paul, 1963), 6.

[71] Indeed, some commentators think Lindbeck polarizes too sharply the different models. For instance, Daphne Hampson, *After Christianity* (London:

in terms to first admit to a dialectical and reciprocal relation, and
then to proceed to argue, as Lindbeck has done, that there are two
clearly defined *options* from which one can choose.[72] This, perhaps, is one of the most difficult aspects of Lindbeck's enterprise.
In view of his stated aim of proposing a theoretical scheme that
could be put into service for solving complex practical problems
(of ecumenism and theology), Lindbeck's concern is to devise a
well-defined and intelligible scheme. However, in his attempts to
do this, he resorts to an oversimplification of opponent models.
Occasionally, the language of disapproval becomes strong, giving
the impression that certain positions are being condemned. Indeed,
his occasional polemic against opponent models gives the impression of a procrustean bed into which he tries to force the entire
debate. And yet, precisely here, a point is emerging: properly
read, Lindbeck does not claim that any single theory is able to
account for the complex reality. He does not deny other substantial positions, while stressing the superiority of his own. This point
is a key to a proper reading of his presentation of the viability of
different theories of religion and of doctrine. On the other hand,
we shall take a step further when we deal with theories of doctrine, and see whether this might not entail the conclusion that the

SCM, 1996), 316 n.20 suggests that it is "possible both to say that religion is a
response to something which is experiential and also to acknowledge that that
experience can never be separated from our linguistic cultural matrix."

[72] Our remark has been arrived at independently of D. Z. Phillips' elegant comments. He raises two fundamental objections to any suggestion of options being
available here. "First, those in the grip of these ways of thinking do not regard
them as options. On the contrary, although they are confused, they, not seeing this,
think they are giving a faithful conceptual account of the religious practices they
are talking about. Second, those no longer in the grip of these ways of talking, who
have seen the confusion involved in them, certainly cannot view them as options
which they can take up again. The difficulty I have with Lindbeck's strategies is
that he claims to see the confusion and yet continues to talk of these ways of talking as options." See his "Lindbeck's Audience," *ModTh* 4 (1988) 144.

sharp contours of Lindbeck's typology need to be blurred because his fostered cultural-linguistic model is intelligible only if it is explicitly portrayed as parasitic on the other models.

As a *fifth* comment, we turn to the cultural-linguistic model which Lindbeck fosters. Consistent with his laudable goal of keeping a Christian way of life from being simply subsumed under the dominant host culture – particularly as a mere instance of the general liberal culture of the day – Lindbeck rejects the claim to universality ingredient in both the cognitive-propositionalist and experiential-expressivist approaches. But "culture," as the first component in Lindbeck's model, is, according to Tanner, often erroneously regarded as a "self-contained and self-originating Christianity in virtue of a cultural boundary."[73] What is objectionable is the presumption of an unnuanced form of cultural-linguisticism that harps on the sharpness of the cultural boundary that divides Christians from non-Christians, insiders from outsiders. History shows that Christian identity is essentially *relational*. Right from its inception, Christianity's engagement with the surrounding culture rarely involved a "face-off between distinct wholes." Instead of a sharp boundary of independent cultural content as the cultural-linguists presume, the boundary has always been "one of use that allows Christian identity to be essentially impure and mixed, the identity of a hybrid that always shares cultural forms with its host culture and other religions (notably Judaism)." That the drawing of sharp boundaries is inconsistent with history is evident, for instance, in the way Christian institutions are organized in the West. Is such structural organization a *religious matter*, or a consequence of following the existing social norms? Only if the structures were set up on account of religious imperatives would it make sense to argue that they are essential to

[73] Tanner, *Theories of Culture*, 107.

a Christian identity determined by a religious boundary. Indeed, as Tanner points out, instead of operating on a strategy of exclusion, the early Christians incorporated a great deal of, for example, the shame/honour code of Greco-Roman morals. She writes: "Rather than establishing Christian identity by its exclusion, a cultural difference was maintained by changing the goal of such a moral code (the goal is now to do the will of God), by substituting different warrants for the practices (scriptural ones), by making odd content substitutions (humility is now to be honored), and by seeking moral achievement on those terms not as individual accomplishment of the philosopher but something requiring sustenance from a particular religious community and guaranteed only by God."[74] Tanner perceptively suggests that "the distinctiveness of a Christian way of life is not so much formed *by* the boundary as *at* the boundary."[75] What is happening is a *cultural process* in which a distinctive identity emerges through the distinctive use of cultural materials shared with others. The validity of "spoiling the Egyptians," that is, culling from the ancient world those ideas and culture that would serve the new Christian dispensation should not require much debate; the Church has always been doing that. In their effort to maintain Christian identity, the cultural-linguists evince a danger of "confusing subordination to the Word with subordination to human word." Christianity does not always need to keep the upper hand in relation to external materials; the Word does. The cultural-linguists are correct in suggesting that, in order to be open to the Word, "borrowed materials must lose their fixity." The idea being to transform borrowed materials in service of the Word, the proposal by cultural-linguists to keep them from being the interpretive lens is quite unnecessary. After all, the lens one employs, however apt it may be, remains a human construct;

[74] Tanner, *Theories of Culture*, 108-09.
[75] Tanner, *Theories of Culture*, 115.

it is never "adequate" to the Word it seeks to interpret. Tanner thus reminds us that instead of always subordinating borrowed materials to Christian claims, the former should be permitted, instead, to shake the latter up where necessary.[76]

The second component in Lindbeck's fostered paradigm is "language." Here, a crucial question is the legitimacy of Lindbeck's use of Wittgenstein. In the philosophy of religion, it is commonly accepted that language games may be construed as expressive of worlds, in the sense of horizons relevant to a particular standpoint. Interpreters generally go further and agree, allegedly with Wittgenstein, that language games are also expressive of "forms of life." Just what Wittgenstein meant by the phrase "forms of life," however, is rather complicated and a matter of controversy. Part of the problems has to do with the different senses for which the phrase is used.[77] In J.F.M. Hunter's classification of interpretations of "form of life," the "language-game account" suggests that a form of life is virtually the same as a language, so that a close observation discloses what the "game" is. On the other hand, a form of life may also be a package of language and behaviour. Since language games and behaviour may be logically distinct, the "behaviour-package account" then suggests that not all language games are forms of life.[78] But is that how Wittgenstein uses the two terms? And, further, how does his concept of "forms of life" compare with what others might call "culture?" In proposing his cultural-linguistic theory of religion, Lindbeck draws on Geertz's theory of culture and Paul Holmer's

[76] Tanner, *Theories of Culture*, 149-50.

[77] For an analysis of the seven passages in Wittgenstein's works in which the phrase is found, see B. Haymes, "The Knowledge of God as a Form of Life," in *The Concept of the Knowledge of God* (London: Macmillan, 1988), ch. 4, 150ff.

[78] J. F. M. Hunter, "Forms of Life in Wittgenstein's *Philosophical Investigations*," *AmPhQ* 5 (1968) 233-43.

reading of Wittgenstein's theory of language games.[79] Holmer's interpretation, however, is said to be open to serious question.[80]

Fergus Kerr, for instance, addresses the issue of "Wittgenstein-ian fideism" introduced into philosophy by Kai Nielson. Kerr offers a concise account of the mistake committed by those who deploy the concepts "language game" and "form of life" to sub-stantiate the case that religious talk "constitutes a distinctive and autonomous 'language game' which outsiders could not under-stand, let alone expose as incoherent or erroneous."[81] In Kerr's analysis, two points stand out. *First*, religion is erroneously seen as a "form of life" that just "has to be accepted." Wittgenstein's name has thus been wrongly associated with the view that familiar religious concepts are presumed to be available only to those who share the "form of life" in which they are employed, that is, those who are adherents of the same religion. *Second*, religious talk is wrongly taken to be a "language game," with its autonomous rules and hence "intelligible only to the players."[82] Kerr excludes, *on textual grounds*, any attempt at associating with Wittgenstein the application of these central analytic tools to a large phenome-non like religion. Correspondingly, of course, once this is under-stood, any claim that a language-game is autonomous, so as to impute a so-called "Wittgensteinian fideism," will prove vacu-ous.[83] Whenever Wittgenstein spoke of forms of life and the lan-guage-games embedded in them, he had "very basic small-scale activities in mind." In Kerr's judgment: "Nothing could be plainer than the *level* of micro-practices with which Wittgenstein

---

[79] See P. Holmer, "Wittgenstein and Theology," in *New Essays on Religious Language*, ed. D. M. High (Oxford: Oxford University Press, 1969).

[80] See J. A. Martin, *Beauty and Holiness* (Princeton: Princeton University Press, 1990), 210 n.67.

[81] F. Kerr, *Theology after Wittgenstein* (Oxford: Blackwell, 1986), 28.

[82] Kerr, *Theology After Wittgenstein*, 29.

[83] Ibid.

is concerned when he speaks of 'forms of life'. He means the open-ended multiplicity of social skills embodied in our workaday interaction with one another and consequently with things."[84] Challenging what he perceives to be a widespread assumption in religious studies that the concepts of "form of life" and "language-game" refer to large scale practices and institutions constitutive of our whole social order, Nicholas Lash takes on the burden of proving that, in Wittgenstein's primary usage, these concepts refer only to "micro practices."[85] Kerr's and Lash's conclusions seriously challenge Lindbeck's theory on three counts: [a] Wittgenstein's work has been wrongly used "to license the doctrine that religious discourse might be an autonomous 'language game', with its own rules intelligible only to the insider." "Religion as such can not be a 'form of life' in Wittgenstein's sense" and "religious discourse could not be a 'language game' either."[86] [b] The same conclusions are hence applicable to individual religious traditions. [c] It is not advisable to ignore Wittgenstein's insights, disengage from any association with his name, and proceed nonetheless to use the terminology "to describe large-scale practices, institutions and 'conceptual schemas'."[87]

Given the above analysis of Wittgensteinian micro practices, and the Geertzian call for "depth description" appropriate to each culture, our *sixth* comment focuses on one complicated aspect of reality in the religious domain. It concerns the distinction between learning the idiom of a religion and becoming religious. In other words, persons, and even communities, can have at most a sort of latent religion if they have learnt the "language" (the *form*) but do

---

[84] F. Kerr, "Wittgenstein and Theological Studies," *NewBf* 63 (1982) 501.
[85] N. Lash, "How Large Is a 'Language Game'?" *Th* 87 (1984) 19-28.
[86] Kerr, "Wittgenstein and Theological Studies," 500-02
[87] Lash, "How Large Is a 'Language Game'," 25, 27-28.

not have the spirit or power (the *substance*) of the faith within them. They may appropriately be described as potentially religious, but they need to respond to the message in the language to be positively religious. Lindbeck is acutely aware of the need for Christians to respond to the proclamation of the Christian message. A Christian, he writes, "becomes a new creature through hearing and interiorizing the language that speaks of Christ." Obviously, Lindbeck must mean considerably more than accepting language rules; what he undoubtedly advocates is the necessity of embracing the deeper message in the idiom. If this reading of Lindbeck is correct, the cultural-linguistic or "language-game" theory of religion must imply a more complex model, of which it is only a part. The cultural-linguistic components are important, but they are not the only components, of religion.[88] For instance, in keeping with his cultural-linguistic analysis, Lindbeck suggests that the only possible avenue for persuading others of the Christian truth is that of "socializing" them into a Christian linguistic enclave and its corresponding form of life. Apart from the danger of unwittingly equating gospel-proclamation with indoctrination, Lindbeck's scheme also fosters a rather passive view of religious understanding and faith. For, curiously silent in his analysis is the *active process* of coming to belief. "Believing," Hollenbach points out, "is an act of judgment and commitment." Christian truth and meaning eludes the believer who does not actively enter into a quest for ultimate meaning and find answers in the story of Jesus of Nazareth. Without this active engagement of the self, what seems like religious faith may in fact "not be faith at all but rather a mere piece of cultural baggage."[89]

---

[88] The line of argument in this paragraph is drawn from C. J. Sommerville, "Is Religion A Language Game?" *ThT* 51 (1995) 594-99.

[89] In which case, "Lindbeck's 'communal enclave' will have to have very high walls indeed if they are to survive in our pluralistic culture." See Hollenbach, ""Fundamental Theology and the Christian Moral Life," 173 and 178.

Seventh, Lindbeck's metaphors, "language" and "culture," while fecund in certain ways, are extremely limited in others. In Kelsey's insightful analysis, for example, while Church discourse and Church life may be likened to a culture and a language, "Christianity is not *a* culture or *a* language, and in some important ways it is unlike them." More importantly for this chapter, Kelsey points out that a major limitation to the usefulness of these metaphors for Christianity is that they hold the Church "ideologically captive, so that its teachings and practice are in some ways in support of its own material interests, a state of affairs that the church's very identity requires it to name and repent as idolatry." Arguably, if any part of Christian discourse gets deformed, its "grammar could not logically be its own principle of reform and change."[90] We must be open to a critical conversation with novel and dissonant experiences to allow a dialectical disclosure of truth.

Eighth, if Lindbeck's system is to be coherent, the cultural-linguistic view of religion must be consistent with his emphasis on the irreducibility of Scripture narrative within the particularity of the Christian communal context, as against a totalizing foundationalist metadiscourse. This, to be sure, parallels Lyotard's philosophical portrait of the postmodern condition where narratively-shaped particularity constitutes the universal human condition. For Lindbeck the theologian, naturally, a similar interest finds expression in a focus on the "particular particularity of the Christian community and its narrative."[91] The experiential-expressivist model's emphasis on common inner experience tends to eclipse the distinctiveness of each religion. In contrast, by stressing communal particularity, Lindbeck's cultural-linguistic model is more efficacious in preserving the difference. The cultural-linguistic

---

[90] D. H. Kelsey, "Church Discourse and Public Realm," 27.

[91] Watson, *Text, Church and World*, 135.

lens may not solve all the problems, and may even be found wanting when it comes to specific theological issues. But it promotes
the vision that language creates the fact, and not the other way
round, and is better able to account for the complex diversity in
contemporary society. Of relevance to our discussion is a point
Watson perceptively discerns as keeping Lindbeck's scheme in a
peculiar tension: "The plea for a return to the particularity and
concretion of the Christian communal and linguistic matrix is
dependent for its credibility as a theological proposal on the non-
theological, postmodern view of particularity as a universal."[92] It
is a different kind of universalism, but a universalism nonetheless.

Finally, Lindbeck's focus on the grammatical function of religion or theology is viewed by some as a reductionist error. Lindbeck constructs a postliberal way of conceiving religious doctrine
which is "more concerned with how to think than with what to
assert about matters of fact" because this way is "religiously neutral."[93] But such an approach may well be too abstract to be of
service to the Christian community. In particular, so it has been
argued, "in refusing to take the claims of Christian experience as
the primary data to be understood, Lindbeck insulates his proposal
from being useful to the widest community of Christian believers."[94] Further, as William Stack Johnson pointedly observes, "It
will not do to reduce God to a single dimension of reality that is
beyond critical inquiry. Not even the biblical story itself can function as a proxy for the living God. There is more to theology than
plumbing the cultural-linguistic system of the Christian West."[95]

[92] Watson, *Text, Church and World*, 136.

[93] ND, 7 & 9.

[94] K. R. Trembath, *Divine Revelation* (Oxford: Oxford University Press, 1991), 187 n.33.

[95] W. S. Johnson, *The Mystery of God* (Louisville: Westminster John Knox, 1997), 4.

4.3 The Theological Viability of Different Theories of Religion

Lindbeck is rightly conscious that an empirical comparison of theories of religion is anything but conclusive. Even if experiential-expressivism, in his estimation, fares poorly in a scientific study of religion, it could still prove to be of superior quality theologically, compared to cultural-linguisticism. *To be religiously useful*, Lindbeck declares, even a nontheological theory of religion ought to be able to tackle the claims religions make about their superiority and be able to interpret what these claims mean.[96] A transition to a theological evaluation is hence an inevitable second step. He therefore attempts to tackle three interreligious problems — unsurpassability, dialogue, and the salvation of non-Christians, which we now examine in turn.

4.3.1 Unsurpassability

In line with his typology, Lindbeck suggests that religions may be compared with each other in light of their propositional truth, their symbolic efficacy, or their categorial adequacy.

Cognitive-propositionalism tends to compare religions by a sort of correspondence theory of truth. This theory, according to Lonergan, asserts an ontological correspondence or "isomorphism" of the "structure of knowing and the structure of the known."[97] In this mode of thought, Lindbeck suggests, a religion is judged to be superior which "makes the most significant veridical truth claims and the fewest false ones." It is a mark of orthodoxy to maintain superiority in terms of absence of error. Further, this model makes it a *conditio sine qua non* of unsurpassability that the unsurpassable religion "contain the highest of what Aquinas called *revelabilia*

---

[96] For what is essentially Lindbeck's declaration of intent, see ND, 46.

[97] B. Lonergan, *Insight* (New York: Harper & Row, 1978), 399.

(i.e., religiously significant truths capable of being revealed within the space-time world of human experience)." To fail to possess *revelabilia* to this highest degree may mean that a religion is wholly, yet incompletely, true: wholly, because none of its truth claims is false; incompletely, because its truth-claims are limited in stock, scope, and actual significance. According to one traditional Christian attitude, this aptly describes the religion of Israel: the Old Testament religion contains no falsehood, but is nevertheless surpassed by higher revealed truths in the Christian faith. Religions, Lindbeck suggests, are "a mixture of truth and error," and a religion, partly false, may contain truths not present in other religions which could profit from them.[98]

Truth is viewed by the experiential-expressivist as a function of "symbolic efficacy." Religions are to be judged on the yardstick of their efficacy at articulating and communicating the inner experience of the divine common to them all. In light of its symbolic and nondiscursive perspective, all religions are perceived as capable of functioning truly, the difference being only a matter of degree of truth either in potentiality or actuality. Again, Lindbeck doubts the usefulness of this model for the reason that it is hard put to come up with a specific meaning for the notion of "unsurpassably true." He spots the Achilles' heel of this model in the fact that a symbol-system is a variable quality that logically has no intrinsic upper limit to its adequacy and effectiveness. Lindbeck would admit of unsurpassable expressive truth only in a *weak sense*: historical accident decides definitively whether or not the religion in question is in fact unsurpassable. But that is only a scenario posited for the end of history. In Christian terms, it is a matter of "eschatological finality."[99]

---

[98] See ND, 47 & 49. See also K. Surin, "Many Religions and the One True Faith," *ModTh* 4 (1988) 190-91.

[99] See ND, 47, 49-50. Lindbeck refers to Wiles who regards eschatological finality as the only finality the early Christians knew: history and the world as

Lindbeck, in contradistinction to the other two approaches, introduces the idea of *categorial adequacy*. Because religions are, under the cultural-linguistic lens, primarily thought of as "different idioms for construing reality, expressing experience, and ordering life," questions of truth are correlated with the *categories* that encapsulate truth claims and convey symbols. Questions raised in comparing religions have to do, not with propositional truth, nor with symbolic efficacy, but with the adequacy of the categories employed. Categories are adequate "which can be made to apply to what is taken to be real, and which therefore make possible, though they do not guarantee, propositional, practical, and symbolic truth." A religion evincing such categories is adjudged to be *categorially true*. Notions of truth, of experience, of categorial adequacy, and of God, may well be *incommensurable* within different religious or philosophical systems. In one respect, the cultural-linguist is able to account for a claim to unsurpassable truth in a more forceful way than the expressivist or the propositionalist. It is conceivable that only one religion might possess adequate *categories* for describing the religious object, i.e., the object of ultimate significance in the universe. The cultural-linguist is alone able to affirm *this religion* as the only one in which any form of propositional and expressive religious truth or falsity is present, and to regard all other religions as categorially false, although they remain propositionally and expressively neither true nor false. They would be religiously meaningless, just as talk about light and heavy things is meaningless when one lacks the concept of 'weight.' A weaker version of the cultural-linguistic claim to better account for the unsurpassability of a religion consists in the argument that "categorial truth

they knew it would end. Because Christians no longer expected an imminent parousia by the time the Council met at Nicaea, Wiles contends that it was not legitimate for Nicaea to affirm an unsurpassable finality of Christ. See his *Working Papers in Doctrine* (London: SCM, 1976), 156-57.

does not exclude propositional error. Rather it makes error as well as truth possible. Even if there is only one religion in which reference to God can occur... yet it will be open to all sorts of falsehoods in what it affirms of him."[100]

When a religion is thought of as comparable to a cultural-linguistic system, that is, as a particular set of language games correlated with a particular form of life, Lindbeck suggests that, *as a whole*, a religion may then be assessed for its correspondence, or otherwise, to God's will. Stressing a dimension which he will consistently reiterate, Lindbeck suggests that a religion, *as actually lived*, may be likened to a *single gigantic proposition*. "It (a religion) is a true proposition to the extent that its objectivities are interiorized and exercised by groups and individuals in such a way as to conform them in some measure in the various dimensions of their existence to the ultimate reality and goodness that lies at the heart of things. It is a false proposition to the extent that this does not happen." The "categorially and unsurpassably true religion" is, therefore, one that is capable of engendering the thought, passions, and action that correspond to the ultimate reality, although it may not in practice be so employed.[101]

In his critical assessment of Lindbeck's arguments, Kenneth Surin begins with the observation that, even as Lindbeck argues for the superiority of the cultural-linguistic model in accounting for religious unsurpassability, he is keen to demonstrate that his account is likewise consonant with a modest and qualified propositionalism. While he rejects a strict propositional approach, therefore, he finds utility in the notion of truth as correspondence. If this sounds incongruous in the light of Lindbeck's outright rejection of the correspondence theory associated with the cognitive-propositional approach to religion, it is because now "Lindbeck wants to reconcile his categorial

---

[100] See ND, 48-51.
[101] ND, 51 & 52.

account of religious truth with an ingenious hybrid truth-theory which combines the correspondence, coherence and pragmatic theories of truth." Hence, the equation of religion with a single giant proposition. We may therefore note an implicit, albeit muffled and faint, propositional dimension in Lindbeck's argumentation – a point we shall explore further in the next chapter.

Next, skeptics would want to question whether Lindbeck's claim to unsurpassable status for Christianity stands up to historical scrutiny. Christianity, to be sure, must fare poorly. The Nazi death camps, and the Rwandan and Bosnian holocausts are graphic testimonies to its "uselessness." Certainly, martyrs like Maximillian Kolbe and Dietrich Bonhoeffer are shining examples of the correct 'utilization' of the Christian category in Lindbeck's sense, but such examples are few and far between in comparison with the atrocities perpetrated by Christians. Lindbeck only belatedly discloses his awareness of the incongruity of the match between his theory and the actual application thereof. He admits, at the end of his presentation, that even if his theory is sound, it may not actually be reflected in practice. Surely, this admission must seriously compromise the claim for superiority for his model. So Surin can pointedly remark: "To provide a definition of 'unsurpassability' which seemingly evinces no recognition that Christianity would betray or erode its mainsprings if it were to possess this 'capacity' in a merely 'theoretical' way, is inevitably to sanction a form of Christianity that is prey to illusion and distortion." And yet, Lindbeck will rely heavily on "Christianity's irreducibly 'performative' aspect" in support of his rule theory of doctrine which we shall see in the next chapter. The reader soon realises that there is much ambiguity in Lindbeck's presentation, occasioned by his zeal, firstly, to argue the case for a theory that is consistent with his intratextual theology and, secondly, to preserve the doctrinal truth claims of the Christian Tradition.[102]

[102] For much of the discussion in these comments, see Surin, "Many Religions and the One True Faith,"192-93.

4.3.2 Salvation and Other Faiths

Lindbeck is concerned with the dilemma of reconciling the salvation of non-Christians and the *sola Christi*. He goes along with the dominant contemporary view which repudiates theological exclusivism. This leaves two other basic modes of explanation: [1] the saving grace of Christ is present in all religions and is effective for all human beings in their *present life*, a position best exemplified by Rahner's anonymous Christianity; [2] the destiny of human beings is pictured *prospectively* in eschatological terms, Christ being the life of the world to come.[103] To the cultural-linguist, the only viable account of salvation for non-Christians is a prospective one.

For Rahner and Lonergan, according to Lindbeck, a response in diverse ways to the saving grace of Christ constitutes a present reality: non-Christians have made an implicit, and Christians an explicit, response to Christ. Denying any implicit-explicit distinction,[104] Lindbeck suggests that "just as a person becomes human by learning a language, so he or she begins to become a new creature through hearing and interiorizing the language that speaks of Christ." At least eleven years before publishing his 1984 book, the basic framework of Lindbeck's cultural-linguistic theory of religion had already been worked out. Relying on contemporary history,

---

[103] See ND, 56. This prospective account of the salvation of non-Christians is also favoured by DiNoia who further undergirds it with his exposition of the doctrine of purgatory. See J. A. DiNoia, *The Diversity of Religions* (Washington: Catholic University of America Press, 1992), especially pp.103-08.

[104] Relying on Aquinas' analysis of faith, DiNoia, too, objects to the idea of a universal pre-reflexive experience of the grace of Christ. See J. A. DiNoia, "Implicit Faith, General Revelation and the State of the Non-Christians," *Thomist* 47 (1983) 209-41. One noted difference between DiNoia and Lindbeck is that DiNoia, probably because of his Catholic background, ascribes saving value to the loving lives led by non-Christians (p. 238).

phenomenology, sociology and psychology of religion, he arrived at the conclusion that "the faiths by which [we] live, whether Christians or non-Christians, are always acquired *ex auditu*."[105] One might perceive Lindbeck's Lutheran background at work in this analysis, with its emphasis on the *fides ex auditu*, that is, the faith which comes through hearing the Gospel proclamation (Rom. 10:17).

In Lindbeck's eschatological perspective, the "final die is cast beyond our space and time, beyond empirical observation, beyond all rootage in this world and passes into the inexpressible transcendence that surpasses all worlds, images, and thoughts." At the point of death, the final decision for or against Christ is made. This applies as much to non-Christians as it does to Christians. This is *fides ex auditu* in future tense, "applied to ultimate completion when faith passes into the beatific vision."[106] Salvation for non-Christians becomes an eschatological prospect. Lindbeck believes this view can serve to curb boasting and an arrogant sense of superiority on the part of the Christians and even pave the way for open, and mutually enriching dialogue.

Having said that, Lindbeck then has to concede two things, which he does. *First*, by grounding his scheme in a future eschaton, Lindbeck renders it mythical and unreal in philosophical and scientific terms, the very same charge he makes against the notion of an anonymously Christian, preconceptual and prelinguistic experience of salvation. *Second*, Lindbeck is compelled to concede that since mythological elements are integral to every religion, the salvation of non-Christians may arguably be affirmed in the light either of Rahner's anonymous Christianity with its primordial, prelinguistic experience of the *gratia Christi,* or of

[105] See ND, 62 & 60. See Lindbeck, "Unbelievers and the 'Sola Christi'," *Dialog* 12 (1973) 182-89.
[106] ND, 60.

eschatological fulfilment with its attendant *fides ex auditu* component.[107]

Two comments may be made. *First*, Lindbeck's denial of the necessity of a primordial, prereflective experience of Christ's grace is consonant with his rejection of experiential-expressivism. That, in turn, impels him to criticize Rahner's theory of anonymous Christianity. It should be pointed out that, in a 1973 article, Lindbeck's assessment of Rahner was positively different. There, he was impressed with Rahner's success in having thoroughly reconciled the *sola Christi* and the salvation of non-Christians, in a way which, Lindbeck pointed out, Rahner's Protestant counterparts had not been able to do. The latter were said to lack Rahner's categories of infused grace, implicit faith and, most crucially, *incarnational realism*.[108] Some aspects, at least, of Lindbeck's argumentation, may therefore seem to have been made pliable to suit different occasions.

Second, the coherence between Lindbeck's eschatological *fides ex auditu* and his definition of unsurpassability may not bear close scrutiny. In his metaphorical description of transcendence and eternity, Lindbeck speaks of a loss of rootage in this world, and posits a location that lies beyond our space and time. In effect, a disjunction is posited between an existential rootage in this world and an existence some place else. This is not an eschatological image subscribed to by all theologians. Lindbeck knows he has to take a clear stand so as to preserve a universal scope for his notion of *fides ex auditu*. An opportunity has to be postulated for the whole of humanity, without exception, to hear the offer of salvation by the crucified and risen Lord, and this he consigns only to the eschatological realm. Surin concludes from this, that "Lindbeck's position, while it requires an explicit confession of Christ on the part of all

---

[107] See ND, 59, & 62-63.
[108] See Lindbeck, "Unbelievers and the 'Sola Christi'," 184.

who are candidates for salvation, can appropriately be described as an eschatologically-qualified 'universalism'." This is precisely where Surin accuses Lindbeck of evacuating the unsurpassability of Christianity "of any real point or urgency." Within the cultural-linguistic perspective, religion is "irreducibly communitarian," so that "any attempt to reconcile the *Christus solus* with the salvation of non-Christians will involve the positing of an extension or a dismantling of the visible boundaries of the Christian community." At the *eschaton*, all human beings will be accorded the capacity for hearing, and the opportunity for accepting, the true religion. As required by the 'cultural-linguistic' model, all would then be incorporated into the Christian linguistic community. His insistence on *fides ex auditu* being closely tied to the eschatological unsurpassability of Christianity, Lindbeck's scheme presupposes that there could logically be only one historical system that would be isomorphic with the ultimate reality. That being the case, Surin claims that Lindbeck's whole discussion of the 'categorial adequacy' of factual, historical systems becomes quite superfluous. Surin's conclusion is perceptively pointed: "So while Lindbeck starts off by furnishing an exposition of the connection which — ostensibly — obtains between 'categorial adequacy' and 'unsurpassability', thereby giving the impression that this connection is designed to shoulder a not insubstantial conceptual and theological burden, his subsequent advocacy of a 'prospective *fides ex auditu*' theory — especially one so tightly harnessed to the *solus Christus* — ensures that in the end this putative connection really has no work to do!"[109]

Once again, we encounter in Lindbeck a certain anthropological timidity. He shies away from the Augustinian innate human yearning for God. He also lacks the Rahnerian conception of

[109] See Surin, "Many Religions and the One True Faith," 193-97.

human capacity to lead authentic human lives by positively responding to love as the essence of the Transcendent Mystery. Augustine, Rahner and Lindbeck may conceivably agree that because a contrite heart of a repentant sinner is pleasing to God, a penitent heart at the point of death would bring the person close to the Creator. Yet, there is an immense difference in the ways they understand how salvation is achieved *at the point of death*. Lindbeck, as a good Lutheran, postulates that a person's eternal future is solely decided by faith in response to hearing the Word, if not during one's lifetime, then at the point of death. Even the term "repentance," in distinction from "remorse," is, for Lindbeck, biblically determined. Rahner, on the other hand, with his Catholic background, would find Lindbeck's strict insistence on *fides ex auditu*, at the point of death, somewhat artificial and unduly restrictive. While not ruling out the possibility, as Lindbeck seems to suggest, of Christ appearing to a dying person and offering him/her an opportunity to make an explicit profession of faith, Rahner understands conversion to God as a gradual process with which one struggles throughout one's lifetime. To be sure, it is God who judges the activities in one's biography. But Rahner is hopeful that, because grace has been given through Christ, there will be some validation by the Lord of every human effort in making an authentic and positive response to the movement of that grace in human lives. Christocentricity is evidently operative in both Lindbeck's and Rahner's schemes, but their underlying differences in theological anthropology would lead to very different theological constructions as to what might happen to a person at the point of death. There, the old debate on grace and nature continues to exert an obstinate influence.[110]

[110] Lindbeck's eschatological universalism also seems to operate on a presupposition of some clear dichotomy between heaven and hell in Christian eschatology. Rahner's caveat seems appropriate: "From the perspective of Christian

4.3.3 Interreligious Dialogue

Lindbeck acknowledges with candour the "popularity," not necessarily the actual efficacy, of the experiential-expressive approaches in affirming dialogue and the possibility of salvation for adherents of other religions. He appreciates an "enthusiasm and warm fellow-feelings that can be easily promoted in an experiential-expressive context," but proposes, in keeping with a cultural-linguistic outlook, to develop viable "theological rationales" for difficult but "sober and practically efficacious" interreligious dialogues.[111] The question for Lindbeck is how the cultural-linguistic approach is able to attend to all these matters as well.

The current interest in exploring common experience, although not discarded, does not have to take centre stage. Without assuming that religions share a common experiential core, thereby disguising a multiplicity of problems, Christians can look on other religions as cultural-linguistic systems just like Christianity. There are a few advantages to this approach. *First*, particularities are respected at the start of a dialogue. DiNoia capitalises on this insight and shifts the issue of salvation from the centre stage in interreligious dialogue, making a convincing case instead for the respectful study of the doctrinal tradition of each partner in dialogue. But, we could go further, as Paul Griffiths has done, and challenge the anti-apologetical view that "the active defense of the truth of those beliefs and practices to which one's community appears committed is

anthropology and eschatology, and in a serious and cautious interpretation of scripture and its eschatological statements, we are not obliged to declare that we know with certainty that in fact the history of salvation is going to end for certain people in absolute loss. As Christians, then, we do not have to regard statements about heaven and hell as parallel statements of Christian eschatology." See *Foundations of Christian Faith*, 435.

[111] ND, 55.

always to be shunned."[112] Griffiths insists that doctrinal differences must be brought out into the open and soberly challenged. For the time has come, he argues, when representative intellectuals from each religious tradition are obliged to engage in both "positive and negative apologetics" vis-à-vis religious claims that are incompatible with their own.[113] To be sure, this presumes an element of commensurability. *Second*, when what it takes to be a true adherent of a given religion means becoming skilled in the language or the symbol system of that religion, religions have, on that ground, a better chance at interreligious dialogue without sacrificing claims to unsurpassability. *Third*, Christian participation in interreligious dialogue may then be diverted away from an undisclosed agenda aimed at recruiting converts and, as Vatican II declares, may be to the benefit of other religions.[114]

Interreligious dialogues are not envisaged by Lindbeck as tough debates on contentious doctrinal issues. This runs counter to the point advocated by Paul Griffiths that the time has come for representatives of all the world religions to clearly argue for the validity of their doctrinal traditions at the interreligious level. Lindbeck confines himself to suggesting what amount to interreligious contacts rather than dialogues. In the context of such contacts, Christians can offer selfless service in imitation of their Lord in helping members of other religions to actualize their potentialities. The underlying rationale is that, even though adherents of other religions are "not within the direct purview of the peoples of

---

[112] P. J. Griffiths, *An Apology for Apologetics* (New York: Orbis, 1991), xi.

[113] Griffiths, *An Apology for Apologetics*, 3. The entire book is a sustained articulation of this thesis.

[114] *Nostra Aetate*, 2 reads: "Let Christians, while witnessing to their own faith and way of life, acknowledge, preserve and encourage the spiritual and moral truths found among non-Christians."

Messianic witness," they are nevertheless "God-willed and God-approved anticipations of aspects of the coming kingdom," and, hence, equally "elected" though they, too, like us, perhaps fail "to carry out their own distinctive tasks within God's world."[115]

4.3.4 The Flight from the Modern to the Postmodern

Lindbeck's agenda is by now crystal clear. He is seeking what Stanley Hauerwas and Gregory Jones describe as "a clear alternative to liberalism." His agenda is deeply affected by his disagreement with what he takes to be a current pervasive concession to liberalism as regards the nature of religion. Charles Hefling seems accurate in diagnosing the current liberal mood, even if he is not altogether on target in suggesting that "theologians today, whatever their confessional loyalty, still do their thinking and writing within a cultural environment to which Schleiermacher's way of understanding religion is very well adapted."[116] Lindbeck's trenchant disaffection for this liberal mood deserves attention. In this context, it is useful to examine his criticisms of the theology of a fellow Lutheran, Gerhard Ebeling, as an example of the liberal experiential-expressivist approach that he seeks to dethrone.

His assessment of Ebeling may be conveniently summarised in four points. *First*, he is surprised that, as a Lutheran, Ebeling has favourable things to say about some aspects of the Hellenization of Christianity, and even the medieval use of Aristotle. *Second*, and worse, Ebeling regards as sound, Schleiermacher's systematic development of a "methodological premise that theological concepts should be formulated in correspondence to experience." Ebeling has used this method to "move from Luther's insight into the experience of being as relational to a corresponding relational

115 ND, 53-55.
116 Hefling, "Turning Liberalism Inside Out," 51.

ontology." This leads Lindbeck to conclude that, while *materially*,
Ebeling is a follower of Luther, *methodologically*, he is a nineteenth century liberal.[117] *Third*, this methodological liberalism has
in fact taken a linguistic turn: "The progressing from experience
to God now takes place via language, and more specifically, via
the language of prayer." Along this line, theologians are encouraged to conceptualise God "in correlation to the fusion of experience and language which is prayer."[118] This is in stark contrast to
the intratextual emphasis on the living Word which entails "applying the language, concepts, and categories of Scripture to contemporary realities, and is different in its intellectual, practical, and
homilectical consequences from liberal attempts of which Ebeling's is the most notable, to understand the Reformation notion of
the word of God in terms of an experiential 'word event'."[119]
Despite his special emphasis on language, Ebeling is assessed by
Lindbeck as being typically liberal. What makes Ebeling's linguistic shift different from other phenomenological or existential
methods is that his practice of correlating theological concepts
with "speech events" rather than directly with experience saves
him from taking "a universally valid phenomenological account
of religious or common human experience as his starting point."
This is a big plus, in Lindbeck's reckoning. However, a major
error in Ebeling's work, Lindbeck diagnoses, is that his linguistic
turn resembles Wittgensteinian thoughts only superficially, and
masks a difference at a fundamental level. On the one hand, the
fusion of language and experience in prayer, for instance, bears

---

[117] Lindbeck, "Ebeling: Climax of a Great Tradition," *JR* 61 (1981) 310-11.
The work which Lindbeck is discussing is Gerhard Ebeling, *Dogmatik des
christlichen Glaubens*, vol. 1, *Der Glaube an Gott den Schöpfer der Welt* (Tübingen: J. C. B. Mohr [Paul Siebeck], 1979).
[118] Lindbeck, "Climax of a Great Tradition," 311.
[119] ND, 119.

some semblance to the relation between language games and forms of life, in Lindbeck's interpretation of Wittgenstein. On the other hand, language seen as ruled behaviour is absent in Ebeling. Rather, languages are regarded as "collections of evocative and expressive symbols," a view that represents a clear departure from that which identifies God as Agent in the Scripture narratives. When Ebeling identifies as normative for all human beings, a "despair of self and trust in God," this epitomizes his inclination towards the private and affective dimensions rather than the behavioural and the communal form of life.[120] *Finally*, Lindbeck regards the whole theological tradition stemming from Schleiermacher as being deeply flawed due to its patent inability to identify a universally normative pattern of Christian experience. The resultant picture is a cacophony of theologies inspired by different experiential starting points. Lindbeck thus presses the argument that if God is not conceived as a correlate of experience, the need for a single normatively expressive pattern is then obviated. One can then account for diverse and different, but equally authentic, experiential *responses* to the One God in different cultural settings. This alternative approach, he claims, would be useful for understanding the fundamentally different, and yet authentic patterns of experience in biblical as well as postbiblical Christianity.

Lindbeck's critique of Ebeling links up nicely with his critique of the liberal appeal to experience as providing no means for adjudicating between different theologies. There is no doubt that a realistic assessment of the failures of the liberal theological agenda is essential for a genuine growth in Christian understanding. On the other hand, critics are wary of the danger, inherent in Lindbeck's flight from the modern to the postmodern, of failing to give due credit to some real gains in the nineteenth century, and to

---

[120] Lindbeck, "Ebeling: Climax of a Great Tradition," 313.

the liberal tradition of the twentieth century.[121] In particular, Lindbeck's trenchant denial of a healthy spot for experience may be seen as the focal point for much debate around which a number of issues cohere. Issues which so far surface in this chapter include the following: whether religious traditions are so hide-bound to the particular languages which determine their specific values, cultures and ethos, that they are incommensurable; whether meaningful dialogues between religious communities have not been all but scuttled as a consequence; whether Lindbeck's scheme is incorrigibly fideistic and relativistic; whether we are not all doomed to a pathetic sectarianism? Some of these issues must now be examined, and others postponed to the next chapter.

4.4 The Debate Over the Normativity of Experience

In the ecclesial-communal context, Tradition, with its Scripture, is indispensable for theology. We have thus far not raised the question of the legitimacy of an appeal to *experience* in the theological task. This question bears closely on the issue of the normative significance of experience in the interpretation of Scripture-in-Tradition.[122] It is a question which in any case cannot be avoided in present-day culture in which diverse experiences clamour for theological attention. It is certainly a question that needs to be addressed whenever one reflects on religions and dialogue, where the particular *experiential contexts* of the dialogue partners claim ever greater attention.

---

[121] See, for example, George Newlands who casts Ebeling in better light in *God in Christian Perspective* (Edinburgh: T & T Clark, 1994), 21-24.

[122] The encounter between the Scriptures and contemporary experience is an issue of supreme importance to theology and the life of the Church. See D. Senior, "Living Word or Dead(ly) Letter: A Response to Sandra Schneiders," *CTSAP* 47 (1992) 61.

Many questions press for attention when one attempts to reflect theologically on experience. The debate is significant for this study not simply because Lindbeck's project, as it stands, entails a strict denial of any determining role in theology for present-day experience. There is more. The issue of the appeal to experience constitutes one of the most obstinate and perennial problems for fundamental and systematic theology. In a significant way, an appeal to particular contextual experience defiantly underwrites some new and challenging theologies of the late twentieth century. Do new experiences have a role in religious change? Does increasing cultural pluralism provide an impetus for change? Our aim is not to undertake an adequate study of a very wide field. Rather, we must confine ourselves to a discussion of the correlational, or revisionist approach of the Chicago school of which Lindbeck is trenchantly critical, to see how the debate might inform our critical dialogue with Lindbeck and his postliberal project. We must begin with the basic question of what an experience is.

4.4.1 What Is an Experience?

Experience includes all that contributes to our perception of God, self and world. Experience takes place in our personal, socio-political, historical-cultural, intellectual-spiritual contexts. It includes what Rahner calls the "transcendental experience," where the human subject discovers an orientation towards holy mystery. There, one experiences one's essence as subject and as person.[123] At the other end of the spectrum, and rather different from the more

[123] Rahner describes transcendental experience as "the subjective, unthematic, necessary and unfailing consciousness of the knowing subject that is co-present in every spiritual act of knowledge, and the subject's openness to the unlimited expanse of all possible reality." See *Foundations of Christian Faith*, 20.

speculative philosophical aspects, experience encompasses the concrete *present-day* experiences that plead for recognition. In Roman
Catholicism, in conjunction with its call for attention to the "signs
of the times," the Second Vatican Council has sanctioned experience as an indispensable element for theological reflection.[124] Any
Church teaching that is unrelated to experience risks becoming arid
and "dogmatic" in a derogative sense. In this regard, Rahner's
insight is worth repeating, for he urges that we recognize God's
self-communication within the ordinary experience of ordinary
people so that any authentic experience of the self may be interpreted as an experience of God.[125] In *this* sense, ordinary human
experiences may be called *religious*. Although Scripture is a
medium for encountering the Divine, Scripture is not unique in that
respect. We also encounter God in other experiences.

Still, when we ask what might an experience consist of, John
Coleman is clearly on the mark in referring to experience as an
"elusive" and "evocative" term.[126] Although "preconceptually
the most evident," experience is regarded as "the most difficult
notion in philosophy."[127] As a concept, experience "defies linear

[124] See *Gaudium et Spes* 4 & 46, where the Council drew attention to "urgent
problems deeply affecting the human race at the present day in the light of the
Gospel and of human experience."

[125] Rahner, *Foundations of Christian Faith*, 126-33; "Reflections on the
Experience of Grace," in *Theological Investigations*, trs. K-H and B. Kruger
(London: Darton, Longman and Todd, 1975), 3:86-90. Rahner distinguishes the
ascending from the descending approaches in current Christologies. He also
stresses the validity of doing Christology by beginning with experiences and the
observation and reflection upon these, rather than beginning with dogmatic affirmations. See "The Two Basic Types of Christology," in *Theological Investigations*, trs. D. Bourke (New York: Seabury, 1975), 13:213-23.

[126] J. Coleman, "A Response to Ellen Leonard," *CTSAP* 43 (1988) 62.

[127] J. H. Walgrave, "Faith as a Fundamental Dimension of Religious Experience," in *Religious Experience, Its Unity and Diversity*, ed. Thomas Mampra
(Bangalore: Dharmaram Publications, 1981), 2.

definitions" and can mean a host of different things.[128] A closer examination of the characteristics of an experience may be useful before we take the discussion further.

Gerald O'Collins has undertaken a useful analysis of the notion of "human experience." Realising the complexity of that notion, O'Collins presents a scheme comprising three elements. *First*, there is the *human subject* for whom every experience has a dimension of "*immediacy.*" The subject "experiences" first-hand, for him or herself. There "cannot literally be second-hand experiences." Nor can there be a radical disjunction between experience and abstract reason: we cannot properly speak of "experiencing something which forms the conclusion of our rational argument." Further, there are both active (e.g. when we are "alive" to something) and passive (e.g. when we undergo something that happens *to* us) moments in an experience. Moreover, an experience has the potency to affect "*the entire existence*" of a human person, in the way it touches the imagination, the emotions, the senses, the mind, the will, the memory, and so forth. At the interpersonal level, it is legitimate to speak of the "*collective experience*" of a community where there is "experience not only *of* others but also *with* others."

Second, there is "*the experience itself.*" Every experience has a "*meaning*" and, at some point in time, makes sense for the human subject. When it does make sense, it carries a directional import, "a certain purposefulness," and even "finality." Experience cannot be described in ahistorical general terms: it is *concrete*. Furthermore, an experience, by its very nature, generates a sense of "*newness.*" It can be "*positive, negative, or seemingly ambiguous.*" Borrowing from the terminology of *Gaudium et Spes* 13, we could say that "the call to grandeur and the depths of misery" are both part of the human experience.

---

[128] A. C. Lammers, "The Complications of Experience," *ATR* 75 (1993) 15.

Thirdly, an experience has its aftermath or *consequences*. The question of *discernment* becomes important, that is, the interpretation of the experience through which the subsequent action of the subject and of the community is determined. What is it that is experienced? What criteria can we use to determine the authenticity of that experience? These and other questions call for *conscious interpretation*. As we asked in the last chapter in conjunction with fiduciary interests, what cultural, religious and sociological or, in short, contextual presuppositions are insidiously at work while we carry out interpretations? What specific criteria may legitimately be brought to bear as we carry out conscious, intellectual interpretations? These and other questions have important bearings on theological methodology. Further, when an experience is later 'narrated,' there is a "shift from the immediate and particular level of experience to the mediate and generalized level of language. The verbal account makes experiences and their meaning public." Finally, experiences leave behind memories.[129]

4.4.2 The Contested Status of Experience as a Source for Theology

John Macquarrie makes positive claims for the role of experience: "If anything can be said for the validity of religious statements, it must come from the discrimination and analysis of experience itself."[130] The question of a conscious articulation of

---

[129] For G. O'Collins' detailed analysis, see "Human Experience," in *Fundamental Theology* (London: Darton, Longman and Todd, 1981), 32-52. For another discussion, see D. Lane, *The Experience of God* (New York: Paulist, 1992), 10-21.

[130] J. Macquarrie, *The Scope of Demythologizing: Bultmann and His Critics* (London: SCM, 1960), 217. Presenting the traditional task of theology, Macquarrie has named six formative factors: experience, revelation, Scripture, Tradition, culture and reason. See idem, *Principles of Christian Theology* (New York: Scribner, 1966), 4.

theological methodologies incorporating experience is a relatively recent development.[131] The theological question has not been "*whether* experience is a basic source of theology but *how* we can accurately and critically use it."[132] Edward Schillebeeckx claims that experience may be used as one of "two sources" for contemporary theology: "On the one hand we have the whole tradition of the experience of the great Jewish-Christian movement, and on the other hand the contemporary, new experiences of both Christians and non-Christians."[133] In much the same way, Tracy identifies what he calls two 'constants' in contemporary theology, viz., "the present world of experience in all its ambivalence, contingency and change," and "the Judeo-Christian tradition which is ultimately based on the Christian message, the Gospel of Jesus Christ." He claims that whatever their particular theology may be, each theologian must *interpret* both these constants.[134] However, the claim that experience constitutes one inescapable pole of the theological project is, in the reality of the theological domain, exactly what it is, a claim. For, in reality, the legitimacy of that claim attracts a lively debate in contemporary theology. It is, as

[131] In "Experience as a Source of Theology," *CTSAP* 43 (1988) 44, E. Leonard claims that "experience has always functioned in theology although its function has not always been recognized." If G. P. Schner is right, it is somewhere in this century that the term *experience* makes its regular appearance in theological works and becomes an integral feature in methodological considerations. See idem, "The Appeal to Experience," *TS* 53 (1992) 40.

[132] See B. Cooke, "The Experiential 'Word of God'," in *Consensus in Theology?*, ed. L. Swidler (Philadelphia: Westminster, 1980), 72.

[133] E. Schillebeeckx, *Interim Report on the Books Jesus and Christ*, trs. J. Bowden (London: SCM, 1980), 3. Hans Küng prefers the term "two poles" rather than "two sources". See idem, "Toward a New Consensus in Catholic (and Ecumenical) Theology," in *Consensus in Theology?*, 1-17.

[134] See D. Tracy, "Hermeneutical Reflections in the New Paradigm," in *Paradigm Change in Theology*, ed. H. Küng and D. Tracy (Edinburgh: T & T Clark, 1989), 34-45.

Jeanrond correctly observes, a fundamental "problem of the starting-point of theological thinking."[135]

Tracy of Chicago is committed to a *correlational* strategy
which attempts to correlate Christian beliefs with common human
concerns and experiences, and to defend those convictions in the
public arena by publicly acceptable criteria. But, as Dulles rightly
observes: "It is much debated whether the methods and findings
of theology must be public in the sense of being accessible to persons outside the community of faith."[136] Today, that debate has
polarized into two so-called "schools" of thought. At one pole
stands the revisionist *correlational* approach of which Tracy is a
prominent advocate. At the opposite pole, we find the *intratextual*
approach to theology with which the scholars at Yale are closely
associated. Lindbeck is a clear representative of this latter
"school."

4.4.3 The Relationship between Experience and Language

Of signal importance amongst the issues to be examined is the
relationship, or the correct ordering, of experience and knowledge.

Three elements, in particular, will inform this discussion. *First*,
much of Lindbeck's criticism of Rahner's treatment of the transcendental experience of faith may be critically examined from the
angle of the ordering of religious language and faith experience.
The direction of causality is, for Lindbeck, incorrigibly mapped:
religious experience depends on the doctrinal language specific to
a communal context; doctrinal language never springs from an

---

[135] See W. Jeanrond, "The Problem of the Starting-Point of Theological
Thinking," in *The Possibilities of Theology*, ed. John Webster (Edinburgh: T &
T Clark, 1994), 70-89.
[136] A. Dulles, "Theology for a Post-Critical Age," in *Theology Toward the
Third Millenium*, ed. D.G. Schultenover (Lewiston: Edwin Mellon, 1991), 18.

implicit, or as yet unfocused, unthematised religious experience. Although he includes a group of major theological figures for a common criticism, a group which includes Schleiermacher, Otto and Eliade, Lindbeck's prime targets are the transcendental Thomists, notably Rahner and Lonergan. Whatever may be the variations in articulations, Lindbeck pronounces, these thinkers "all locate ultimately significant contact with whatever is finally important to religion in the prereflective experiential depths of the self and regard the public or outer features of religion as expressive and evocative objectifications (i.e., nondiscursive symbols) of internal experience."[137] On this score, Lindbeck accuses Rahner of confusing the proper ordering of the inner and the outer. The entire picture seems "more than doubtful" to Lindbeck when a private, inner experience is posited as the origin and starting point for an expression that has to assume a public and intersubjective form. The experiential-expressivists, in deriving the "external features of a religion from inner experience," have, according to Lindbeck, culpably overlooked the reality that it is the inner experiences that are derivative.[138] In positing a linear causality, Lindbeck is claiming for his cultural-linguistic model of religion a coherence with his intratextual theology which insists that it is the text that absorbs the world of experiences and not the other way around. In other words, experiences are derivative from the particular language of religion, which functions primarily neither as propositional truth, nor as expression of inner experience, but "in the story it tells and in the grammar that informs the way the story is told and used."[139] In questioning whether this criticism of Rahner is accurate, our aim here is to draw out the implications on the relationship between language and experience.

[137] ND, 21.
[138] ND, 39
[139] ND, 80.

Doctrines, or dogmatic statements, in Rahner's understanding, are indeed linguistic symbols of what God reveals and of what the Church experiences of God. However, to suggest, as Lindbeck does, that Rahner regards dogmatic statements as the symbols of the Church's reception of the truth communicated in Christ, is to seriously misrepresent Rahner. As a confession of faith, a dogmatic statement is for Rahner never merely a verbal "evocative objectification" of the content of faith, but actualizes both the revealed content of faith as well as the Church's act of faith.[140] Crowley rightly exposes Lindbeck's error in suggesting that Rahner regards the relationship between language and experience as simply a correlation between the outward expression of some inner event and the inner event itself. Capturing an essential dialectical relationship, Crowley observes: "Although dogmatic statements function as one specification of the linguisticality of the transcendental experience of faith, the experience always exceeds the verbal expression. At the same time, the verbal expression informs the experience."[141] Of great significance is the distinction between, and the ordering of, the knowledge of faith and its articulation. The truth of faith is known *before* it becomes the explicit object of intellectual articulation. However, this does not mean there is a pre-reflexive experience, or unthematic knowledge, that is wholly independent of its reflexive articulation in faith consciousness. While, therefore, the articulation is carried out in full knowledge of that which is being articulated, the articulation is an exercise essential to the knowledge itself. Further, insofar as we speak of an act of faith, we cannot regard the act as having been finalised upon the completion of the articulation of faith. Rather, in Aquinas' scheme of things, the act of faith tends

---

[140] See Rahner, "What Is a Dogmatic Statement?" in *Theological Investigations*, trs. K-H Kruger (Baltimore: Helicon, 1966)), 5:48-51.

[141] Crowley, *In Ten Thousand Places*, 87.

towards the source and goal of the knowledge of faith, which is
the divine mystery revealed in Jesus Christ.[142]

Second, Crowley threads together a few major theologians to
draw out a few points germane to our discussion. He flushes out
some interesting points of agreement and disagreement between
Lindbeck and Lash. On the one hand, Lash and Lindbeck are in
basic agreement insofar as both display an unease with the suggestion that "the essence of personal religion [is] to be sought in
abstraction from all considerations of structure, narrative, history
and social relations."[143] Nothing is more offensive than the idola-
trous and variegated "forms of the illusion that the nature of God
lies within our grasp."[144] Resonating with Lindbeck's cultural-linguistic understanding, Lash suggests that "the concept of the
Christian doctrine of God be taken to refer to the declaration, by
the Christian community, of identity-sustaining rules of discourse
and behaviour governing Christian uses of the word 'God'."[145] On
the other hand, Lash keeps clear of the inner-outer dichotomy for
ordering experience and language that is so central to Lindbeck.
Against Lindbeck, Lash affirms Rahner's rejection of the idea that
the doctrinal elements of Christian faith are merely the result of a
subsequent reflection on the transcendental salvific relationship of
humans to God. "Religious experience" is all too often erroneously distinguished from the common phenomenon of conscious experience whereas, for Lash, religious experience is, like
all experience, essentially "hermeneutical."[146]

Third, and following from this, Crowley flushes out some
thoughts on the hermeneutical aspect of experience which is at

---

[142] For this rendering of Aquinas's scheme, see Crowley, *In Ten Thousand Places*, 88.

[143] Nicholas Lash, *Easter in Ordinary* (London: SCM, 1988), 61.

[144] Lash, *Easter in Ordinary*, 261.

[145] Lash, *Easter in Ordinary*, 260.

[146] Crowley, *In Ten Thousand Places*, 104-05

once relevant to our discussion. To start with, resonating with our discussions in the last chapter, Crowley locates the relationship between religious experience and religious language right in the *dialectic of interpretation*. Participation in the life of the community constitutes the key here, for the dialectic of interpretation begins with one's "participation in the totality of a religious tradition, not only in particular experiences labelled religious."[147] Lindbeck has acutely pressed the point that any kind of common life and community wisdom — in our present discussion, positive faith professions — have basic characteristics in common with languages: they must, and can, be learned, and understood, and the process of learning is best envisioned as participation within a communal way of life. God cannot be known, as Lash explains, through "gazing" at various representations, be they pictorial, narrative, abstract, or otherwise, but by *participation* in what Hegel calls the historical movement of "utterance and love" that seeks to represent the eternal essence of God. It is only when we accept the claim that the dialectic of interpretation properly begins with participation in the Church's communal life that we can accept Lash's enigmatic assertion: "And it is this participation which constitutes the reality of human life and history, a reality which achieves representational expression in Christian symbolism."[148] It makes no sense to speak about the life of faith unless we stand within the tradition that transmits that faith. Lash is keen to hold in healthy tension the complexity of "Christian experience" as

[147] Crowley, *In Ten Thousand Places*, 105.

[148] Lash, *Easter in Ordinary*, 111. Lash's work has been described by Van Beeck as the most sustained recent argument to illumine the central Judeo-Christian thesis that "God is to be found in the world and beyond it, but never apart from it, and that the world cannot be understood apart from God." Lash succeeds brilliantly in unmasking the critical weakness in William James' theological anthropology where "religious experience" is a totally separate, privileged, inner event. See Van Beeck, *God Encountered*, II/1:159.

"lived, refracted, and interpreted in faith." Bringing experience to speech is by no means an easy task. There is, on the one hand, the call for a critical alertness to *a sense of limit* to all talk of experience that Lash ascribes to Jean-Pierre Jossua. On the other hand, there is the "naïveté" of Baron Friedrich von Hügel's use of the language of affirmation. Von Hügel is apparently inspired by his conviction of the "prevenient, accompanying and subsequent power and help of God" upon which every one of our acts depends. The "dauntingly difficult" interpretive task of bringing the effect of experience into speech, Lash suggests, "requires the reworking into fresh, accurate, and accessible language of stories and symbols that have – through use, misuse, and dislocation from the common conversation of the culture – become, in fact (for Christians and non-Christians alike) an obstacle to that hearing and proclamation of the Gospel of which they remain, nevertheless, the indispensable medium."[149]

The term "hermeneutical," in Lash's usage, would then imply a "mutually critical correlation" in the interpretation of experiences. Whatever accounts we give, whatever interpretations we render, would redound to the internal constitution of that experience, and hence make a difference to the experience itself.

Properly understood, none of the authors Lindbeck criticizes as espousing the experiential-expressive model is claiming that members of all the world religions have the same religious experience, as he crudely suggests. In specific reference to the relationship between experience and language, many of these key thinkers subscribe to the notion of *mutual conditioning* – a necessary

---

[149] Lash, *Easter in Ordinary*, 174-75. Lash suggests that Joshua's definition of experience as "lived, refracted, and interpreted in faith" summarizes Hügel's account of the dialectical interplay of "forces and elements woven from a vast array of information from ancient philosophy, from the history of the Christian Church, and from modern thought."

corrective notion to Lindbeck's radically one-directional causality. Lash, for instance, correctly perceives this underlying commonality in the understanding of Schillebeeckx and Rahner. Schillebeeckx posits a reciprocal relationship between experience (i.e., "the ability to assimilate perceptions") and the "already given framework of interpretation." Significantly, Schillebeeckx suggests in this schema that the given framework of interpretation is also "exposed to criticism and corrected, changed or renewed by new experiences." The difference with Lindbeck on this point is acute, for Lindbeck absolutely denies any hermeneutical role for novel experiences. But, a parallel with Rahner is evident. For Schillebeeckx: "We experience in the act of interpreting, without being able to draw a neat distinction between the element of experience and the element of interpretation."[150] In the case of Rahner, revelation is the "answer" to the "question" that a human being is. Far from postulating the transcendental level as the privileged locus where revelation first occurs as some mysterious process, and later receives its objectification in human speech, as Lindbeck accuses Rahner of suggesting, Rahner understands revelation as the name for that experience where the human subject receives an answer to the question arising from the depth of one's being, and where this "answer" finds its elucidation within the languages of diverse cultures and histories. These languages are, in turn, shaped by the answer itself. Lacking a genuine dialectical scheme like this, Lindbeck uses Ockham's Razor too hastily, and ends up with a "crew-cut," a neater and vastly more manageable scheme of one-directional absorption of all experiences into religious language. William of Ockham argued that, all things being equal, the simpler explanation is preferable to the more complex. But "all things" are anything but equal with regard to the complex reality

---

[150] E. Schillebeeckx, *Christ: The Christian Experience in the Modern World*, trs. John Bowden (London: SCM, 1980), 31-33.

of religion and experience. A premature use of the Razor only offers a scheme of understanding that impoverishes the living Tradition and the dialectical nature of truth-disclosure and human understanding.

This discussion again recalls our first chapter where we drew on the hermeneutical insights of Gadamer, in which the essence of human beings is defined in terms of an ongoing process of language formulation and interpretation. The "linguisticality of being" acts as the central motif and condition for the possibility of the transmission of tradition: "Language is the fundamental mode of operation of our being-in-the-world and the all embracing form of the constitution of the world."[151] Gadamer's characterisation of language as both speculative and dialectical yields an understanding of human experience that is inevitably hermeneutical. The progressive nature of human understanding is best described as a spiral movement.

4.4.4 The Need for a Methodological Shift?

"Christians are commanded," Lindbeck exhorts, "to bring all thoughts into captivity to Christ."[152] This is scripturally and religiously sound, and hence warrants acceptance by members of every Church denomination. But this sound exhortation must not be confused with Lindbeck's intratextual theology or the cultural-linguistic theory which functions to shore up his intratextual claims. The one may not be identical with the other. Lindbeck argues for the immense possibilities of his intratextual approach in the current postmodern climate. And yet, while many authors

---

[151] Gadamer, "On the Universality of the Hermeneutical Problem," in *Philosophical Hermeneutics*, trs. D. E. Linge (Berkeley: University of California Press, 1976), 4. See also *Truth and Method*, 395-405.

[152] Lindbeck, "Barth and Textuality," *ThT* 43 (1986) 369.

agree with Lindbeck's observation that the modern era is passing away, they are, according to Williamson, also uneasy with "his general tendency to distort the tension that does and should exist between 'Christ and culture.'"[153] For a theologian who stresses contextuality, Lindbeck is surprising in his palpable neglect of the contextual and the historical dimensions of the human condition. The vicissitudes of complex human existence do not seem to get an adequate hearing. More precisely put, his cultural-linguistic intratextual theology *a priori* disqualifies present experience as a source. For Lindbeck, religion makes experience possible, and not the other way around. So Jeanrond can conclude that, for Lindbeck, "experience is no longer the first source of religious insight, but rather experience is always already based upon a certain religious praxis."[154] To be sure, this is not attributable to any lack of an acute awareness of the need to adequately tackle the urgent voices of the marginalised. For, in an article in 1986, Lindbeck sounds the clarion call: Postliberal theology must "at all costs" avoid leaving the concern for the victims of oppression to extra-textualists.[155] But it is uncertain how he could avoid that under his scheme, in which newness in present experience is totally subservient to the biblical world? Again, Williamson is on the mark in his observation that "Christian faith requires 'Christ and culture' positioned in dynamic interaction if human beings and churches and societies are to exist — let alone be transformed."[156] If he is to accommodate the experience of the oppressed and the marginalised, Lindbeck would seem to require a methodological

[153] See J. C. Williamson, "Challenging Lindbeck," *Ch&Cr* 50 (1990) 299-301.

[154] Jeanrond, "The Problem of the Starting Point of Theological Thinking," 74.

[155] Lindbeck, "Barth and Textuality," *ThT* 43 (1986) 367.

[156] See Williamson, "Challenging Lindbeck," 299-301.

shift or, at the least, a tempering of some of the more radical
aspects of his methodology.

4.4.4.1 A Role for Ideological Critique

Lindbeck does not specifically discuss how exactly particular
theologies born of deep-seated human experiences, such as liberation theology, feminist theology, or black theology, can be neatly
absorbed into the biblical world. He allows for no dialectical play
where the text, and novel experiences, engage each other in a critical tension, informing each other, and thereby enriching each
other. In her 1982 Père Marquette Theology Lecture, Monika
Hellwig argues for a place in the sun, so to speak, for "present and
unique" experiences. Unless the Christian community is prepared
to validate theological reflections that are grounded, *in the first
place*, in present experience, many deeply Christian forms of particular theologies that stem from present and unique experience
will *never* be officially legitimated. These particular theologies are
identified by Hellwig as the political theology of J. B. Metz, the
liberation theology of the Third World, black and other ethnic theologies, feminist theology, claims for the hermeneutic privilege of
the poor and the oppressed, and claims by the heavily present-
experience-oriented social action groups.[157] Hellwig observes a
"real revolution in Christian theology." Hitherto, the theological
task involved a retrieval of data from the past for purposes of formulating doctrines suitable for communication to the present. Theology, in this mould, proceeds from Tradition to a communication
in present categories. While she acknowledges that such a movement from past to present is "*an* inevitable task of a theology that

---

[157] M. Hellwig, *Whose Experience Counts in Theological Reflection?* (Milwaukee: Marquette University Press, 1982), 6-7.

claims to be Christian (as it would be indeed of a theology that claimed to be Jewish or Muslim)," Hellwig doubts if this approach to theology is *the* only valid, or even ought to be the central, method. For while experience is honoured in such a scheme, it is the experience of the past and not of the present. The shift in approach that she identifies consists in a "contrapuntal perception of theology — simultaneous processes of ascending and descending theologies that need to be combined in such a way that one does not simply subsume and dominate the other." Within that shift, she finds a movement that claims equal recognition with the old approach. This movement proceeds "from present experience to reflection and evaluation first in existential terms and then by correlation with the tradition and its established formulations."[158]

Religions are *living* traditions, and not simply philosophical systems embalmed in fossilised texts. When Macquarrie, for example, refers to the proliferation of the different theologies just described, he does so in light of the challenge of ideology. For centuries, he notices, Christian theology was the sole preserve of European, and later North American, middle-class or upper-class white males, steeped in the traditions of Western classical learning. This lengthy dominance of theology by one particular segment of society cannot but have harmed theology in two respects: the infiltration into theology of particular ideas and values extraneous to Christianity itself; and the (largely unconscious) suppression of other elements which are proper to the Christian message. In any case, the theological world today is witnessing a crisis, as hitherto silent and inarticulate groups are demanding their right to be heard in shaping the theological outlook of the faith community. In addition to the theologies listed by Hellwig, Macquarrie

[158] Hellwig, *Whose Experience Counts*, 5-9.

mentions indigenous theology expressed in the images and concepts native to India, China, Africa and the Caribbean. Plurality does not bother Macquarrie in the least, for there cannot ever be "one all-embracing theology, expressing in proper proportion all the truths of Christian faith." Neither does he rejoice in sheer pluralistic fragmentation, however. Rather, his concern is to point out that value-free theology is a chimera, and that, instead of seeking to harmonise the different strands into one all-encompassing statement, theology would profit from the mutual correction and enrichment of diverse strands that spring from unique and present experience.[159]

Today, arguably the most disturbing issue raised by the encounter between Scriptures and contemporary experience is the role of the Bible in legitimating the discrimination against women in family, society and Church. The seriousness of the problem is argued on two counts: *first*, half of the Christian community is adversely affected by the anti-woman bias of the text; *second*, the androcentric and patriarchal bias pervades the entire Scriptures and not just selected writings.[160] Much has been written on feminist ideology criticism, creating a veritable new horizon in hermeneutics where almost every major issue in hermeneutical theory is canvassed.[161] Lindbeck, who advocates a Word-to-world

---

[159] See John Macquarrie, *Theology, Church and MInistry* (London: SCM, 1986), 16-19. For an example of Asian indigenous theology, see Aloysius Pieris, *An Asian Theology of Liberation* (Edinburgh: T & T Clark, 1988); *Love Meets Wisdom* (Maryknoll, NY: Orbis, 1988). For an analysis of liberation and black theologies, see Thiselton, *New Horizons in Hermeneutics* (Grand Rapids: Zondervan, 1992), 410-27.

[160] Sandra Schneiders, "Living Word or Dead(ly) Letters: The Encounter between the New Testament and Contemporary Experience," *CTSAP* 47 (1992) 57.

[161] For an instructive exposition and bibliography, see Thiselton, *New Horizon in Hermeneutics*, 430-62.

absorption of contemporary experience, ignores ideological problems.[162] In sharp contrast, feminist writers espouse a deep
hermeneutic of suspicion aimed at exposing the fallacy in the presupposition that conventional constructions of God's message to
humanity, as embodied in biblical texts, represent *value-neutral*
descriptions of biblical history, traditions and texts. All past interpretations, so the feminists argue, have been fatally tainted on
account of their mediation through Christian traditions that were
generated by male-dominated reading communities. Objected to
are the transpositions of these traditions into instruments of power,
domination, and social control. Feminist writers may approach the
problem at a variety of hermeneutical levels, but they share a common and deep instinct for emancipation from suffocating "norms"
and thus seek a critical hermeneutical principle that will effectively unmask the social-functional, male-legitimating, cultural-
linguistic reading tradition.

Elizabeth Schüssler Fiorenza argues that feminist hermeneutics
is a liberation hermeneutics, and attacks "the dogma of value-neutral detached interpretation."[163] It is difficult to visualise how
Lindbeck's narrative-reading based on intratextual terms can
escape the conceptual critique of the feminist socio-critical
hermeneutics advanced by Rosemary Radford Ruether: "The
androcentric bias of the male interpreters of the tradition, who
regard maleness as normative humanity, not only erase women's
presence in the past history of the community, but silence even the
questions about their absence. *One is not even able to remark*

---

[162] Wiles, wary of reading regulations in Lindbeck's rules of engagement
with the text, asserts that "the grammatical rules for reading the Christian story
(as Lindbeck regards them) have served the cause of institutional control at least
as much as the cause of religious truth." See Wiles, "Scriptural Authority," 51.

[163] E. Schüssler Fiorenza, *In Memory of Her* (New York: Crossroad, 1983), 5,
6, 16. See further, Sandra Schneiders, "Feminist Ideology Criticism and Biblical
Hermeneutics," *BTB* 19 (1989) 3-10.

upon or notice women's absence, since women's silence and absence is the norm."[164] The acute relevance to our discussion is that the ideological critique of feminist hermeneutics is defined by Ruether as "the appeal to *women's experience*. It is precisely women's experience that has been shut out of hermeneutics ... Women's experience explodes as a critical force, exposing classical theology, including its foundational tradition in scripture, as shaped by male experience rather than human experience."[165]

Paradoxically, the respect for particularities in Lindbeck's cultural-linguistic paradigm is undercut by his intratextual insistence since, inherent therein, is a universalising dimension that is objectionable to feminist hermeneutics. In the words of Isasi-Díaz, "the locus and source of women's liberation theologies" reside in women's experiences, not in the patriarchal culture and language of the Scripture texts, nor in the androcentric traditions of interpretation of these texts. Feminist theologies appeal to the "experiences of particular women whose very existence is constantly thwarted and endangered," not to the standard communal experiences encoded in Holy Writ which are socially-located, power-connected, value-defined and interest-laden.[166] To appeal to the latter is to subscribe to a patriarchal hermeneutics whose perceptions are grounded in the ideological assurance of "reality" or "the way things are" or what we have earlier described as the "status quo." Feminist hermeneutics would consciously ground its perception in the actual experience of women's oppression: "It is only those whose very being (e.g., black, female, Native American) prevents them from fully participating in the dominant

---

[164] R. R Ruether, "Feminist Interpretation: A Method of Correlation," In *The Liberating Word*, ed. L. M. Russell (Philadelphia: Westminster, 1976), 113.

[165] Ruether, "Feminist Interpretation," 112-13.

[166] See A. M. Isasi-Díaz, ""Experiences," in *Dictionary of Feminist Theology*, ed. L. M. Russell et al. (London: Mowbray, 1996), 95-96.

cultural structure regardless of ability or achievement who experience the *aporia* of life and who consequently understand 'reality' to be ideologically formulated."[167] It is thus the sort of disjunctive and anomalous experience of women, rather than the androcentric culture and language in which they find themselves, that impel them to deviate from the male norm. And it is this particular experience that constitutes the bedrock on which feminist hermeneutic is built.

Contemporary experience thus constantly challenges both the relevance and authority of the Bible for believing Christians. Schneiders advances a thesis that provides a hermeneutical framework comprising resources which would preserve both the integrity of contemporary experience and the biblical text as revelatory. These resources are: [1] Gadamer's notion of "effective history" which avoids a positivistic understanding of history as independent, fixed events of the past, but as events influencing and being influenced by the present; [2] Ricoeur's theory of text and interpretation which allows a distanciation from the original author's "restricted intentional horizon," the original socio-historical context, and the original ostensible reference. Thus, the text is freed for multiple meanings, ruled only by the linguistic structures of the text and the engagement of the contemporary reader; [3] Feminist ideology criticism which suggests that the "ultimately serious question" is what it means to be a woman and a Christian of today. Schneiders' scheme includes all of the biblical text, not just selected parts of it, as revelatory, so as to facilitate a "life-giving interaction between Scripture and ongoing Christian experience." She rejects the image of the Bible as a "definitively fixed propositional revelation or as a blueprint for contemporary Church

---

[167] M. A. Tolbert, "Defining the Problem: The Bible and Feminist Hermeneutics," *Semeia* 28 (1983) 119-20.

life." When the meaning of the Bible is seen as emerging in the "interpretive engagement by the reader within the horizon of contemporary experience," then Christians are called to "wrestle incessantly" with the text until it blesses them with "liberating truth."[168] In his response to Schneiders' proposal, Donald Senior acknowledges the penetrating challenge posed by contemporary feminist experience. However, for an adequate and comprehensive hermeneutical framework that enables the Christian to hold in balance the integrity of contemporary experience as well as the authority of the Bible, Senior proposes two resources in addition to Schneiders' renewed sense of history and a recognition of the potential for multiple meanings: [1] A rigorous historical-critical methodology aided by the contemporary insights into the historical context constituted by the cultural, social and economic systems of the New Testament times. This method is useful to prevent us from straying too far from the historical events and personages of the original context and their impact on the original author as well as on the literary structure of the text. Senior argues that the range of meanings prompted by contemporary experience should be brought into a *dialectic* with the range of meanings that are socio-culturally bound to the original historical contexts in which the texts were composed; [2] A moderating role in the wisdom of the faith community and its tradition. Here, Senior is not suggesting that we adhere to a fixed layer of Christian tradition. Rather, he envisages every reading of the biblical text ultimately having to meet the test of "the collective wisdom of the Christian community as a whole and over time." While he is optimistic about the capacity of the community, within the deepest currents of its life and thought, to provide the crucial check and control on what constitutes a legitimate interpretation of Scripture, he also

---

[168] Schneiders, "Living Word or Dead(ly) Letter," 45-60.

claims that this wisdom ultimately comes from "the life of the Spirit within the community and the full span of the Christian tradition."[169]

An appeal to experience in theology essentially claims that revelation is located in experience. And yet, such a claim is problematic, not least because it is "notoriously difficult to clarify."[170] Despite the problems, one crucial insight that feminist criticism has surfaced is to cast doubt on the implicit suggestion by Lindbeck that the biblical narrative is really a panacea. As Lauritzen would put it, the issue of how to judge the truthfulness of a story demands that we ask not only, "which narrative?" but also "which interpretation?"[171] According to Rebecca Chopp, feminist theology differs from Lindbeck's theological model on two counts. *First*, feminist theology objects to Lindbeck's stress on the task of theology as a "redescription" of the internal logic of the Christian faith. This objection is based on the claim by feminist theology that the faith has already been corrupted by patriarchal interpretations. There is a need for transformation away from patriarchal distortions, rather than simply to describe a patriarchal tradition. *Second*, feminist theology agrees with the cultural-linguistic model that "Christianity involves certain symbolic patterns as a kind of grammar or logic of the faith." The two models share the understanding that the symbols of Christian faith provide the continuity for the inner life of the faith-community and for its life in the world. But their differences are immense. At issue, in particular, is how Christians construe the grammar of faith. The

[169] See D. Senior, "A Response to Sandra Schneiders," *CTSAP* 47 (1992) 61-68.

[170] M. C. Hilkert, "Experience and Tradition – Can the Center Hold?" in *Freeing Theology: The Essentials of Theology in Feminist Perspective*, ed. C. M. LaCugna (New York: HarperSanFrancisco, 1993), 77.

[171] See P. Lauritzen, "Is Narrative Really a Panacea?" 336-39.

cultural-linguists presuppose "a unified textual narrative that provides a kind of timeless grammar of faith." In contrast, the feminists construct the grammar, or the symbolic logic of the Christian faith, in terms of "emancipatory praxis."[172] On this score, Lindbeck's insistence on locking out contemporary experience is objectionable. On the other hand, Lindbeck is clearly right in his basic intuition that the truthfulness of the Christian message cannot be dependent on individual experiences in the way modern liberal society insists on personal freedom of choice. As Outler has argued, "The interpreter cannot be the sole judge of what is edifying in the remarkable miscellany in the Bible."[173] The collective sense of the faith community and the full span of the Christian tradition ought to be brought to bear in determining the true meaning of Scripture texts.

In sum, present experience constitutes a category which

[172] Rebecca S. Chopp, *Saving Work: Feminist Practices of Theological Education* (Louisville: Westminster John Knox, 1995), 82-83. Mary M. Fulkerson, too, sees Lindbeck's postliberal theology as failing to "allow assessment of the ideological and occluded discourses in Christian communal life and sedimented traditions, which is necessary to a feminist theological interpretation of scripture." See idem, "'Is There a (Non-Sexist) Bible in This Church?'," *ModTh* 14 (1998) 230. Linell Cady uses Lindbeck's typology to unravel some of the complexities and limitations in feminist appeals to experience. See idem, "Theories of Religion in Feminist Theologies," *AJTP* 13 (1992) 183-93. There is, to be sure, a need to be conscious of the tension in much of current feminist theologies between their acknowledgment of the historical situatedness of all human knowledge and their appeals to women's experience as a kind of Archimedian point from which to judge the Christian faith. See Sheila G. Davaney, "Problems with Feminist Theory," in *Embodied Love*, ed. Paula M. Cooey et al. (New York: Harper, 1987), 79-95. On the possibility of developing Lindbeck's cultural-linguistic approach that avoids reading it narrowly and applying it to feminist theology, see Amy P. Pauw, "The Word Is Near You, A Feminist Conversation with Lindbeck," *ThT* 50 (1993) 45-55.

[173] A. C. Outler, "Toward a Postliberal Hermeneutics," *ThT* 42 (1985-86) 286.

theology — and, *a fortiori*, a context-specific cultural-linguistic approach to theology — must seriously take account of. The questions that arise are the methodological questions of *how* experience may be assessed to be authentic, and how authentic experience may be integrated into the theological enterprise to guide our progressive understanding of truth. We turn to examine Tracy's sustained methodological approach, one that seems diametrically opposed to Lindbeck's, and to draw some insights from it.

4.4.4.2 The Need for a Mutually Critical Correlation

Inspired by the desire to clarify the postmodern experience of radical religious and ideological plurality and relativity, Tracy has reworked the correlational approach of Paul Tillich, and turned hermeneutical method into a new paradigm for explicating the integrity and normative claims of Christian faith. This paradigm, he says, is "the attempt to establish mutually critical correlations between an interpretation of the Christian tradition and an interpretation of contemporary experience."[174] Tracy thus operates on two assumed constants: on the one hand, "the present world of experience and all its ambivalence, contingency and change" and, on the other, "the Judaeo-Christian tradition which is ultimately based on the Christian message, the Gospel of Jesus."[175] Clearly, this approach aids our case for the inclusion of contemporary experience to inform theological reflections. The question is how might it be envisaged as appropriate for the interpretation of Christian Tradition.

Most religions, John Haught suggests, may be regarded as responses to the revelatory disclosure of sacred mystery. Although Christianity is founded on a distinctive revelation, it is linked to a common human search for meaning and mystery that dates back

---

[174] Tracy, "Hermeneutical Reflections in the New Paradigm," 35.
[175] Tracy, "Hermeneutical Reflections in the New Paradigm," 35.

to time immemorial. Before the Christ-event, humanity was in search of God. Christians understand that with the coming of Jesus Christ, God has come in search of humanity.[176] There is a continuity from common human search for meaning to Christian revelation which suggests that we cannot exclude from our considerations the broader religious and social contexts that saw the historical genesis of Christianity. The uniqueness of the Christian revelation can only be appreciated in relation to the wider religious and secular culture of which it forms a part.

Christian theology is a conversation between our situation and the revelatory sources. Theologians, however, disagree on what constitute the sources and on how a proper conversation ought to proceed. The postliberals virtually restrict the revelatory sources to the written Scripture, and reduce the conversation to a monologue. Others view these sources as primarily the Bible, but they also include the deposit of interpretations of revelation known as tradition, and suggest a critical conversation between the contemporary situation and those classic texts, persons, symbols, and events in which the divine promise is perceived to be embodied. By "critical" is meant the need to guard against carelessly formulated interrogations to which the classic sources may be subject, lest we miss the real substance of the sources altogether. Further, a critical theology maintains a genuine openness to the sources so as to be challenged by their "otherness." A method of conversation dominant in contemporary theology is the correlational method.[177] Although there are obvious variations in actual details

[176] See Pope John Paul II, *Tertio Millennio Adveniente*, *Origins* 24:25 (1994) 402-16.

[177] See F. S. Fiorenza, *Foundational Theology*, 276-84, and "Systematic Theology: Task and Methods," in *Systematic Theology*, I:55-61. He identifies an impressive list of practitioners of this method that includes M. Blondel, P. Tillich, K. Rahner, P. Hodgson, S. Ogden, D. Tracy, E, Schillebeeckx, L. Gilkey, and H. Küng. B. Lonergan can be added.

amongst different theologians, the method of correlation having been incorporated into phenomenological, existential, and transcendental interpretations, there are basically two distinct steps involved. The first step entails a critical analysis (transcendental, existential, or phenomenological) of the religious dimension of human experience; the second is to attempt to correlate this experience with Christian revelation.

Christian theologians, whatever be their particular shade of correlational theology, must concede that the formal understanding of the situation in which we find ourselves has, to some degree at least, been shaped by a history and tradition that emerged from the classic texts and events associated with the biblical revelation. In this regard, Lindbeck's arguments on the conditioning power of culture and language are perceptive. The biblical world and doctrinal tradition have impacted on the culture and language of the West for so long that hardly any body conducting reflections on mystery, nature, history and self within the Christian world can claim to be wholly innocent of the interpretations embodied in the biblical stories. The correlational approach hence is destined to be somewhat circular. And yet, in all serious reflections, such a gaping hole of unintelligibility constantly plagues our understanding of both the present situation and the depth of God's self-disclosure that conducting critical conversations anew between experience and traditional sources remains a constant challenge. In this light, a method of correlation between experience and the sources of revelation seems to be a potentially fruitful approach for the theological task. Any theology that strives to be relevant to the contemporary situation, it has been claimed, must practice some form or other of the method of correlation, whether it is aware of it or not.[178]

---

[178] Haught, *Mystery and Promise*, 21.

In essence, Tracy's revisionist theological method presupposes two sources for theology, common human experience and language, and the Christian Tradition, primarily in texts. The first source may be investigated by a *hermeneutical* phenomenology of the religious dimension in all human experience, while the second source may be investigated by historical and hermeneutical methods; the results of these investigations are to be correlated to determine their similarities and differences, and their truth value is to be further determined by an explicitly *transcendental* or metaphysical reflection.[179] It is, for Tracy, not a question of the capitulation of traditional religious beliefs to contemporary secular beliefs. What he, and others like him, are suggesting as an indispensable task of theology is the *"mutually critical* correlations of an interpretation of the meaning and truth of the tradition and the interpretation of the meaning and truth of the contemporary situation."[180] How does this method, which operates as a *heuristic guide* for the enquiry into concrete issues, further our discussion of Lindbeck's programme?

First, Tracy's "revisionist" enquiry renders itself closely relevant to any attempt that seeks to grapple and converse with the vexing pluralism of today. For it is an enquiry that seeks to confront, mutually illuminate, correct and conciliate between "the principal values, cognitive claims, and existential faiths of both a reinterpreted post-modern consciousness and a reinterpreted Christianity."[181] Short-range "relevance," we have been told, is

---

[179] Tracy, *Blessed Rage,* 53. In order to correlate and ultimately to validate the interpretations one gives to the two sources, Tracy lays down three criteria: (1) meaningfulness as disclosive of our actual experience, as speaking in powerful symbols to our existential situation; (2) meaning-as-internal-coherence which can be expected of any cognitive claims; and (3) truth as when critical analysis shows its "adequacy to experience." See *Blessed Rage,* ch. 4.

[180] Tracy, "Lindbeck's New Program for Theology," 468-70.

[181] *Blessed Rage,* 32. First introduced by Tracy, the term "revisionist" means the necessity of "revisioning" all the central claims of Christian faith in light of

precisely what Lindbeck rejects as a flawed strategy of accommodation to the secular culture. But it would be an utter misunderstanding to accuse Tracy (along with Gilkey and Ogden) of reducing Christianity to the modern secular spirit, when, as Sanks points out, the whole burden of Tracy's *Blessed Rage for Order* is to argue that "a purely secularist interpretation of our common human experience" is inadequate.[182] Nor, clearly, is Tracy denying the transcendent element, the reclamation of which was the declared intention of the controversial Hartford Appeal.[183] Rather, the key to the correlational method is to accord present experience special attention in an attempt to address the question of the relationship of traditional Christian claims to the vicissitudes and perspectives of contemporary life and culture. In this approach, there are two clear sources of information for theological reflection: the basic values and faith tenets that reside in the authentic Christian Tradition, and the values and belief systems of the secular

the critical questions raised by the contemporary world. The theologian must face the dilemma of dual commitments: to faith in the God of Jesus Christ, and to the fundamental ethical commitment of the theologian qua theologian to the "community of scientific enquiry." See *Blessed Rage*, 7. Revisioning is targeted towards releasing anew the potentiality of these claims for redemptive transformation. See P.C. Hodgson, *Winds of the Spirit* (London: SCM, 1994), 16.

[182] T. H. Sanks, "David Tracy's Theological Project," *TS* 54 (1993) 711. For the accusations, see P. Berger, "Secular Theology and the Rejection of the Supernatural," *TS* 38 (1977) 39-56; A. Dulles, "Method in Fundamental Theology," *TS* 37 (1976) 304-316; *The Resilient Church* (New York: Doubleday, 1977), ch. 4. For the rebuttals, see L. Gilkey, "Anathemas and Orthodoxy," *ChCent* 94 (1977) 1026-29; M. E. Marty et al., "We Still Have Some Unresolved Theological Differences," *NCR* 14 (1977) 9-10, 15-16; L. Gilkey et al., "Responses to Peter Berger," *TS* 39 (1978) 486-507; P. Lakeland, "Accommodation to Secularity," *The Month* 239 (1978) 162-66; J. Nash, "Tracy's Revisionist Project," *AmBenR* 34 (1983) 240-67.

[183] At which Berger, Dulles and Lindbeck were signers, but Tracy and Ogden were not. For a historical account of the controversial event, see Lindbeck, "A Battle for Theology," in *Against the World for the World*, ed. Berger and Neuhaus (New York: Seabury, 1976), 20-43.

world.[184] In other words, the vocation of the Christian theologian includes a two-fold task of *interpretation*: the interpretation of the Christian Tradition and the interpretation of the world in which this Tradition develops and is lived.[185]

Tracy is, to be sure, fully aware of the Catholic interpretations of Tradition as *traditio* and not merely *tradita*, and makes clear that the category of "Christian fact" includes not only texts, but also symbols, rituals, events, and witness.[186] As for his choice for the second source, that is, *common human experience*, Tracy argues that it is the task of theology to show the adequacy of the major Christian theological categories for all human experience. The very logic of Christian affirmations demands the formulation of adequate methods and criteria to render them intelligible. But, more significantly, since the Scriptures claim that Christian self-understanding expresses authentic *human* existence, theology is called upon to test that universalist anthropological claim. Since at least the time of Schleiermacher, Tracy suggests, intellectual integrity demands that human experience be taken as a source of theological reflection, over and above the "inner theological" demands of Tradition. In this regard, Tracy finds an echo in Schleiermacher's slogan for the task of theology: "The theses of faith must become the hypotheses of the theologian."[187] The

[184] For a sketch of Schleiermacher's thought, as a precursor to Tracy, see W. Jeanrond, "Theology in the Context of Pluralism and Postmodernity: David Tracy's Theological Method," in *Postmodernism, Literature and the Future of Theology*, ed. D. Jasper (New York: St. Martin's, 1993), 143-63.

[185] Tracy, *Blessed Rage*, 3. "Interpretation" is a basic human activity in participatory understanding and forms the leitmotif of Tracy's work. See J. P. McCarthy, "David Tracy," in *A New Handbook of Christian Theologians*, 468-78.

[186] Tracy has earlier in the book clarified two points: (1) "Christianity as a religion of the Word clearly involves written texts (the Scriptures) as at least its charter document;" (2) "further investigation is clearly needed to interpret the fuller meanings of the 'Christian fact.'" See *Blessed Rage*, 15 n.5.

[187] *Blessed Rage*, 43-44.

methodological question is *how* to go about examining the meanings present in the two sources, human experience and Christian
texts. "The final appeal to our experience," writes Tracy, "is an
appeal not so much to what we may verify through our senses as
to what we may validate as meaningful to the experience of the
self as an authentic self, to what phenomenologists call our 'lived
experience.'" The theologian's responsibility is "to show how his
or her present categories are appropriate understandings of the
Christian understanding of existence."[188]

Second, as might be expected, the evangelicals would find
Tracy's position uncongenial to their perspective on the dynamic
between text and context. They would object to the idea of *mutual*
correlation which is so crucial in Tracy's model, particularly when
Tracy posits these sources (i.e., text and context) as the "mutually
corrigible constants." In Gabriel Fackre's view: "All translation
and interpretations proffered for the modern context must pass
muster before the authority of Scripture. Scripture is the *source*,
and the world of human experience is the *setting*. There are not
two sources in mutual correlation."[189] One must, however, question whether Lindbeck and the evangelicals are not claiming too
much for Scripture. In relation to the principal aim of this chapter,
the key question is whether one acknowledges new experience and
mediations of God's mysterious presence in this universe. Lindbeck and his colleagues do not reckon with the category of newness, a result that seems congruent with a "sovereignty of faith"
which Jeanrond identifies as "exclusively grounded in the biblically mediated Christological process of salvation." When this
exclusivity is bracketed in an attempt to grapple with the pluralistic religious situation of our time, a more encompassing approach

---

[188] *Blessed Rage*, 66 and 72.

[189] G. Fackre, "David Tracy, Evangelically Considered," in *Ecumenical
Faith in Evangelical Perspective* (Grand Rapids: Eerdmans, 1993), 211.

emerges.[190] One may then, unlike Frei and Lindbeck, presuppose
that the God of Abraham, Moses and Jesus Christ has revealed
himself in different prophetical and mystical ways, and that he
continues to reveal himself today. In this light, while Tracy's theological starting-point is not exclusively Christological, he is, "on
the basis of Christological experience, open for ever-new and surprising experiences of divine presence." Plurality is not something
to be feared and avoided, but to be confronted and challenged by.
"Because God has begun a relationship with this world, theology
must do the same without fear of compromising itself in the
process." Christian identity is thus not a given but a task, which is
carried out "in the long and expensive process of following Christ
within this world. Theology reflects on the possibility of coping
with this task."[191]

Third, however, in announcing a two-source theory, Tracy runs
the risk of conveying the impression that "both are mutually independent agents."[192] Such an impression is clearly unintended by
Tracy, of course. For the very fact that Tracy undertakes an
extended treatment of the religious dimension looming behind
everything existing and happening in the world undercuts any suggestion that Tracy might view the world as independent. Nevertheless, Stephen Stell makes a valid point in claiming that "Tracy
not only affirms two sources for theology, but two *polar* sources,
two *poles* of tradition and experience."[193] That Tracy presents a

[190] See, in this connection, D. Tracy, *Plurality and Ambiguity* (New York:
Harper and Row, 1987); *Dialogue with the Other* (Louvain: Peeters, 1990). See
also "The Uneasy Alliance Reconceived," *TS* 50 (1989) 548-70; "On Naming
the Present," *Concilium* (1990) 1:66-85.

[191] See Jeanrond, "The Problem of the Starting-Point of Theological Thinking,"
85-86. On Christian identity as a task, see Tanner, *Theories of Culture*, 151-55.

[192] See Schwarz, *Method and Context as Problems for Contemporary Theology*, 26-27.

[193] Stell, "Hermeneutics in Theology and the Theology of Hermeneutics," 684.

dichotomous framework for his method of correlation is further reflected in his bifurcating the two sources of theology into "two distinct phenomena."[194] Stell therefore identifies a common inadequacy in both Lindbeck and Tracy, although in opposite directions. Lindbeck's proposal betrays an underlying assumption of a "dichotomous split" in the relation between experience and Tradition. Such an assumption of polarity precipitates two features in Lindbeck's scheme: [1] the tendency to overlook the interrelationships between experience and Tradition; and [2] the tendency to impose unilateral interpretations on substantive issues. Lindbeck's programme is inadequate, not for failing to incorporate experience, for he in fact attempts to funnel the entire spectrum of human experience into the biblical world. Rather, it is inadequate because human "experience is itself defined within this deficient (polarised and unilateral) interpretive framework." Stell correctly accuses Lindbeck of an *exclusive* value-concentration on the text as against experience, thereby distorting both, and ignoring the "actual creative interplay *between* tradition and experience." In the case of Tracy, his dichotomous framework for his method of correlation has also imposed a structural polarity of tradition and experience, only this time the result is an "imbalance to their mutual relationships which, for Tracy, is tilted toward human experience." Stell then claims that "the possible interaction between tradition and experience is thwarted by this premature structuring of differences."[195] In essence, Stell seeks theologically to question any proposal which manifests a structured polarity between Tradition and experience, with a resultant struggle for priority and a concomitant neglect of their inherent interconnectedness. On the one hand, he questions "any commitment to the

---

[194] See Tracy, *The Analogical Imagination*, 88 n.44.

[195] Stell, "Hermeneutics in Theology and the Theology of Hermeneutics," 684-85.

specificity of the tradition of Jesus Christ at the expense of the universality of God's work in creation and the present experience of the Holy Spirit." This, he diagnoses, is the crux of the problem with Lindbeck's intratextual theology. Conversely, he also questions "any commitment to God's universal work in creation which overlooks the specificity of God's revelation in Jesus Christ or denies the way in which present experiences of God's Spirit are shaped by particular traditions." This, he suggests, characterizes Tracy's correlational approach.[196] Is Stell right and, if so, to what extent?

Stell is keen to work out an appropriate hermeneutical structure that would "facilitate the mutual interactions between experience and tradition, and thereby enable their accurate conjoining in the imaginative process of interpretation."[197] In a significant way, Stell's project supports our own proposal to include not only Tradition, with its Scripture and doctrines, but also experience, as valid components for essential consideration by theologians seeking to adequately address the pluralistic reality of the contemporary world. Furthermore, his critiques of Lindbeck and Tracy expose the weaknesses in their programmes and the risk factors to which these are prone. Stell's assessment seems to support our unease with Lindbeck's radical insistence on an *exclusive scriptural-causality*. However, can Tracy similarly be accused of claiming *exclusivity* in the direction opposite to Lindbeck's? To so impugn Tracy would be to overlook too much of what he himself has sought to emphasize. To be sure, even after *Blessed Rage for Order*, Tracy continues to speak of the two constants, insisting that "whatever the de facto situation, de jure any theologian who has interpretations of *two distinct* phenomena

---

[196] Stell, "Hermeneutics in Theology and the Theology of Hermeneutics," 696.
[197] Stell, "Hermeneutics in Theology and the Theology of Hermeneutics," 688.

(tradition and *situation*) must somehow correlate those interpretations."[198] Stell is clearly correct in concluding that Tracy not only affirms two sources for theology, but "two *polar* sources, the two *poles* of tradition and experience." In addition, Tracy's formulation of the cause and effect of religious language and experience stands diametrically opposed to Lindbeck's: "We misunderstand the function of religious language if we claim that it *causes* (presents) our general confidence or trust in the meaningfulness of existence. We understand such language correctly only when we recognize that the use of religious language is *an effect* (a *re*-presentation) of an already present basic confidence or trust."[199] Nevertheless, and this is what Stell omits mentioning, Tracy has significantly noted his taking an "explicitly hermeneutical turn in *The Analogical Imagination* in contrast to the hermeneutically informed but undeveloped position on 'common human experience' in *Blessed Rage for Order*."[200] Two things must here be stressed: [1] Tracy's explicit reliance on the hermeneutical insights of Gadamer and Ricoeur at once reminds us of his healthy respect for Tradition, coupled with an acute sense of "distance;" and [2] Tracy is explicitly interested in affirming the full plurality of interpretive frameworks which define our contemporary world. It is to seriously misunderstand Tracy if we ignore his principal concern, which is to *mutually* correlate in a critical fashion the results of rational investigations of the contemporary culture with the truth of traditional faith expressions.

[198] See, e.g., Tracy, *The Analogical Imagination*, 88 n.44; "Hermeneutical Reflections in the New Paradigm," 35.

[199] Tracy, *Blessed Rage for Order*, 103.

[200] Tracy, "Lindbeck's New Program for Theology," 464. In Tracy's revised correlational method, both the contemporary situation and Tradition provide answers as well as questions. He stresses the qualifier "mutually critical." See "God, Dialogue and Solidarity," *ChCent* 107 (1990) 900-04.

Evincing essentially a similar line of thought, but offering a different argumentation, Robert Gascoign has also taken on the burden of presenting a critique of the narrative theology of revelation developed by Thiemann and Lindbeck. In contrast to these two, he argues for a dialectical conception of the relationship between experience, text, and Tradition so as to do justice to the character of biblical revelation.[201] In both Stell and Gascoign, the validity of introducing experience for interpreting Scripture is explicitly argued for. Geoffrey Wainwright, too, argues the thesis that a cultural-linguistic approach to the Christian faith would not be misplaced, "provided the approach allowed for a recuperation of doctrinal realism and even the reintegration of a certain active role for experience."[202]

Fourth, also of significant import is perhaps the need to consider, as Jeanrond does, the much-needed mutual correlation between theology and the contemporary context. This calls for reflection not only "upon the manifold experiences of God within the community of believers," but also "upon the possibilities of the church's action in this world." For Lindbeck, the given Church praxis largely determines theological thinking. For Tracy, interpretation theories influence the understanding of religion, and create "the possibilities of insight, of resistance and of change." But Tracy's proposal seems rhetorical, which in a way is inevitable when the preponderance of attention is concentrated on

---

[201] Gascoign, "The Relation between Text and Experience in Narrative Theology of Revelation," *Pacifica* 5 (1992) 43-58.

[202] G. Wainwright, "Ecumenical Dimensions of Lindbeck's 'Nature of Doctrine'," 121 and 124. The exact nature of the experiential role is not worked out by Wainwright. In analysing the way in which the cognitive and experiential aspects of Christian theology relate to one another, McGrath renders special attention to the "significant experiential component," but in a way that consciously avoids radically liberal recommendations. See idem, "Theology and Experience," *EuroJT* 2 (1993) 65-74.

methodology. One could ask Tracy, since reflections never take
place in a vacuum, "where exactly the global search for better
possibilities of understanding and change takes place concretely
and institutionally?" To the extent that a correlational theology
risks losing itself on one side of the correlation, Lindbeck and his
colleagues offer a sound corrective by providing a useful reminder
of the narrative data of Christian identity. Jeanrond suggests that
the "starting-point of theological thinking is always to be found in
concrete praxis." The problem with Lindbeck's intratextual theology lies in its insistence upon determining such a praxis "monisti-
cally, that is, by one particular religious community or tradition."
Jeanrond rightly asks whether, in the case of Lindbeck and his colleagues, "the unified praxis which they defend as the place of theology does not contain a seed of potential sectarian terror."[203]

Lindbeck's vision strengthens the particularity-dimension of
Christian confession, but it lacks a more universal, world-engag-
ing significance. The problem is most acute in his controversial
proposal for communal enclaves in a sectarian Church.

4.4.4.3 Particularity of Confession and World-Engaging
Significance

We might thus further our discussion from an ecclesiological
perspective. Even without explicitly referring to those categories,
theologians betray an implicit espousal of either of two divergent
ecclesiological models, namely, a *contrast society* model or an
incarnational model. Theologians favouring the contrast-society
model envision the Christian faithful living in a Christian society
within, but clearly separate from, the larger society. This is God's
solution; it is a political fact. The Christian vocation is to transform

---

[203] Jeanrond, "The Problem of the Starting-Point of Theological Thinking," 88-89.

the world and Christians fulfil their vocation most efficiently by distancing themselves from the surrounding world, building a counter society and living differently. By contrast, theologians who subscribe to the incarnational approach perceive the Christian role to be squarely situated within human society. The Christian objective is better served by placing the Gospel in the midst of human activities, not away from them. Christians are to fully penetrate all domains of everyday life. The world has to be transformed from within. We need to get our hands dirtied, as it were, through engagement rather than living some high ideals and observing from a distance. We need to go public, so to speak, and meet the public which is pluralistic and different. We need to confront the "other" and be prepared to be challenged by it. We are faced with a deadly dilemma when options are articulated in stark alternatives: to be relevant or to maintain our confessional identity; complete involvement in culture or complete withdrawal; and, hence, social responsibility or sectarian retreat. The debate is most acute between two ethicists, James Gustafson and Stanley Hauerwas as they investigate sectarianism. Mindful of a risk of caricature here, a brief look at the controversy occasioned by their debate may shed light on the debate between Tracy and Lindbeck.

Michael Quirk provides a useful definition: "Sectarianism" connotes "the impossibility of any rational dialogue with those outside the 'sect,' on grounds that their epistemically and morally central convictions are corrupt and diametrically opposed to those of 'insiders.'" [204] Attempts at forging a consensus are shunned for its futility and inherent danger: any argument on "their" terms would only serve to undermine "ours." Rather than proclaiming their confession to a world that can not listen, sectarians retreat to their own enclaves and articulate among themselves the truth to

---

[204] For the materials in this paragraph, see Quirk, "Beyond Sectarianism?" 81-82.

which they bear witness in a life set apart from the rest of society. This is a vision that seems inevitably to slide into fideism, a vision to which Hauerwas says he does not subscribe. Theology is then reduced to an "in-house" affair, culturally marginal, and lacking in robust rationality, dangers which Hauerwas claims he avoids. He does so by embracing an antifoundationalist religious epistemology.

The connection between the *epistemological issues* and the *correct social stance of the Church* define Hauerwas' proposal. Resonating Lindbeck's thoughts, Hauerwas has for years now been insisting that the Church, with her cultural-linguistic particularities, ought to stand apart in order to witness to society.[205] This strategy of standing apart, however, in no way suggests that Hauerwas thinks the Church has nothing to say on important social and political issues, or that she should be silent even if she had something to say. Rather, the strategy stems from deep convictions that the particularity of the Christian story, and the corresponding particularity of the story-shaped Church, are necessary presuppositions for Christian contribution to social ethics. Consistent with this view, Hauerwas chooses to repeatedly advocate that the primary task of the Church is not to jostle for involvement in policy-making in society, and risk compromising its distinctive convictions, but to be ever-mindful that the Church serves society best through training virtuous people — people of true Christian character. The first social task of the Church, in other words, is to be herself.[206] This, he contends, is neither "a formula for a

---

[205] See, for example, S. Hauerwas, *A Community of Character* (Notre Dame: University of Notre Dame Press, 1981), esp. 89-110; *The Peaceable Kingdom* (Notre Dame: University of Notre Dame Press, 1983), esp. 96-115; and J. H. Yoder, *The Priestly Kingdom* (Notre Dame: University of Notre Dame Press, 1984); *The Politics of Jesus* (Grand Rapids: Eerdmans, 1994[2].)

[206] Hauerwas, *A Community of Character*, 73.

withdrawal ethic" nor "a self-righteous attempt to flee from the
world's problems." Rather, it is a call to the Church to witness
first to the "peaceable kingdom" by being a community that tries
to "develop the resources to stand within the world."[207] This
means, *inter alia*, that the Church must live its true self, as a particular community (a "servant community") rendering universal
service. The Church, through a faithful living out of its particular
convictions, which entails a total refusal to align itself to narrow
national loyalties, for instance, approximates itself to a universal
society. The idea hence is to so position the Church that "it can
serve society imaginatively" with its distinctive story-inspired values and judgments without being "captured by societal options or
corresponding governmental policy;" only then, will it stand in
good stead to "help the societies in which it lives to have alternatives that are not part of the current social and political agenda."[208]
Christians must, of course, relate both to the cultures and the corresponding political forms in which they find themselves; the
question is how to do so discriminatingly. In proposing his contrast model of the Church, therefore, Hauerwas denies that his
ecclesiology is sectarian.[209] The criticisms of Gustafson, who
labels Hauerwas' work as "sectarian, fideistic, tribalist," for calling the Church to beat a retreat from the world, and Miscamble,
who accuses him of sectarianism because a "standing-apart" posture pits the Church "against culture," have accordingly been dismissed as caricatures.[210] How do we assess this debate? What
insights can we draw for our discussion?

[207] Hauerwas, *The Peaceable Kingdom*, 102.

[208] See Hauerwas, "Will the Real Sectarian Stand Up?," *ThT* 44 (1987) 89-90.

[209] See *A Community of Character*, 253 n.37; *Against the Nations*, 7; *Christian Existence Today*, 3-21; "Will the Real Sectarian Stand Up."

[210] K. Tanner, in *Theories of Culture*, 104 n.11, treats J. M. Gustafson's "The
Sectarian Temptation," *CTSAP* 40 (1985) 83-94 as the *locus classicus* of the alle-

Like Lindbeck, Hauerwas does not dismiss "secular civilization" or even liberalism as utterly bad. Much good has come of
liberalism, not least in promoting limitations on state power which
has yielded corresponding freedom for individuals and in encour-
aging public cooperation in promoting good community. But liberalism generates its own difficulties, tending to set up "destruc-
tive" policies for individuals who lack the means to say "no" to
the state.[211] Hauerwas also questions the compatibility between
political liberalism and the way of life that embodies Christian
belief and practice. In all this, the term "liberalism" in Hauerwas'
usage, and thus the project of liberalism that he rejects, assumes a
slant different from common parlance: it is the belief that "society
can be organized without any narrative that is commonly held to
be true,"[212] or "that impulse deriving from the Enlightenment project to free all peoples from the chains of their historical particularity in the name of freedom."[213] This is why Hauerwas is particularly critical of theologians who uncritically appropriate a
justification for liberal democracy. Central to his critique of this
appropriation is the assumption that "democratic societies and
governments are the most natural expression of Christian convictions."[214] He finds it objectionable when Christian social ethics
uncritically underwrites Christian engagement in the world as a
way of sustaining "democracy as a universal achievement."

gation that postliberalism recommends a kind of Christian cultural insularity.
Hauerwas himself dismisses the criticisms of Gustafson (see Hauerwas, *Christ-
ian Existence Today*, 3-21) and W. S. Miscamble [see Miscamble, "Sectarian
Passivism?" *ThT* 44 (1987) 69-77; Hauerwas, "Will the Real Sectarian Stand
Up?"] as a complete misunderstanding of his work.

[211] Hauerwas, "Will the Real Sectarian Stand Up?" 93.

[212] Hauerwas, *A Community of Character*, 12.

[213] Hauerwas, *Against the Nations*, 18.

[214] See Hauerwas, *Dispatches from the Front* (Durham: Duke University
Press, 1994), 93-96.

Implicit in all this is an assumption of a legitimate role in democratic policing by Christianity. What becomes offensive to Hauerwas is the progression, from there, to the assumption that "a world-affirming 'church' or a world-denying 'sect'" are the only options available to Christians. The Church-world or Church-culture relationship is, from the outset, defined by the deadly dilemma, and recalls Niebuhr's influential Christ-culture typologies.[215] However, stark alternatives here suggest that Christianity cannot avoid the sectarian label unless it makes itself "useful" by helping to prop up state programmes by its social strategies and pastoral guidelines. In this regard, sociological defences of a civil religion are advanced by Bellah who advocates a role for the Church not only in sustaining a democratic public ethos, but also as a critical agent within the polity.[216] The danger with this strategy, in Hauerwas' vision, is that it leads the Church to a new Constantinism — uncritical, and neglecting the historical and particular nature of the Church.[217]

Clearly, while he acknowledges his alignment with such social theorists as Alasdair MacIntyre, Michael Sandel, Michael Walzer and Charles Taylor, whose historicist starting point as well as their more communitarian and antiliberal political and social theory he shares, Hauerwas' own thoughts represent some important differences from theirs. The crucial factor, for Hauerwas, is that even a

[215] In *Christ and Culture* (New York: Harper & Row, 1965), R. Niebuhr assesses Christianity's relation to society through an all-encompassing five-fold typology: Christ-against-culture; Christ-of-culture; Christ-above-culture; Christ-and-culture; and Christ-the-transformer-of-culture. Presupposing the normative superiority of the last-named of the five, he sees the Christ-against-culture typology as sectarian and the Mennonites as the best example of this position.

[216] See R. Bellah, "Public Philosophy and Public Theology in America Today," in *Civil Religion and Political Theology*, ed. R. Bellah et al. (New York: Clarendon, 1989), 79-97.

[217] See Hauerwas, "Will the Real Sectarian Stand Up?," 87; *Against the Nations*, 71.

revival of the tradition of a greater "civic republicanism" which these authors argue for, is still a form of *humanism*. Hauerwas is not bashful about using explicitly Christian categories informed by a distinctive story about Jesus Christ and his Kingdom. Impelled to distance the Church from society on account of his commitment to the Christian story, his route leads "not to the *polis* but to the church, not to *solidarité* but to *agapé*."[218] The Church, then, is the only true polity for the world. This is a vision of the Church founded, not on a critique of liberal society, but on the integrity of the story-formed Church so that Christians might be better able to negotiate the challenges of a liberal society. The cultural-linguistic particularities of the Christian religion constitute the key.

Without elaborating his specific understanding of religion, Hauerwas generally endorses Lindbeck's analysis and explicitly aligns himself with the cultural-linguistic model, hailing it as "extremely helpful" in assisting him to clarify some "primary presuppositions" in his work.[219] His attraction to the cultural-linguistic model is readily understandable. Experiential-expressivists assume some universal core to religious experience that is differently expressed in various religious texts; theologians read those texts into contemporary experience and give them intelligibility. But this approach depends on a moribund epistemological foundationalism. Neither can we have a pure presuppositionless experience to act as faultless touchstone for interpreting texts, nor can we ignore the possibility that the dominant experience in a culture is false and distortive. To accommodate the canonical texts to such experience would, for Hauerwas, be to "denature" the Christian

[218] Quirk, "Beyond Sectarianism?" 79.
[219] See Hauerwas's explicit alignment to Lindbeck in *Against the Nations*, 1-22; "Embarrased by God's Presence," *ChCent* 102/4 (1985) 98-100; "Seeking a Clear Alternative to Liberalism," *B&R* 13/1 (1985) 7.

message. In contrast, the cultural-linguists regard religions as attempts by faith communities to incorporate the world into their sacred texts. Contemporary experience must, under this vision, be subordinated to and interpreted in light of religious texts and traditions. It is this narrative-formed perspective, not any external experiential standard, that determines belief and practice, their extension and revision. A cultural-linguistic textualist orientation can thus work to save Christianity from the acids or contagions of modernity and to prevent a slide into irrationalism. This orientation does not, in Hauerwas' view, entail fideism and relativism, for all theological claims made on nonfoundational ground can be challenged, tested and argued about. There is no necessity to collapse Christianity into sectarianism, or impute to it any inability to rationally defend itself in a dialogue with the world. And yet, Hauerwas argues against such a dialogue, convinced of its futility on two counts: the corrosive nature of liberalism as a dialogue partner; and the coercive nature of secular politics. In keeping with his epistemological principles, what Hauerwas recommends is not a withdrawal of Christians or the Church from social or political affairs, but for them to be *simply there*, "as Christians and as Church."[220] For him, the distinctiveness of the Christian story entails the distinctiveness of Christian ethics which, in turn, prohibits its sublimation in ways that seek to accommodate secular sensibilities. The Church, he insists, "does not exist to provide an ethos for democracy or any other form of social organization, but stands as a political alternative to every nation, witnessing to the kind of social life possible for those that have been formed by the story of Christ."[221] The Church's social task is "first of all its

---

[220] For the arguments in this paragraph, see Quirk, "Beyond Sectarianism?" 82-83.

[221] Hauerwas, *A Community of Character*, 12.

willingness to be a community formed by a language the world does not share." Christian social ethics is concerned not with making the world more just, but with the formation of a society shaped and informed by the truth of the biblical stories.[222] The Church is the only "true polity" in this life.[223]

Given all this, one may be forgiven for questioning whether Hauerwas has not, in effect, advocated the proper posture of the Church to be in "antagonism and opposition to the world," and whether his position is not, after all, a "wholesale rejection of the claims of secular civilization?"[224] Even though he does not explicitly recommend an active withdrawal from the world, has he not, in effect, insisted on an active standing-apart-from the world? Is non-engagement not, in some form, a withdrawal? Despite Hauerwas' denial of any sectarian appellation, therefore, and even if one does not tax him with narrow sectarianism, one may conclude that it is difficult to see how he can escape some form of sectarianism.[225]

It is therefore not surprising to find that Jean Bethke Elshtain, who, though agreeing with Hauerwas that Christianity's task is not primarily to help politics, including democratic politics, insists that there is no denying that Christians "unavoidably *must* engage politics." He thus taxes Hauerwas on what better and more

[222] Hauerwas, *A Community of Character*, 92.

[223] Hauerwas, *Against the Nations*, 11.

[224] So questioned by Quirk in "Beyond Sectarianism?" 83.

[225] We must of course point out that specialist studies on Hauerwas, which reject the charge of sectarianism against him, have embarked on an "archeological" survey into the genealogy of the language of "sectarianism." Their conclusion is that the continued use of the term "sectarian" tends to confuse the issues rather than help to clarify them. See Arne Rasmusson, *The Church as Polis* (Lund: Lund University Press, 1994), 231-47; Emmanuel Katongole, *Particularity and Moral Rationality* (Ph. D. dissertation, Catholic University of Leuven, 1996), 231-34, now forthcoming as *Beyond Universal Reason* (February, 2000, University of Notre Dame Press).

sustainable proposals the latter actually does offer Christians to engage the liberal democracies under which we live. For there have to be better ways "to promote social and political decency and human dignity ... than does the combination of prophecy and denunciation of which Hauerwas is a master." Acutely interested in "the identity and clarity of 'the Church'," as Hauerwas is, rather than in "sustaining the engagement over-time with the wider culture," one cautiously wonders if his views do not, in fact, encourage another "identity politics," heavy on the call for "militant affirmation of identity," but light on empowering Christians to be leaven and goad. What is arguably a good end which Christianity can help to promote would, for Hauerwas, be at best a side issue. The end result may well be that Christians are reduced to salt that has lost its flavour.[226] Hauerwas diligently guards against any project that risks compromising or diluting the Gospel message, and to seek to contribute to public policy formation does run that risk. On the other hand, Hauerwas' standing-apart posture actually consigns decision-making about important social issues — even the life and death policy issues of the human community — to those neither formed nor informed by Christian faith. This is a veritable abdication, an escape from responsibility which Miscamble correctly judges as culpable on the part of Christians who have a message to offer.

Elshtain introduces to this discussion a powerful argument by Albert Camus[227] who, like Hauerwas, also insisted that what the world needs most today is "Christians who remain Christians." Camus' challenge, however, represents a world of difference from what Hauerwas advocates, for Camus strenuously called for Christian engagement in the world and work to lessen rampant suffering

[226] See J. B. Elshtain, "Theology and Political Life," *ModTh* 12 (1996) 367-76.
[227] See Albert Camus, "The Unbeliever and Christians," in *Resistance, Rebellion and Death*, trs. Justin O'Brien (New York: A. A. Knopf, 1961), 69-74.

and injustices. Elshtain's succinct summary of Camus' arguments is instructive: Christians are called to be, "at one and the same time, faithful to their own identity and, from that identity, to reach out to the world in a way that promotes clarity rather than opacity on grave moral questions; in a way that is open-hearted and compassionate yet, if needs be severe. The severity Camus calls for is a robust condemnation of earthly powers when they transgress certain ethical lines and commit evil deeds, by contrast to fomenting sharp judgments *within* the Christian community, judgments Camus found all too often to be harsh and unforgiving."[228]

We cannot stop at a dichotomous split between individual morality (changing one's heart) and working to alleviate the structural and social sins that beset the world. Nor should we stop at the communal (corporate) ethic of disposition and disavow all interest in the ethic of action. Catholic ecclesiology traditionally places the Church directly in history and regards the Church as having "an integral role in the development and defense of societies and cultures." The point is not to attempt to influence decisions "at the top," which Hauerwas judges to be an inadequate strategy; rather, while Christian faith does not require us to start at the top, it should lead us to make contributions at this level.[229] Would a revision of Hauerwas' and Lindbeck's views on modern experience be in order?

We agree that the Christian Scripture has much to offer for the transformation of "corrupted modern experience." But this modern experience did not arise out of a vacuum. History shows that Christianity has had much to do with the fortunes (and misfortunes) of the secular world. So, too, this "corrupted modern experience" may also have something to do with the "twists and turns of the interpretation of Christian narrative." In other words, the

---

[228] Elshtain, "Theology and Political Life," 369.
[229] See Miscamble, "Sectarian Passivism," 74.

chasm between Church and world may not be as great as Hauerwas' and Lindbeck's programmes suggest. The upshot of this discussion is that a postliberal, cultural-linguistic, intratextual
approach to ethics "can be augmented by an awareness that moral
particularism does not require that public moral argument be conducted in *exclusively* particularistic terms."[230] In an important
sense, the issue seems again to turn on the question of commensurability. There is no good reason to suggest that the content of a
distinctively Christian ethical perspective, insofar as it is ethical,
eludes all comprehension by non-Christians. Its persuasive rational force to those who inhabit the "secular world" may be something else.

Whereas Hauerwas strenuously seeks to ward off the sectarian
label, Lindbeck, in sharp contrast, explicitly insists on the sectarian nature of a true Church, thus prompting Tracy's accusation of
confessionalism, fideism and relativism. To recap briefly, Lindbeck's provocative writings, too, stem from a conviction that we
need to arrest the gradual erosion of the distinctive Christian identity caused by liberalism. What he advocates is some kind of
"sociological sectarianism," one by which members of the Christian faith can stand apart from the secular world in communal
enclaves. The future of the Church requires a sectarian strategy
whose rationale and purposes may be briefly enumerated: [1] the
tide of de-Christianization requires, "for the sake of survival," the
formation of "communities that strive without traditional rigidity
to cultivate their native tongue and learn to act accordingly;" [2]
the tide of advancing debiblicization requires the socializing of
members into highly particular outlooks informed by the distinctive message of the Christian Gospel; [3] the temptations to be relevant, the "acids of modernity," are better resisted in a mutual

[230] Quirk, "Beyond Sectarianism?" 84.

support group which concentrates in the first place on its own traditional intratextual outlooks and forms of life; [4] the "viability
of a unified world" may well depend on Christians forming "networks of socially deviant groups of the deeply committed ... [as]
... the seed-beds of new life."[231]

However, like Hauerwas, Lindbeck also stresses that such sectarian groups must be "supportive of concern for others rather
than for individual rights and entitlements." Further, he emphasizes "a sense of responsibility for the wider society rather than
for personal fulfilment."[232] In sum, Lindbeck and Hauerwas echo
the Barthian theme "Let the church be the church," and argue for
the impact of sectarian faithfulness on the part of the Church. Public commendation or argument of faith is decried.

The characteristic of sectarianism is precisely that which James
Gustafson explicitly warns against. He states his thesis succinctly:
"It is very tempting in our cultural era to isolate Christian theology and ethics from critical external points of view in order to
maintain the uniqueness or historic identity of Christianity. I call
this a sectarian temptation... because the separation of theology
from other ways of construing the world in the culture is somewhat similar to the sharp separation of the Christian community
from the world that has always characterized sectarianism."[233]
Lindbeck, it seems to Gustafson, ascribes to doctrine a task of
maintaining an aspect of culture called Christianity. Doctrine
serves to maintain a distinctive language or culture, and to socialize persons into a particular form of life. Lindbeck posits no interaction with other ways of viewing the world, nor any openness to
outside creative offers of ways to 're-vision' one's world view.

---

[231] See ND, 127, 128 & 133; "Ecumenism and the Future of Belief," 6; "The
Sectarian Future of the Church," 231; "Barth and Textuality," 372.

[232] ND, 127.

[233] J. M. Gustafson, "The Sectarian Temptation," *CTSAP* 40 (1985) 83.

The Biblical way is "untouchable"; the entire universe is to be absorbed into the Biblical world. Even the "truth claims of theology are ignored, except insofar as they are *subjectively true* for persons socialized into the Christian culture and language." Because Lindbeck's outlook is sectarian, it is also defensive. Doctrine, in his hands, has all but become ideology; and theology, too, is beyond any correction by other modes of construing reality. So Gustafson can pronounce against Lindbeck in theology and Stanley Hauerwas in ethics: "Fidelity to the narratives becomes virtually self-justifying in the sectarian temptation and both theology and ethics become incorrigible by anything outside the community itself." Gustafson agrees that "theology ought not to succumb to the immediately fashionable." But he sounds the clarion call by alerting people to "the denigration of the intelligible" in a sectarian movement bent on remaining "cognitively dissonant."[234] In this regard, Thiemann, who shares Lindbeck's commitment to a nonfoundational approach to theology, is unwilling to describe his own work as postliberal. He is concerned that Hauerwas is unduly blind to "the resources that liberalism might provide for the reconstruction of a political ethos that honors the pluralism of contemporary public life." He fears, too, that Lindbeck's "pessimistic reading of our postmodern culture will engender such skepticism about the possibility of Christian involvement in public life as to render a public theology virtually impossible."[235] In a similar critique, Rowan Williams fears that unless Lindbeck's 'enclaves' participate to restore an "authentically public discourse" in their

---

[234] Gustafson, "Sectarian Temptation," 86 and 88. For Hauerwas's objections against the sectarian label, see idem, "Will the Real Sectarian Stand Up?" *ThT* 44 (1987) 87-94; *Christian Existence Today* (Durham, N. Carolina: Labyrinth, 1988).

[235] R. Thiemann, *Constructing a Public Theology* (Louisville: Westminster, 1991), 24.

cultural setting, they would inadvertently collude with "the dominant consumer pluralism" and end up trivializing themselves into
"stylistic preferences."[236]

In this light, Tracy's vision poses a constructive contrast. Theology, in Tracy's programme, is best undertaken by placing ourselves
in the secular world in which we live and seeing how our faith
comes to bear in this world. In the larger society, there is a diversity of religious traditions. A concern for the truth claims of each
particular religious tradition has led Tracy to his understanding of
the public character of all theological claims. Howland Sanks sums
up the possibilities well: "Radical pluralism need not lead to radical relativism or narrow sectarianism. Tracy's strategy for doing
theology publicly allows us to avoid both."[237] Having said that, two
cautionary remarks are in order. *First*, the notion of "publicness"
comes in different shades as Kelsey points out. In a nuanced presentation, he positively sees the churches' self-description as being
constituted by its relationship with God. That relation, marked by
"calling" and "sending," "vocation" and "mission," is the condition of the possibility of the churches' engagement in the public
sphere, that is, of the larger society.[238] *Second*, as Placher points
out, the effort to find a universally "public" theology risks turning
the world in which we live into *one* culture in which Christian theology finds justification for its public character. It is precisely in
view of this concern that we have, earlier in this chapter, stressed
the importance of the present cultural experience of Africa and
Asia, feminists and others, as an essential critique against the
(unconscious) Western notion of "culture."[239]

---

[236] Rowan D. Williams, "Postmodern Theology and the Judgment of the
World," in *Postmodern Theology*, 101.

[237] Sanks, "David Tracy's Theological Project," 725.

[238] See Kelsey, "Church Discourse and Public Realm."

[239] See William Placher, *Unapologetic Theology*, 158.

A "critical-conversational process" is Tracy's treasured aim for the theological enterprise. It is difficult to picture how Lindbeck's cultural-linguistic approach could make room for conversation. More than the Gadamerian "fusion of horizons" in an interpretive-conversation is discarded when truth is fixed in one direction only, that is, from the textual-language to experience. Lindbeck has effectively moved to the other extreme of harbouring prejudices against the present. In the current debate concerning the precise nature of this conversation with the text, one key question concerns the interpreter's ability or otherwise to know what is true about the text. Lindbeck's cultural-linguistic approach is most concerned with the functional dimension of the text for and within a particular community of believers. Scripture, on this reading, pre-eminently functions as a "sociolinguistic framework that defines and gives identity to the Christian community."[240] But, to hold that theological discourse is only available to those *within* a particular confessional tradition is unacceptable to Tracy. The key to his argument is the "classics." Tracy's appeal to the classic is crucial to his argument.[241]

For Tracy, "certain expressions of the human spirit so disclose a compelling truth about our lives that we cannot deny them some kind of normative status," which alone we name "classics."[242]

---

[240] See R. Lints, *The Fabric of Theology* (Grand Rapids: Eerdmans, 1993), 229.

[241] According to Vissers: "What we find in Tracy's program is a revisionist attempt to rehabilitate and reappropriate Schleiermacher's basic program... Where Schleiermacher employed the notion of piety to explicate the relationship of culture, religion, and Christianity, Tracy employs the notion of the classic." See idem, "Interpreting the Classic," 202. Sanks also affirms Tracy's theory of the "classic" as the key to the possibility of public theological discourse from a particular religious tradition. See idem, "David Tracy's Theological Project," 714. Likewise, Jeanrond, "Theology in the Context of Pluralism and Postmodernity," 150.

[242] See Tracy, *The Analogical Imagination*, 68 and 107-08.

They exist in every culture as events, images, persons, rituals, written texts, and symbols (conveniently referred to as "texts") of a tradition. Empowering his hermeneutical approach is a set of convictions about the power of "texts" that constitute religious traditions. His crucial contribution to our discussion consists in the claim that such "texts" constitute sources of *present revelation*. *First*, a classic in any literature is an "expression of the human spirit" born of a particular age and context. "The classic opens up and focuses some dimension of experience with such engaging power and depth that persons from other times and contexts find themselves addressed, expanded, and informed by it."[243] Classics display first a powerful claim to one's attention and, with what Ricoeur calls "a surplus of meanings" that resist definitive interpretation, transcend their original temporal-cultural background to speak to people across the ages. They naturally engender insights in new situations and give rise to conflicts of interpretation. Every classic thus has two poles: the classic text of the past and the present world of the interpreter. Every encounter with a classic generates a new interpretation and opens out to a lived experience. But a genuine encounter does not take place if one merely repeats a previous interpretation. One who acknowledges the authority of a classic allows it to challenge one. This can lead to a disclosure, and may provoke personal transformation. A classic can neither simply be repeated nor rejected, but demands engagement and interpretation.[244] *Next*, the religious classics, as a special instance of the larger idea of classic, are characterized by the same structure

---

[243] As described by J. W. Fowler, *Faithful Change* (Nashville: Abingdon, 1996), 185.

[244] See Tracy, *The Analogical Imagination*, 154. W. Shea thus comments: "The classic is by nature a particular carrier of a universal meaning that requires interpretation in a culture." See idem, "Review Symposium: The Analogical Imagination," *Horizons* 8 (1981) 316.

just described, with one important difference. Content-wise, "explicitly religious classic expressions will involve a claim to truth as the event of a disclosure-concealment of the whole of reality *by the power of the whole* — as, in some sense, a radical and finally gracious mystery."[245] Allowing for disclosure-concealment is to acknowledge not only that God's self-disclosure never exhausts God's being, but also the inevitable limitation and incomplete apprehension and articulation of the disclosure events that are offered to us. Three important consequences follow from this: [1] There is the hermeneutical opening of access to the disclosive power of religious traditions *in relation to* the situated issues of the present time. Acknowledging the possibility of *present revelation* through the mutually interpretive dialectic of religious classics with present contexts helps to clarify — intellectually and spiritually — the dynamic relationship between religious traditions and present-day experience; [2] There is the possibility of "asserting the integrity of particular religious traditions as mediating relatedness to the Ultimate."[246] Thus, although systematic theology proceeds from Scripture-in-Tradition to work out its implications, this does not render it meaningless for non-Christians. The Bible being a religious classic in our culture, non-Christians can also profit from reflection on it. Significantly, the notion of the religious classic as a cultural classic thus assures a valid entry of all theological classics into the public realm of culture. Without that entry point, Tracy claims, "systematic theology would be eliminated."[247]

For Tracy, the *event and person of Jesus Christ* normatively judges and informs all other Christian classics, and serves as *the* classic Christian focus for understanding God, self and the larger

[245] Tracy, *The Analogical Imagination*, 163.
[246] Fowler, *Faithful Change*, 186.
[247] Tracy, *The Analogical Imagination*, 68-69.

world.[248] Christology mediates the past and the present. The Christ event has decisively graced the world. And yet, it is an event that still needs to be internally made real by each person and for all history.[249] The real fate of a classic, Tracy says, is its constant reinterpretation by later finite, historical, temporal beings. In "critically and tactfully" taking the risk of questioning and listening to the responses of the classic, we can "actualize the event of understanding beyond its present fixation in a text." The resulting conversation with the text itself, and among those responding to the classics' claim for attention, becomes a living tradition of interpretation.[250] Understandably, therefore, Tracy's approach substantially contradicts Lindbeck's in that Tracy insists on the legitimacy and desirability of a critical role for the theologian. The theologian must engage in argument to establish what is finally true about the text.[251]

Tracy is always mindful of the human need for *traditio* and the sort of discernment possible in a particular community where its members continue to appropriate critically their original memories. Classics become an indispensable bridge that links the particular character of a community of faith to a mode of discourse which is potentially open to all. The continued reception of a classic persuades Tracy to aver that "for the Christian, the present experience of the spirit of the Risen Lord who is the crucified Jesus of Nazareth *is* the Christian religious classic event."[252]

[248] Tracy, *The Analogical Imagination*, 233.

[249] Tracy, *The Analogical Imagination*, 234. Tracy identifies Jesus as "the Jesus remembered by the tradition which mediates the event in the present through word, sacrament, and action; the Jesus remembered as the Christ, the presence among us of God's own self."

[250] Tracy, *The Analogical Imagination*, 102.

[251] Tracy, *The Analogical Imagination*, 14-21. In Cady's estimation, a "naturalist model" for hermeneutics is one that "continues to view the past as disclosive of truth but which refuses uncritically to capitulate to it." See idem, "Hermeneutics and Tradition," 460.

[252] *The Analogical Imagination*, 265. D. Burrell makes some apposite comments in "From Particularity to a Discourse for All," *Com* 108 (1981) 310-11.

It is thus important to note that the liberals and revisionists continue a broadly Christocentric tradition. In the case of Tracy, there is no question "*that* the particular figure Jesus requires some prior context to be applicable or intelligible." What he likes to leave open is the question whether "Christ *is* the adequate context of Christian theology." In this light, it is obvious that he differs markedly from Barth and his followers who steadfastly refuse to place Christ within some allegedly more comprehensive context.[253] It is quite legitimate for commentators to find in Tracy's "christological construction of the Christian classic" some "structural weaknesses." For instance, in admitting a plurality of interpretations of the Christ-event-person within Scripture and within Tradition, Vissers thinks Tracy has effectively denied himself the sort of biblical Christology which could undergird his claim regarding Christology as cultural classic.[254] Vissers' point is not without merit. With an obvious liberal inclination, Tracy's work is, according to Kaufman, "in fact determined throughout by the *liberal* problematic."[255] Tracy accepts the "distinctively modern commitment to the values of free and open inquiry, autonomous judgment, [and the] critical investigation of all claims to scientific, historical, philosophical, and religious truth." But it is erroneous to conclude that the liberal reception of modernity is simply at the expense of traditional Christian faith. Quite the contrary; the real concern of the liberal is, in Tracy's own words, "to show how a proper reinterpretation of modernity's most basic value commitments and a proper reinterpretation of Christianity's historic claims to truth and value can be — indeed must be —

---

[253] See Buckley, "Revisionists and Liberals," 98. Buckley makes an instructive survey of four revisionist authors.

[254] See Vissers, "Interpreting the classic," 204-05.

[255] G. Kaufman, "Review of Blessed Rage for Order," *RSRev* 2 (1976) 8.

reconciled."[256] In a liberal mould, plurality is unavoidable. Nevertheless, too much weight cannot be ascribed to Vissers' argument since there is no denying that plurality was already present in the New Testament itself. Further, Vissers may not have given due weight to what Tracy rightly affirms, namely, that the "original and normative responses to the Christ event are those expressions of the earliest communities codified in the texts named the New Testament." This means that there is scriptural warrant for the most fundamental truth in the Christian faith, the Christ-event-person. The original testimonies have become, in Tracy's words, "not just more texts, more expressions, but *Scripture.*" (Emphasis added.)[257] Vissers, it seems, regrets the fact that Tracy, in naming the event and person of Jesus Christ as the Christian classic, has effectively relativised the normative status of the Bible. Perhaps Vissers' objection stems from a deep-seated problem: his fundamental preference may well be to accord a primacy to Scripture, *even if* that entails subordinating the Christ event and person to which Scripture bears witness. If this is the case, Vissers' vision may be seen as Scriptural absorption of the entire universe, *Christ included.*

At any rate, the issue of import for the direction of our discussion is that, according to Bruggemann, "the classic has drawing power not because of manipulative management, but because of the inherent, intrinsic power of the text." A text is classic not only because it is revelatory in a "close and direct

---

[256] Tracy, *Blessed Rage for Order*, 25-26.

[257] See Tracy, *The Analogical Imagination*, 248-49. Kelsey has explained that to call a text or set of texts "scripture" is to make a "self-involving" statement, and to ascribe to it a "wholeness," an "authority" for the common life of the Christian community, and an essential role in establishing and preserving the community's identity. See Kelsey, *The Uses of Scripture in Contemporary Theology*, 89.

way" for the immediate community whose obligation it is to assent to the authority of that text (with appropriate, consequential, obedient activity), but also because all manner and conditions of women and men through the ages can refer to what is given in the text. The Scripture of Christianity, for instance, speaks not only to the ongoing faith community, who, as Lindbeck and Hauerwas correctly suggest, "must keep relearning its own peculiar grammar and dialect, in order that it may maintain itself through time and have the courage and energy for the obedience inherent in its identity," but also to a "second listening community: the larger public that is willing to host many alternative construals of reality."[258]

Once again, the issue turns on the degree of epistemological difference which is necessary to warrant Lindbeck's claim of incommensurability between the Christian message and non-Christian rationality. With the help of Tracy's notion of the classic, it would seem that, even when one explicitly begins from particularity, one must be able to proceed, from there, to participation in public discourse. The problem of incommensurability continues to loom large as a major stumbling block that requires to be addressed. However, in view of the fact that this issue can only be adequately addressed not by isolating some remarks that Lindbeck makes in different contexts, but by attending to the "total package"[259] that he offers in his programme, the issue is best deferred till the next chapter, after we have examined his regulative theory of doctrine — one where Lindbeck's reliance on pragmatism and performative arguments are very relevant.

---

[258] Bruggemann, *Theology of the Old Testament*, 87-88.
[259] Michaelson, "The Response to Lindbeck," 116.

4.4.4.4 An Anthropological Implication

Apart from the ecclesiological element, we further suggest that
there is a potent underlying anthropological paradigm espoused by
every theologian. The sort of anthropological image with which
one begins often makes a crucial difference in one's theology.
Karl Rahner, for example, from the beginning, conceives of
human beings as spirits, namely, as the desire for Absolute Being.
Spirit, understood as the principle of transcendence, implies an
affinity to God and a *capacity* for receiving God. In his famous
formulation, human beings are constituted with a "supernatural
existential:" God's offer of self-communication belongs to all
human beings as a characteristic of their transcendentality. The
human person is characterised by an existential ordination towards
grace.[260] So Rahner starts with *human potentiality*. His Catholic
background, and, more specifically, his Ignatian spirituality, has
much to do with this optimistic view of human beings,[261] a view
which contrasts with the more pessimistic Protestant starting point
of the human person as sinner.[262] We are created with an in-built
yearning for, and a capability of knowing, God, however inchoate
or unthematic that knowledge might be. We have those given
structures for experiencing God's self-communication; otherwise,
we would not be able to say anything about God.

[260] See Rahner, *Foundations of Christian Faith*, 172.

[261] A humanistic and optimistic flavour in Rahner's theology is noted in J.
Macquarrie, *Twentieth Century Religious Thought* (London: SCM, 1988), 381.

[262] A basic principle in Evangelicalism insists on the total depravity of
humanity. As the ERCDOM report expresses it: Roman Catholics think Evangelicals overstress the corruption of human beings by affirming their 'total
depravity' ... while Evangelicals think Roman Catholics underestimate it [i.e.
human corruption] and are therefore unwisely optimistic about the capacity, ability and desire of human beings to respond to the grace of God." See *The Evangelical Roman Catholic Dialogue on Mission 1977-1984*, ed. B. Meeking and J.
Scott (Grand Rapids: Eerdmans, 1986), 40.

Paul Tillich labels this optimistic emphasis of human experience to mediate the presence of God as the "Catholic substance" in contrast with what he calls the "Protestant principle," which protests any attempt to elevate what is human, finite, and limited to the status of the divine.[263] Carl Peter sees a need for a "Catholic principle" to safeguard the substance of faith from erosion by an unrestrained application of the "Protestant principle." The "Catholic principle," he proposes, enjoins us: "Be not so prone to expect abuse that you fail to recognize God's grace as working, as having worked, and as hopefully going to work again" through the means that have been given.[264] To underscore the positive element in each of these positions, Dulles offers a balanced view when he urges that we speak of

> A Christian substance and two principles. The Protestant principle, as a critical norm, prevents one from blurring the distinction between God and creature and from attributing divine status to that which is finite and defectible. The Catholic principle, conversely, criticizes the critics. It warns them not to banish God from his creation and not to minimize the gifts of God in Christ and in the Holy Spirit.... The Catholic principle thus keeps Christianity, whether Protestant or Catholic, from falling into the sins of irreverence, scepticism, and sacrilege, which are no less deleterious than magic, superstition, and idolatry.[265]

[263] See Paul Tillich, "The Protestant Principle and the Proletarian Situation," in *The Protestant Era* (Chicago: University of Chicago Press, 1948).

[264] Carl J. Peter, "Justification and the Catholic Principle," *Lutheran Theological Seminary Bulletin* 61 (1981) 22.

[265] Avery Dulles, *The Catholicity of the Church* (Oxford: Clarendon, 1985), 6-7. Working with the concept of a symbolic order proper to the faith of the Church, Louis-Marie Chauvet paints a tripod-structure of Christian identity comprising Scriptures, sacraments and ethics. An over-exaggeration of any one or two of these pillars is to attempt to stand the tripod on one or two of its legs, resulting in tipping it over. See idem, *Symbol and Sacrament* (Collegeville: Liturgical, 1995), esp. Part Two.

One is tempted, then, to say that perhaps Jeanrond has correctly located a raw nerve. He observes the extent to which the modes of thought at Yale and Chicago are characterized by a very different religious ethos. He describes the difference thus: "Behind Yale we identify chiefly the concern for salvation; behind Chicago we see the joyful response to God's self-revelation in creation. Yale is thus more pessimistic with regard to the world as the location of theology, Chicago more optimistic." The postliberals, Tanner points out, are no fans of any positive claims of God's purposes being generally evident in the world of nature or in the structures of human life. When it comes to the knowledge of God, the particularities of the unsubstitutable personage of Jesus "always outweigh discussions of a universal Logos or the possibly far-flung pereginations of the Holy Spirit; and that preference is backed up by a weighty pessimism about the effects of sin."[266] And yet, the contemporary theological scene yields a far more complicated picture than a simplistic Catholic/Protestant dichotomy or the clear divide of salvation/creation categories. Jeanrond is more on the mark in his thesis that such fundamental moods, detectable behind all theological projects, may well be more decisive for theological thinking than is generally assumed. He concludes to the necessity of a methodological reflection helpful for a critical assessment of all theological proposals, "including the ruling, though not always explicitly discussed, moods of the day."[267]

Perhaps, then, the question of the status of experience in theology may also be approached from the perspective of the relationship between theology and anthropology. This relationship has captured the attention of theology since the time of liberal theological giants such as Schleiermacher. Can anthropology form a

[266] K. Tanner, *Theories of Culture*, 149.

[267] Jeanrond, "The Problem of the Starting-Point of Theological Thinking," 86 n.51.

basis for doing theology without compromising the traditional understanding of the *Theos*? Whatever else one may wish to say regarding the definition of theology, faith as an element is clearly implied.[268] Barth stressed God's sovereign action in the matter of faith: faith must not appear to be something that human beings could perfectly well have provided for themselves. On the other hand, contemporary theology demands the giving of a rich human content to theology; Christian faith must be demonstrated to be intelligible and relevant to people. The problem lies in holding a proper balance of the two. In a lecture delivered at a theological symposium in Chicago in 1966,[269] Rahner's basic thesis is that, in view of the Incarnation, theology and anthropology cannot in principle be separated.[270] Rahner explicitly states that dogmatic theology today must be theological anthropology. This anthropocentric turn[271] focuses attention on human beings as they concretely experience themselves in their own incomprehensibility and amidst the

[268] For an explanation of the difference and the link between theology and faith, see Macquarrie, *Theology, Church and Ministry*, 12-13.

[269] See Rahner, "Theology and Anthropology," in *Theological Investigations*, trs. Graham Harrison (London: Darton, Longman and Todd, 1972), 9:28-45. For an explanation of Rahner's contribution towards turning human experience into an explicit source in Catholic theology, see A. Carr, "Theology and Experience in the Thought of Karl Rahner," *JR* 53 (1973) 359-76. Vatican II's anthropological turn, it has been argued, does not displace the centrality and priority of the divine self-communication in Christ and that anthropocentrism and christocentrism are complementary rather than mutually exclusive. See Gerald O' Collins, *Retrieving Fundamental Theology* (London: Chapman, 1993), 26-27.

[270] For an exposition of Rahner's thoughts on theological anthropology, see J. R. Sachs, "Transcendental Method in Theology and the Normativity of Human Experience," *Ph&Th* 7 (1992) 213-25.

[271] For a brief history of philosophy leading to the modern-day anthropocentric shift, see J. Moltmann, *Theology Today* (London: SCM, 1988), 67-69. On the Thomistic and Kantian influence on Rahner, see F. P. Fiorenza, "Karl Rahner and the Kantian Problematic," in the Introduction to Rahner's *Spirit in the World*, xix — xlv.

vicissitudes of human existence. Insisting that theological statements are *not* simply deduced from human experience, Rahner
nevertheless stresses the experience of grace as the "real, fundamental reality of Christianity itself."[272] Thus, in Rahner's vision,
anthropology may not be regarded as an area of study separate
from other areas of theology: in scope and content, it ought to be
regarded as the whole of dogmatic theology itself. When Rahner
says "dogmatic theology today must be theological anthropology," he means we know about God only by knowing about ourselves and our humanity. Only by plumbing human experience in
all its depth do we come to grasp the significance of particular
Christian doctrines. Human beings constitute the arenas where
encounters with God take place; theology *is* anthropology in a real
sense.[273] To be sure, Catholics are not alone in stressing the
anthropological dimension of theology. Protestant theologians
abound who place strong emphasis on human self-understanding.[274] In the case of Lindbeck, however, the picture seems rather
different. Wainright suggests that by giving priority to the exter-
nality of the cultural-linguistic patterns, Lindbeck denies any role
for human experience in the foundation of Christianity. In this,

[272] 'Grace' is a key category in Rahner's theology. He has expended a great
deal of energy on this topic, earning himself the title, amongst others, of a "theologian of the graced search for meaning. See G. B. Kelly (ed.), *Karl Rahner*, in
The Making of Modern Theology series (Edinburgh: T & T Clark, 1992).

[273] See J. J. Mueller, *What Are They Saying About Theological Method?*
(New York: Paulist, 1984), 12.

[274] For example, S. Ogden writes: "A theology is mythological and so untenable to the extent to which it denies that statements about God may be interpreted
as statements about man. By this we mean not that theology may not speak
directly about 'God and his activity', but simply that whenever it does so speak
its statements must at least be implicitly about man and his possibilities of self-
understanding if they are not to be incredible and irrelevant. In this human sense,
statements about God and his activities are statements about human existence,
and vice versa." See idem, *Christ Without Myth* (London: Collins, 1962), 160.

Lindbeck is seen to have been "over-influenced by the Lutheran insistence that, whereas all other Christians are content with the *Allwirksamkeit Gottes* ('God does everything'), God's glory and human salvation require that God 'does everything alone' (Allein-wirksamkeit)."[275]

Tiina Allik has focused attention on the anthropological implications of Lindbeck's typology. She suggests that, apart from anything else by which Lindbeck may have been motivated, the most basic issue that impacts on his theoretical scheme and theological implications is his anthropology.[276] She offers a sustained argument for the thesis that the anthropology of the cultural-linguistic model elaborates the radical materiality, historicity, and contingency of religious experience in a way that the expressivist model does not. In the cultural-linguistic view, there are no experiences prior to language (conceptualization or symbolization). In acknowledging the prereflective depth dimension of human experience, Lindbeck only allows this as a quasi-transcendental *a priori* on account of its cultural ancestry — a "precondition, a kind of quasi-transcendental (i.e., culturally formed) *a priori* for the possibility of experience."[277] Allik's case for granting a superior rating to this vision's ability to affirm human finitude hinges on a notion of human finitude "not only as a way to refer to the limits of human powers, but also as a way to characterise the basic openness, vulnerability, and contingency of the human capacities."[278] If human finitude is described as the limitedness of human

---

[275] G. Wainwright, "Ecumenical Dimensions of Lindbeck's 'Nature of Doctrine'," 124.

[276] This analysis parallels Watson's view that Hauerwas' "rooted dislike of Christian socio-political engagement" is the appeal to an ethic grounded in universal human nature. See Watson, *Text, Church and World*, 132.

[277] ND, 36-37.

[278] T. Allik, "Religious Experience, Human Finitude, and the Cultural-Linguistic Model," *Horizons* 20 (1993) 244.

creatures whose innate capacities, on account of their material-bodily existence, never attain perfection, this negative construal must be rejected for locating the *telos* for human perfection in an immaterial, non-bodily, angelic mode of existence. Allik thus chooses an alternative construal, one that regards human finitude and materiality, in positive terms, as an openness to the world, but an openness that includes both contingency and vulnerability. She proposes this basic openness, vulnerability and contingency as the basis for the creativity and spontaneity of human existence. She criticizes experiential-expressivist anthropologies for compromising human finitude in line with the modern assumption "that human autonomy is diminished or invalidated by explanations of human behavior in terms of psychological, sociological, and physiological analysis."[279] Four points in Allik's instructive analysis may be called into question for purposes of our dialogue with Lindbeck.

First, the usefulness of her thesis, grounded in an argument against those thinkers who allegedly compromise human finitude, is limited to the extent that she targets her argument on those whom Lindbeck labels as experiential-expressivisits in his typology but whom, as we saw, are strawmen. *Second*, in choosing from two alternative construals of the human person, her description exposes itself to the risk of being found inadequate in light of a list of eight *continuous dimensions* proper to the "human person adequately considered" ('HPAC'), as drawn up by Louis Janssens.[280] *Third*, her prime interlocutor is evidently Rahner whom, she rightly acknowledges, is keen to affirm the historical and contingent character of human knowledge. However, Rahner,

[279] Allik, "Religious Experience," 245.

[280] See L. Janssens, "Artificial Insemination: Ethical Considerations," *LS* 8 (1980) 3-29. See further, D. L. Christie, *Adequately Considered: An American Consideration of Louis Janssens' Personalist Morals* (Louvain: Peeters, 1990).

in her view, does not only describe human transcendental orientation as *a priori* basis for human experience. He even posits it as a
core experience of self and God that is unthematic and preconceptual, thereby elevating human core and religious experience to a
level that is invulnerable to the vicissitudes of contingent experience in the world. This, in her view, is to disregard the material,
social, and historical complexity and amplitude in the world.[281] An
underlying motivation for such an experiential-expressivist construal of the human core is said to be the desire to find a sure foundation for the validity of religious experience and theistic belief,
apart from a desire to affirm the human capacity, despite its finitude, to know God. However, Allik overlooks the fact that much
of Rahner's theology is explicitly done in recognition of human
creatureliness as, for example, his understanding of concupiscence, which is rooted in human materiality.[282] Moreover, she
seems to overlook the fact that, the transcendental and categorial
are indispensable, co-existing, dimensions in Rahner's thought,
and that he conceives of dialectical dynamics as always at work
between transcendental experience and its verbal expression.[283]
Besides, if she objects to Rahner's positive assessment of human
capacity, has she not thereby disclosed her own espousal of a
more pessimistic sinner-image of the *homo sapiens*, an image
objectionable to the opponents? An oversight is again evident, at
the opposite end, as she praises Lindbeck's cultural-linguistic

[281] Allik, "Religious Experience, Human Finitude, and the Cultural-Linguistic Model," 246. See further, T. Allik, "Karl Rahner on Materiality and Human
Knowledge," *Thomist* 49 (1985) 367-86; "Nature and Spirit," *JRE* 15 (1987) 14-
32; "Narrative Approaches to Human Personhood," *Ph&Th* 1 (1987) 305-33.

[282] See Karl Rahner, "The Theological Concept of Concupiscence," in *Theological Investigations*, trs. Cornelius Ernst (Baltimore: Helicon, 1961), I: 347-
82; Stephen J. Duffy, "Justification by Faith," in *Church and Theology*, ed. Peter
C. Phan (Washington, DC: Catholic University of America Press, 1995), 211.

[283] See Crowley, *In Ten Thousand Places*, 87.

approach which grants *no inalienable ability* to the human agent
to see oneself as agent, or to be aware of oneself as having certain
intentions, or to be able to experience any event whatsoever.
There is, in other words, no given human nature that is invulnerable to one's environment. Hence, the cultural-linguist is right to
portray human agency and human experience as being constituted
by a semiotic system that is "created, appropriated, and maintained in social and cultural settings."[284] However, an oversight is
evident here in that Lindbeck has actually posited a textual language that is constant and unchanging through time, virtually
"untouchable" by different historical and cultural contexts, and a
religious language that remains wholly inviolate amidst a sea of
diverse and emerging experiences, in order to maintain the one-
directional causality that we have discussed. Paradoxically, Lindbeck has elevated text and language to a level that is a-historical.[285] Not only are texts posited as being untouched by novel
experiences, the fact that they were products of experiences at
their archaic origins also gets ignored.

Fourth, Allik credits the cultural-linguistic vision on a specific
theological point, namely, for positively affirming the human
capacity to know and experience things as being dependent on
providence (i.e., the "particular contingencies of an individual's
cultural and linguistic environments"), and not on "the security
provided by the concept of an inviolable core of human nature."[286]
Three matters militate against the accuracy of her assessment. [1]
Her remark risks becoming a mere assertion in the absence of
cogent arguments to support the claim that human placement

[284] Allik, "Religious Experience, Human Finitude," 248-49.
[285] See D. Bryant, "Christian Identity and Historical Change," *JR* 73 (1993)
35. Milbank, as we saw, also criticizes Lindbeck's "metanarrative realism" for
being "dangerously ahistorical." See his *Theology and Social Theory*, 386.
[286] Allik, "Religious Experience, Human Finitude," 248.

within particular cultures and languages is providential, while a fundamental human openness to God as part of the created structures of the human person is not. [2] She overlooks the fact that in his polemic against liberalism and in his despair over a de-Christianised culture, Lindbeck's cultural-linguistic vision does not "function to nurture a sense of hope about God's reconciling action on behalf of the entire cosmos."[287] [3] Most seriously, Allik implies that Rahner, with his a-historical transcendental method, is weak on acknowledging providence. And yet, is not Rahner's incessant emphasis on grace and Divine Mystery precisely one of glorifying Divine Mystery — that which *provides*, and beckons, our "inviolable core of human nature" to authentic human life? Is not Rahner doing what precisely the cultural-linguists have failed to do, namely, to draw the attention of secular moderns away from the scientific-atheistic view that what we can see, feel, hear and touch, or linguistically analyse and culturally influence, is all there is? What is missing in Allik's critique is the powerful religious message of Rahner's theology: What is immediately available to physical perception, including, we may add, the diverse cultures and languages, is *not all there is*; particularities, in whatever manner and form, and however strong and respectable, do not exhaust the inexhaustible Infinite Reality. In arguably the clearest analysis of the contemporary distinction between *transcendental* and *historical* experiences, Rahner offers a fundamental and fecund insight that all knowledge and experience tie us to the Infinite Reality disclosed by these two "horizons." And around this Reality, faith and unfaith revolve. "Religious faith does not see what is not there to be seen, as has so often been claimed in the past. It sees precisely what is there, but 'there' as the invisible ground of what is there and visible. It is unfaith that resists the opportunity

[287] Thiemann, *Constructing a Public Theology*, 25.

to look beyond what is seen to that which makes the seen and known both seeable and knowable, and thus it is unfaith, and not faith, that ultimately distorts the reality of the world."[288]

4.5 Concluding Remarks

Some implications result from our discussion of the relationship between religion and experience. A few concluding remarks are now in order.

First, Lindbeck is concerned with safe-guarding a Christian faith that has its own internal logic, language, thought forms and practices, according to which it would be illegitimate to correlate the Christian message with external criteria, such as new experiences. In line with this concern, Lindbeck's theoretical argument takes the conditioning force of language and culture seriously, and forcefully articulates the case for a cultural-linguistic description of religious thought and religious doctrine. While his approach enhances Christian distinctiveness, this enhancement is, in part, purchased at the expense of inadequate descriptions of other models of viewing religion. Further, his assessment of some major authors as experiential-expressivists, including Schleiermacher, Rahner, Lonergan and Tracy, are less than accurate. Finally, in his fostered paradigm, the "culture" component seems to have been unduly weighted on the side of fixity, ignoring the fact of the variety and fluidity, geographical as well as historical, of the early church. Also ignored is the fact that identity is constantly evolving, and established not *by* the boundary, but *at* the boundary, as *relational.* The "language" component, and its corresponding "form of life," is explicitly based on Wittgenstein's work. However, Wittengstein did not address macro institutions and probably

---

[288] K. R. Trembath, *Divine Revelation* (Oxford: Oxford University Press, 1991), 91.

would not describe a religion as a "language game" or a "form of life." The value of the triumvirate that Lindbeck discusses is thus somewhat diminished. Still, his typology offers a convenient starting point for discussing views on religion.

Second, it is by no means evident that Lindbeck has effectively stepped out of the current regnant, and seemingly all-encompassing, albeit shorthand, tripartite description of approaches to Christian theology of religions, namely, exclusivism-inclusivism-pluralism. To be sure, Lindbeck's disclaimer regarding 'common ground,' confession of particularity, and critique of foundationalism, place him squarely within the current postmodern intellectual climate.[289] On epistemological grounds, he acknowledges the diversity of religious traditions. But he fixes the source and impulse for belief squarely in the cultural-linguistic particularities of each religious tradition. This has two divergent implications worthy of note. On one hand, his emphasis on particularity engenders respect for the religious experience and theological doctrine specific to each of the diverse systems of religious language and culture. His cultural-linguistic lens thus resonates with the postmodern suspicion of theologians who presuppose some common experiential touchstone concerning cultural and religious differences.[290] On the other hand, consonant with his emphasis on *Christian* cultural-linguistic particularities, Lindbeck, as we saw, upholds the doctrine of *sola Christi*, insists on *fides ex auditu*, and proposes a prospective eschatological salvation for all — Christians and non-Christians alike — to hear and accept the *Christian Word*, in order to be saved. All this clearly identifies Lindbeck

[289] See M. K. Taylor, "In Praise of Shaky Ground," 37.

[290] In his judgment, Terrence Merrigan concludes that "the pluralists' understanding of religious knowledge cannot be ultimately integrated into any recognizable version of orthodox Christianity." See idem, "Religious Knowledge in the Pluralist Theology of Religions," *TS* 58 (1997) 706.

with the exclusivist and inclusivist camps — albeit an identification with some remainder, on account of his distinctive arguments. While, therefore, Tilley has correctly labelled Lindbeck a "particularist," thereby distinguishing him from the current dominant tripartite division,[291] this label can mislead if it is taken to suggest that Lindbeck's position is so fundamentally different from the exclusivists and the inclusivists as to fall outside the tripartite division altogether. Lindbeck's critical orthodoxy does not warrant such a suggestion.

Third, consistent with his intratextual theology, the underlying polemic in Lindbeck's cultural-linguistic vision consists of a critique of the liberal appeal to experience. In the way he presents his theoretical argumentation, this critique finds expression in an insistence on a uni-linear direction of causality between religion and experience: it is the sources of Christianity, namely, its culture and language, that informs and nurtures religious experience, never the other way around. Effectively, Lindbeck is saying the same thing here as when he argues for scriptural absorption of the world. What is at once objectionable here is his neglect of ideological critique and his exclusion of novel experience which hitherto have had no voice within the existing power structures in the Church. The absence of a dialectical emergence of truth through a critical interpretive act of the reader, seriously calls Lindbeck's exclusion of contemporary experience into question. Feminist theologians, for example, may pertinently ask not only by "which text?" but also by "whose interpretation?" are our faith and practice to be shaped. Non-Western theologians may also ask whether there should not be more to theology than plumbing the 'cultural-linguistic system' of the Christian West. Is Lindbeck's programme

[291] T. W. Tilley, "The Challenge of Religious Diversity," in *Postmodern Theologies* (New York: Orbis, 1995), 165.

not unwittingly urging the view that "orthodoxy" is what is con-structed by the dominant party in the Church? This is the risk we run when God is reduced to a single dimension of reality that is beyond critical inquiry. Wiles puts it well: "The combination of faith and critical detachment is a difficult but possible role. It is also a very necessary one, for uncritical religion is a dangerous phenomenon."[292] The danger, critical voices remind the Church, is that the *status quo* in the cultural-linguistic system of Christianity perpetuates the illegitimate exclusion of experiences from certain sectors of the Church which hitherto have had no voice. Feminist theology, in particular, has unmasked a systematic exclusion of women's experience from the Christian story down the ages. Its analysis surfaces the need to incorporate a whole new dimension to the cultural-linguistic system of the Church that has existed for the last two millennia. Donald Senior may be right in being opti-mistic that *the community as a whole*, sustained by the Spirit, will, in the course of history, continue to rectify major errors. However, that optimism should in no way suggest that theologians who see the problems should be reticent, or that their effort at pressing the issues is not part of the working of the Holy Spirit. But more importantly for purposes of this chapter, when Lindbeck insists that experience is formed by culture and language, and never the other way around, his theoretical argumentation may have effec-tively reduced God, or, better, the proper and legitimate under-standing of God, to a single dimension of reality. In that light, it is pertinent to reiterate that "not even the biblical story itself can function as a proxy for the living God."[293]

Fourth, Lindbeck has done right by the Church in his attempt to create a community whose ethos, worldview and sacred symbols (to use Geertz's famous trilogy) are shaped by the distinctive

---

[292] M. Wiles, *What Is Theology?* (Oxford: Oxford University Press, 1976), 9.

[293] Johnson, *The Mystery of God*, 4.

Christian culture and language. Taking this line of argumentation to its radical end, Lindbeck makes the provocative assertion that "the only kind of Christian community which might respond adaptively and faithfully to the signs of our times is a paradoxical form of sect: intent on its internal norms and forms of life, but open to the world."[294] Echoing the Barthian slogan "Let the Church be the Church," Lindbeck and theologians of the cultural-linguistic mould argue for the public impact of sectarian faithfulness on the part of the Church. Amongst the things that are commendable about their arguments are their zeal for Christian identity, their effort at safe-guarding the specificity of the Christian message against unmitigated adulteration by liberal culture, and their view of the primary task of the Church as the training of faithful disciples. On the other hand, the relation of the Church to the world gets subsumed under the debate over "purity" against "engagement." But, as Daniel Hardy rightly points out: "The very activity by which those who gather in worship are a community in contrast to the world also identifies them with the world, those who are not so gathered. In their common worship they are constituted as ethically responsible before God, but ethically responsible in and for the world."[295] Ethics and ecclesiology are inseparable; "segregation" is not the answer. The powerful rhetoric of the postliberals may be seen as resolving matters a little too easily. Unless the Church is more than an aloof contrast-society, she risks failing to positively contribute to the world in which she forms a part. A sharp either/or understanding (i.e., *either* "purity" *or* contamination through "engagement") of the true role of the Church vis-à-vis culture is to misconstrue the

[294] Meeks, "Social Embodiment," 184.
[295] D.W. Hardy, "A Magnificent Complexity: Letting God be God in Church, Society and Creation," in *Essentials of Christian Community*, ed. D. F. Ford and D. L. Stamps (Edinburgh: T & T Clark, 1996), 313.

public role of the Church.[296] Not least among its results is that Christians are no longer leaven in society. Furthermore, a sectarian ecclesiology also ignores the fact, as Michael Perry trenchantly observes, that while the world may need the Church, the Church also needs the world. "Religious communities need a robust external deliberation to protect them from themselves."[297]

Fifth, the discussion in this chapter also impinges on the lively debate over the public character of theology: Is this unpacking of the intelligibility and credibility of faith directed to the inner community of the faithful, or to the community at large? Do universities and theological faculties have a role to play? Jeanrond reflects on some implications in the contemporary scene:

> Theology has achieved a public and publicly-funded institutional position within the university on the basis of which it can do what it is charged with as *theo-logy*, namely reflection upon God carried through in a spirit which is fearless, rigorous, public, critical and self-critical .... Theology has for the first time the chance of truly becoming a theology of the world, not an imagined world, but the real world, our world and that of our fellow human beings. This new way of engaging in theology — free of colonial ties and no longer eurocentric — has widened the opportunities for theological discourse and invited every human being to become a genuine participant in a global conversation on the religious dimension of reality. In this process, Christian theology has learnt anew how to respect human experience in all its diversity and plurality.[298]

---

[296] In attempting to identify the proper stance which Christians should adopt toward the secular order, Archbishop Joseph Bernardin writes: "Engagement with the secular order, which is after all part of God's creation and the environment in which human life is lived, has been simplistically equated with "secularism," the error which supposes that the reality of life is exhausted by this life." He takes note of individual Christians and the institutional Church's significant contributions to human progress in the world in many ways. See "What Can the Church Expect from Catholic Universities?" *Origins* 4 (1975) 518.

[297] M. Perry, *Love and Power* (New York: Oxford University Press, 1991), 106.

[298] W. G. Jeanrond, "Thinking about God Today," *D&L* 47 (1997) 14-21.

Sixth, our research shows that a mere retrieval of Tradition is clearly insufficient. An aspect of Gadamer's hermeneutics is a refusal to treat the past as fossilized; understanding entails a fusion of both the horizon of the past and the horizon of the present-day interpreter. Although we have, from the start, sought to show the logical necessity of adopting Tradition as a category and overriding perspective in Christian theology, our thesis has been that not just Christian Tradition, with its Scripture and core doctrines, but *present experience* as well, has to be taken seriously by Christian theologians. Present experience is most assuredly pluralistic in the cultural, political, social, religious and intellectual domains. Authentic experience in every one of these domains must be incorporated into the Christian understanding. Pluralism is to be confronted and not avoided.

The importance of this concern for present experience is underlined by a serious debate and a growing body of literature centred around the opposing "Yale" and "Chicago" schools.[299] There is

---

[299] While there are certainly some major differences in emphasis, Dan Stiver, *The Philosophy of Religious Language: Sign, Symbol and Story* (Oxford: Blackwell, 1996), 134-62 finds that the lines between the so-called Yale and Chicago schools are overdrawn. Placher, for example, has earlier given a clear account of the differences between Yale and Chicago thinkers in "Revisionist and Postliberal Theologies and the Public Character of Theology." Along with other commentators, however, he has grown increasingly aware of more continuity between the two schools. See, in this regard, his *Unapologetic Theology*, ch. 5; "Paul Ricoeur and Postliberal Theology," *ModTh* 4 (1987) 35-52; and "Introduction" to Han's Frei's *Types of Christian Theology*, x. See also Wallace, *The Second Naiveté*; Charles J. Scalise, *Hermeneutics as Theological Prolegomena: A Canonical Approach* (Macon, GA: Mercer University Press, 1994); Tilley, "Incommensurability, Intratextuality, and Fideism;" T. Guarino, "Postmodernity and Five Fundamental Theological Issues," *ModTh* 57 (1996) 680; Barry Harvey, "Insanity, Theodicy, and the Public Realm," *ModTh* 10 (1994) 27-57; Gary Comstock, "Two Types of Narrative Theology," *JAAR* 55 (1986) 687-717; Stell, "Hermeneutics in Theology and the Theology of Hermeneutics;" Lints, "The Positivist Choice;" Tanner, *Theories of Culture*.

no doubt about the validity and importance of the postliberal concern that courting modern liberal culture is to risk losing our Christian identity. Yet the postliberal insistence on cultural-linguistic particularities seems exposed to serious dangers as well. Most serious of all, in proposing to absorb the entire universe into the Scriptural world, it effectively denies the validity of present experience as a source. Too many modern-day hermeneutical insights and ideological critiques have been ignored. Postliberalism's dichotomous splitting of Tradition and experience misses the reality of an interplay between the two. Lindbeck's understanding of the incommensurability of religious traditions within his intratextual programme leads to a new form of fideism. This has practically scuttled any meaningful interfaith dialogue. Christians end up having no grounds to criticize their religious cultural-linguistic system. They are positively asked to espouse some form of sectarianism. In isolation, they are no doubt protected from the criticisms and suspicions of others, but they are also denied the opportunity to learn from the wisdom available from the rest of God's creation. We have suggested that perhaps there are basic anthropological and ecclesiological presuppositions at work. The revisionist correlational approach offers useful correctives. And yet, correlational methods are not without their own limitations as well. If we need to overcome the risk of one-dimensional tendencies in Lindbeck's cultural-linguistic proposals, similarly, we need to overcome the dichotomous splitting of experience and Tradition in Tracy's programme. Christian theology ought to begin with Christian particularity which, for all practical purposes, is a return to its traditional sources. Hence we agree with that part of Lindbeck's programme that stresses the cultural-linguistic specificities. But Tradition is only correctly embraced with an attitude of critical openness. Faithfulness to the original witness, coupled with a critical integration of fresh insights, provide the key. But a critical openness also means the work is not yet done. The search continues. Conversation and dialogue are legitimate. Incommensurability is not the last word.

The question of commensurability of different epistemological schemes in diverse religious traditions persists. Are various religious traditions so irreducibly different? Are they so static and impermeable in their doctrinal articulations that one cannot learn another tradition as one learns another language? How does Lindbeck's cultural-linguistic approach impact on his theory of doctrine? And how does all this impact on our understanding of the Church? These issues constitute the subject matters of our final chapter.

CHAPTER V

DOCTRINE AND TRUTH

5.1 Preliminary Remarks

5.1.1 The Aim and Burden of This Chapter

It is a truism that, in the religious as much as in the secular domains, faith-statements claim to refer to what *is*. Faith unabashedly asserts the truth, or correspondence with reality. The Christian faith is a case in point. Christians understand their faith to lay claim to truth, and find support in their Tradition, according to which, "the Word was made flesh and dwelt amongst us, full of grace and truth" (John 1:14). It is no surprise to find anthropologists remark that, "when it comes to making cognitive claims, Christianity may be the most ambitious of world faiths."[1] As Luther once put it against Erasmus: "Take away assertions, and you take away Christianity."[2] In like manner, Karl Rahner, reflecting on the predicament Christianity faces in a world characterized by a plurality of religions, states the problem this way: "This plurality is a greater unrest for Christianity than for any other religion. For no other religion — not even Islam — maintains so absolutely that it is the religion, the one and only valid revelation of the one living God as

---

[1] See Paul Sponheim, "The Word in the World," *Dialog* 25 (1986) 167.

[2] See Geoffrey Wainwright, "Ecumenical Dimensions of Lindbeck's 'Nature of Doctrine'," *ModTh* 4 (1988) 130.

does the Christian religion."[3] This "absolute" claim is not a modern-day invention. We saw from the first chapter that the Christian faith is founded upon the belief of the community. The foundational stage of the Tradition disclosed the community-faith that "Christ died for our sins, in accordance with the scriptures; that he was buried; and that he was raised to life on the third day, in accordance with the scriptures" (1 Cor. 15:3-4). Transmitted down through the ages is the belief "that God has made him both Lord and Christ, this Jesus whom you crucified" (Acts 2:36). Ever since the first disciples of Jesus, this *kerygma* has been the *basic doctrine* of the Christian Church.[4]

The Christian community develops its doctrinal tradition in the course of time. Doctrinal statements, which Paul Griffiths calls "doctrine-expressing sentences," are: *sentences in some natural language... which are taken by the community either to make or to entail claims about the nature of things*, or *claims about the value of certain courses of action;* and which are *regarded by the community as of some significance for its religious life, and for the salvation of its members*.[5] In ecumenical and interreligious dialogue, it is at the doctrinal level that the going gets tough, because dialogue-partners come convinced that what they believe is true. People from other faiths have come to expect that Christians make their doctrinal assertions on matters of salvation, the

---

[3] Karl Rahner, "Christianity and the Non-Christian Religions," in *Theological Investigations*, trs. Karl-H. Kruger (Baltimore: Helicon, 1966), 5:116.

[4] See Nancy C. Ring, "Doctrine," in *The New Dictionary of Theology*, ed. Joseph A. Komonchak et al. (Collegeville, MN: Liturgical, 1987), 129. The term "kerygma" generally means proclamation, as distinct from *didache* or instruction. In the New Testament, kerygma includes the following: (i) the content of Christian proclamation (Rom. 16:25; 1 Cor. 1:21); (ii) the activity of proclamation (1 Cor. 2:4; 15:14); and (iii) the task given to a preacher or herald (Tit. 1:3; Matt. 28:19). See John F. Craghan, "Kerygma," in ibid., 556.

[5] Paul J. Griffiths, *An Apology for Apologetics* (Maryknoll, NY: Orbis, 1991), 9.

unicity of Christ, and the Holy Trinity, all of which are enshrined in the Nicene creed. But what are the *nature* (what they are) and *function* (what they are for) of doctrinal formulations within the Christian Tradition?

Not only does Lindbeck discuss the nature and function of religious doctrines at length, but he announces early in *The Nature of Doctrine* that, by means of the cultural-linguistic model of religion which he fosters, and its implied regulative/rule theory of Church doctrine,[6] he plans to show that the christological doctrine of Nicaea "in its role as a communal doctrine does not make first-order truth claims."[7] He posits Church doctrines as functioning most prominently "not as expressive symbols or as truth claims, but as communally authoritative rules of discourse, attitude, and action."[8] The significance of Lindbeck's claim seems obvious. On the surface, it at once suggests that the christological definition of Nicaea *does not* claim ontological truth about Christ. If this initial reading of Lindbeck is on the mark, and, if Lindbeck is right, this will revolutionize the whole understanding of Christian beliefs.

First, it would certainly call into question a great deal of what we have said about the Christian belief in the uniqueness of Jesus Christ as witnessed in the Tradition. Second, in turn, this would lend immense support to John Hick, the doyen amongst the Christian theologians who espouse the pluralist paradigm for a theology of religions. Hick has proposed that what appear to be cognitive

---

[6] Lindbeck insists that theories of doctrines and of religion are interdependent and, further, that the cultural-linguistic perspective on religion implies a regulative or rule theory of doctrine. See ND, 7 & 18. Tracy disputes a necessary implication, in "Lindbeck's New Program for Theology," 461-62.

[7] ND, 19. This is at once at odds with Griffiths who argues that to ignore the fact that doctrines typically make absolute truth-claims, is to "eviscerate them, to do them the disservice of making them other than what they take themselves to be." See *An Apology for Apologetics*, 3.

[8] ND, 18.

truth-claims within any given religious world-view are, in fact, only "linguistic pictures or maps of the universe, whose function is to enable us to find salvation/liberation, the limitlessly better quality of existence that the nature of reality is said to make possible."[9] A *plain reading* of Lindbeck's understanding of Christian doctrine would go a long way towards enhancing Hick's project which seeks to dissolve incompatibility between religious systems through evacuating them of truth claims.[10] But, is this a correct reading of Lindbeck?

As we saw earlier, Lindbeck's book is, in the shared view of his commentators, a complex study, so much so that a proposed plain reading of it is liable to mislead. Part of the complexity stems from the fact that, in this book, he tackles three complex subjects — religion, doctrine and theology — which he unifies by means of the proposal that the cultural-linguistic view of religion, which enjoys a long pedigree in the social sciences, is a useful category for understanding doctrines *and* can serve as a cogent model for ecumenical theology and for defending an intratextual theology in contemporary society. Indeed, his insistence on an intratextual theology, aided and abetted by his steadfast rejection of apologetics, his sustained, and occasionally vehement, onslaught against modern liberal culture throughout the book, his proposal for Christian enclaves and a prolonged and assiduous catechumenal model of catechesis for introducing catechumens to the distinctive language and practice of authentic Christian faith, his provision of a prospective eschatological salvation for non-Christians contingent

---

[9] John Hick, "On Grading Religions," *RelSt* 17 (1981) 461. Hick goes on to say that the test for these religions lies in their "successes or failure in fulfilling this soteriological function." Meanwhile, the jury is out, and stays out, for the final judgment can only be an "eschatological verification."

[10] See Paul Griffiths and Delmas Lewis, "On Grading Religions, Seeking Truth, and Being Nice to People – A Reply to Professor Hick," *RelSt* 19 (1983) 76.

upon a *fides ex auditu*, and so forth, have all but laid bare his operative methodology as "a sophisticated version of Barthian confessionalism."[11] This should at once alert us to the risk of any hasty claim of affinity between Lindbeck and Hick. In fact, the common question raised by discussions of Lindbeck's proposal is: "Has he abandoned the truth claims of the Christian faith?"[12]

In light of Lindbeck's claims regarding the truth-status of the Nicene doctrine, and indeed of the overarching context of his postliberal theology, we shall direct attention in what follows to two major elements, addressed separately in two sections, using the notion of truth as the principal analogue. In the first section, our leading questions are: Is Lindbeck abandoning Christian truth-claims or suggesting that Church doctrines do not make propositional assertions at all? Would his regulative model be more intelligible if it were more explicitly parasitic on other models? Furthermore, can his theory be complemented by our thesis that theology is possible because truth is revealed dialectically? In the second section, our leading question is how Lindbeck's observations regarding the meaning of "Church" and their affinity with specific models for doctrine impact on ecclesiology. The implications of the postliberal project will thus be collated for a critical ecclesiological synthesis.

[11] The argument is ours, but the label comes from Tracy, "Lindbeck's New Program," 465. Gordon D. Kaufman holds the view that Lindbeck wishes to put his theory to "conservative establishmentarian" uses. See his review of Lindbeck in *ThT* 42 (1985) 240-41.

[12] See Michael Root, "Truth, Relativism, and Postliberal Theology," *Dialog* 25 (1986) 175. In fact, Lindbeck has, on critical criteriological grounds, challenged Hick, in the volume the latter edited, *The Myth of God Incarnate* (Philadelphia: Westminster, 1977), for turning to "the old liberal assumption that enlightened reason and conscience have access to independent or transcendent criteria which enable them to pick and choose what is of highest value from within various religious traditions." See Lindbeck's review in *JR* 59 (1979) 248-50.

5.1.2 Clarifications of Terms

A clarification of two recurring terms may be useful at this point. Lindbeck distinguishes between "propositions" and "rules." The function of propositions is to express first-order statements, or, in other words, to make truth claims about objective (extra-linguistic) realities. Rules, by contrast, are second-order statements that identify, regulate, and govern the proper use of concepts (including first-order truth claims) in a particular domain, that is, in community discourse.[13]

We would do well to note that Lindbeck is not using the term "doctrine" in its broad sense in the line of traditional "teachings" or "beliefs." Rather, right at the outset, he describes as "those norms of communal belief and action," what we generally call "doctrines or dogmas." It is crucial to note that the objects of his attention are *normative* statements employed in the religious context, particularly as they concern the *"belief and action (credenda* and *agenda,* faith and morals, *mythos* and *ethos*) of religious communities."[14] In that context, doctrines are best regarded strictly as 'rules.' These rules are, for Lindbeck, *second-order* normative statements *concerning* proper beliefs and right actions, in accord with a performative theory of religious language, rather than first-order propositions *of* belief.[15] His principal concern centres on the need of the faith community to develop and articulate a theory of the nature of doctrine that will do a better job than those currently on offer for resolving doctrinal disputes. This concern is born of

[13] ND, 16, 18 & 69. See also Wayne Proudfoot, *"Regulae fidei* and Regulative Idea," in *Theology at the End of Modernity,* ed. S. G. Davaney (Philadelphia: Trinity Press International, 1991), 101.

[14] Charles M. Wood, "Review of *The Nature of Doctrine," RSRev* 11 (1985) 235.

[15] See ND, 7. The emphasis here is taken from Wood, "The Nature of Doctrine," 235.

his experience in ecumenical discussions which generally stagnate on account of the incongruity between the ways doctrines actually function and the ways their nature has ordinarily been conceived. Lindbeck believes that the rule theory of understanding doctrines, compared with alternative models, is better able to resolve hitherto intractable problems concerning doctrinal development, conflict and reconciliation.

In regard to Lindbeck's rule theory, an explicit caveat is entered that announces a restriction on its application. His rule theory, he cautions, is concerned with *doctrines qua doctrines* which are *not* first-order propositions, but are *rules* for appropriate Christian speech and truth-claims.[16] The novelty of Lindbeck's approach lies in his insistence that doctrines as such do not have any first-order function – assertorial, symbolic, or doxological. He will insist that doctrines, in his project, are to be construed as second-order statements that make "intrasystematic" rather than ontological truth claims. On the other hand, and this is crucial, he will agree that, in suitable contexts, doctrines *also* function symbolically or as first-order propositions but, when so employed, they are not being used as Church doctrines. One misses Lindbeck's entire argument when one does not follow this distinction closely. One will then inevitably end up frustrated with his seeming oscillations, as some commentators do.

5.1.3 The Factors Motivating Lindbeck's Work

To be cognizant of Lindbeck's basic motivations is important for a better understanding of his line of argument. To recap what we have seen so far, Lindbeck has schematically arranged theologians into three kinds, namely, preliberal (premodern), liberal[17]

---

[16] See ND, 19, 80, 106.

[17] Delwin Brown has called into question the accuracy of Lindbeck's characterization of liberal theology and of experiential-expressivism as the common

(modern), and postliberal (postmodern) theologians. In essence, this scheme suggests that preliberals take a "cognitive-propositional" approach to doctrine, liberals espouse an "experiential-expressive" approach, and postliberals advocate a "cultural-linguistic" approach. In terms of what the *nature and function* of doctrines are, these theologians offer three different answers. Preliberals see doctrines as propositions that express revealed and therefore unchanging truths. Liberals view doctrines as symbolic expressions of universal and unchanging religious experiences. Postliberals align doctrines to "rules" that reflect the "grammar" of specific religious traditions. Given their disagreement with a perceived liberal accommodation to the "acids of modernity," postliberals tend to be more critical of the liberals than of the preliberals. The reason, quite simply, is their shared discomfort over a liberal strategy that threatens to render vacuous the normative status of Christian doctrines.[18] To be sure, an adherence to Christian doctrinal norms necessarily suggests an espousal of their truth-claims. And yet, not only does Lindbeck not propose a return to preliberalism, but, more importantly for this chapter, Lindbeck strategically ranges his attack on both the symbolist and the propositionalist understandings of doctrines. His rule-theory necessitates such a strategy.

Lindbeck's main thesis is clear: of the different approaches to religions and, relatedly, Church doctrines, he advocates the

basis of nineteenth and twentieth-century liberal theology in America. See Delwin Brown, *Boundaries of Our Habitations*, 200 n.29; Delwin Brown and Sheila Greeve Davaney, "Liberalism: USA," in the *Encyclopedia of Modern Christian Thought* (Oxford: Blackwell, 1993), 325-30.

[18] Lindbeck's technical arguments have met with severe resistance. Thiel points out that Lindbeck "advances a strategic argument: unless that argument is appreciated as a counterpoint to the presuppositions of the liberal tradition, its principal achievements will be overlooked." See Thiel, "Review of *The Nature of Doctrine*," 109.

superiority of the cultural-linguistic view of religion and its regulative theory of doctrine. From the outset, he identifies three familiar theological theories of doctrine. These are, in his terms, the propositionalist, the symbolist, and a hybrid combination of the first two. Again, Lindbeck's strategy is transparent. He sets up these crisply defined models, and promptly dismisses them as ill-suited for his *central purpose* of intelligibly untying the doctrinal knots in ecumenism.[19] This paves the way for his alternative, the rule-theory of Church doctrine. The centerpiece of his proposal consists of an interest in those respects in which doctrines are analogous to the grammar and rules of languages, together with their correlative cultural forms of life. Cultures are semiotic realities and value systems. Under this perspective, Church doctrines function prominently as idioms for communally authorized discourse, attitudes, and actions.[20] In other words, Lindbeck wishes to effectively bring the theories of grammar and sociology into service in ecumenism and in theology. Regarding this strategy, four points are noteworthy.

First, an evaluation of Lindbeck's enterprise is rendered difficult on account of what he calls the "characteristics of the argument." His is a *theoretical inquiry* that is "more concerned with how to think than with what to assert about matters of fact." With an emphasis on providing a *framework* for settling issues, rather than actually settling particular issues, he wants to stress that, quite simply, the logic of rules and the logic of propositions are quite different from each other.[21]

Second, Lindbeck analyses other models not congenial to his own in the form of critiques. Such a procedure, as we saw in his

[19] See ND, 17.
[20] See ND, 17-18. The description, "centerpiece," comes from James J. Buckley, "Doctrine in the Diaspora," *Thomist* 49 (1985) 443.
[21] ND, 8, 9, 10 & 103; see also Buckley, "Doctrine in the Diaspora," 444.

discussion on theories of religion, is liable to deny an adequate
hearing to opponent models. That said, some commentators have
also noted that Lindbeck's intention is to call attention to a general, pervasive tendency, and not to offer a detailed analysis of any
one of its manifestations.[22]

Third, Lindbeck's theories are *explicitly* articulated in furtherance of his ecumenical goals. His work begins with the following
observations about the ecumenical matrix: (1) ecumenical reports
repeatedly indicate substantial convergence on many issues, and
yet denominational theologians continue to adhere to their once-
divisive convictions; (2) people generally, but wrongly, presume
that doctrinal reconciliation entails capitulation; (3) they also
believe that ecumenical openness conflicts with denominational
loyalty; (4) and yet, dialogue participants are agreed that radically
opposed positions of the past are now truly reconcilable, without
changing the original formulation; (5) the reason for the lack of an
official breakthrough stems from an inability to specify *the criteria for conceptualizing doctrines*; (6) the task ahead must surely
be to formulate categories efficacious for doctrinal reconciliation
without requiring capitulation on the part of any dialogue partner.[23] Such being the case, we are put on notice, as it were, that his
arguments may have been constrained by his ecumenical orientation. Avowedly instrumentalistic, his theoretical project aims to be
ecumenically and religiously neutral.[24]

[22] See, for instance, Wood, "The Nature of Doctrine," 236.

[23] ND, 7 & 15. Lindbeck stresses at the outset that the novelty of his work lies
in the application of the cultural –linguistic model and its implied rule theory,
borrowed from other disciplines, to theology, particularly to the task of the conceptualization of doctrine. His inquiry is targeted towards seeking concepts that
will remove the *anomalous* situations of lack of official breakthrough in ecumenical effort, despite an apparent removal of doctrinal conflicts (p.8).

[24] ND, 9. The ecumenical future, Lindbeck insists, belongs to those who
take doctrines seriously. His position calls for the recognition of each tradition

Fourth, the potency of Lindbeck's concern to defend the Christian faith has not escaped the attention of some authors. We have emphasized the significant extent to which his work is driven by his post-liberal, intratextual theology, a point alluded to in the subtitle of *The Nature of Doctrine*. "Prompted by convictions about the kind of theological thinking that is most likely to be religiously helpful to Christians and perhaps others in the present situation," he declares, his motivations are "ultimately more substantively theological than purely theoretical."[25]

Given that Lindbeck's approach is defined by his preoccupation with these four matters, he is inclined to reject models not congenial to his own. This, in turn, has persuaded some scholars to look more closely at these other models before assessing his. Space constraint deters us from taking the same course; instead, we shall concentrate more on Lindbeck's own model and *his* characterization of the others. Keeping in mind the onus this chapter seeks to discharge, it is pertinent to point out that a plain reading of Lindbeck runs the risk of a double-jeopardy of misconstrual: one, for failing to notice that his *theoretical* project centres on "how to think," and is aimed in the first place at ecumenical fruitfulness;[26] two, for failing to heed the fact that

---

as distinct and authentically Christian. He rejects any attempt at synthesis of competing formulations and their integration "from a new and common perspective into a larger and universally accepted whole." See Lindbeck, "The Future of the Dialogue: Pluralism or the Eventual Synthesis of Doctrine," in *Christian Action and Openness*, ed. J. Papin (Villanova, PA: Villanova University Press, 1970), 41, 37.

[25] ND, 10. The whole burden of Gordon E. Michaelson's article, "The Response to Lindbeck," *ModTh* 4 (1988) 107-20, is to show that, in fact, Lindbeck's real agenda lies in advancing postliberal intratextual theology, in radical opposition to the strong liberal-revisionist orientation in the contemporary theological scene.

[26] We therefore agree with Michael Root's observation that many commentators fail to note that Lindbeck only denies that doctrines, *used as doctrines* (i.e., as rules for appropriate Christian speech), make truth claims. See his "Truth,

464   J.C.K. GOH

he is a faithful Lutheran, who writes with an overriding theological interest, to which even his theoretical project is subordinated.[27]

Section I: Speaking of Truth

5.2 Truth and the Ecumenical Efficacy of the Theories of Church Doctrine

Communal norms do not seem to sit well with contemporary
people. Their daily perception is one of broken consensus and
changing views. Where individual freedom, autonomy and
authenticity rank high in personal values, communal loyalty
weakens: communal norms are regarded as stifling, and objective realities are only experienced in personal terms.[28] In an
atmosphere averse to doctrinal standards, what positive roles
do theories of doctrine play? And, in what ways do these theories contribute to, or impede, the ecumenical task?

Relativism, and Postliberal Theology," 180 n.4. For relevant passages in Lindbeck's book, see ND, 19, 80, 106.

[27] We are therefore unable to agree with Root when he argues that,
because Lindbeck develops his theological argument by borrowing from
social science, his proposal is hardly "Barthian." See Root, "Truth, Relativism, and Postliberal Theology," 180 n.15. But, if George Hunsinger's
searching analysis is correct, even Tracy's description of Lindbeck's scheme
as "Barthian confessionalism" may have to be qualified. Hunsinger writes:
"When it comes to stipulating the conditions for cognitive truth, the words are
the words of Lindbeck, but the voice is much more nearly that of Aquinas
than of Barth." See Hunsinger, "Truth as Self-Involving: Barth and Lindbeck
on the Cognitive and Performative Aspects of Truth in Theological Discourse," *JAAR* 61 (1993) 56.

[28] See ND, 77.

5.2.1 Three Opponent Models

5.2.1.1 The Propositionalist Theory of Doctrine

The propositionalist view, with its special interest in the cognitive meaningfulness of religious utterances, holds that Church doctrines are descriptive of ontological realities.[29] The doctrine of the Trinity, for instance, is held to describe the being of God ('Immanent' Trinity).

The traditional propositionalist notions of authoritative teaching have, in Lindbeck's assessment, contributed to giving doctrine a bad name. He notes three weaknesses. *First*, these notions or truth-claims promote rigidity by making it difficult to see how new doctrines can emerge and how old ones can become peripheral. *Second*, they offer an unconvincing account of how old doctrines may be reinterpreted to suit new settings. *Third*, they fail to deal with the specific ecumenical problem of reconciling opposing doctrines without capitulation. The controlling question for Lindbeck is how it might be possible "for doctrines that once contradicted each other to be reconciled and yet retain their identity?"[30]

Intellectually equating doctrines with axioms and definitions, propositionalism insists that "if a doctrine is once true, it is always true, and if it is once false, it is always false." Inflexibility being its hallmark, propositionalism admits of "no degrees or variations in propositional truth."[31] Since it accommodates no doctrinal

[29] See ND, 16.

[30] ND, 78.

[31] See ND, 64, 16 & 47. Lindbeck cites (p.26 n.3) this particular view of doctrine as the focus of Hans Küng's attack on the doctrine of infallibility, in Küng's *Infallible? An Inquiry*, trs. Edward Quinn (New York: Doubleday, 1971), 157-73. Lindbeck does not discount infallibility, but notes the problems it poses to Christian unity. See Lindbeck, *Infallibility* (Milwaukee: Marquette University Press, 1972); "The Infallibility Debate," in *The Infallibility Debate*, ed. John J.

change in any significant sense without varying the traditional for-mulation, *no doctrinal reconciliation* under this model is possible *without capitulation*. It is a position wholly unsuited for ecumeni-cal use. It would, for instance, be futile to seek to harmonize the "historic affirmations and denials of transubstantiation" under this model.[32]

5.2.1.2 The Symbolist Theory of Doctrine

The symbolists regard doctrines as "noninformative and non-discursive symbols" of inner states, feelings, and experiences. Doctrines are perceived as historically relative and malleable attempts to express the universal "inner experience of the divine" that everywhere has a common character.[33] The Trinity is here interpreted as a transcript of the Christian experience of God.

Lindbeck locates the error of this liberal view in its post-Enlightenment tendency to identify the essence of all religions with common human experience. Particularly objectionable to him, is the propensity on the part of the symbolists to suggest that doctrines are derivative articulations of religious experience,

Kirvan (New York: Paulist, 1971), 35-65; "Papal Infallibility: A Protestant Response," *Com* 102 (1975) 145-46; "Problems on the Road to Unity: Infalli-bility," in *Unitatis Redintegratio: 1964-1974: Eine Bilanz der Auswirkungen des Ökumenismusdekrets*, ed. Gerard Békés and Vilmos Vatja (Frankfurt: Verlag Otto Lembeck, 1977), 98-109; "The Reformation and the Infallibility Debate," in *Teaching Authority and Infallibility in the Church*, ed. Paul C. Empire et al. (Minneapolis: Augsburg, 1980), 101-19.

[32] See ND, 16. Given their rigid view of doctrines, preliberals are under-standably sceptical about the ecumenical effort. Ecumenical agreements, if any, could only have come about through one party or the other, or both, selling out. If previously there was a doctrinal disagreement, a later reconciliation could only have resulted from one party changing its position. See Neuhaus, *The Catholic Moment*, 151.

[33] See ND, 16 & 47.

rather than the other way around. Even as he acknowledges the popularity of the symbolic interpretation of doctrines, and admits it will continue to hold sway, he insists this popularity is purchased more by compromise with culture than reaffirmation of authentic Christian identity.

Lindbeck again dismisses this theory as a candidate for the ecumenical task. At first sight, there seems to be a lack of internal coherence in Lindbeck's reasoning on this point. Might not one argue that, even on the basis of Lindbeck's description, the symbolist model is useful in relativising what seems like an uncompromising reality of opposing doctrinal traditions, by grounding them all in a more fundamental solidarity, in this case, the common primordial experience of the Transcendent? Has not Lindbeck himself conceded that, for the symbolists, "religiously significant meanings can vary while doctrines remain the same, and conversely, doctrines can alter without change of meaning"? Has he not granted that, logically pursued, confirmation or denial of transubstantiation are not, for the symbolists, necessarily diametrically opposed at the experiential level? Similarly, has he not declared that, logically, in the eyes of the symbolists, Buddhists and Christians might be said to have the same faith, although expressed differently?[34] However, Lindbeck reserves for this model a precise warrant for dismissal. The symbolist view, he argues, may be put into service as long as the dispute is defined by underlying feelings. But, he insists, this is not the case in ecumenism. In positing doctrines as polyvalent, nondiscursive symbols, the symbolist view portrays doctrines as "subject to changes of meaning or even to a total loss of meaningfulness." As a result, *no doctrinal constancy* is envisaged here; it is a view that can play no

---

[34] See ND, 17.

meaningful role in ecumenical disputes at the very level where disputes are at their most acute, namely, the insistence upon doctrinal objectifications.[35]

Proponents of the symbolist model erode Christianity's claim to preserve "the faith which was once and for all delivered to the saints (Jude 3)." If this model is used to placate the modern antipathy towards age-old doctrines, by the simple expedient of viewing these doctrines as merely expressive of deeper experiences that require reformulation in new contemporary settings, it may well lead to a relativising trend under the social pressure of the day. It cannot be taken seriously in view of its tendency "to exclude *a priori* the traditional characteristics of doctrine." By way of illustration, Lindbeck observes that while the Resurrection may be affirmed, it ceases to be an abiding norm of communal faith if it is the symbol of an experience which can, in principle, be expressed in different ways. In consequence, what Lonergan calls the "classical" propositional views of doctrine would be neglected.[36]

In a passage that epitomizes Lindbeck's disdain for what he perceives to be a liberal marketing strategy for the spread of the Christian faith to the present generation, he describes how past doctrines that now appear absurd to modern minds, are conveniently treated as items that were "never important in themselves, but were only expressive symbolizations of deeper experiences and orientations that ought now to be articulated in other and more contemporary ways." In this portrayal, experiential-expressivism is very handy for legitimizing "the religious privatism and subjectivism that is fostered by the social pressures of the day."[37] In

[35] See ND, 16 & 17.
[36] See ND, 77-78, 79 & 80.
[37] ND, 77. In a similar vein, Neuhaus attributes liberalism's failure to be of any help in attaining ecumenical agreement or even disagreement, principally to

sum, so long as religious experience is understood as subjective, it will remain a "vacuous and nebulous concept." The "diachronic continuity and constancy" of this experience will necessarily be beyond verification or falsification.[38]

5.2.1.3 A Hybrid of Two Perspectives

A third approach, which combines the grounding in experience of the second with the objective reference of the first, is said to find favour with ecumenically-inclined Catholics and is, according to Lindbeck, best exemplified by Lonergan and Rahner.[39] Even though this hybrid approach has its advantages over "one dimensional alternatives," for the purposes of Lindbeck's scheme it gets subsumed under the first two approaches. In fact, more often than not, Lonergan and Rahner serve, along with Tracy, as representatives of the second type, the symbolists, in the contemporary liberal context, with Schleiermacher's theology representing the prototype. Though they are better able than the first two groups to account for doctrinal changes, the proponents here are nevertheless said to have difficulty in coherently combining the two approaches. Using "complicated intellectual gymnastics," they are unpersuasive, their arguments "too awkward and complex,"

the fact that different doctrinal formulations under the liberal lens are regarded as different ways of saying the same thing. "Liberal ecumenism," he judges, "thus tends to produce a type of lowest-common-denominator dialogue that is depressingly vacuous. Successful ecumenical dialogue must produce not a synthetic new tradition but a confession in which both parties to the dialogue can recognize their own tradition." See Neuhaus, *The Catholic Moment*, 151.

[38] See McGrath, *The Genesis of Doctrine*, 22.

[39] Rahner and Lonergan may have been cited on account of a symbolic realism that they hold, founded on notions of veridical insight arising out of the impact of experience. See Paul Avis, "Theology in the Dogmatic Mode," in *Companion Encyclopedia of Theology*, ed. Peter Byrne and Leslie Houlden (London: Routledge, 1995), 994.

not easily intelligible and thus lacking in their ability to convince. Lindbeck thus applies Ockham's razor.[40]

Furthermore, Lindbeck assesses them as lacking in criteria for deciding when a doctrinal development might be consistent with the sources of faith, which explains their "rather greater reliance on the magisterium" in such matters.[41]

5.2.2 The Rule-Theory of Doctrine and Its Superiority

5.2.2.1 Lindbeck's Rule Theory

In Lindbeck's observation, a cardinal rule in ecumenical theological dialogues is the avoidance of any hint of a "compromise." From his lengthy association with the ecumenical enterprise, Lindbeck has come to the conclusion that ecumenical discussions have been hindered by the lack of "adequate categories" to account for "doctrinal reconciliation without doctrinal change."[42] The critical issue in Lindbeck's scheme is whether the dialogue partners can recognize from the new formulation that has been reached, not a synthetic new tradition, but a position that reflects their own as well as that of the interlocutor.[43] In a situation of radically opposed models, Lindbeck proposes something significantly different. He seeks an ecumenical theory of doctrine which can operate as the neutral "grammar" of varied Christian speech and

---

[40] For Lindbeck's recourse to Ockham's razor as a simple expedient, see ND, 38. The implications go much deeper. This recalls, amongst other things, even the old grace and nature controversy which we shall revisit in sections 5.3.3 and 5.4.5 below.

[41] ND, 77. Lindbeck stresses the complexity of the hybrid scheme as the paramount factor that defines his judgment against this perspective. See ND, 26-27 n.5.

[42] ND, 7 & 15.

[43] See Neuhaus, *The Catholic Moment*, 238.

action, and suggests that a "functional" or "regulative" model of doctrine that uses the linguistic "rule-theory" is best suited for the job. He further claims such a model can accomplish the impossible: it would allow for variability in the doctrines of faith without compromising the transcendent value those doctrines purport to contain.[44]

For the theoretical underpinnings for this rule-theory, Lindbeck returns to the cultural-linguistic analysis of religion. The relationship of doctrines to religious belief and practice, he postulates, is best reflected in the relationship of grammatical rules to a natural language: just as grammatical rules are norms for proper linguistic usage, so doctrines are normative illustrations of proper belief. Under a cultural-linguistic lens, doctrines are not presumed to present ontological truth-claims (as they must in the cognitive model) nor to contain only subjective symbols and experiences (as they do in the symbolist model). According to the rule-theory, the *most prominent* function of Church doctrines is their use as "communally authoritative rule of discourse, attitude, and action."[45] Saying the same thing in a different way, within a religious system, Lindbeck argues, doctrines operate not as first-order statements about what there is but as second-order *rules* determinative of the way their adherents are to speak, act and shape their lives. In this specific sense, doctrines are like the "deep" grammar of a language which determines what is a correct performance of the language.[46]

---

[44] ND, 17. For an attempt to trace the salient features of Lindbeck's regulative proposal to Kierkegaard, see Steven M. Emmanuel, "Kierkegaard on Doctrine: A Postmodern Interpretation," *RelSt* 25 (1989) 363-78.

[45] Rahner, "What Is a Dogmatic Statement?," *Theological Investigation* 5:54 has also described a dogmatic statement as "a communal linguistic ruling on terminology."

[46] The kernel of this programme was already in place fifteen years earlier in a paper Lindbeck delivered to an International Lonergan Congress in 1970. See Lindbeck, "Protestant Problems with Lonergan on Development of Dogma," in *Foundations of Theology*, ed. Philip McShane (Dublin: Gill & Macmillan, 1971), 115-23.

The novelty of the rule theory thus lies in its view of religion as a *story* to be told and its regard for the *grammar* that informs the proper retelling and use of that story. Every religion presents a comprehensive framework of categories for interpretation. In the case of Christianity, the story, as it is related by the biblical narratives, is Christocentric.[47] Doctrine, then, acts as a guardian, as it were, of that story, defining the categorial framework of the biblical narrative, delimiting it, giving the grammar by which it can be properly told and lived, and specifying the ways in which any claims can be true intrasystematically. Church doctrines thus provide lexical, syntactical and semantic rules for the Christian narrative. The rules are not truth-statements; properly applied in varied situations, they lead to and help manifest truth. They are the conditions of possibility for truth to reign in our lives. The linguistic analogy entails both grammar and vocabulary which are distinct but related. Vocabulary includes "symbols, concepts, rites, injunctions, and stories," all of which are coherent in their being leashed to a lexical core.[48]

Communal identity lies in *operative* doctrines, officially pronounced or otherwise, which regulate the practices of a distinctive body. Doctrines play an important role in establishing and regulating our Christian culture and hence in shaping our identity as Christians. In Lindbeck's "noncontroversial" description, doctrines are thus seen as "communally authoritative teachings regarding beliefs and practices that are considered essential to the

---

[47] See ND, 18 & 80.

[48] For illustration, Lindbeck refers to a particular doctrine: "The doctrine that Jesus is the Messiah, for example, functions lexically as the warrant for adding the New Testament literature to the canon, syntactically as a hermeneutical rule that Jesus Christ be interpreted as the fulfillment of the Old Testament promises (and the Old Testament as pointing toward him), and semantically as a rule regarding the referring use of such titles as 'Messiah.'" See ND, 81.

identity or welfare" of each group.[49] He argues that the structural coherence of the system of meaning within each group is defined largely by the rules which govern its functioning and thereby regulate the dynamics of legitimate participation within its boundaries of meaning. The authority of these rules coincides with their intrasystematic coherence. Evidently, a rule-theory of doctrines is highly particularistic in its orientation: doctrines are an integral part of a religion in guiding the nurture and instruction by which members of a community are shaped into a particular identity with a particular way of seeing and dealing with reality.[50]

One obvious advantage of *rules*, as opposed to propositions, according to Lindbeck, is their resilience. While rules possess intrasystematic normativeness, they are not invariable but responsive to the movement of historical experience. Their meanings remain unchanged even as they confront changing or conflicting situations. Lindbeck uses the example of radically conflicting traffic rules: "Drive on the left" for the British, and "Drive on the right" for the North Americans. Both are invariant, unequivocal, diametrically opposed, and yet equally binding to the users on their respective roads. A regulative conception constitutes an ideal tool for resolving the oppositions between these rules, without requiring any alteration to either of them. In a similar fashion, once cultural context and cultural change are appreciated, the implication for ecumenism can be immense: all we need to do is indicate when and where doctrines appropriately apply, or specify their order of precedence. *To the degree that doctrines function as*

[49] See ND, 18 & 74.

[50] See Ronald Burke, "Newman, Lindbeck and Models of Doctrine," in *John Henry Newman: Theology and Reform*, ed. Michael Willsopp and Ronald Burke (New York: Garland, 1992), 32. Lindbeck's main concern is thus "to give an account of doctrine which allows for pluralistic particularity." See Patrick Heifert, "Labor Room or Morgue: The Power and Limits of Pluralism and Christology," *Word & World* 5 (1985) 84.

rules, Lindbeck announces, historically opposed positions can be logically reconciled, while remaining unchanged. He takes the controversy surrounding the Eucharist as an illustration. The Roman Catholic doctrine of transubstantiation and other doctrines that seem to contradict it may be interpreted as "embodying sacramental thought and practice" that appeared irresolvably opposed and that was deeply entrenched in certain historical contexts. But, in changed circumstances, they can be "harmonized by appropriate specifications of their respective domains, uses, and priorities." Thus, unlike the propositional or the symbolist views, doctrinal reconciliation without capitulation becomes a coherent notion under the regulative theory.[51]

5.2.2.2 Testing the Rule Theory

Lindbeck notes that a conflict or controversy precipitates doctrinal articulation, with two notable consequences: [1] particular doctrines that become officialised can only be authentically understood contextually and in reference to what was being opposed (that is to say, they tend to deny, rather than to affirm); [2] at a time of conflict, exaggerated attention lends an inflated significance to matters otherwise trivial in relation to a community's most important beliefs. The latter, because they are not seriously challenged, are not the object of an official effort towards doctrinal clarification. Doctrines, in other words, are basically guiding us in what we are allowed to say and not say in a very particular context.

[51] ND,18. See William C. Placher, "Postliberal Theology," in *The Modern Theologians*, ed. David F. Ford (Oxford: Blackwell, 1989), II:120: "On the propositionalist model, if Lutheran and Catholic doctrines were in contradiction in 1541, then they still are. But on a regulative model, rules could apply in one circumstance but not another. They could still disagree about what it was essential to the health of the church to say in 1541, while agreeing on what needs saying now."

Lindbeck tests his model for ecumenical usefulness on three doctrines: Christological (and Trinitarian) affirmations, the irreversibility of doctrinal developments regarding Mary, and the infallibility of the teaching office. Here, we shall only examine Lindbeck's attempt to test the theological usefulness of his rule theory in relation to his most significant example, namely the Nicene dogma. He admits the distinction between form and content in doctrinal formulation. From its inception, Christianity sought to express the same faith, the same teaching, and the same doctrine in diverse ways, as the multiplicity of Christological titles testifies. Lindbeck maintains that other formulations and terms are possible than the ones provided by the bishops who formulated the Nicene Creed in A.D. 325 and the Chalcedonian Definition which qualified it in A.D. 451. He does not think the concepts employed in formulating these titles are "uniquely sacrosanct." His line of argumentation proceeds as follows: First, because Scriptures came into being over a long period of time, through the hands of many authors, and made use of Hebrew and Greek categories for their respective readers, there can be no unity to the canon *unless* we accept a *nonliteralistic* approach. Next, to account for the diversity of expressions and to preserve the distinctiveness of a given doctrine requires *either* a propositional *or* a regulative interpretation, since the symbolic view is impotent in the matter of distinguishing between doctrines. However, in order to achieve parity between different doctrinal formulations, it is "better" to regard doctrines as "second-order guidelines for Christian discourse rather than first-order affirmations about the inner being of God or Jesus Christ." Finally, Lindbeck conscripts an ancient authority for support, namely, Athanasius, and adopts his dictum for expressing the meaning of consubstantiality: *eadem de Filio quae de Patre dicuntur excepto Patris Nomine* ("whatever is said of the Father is said of the Son, except that the Son is not the Father") and adds:

Thus the theologian most responsible for the final triumph of Nicaea
thought of it, not as a first-order proposition with ontological reference, but as a second-order rule of speech. For him, to accept the
doctrine meant to agree to speak in a certain way. He and other early
fathers did not deny first-order interpretations, but according to Lonergan, these were at first only 'incipient'. It was only later, in
medieval scholasticism, that the full metaphysical import of the doctrine was asserted.[52]

Why is Lindbeck doing all this? The propositional view of doctrine succeeds well in portraying doctrines as unconditionally and
permanently true.[53] The Nicene doctrine *is* interpreted in that manner within the Church. The question for Lindbeck is whether his
regulative view can likewise *allow for* unconditional permanence.
But, with regard to the rule-theory, can we think of the Nicaenum
as primarily embodying a rule, a second-order proposition which
regulates community discourse, and not a first-order proposition
that refers to extra-linguistic reality? Stephen Williams denies that
any good grounds have been offered by Lindbeck to substantiate
his reconceptualization of the Nicaenum. Even from the quotation
given above, Lindbeck is documenting "a claim already heralded"
by the early Fathers, and "unpacking a surprise whose content has
already been described."[54] Moreover, to rely on Lonergan's
research on Athanasius, as Lindbeck has done, is problematic in

[52] See ND, 92-94. See also Bernard Lonergan, *Method in Theology* (York:
Herder & Herder, 1973²), 307-09. For some of Lindbeck's early reflections and
questions, see *The Status of the Nicene Creed as Dogma of the Church*, ed. P. C.
Empie and W. C. Baum (Washington, DC: National Catholic Welfare Conference, 1965), 11-15.

[53] For Lindbeck's "taxonomy of doctrines," see ND, 84-88.

[54] It is anachronistic to view the Nicene and Chalcedonian symbols as rules
only, Proudfoot pointedly observes in "*Regulae Fidei* and Regulative Idea," 112.
To consider the Nicene Creed as a second-order rule of speech is to project
"post-Kantian scepticism onto the Fathers," says Coleman E. O'Neill in "The
Rule Theory of Doctrine and Propositional Truth," *Thomist* 49 (1985) 439.

view of the doubtful reception of Lonergan's work among patristics specialists. But most crucially, Lindbeck overlooks the very focus on the "goal of conceptual and verbal analysis" undertaken in Lonergan's interpretation of Athanasius' dictum, namely, "as the outcome of an attempt to formulate the relation of Father and Son so that their ontological relation, or the ontological status of the Son, should be adequately protected." In formulating the rule comprised in the dictum, Athanasius takes special account of biblical titles like 'God', 'Omnipotent', 'Lord', and 'Light' which applied as much to the Son as to the Father.

> Indeed, Alexander of Alexandria was ahead of Athanasius in teaching this doctrine: before the Council of Nicea, he had affirmed that 'the Son is less than the Father only in this, that he is not unbegotten', and he ruled out every element of materialism, in the manner of understanding how the Father generated the Son.[55]

Wainwright advances the same view, emphasizing that a "*subsistent trinitarian relation* is being declared by Nicaea and by Athanasius. It is with this substantive content that the conciliar declaration is intended to give guidance to Christian language concerning God and Jesus Christ." Athanasius cannot be interpreted as merely enunciating a logical or grammatical rule.[56]

To be sure, the Athanasian dictum, as a "rule of discourse," does not insist that the Father and the Son must be spoken of in substance language every time. But the key question Lindbeck addresses is whether the regulative function developed in the early Church is *independent* of first-order reference to extra-linguistic reality. Here again, Williams finds that Lindbeck has clearly misread Lonergan.

[55] Stephen Williams, "Lindbeck's Regulative Christology," *ModTh* 4 (1988) 173, 174 & 176.

[56] See Geoffrey Wainwright, "Ecumenical Dimensions of Lindbeck's 'Nature of Doctrine'," 125-26.

The dictum validly regulates christological discourse as an analysis of scriptural data which predicates *de facto* omnipotence (e.g.) of the Father and Son. So the move to the concept of substance that emerged from [the] variegated multiplicity of titles to the sunlight of conceptual clarity was theologically serviceable for church doctrine and historically describable as such in the context of the ontological question.

Clearly, then, insofar as Lindbeck attempts to describe the Nicene creed as a Church 'rule', and, insofar as a 'rule' is defined by him as being innocent of any first-order reference, his proposal is anachronistic.[57] What Lindbeck suggests, however, is that if we allow a theoretical distinction between form and content, we may have new possibilities for developing contemporary formulations — provided, of course, these different formulations are not guided by any inner meaning, intentions, or positive propositional assertions from Nicaea and Chalcedon, but by certain *rules* which determine what it is we are allowed to say or not say while still being definable as the Church. The Nicene Creed and Chalcedonian Definition, as doctrines, function not to assert certain extralinguistic "truths," but to authoritatively *exemplify* rules of correct discourse.

Lindbeck then abstracts from historical evidence, and posits three regulative principles at work in the ancient (even in the New Testament period) trinitarian and christological affirmations, to which he attributes "unconditionality and permanence." These are:

[i] *The monotheistic principle*: "there is only one God, the God of Abraham, Issac, Jacob, and Jesus."

[ii] *The principle of historical specificity*: "the stories of Jesus refer to a genuine human being who was born, lived, and died in a particular time and place."

---

[57] See Stephen Williams, "Lindbeck's Regulative Christology," 177-78. Williams implies that since the validity of Lindbeck's theory in part rests on its demolition of the alternatives, the fact that arguments on behalf of his own model

[iii] *The principle of Christological maximalism*: "every possible importance is to be ascribed to Jesus that is not inconsistent with the first rules."[58]

These rules are a part of what Lindbeck calls the *grammar* of the religion that Church doctrines seek to reflect. Teachings that came to be rejected as heresies (e.g., docetism, gnosticism, adoptionism, arianism, nestorianism and monophysitism) met their fate on account of their cognitive dissonance under the joint pressure of these three criteria, and what "ultimately became Catholic orthodoxy was a cognitively less dissonant adjustment" to these rules. Hence, Lindbeck's main contention, in furtherance of his ecumenical aim, is that "if the same rules that guided the formation of the original paradigms are operative in the construction of the new formulations, they express one and the same doctrine."[59] In other words, terms and concepts used in christological discussions can change radically according to circumstance and need, while yet remaining faithful to the fundamental intention of the original impulse of faith. Even though these are but a first approximation, and more rules are needed, Lindbeck's point is clear enough. The creeds embody doctrines that are not to be regarded as truth assertions. As rules that are communally authoritative in different historical contexts, they explain doctrinal diversity and development. Lindbeck grants that an ontological interpretation of the Trinity is *possible* and not prohibited by the rule-theory, although he does not

suffer a severe setback under close scrutiny must, *ipso facto*, raise the question of viability of those alternatives.

[58] ND, 94. In addition to these three basic regulative principles identified by Lindbeck to be at work in the shaping of the classic doctrines of Incarnation and the Trinity, Graeme Garrett, in service of the feminist interest, advances a fourth rule, viz.: "Rule 3 may not be so interpreted as to yield non-equivalent theological consequences in relation to matters of gender difference." See idem, "Rule 4? Gender Difference and the Nature of Doctrine," *Pacifica* 10 (1997) 182.

[59] ND, 95.

concede that such an interpretation is either "doctrinally necessary" or "binding."[60] And yet, it must be argued that the application of the principle of christological maximalism would seem to be anything but a matter of choosing an ontological *option*. Clearly, the principle must *require* an ontological Trinity, for "presumably one cannot ascribe to Jesus the highest *possible* importance unless one accords his Person eternal, trinitarian divinity."[61]

This analysis points to the problem we raised at the beginning of this chapter, namely, whether Lindbeck's regulative model might not be more intelligible if it were more explicitly parasitic on other models. Lindbeck wishes to preserve the possibility of believers reading the creeds ontologically. If that is the case, Jay Wesley Richards suggests, we must not regard credal formulae as mere rules, but as *propositional attitude statements*. These are statements that assert certain epistemic attitudes with respect to certain truth-claims embedded in propositions. Yet, at the same time, Lindbeck's principal interest lies in articulating what doctrines *do*. Doctrines are rules, he insists. Clearly, to deny the propositional nature of the Nicaenum in exchange for a rule function is to commit the fallacy of an anachronistic reversal. Richards, in our view, correctly concludes that "even any plausible *rules* will be parasitic on the truth (or presumed truth) of particular propositions."[62]

5.3 Assessing Lindbeck's Typology

In view of the fact that debates over specific, controversial doctrines usually generate more heat than light, commentators appreciate Lindbeck's call for prior attention to the nature of doctrine

---

[60] See ND, 106.

[61] Stephen Williams, "Lindbeck's Regulative Christology," 184.

[62] See Jay Wesley Richards, " Truth and Meaning in George Lindbeck's *The Nature of Doctrine*," *RelSt* 33 (1997) 48-9.

itself.[63] However, as a general observation, Macquarrie questions the validity of Lindbeck's comparison of the three theories of doctrine, doubting the presupposition that they are of the same order.[64] Lindbeck's typology has come under severe criticisms.

5.3.1 The Historicised Propositionalists

A first critical comment on Lindbeck's typology is the doubt that must be cast on his characterisation of the approach he is most concerned to refute, when it comes to the question of the most adequate theory of doctrine, namely, the propositionalist approach. He suggests that only those who "combine unusual insecurity with naiveté" can subscribe to the propositionalist view that "if a doctrine is once true, it is always true, and if it is once false, it is always false."[65] A question commentators raise is whether the propositionalist view, as it is presented by Lindbeck, has ever been a theological position seriously held? He ascribes to the propositionalists the view that objective truth about God *can be stated* "definitively, exhaustively and timelessly in propositional form." And yet, such a portrayal does not adequately describe either the "classical or post-critical forms" of this position.[66] It is an unwarranted imputation of inflexibility to describe

---

[63] Robin W. Lovin, "When the Church Is a Church: Doctrinal Standards in Denominational Contexts," *The Drew Gateway* 57 (1986) 2.

[64] John Macquarrie, "Usefulness of Doctrines," *ExpT* 96 (1985) 316.

[65] See ND, 16, & 21. D. Z. Phillips comments in "Lindbeck's Audience," *ModTh* 4 (1988) 138 that Lindbeck "rightly wants to oppose that strong tradition in which propositions about the existence of God are treated as *presuppositions* of religion. On this view, those propositions stand in isolation, their sense being entirely unmediated."

[66] See McGrath, *The Genesis of Doctrine*, p.16. In "Ecumenical Dimensions of Lindbeck's 'Nature of Doctrine'," *ModTh* 4 (1988) 122, Geoffrey Wainwright makes an earlier remark to the same effect: "Responsible cognitivists have never held that their propositions speak the truth about God exhaustively."

doctrines under the propositionalist view as invariant, eternal truths. Scholars record a culpable negligence on the part of Lindbeck for failing to give credit to the propositionalist for a linguistic and historical sensitivity. This is an important observation; more so, because in the ecumenical context in which our discussion is presently situated, gatherings are more likely to be attended by dialogue-partners who are "*historicized* propositionalists."[67]

In fact, even in medieval times, dogma was perceived not in a wholly static fashion; rather, it was associated with a dynamic concept of a movement tending *towards* divine truth. Theologians were aware that while they were reliable, doctrines were incomplete descriptions of reality. The usefulness of doctrines was not so much defined by what they were in themselves, but by what they represented. What was intended in doctrinal formulations was not so much "to reduce experience to words," as to attempt to convey communal insights through words.[68] Lindbeck does not mention that cognitive-propositional statements do operate at different levels. Further, Lindbeck neglects the fact that cognitive approaches to doctrine take, as their point of departure, the "theological truism that no human language can be applied to God univocally."[69]

A crude correspondence theory of truth laid at the door of the propositionalist is clearly unjustified.[70] One of the weaknesses of

[67] This does not suggest that there are no more "linguistic absolutists" among the propositionalists. One clear example is Paul VI, as his 1965 encyclical, *Mysterium fidei*, shows. See B. A. Gerrish, "The Nature of Doctrine," *JR* 68 (1988) 88.

[68] See McGrath, *The Genesis of Doctrine*, 16-17.

[69] McGrath, *The Genesis of Doctrine*, 18.

[70] O'Neill correctly puts his finger on what, in fact, is a caricature by Lindbeck, when he calls it doubtful that any theory of religion or doctrine exists, at least within Christianity, which corresponds to the description given of cognitivism. See "The Rule Theory of Doctrine and Propositional Truth," 428.

Lindbeck's typology lies in his failure to attend to the principle of *analogy*. In an analogy, the issue is not one of the adequacy of *any* statements concerning God, for *no* statement can, strictly speaking, be adequate. The issue is how to speak of analogous uses of language and the analogical potential of linguistic expressions. To cite an illustration from Wainwright: "When we speak of the goodness, justice or love of God, the usage is not equivocal but, precisely, analogical."[71]

5.3.2 The Schleiermachian Communal Dimension

A second comment focuses on Schleiermacher's position which Lindbeck seems to have forced into a strait-jacket which is not true to its complexity. According to B. A. Gerrish, Schleiermacher does use a language that resonates with Lindbeck's depiction of experiential-expressivism. Schleiermacher

> does assert the presence of a common prereflective moment in every religious consciousness; he sometimes appears to picture religious experience as going on before and behind the language that tries to express it; and, sometimes, he writes as though religious communities came into being through the clubbing together of religious individuals. But none of this tells us what he took Christian doctrines to be.[72]

---

[71] Lindbeck's lack of attention to analogy is noted by Wainwright, "Ecumenical Dimensions of Lindbeck's 'Nature of Doctrine'," 123 and Richard Viladesau, "The Cultural Linguistic Model for Theology," *Jeevadhara* 21 (1991) 377. Guarino traces four major axial developments in twentieth-century thought on analogy and demonstrates its usefulness for systematic theology in "The Truth-Status of Theological Statements: Analogy Re-visited," *ITQ* 54 (1988) 140-55. For another historical account of the principle of analogy, see David B. Burrell, "Analogy," in *The New Dictionary of Theology*, ed. Joseph Komonchak et al. (Collegeville, MN: Liturgical, 1987), 14-16. Lindbeck's alleged lack of attention to analogy will be qualified later in reference to David Fergusson's analysis of Lindbeck's different analogical scheme.

[72] B. A. Gerrish, "The Nature of Doctrine," *JR* 68 (1988) 89.

It is thus necessary to state at once two points about the
Schleiermachian scheme germane to this discussion. *First*,
Christian doctrines "are not about the prereflective experience
underlying all religions but about the distinctively Christian
way of believing, in which everything is related to the redemption accomplished by Jesus of Nazareth." *Second*, it is to culpably ignore that Schleiermacher's dogmatic writings bear specifically upon the Protestant evangelical faith, for any reader to
insist on an element of "ubiquitous private experience" in his
work. What is emphasized is the communal and not the individual dimension in Christianity. Doctrines are "accounts of a particular community's faith, a faith that the individual comes to
experience only through participation in the community." Far
from expressing a prelinguistic experience, doctrines testify to
"an experience that has already been constituted by the language of the community." Consonant with Peter Berger's
analysis, Gerrish acknowledges a universal anthropological
ingredient in Schleiermacher's formulation of a "feeling of
absolute dependence." But a crucial distinction cannot be
glossed over without missing Schleiermacher's point: it is
never Schleiermacher's intention to reduce Christian faith to
this formulation or, for that matter, to any other private experience. In fact, the "entire movement of his theology is *away
from* what Lindbeck terms 'the homogenizing tendencies associated with liberal experiential-expressivism' (p. 128); even the
famous analysis of the universal, prereflective element in religious consciousness actually occurs within a line of thought
intended to define the Christian church."[73]

---

[73] Gerrish, "The Nature of Doctrine," 89-90.

5.3.3 The Dialectic in Rahner's Dogmatic Understanding

In conjunction with our discussion on the ordering of language and experience in the previous chapter, we have noted that, as a confession of faith, a dogmatic statement is for Rahner never merely a verbal "evocative objectification" of the content of faith, but actualizes both the revealed content of faith as well as the Church's act of faith. Rahner does not regard the relationship between language and experience as simply a correlation between the outward expression of some inner event and the inner event itself. There is always an essential dialectical dimension in that relationship, so that, just as the experience always exceeds the verbal expression, the verbal expression always informs the experience as well. Thus, in the ordering of the knowledge of faith and its articulation, the truth of faith is known *before* it becomes the explicit object of intellectual articulation. What Rahner posits is not a pre-reflexive experience, or unthematic knowledge, that is wholly independent of its reflexive articulation in faith consciousness. What he does say is that, while the articulation is carried out in view of an unthematic knowledge of that which is being articulated, the articulation is an exercise essential to that knowledge itself. Furthermore, insofar as we speak of an act of faith, Rahner does not regard it as having been finalised upon the completion of the articulation of faith. Rather, in Aquinas' scheme of things, the act of faith tends towards the source and goal of the knowledge of faith, which is the divine mystery revealed in Jesus Christ.

Our earlier discussion points to the fact that Lindbeck's analysis seeks to be consistent with his anti-foundational alternative to knowing-by-faith. What he develops is a Wittgensteinian model of knowing as knowing-how, with grammar functioning as guide in our correct use of language. Grammar-in-use is offered as a plausible way of getting round the pitfall of a foundationalist grounding of the life and language of faith in common inner experience to justify to unbelievers and believers alike. Lindbeck realizes that Rahner's affirmation of an experience of *"Vorgriff auf esse"* is distinguishable, though not separable, from its conceptual thematization and is the transcendental condition of all human knowing and willing.[74] He further assesses Rahner's position to be in agreement with that of Aquinas. Lindbeck's point is that the transcendental argument is invalid and thus transcendental experience is wholly impossible.[75] What is at stake, in David Burrell's view, is the old debate concerning the *preambula fidei*. In Lindbeck's reading of Aquinas, the *preambula fidei* function retrospectively for believers, and not as stepping stones for faith, for it is the community of faith that impels one to the threshold of faith.[76] This is markedly different from the traditional Catholic understanding where faith and reason can co-exist, even though reason depends for its origin and existence upon the grace of God. Faith arises out of a process in which human reason is involved at every step of the way. Thus, medieval theologians perceived the *preambula fidei* as naturally knowable by the normal exercise of human reason.[77]

Once again, we note an interesting difference that Lindbeck's Lutheran heritage makes. As a Protestant nonfoundationalist, he finds fault with foundationalism on the ground that it gives

[74] Despite Rahner's keen attention on "historicity, difference, otherness and absence," Guarino has no difficulty chracterising him as a foundationalist. While he disputes Lindbeck's label of propositionalist on Rahner, Guarino accepts that Rahner "remains reliant on transcendental grounds that posit an invariant metaphysical and epistemological structure common to all humanity." See Thomas G. Guarino, *Revelation and Truth* (Scranton: University of Scranton Press, 1993), 53

[75] See the page-length footnote 18 on ND, 43-44, and Lindbeck, "The *A Priori* in St. Thomas' Theory of Knowledge," in *The Heritage of Christian Thought*, ed. R. E. Cushman and E. Grislis (New York: Harper & Row, 1965), 41-63.

[76] See David Burrell, "Review of *The Nature of Doctrine*," *USQR* 39 (1984) 324.

[77] See Avery Dulles, "The Cognitive Basis of Faith," *Ph&Th* 10 (1998) 21.

priority to human reason over the divine initiative – the prevenient grace. The prevenience of God, whose gratuitous presence to potential believers, according to His promises encapsulated in the biblical narrative, is exclusively *constitutive* of faith, grace, merit, justification and so forth. From the Catholic perspective, the complexity of the matter cannot be resolved in the terms that have characterized the longstanding disputes between evidentialism and fideism, and which have recently found new echoes in the disputes between foundationalism and nonfoundationalism. Faith is a gift. There is no question of Catholics, who reject Pelagianism, claiming that sanctification and justification are purely achievements of human striving, or that faith is attainable by natural powers. It should also be without doubt that Catholics accept the primacy of God's work and of His word as they address us through Scripture and Tradition. However, Catholics, consistent with the tradition witnessed by such authorities as Augustine, Aquinas and Trent, would also give a prominent place to the action of grace in human mind and heart. Thus, Dulles advances the thesis that the approach to faith cannot be adequately undertaken without rendering attention to its different aspects, namely, the metaphysical, the historical, the religious and the theological.[78]

Lindbeck's propensity to wield Ockham's razor recalls Luther's ready recourse to the same expedient in removing Aquinas' 'infused grace' which served as an intermediary bridging the deep chasm separating God and humans. The rationale was, if one could go directly to God, why did one need an intermediary? However, Hunsinger makes the surprising observation that Lindbeck's use of Aquinas takes him to a "sophisticated version of the idea that grace perfects but does not destroy nature."[79] This

---

[78] See Dulles, "The Cognitive Basis of Faith," 29.
[79] Hunsinger, "Truth as Self-Involving," 49.

reading is rather different from our own which sees Lindbeck, with an antifoundationalist posture, stressing the prevenience of God. But it serves as an interesting pointer to Lindeck's anthropological ambivalence to which we shall return when we consider the notion of "constitutive truth."

5.3.4 A Flawed Application of Wittgenstein

A critical comment, repeatedly advanced by D. Z. Phillips, questions Lindbeck's proposed application of Wittgenstein's notion of grammar. Phillips deems it erroneous to assume that "the language in which we make judgments regarding what is true or false, is *itself* a description of the nature of reality." It is tempting, but quite wrong, to imagine that Wittgenstein's notion of grammar can "*itself* be used to determine the direction in which theological doctrines should develop," or that it can "*itself* become the handmaid of a *particular* theological development." Lindbeck, he suggests, has succumbed to this temptation.[80]

Tanner contributes to the discussion by examining rules and change. In the face of diverse Christian practices, a hallmark of postliberal theology is to ascribe the unifying factor in Christian identity to rules. Christian speech and action may vary according to situations, so the argument goes, but there may be an underlying unity with respect to the rules governing such speech and action. Such an argument presupposes that rules stay constant while historical change affects everything else: rules are insulated from the

---

[80] See D. Z. Phillips, *Faith After Foundationalism* (New York: Routledge, 1988), 195 & 213. Chapters 15 and 16 of this book together constitute a reprint of Phillips' article, "Lindbeck's Audience," *ModTh* 4 (1988) 133-54, with introductory remarks and some minor adjustments. Paul Rigby et al. contribute to the discussion by identifying a fundamental flaw in Lindbeck's appeal to Kuhn's concept of paradigms in the philosophy of science. See idem, "The Nature of Doctrine and Scientific Progress," *TS* 52 (1991) 669-88. See section 5.4.3.4 below.

vicissitudes of history. The postliberal alertness to historical and cultural particularities, and its treasured-insight that rules are produced by historical agents falters when a disjunction is made between "historically changing materials and abiding rules." Tanner reverts to a postmodern reading of Wittgenstein to deflate the postliberal account of Christian identity in terms of rules. Denying that the use of the same rules can serve as the linchpin of Christian identity, Tanner's point is fundamentally grounded in the fact that the object of Wittgenstein's philosophy was "to problematize what it means to follow a rule." Wittgenstein points up the fact that observing and enumerating purported instances of the application of a rule does not vouchsafe the accurate abstraction of "the" rule being applied. The postliberals are right in their claim that it is the rules which, correctly followed, lead to uniformity. Tanner's analysis, however, raises two questions as to how far this claim validly takes us. *First*, like a chess-game, knowing the rules only means one knows what moves one can legitimately make, without ensuring that one knows the best move to make at any given point of the game. *Secondly*, the Wittgensteinian point similarly affirms that appeal to communal norms does not guarantee stability, not least because these norms are liable to change in the course of decisions by human agency.[81]

5.3.5 An Amazingly "Liberal" Outcome

Lindbeck's avowed aim is to draw an important implication of his model of doctrine for ecumenism. Stressing cultural contexts and cultural change, his *functional* model recognizes that the first thing doctrines "do" is to teach the faithful how to speak and how

[81] See Tanner, *Theories of Culture*, 138-41. Hans Zorn, "Grammar, Doctrines, and Practice," *JR* 75 (1995) 509-20 contends that the role of religious

to properly tell their sacred story. Both of these, he claims, are logically prior to and independent of debates about the ontological truthfulness of doctrines. Doctrinal agreements among different denominations can, on this view, be understood as correlations of different but not contradictory regulative principles. Denominational differences can thus be "tamed" and accounted for as historical differences.[82] The weakness of his claim becomes apparent when Lindbeck draws a parallel with the contradictory British and American traffic rules. There, he overlooks one crucial datum, namely, the fact that traffic rules are conventions upon which people in a particular locale agree *or* laws they are obliged to observe while they find themselves in that locale, on pain of penal and civil sanctions operative within that locale. However, in Lindbeck's model, doctrinal agreement will be dependent *only* on the goodwill of the dialogue-partners; such an agreement is predicated neither on a real resolution of differences in substantive issues nor on pain of a legal enforcement like the traffic rules. In effect, Lindbeck's suggestion amounts to saying that "if we want to agree, we can, because we choose in what ways to use ... religious language." Such a theory of doctrine would be "liberal to the extreme."[83] Quite apart from the fact that Lindbeck's rule-theory of doctrine fails to take account of the doxological character of credal and conciliar statements of the early Church,[84] it certainly does not address the fact that religions deal with what *is*, with truth-claims.

practice in Lindbeck's account differs significantly from the role it plays in a Wittgensteinian analysis of language and doubts whether the Wittgensteinian framework plays a substantial role in Lindbeck's account as may at first appear.

[82] See Ronald Burke, "Newman, Lindbeck and Models of Doctrine," 35-36.

[83] See Georg Behrens, "Schleiermacher *contra* Lindbeck," 414-15.

[84] Kasper, "Postmodern Dogmatics," *Communio* 17 (1990) 186.

We are thus at once confronted by Hunsinger's pointed observation: "Surely no question stands closer to the core of any theological position than that of how truth is conceived."[85] How, then, does Lindbeck account for the truth of, and in, the Nicene creed or statements like "Christ is Lord"? To the question of doctrinal truth we must now turn.

5.4 On the Question of Truth and Meaning

Much is made of the notion that even though they look like first-order affirmations, doctrines actually function *as doctrines* only when they are taken as examples – that is, when the rules which they instantiate are learned and properly applied to life situations. The analogy of language and cultural rules offers Lindbeck the possibility of describing doctrines as malleable categories that do not function as objective truths *per se*, but frame the context within which a particular way of life is properly lived.[86] The downside of this approach is the obvious eclipse of the assertive dimension of religious faith. To appreciate his vision, a few interlocking arguments must first be in place.

5.4.1 An Option for Intrasystematic Truth

In keeping with his triumvirate typology, Lindbeck first speaks of propositional, expressive, and categorial truths. *Propositional* truths refer to the ontological correspondence of religious cognitive statements to objective reality. Terms of related effect are "ontological" and "veridical" truths. *Expressive* truths pertain to symbolic efficacy in communicating the inner experience of the

[85] Hunsinger, "Truth as Self-Involving," 42.
[86] See reviews of *The Nature of Doctrine* by Thiel in *HeyJ* 29 (1988) 107 and Wood in *RSRev* 11 (1985) 240.

divine. But, in a cultural-linguistic outlook, religions are seen as "different idioms for construing reality, expressing experience, and ordering life." In religions, truth claims are made and expressive symbols are employed, Lindbeck suggests, on the basis of what he calls "categories," i.e., "grammar" or "rules of the game." *Categorial* truth is dependent on the adequacy of truth claims made to the religious system in its entirety. When we compare religions, he claims, the first question has to do with the adequacy of their categories. *Categorial* truth is a precondition for propositional, practical or symbolic truth but does not guarantee it.[87] In relation to these three visions of truth, two distinct but related questions call for attention. The first pertains to *how* we can *justify* a truth-claim (i.e., the question of justification). The second pertains to *what* it *means* to say that something is true (i.e., the question of meaning).[88]

Firstly, in every theory that aims to justify the truth of a religious doctrinal tradition, a comprehensive interpretive structure is erected which purports to operate as the context within which truth claims are somehow justified. Within an experiential-expressive vision of religion, a comprehensive anthropology forms an overarching context within which the truth of Christian faith in the modern world is understood. It is the interpretive context that reveals *the point* or "truth" of the faith. But, a comprehensive context that embraces both religion and modernity is a continuation of the liberal Enlightenment programme which Lindbeck

---

[87] See ND, 48-52. For a brief but incisive criticism of Lindbeck's "categorial truth" as a condition for ontological truth, see Paul Griffiths, "An Apology for Apologetics," *F&Ph* 5 (1988) 409-11. Murphy, *Anglo-American Postmodernity*, 122 argues that Lindbeck ought to have employed "categorial adequacy" rather than "categorial truth."

[88] In the following analysis, much is drawn from Michael Root, "Truth, Relativism, and Postliberal Theology."

feels obliged to reject.[89] Moreover, a commitment to Christian
particularity being the defining feature of his theological programme, Lindbeck is bound to reject any comprehensive interpretive context that ends up subsuming the Christian message under a
scheme of interpretation that is extraneous to that message. The
problem for Lindbeck, then, is that the question of the justification
of the Christian faith will now have to be achieved in a complicated way.[90] In particular, three aspects of Lindbeck's demonstration and argument stand out: a non-foundationalist epistemology;
seeing religion as a comprehensive whole that shapes our entire
life and thought; and taking the lived comprehensive religion as a
whole, not its individual parts, as needing justification. "As actually lived," Lindbeck suggests, "a religion may be pictured as a
single gigantic proposition."[91] Lindbeck knows that his argumentation is circular at this point, rendering it suggestive but quite
impossible to demonstrate or refute: "theoretical frameworks
shape perceptions of problems and their possible solutions in such
a way that each framework is in itself irrefutable."[92] This, as we
saw, inevitably draws a debate on the relativistic and fideistic
aspects of his claims.

Next comes the question of the nature of truth, a question that
ties in closely with the debate on truth and reference. From our
discussion on referentiality in regard to the postliberal, intratextual

[89] The proposal that the liberal Enlightenment project is, or ought to be, long
over, is receiving anything but a universal support. For a recent discussion, contra MacIntyre, see Mark D. Chapman, "Why the Enlightenment Project Doesn't
Have to Fail," *HeyJ* 39 (1998) 379-93.

[90] To be sure, some commentators have noted that Lindbeck himself may not
have escaped the very accusation of over- intellectualizing the Christian communal faith which he leveled at Rahner and Lonergan, on basis of which he wielded
Ockham's Razor. See, for example, Martin R. Tripole, "Review of *The Nature of
Doctrine*," *TS* 46 (1985) 384.

[91] ND 51 and 33.

[92] ND, 10.

reading of Scritpures, it is to be expected that Lindbeck is not anxious to articulate the case, or even preserve the idea, that truth is correspondence or reference to a reality beyond language. When he comes to discuss doctrinal truth, Lindbeck does not think we can know the transcendental reality of God in itself. Since the cognitive content of truth claims about God is, for him, "minimal," he wishes to stress the "informational vacuity" of much of our religious truth claims. Take, for example, the assertion "God is good." Lindbeck accepts that "God truly is good in himself is of utmost importance because it authorizes responding as if he were good." But, he insists, the fact that God's goodness is meaningful and true in Christian life does not mean we know the meaning of "God is good." His aim is to show that to really have propositional force, religious utterances must be put to performatory use.[93] In keeping with his holistic vision of religion as a single gigantic proposition, Lindbeck thus radically extends this holism to his discussion on truth, insisting that correspondence must be grasped in relation to a religion in its totality rather than to any of its parts. That totality is understood in the most global sense possible, to include all Christian assertions and practices, that correspond to something which lies beyond them, but with special emphasis on practice. This is an approach that is functional and pragmatic, but the line of reasoning points up the importance of coherence between faith and life: if the faith embodied in the credal formula "Christ is Lord" is used to shape an authentic Christian life, it is a true utterance; but if it is used to authorize a crusader crushing the skull of an infidel, it is false.[94] Truth is considered as the intelligibility of the categories in terms of which a particular vision of reality is framed. In sum, a religious statement is *categorially* true if its faith-claim is coherently enacted in life.

---

[93] ND, 66-67.

[94] ND, 64. Michael Root draws an analogy between the murderous crusader

Lindbeck is all too aware that Christians generally affirm "Jesus Christ is Lord" as more than a merely categorial truth: the Jesus Christ of the Gospels "is, was and will be definitively and unsurpassably the Lord." The propositionalist model admits this with ease and its strength here is obvious. The crucial challenge for the rule-theorist alternative is to show that it, too, has the capacity to account for such truth claims. To that end, Lindbeck follows the trajectory of *intrasystematic* truth, which he distinguishes from ontological truth: the former is the truth of coherence with context; the latter is the truth of correspondence to reality. Intrasystematic truth occurs in a religious context whenever a confessional utterance is made which coheres with the religion as a whole, i.e., when it coheres not only with other statements, but also with the correlative forms of life.[95] A statement uttered out of context is incoherent and thereby false. While this differs sharply from *ontological truth* — "that truth of correspondence to reality which, according to epistemological realists, is attributed to first-order propositions," Lindbeck wishes to affirm *the possibility* of ontological truth alongside his intrasystematic option. He locates the primary mistake of a propositional theory in neglecting that "a religious system is more like a natural language than a formally organized set of explicit statements, and that the right use of this language, unlike a mathematical one, cannot be detached from a particular way of

crying "Christus est Dominus" and the unbelieving recipient of the Eucharist. "Precisely because the words refer to the Jesus who is indeed Lord, precisely because they are true despite the life in which they are uttered, they are words that expose sin, words of judgment." See Michael Root, "Truth, Relativism and Postliberal Theology," 179.

[95] ND, 64. Timothy Jackson sees intrasystematic truth as "a matter of verbal or logical consistency, rather than of correspondence between language and reality." See "Against Grammar," *RSRev* 11 (1985) 242.

behaving."[96] What he must do, is to make *contextual* and *performative* aspects essential requirements for the *ontological* truth of statements. "If the form of life and understanding in the world shaped by an authentic use of the Christian stories does in fact correspond to God's being and will, then the proper use of '*Christus est Dominus*' is not only intrasystematically but also ontologically true."[97] Performance, ultimately, is the key.

5.4.2 Truth as Performance: A Reliance on Pragmatism

We set out to show that Lindbeck never intended to deny the doctrinal truth claims of the Christian Tradition. His insistence upon the *sola Christi* and the eschatological salvation of non-Christians contingent upon a *fides ex auditu*, are sufficient to disclose his deep-seated faith in the Christian economy of salvation. He is not concerned with the project of legitimating or denying the propositional content of doctrines as such. As we saw earlier, Lindbeck prefers to give to the term "doctrinal truth" a pragmatic signification. His principal focus is not the cognitive content of religious utterances, but only the *function* they have in "constituting a form of life, a way of being in the world." Truth is the structural coherence of a symbol system, the key to that coherence being right performance. Throughout, a certain consistency is maintained in Lindbeck's scheme. Just as the task of theology is to assist the formation of Christian identity, the correlate for theological "truth" is seen in terms of faithfulness to the fundamental

---

[96] See ND, 64. So Lindbeck is here trying to show that: "To have truth values, the Christian assertions must be used to shape lives in specific ways... Here the emphasis is not upon the formal rules considered in isolation, but upon the technique of applying them in determinate contexts." See L. C. Barrett, "Theology as Grammar," 161.

[97] ND, 65.

Christian narratival portrayal. To participate in the Christian tradition is to interiorize its story and to learn its way of life by practice. His epistemologically non-realist view of religions thus
issues in a preference for the performative: performance is the
ultimate test, not metaphysical analysis. Hence Christianity is one
gigantic proposition. As a comprehensive scheme or story used to
structure all dimensions of existence, Christianity is "not primarily a set of propositions to be believed, but is rather the medium in
which one moves, a set of skills that one employs in living one's
life."[98]

Lindbeck's interest in the *performative* aspect of religious language is consistent with a commitment to a particularistic understanding of the meaning and truth of the Christian faith.[99] Given
that commitment, ontological truths are de-emphasized. Commentators miss the point if they "fail to note that Lindbeck only denies
that doctrines *used as doctrines*, i.e., as rules for appropriate
Christian speech, make truth claims."[100] Lindbeck's agenda is "to
suggest the 'availability' of cultural-linguisticism as a 'serious
option' whose ultimate test is 'performance'."[101] Just as we have
criticized Lindbeck for wrongly truncating the theologies of
Schleiermacher and Rahner, so too, we must dissent from critics
who truncate Lindbeck's. In sum, doctrinally, Lindbeck's scheme
does not detract from our findings in chapter one. Christian doctrines do make truth claims about Jesus Christ and God. Lindbeck's contribution consists in an insistence that we neither sell
the Christian faith short by simply accommodating it to modernity,

[98] ND, 35.

[99] Bruce Marshall, "Truth Claims and the Jewish-Christian Dialogue,"
ModTh 8 (1992) 221.

[100] Michael Root, "Truth, Relativism, and Postliberal Theology," 180 n.4.
See ND, 19, 80, 106.

[101] James J. Buckley, "Doctrine in the Diaspora," 445. See also ND, 134, 73, 91.

nor speak inconsequentially of the Christian truth. Church doctrines not only present the truth claims of the Tradition, they also
articulate the Christian experience, and, as Lindbeck correctly suggests, they are also rules for group identity and authentic practice.

What scholars question is the real substance of his allocation of
importance to the work the propositional side of religion does.
When Lindbeck compares religions, his focus is not on truth
claims, but on the power of religion to conform people "to the
ultimate reality and goodness that lies at the heart of things."
Truth, for him, consists in a correspondence between the way a
religion is lived and what a theist calls "God's being and will."
What matters is the performative side of religion, for a religious
utterance "acquires the propositional truth of ontological correspondence only insofar as it is a performance, an act or deed,
which helps create that correspondence."[102] Lindbeck preempts an
objection and admits that, for Paul and Luther, Christ's Lordship
is objectively real in the very utterance of the credal formula
"Jesus is Lord." This advances the case for the cognitivists,
whose impact he attempts to weaken by capturing Paul and
Luther's emphasis on *doing*, or committing oneself to a way of
life, as the only authentic way for asserting that "Jesus is Lord" –
an emphasis he presumes to be wholly congruent with his thesis
that "it is only through the performatory use of religious utterances that they acquire propositional force."[103] How, then, are

---

[102] ND, 51 & 65. For this point, Lindbeck draws a parallel with John A.
Austin's famous notion of the performatory use of language in *How to Do Things
with Words* (Oxford: Clarendon, 1962); "Performative Utterances," in *Philosophical Papers* (Oxford: Clarendon, 1972[2]), 232-52. Of interest too is Ian T.
Ramsey's analysis of the language game as a language of discernment and commitment, in his *Religious Language* (London: SCM, 1957).

[103] See ND, 66. The performatory approach to religious utterances is also
favoured by Hermen-Emiel Mertens in his christological study, *Not the Cross,
But the Crucified: An Essay in Soteriology* (Leuven: Peeters, 1992).

intrasystematic and ontological truth related? Lindbeck's thesis betrays a tension: *first*, he suggests that intrasystematic truth is a necessary but insufficient condition for ontological truth, thereby affirming that the latter is *more than* the former; *second*, he suggests that ontological truth co-exists with religious language if and only if it belongs to a form of life which "itself corresponds to the Most Important, the Ultimately Real,"[104] thereby affirming that ontological truth is intrasystematically dependent. Thus, when Lindbeck describes the ontological truth of a religious statement as "correspondence to reality," he is not expounding on an attribute that the statement has in and of itself, but only a function of its role in constituting a form of life, a way of being in the world.

Lindbeck further seeks to hold the conjunction of the intrasystematic and ontological notions of truth together by a Thomistic theory of meaning, arguing that his preferred model need not exclude, even though it does not imply, a kind of modest propositionalism espoused by classical theists epitomized by Aquinas.[105] Here, Lindbeck appears to have developed a rather different kind of a principle of analogy grounded in a conjunction of the ideas of truth and use.[106] He presents Aquinas as holding that, "although in statements about God the human mode of signifying (*modus significandi*) does not correspond to anything in the divine being, the signified (*significatum*) does."[107] The claim that "God is good,"

---

[104] ND, 65.

[105] Even as he creates a space for ontological truth in religious discourse, therefore, Lindbeck narrows it significantly. His reliance on Aquinas for support of what he calls a "modest propositionalism" is described by Jay Wesley Richards as both tendentious and agnostic. See "Truth and Meaning in George Lindbeck's *The Nature of Doctrine*," *RelSt* 33 (1997) 39.

[106] For this important observation and the subsequent analysis, see David Fergusson, "Meaning, Truth and Realism in Bultmann and Lindbeck," *RelSt* 26 (1990) 196.

[107] See ND, 66. Lindbeck's misreading of Aquinas is treated by Colman E. O'Neill in "The Rule Theory of Doctrine and Propositional Truth," *Thomist* 49

for instance, means there is a notion of goodness unavailable to us which applies to God. But while we do not affirm that any of our concepts of goodness (*modi significandi*) apply to God, and that the notion of "God is good" cannot be comprehended by us in and of itself, we nevertheless do assert that the statement "God is good" is both meaningful and true and is something that we urge the community to interiorize and exercise in all dimensions of our existence. It follows that even though the human mode of signifying is analogous to something in itself unknown, it nevertheless functions performatively in enabling us to live and act *as if* God were good, according to goodness in common parlance. The end result is a theory of analogy that qualifies a religious utterance as true if it is properly used in context and its *significatum* corresponds to God, as the community understands God.

5.4.3 An Assessment

5.4.3.1 Rule-Viability and a Price Tag

Lindbeck's particularist focus on doctrines has much to recommend it. At the inter-religious level, respect for the diverse but particular doctrinal-traditions of dialogue partners urges a doctrinally-specific approach to dialogue. If the way to become religious is to be skilled in the language and symbol system of a religion, then the point is not to interpret doctrines but to develop the sort of skills it takes to follow or not follow them as circumstances arise. Religions can on these grounds engage in interreligious dialogue, concentrating more on appreciating how each religion

(1985) 417-42. O'Neill's critique is resisted by Bruce D. Marshall in "Aquinas as Postliberal Theologian," *Thomist* 53 (1989) 353-402, whose rebuttal is gratefully received by Lindbeck in "Response to Bruce Marshall," *Thomist* 53 (1989) 403-06.

attempts to develop its own skills, without sacrificing claims of
unsurpassability.[108] Within the Christian fold, the focus on performance promotes the important insight that religious language aims
at correspondence not only of the mind, but of the whole human
being, to the reality of God.[109] What is crucial, in this context, is
to appreciate the contribution Lindbeck makes concerning religious truth, for he forcefully brings to centre-stage what it means
to be Christian: Is it to utter meaningless and incoherent truth-
claims, or to live the truth that has been once and for all delivered
to the saints?

As for his explicit agenda of furthering the cause of ecumenical
progress, Lindeck assumes the staggering task of reconceptualiz-
ing the nature and function of ecclesiastical doctrine, its claims to
authority, and the manner in which it reveals truth. The rule-theory through which he chooses to unpack his scheme is a functional
analysis of doctrine by which validity is assessed contextually
rather than ontologically. He has no intention of challenging
Luther's statement against Erasmus: "Take away assertions, and
you take away Christianity." Rather, in his conceptual scheme,
truth is considered as the intelligibility of the categories in terms
of which a particular vision of reality is framed, rather than as the
correspondence of that vision to an objective metaphysical referent. There, the cultural-linguistic model is appealing for its capacity to account for Christian truth claims while avoiding the mire of
reductionistic subjectivity and the criticism that has befallen meta-
physically-grounded models of truth.[110] While his rule-theory

---

[108] See, e.g., J. A. DiNoia, *The Diversity of Religions: A Christian Perspective*
(Washington, DC: Catholic University of America Press, 1992). For Lindbeck's
own argument concerning the point of dialogue, see section 4.3.3 of chapter 4.

[109] A point made by Miroslav Volf in *Theology, Meaning, and Power*, 106.

[110] See Thiel, "Review of *The Nature of Doctrine*," 108 and Michaelson,
"The Response to Lindbeck," 118.

strengthens the hands of non-cognitivist theories of religion, it remains compatible with theological realism.[111]

But is a rule-theory of doctrines at all viable for resolving long-standing doctrinal differences? The reality is that dialogues, ecumenical or inter-religious, are at their most difficult at the doctrinal level precisely because dialogue-partners come convinced of the truth of their doctrinal traditions. The viability of Lindbeck's project in part entails convincing the parties that they have been fighting over nothing really, for resolution is at hand if only they would see their doctrines not as embodying truth-claims but as linguistic rules. But doctrinal agreements or conflicts can only superficially be attributed to disputes about how religious language ought to be used. More often than not, doctrinal differences are located at the fundamental level of the rational explanation of particular doctrines. There, the inadequacy of the regulative theory is disclosed in its inability to account for this deeper level of disagreement. Consider, for instance, the question, "Why does Christ have two natures?" Georg Behrens suggests that the propositionalist account is unequivocal: it is because Christ has two natures. For the expressivist, it is because the formulation 'Christ has two natures' better expresses our religious experience than its negation. What explanation can the proponent of the regulative theory give? Lindbeck is at a loss, for the regulative model has no definitive response at this juncture.[112] Behrens concludes that Lindbeck's model must "either take refuge in propositionalist or expressivist reasonings, or open itself to the charge of irrationality." Two problems confront Behrens, however. In the first place, the regulative model helpfully points out that we cannot say of

[111] See David Fergusson, "Meaning, Truth and Realism," 195.

[112] Nancey Murphy, too, contends that Lindbeck, unlike MacIntyre, has no answer to the question of how one is to know which religion or moral standpoint is (ontologically) true. See her *Anglo-American Postmodernity*, 123.

Jesus that he is only man or only God. Additionally, it would be wrong to suggest that the cultural-linguists have no response to the charge of irrationality. Lindbeck assesses truth-claims on the basis of a complicated analysis of their practical "consequences." What Behrens has succeeded in doing is, perhaps, to imply that which we have explicitly contended in this study, namely, that to be rational, Lindbeck's scheme has to be parasitic upon the other two models.[113]

Commentators are agreed that while Lindbeck's ecumenical motivation may be laudable, the potentials of his project for resolving doctrinal disputes are doubtful. Lindbeck erroneously presumes that recognising doctrines as grammatical statements *necessarily* renders ecumenical discussions easier. In the doctrinal context, resolving the grammatical tension usually entails doctrinal capitulation. The logic of capitulation seems simply to have shifted from a capitulation with regard to objective description, to a capitulation involving an understanding that the speech of other times (e.g., Counter-Reformation) was adequate then but may not be now. Phillips, however, insists that if the tensions are to be resolved, there will have to be doctrinal capitulation. The logic of this capitulation may not be "the logic of capitulation where one man sees that a description of an object he has provided is incorrect." But now, capitulation takes the form of "the admission that one had not been speaking properly about God." Given the close relationship between theology and the life of worship, Phillips points out that such an admission must come as a result of "a new

---

[113] This criticism is advanced by Georg Behrens in, "Schleiermacher *contra* Lindbeck," 415. See also L. C. Barrett, "Theology as Grammar," 161-62. John D'Arcy May does not think Lindbeck has done enough to show how his cultural-linguistic model might integrate the other two models. Nevertheless, he assesses Lindbeck's approach to doctrine positively for providing a "timely reassessment of our ecumenical priorities." See "Integral Ecumenism," *JES* 25 (1988) 586.

awareness of spiritual truths." He thus emphatically points out, "just because the grammar of capitulation is different, it is no less capitulation." Part, at least, of Lindbeck's problem lies in his "oscillating" between two different grammars: one, where a statement merely provides a rule for the use of, say, the term 'God'; the other, where a statement refers to a reality independent of the grammatical rules.[114]

What Lindbeck seeks to do is to refocus the discussion; his intention is never to empty the idea of truth. However, the rhetoric that accompanies much of Lindbeck's discussion is generally perceived by his commentators as attaching too heavy a price tag to the viability of his rule-theory. The rule-theory seems to operate, in the way Lindbeck presents it, by doing great violence to "the common use of truth and the truth predicate," emptying a religion of its "vital *assertive* use of language and doctrines," and, ironically, stripping his scheme of "the peculiar grammar of Christian faith."[115] The notion of *regulae fidei* does go back to Christian antiquity, but to propose the "novel" hypothesis that the regulative function "becomes the *only* job that doctrines do in their role as Church teachings" is, according to Dulles, to *unduly minimise* their "cognitive and expressive content."[116] To Fackre, the weakness of Lindbeck's theory of doctrine as "rules of discourse, attitude and action" is most pronounced in its unclarity about doctrine's relation to "objective reality."[117]

---

[114] See D. Z. Phillips, "Lindbeck's Audience," 146-47.

[115] Jay W. Richards, "Truth and Meaning," 53; Stephen Williams, "Lindbeck's Regulative Christology," 182.

[116] Avery Dulles, "Paths to Doctrinal Agreement: Ten Theses," *TS* 47 (1986) 43. Lash accepts the legitimacy of this criticism "without undermining the central contention that the *primary* function of Christian doctrine is regulative rather than descriptive." Lash, *Easter in Ordinary*, 260.

[117] Gabriel Fackre, *The Christian Story*, vol. 2 (Grand Rapids: Eerdmans, 1987), 219 n.7. He cites Dulles, who wrote in "Observations on George

5.4.3.2 Pragmatism and Lindbeck's Equivocations

Lindbeck's rule theory of doctrine is fundamentally grounded in the thesis that "doctrines are not first-order propositions, but are to be construed as second-order ones," because they make "intrasystematic rather than ontological truth claims."[118] Two related questions in this regard are particularly engaging for commentators: Has Lindbeck, through what appear like repeated equivocations, oscillated away from traditional Christian truths? Are doctrines in Lindbeck's proposed reconceptualization simply devoid of ontological claims? The first is trying; the second unsettling.

Readers are treated to an obstinate ambivalence in Lindbeck's critique of the cognitivist account that could confuse more than clarify. The following quotations may help illustrate the point:

> "The Nicaenum in its role as a communal doctrine does not make first-order truth claims." The regulative function "becomes the *only* job that doctrines do in their role as church teachings." _Compare_: "A religion's truth claims are often of the utmost importance to it (as in the case of Christianity)."[119]
> "The crusader's battle cry '*Christus est Dominus*' ... is false when used to authorise cleaving the skull of the infidel." _Compare_: "If we are to do justice to the actual speech and practice of religious

Lindbeck, *The Nature of Doctrine*," (an unpublished paper delivered at the Divinity School, Yale University, September 4, 1984): "For me, the church's claim to impose a doctrine in the name of revelation implies a claim of conformity to the real order, rather than a mere claim or a power to regulate language." McGrath also takes issue with Lindbeck on the latter virtually reducing truth to internal consistency. Evangelicalism is "insistent that Christian 'truth' must designate both a reality outside the language game and the adequacy of that language game to represent it." See idem, "An Evangelical Evaluation of Postliberalism," in *The Nature of Confession*, ed. T. R. Phillips and D. L. Okholm (Downers Grove, IL: InterVarsity, 1996), 36 & 39.

[118] ND, 80.
[119] ND, 18 & 19; cp. ND, 35.

people ... we must also allow for its possible propositional truth. Christians for example, generally act as if an affirmation such as 'Jesus Christ is Lord' is more than a categorial truth." "The proper use of *Christus est Dominus* is not only intrasystematically but also ontologically true."[120]

One scholar thus bluntly admits to his frustration at Lindbeck's propensity to vacillate and shift ground.[121] And yet, we suggest, much of that frustration can be avoided, if one is attentive to Lindbeck's underlying motivations and the novelty of the reconceptualization that they inspire. Notice, for example, that, even though he appears to have uncovered the grammatical confusions of the cognitivist theory, Lindbeck nevertheless proceeds with attempting to validate that category from the view point of his new paradigm. He thus avers:

There is nothing in the cultural-linguistic approach that requires the rejection (or the acceptance) of the epistemological realism and the correspondence theory of truth, which, according to most of the theological tradition, is implicit in the conviction of believers that when they rightly use a sentence such as 'Christ is Lord' they are uttering a true first-order proposition.[122]

The ambiguity in Lindbeck's position may then, in part, be examined from the angle of the two extremes he seeks to avoid: one is a radically relativistic view of Christianity that pictures everything in a state of flux, devoid of a central core; the other is a static view that holds on to old forms as fossilized truths, historically valid, but unable to speak to the present situation.[123] These,

[120] ND, 64; cp. ND, 63 & 65.
[121] See Richard Viladesau, "The Cultural Linguistic Model for Theology," 376 n.26.
[122] ND, 68-69.
[123] See D. Z. Phillips, "Lindbeck's Audience," 147-48.

as we saw in chapter one, are elements that concern Gadamer as well. Lindbeck's scheme would have been strengthened had he incorporated Gadamer's hermeneutical insights, especially on the dialectical tension between text and reader. His omission of Gadamer, as we saw, has also resulted in his steadfast exclusion of contemporary experience as an authentic source for theology.

We could observe, from a different angle, Lindbeck's refusal to abandon epistemological realism or truth by correspondence altogether. In a sense, his work, however influential, does not actually provide new ways of reading theology. What he has essentially done, is to validate traditionally recognizable theological interests with the help of postmodernist assumptions, including structuralist and poststructuralist insights. Taking his cue from cultural-anthropologists and linguistic modes of thought as defining the limits or linguistic conditions within which theology ought to be done, Lindbeck attempts to work out his key concern to disqualify from serious consideration the "liberal" mode of theologies. These theologies, wedded as they are to modernist modes of thought and thus undergirded by foundationalist concepts, are, in his view, seriously flawed: they postulate a-historical, unchanging universals and rely on shared human experience. In sharp contrast, he tightly latches doctrines onto particular, historically defined cultures and languages. Christian doctrines, under this proposal, at once become *communally-located* rules directing the community of believers' discourse, attitudes and actions. Lindbeck is well aware that the price for a reliance on postmodernist assumptions is the corresponding eclipse of the referential force of doctrines. The fact that he does not pursue this more objectivist consequence as relentlessly as he does the more subjectivist equation, betrays three dimensions of his work germane to our discussion. *First,* Lindbeck's distaste for liberal theologies finds expression in his attempt to discredit the symbolist theories of doctrine. *Second,* his

Protestant fiduciary interest ultimately operates to displace even
the admittedly more nuanced and hybrid positions of Rahner and
Lonergan. And, *thirdly*, most important of all in the context of this
chapter, he knows that a faithful Christian must preserve the
objectivist thrust of Christian doctrines. He thus explicitly declares
that "a religion can be interpreted as possibly containing ontologically true affirmations, not only in cognitivist theories but also in
cultural-linguistic ones." Hence, he goes on to say: "There is
nothing in the cultural-linguistic approach that requires the rejection (or the acceptance) of the epistemological realism and correspondence theory of truth."[124]

Still, the problem does not go away. One gets the distinct
impression that while it makes for a forceful advocacy, Lindbeck's unbending rhetoric often does his proposal much harm.
What interpreters find deeply unsettling is the large role the
minute word "only", twice repeated in the same context, is made
to shoulder:

> [A] religious utterance ... acquires the propositional truth of onto-
> logical correspondence only insofar as it is a performance, an act or
> deed, which helps create that correspondence.

> [I]t is only through the performatory use of religious utterances that
> they acquire propositional force.[125]

All this, to be sure, ties in well with his announcement at the
outset:

> Doctrines regulate truth claims by excluding some and permitting
> others, but the logic of their communally authoritative use hinders
> or prevents them from specifying positively what is to be
> affirmed.[126]

[124] ND, 68-69.
[125] ND, 65; cp. ND, 66.
[126] ND, 19.

In arguing this way, Lindbeck (perhaps unwittingly) implies that propositionally true claims (such as "Christ is Lord," according to traditional Christian belief) are *propositionally false* when they are not accompanied by corresponding performance. Conversely, propositionally vacuous claims (such as "God is good", according to Lindbeck) are *propositionally true* if, through them, we commit ourselves "to thinking and acting as if God were good."[127] It would seem that, in Lindbeck's scheme, the epistemological side of the Christian faith is entirely performance-oriented. Miroslav Volf thus judges that Lindbeck has all but reversed the order of things: doctrines are true not because they are adequate to reality, but *only if* they make reality adequate to them. Such an epistemology, he argues, equates religion with "a free floating semiotic system that seeks to absorb the world."[128]

However, Bruce Marshall has argued that scholars who share in this interpretation of Lindbeck are quite mistaken. Rather, he insists, and Lindbeck concurs, that *adequate performance does not make a statement ontologicaly true.*[129] Two pressing problems are implicated here. *First*, according to Paul Griffiths, "if this is all that is meant by categorizing religious utterance as performative, not enough has been said to support the rule-theorist's third requirement for the possession of ontological truth by a religious utterance — that such an utterance be given voice to in an appropriate confessional context."[130] *Second*,

---

[127] ND, 67.

[128] Volf, *Theology, Meaning, and Power*, 106.

[129] See Marshall, "Aquinas as Postliberal Theologian," 364; Lindbeck, "Response to Bruce Marshall," 403. For arguments that Marshall's attempt to enlist Aquinas in defense and support of the postliberal view of truth, meaning and epistemic justification is unpromising, see Louis Roy, "Bruce Marshall's Reading of Aquinas," *Thomist* 56 (1992) 473-80; Frederick J. Crosson, "Reconsidering Aquinas as Postliberal Theologian," *Thomist* 56 (1992) 481-98. For Marshall's reply, see "Thomas, Thomisms, and Truth," *Thomist* 56 (1992) 499-524.

[130] See Paul Griffiths, *An Apology for Apologetics*, 42.

Volf then argues that, based on Marshall's interpretation, endorsed by Lindbeck, the logical conclusion ought to be that "one *can* speak of the ontological truth of religious utterances apart from the concrete performance of what they affirm." That being the case, the assertive, cognitive aspect of religion is no longer idle, precisely on which point many authors take issue with Lindbeck.[131] Hans Zorn compellingly suggests that Lindbeck's "minimal propositionalism" is the central feature in the overall thrust of his regulative view of doctrines.[132] This sits well with Marshall's contention that Lindbeck is not concerned with giving an analysis of doctrinal truth, but rather an account of how religious truth-claims are to be justified.

Tracy assesses the difficulty inherent in Lindbeck's position to lie in the fact that it amounts to a "new linguistic version of one side of classical pragmatism." To speak more specifically, because Lindbeck defines truth-claims by how those claims "perform" to order a whole life, the one aspect of pragmatism's assessment of truth-claims which he adopts has to do with the analysis of "consequences" in life as criterion of assessment. Given this to be the case, Tracy remains unpersuaded that Lindbeck's "epistemological realism" is anything more than "relativism" under a new name. Hence, while Lindbeck aligns himself in some way with the pragmatism of William James, Tracy concludes that he fails to make clear that even James had three criteria for assessing religious truth-claims. These criteria are [i] their consequences in life and action, [ii] their power of illumination (or, as James put it, their "luminous possibility," or, as Tracy is

---

[131] Religions and theology are, for Volf, propositional at their core. See *Theology, Meaning, and Power*, 107-08. Walter Kasper asserts that: "Without a transcendent ground and point of reference, statements of faith are finally only subjective projections or social and ecclesial ideologies." See "Postmodern Dogmatics," *Communio* 17 (1990) 181-91.

[132] Hans Zorn, "Grammar, Doctrine, and Practice," *JR* 75 (1995) 509-20.

fond of saying, the "manifestation" of hermeneutical truth), and
[iii] their coherence with what "we otherwise know, practice and
believe" to be true.[133]

Terrence Reynolds contends that ambiguity arises in Lindbeck's
presentation in the way he attempts to relate the *ontological* and
practical dimensions of claims to truth. He recognizes that the
logic of Christianity demands something more than a sheerly prag-
matist understanding of truth; Christianity does intrinsically claim
to be true to the way things really are and make true propositional
statements.[134] Given that the Christian faith and its Scripture
require a claim upon truth, doctrines cannot be only "intrasystematic"; Christians are driven by the very inner logic of their own
talk to epistemological realism. Thus, Lindbeck wants to say that
doctrines are both metaphysical and moral, descriptive and prescriptive. But, he also wishes to suggest that moral actions serve
as benchmarks to *justify* belief in the ontological claims that produce these fruitful actions. And yet, he often confuses actual conduct with truth itself, as he does in the crusader example. The fact
that *both* interpretations can be supported by the text gives rise to
charges of ambiguity, ambivalence and equivocation. But, attention to Lindbeck's underlying motivations would suggest he
intends that "confessing Christ commits one to act in accord with
His Lordship and that the fruits of that commitment serve as subsequent justification for believing the claim itself." What must be
stressed, however, is that moral fruits can only serve as criteria for
justifying belief, *not* criteria for truth.[135] What Lindbeck has not
done, is to provide more clearly for an underlying framework of

[133] Tracy, "Lindbeck's New Program for Theology," 470.
[134] David Yeago, "A New Paradigm for Theology and Church," *Lutheran
Forum* 18 (1984) 32.
[135] Terrence Reynolds, "Walking Apart, Together: Lindbeck and McFague
on Theological Method," *JR* 77 (1997) 51.

truth to which theological realism can appeal without retreating into fideism. In the absence of such a framework, Lindbeck's refusal to abandon notions of truth in favour of pragmatism creates a dilemma. This dilemma, Jackson points out, arises from Lindbeck trying to do the impossible, namely, to balance "two quite irreconcilable intuitions about truth: realism and pragmatism. Propositional or ontological truth is essential to realism, while the rejection of such truth in favor of social convenience or linguistic convention is essential to pragmatism."[136]

It thus seems, apart from Lindbeck's unbending language, that an unresolved tension characterizes his project: he does acknowledge the propositional content of Christian doctrines, but he is keen only to show *the conditions under which propositional truth can be validly attained*. To accommodate ontological truth, Lindbeck supplies a definition of first-order propositions thus:

> For the cognitivist, it is chiefly technical theology and doctrine which are propositional, while on the alternate model, propositional truth and falsity characterize ordinary religious language when it is used to mold lives through prayer, praise, preaching, and exhortation. It is only on this level that human beings exhibit their truth or falsity, their correspondence or lack of correspondence to the Ultimate Mystery. Technical theology and official doctrine, in contrast, are second-order discourse about the first-intentional uses of religious language.[137]

It is in keeping with this distinction that, ultimately, Lindbeck is able to make his highly controversial suggestion that "the Nicaenum in its role as communal doctrine does not make first-order truth claims." In making that suggestion, his intention lies in

---

[136] Timothy Jackson, "Against Grammar," *RSRev* 11 (1985) 242. For the plausibility of "a mild-mannered pragmatism," see the argument of Mark S. Cladis, "Mild-Mannered Pragmatism and Religious Truth," *JAAR* 60 (1992) 19-33.

[137] ND, 69.

demonstrating that doctrines are second-order rules that regulate our talk of God, Christ and Church, and "for the imagining of God and world, in our story-telling, pray-acting and in our common-living."[138]

It comes as no surprise that authors abound who take Lindbeck to task for seemingly concluding that believers do not make onto-logical assertions about the order of reality, but merely utterances which are intrasystematically coherent or incoherent with their religious vision.[139] That said, however, it is to seriously misread Lindbeck if we fail to observe a crucial distinction, namely, that Lindbeck attempts to "give an account not only of the *truth* of Christian beliefs ('correspondence to reality') but also of their *justification* (adequate categories used in ways that are intrasystematically true)." Commonly, authors object to Lindbeck's suggestion that the truth or reality of Christ's lordship *depends* upon the practices and dispositions of believers. In part, critics who take this position, though in some way correct, fail to give him credit for the *practical* relationship he seeks to introduce between intrasystematic and ontological truths. Intrasystematic truth is not, in the first place, a matter of clarifying the *meaning* of propositional truths. The point is *not* to establish whether there are true propositions but, rather, "to clarify one of the essential *criteria* of truth in the religious domain." In other words, Lindbeck seeks to establish "what the conditions are under which one can state a sentence which is a true proposition." One such condition is the intrasystematic coherence of statements with one another and with appropriate practices. One can only lament Lindbeck's brevity, not his accuracy, when he concludes that "the intrasystematic falsity of

---

[138] Loughlin, *Telling God's Story*, 19.

[139] For examples, see Mark Wallace, "The New Yale Theology," 168-69; Michael Root, "Truth, Relativism, and Postliberal Theology," 179; O'Neill, "The Rule Theory of Doctrine and Propositional Truth," 437-38.

the crusader's battle cry lies precisely in the meaning the utterance has in this practical context." Lindbeck can thus assert: "When thus employed, it contradicts the Christian understanding of Lordship as embodying, for example, suffering servanthood." Bruce Marshall summarises Lindbeck's discussion in three points: (1) *Categorial truth is a necessary but not sufficient condition for ontological truth.* (2) *Intrasystematic truth is also a necessary but not sufficient condition for ontological truth.* (3) *Categorial and intrasystematic truth together are the necessary and sufficient conditions of ontological truth.* Marshall's analysis culminates in a claim which we can endorse, namely, that Lindbeck's "account of religious truth does not at all exclude the claim that Christian beliefs are ontologically true."[140]

5.4.3.3 Truth: Meaning and Use

Marshall's gallant support notwithstanding, many commentators have noted a serious lack of attention by Lindbeck to the difference between meaning and use. Wallace, for example, claims that a confusion over notions of *truth and reference* with notions of *meaning and use* plagues Lindbeck's scheme, which conflates them to a singular notion of *coherent usage*. Wallace points to the fact that Wittgenstein has himself noted[141] that, although the correct *use* of a theological proposition is generally measured intrasystematically in the context of a particular theological "language-game," this does not represent the whole story. To

[140] See Marshall, "Aquinas as Postliberal Theologian," 363-67, from where this paragraph draws its material. See also ND, 64-5. Marshall's assessment has been explicitly affirmed by Lindbeck. For a dissenting voice that doubts if Lindbeck has paid sufficient attention to a distinction between "meaning" and "use," see Charles Wood, "The Nature of Doctrine," 237.

[141] See L. Wittgenstein, *Philosophical Investigations*, trs. G. E. M. Anscombe (New York: Macmillan, 1959), 95-145.

adequately account for the success of a given language-usage, one needs to give attention to "the capacity of some statements to refer appropriately to certain states of affairs." That success, according to Hilary Putnam, often depends on *how* a given language is employed, as well as *whether* there is correspondence with particular extralinguistic objectives for which this language-using programme is intended. Wallace is led to conclude that in studying how language actually works when it attains certain ends, "meaning as *use*" and "truth as *reference*" are complementary, not contradictory, aspects. This sense of complimentarity is omitted by Lindbeck when he concludes that believers do not make ontological assertions about objective reality, but only utterances intrasystematically coherent with their tradition-specific Christian vision of God and world.[142]

Richards accuses Lindbeck of conflating what doctrines *do* with what their confessors *believe* or *intend* that they do. In the case of the two-natures doctrine of Christ (summarised as "Christ is fully human and fully divine"), whether it is true or false, the doctrine makes a substantive claim. It is manifestly confused to ask whether a confessor of this doctrine is affirming a first-order proposition about Christ, or is uttering a rule on what one should or should not say. This doctrine is a *"propositional attitude statement."* Its fundamental meaning is rendered vacuous in Lindbeck's scheme once it is identified with a *"performative utterance"* which depends on some externally-construed notion of use. Richards is thereby persuaded that "the modicum of plausibility in Lindbeck's theory of the meaning of doctrine stems from a subtle but improper confusion" over meaning and use, and his improper categorization of doctrines in performative terms, rather than propositionally. When a believer makes doctrinal claims, s/he

---

[142] See Mark Wallace, *The Second Naiveté*, 106-07.

"means them to refer to an extra-linguistic Reality not beholden to the wiles of human action or speech."[143]

Presenting a realist critique, Fergusson maintains that every theological realism acknowledges a gap between truth and the reasons which one may give to substantiate truth. In other words, whatever my reasons for making a particular statement, these reasons by themselves do not constitute the truth of the statement I make. To make an assertion is to claim the truth of its content, not that there are warrants for the claim. We cannot understand what constitutes proper warrants, unless we have already grasped what it would be for the assertion to be true. An epistemological realist would thus insist that truth is *logically prior* to warranted assertibility. Applied to Lindbeck, Fergusson finds that his account founders over a confusion of use and truth. The proper *use* of a religious doctrine may indeed, as Lindbeck has pointed out, depend on context and proper warrants for its assertion. But if the statement is ontologically true, that *truth* is not derivative of its being properly used. Thus, on the example of the crusader asserting "*Christus est Dominus*," the *truth* of that assertion in Christianity cannot possibly be displaced by its grotesque *use*.[144]

Inadequacy in Lindbeck's scheme also arises in the way of epistemological content. He accepts that, traditionally, Christians have made truth claims for their message and teaching. He acknowledges

---

[143] See Jay W. Richards, "Truth and Meaning in George Lindbeck's *The Nature of Doctrine*," 46 & 53.

[144] See David Fergusson, "Meaning, Truth and Realism," 196-97. Frei, too, expresses some anxiety over Lindbeck's rule theory in "Epilogue: George Lindbeck and *The Nature of Doctrine*," 279. In his exposition of Barth, Frei declares that "justification by faith is a doctrine that functions as a rule in, let us say, orthodox Christian discourse. Not only does it function as a rule but it looks as though it were asserting something about how God deals with human beings, and to that extent it is a statement that holds true regardless of the attitude of the person or persons articulating it" [*Types*, 42].

the *fact* of this traditional cognitive dimension. Lindbeck's concern
is by now crystal clear: he wishes to emphasize an "active receptivity" of faith. Wainwright rightly observes that to speak of an
active reception of faith necessarily implies an ecclesial consensus
on what that faith consists in. There is an epistemological content to
that faith. In other words, a consensus theory of truth makes no
sense within the particular Christian context *"without a veridical
God."*[145] Stell's argument thus seems apt when he casts doubt on
Lindbeck's attempt to separate doctrinal form (i.e., the transient,
culturally-dependent terms) from content (i.e., epistemic verity).[146]

5.4.3.4 Sensus Fidelium

Giurlanda accurately observes that, "when pushed on the subject of fidelity, Lindbeck will appeal, finally, to the *consensus
fidelium*, just as the ultimate test of whether you're speaking Eng-
lish is whether a native speaker understands you."[147] The question
of the *consensus fidelium* is of signal importance in Lindbeck's
overall scheme in which it is comparable to that universal agreement about language, the common grammar and vocabulary, that
makes communication possible.[148] A cultural-linguistic view of
religion suggests that issues regarding Christian doctrine ought to
be referred neither to Scripture (under classical Protestantism's
sola scriptura) nor to an institutional *magisterium* (under classical

[145] See Geoffrey Wainwright, "Ecumenical Dimensions of Lindbeck's
'Nature of Doctrine'," 124-25. This is one of the reasons upon which Wainwright builds his argument for a recuperation of the cognitive-propositional
dimension.

[146] Stell, *Hermeneutics and the Holy Spirit*, 146-50.

[147] Paul Giurlanda, "Post-liberal Theology," *CrCur* 35 (1985) 323.

[148] See Lindbeck, "Reflections on the New York Forum: From Academy to
Church" *ThEd* 19 (1983) 68; "Ecumenical Theology," in *The Modern Theologians*, ed. David F. Ford (Oxford: Blackwell, 1989), II:255-73.

Catholic doctrine of the Church's teaching office), but to the
whole community of those who competently speak the Christian
language.

Given this to be the case, there is, then, an inherently insuperable difficulty that confronts Lindbeck's constructive thesis. We
have seen the practical orientation he ascribes to doctrines, i.e.,
how doctrines, *qua* doctrines, function in the Church. At the end
of the book, he again reiterates what is doctrinally *reasonable*:
"Credibility comes from good performance, not adherence to
independently formulated criteria." In ecumenism, we are dealing
with doctrinal change and development. The question that presents
itself here is, who is to decide which are valid changes and which
are not? Lindbeck's first answer is easy enough to identify: the
task of deciding which of the changing forms is faithful to the
"putatively abiding substance," he says, is the job of the "consensus fidelium," or the "consensus ecclesiae." Two elements in this
answer seem actually to be in line with our findings in the first
chapter: (1) there is a core, an "abiding substance," in the Christian Tradition; (2) the ecclesial Tradition is the proper setting for
theology. The next question is, who are these *fideles* who would
constitute the "consensus ecclesiae?" Again, Lindbeck's answer
is clear: those whose opinions count, and who make up this body,
are those "who have effectively interiorized a religion." But, the
third question is, where can these *fideles* be found? There, Lindbeck flounders. He finds that while he can theoretically identify
the *fideles* in the "consensus ecclesiae," he cannot, in practice,
locate them in "highly variegated religions such as Christianity."[149] The point is that if Lindbeck is unable to draw a "sample"

---

[149] See ND, 131 & 99; Paul Rigby et al., "The Nature of Doctrine and Scientific Progress," *TS* 52 (1991) 670, 676-77. In any case, what would "consensus ecclesiae" really mean unless the languages of "popular faith" and "profes-

of the necessary *fideles*, talks of consensus must remain purely theoretical. For a theory which is targeted for practical solutions, Lindbeck's scheme must surely be judged to be quite inadequate. To be sure, Lindbeck does see the shortcomings of his project, if for no other reasons, because the modern world is inhospitable to it. We moderns have a penchant, he laments, for the liberal and propositional-dogmatic approaches. This has contributed to our loss of community as a principle of meaning, truth, and action.

Through a research project funded by The Social Sciences and Humanities Research Council of Canada, Paul Rigby and colleagues uncover a few points closely relevant to our discussion. *Firstly*, they call into question Lindbeck's reliance on Thomas Kuhn. Lindbeck insists that the institutional ecclesial tradition constitutes the proper setting for theology. This is legitimated by the fact that a religion's identity is constituted by its basic paradigm, the effective use of which depends on respecting "its inner logic, its deep grammar."[150] He understands ecclesial doctrines as abiding *regulae fidei* which permit certain usage and exclude others. As such, these doctrines are validly used only by those religiously competent to do so whom he calls the *fideles* – people who possess special skills associated with the linguistically competent. In all this, to be sure, Lindbeck manifests a skilful adaptation of Kuhn's thesis that theories belonging to different paradigms cannot be translated or compared. Hence, doctrines function meaningfully only in relation to their tradition-specific communities and their particular world views. Non-theological paradigms have at most a supporting role, the import of their normativity into theology being

sional theologian" come nearer to each other and theological discourse is directed to a wider public? See Thomas Corbett, "Teaching Dogmatic Theology," 55.

[150] Lindbeck, "Theological Revolutions and Present Crisis," *TD* 23 (1975) 318.

barred by the Kuhnian stricture. Against Lindbeck's constructive thesis, however, Rigby and company identify two "insuperable difficulties." *First*, as we saw, Lindbeck's *fideles* exist in *consensus ecclesiae* only in theory. *Second*, recourse to the social sciences to draw an "empirically recognizable" sample would lead to category mistakes invalidated by the same Kuhnian theory he seeks to align his cultural-linguistic paradigm with. In order to identity the *fideles* who can attest to the truth of doctrinal language game, it is more fruitful to have recourse to psychology of religion instead. There, research yields a profile of the *fideles* as "intrinsically" religious, in contrast to those only "extrinsically" so. Whereas the extrinsically motivated person *uses* religion for "comfort and social convention," the intrinsically motivated *lives* his/her religion as a "proto-point." Further, a "quest" orientation may be usefully added, which concerns the "degree of open-minded, critical struggle with existential questions." The drawback is that coupling the "intrinsic" and "quest" orientations would take the rule theory *out of a confessional paradigm into a dialectical or correlational paradigm.* This latter paradigm is not populated by mere "quest" strawmen as the Chicago School accuses Lindbeck's typology of suggesting, for it is made up of persons who display an egalitarian commitment to Church and society.[151]

Much of this discussion, like other discussions on Lindbeck's project, has a tendency to gravitate towards the debate on commensurability.

5.4.4 Truth and the Incommensurability Thesis

That commensurability poses a focal point for much discussion is understandable. We have raised the question in the last chapter

---

[151] See Paul Rigby et al., "The Nature of Doctrine and Scientific Progress," *TS* 52 (1991) 669-88.

whether, if religious traditions are so hide-bound to the particular languages which determine their specific values, culture and ethos, as Lindbeck suggests they are, they are not incommensurable? In distinguishing different senses of truth, Lindbeck makes good his claim that we live amidst a plurality of incommensurable norms and standards where different religions and philosophies "have incommensurable notions of truth, of experience, and of categorial adequacy,"[152] and his project is elucidated in a way consistent with that view. Commentators, sympathetic and otherwise, are correct to hold that his formal proposal of the cultural-linguistic lens for viewing religions and the rule-theory of doctrine are motivated primarily by his intratextual theological concern to affirm the incommensurability between the Christian Gospel and other religious and secular traditions.[153] The issue is one of epistemological differences. Are the different epistemological schemes in diverse religious traditions so irreducibly different? Are they so static and impermeable in their doctrinal articulations that one cannot learn another tradition like one learns a new language?

In holding the theological view that the Christian Gospel is an external word that comes to human beings as an alien force, rather than in continuity with internal human consciousness, Christian religion becomes for Lindbeck a *verbum externum* that moulds and shapes the self and its world. Gordon Michaeson thus identifies Lindbeck's incommensurability principle with his proposal of a model that sees religions primarily as external, cultural-linguistic symbol systems that one must appropriate in a way similar to

[152] ND, 49 & 130.

[153] Tiina Allik's special contribution consists in her thesis that Lindbeck's denial of a continuity between the Christian faith and other modes of human consciousness is more fundamentally inspired by a radical aspect of his anthropology — that the self is always mediated through the culture and language of the communities in which one participates. See "Religious Experience, Human Finitude, and the Cultural-Linguistic Model," *Horizons* 20 (1993) 241-59.

the way one learns the grammar and vocabulary of a foreign language. Lindbeck contrasts sharply with revisionist theologians in the classical liberal tradition in his denial that Christianity may be explained in terms of what Michaelson calls "natural modes of human consciousness," "anthropological givens," or the "immediately intelligible."[154] To Mark Corner, Lindbeck effectively shuts the door on the criticism of religion. When a community's self-understanding is independent of what lies outside, it rules out of court any critique which seeks to expose the inadequacy of its truth claims.[155]

An assertion of some form of incommensurability among the doctrines of different religious communities may be one way of denying cognitive realism with respect to doctrines. But the decisive question is whether the distinct ways diverse religions shape their adherents' beliefs and judgments imply that no rational discussion can proceed between them. If, by his denial of commensurable "notions of categorial adequacy," Lindbeck implies that indeed no rational discussion is possible, then there could be no common comprehensive interpretive scheme which could function as neutral adjudicator of inter-religious discussions. This is a strict incommensurability view. But, then, is a neutral comprehensive structure strictly necessary for arbitrating rational disputes? Is rationality not heuristic, creative or exploratory? Cannot dialogue-partners from diverse traditions seek points of similarity-in-difference and areas of overlap, partial or otherwise, despite their vastly different perspectives?[156] A strict incommensurability tends to be

---

[154] Gordon Michaelson, "The Response to Lindbeck," *ModTh* 4 (1988) 111, 112 & 116. He sees "the most sensitive nerve ending touched by Lindbeck concerns the question of the sheer intelligibility of the Christian faith," i.e., "the degree to which Christian faith can be placed in correlation with natural modes of human consciousness."

[155] Mark Corner, "Review of *The Nature of Doctrine*," *ModTh* 3 (1986) 112.

[156] Michael Root, "Truth, Realism, and Postliberal Theology," 177

an *empirical thesis* concerning criteria applicable across community-boundaries for assessing doctrines. Aided by significant counterexamples, Griffiths argues against any strong version of the incommensurability thesis. But conceptual relativists go beyond the empiricism of the incommensurability thesis. They press theoretical reasons for the case that the application of any empirical criteria does not yield the kind of truth-knowledge that the cognitive realist would claim.[157]

Lindbeck's postliberal position thrives on a dichotomy of *either* reading religions and their sacred texts intratextually, *or* attempting to translate them into popular categories. Tilley sees this as a false dichotomy, for there is an operative presumption in both cases that "Christian discourse is *essentially* a normal, commensurable, discourse which requires only instantiation." Furthermore, on the question of commensurable frameworks, Lindbeck maintains two different positions all at once. On the one hand, he insists that no framework can commensurate Buddhist compassion, Christian love, and French revolutionary *fraternité*. Yet, on the other hand, in dealing with ancient Christian creeds, he holds that one framework can commensurate such notions as "ousia," "hypostasis," "persona," "nature," and so forth. In Tilley's opinion, Lindbeck's analysis, which draws on mathematics and cultures for illustration, displays a conflation of the necessary incommensurability of mathematical systems with the contingent incommensurability of cultural systems. The Scripture texts, the scriptural world, and the worlds in which we live are all internally plural, and the influences upon their genesis complex. Even when we are absorbed into the worlds of masterpieces such as *Oedipus Rex* and *War and Peace*, we do not dwell in singular texts, but

---

[157] See Paul Griffiths, *An Apology for Apologetics*, 27-32. He does not identify Lindbeck as a conceptual relativist.

ones which we read in extratextual contexts. "Pure incommensurability is a practical impossibility."[158] Tilley calls into question Lindbeck's presumption of a linear or pure intratextuality predicated on the notion of an easy access to a privileged framework which is already given. By thus positing "a 'pure' text immune from shaping by ongoing conversation," such an intratextuality banishes conversation and invites particularistic isolationism. Even if one is mindful of advocating a cultural-linguistic system as providing the conditions-of-possibility for any experience at all, and thereby ruling out the possibility of an unmediated primary or core experience, there is no persuasive reason for suggesting that we live in a hermetic system which allows no "new" experience to break through its boundaries. What we need to postulate is a dialectical, "dirty" intratextuality which rejects a strict linear relationship between text and experience.[159]

At this juncture, David Kamitsuka makes an important contribution. He notes that, properly read, Lindbeck does not reject the notion of translation *per se*. He draws attention to qualifications inserted by Lindbeck, and underlines the fact that Lindbeck's criticisms concern translations which are done "systematically" and

---

[158] Terrence Tilley, "Intratextuality in a Postmodern World," 104. Tilley relies on Richard Rorty, *Contingency, Irony, Solidarity* (Cambridge: Cambridge University Press, 1985), 9: "Alternative geometries are irreconcilable because they have axiomatic structures, and contradictory axioms. They are *designed* to be irreconcilable. Cultures are not so designed, and do not have axiomatic structures."

[159] Terrence W. Tilley, "Incommensurability, Intratextuality, and Fideism," *ModTh* 5 (1989) 105. James Buckley finds Tilley 's distinction between "pure" and "dirty" intratextualism useful, but thinks Lindbeck is more a "contextualist" than a "pure intratextualist." The confusion in Lindbeck's hermeneutics arises because "he does not seek a full blown theory of subject matters and contexts and texts but a set of rules 'essential to Christian identity' on such issues." See Buckley, "The Hermeneutical Deadlock between Revelationists, Textualists, and Functionalists," *ModTh* 6 (1990) 333.

where the "contemporary framework is controlling" in such a way
that the Christian semiotic system is distorted. When he describes
religions as "incommensurable," his remark is targeted specifically at driving home the point that "no common framework"
exists "within which to compare different religions." Incommensurable, then, is not equated with incomparable or wholly untranslatable. It only means the absence of an easy solution, for there
"cannot be any neat and simple way of settling the issues"
between two very different religious paradigms on a systematic,
"point after point" basis.[160] Kamitsuka thus contends that Lindbeck has not abandoned any notion of a "shared rational space"
which Tracy insists must be affirmed if theological claims to
validity are to be redeemed rationally in the public realm.[161]
Kamitsuka's point finds an echo in Charles Hawkins who distinguishes "soft" and "hard" readings of Lindbeck by commentators. A "soft" reading of Lindbeck, one preferred by Placher,
would release him from the "aporias of a self-referential critique
of reason." A "hard" reading of Lindbeck's postliberalism sees
him as being hermetically imprisoned within the language game of
the Christian faith. He is, in Tilley's term, a "pure" intratextualist,
one who — to borrow an image from Seyla Benhabib — is
trapped inside "the parish walls."[162]

No matter which way Lindbeck is read, commentators display a
pervasive impulse to recommend a lowering of his "parish walls"
so as to facilitate a greater outreach. We take four examples. *First*,
given this impulse, Placher, who is deeply sympathetic to the
postliberal insistence on fidelity to the internally-authenticated

---

[160] ND, 49; Lindbeck, "Scripture, Consensus, and Community," 87-88;
"Theological Revolutions and the Present Crisis," 315.
[161] David Kamitsuka, "The Justification of Religious Belief in the Pluralistic
Realm," *JR* 76 (1996) 588-606.
[162] Hawkins, *Beyond Anarchy and Tyranny in Religious Epistemology*, 21ff., 173.

particular world-view,[163] urges that Christians make wider connections while still speaking faithfully in their own voice. Adopting the method of *bricolage*, he assumes the burden of forging for
Christian theology a middle ground between the Enlightenment
ideal of universal rationality on the one hand and some form of
radical relativism on the other.[164] *Second*, in place of what he calls
the "ideology of particularism" of the 'new Yale School,' Tilley
suggests that a "true particularity" entails a *"dirty intratextuality"*
– one that assumes no privileged framework, but attempts each
commensuration and comparison in an *ad hoc* fashion from within
a particular conversation.[165] *Third*, to extend Lindbeck's postliberal outreach, Hawkins proposes the integration of Benhabib's
"interactive universalism," understood as "the practice of situated
criticism for a global community that does not shy away from
knocking down the 'parish walls'."[166] While the theologian begins
properly not with a search for a universal foundation on which to

---

[163] Placher writes: "Christians must remain faithful to their own vision of
things for reasons internal to Christian faith, and if, in some contexts, that means
intellectual isolation, so be it." See his *Unapologetic Theology*, 13.

[164] In *Ethics After Babel*, Jeffrey Stout calls a creative integration of competing traditions a "bricolage." We are all bricoleurs, he says (pp. 74-7, 292), borrowing from a favourite image of the anthropologist Claude Leví-Strauss in *The
Savage Mind* (Chicago: University of Chicago Press, 1966), 17. A bricoleur does
odd jobs and always squirrels away tools and bits and pieces of materials for possible future use. Placher uses this concept to urge that as theological bricoleurs,
we should employ whatever tools and materials are at hand, without undue concern that philosophy has been prioritised over theology. See Placher, *Unapologetic Theology*, 13 & 67. Understandably, Placher proposes authentic interdisciplinary conversation as a model for meaningful interaction between theology and
culture, science and philosophy, and between different theological traditions. In
doing so, however, one may see him as having already moved beyond his self-
confessed postliberal leanings. See, for this assessment, J. Wentzel van
Huyssteen, "Tradition and the Task of Theology," *ThT* 55 (1998) 223.

[165] Tilley, "Incommensurability, Intratextuality, and Fideism," 105.

[166] Seyla Benhabib, *Situating the Self* (New York: Routledge, 1992), 227.

build a systematic theology, but with speaking faithfully in the voice of the Church, s/he is on good ground in assuming the public and interactive nature of language and knowledge.[167] *Fourth*, to help move the postliberals out of an image of strict confessionalism, uninterested in debate in the pluralistic public realm or lacking in rational arguments for the credibility of Christian discourse, Kamitsuka proposes a *coherence approach* which in philosophical circles is known as "wide reflective equilibrium."[168] It is a fallibilistic rather than a perfect approach, but it is contextual in casting a wide net to include (a) the stable beliefs which the individual or community holds as normative which, for the postliberals, would be the "plain sense" of Scripture, (b) a set of general principles as in the "regulative" doctrinal principles, as well as (c) the use of various background theories, including non-Christian-specific apologetics and Christian-specific apologetics.[169] In their rich diversity, all these proposals find a resounding, if varying degree of, echo in Tracy's critical correlation and analogical imagination.

5.4.5 Constitutive Truth: An Anthropological Implication

Hunsinger captures the very rationale that underlies our attention to doctrinal truth when he vehemently avers: "Surely no question could stand closer to the core of any theological position

[167] Hawkins, *Beyond Anarchy and Tyranny*, 167 & 171.

[168] Francis S. Fiorenza has also constructed a model of theological rationality based on the notion of a "wide reflective equilibrium" borrowed from moral philosophy, especially that of John Rawls'. There, tradition is set in interaction with modern cognitive and normative claims understood nonfoundationally and mutually critical of each other. In this approach, distortions can be identified and prejudices criticized. Theology is portrayed as depending, not on stable foundations, but on a "diversity of judgments, principles, and theories, each entailing different kinds of justification that come together to support or criticize, to reinforce or to revise." See his *Foundational Theology*, 302ff.

[169] Kamitsuka, "The Justification of Religious Belief," 590-94.

than that of how truth is conceived." Lindbeck's proposal leads to
the idea that truth is *not* a property that pertains to Church doctrines so much as to the forms of life in which these doctrines are
used. Truth is correlated with performance. In this respect, Lindbeck diverges from Barth very significantly.[170] But the difference
goes deeper. In ascribing a strong role to human agency in *causing* a religious utterance to be either true or false, truth is articulated in terms of *self-involvement*. In this light, Hunsinger's surprising indictment of Lindbeck for attributing an inordinate role to
human agency, correspondingly muting divine providence, does
not seem misplaced. He rhetorically asks: "Can it be irrelevant ...
that Lindbeck finds it possible to define the necessary and sufficient conditions for the truth of a theological assertion without
once referring to the role of the divine agency?"[171] What is particularly interesting are two matters that are at once related.

First, there is a disturbing degree of inconsistency in the anthropological element of Lindbeck's analysis. In the context of discussing doctrinal truth, when Lindbeck defines truth in terms of self-
involvement, he accords so much space for human agency that,
ironically, truth is achieved at the price of eclipsing divine agency.[172]
This calls into question Allik's characterisation of Lindbeck's attention to divine providence, in alleged contrast to Rahner, which we

[170] George Hunsinger, "Beyond Literalism and Expressivism: Karl Barth's
Hermeneutical Realism," *ModTh* 3 (1987) 222 n.20. Bruce Marshall tends to
emphasize the "particularism about truth" which Lindbeck and Barth share in
common. See idem, "Truth Claims and the Possibility of Jewish-Christian Dialogue," *ModTh* 8 (1992) 221-40.

[171] Hunsinger, "Truth as Self-Involving," 49.

[172] In treating the notions of God as "the Giver, the Given and the Giving" as
"rules," Stephen Webb adopts Lindbeck's strategy to mark the boundaries to,
and provide the conditions for, any proper discourse on divine benevolence. Yet,
he finds Lindbeck's position inadequate in its tendency "to give religion over to
social construction, so that human behavior is governed by reciprocal agreements

discussed in the last chapter. Yet, the picture is not entirely clear. As we saw, in the case of text-reading in Lindbeck's intratextual theology, the dialectics of human involvement is contrarily muted, absorption into the narrative world of the text being postulated as a linear, one-dimensional affair. There, we have raised the question as to how human agency could possibly be positively described when "novel" experiences are steadfastly locked out.

Second, in the context of our overarching framework of the hermeneutic of Tradition, it ·is even more urgent that we clarify whether truth *resides* in what we inherit from Tradition or in a truth-producing-process of self-involvement. Throughout this study, our overriding thesis is the *dialectical revelation* of truth where human agency, inescapably conditioned though it is by the particular communal tradition in which it exists and functions, plays an active role. To be sure, in a valid theological anthropology, personhood cannot be defined in terms of freedom and agency without due regard to such severe limitations as human creatureliness, the vicissitudes of life and the facticity of communal history. But, we are as much active agents in authoring our stories as passive recipients and narrators of an external communal story. The creative dynamics of Tradition would suggest that it is only in acknowledging *both* the active and passive dimensions that one can account for the normativity of truth as a given in Tradition, *and* the dialectical revelation of truth in human history.[173]

and spiritual practice is bounded by communal norms, leaving little room for the surprise of grace." See idem, *The Gifting of God* (New York: Oxford University Press, 1996), 91-94, 124.

[173] As Stephen S. Duffy sees it, an anthropology is more adequate if it *dialectically* takes into account "the labyrinthine interplay of action with passivity and suffering, the voluntary with the involuntary, intentions and meanings with energies and forces, the deliberate with the spontaneous, the planned with the unexpected." See "Justification by Faith," in *Church and Theology*, ed. Peter C. Phan (Washington, DC: Catholic University of America Press, 1995), 211-12.

"Truth" is an ambiguous word. Its meaning ranges from something that is expressively meaningful, to something that corresponds to the really real. The expressive pole of truth implies that the more deeply interior the meaning is experienced, the more truthful it is. The correspondence pole implies that the more precisely the correspondence can be objectively encoded in words, the more true the proposition. Lindbeck speaks of a third, categorial truth, which implies that what is said must correlate with the reality in the overall framework. His view of truth as 'categorial adequacy' seems, according to Thiel, to assume "the modest limitation that truth only flourishes within the defined context of a particular meaning system."[174] There is, as it were, a "particularism" about truth. But, it is a *particular*, "Lindbeckian" particularism, predicated on [1] a pointed departure from the traditional cognitivist view[175] that the "meaning, truth, and falsity of propositions are independent of the subjective disposition of those who utter them," and [2] the thesis that it is only through performance that religious utterances acquire propositional force. It seems legitimate to draw a parallel between such a performatory view of truth and the pragmatic notion that truth is "made" rather than discovered.[176] To claim that truth is "made" is much more than to say that truth "flourishes": the former cannot square with the acceptance of an unchanging truth that was once and forever delivered to the saints in a way that the latter can. Which view does Lindbeck actually espouse? Marshall has stated, and Lindbeck has agreed with him, as we saw, that *adequate performance does not*

---

[174] See Thiel, "Review of *The Nature of Doctrine*," 108.

[175] Jackson's assessment of Lindbeck's "relative insouciance about ontological truth" is well-accepted by commentators. See idem, "Against Grammar," 241.

[176] See ND, 66 and the parallel drawn by Michael W. Nicholson, *A Theological Analysis and Critique of the Postmodern Debate* (Lewiston: Edwin Mellon, 1997), 240.

make a statement ontologically true. We ought to accept what they
say they have in mind. Still, commentators continue to be exercised by the confusing ambivalence and ambiguity in Lindbeck's
text. Greater clarity, it seems, is called for than Lindbeck has
given thus far. Towards greater clarity, the introduction of *constitutive* truth as a fourth understanding of truth may be helpful.[177]

By *constitutive* truth is meant reality as constituted by its
events. Reality, similar to the notion of Tradition that purports to
encapsulate some aspects of it, is not conceived of as fossilized
layers of truth. Rather, reality comes to us as a dynamic horizon
that we cannot do without. Our language of faith, which speaks of
what is yet to be, does not merely report; it creates – by performing what it promises.[178] This description suggests William James'
pragmatic theory: "The truth of an idea is not a stagnant property
inherent in it. Truth *happens* to an idea. It *becomes* true, is *made*
true by events. Its verity *is* in fact an event, a process: the process
namely of its verifying itself, its veri-*fication*. Its validity is the
process of its validation."[179] In its dynamism, Tradition encompasses the past and the present and is already driving towards the
future. It is in this striving towards the future that hermeneutics
correctly postulates an active role for the reader of a text. To be
sure, the authority of Scripture-in-Tradition is preserved. But now,
the normativity of Scripture-in-Tradition is better described in the
"future" tense, as a necessary corrective to an overemphasis on
fossilized layers of truth residing in the past.[180] Indeed, to

[177] This line of thought is adopted from Paul Varo Martinson, "Speaking the
Truth: Contemporary Approaches to Religious Pluralism," in LWF Report No.
23-24 (1988) 54-57.

[178] Paul Sponheim, "The Word in the World Is True," *Dialog* 25 (1986) 169.

[179] William James, *Pragmatism: A new Name for Some Old Ways of Thinking* (New York: Longman, Green, 1970), 201.

[180] Hence, see Reimund Bieringer, "The Normativity of the Future," *Bulletin
ET* 8 (1997) 52-67.

seriously embark upon unpacking the notion of doctrinal truth is
to risk what Jacque Haers describes as an encounter with God:
"an encounter which can only be understood within the hermeneutical play of receptivity and creativity."[181] Truth is neither created
ex nihilo nor given as a static achievement. We struggle to give
birth to what a doctrinal truth really means. Truth is *revealed*
dialectically in that struggle; truth flourishes.

5.4.6 The Rule-Theory and Postmodernity

Finally, we are in a position to stitch together a few major
strands of Lindbeck's thought and view them in relation to his
claim that his rule-theory, his fostered cultural-linguistic vision,
and the postliberal theology that inspire them are postmodern.
How does his claim of affinity with postmodern thought compare
with recent definitions of postmodernity? We take three examples.
    First, the impetus of postmodernity has been underscored in
terms of its radicalizing of the insights of modernity and issuing in
[i] historical relativity, [ii] accentuation of experience as the measure of all things, and [iii] openness to alterity.[182] In this light,
Lindbeck's postmodern slant manifests itself in his steadfast
refusal of any common experiential touchstone, emphasizing,
instead, particular experience; but it is a particularity that is tradition-bound, communally regulated and normatively verifiable for
commitment and action. In his scheme, every religious experience
and theological doctrine is specific to systems of language and
culture. As Lindbeck distances himself from the cognitive-propositionalist and experiential-expressive approaches, he evinces a

---

[181] Jacques Haers, "A Risk Observed," *LS* 21 (1996) 48.

[182] As proposed by Terrence Merrigan, "The Anthropology of Conversion:
Newman and the Contemporary Theology of Religions," in *Newman and Conversion*, ed. Ian Ker (Edinburgh: T & T Clark, 1997), 117-18.

postmodern turn which frees theology from subservience to the
harsh master of modern historical facts which had seemingly
forced it into an either/or of blind dogmatism or liberal experien-
tialism. *Second*, in a somewhat more familiar account, postmodernity has been defined in relation to the manifest loss of the plausibility of all overarching master narratives, concomitant with a
growing consciousness of [i] the fundamental plurality that characterizes the present-day human condition; [ii] the radical particularity and contextuality of all narratives; and [iii] the resultant
irreducible heterogeneity wedded to a contemporary critical consciousness.[183] Viewed against this account, Lindbeck is a postmodern thinker principally in the way he rejects the Enlightenment optimism that all rational agents can come to the same
conclusions; he is particularly suspicious of the liberal idea that
there can be a single set of tradition-independent rational ground
rules capable of settling debates between different religious traditions. He thus eschews universal claims and provides no warrant
for universal truth-claims or claims that transcend a culture or subculture. Postmodernity's epistemological relativism is, in this
light, congruent with his aim to take the particularity of Christian
language seriously and to espouse Christian faithfulness as our
first task. This is most evident in his battle against the liberal theological agenda and its assumption of a universal rationality. For
Christians, the hope for a resolution of the cacophony of our pluralistic time emphatically resides in the intratextual particularity of
its Scripture-in-Tradition. *Third*, a postmodern theologian has also
been classified as one who successfully leaves the space defined
by three 'modern' axes without reverting to premodern categories.
These axes are [i] an epistemological axis (ranging from founda-

---

[183] As defined by Lieven Boeve, "Postmodern Sacramento-Theology:
Retelling the Christian Story," *ETL* 74 (1998) 326-43.

tionalism to scepticism), [ii] a metaphysical axis (ranging from
individualism to collectivism) and [iii] a linguistic axis (ranging
from representationalism to expressivism).[184] Here, Lindbeck's
disclaimer regarding 'common ground', confession of particularity, and critique of foundationalism, place him squarely within the
current postmodern intellectual climate.[185] But if, as some suggest,
Lindbeck's attempted departure from the linguistic axis most characterizes his thought, then three points of congruence may be
identified between him and postmodern thinking: [i] truth and
understanding conceived in terms of intratextuality; [ii] language
regarded not as descriptive of reality but in terms of meaning-as-
use; [iii] religious language and doctrines perceived as undergoing
change without becoming 'untrue' to the language game.[186]

Indeed, when different strands of Lindbeck's thought are woven
together, the resultant fabric does recall Lyotard's view of the
postmodern condition.[187] Thus, Lindbeck [i] eschews experiential-
expressivism on account of its metadiscourse behaviour which
subjects heterogeneity (i.e., diverse religious experiences) to a
totalising sameness (i.e., a common core experience of the Ultimate) under the illusion that it can transcend language (i.e., to gain
access to this core experience) while ignoring the fact that language precedes experience; [ii] espouses a highly particularistic,
cultural-linguistic outlook which insists that one can "no more be

---

[184] See the oft-quoted classification by Nancey Murphy and James Wm.
McClendon, "Distinguishing Modern and Postmodern Theologies," *ModTh* 5
(1989) 191-214. For an overview of postmodern thinkers, see George de Schrijver, "Postmodernity and Theology," *Philippiniana Sacra* 27 (1992) 439-52.

[185] See M. K. Taylor, "In Praise of Shaky Ground," 37.

[186] As so identified by Brad J. Kallenberg ["Unstuck from Yale: Theological
Method after Lindbeck," *SJT* 50 (1997) 191-218] who also suggests that Lindbeck's reluctance to make positive affirmations about God not only places his
faithful exegesis of Wittgenstein in doubt, but also brings into question his success in leaving the representational-expressivist axis.

[187] So judges Watson, *Text, Church and World*, 133-36.

religious in general than one can speak language in general;"[188] [iii] construes the dynamics of Christian faith wholly within Christian language and is reticent on the view that Christian faith is *not only* a sociological reality; [iv] maintains that it is language rather than 'truth' that is primary, for "to become a Christian involves learning the story of Israel and of Jesus well enough to interpret and experience oneself and one's world in its terms;"[189] [v] locks on to the argument that religions, as different language games and forms of life, are fundamentally incommensurable, there being no common framework to compare them; [vi] claims that truth is intrasystematic, that is, dependent on locally-operative grammatical rules for correct and incorrect utterance; [vii] accepts that doctrines function most prominently, "not as expressive symbols or as truth claims, but as communally authoritative rules of discourse, attitude and action;"[190] [viii] elevates the regulative function of doctrine, wields Ockham's razor against the alleged superfluity of propositional interpretations, and strenuously dismantles the various ramifications of a correspondence theory of truth;[191] [ix] differs from the symbolist model by suggesting that "it is the Christian story which alone is able to identify what for Christians is true love,"[192] thereby concretizes a supposed universal (love) by way of a particular language and reduces its significance to a small-scale locality specific to a single linguistic community; and [x] insists on the irreducibility of narrative *within* its small-scale communal context to support the argument that narratives cannot be *about* something any more than languages can, thereby concluding

[188] ND, 23.

[189] ND, 34.

[190] ND, 18.

[191] The latter being identified by Watson, *Text, Church and World*, 134 as typical of postmodern theorizing.

[192] ND, 83.

that, like languages, narrative plays the role of providing the
means to talk about things.

And yet, commentators abound who note that Lindbeck
does not arrive at postmodern theology, his postliberal project
failing to really engage postmodernity or follow through with
the radical implications ingredient in the postmodern position.[193] Concretely, his project evinces "a postmodernity that
is really a nostalgia for a premodern world" principally
because he incorporates postmodern thought only in a tactical
or pragmatic way without a willingness to engage the secular
world in any wholesale dialogue.[194] There are, to be sure, a
conflict of assessments here: some regard his overall scheme
as evincing a meta-narrative realism which lacks congruence
with the standard postmodern mindset;[195] others view his pre-
Enlightenment meta-narrative as but "a glittering gem in the
mosaic of pluralistic culture" in which the Enlightenment
quests for human justice and dignity are abandoned, replaced,
as they are, by a web of non-privileged discourses of equally
valid linguistic constructions of reality.[196] Similarly, his emen-
dation of Wittgenstein, which demands that a Christian 'form
of life' be regulated by the Gospel, comes at the cost of abandoning all truth-claims, and contrasts with his overarching
vision of the eschatological salvation of non-Christians via
fides ex auditu. One must presume that Lindbeck is astute
enough to realize that pitfalls await the theologian who
embraces the postmodern turn, for one implication is that

---

[193] Tilley, "Intratextual Theology," 104; Reader, *Beyond All Reason*, 70-71.

[194] Paul Lakeland, *Postmodernity: Christian Identity in a Fragmented Age*,
(Minnesota: Fortress, 1997), 48.

[195] Thus judges Milbank, *Theology and Social Theory*, 386.

[196] As Andrew Walker, *Telling the Story* (London: SPCK, 1996), 178-79
assesses Lindbeck's scheme.

Christianity can no longer claim to be normative.[197] He wants, after all, to fit the smaller human narratives into a much larger perspective — the Christian story. How else could his intratextual theology function to endorse a single text — the Christian biblical text — for the absorption of the entire universe, as a resolution to the prevailing cacophony?[198] Perhaps, then, in advocating a return to a pre-modern version of Christianity, Lindbeck may be seen as attempting to have the best of both worlds, that is, regarding Christianity as a meta-narrative which offers a universal explanation of human existence and thus discounting any validity to alternative explanations, *and* presenting Christianity as one local narrative alongside many others and even in competition with, or sealed off from, all of them. He thus evinces an irreconcilable contradiction born of a selective use of philosophical ideas while ignoring their wider implications, especially the postmodern insight that there is a plurality of discourses and languages in which there can be no one dominant narrative.[199] It is this selective appropriation of the postmodern framework, in the service of promoting a "narrowly confessional" proposal, instead of using the framework to critique and interpret the Christian Tradition, that most exposes his constructive position as manifesting "little affinity

[197] Paul O'Shea, "Theology, Pluralism and Postmodernity," *Miltown Studies* 36 (1995) 37. Indeed, when placed under scrutiny by Lyotard's postmodern critique, modern, pre-modern and even so-called postmodern neo-conservative theologies would be negatively exposed as operatively presupposing a closed master-narrative of Christianity. See Lieven Boeve, "Bearing Witness to the Differend: A Model for Theologising in the Postmodern Context," *LS* 20 (1995) 362-79.

[198] Lindbeck's intratextual reading of Scripture that absorbs the world projects the Christian story as an "overarching story" — a feature in Lindbeck's theology which Fackre characterizes as "high-profile" in *The Doctrine of Revelation*, 4.

[199] John Reader, *Beyond All Reason*, 66-67.

with the animating impulse of postmodernism."[200] In any event, it is clear that Lindbeck does not examine, as postmodern authors do, the historicity of human life "in terms of power and the interconnection between power and the overarching interpretive schemas."[201]

Section II: Speaking of Church

5.5 Doctrine and the Church

Doctrines draw their meaning from, and are ultimately intended to have some effect on, the practices of the believing community. Doctrines are not formulated as an end in themselves, but as communally authoritative teachings which bear closely on the identity of the Church. Vanhoozer correctly suggests that the real issues in the debate between the so-called Chicago and Yale "schools" concern not merely the interpretation of narrative but the task of theology, the nature of theological method and the judgment as to what Christianity is all about. It is to this last issue, namely, the question of what it means to be a Christian Church, that we now turn to round up our discussion.[202]

5.5.1 A Prolegomenon for Constructive Ecclesiology

When we take stock of the many questions raised by commentators, the more clearly we see Lindbeck's works for what he says

[200] Linell Cady, "Resisting the Postmodern Turn," 90.

[201] S. G. Davaney, "Options in Post-modern Theology," 200. For other arguments against Lindbeck's claim of affinity with the postmodern intellectual climate, see Tanner, *Theories of Culture*, 107-110.

[202] Vanhoozer, *Biblical Narrative in the Philosophy of Paul Ricoeur*, 157.

they are, namely, prolegomena which require much enfleshment. Much still needs to be developed, as Tracy points out.[203] But that in no way takes away the potency of many of his proposals. In fact, one immediate advantage is that a programmatic proposal leaves plenty of room for others to make their contributions from within their own respective contexts. As Buckley points out, there are simply too many ways to describe and explain how the scriptural text does in fact tie its language to the world of a believer in any particular communicative situation, to warrant any theology suggesting it alone has done so.[204] One point throughout this study is that inadequate though his theological arguments may be in some respects, Lindbeck's prolegomena can nevertheless act as a powerful impetus for much constructive possibilities across the whole spectrum of Christian theology. One area of theology where little has yet been published in explicit dependence on, or dialogue with, Lindbeck's postliberal programme, is ecclesiology.

5.5.2 The Implications of Postliberal Theology for Ecclesiology

When doctrine is taken as a rule, to be followed rather than interpreted, attention is focused on the concrete life and language of the faith community. Lindbeck is candid about the modern world being inhospitable to his method, on account of its penchant for the liberal and propositional dogmatic approaches, as well as its loss of an experience of community as a principle of meaning, truth and action. What he has done is to shift the locus of criticism

---

[203] See allusion to this effect in Lindbeck, "The Gospel's Uniqueness," 423. In "Seeking a Clear Alternative to Liberalism," *B&R* 13 (1985) 9, Stanley Hauerwas and Gregory Jones speak of much hard work ahead if the implications of Lindbeck's alternative vision to liberalism are to be fully charted. See also Tracy, "Lindbeck's New Program."

[204] Buckley, *Seeking the Humanity of God*, 195 n.28.

from proposition and experience to practice, as the locale for grasping meaning and truth. The task of theologians is then to specify the circumstances in which Church doctrines apply. "The gears mesh with reality," Lindbeck suggests, "and theological reflection on doctrine becomes directly relevant to the praxis of the church."[205] Although lacking in detail, an outline of the postliberal ecclesiology that reflects Lindbeck's thought can be traced. We present this ecclesiology by critically enumerating nine "postliberal pleas." In doing so, we shall incorporate materials from sources other than Lindbeck, which are either directly inspired by him or which dovetail with his postliberal vision. And, where applicable, a comparison with a Catholic perspective will be noted.

5.5.2.1 A Story-Shaped Church: A Plea for a Narrative Ecclesiology

In Lindbeck's project, the canonical Scripture provides the basic narratives for how the Church imagines and interprets the world and itself in the world. The Church is fundamentally a story-shaped Church,[206] in relation to which four related points may be briefly noted.

First, the Church serves as the memory of Jesus and is constituted as the continuation of Christ's story. In this capacity, the Church is the community that tells Christ's story and lives a communal life that witnesses to the truth of that story. The Church, if it is to be the continuation of Christ's story, must, in Lindbeck's

---

[205] ND, 107.

[206] Adopting Kelsey, Tanner writes: "To call a text scripture is to say, in a Christian context, that the text is to be used (in some fashion or other) to shape, nurture, and reform the continuing self-identity of the church." See Tanner, "Theology and the Plain Sense," 62; and Kelsey, *The Uses of Scripture*, 90ff., 207ff.

terms, be shaped by and embody the story of Christ. The story of
Christ defines the fundamental identity and characteristic of the
Church.

Second, an ecclesiology that focuses on the story of Christ takes
seriously the entire salvation history, beginning with the story of
Israel, and accepts it as necessarily prior to any distillation of distinguishing "marks" or "images" of the Church. "Images such as
'body of Christ,' or the traditional marks of 'unity, holiness,
catholicity, and apostolicity,' cannot be first defined and then used
to specify what is and what is not the church. The story is logically prior. It determines the meaning of images, concepts, doctrines, and theories of the church rather than being determined by
them."[207]

Third, there are, of necessity, rules for telling and retelling the
story of Christ and of the Church, the story that embodies the truth
by which Christians hope to live and in which they hope to die.
The doctrinal regulative approach suggests that the story is validly
told only in the performative sense. In this light, Church doctrines
are primarily regarded as rules for our perception of God and the
world, which function to guide our "story-telling, pray-acting and
common-living."[208] In addition to rules, we also need a vocabulary that facilitates the ruling function of the story. This vocabulary of "symbols, concepts, rites, injunctions and stories" that

[207] Lindbeck, "The Story-Shaped Church," 165. Wesley Kort suggests that
the principal object of Lindbeck's theology is "the Church identified as Christian
community and projected as generative of doctrine, a reality whose unique significance and authority must be protected from the generalizing and compromising consequences of 'experiential-expressive' theologies. 'Cultural-linguistic'
and other poststructuralist terms are used to establish a traditional ecclesiological
interest: the Church as 'one, holy, universal, and apostolic'." See idem, *Bound to
Differ: The Dynamics of Theological Discourse* (University Park, PN: Pennsylvania State University Press, 1992), 38-39.
[208] Loughlin, *Telling God's Story*, 19.

underpins a doctrinally ruled Christian worldview is predominantly derived from the Scripture narratives.[209] Thus, under a postliberal ecclesiology, a comprehensive *performatory* (versus *propositional*) view of doctrine that is informed by the scriptural text, constitutes a key *rule* for Christian reading, imagining and retelling.

However, *fourthly*, if the Church is shaped by the story of Jesus Christ, it is formed by a language which, essentially, the world does not share: "a stumbling block to Jews and foolishness to Gentiles" (1 Cor. 1:23). The Church that performs the Jesus-story by which it is shaped, must, in the first place, fix its gaze on Jesus. A postliberal hermeneutics suggests that the Church should, above all, constantly return to the canonical Scriptures as its primary source where it locates a basic narrative framework with which it imagines and interprets its existence in the world. The Bible provides the fundamental story by which all other stories are to be judged. The Church is urged to "inscribe" itself in the narrative-world of the Bible, seeking only to understand the world in biblical terms and never allowing its primary communal text to be understood in worldly terms. This methodological proposal to renew the ancient practice of "absorbing the universe into the biblical world" is intended both "to instruct and to empower theologians to perform — to speak authentically to the church and to the culture at large."[210] However, even an intratextual approach cannot do without an external authoritative voice — a role tradition-

---

[209] See ND, 81.

[210] See ND, 135 and Miroslav Volf, "Theology, Meaning, and Power," 99. This approach links up well with the official position of the Catholic Church at Vatican II. We indicated in Chapter I the logic and historical reality of *Scripture-in-Tradition*. In addition, *Dei Verbum*, in reaffirming the indispensable role of the Magisterium in the interpretation of Scripture-in-Tradition, brings into relief a peculiar difficulty attendant on the postliberal intratextual approach which is not accompanied by recommendations for an authoritative arbitrator outside the text.

ally exercised by the Magisterium in the Catholic fold — to regulate or pronounce on normative readings in the face of disputed interpretations. Intratextuality and an external authority are, in this context, complementary elements in the Church. Just as a vigilant Magisterium may be experienced as authoritarian and stifling in some quarters of the Catholic Church, the absence of a Magisterium constitutes a conspicuous *lacuna* in Protestantism in general and is experienced as a recipe for veritable anarchy in some quarters.[211] In this regard, too, a Catholic, postliberal, intratextualist would welcome the Petrine office.[212]

5.5.2.2 A Non-Supersessionist Church: A Plea for a Christocentric Figural Ecclesiology

Ecclesiology in Lindbeck's postliberal paradigm is essentially biblical ecclesiology, one which relies equally on [a] a retrieval of premodern hermeneutics in a critical fashion, and [b] an acceptance of the corrective function of historical criticism as a necessary condition for that retrieval. Whereas the classic or premodern hermeneutics unrestrictedly attempts to capture the entire universe

---

[211] See, for example, *Surprised by Truth*, ed. Patrick Madrid (San Diego: Basilica, 1994). Lindbeck is cognizant of Protestant bodies' lack of competence and interest in magisterial action: "They lack or can no longer effectively use the decision-making structures which are the means by which communities make up their collective minds on what should or should not be taught regarding contemporary issues." See Lindbeck, "Reflection on the New York Forum," 67-68. What Lindbeck clearly disapproves of is an "uncritical and one-sided emphasis on the official magisterium." He has hoped to see a Roman magisterium that is more "visibly subject to the Word of God as witnessed to in Scriptures and tradition." See Lindbeck, "The Ratzinger File," *Com* 112 (1985) 636.

[212] Lindbeck himself holds a minimalist view of the papacy on account of his Lutheran heritage. See "Lutherans and the Papacy," *JES* 13 (1976) 368-78; "Papacy and *ius divinum*: A Lutheran View," in *Papal Primacy and the Universal Church*, ed. Paul Empie and T. A. Murphy (Minneapolis: Augsburg, 1974), 193-207.

in the embrace of biblical language, historical criticism releases this classical hermeneutics from its supersessionist bias and renders the example of Israel once more available to the Church.[213] A postliberal biblical ecclesiology will thus yield a portrait of the Church that is both Israel-like and non-supersessionist.[214] The concrete gathering of people depicted in the New Testament cannot be regarded as antitypical to the gathering of God's people portrayed in the Old Testament.[215]

To be sure, a typological or figuralist approach to reading Scriptures is not at all novel. But Lindbeck takes the project a step further than others before him who used a figuralist approach. Not only does he eloquently retrieve the basic hermeneutical presuppositions lying behind the patristic figuralist identification of Israel and the Christian Church, but he insists on appropriating and applying the *whole* of the figural story to the Church, and not just selecting favourable parts or jettisoning other narrative

[213] See Lindbeck, "The Gospel's Uniqueness," 438-39. Lindbeck adds the proviso that historical criticism is a necessary but not sufficient condition for the retrieval of premodern hermeneutics, provided "its focus is corrective and it is not made into a launching pad for tradition-independent speculations."

[214] The most extreme version of supersessionism was that of Marcion. For him, it was not just a matter of temporal succession in which a better religion followed a worse one with which it had no necessary connection. For Marcion, Israel had never been elect and the God of the Old Testament was not the same as the God of the New Testament. Quasi-Marcionite views had again become pervasive in ecclesiology since the sixteenth century. The ecumenical Council of Vatican II insists that the vocation of the Jews continues, they being the people God addressed first. The Council's *Declaration on Non-Christian Religion* (*Nostra Aetate*), 4 states: "Although the Church is the new people of God, the Jews should not be presented as repudiated or cursed by God, as if such views followed from Holy Scriptures."

[215] Lindbeck has indicated his indebtedness to Jewish writers for his rejection of ecclesiological supersessionism. See "Response to Michael Wyschogrod's 'Letter to a Friend'," *ModTh* 11 (1995) 205-10.

elements of judgment that cause discomfiture.[216] And, most importantly, the *mediating reality* for working out the elements of a narrative ecclesiology is located by Lindbeck in Christ himself. The relation of Israel's history to the Church in the New Testament is not one of "shadow to reality," or "promise to fulfillment," or "type to antitype." In Lindbeck's exegesis, *the kingdom already present in Christ alone* is the antitype, so that Church and Israel are both types of one antitype. "The people of God existing in both the old and the new ages are typologically related to Jesus Christ, and through Christ, Israel is prototypical for the church in much the same way that the exodus story, for example, is seen as prototypical for all later Israelite history by such prophets as Ezekiel."[217]

As Frei would put it, the stories of all are included in the story of Christ, so that the end of Christ's story is the end of all stories.[218] "Christ is depicted as the embodiment of Israel (e.g., 'Out of Egypt have I called my son,' Matthew 2:15), and the Church is the body of Christ. Thus, in being shaped by the story of Christ, the church shares (rather than fulfills) the story of Israel."[219] However, Israel and Church are variously shaped by Christ: Israel precedes, and the Church proceeds from, Christ. Thus, the shape of Israel is known retrospectively while that of the Church prospectively. Through Christ, Church and Israel embody, in different ways, the one body that is "God with us."

Adopting a christocentric figural approach yields great potential on four counts.

First, in suggesting that the Church is shaped by the story of Christ, a logical consequence is that the "Church" must refer to a

---

[216] For this positive assessment, see Radner, *The End of the Church*, 32.

[217] Lindbeck, "The Story-Shaped Church," 166.

[218] See Frei, *Theology and Narrative*, 43.

[219] Lindbeck, "The Story-Shaped Church," 166.

concrete, and not some transempirical, reality. It refers to a community of human beings called by and gathered before God (*qehal Yahweh*). Furthermore, an ecclesiology that explicitly takes the Christian Church's character as essentially explicated in and through the figure of Israel would insist on the ecclesial referent of scriptural figure as concrete and "visible." This has the obvious practical relevance of counteracting claims from some Protestant quarters that insist on the invisible character of the true Church. It is as unbiblical to speak of the invisible Church as it is to refer to an invisible Israel. If such exalted metaphorical descriptions of the Church as "holy" and "bride of Christ" are to bear any meaning at all, they must refer to the body of faithful in all its historical contingency and "actual or potential messiness."[220]

Second, in construing both Israel and Church as types of Christ, Lindbeck is paving a positive way forward in Church-Judaism relation today. "Christendom is passing and Christians are becoming a diaspora," Lindbeck points out. "The antagonism of the Church to the synagogue has been unmasked (we hope definitively) for the horror it always was. Christian pretensions to fulfillment have become obnoxious to vast numbers of Catholics and Protestants alike. Some of the reasons for distorting the story are disappearing, and perhaps its original version is again applicable."[221] To start with, the grammar of the Israel-Church relationship will be articulated in terms of prototype to ectype, rather than antitype to type. It is what is good about Israel of old, not what is bad, which is prototypical of the Church. "The stories of unfaithfulness

---

[220] Lindbeck, "The Story-Shaped Church," 165. We note, in this connection, that Lindbeck clearly takes much more seriously the historical factuality of the scriptural referent when he is doing ecclesiology than, as we saw in chapter 3, when he is presenting his scriptural hermeneutics in support of his intratextual theology.

[221] Lindbeck, "The Story-Shaped Church," 174.

and the thunderings of the prophets were read as directed first against Jews, second against heretics, and third against unrighteousness in professedly Christian societies." [222]

To be sure, the Messianic era has begun *in nuce* in Jesus, so that some of God's past instructions accommodated to particular times, places and persons may never again have renewed application. Nevertheless, "objectionable deeds and happenings in Israel of old 'were written down for our instruction, upon whom the end of the ages has come' (1 Cor. 10:11) precisely because the commonwealth of Israel, now messianically expanded to include gentiles (Eph. 3:11-22), remains one and the same people of God."[223] The wickedness of the Israelites in the desert, their rebellion (Numbers 16) and annihilation for fornication (Numbers 25) and a catalogue of colossal vices and dire punishments are, according to Paul, types (*tupoi*) written for our admonition (1 Cor. 10:5-11). "As of old, judgment continues to begin in the house of the Lord (1 Peter 4:17), and the unfaithful church can be severed from the root no less than the unbelieving synagogue (Rom. 11:21). There is nothing in the logic of this hermeneutic to deny that the bride of Christ, like the betrothed of Yahweh (Ezekiel 16 and 23), can be a whore worse than the heathen."[224]

The Church, like Israel, is not called to be what it is, but is to grow into what it is called to be. This suggests yet another sense in which Christ's story is not over but continuing. Significantly, the Church insists that Jesus Christ is not dead but alive, for He has risen from the dead never to die again. The Church errs if it looks for the living among the dead (Luke 24:5), for Jesus has gone on ahead of them (Mark 16:6-7). The place where Jesus is awaiting those who follow after, is not Jerusalem, a symbol of

[222] Lindbeck, "The Gospel's Uniqueness," 436.

[223] Lindbeck, "The Gospel's Uniqueness," 435.

[224] Lindbeck, "The Story-Shaped Church," 166.

politics and power, but Galilee, a symbol of the workplace where the struggles in life and in faith are lived out in mundane affairs. The Second Vatican Council, at once pastoral and ecumenical, urges sensitivity on the part of the faith community to the struggles in the world: "The joy and hope, the grief and anguish of the men of our time, especially of those who are poor or afflicted in any way, are the joy and hope, the grief and anguish of the followers of Christ."[225]

Third, although Lindbeck himself does not explicitly deal with the pneumatic vocation in addressing Christian division, his christocentric figural approach does help to open an avenue for ecumenical discussion on precisely that point. In this regard, one perspective is provided by Tillard and Ratzinger. In discussing the way the original thrust of the World Council of Church's foundational vision for the reestablishment of unity among the churches has been increasingly pushed to the periphery of the Council's concern, Tillard raises the searching question of whether the Holy Spirit was present at the WCC Assembly at Canberra. He shows willingness to answer in the affirmative only in the sense that the Spirit was there to offer "the grace of clarity which led to the discovery that the ecumenical movement is beginning to go adrift."[226] His answer, dismal though it is with regard to the discussion that actually took place at the Assembly, nevertheless brings into relief the general pneumatic absence from the Church and the recognition that the pneumatic presence was only discerned as "the sobering knowledge of a dissipated vocation."[227] The question naturally arises as to how the Scripture can speak the Gospel of Christ to a community of hearers bound in a condition

---

[225] *Gaudium et Spes*, 1.

[226] J. M. R. Tillard, "Was the Holy Spirit at Canberra?," *One in Christ* 29 (1993) 62.

[227] Radner, *The End of the Church*, 26 n.43.

of division? Radner's answer is emphatic: "it *cannot*, except insofar as it unveils our deaf incomprehension." This leads him to
posit a basic pneumatological obstacle, an "absence of the para-
clete," as a reality in the relationship between Spirit, Scripture and
Church. He thus describes this absence of the Spirit from the
Church as being "constitutive of historical pneumatology" and
declares "that Christian division and scriptural obscurity are themselves pneumatic realities of the historical present."[228]

Contemporary Catholic theologians have for decades been
adopting this figuralist approach in their reflections on Christian
division. For instance, in 1948, Yves Congar offered a basic outline of a figuralist construal of the divided Christian Church after
the type of divided Israel.[229] Ratzinger, too, commenting on the
Anglican-Roman Catholic dialogue as reported in ARCIC I,
makes a remark that highlights two points. *Firstly*, the division of
the churches may be regarded as somehow bearing significance in
the context of salvation history. Ratzinger seems to suggest that
the fact of institutional separation, present as a reality in the path
of the sovereign shaping of history by God, must necessarily point
to the heart of the Gospel of Christ. *Secondly*, this division of the
churches can properly point to the Gospel in the fashion of "the
division between Israel and the Gentiles" in that they should
"make 'each other envious', vying with each other in coming
closer to the Lord (Rom. 11:11)."[230] In like manner, Ratzinger
refers to Paul's remark in 1 Cor. 11:9 that "there must be factions." Agreeing with Augustine and H. Schlier on this "mysterious

---

[228] Radner, *The End of the Church*, 27.

[229] See Yves Congar, "Reflections on the Schism of Israel in the Perspective
of Christian Division," in *Dialogue Between Christians: Catholic Contributions
to Ecumenism* (Westminster, MD: Newman, 1966), 160-83.

[230] Joseph Ratzinger, *Church, Ecumenism and Politics*, trs. Robert Nowell
(Slough: St. Paul, 1988), 87.

phrase in Paul," Ratzinger suggests that it be regarded as "an eschatological and dogmatic proposition," the imperative "must" (*dei*) being understood by exegetes as always referring to "an action of God" or expressing "an eschatological necessity." In this light, even where schisms originate in human sin, they may nevertheless be regarded as bearing "a dimension that corresponds to God's disposing."[231]

Fourth, when its focus and center is Jesus Christ, the Church is better able to give a clear primacy to the *object* of faith. The object of Christian faith is not constituted by a set of propositions, but by a person – the person of Jesus Christ in whom Christian Tradition affirms the definitive revelation of God.

5.5.2.3 The Nature and Mission of the Church: A Plea for Silence in the Public Square

Returning to the sources of the faith, particularly to the Bible and Church Fathers, Vatican II, in its *Dogmatic Constitution on the Church*, employed a vision of the Church as the pilgrim people of God – a people in communion with God and each other, who are the sacramental sign of the Kingdom which has begun and will be consummated in Christ.[232] This picture at once involves the two basic aspects of the Church, namely, its *nature* and *mission*:

[231] Ratzinger, *Church, Ecumenism and Politics*, 138-39.

[232] The understanding that different views of Church – as people of God, Mystical Body, sacrament, communion, institution of salvation and so on – are juxtaposed in the conciliar document is commonplace, thus obviating any need to belabour the point here. Suffice it to affirm Lindbeck's assessment that this ambiguity, frustrating to those who seek a precise definition of the Catholic view of the Church, is deliberate and fortunate in that it "reflects the Council's desire to be 'pastoral,' to make a minimum of doctrinal decisions, and leave room for theological variety and development." See Lindbeck, *The Future of Roman Catholic Theology*, 32-33.

The nature of the church is understood in terms of a pilgrim people. The church is a band of men and women traveling towards the promised land: God's kingdom of justice, righteousness, peace, and love... Second, however, this pilgrim people has a mission. It exists not for itself, but in order to be a concrete witness to the world, a sacramental sign and anticipation in all that it is and does, to Christ and to the kingdom. Apart from this mission, there is nothing which differentiates this people from other peoples.[233]

Given its fundamental missionary character, the Church has, as its primary rationale for existence, the task of mediating transcendence to society. The question is, how is that task discharged in the public square? More appropriately formulated in the negative, postliberal strategy recommends no talkative and confident activism. In this respect, an adverse reflection on the postliberal theological commitment is their lack of attention to justice and political issues. Lindbeck's reflections on two occasions help focus our discussion in this regard.

The *first* occasion is related to the "Hartford Appeal for Theological Affirmation" which is essentially a response to a perceived crisis of transcendence in the theological discipline. Lindbeck, himself a signatory to the Appeal, locates the relevance of that Appeal to theology today in its providing an orientation for theological thinking in a time of flux and transition: "the affirmations for which it calls are forever necessary because Jesus Christ as witnessed to in Scripture and tradition is forever normative for human thought and life." While he is deeply conscious that biblical studies have "opened our eyes to the primacy of praxis and of the struggle for human liberation," Lindbeck will not agree that orthopraxis is more fundamental than orthodoxy, or action than theological affirmation, because "theology is necessary to praxis," like "concepts to precepts" or "doctrine to the discrimination

---

[233] Lindbeck, *The Future of Roman Catholic Theology*, 27.

between true and false liberation." However, in view of Matthew 25:31-46, is not the struggle against oppression and for liberation more basic than the zeal to discourage those engaged in it "by talk of the danger of alien influences, the importance of 'transcendence,' and the need to keep Christian language straight and its grammar uncorrupted?" Lindbeck's vision for theology, then as now, is consistently driven by a desire to counteract the "cultural accommodators" who are especially strong in the academy. Reverting to Luther, Lindbeck indicates his preference for the view that "the cause of Christian faithfulness in every generation is to resist cultural captivity ... and to harken to the biblical story, climaxing in cross and resurrection, which stands in tension with all our human thoughts and wishes."[234] But how ought the Church deal with that tension in the public square? Does it do so by keeping silent, influencing the outside world only through quietly living its own faith-life in a manner coherent with its beliefs? Evidently, Lindbeck's strategy comprises, as its first step, an insistence on the need to harken back to Scriptures *before* we do anything else.

This takes us to the *second* occasion, where Lindbeck indicates his disapproval of what appears to him as an excessive commitment by the World Council of Churches to social-ethical concerns over specifically religious concerns:

> From the 1960s on, the service of humanity, reconceived in liberationist and politically progressive terms, increasingly became the motor driving the ecumenical train. It now dominates the World Council agenda in the form of Justice, Peace, and the Integrity of Creation initiatives. However good these JPIC programs may be, they are more than questionable to the extent they become the goal and motive rather than fruit and by-product of Christian life

---

[234] Lindbeck, "A Battle for Theology," in *Against the World for the World*, ed. Peter Berger and Richard Neuhaus (New York: Seabury, 1976), 23, 40-41.

together. When it is work not worship which unites, human need rather than God's glory becomes central, and justification by service replaces justification by faith.[235]

Evidently, the second step in Lindbeck's strategy is to insist on salvation by faith and not by clamour and busyness (human works) in the public square. However, where the strategy issues in a frequent disparagement of liberation theology, it gives rise to an anomalous situation for, as Paul Lakeland observes, there are elements in liberation theology that renders it the nearest thing in current Christianity which represents a postliberal ecclesiality: [i] it is rooted in the scriptural reflection of local faith communities; [ii] it uses social-scientific method in an *ad hoc* and descriptive manner; [iii] it employs a narrative of the Christian community that stresses continuity with Israel and the practices of the early Church; and [iv] its theology is subordinated to, and comes after, the practice of the community — as "the second act" of religious reflection.[236]

And yet, Lindbeck's position makes sense when it is viewed in relation to the Lutheran tradition to which it is closely attuned. It is a position that is markedly different from even the post-Vatican II Catholic tradition, where the "age-old willingness to wield the secular sword is much reduced." Characteristically more focused and limited in its definition of the mission of the Church, Lutheranism sees the Church as discharging its calling well merely in proclaiming the Gospel purely and administering the sacraments properly. Its "core vision" is attained by forming a people in the central religious and moral vision in response to Word and Sacrament. This people of faith will express itself in

---

[235] Lindbeck, "Tilting in the Ecumenical Wars," *Lutheran Forum* 26:4 (1992) 23.

[236] Paul Lakeland, *Postmodernity: Christian Identity in a Fragmented Age* (Minnesota: Fortress, 1997), 67-68.

society only indirectly, for any form of direct intervention in societal affairs would only confuse its mission and generally put its integrity in jeopardy. The basic rationale here is that "God has given the Church only the power of the Word not the sword."[237] It is an eminently dualistic view which insists as follows: "The gospel has absolutely nothing to do with outward existence but only with eternal life.... It is not the vocation of Jesus Christ or of the gospel to change the orders of secular life and establish them anew.... Christianity wants to change the person's heart, not his external situation."[238]

Among the postliberals, Hauerwas has written most extensively in the area of public theology and active involvement with the world, advocating the negative in each case, the Church's task being primarily one of formation of a community of truthful character, not of vociferous speakers.[239] It is little wonder that he finds fault with liberation theology.[240] His position should be seen in a larger picture where he has articulated over the years an offensive against what he judges to be a Kantianism in which morality is freed from its historical moorings and universalized into a kind of

[237] See Robert Benne, *The Paradoxical Vision: A Public Theology for the Twenty-first Century* (Minneapolis: Fortress, 1994), 101-02.

[238] Carl E. Braaten, *Principles of Lutheran Theology* (Philadelphia: Fortress, 1983), 124.

[239] A preeminent example is Stanley Hauerwas and William H. Willimon, *Resident Aliens: Life in the Christian Colony* (Nashville: Abingdon, 1989). Hauerwas has been influenced by Alasdair MacIntyre who said, "What matters at this stage is the construction of local forms of community within which civility and the intellectual and moral life can be sustained through the new dark ages which are already upon us." See *After Virtue*, 263.

[240] See Stanley Hauerwas, "Some Theological Reflections on Gutierrez's Use of 'Liberation' as a Theological Concept," *ModTh* 3 (1986) 67-76; *After Christendom? How the Church Is to Behave If Freedom, Justice, and a Christian Nation Are Bad Ideas* (Nashville: Abingdon, 1991), 50-55. Hauerwas' reaction is to Gustavo Gutiérrez, *A Theology of Liberation*, trs. Sr. Caridad Inda and John Eagleson (Maryknoll: Orbis, 1973).

"secularized version of Christian hope."[241] In keeping with this judgment, he finds Gutierrez's account of liberation positively at odds with the Gospel and "profoundly anti-Christian," in view of its kinship with Kant and the Enlightenment, rather than with the Kingdom established by Christ.[242]

The Vatican, too, has always been vigilant with respect to potential errors coming from liberation theologians. But this vigilance is decidedly different from the postliberal plea for silence on the part of the Church in the public square. The silencing of Leonardo Boff, it has been suggested, may have to do with what is called a "communion ecclesiology" which the Vatican espouses, the central premises of which Boff was suspected to have violated.[243] Even the Vatican Congregation for the Doctrine of the Faith's instructions issued in 1984, which criticized the liberation theologians for using "concepts uncritically borrowed from Marxist ideology and ... theses of a biblical hermeneutic marked by rationalism," did so because these theologians offered a "new interpretation which is corrupting whatever is authentic in the generous initial commitment on

---

[241] Hauerwas, *A Community of Character*, 100. Another element of basic motivation in Hauerwas' work is the insistence on the necessity of an ecclesially and biblically rooted paradigm, so much so that even the "very sophisticated hermeneutical analyses of the formal significance of narrative" cannot be substituted for a theory of interpretation for the Church. See Hauerwas, "The Church as God's Language," in *Scriptural Authority and Narrative Interpretation*, ed. Garrett Green, (Philadelphia: Fortress, 1987), 179.

[242] For an appreciative critique of Gutiérrez, see George Hunsinger, "Karl Barth and Liberation Theology," *JR* 63 (1983) 247-63. For an attempt to draw out the regulative principles operative in Gutiérrez's work and the complementarity between him and Hauerwas on some aspects, see David G. Kamitsuka, "Salvation, Liberation and Christian Character Formation: Postliberal and Liberation Theologians in Dialogue," *ModTh* 13 (1997) 171-89.

[243] See Dennis M. Doyle, "Communion Ecclesiology and the Silencing of Boff," *Am* 167 (1992) 139-43.

behalf of the poor."[244] Two years later, in its 1986 "Instruction
on Christian Freedom and Liberation," the Congregation abandoned the negative tone of its 1984 predecessor. While it
opposed "the systematic recourse to violence as the necessary
path to liberation," the Instruction now positively endorsed a
preferential love for the poor on the part of the Church and a
"Christian practice of liberation," arguing that "it is perfectly
legitimate that those who suffer oppression on the part of the
wealthy and the politically powerful should take action through
morally licit means, in order to secure structures and institutions
in which their rights will be truly respected."[245]

Thus, from the Catholic point of view, the question of liberation
is germane to the mission of the Church. In any event, it would
seem that an emphasis on liberation ought to emanate naturally
from the narratively-inclined. Stephen Duffy captures the perti-
nence of this comment well:

> We are victims as well as agents, mere narrators as well as, or more
> than, authors. People are often scripted and contribute little to the
> creation of their story; they may even be unaware they have a story,
> and hence are unable to tell it. How vital it is to tell the stories of the
> depersonalized, the losers! The history of suffering wails out for
> narrative and redress. To the credit of the liberationists, they are
> telling the stories of history's victims.[246]

[244] See Congregation for the Doctrine of the Faith, "The Instruction on Certain
Aspects of the 'Theology of Liberation'," *Origins* 14:13 (1984) 193-204. Juan Luis
Segundo accused the Vatican of making "constant allusions to Marxism [as a] mere
publicity gimmick to diminish liberation theology in the eyes of those who are not
sufficiently sensitive to the profound and subtle methods of theology." See idem,
*Theology and the Church: A Response to Cardinal Ratzinger and a Warning to the
Whole Church*, trs. John W. Diercksmeier (Minneapolis: Winston, 1985).

[245] Congregation for the Doctrine of the Faith, "Instruction on Christian Freedom and Liberation," *Origins* 15:44 (1986) 713-28.

[246] Stephen Duffy, "Justification by Faith: A Post-Conciliar Perspective," 212. Lamenting the division of the secular and the religious in the

In sum, we note that the Catholic Church has always incarnated the proposition that the Church's social task is discharged by embodying the truth of Christ's lordship in its internal life (doctrine, liturgy, and practice) as well as by its declarations of moral truth in the public realm. In this regard, we note three related points.

First, there is the contentious issue of the Church's *relevance* to and in society. If the Church is needed by liberal society on account of its inherent orientation to eternity, then it fails both itself and society if it secularizes itself or becomes so preoccupied with the historical that it becomes mindless of the eternal.[247] Far from wondering aimlessly, history, in the Christian understanding, is embraced in divine providence which vindicates and brings to eschatological fulfillment the order of creation to which the Church witnesses. The integrity of the Church can never, ultimately, be measured by its historical effectiveness. The Church, then, is to be subservient not to the demands of society, but only to its call to signify the eschatological Kingdom. Lindbeck thus insists that "religious communities are likely to be practically relevant in the long run to the degree that they do not first ask what is either practical or relevant, but instead concentrate on their own

seminary, Sallie McFague Te Selle said: "In a religion such as Christianity, concern with oppression and poverty in the 'secular' sphere should not be at variance with vitality in the 'religious' sphere, for Christianity is inescapably incarnational, inescapably, as Erich Auerbach has said, set by the pattern of God with us in the story of Jesus, God with us in the historical and everyday dimension of our lives." See "A Report from the Field," *Am* 134 (1976) 257.

[247] For some engaging discussions on the crisis of transcendence in contemporary theology, see *Against the World for the World: The Hartford Appeal and the Future of American Religion*, ed. Perter L. Berger and Richard J. Neuhaus (New York: Seabury, 1976); Paul Crowley, "The Crisis of Transcendence and the Task of Theology," in *Finding God in All Things*, ed. Michael J. Himes and Stephen J. Pope (New York: Crossroad, 1996), 197-214.

intratextual outlooks and forms of life."[248] 'Practicality' or 'relevance' are never the first words to which the Church listens. Projects that seek to be relevant to current trends only raise the risk of increased balkanization.[249] Faithfulness on the part of the disciples of Christ is measured by the degree of their close adherence to the message of the Gospel, rather than to their accommodation to the demands of the world. In thus being faithful in intratextual terms, postliberals trust that the Church can finally never be less than supremely relevant; for the greater our faithfulness, the greater will be our likeness to Christ in whose footsteps we are called to follow.[250]

What then do we make of the much-debated problem of theory and praxis? Lindbeck's line of reasoning leads him to conclude, rather too optimistically, that the problem is dissolved by the (Protestant) communal analogue of justification by faith. Salvation for individuals, as for the religious community, is neither by good works nor by faith in the practical efficacy of intentional effort; rather, all kinds of unforeseeable good works will ensue from faithfulness. In like manner, Hauerwas, in making what is essentially his flagship statement, avers: "The Church's social task is first of all its willingness to be a community formed by a language the world does not share.... The church's social ethic is not first of all to be found in the statements by which it tries to influence the ethos of those in power, but rather ... in its ability to sustain a

---

[248] ND, 130. This is consonant with Barth's refusal to justify theological assertions by making the criterion of meaning and truth their anthropological relevance. When relevance is the overriding criterion, 'God' is made a predicate of human needs, resulting in an abandonment of the "objective constraints of divine self-revelation" and dire relativism. See Hunsinger, "Beyond Literalism and Expressivism," 219.

[249] Lindbeck, "The Gospel's Uniqueness," 427.

[250] See Robert Song, *Christianity and Liberal Society* (New York: Oxford University Press, 1997), 231-32.

people who are not at home in the liberal presumptions of our civilization and society."[251] Bitter disputes, however, stem from this line of argument. As we saw, one contentious issue is the ecclesiological model suitable for adoption by the faith community. The Word/faith paradigm preferred by Lindbeck and many postliberals leads to something like the contrast-society model we discussed earlier. The debate continues as to whether this position is not, ultimately, ghettoish, sectarian, fideistic and relativistic.

Secondly, theologians always need to be attentive to the tensions between the particularity of Christian doctrines and the universal application of certain aspects of their doctrinal tradition. One of these aspects concerns the question of dialogue with others. Dialogue, many would agree, is an imperative in contemporary pluralistic societies. But Lindbeck's vision for dialogue is minimalist and even instrumentalist. He sees the very welfare and survival of the world-wide diaspora of peoples of biblical faith as largely dependent on peace prevailing in the earthly cities. But, without religions, societies become dysfunctional: "morality disintegrates and social viability weakens in the absence of culturally powerful, meaning-conferring, and community-sustaining comprehensive outlooks." Because the malfunctioning of religions only works to diminish the prospects of communal and personal flourishing both inside and outside the churches, the question of how religions actually sustain these societies must therefore be of intimate concern to the churches. As for the Christian contribution, even though history may show that the churches have provided both negative and positive examples to people of other religions, Lindbeck is confident that "the effects of their unwitting servanthood have been volcanic." In proposing "servanthood" as a useful model for Christian religious dialogue, Lindbeck argues

that the Church is called to serve other religions for the sake of [i]
the neighbour, [ii] humanity, and [iii] God's promise to Abraham
that through him all nations will be blessed. To this list he must
now add [iv] communal self-interest.[252] But how, in practice, does
Lindbeck visualize this servanthood to be carried out, when
silence in the public square is desirable to the postliberals?

For Lindbeck, the warrant for dialogue consists in the Christian
churches [i] rendering service to their neighbours in imitation of
their Lord, even free from the proselytizing motive; and [ii]
acknowledging (as passages like Amos 9:7-8 do) that others are
also the elect but have not carried out "their distinct tasks within
God's world." Hence, it is incumbent on us in our missionary task
to assist them towards making better particular contributions.
Lindbeck thus locates his warrant for dialogue with non-Christians
in the idea of *service* to neighbours, through helping them to
"purify and enrich their heritage, to make them better speakers of
the languages they have."[253]

Thirdly, how is evangelism conceived of in a postliberal
Church? The Church of today finds itself in a pluralistic, postmodern world which, Lindbeck suggests, bears potential for bringing us closer to a pre-Constantinian relation to the cultures around
us.[254] As Constantinianism wanes, postliberals regard evangelism
"not simply as declaring a message to someone but as initiation
into the world-changing kingdom of God." Instead of its old category of proclamation, evangelism will once again be understood

---

[252] See Lindbeck, "The Gospel's Uniqueness," 424, 447-48.

[253] See ND, 54-55. Lindbeck cites Vatican II's *Declaration on Non-Christian
Religions* in support of the claim that the aim of dialogue may simply be to benefit, and not convert, the other.

[254] "Constantinian Christendom seems to be definitively ending, and reshap-
ings of ecclesial thought and practice greater than those of the Reformation and
comparable, perhaps, to the fourth century may well be unavoidable," Lindbeck
suggests in "Scripture, Consensus and Community," 90.

as an invitation to people to come into the world of Christ — to "come and see" how Christians live as responsible members of the body of Christ.[255]

Precisely at this point, it seems that the door ought to be held open for a link up of the postliberal mode of thought with an argument, such as the one made by Cornelius Ernst, that articulating the meaning of *the world in Christ* necessarily entails a continuing search for a "total human culture, the progressive discovery of a single human identity in Christ"[256] — "so that God may be all in all" (1 Cor. 15:28). For, conspicuously missing in the postliberal vision for dialogue is the rich dialectics of encounter. Without reducing dialogue to self-understanding, it is in and through the encounter with the other, with what is different from ourselves, that we better understand ourselves. In mutually critical dialogues, we are forced to appreciate the emergence of truth in its different dimensions. Take the case of Ernst's point. There are clearly discernible "totalizing" trends in society which threaten authentic human self-definition. One such trend is the uniform mass-culture of technological manipulation and control. A Church whose essence is missionary must find a potential ally in this human search for liberation from common adversaries. Attending to anthropological questions does not necessarily mean, as the postliberals are wont to suggest, becoming liberal foundationalists, zealous at translating the Gospel into alien terms in response to secular questions. Does the Gospel share not even the remotest interest in secular concerns? Is the Church completely above and beyond the joys and sorrows of the people of the world? Thus, according to Rowan Williams' thesis, the interpretation of the

---

[255] See Rodney Clapp, *A Secular People: The Church as Culture in a Post-Christian Society* (Downers Grove, IL: InterVarsity, 1996), 167.

[256] Cornelius Ernst, "Theological Methodology," in *Multiple Echo*, ed. Fergus Kerr and Timothy Radcliffe (London: Darton, Longman & Todd, 1979), 85.

world within the scriptural framework has got to be intrinsic to the Church's critical self-discovery.[257] He challenges the postliberals thus: "Can we so *rediscover* our own foundational story in the acts and hopes of others that we ourselves are reconverted and are able to bring those acts and hopes in relation with Christ for their fulfillment by the recreating grace of God?"[258]

All this, to be sure, closely ties in with the tension that ought to exist between "Christ and culture." Scholars are uneasy over a general tendency in postliberalism to distort that tension.

5.5.2.4 Church and Culture: A Plea for a Modified "Christ Against Culture" Model

Williamson makes a potent statement when he suggests that "Christian faith requires Christ and culture positioned in a dynamic interaction if human beings and churches and societies are to exist, let alone be transformed."[259] In many ways, this captures the crux of the debate between Lindbeck and Tracy. The critical question is how to work out that contrast, and especially how to concretely spell out the "dynamic interaction" between Church and culture.

---

[257] "In attempting to show the world a critical truth, it shows itself to itself as Church also." See Rowan Williams, "Postmodern Theology and the Judgment of the World," 95.

[258] R. Williams, "Postmodern Theology and the Judgment of the World," 105. Loughlin thus assumes the burden of showing that "doctrine construed as ecclesial grammar is intimately dependent upon that which it rules: the telling of the story." Ultimately, it depends on the ecclesial tradition of discipleship. See idem, "The Basis and Authority of Doctrine," in *The Cambridge Companion to Christian Doctrine*, ed. Colin E. Gunton (Cambridge: Cambridge University Press, 1997), 55. Loughlin finds support in Rowan Williams who teaches that it is only insofar as doctrine brings the Church to the point of "judgment and conversion worked out through encounter with the telling of the Jesus' story," that it finds its proper basis and function. See Rowan Williams, "The Incarnation as the Basis of Dogma," in *The Religion of the Incarnation*, ed. Robert Morgan (Bristol: Bristol Classical, 1989), 87.

[259] Williamson, "Challenging Lindbeck," 300.

Richard Niebuhr dealt with this tension through a five-fold typological conspectus of Christianity's relation to society: Christ-against-culture; Christ-of-culture; Christ-above-culture; Christ-and-culture; and Christ-the-transformer-of-culture. Taking the Christ-the-transformer-of-culture paradigm as normative, Niebuhr viewed the Christ-against-culture model as sectarian, citing the Mennonites as its purest representative.[260] Hauerwas, who regards the Mennonites as the best exemplification of the kind of Church he prefers, has critically noted some specific problems facing Niebuhr's preference for Christ-transformer-of-culture ecclesiology. For instance, it would seem to involve an essentialist reading of "culture" (i.e., that culture is one and given and, like an Aristotelian essence, does not change)[261] which usually ends up in an uncritical underwriting of liberal assumptions and practices in an attempt to render Christ "relevant." "Culture" became a term used indiscriminately to underwrite Christian involvement with the world without differentiating the good from the bad in "culture." The most inclusive ecclesiology becomes the most acceptable, and any church which is too concerned about its identity and the formation of the young in a tradition-specific fashion would be branded "sectarian" and "tribalist." A generously pluralistic approach of this kind underwrote the implicit assumption that pluralism must be superior to more narrow ecclesiology. The Constantinian synthesis between the Church and the world shackled the Church to the idea of unification so as to keep the Empire together. Christianity had aided, abetted or acquiesced in some of

---

[260] Richard H. Niebuhr, *Christ and Culture* (New York: Harper and Row, 1965).

[261] Ironically, Karthryn Tanner, arguing from theological and postmodern cultural grounds, disputes the postliberals' own presupposition of a self-contained and self-originating Christian identity in virtue of a cultural boundary. See *Theories of Culture*, 107f.

the greatest atrocities in the world on account of the Church's eagerness to serve the world, instead of attending to the infinitely more important task of being faithful to the Gospel. Niebuhr had all but created a false dilemma of "whether to be in or out of the world, politically responsible or introspectively irresponsible."[262] Here, as elsewhere, Hauerwas has captured something which the Church would do well to ponder. And yet, there is no denying the dialectical situation in which Christianity finds itself in modern culture. On the one hand, how can Christianity be 'relevant' without becoming 'trivial' or being reduced to a rubber stamp for liberalism? On the other hand, how can Christianity be seriously challenging without becoming 'isolationist'?[263]

The Church often appears to enter the public arena only to pronounce on some religious and moral issues. It assumes the posture of a "teaching" and never a "listening" Church, giving the impression that it is "wired for transmission only, and not for reception."[264] But, on the question of "dynamic interaction" between Christ and culture, the issue is not that Christianity is unwilling to 'listen' to culture. The option has been tried — Vatican II was certainly very optimistic about its prospects. The problem, so it seems to the postliberals, is that modern liberal culture is so caught up in its own self-sufficiency and arrogant moral solipsism that it is unwilling to listen to any "alternative voice" which may challenge it. Postliberals are uneasy with liberal theologians who revise the Tradition, tone down its hard paradoxes, and adapt its liturgies and practices, until it is finally "relevant" to

---

[262] Hauerwas, *Resident Aliens*, 17-18, 39-42.

[263] Lauritzen, "Is Narrative Really a Panacea?," reviews the work of Hauerwas and Metz, particularly their attention to 'narrative' as a way out of this dialectical challenge.

[264] Gabriel Daly, "Theological Analysis and Public Policy Debate in a Pluralist Society," *D&L* 45 (1995) 86.

the culture. When much of liberal theology seems to be engaged in constant revisions and translations of this nature, it can hardly be described as genuine "dynamic interaction." The liberal churches, dancing to the beat of an erratic liberal drum, end up being purveyors of common commodities. The insight uncovered by Lindbeck and Hauerwas is that the way to provide a dynamic interaction between the Church and this unwilling dialogue-partner called modernity, is for the Church to be true to itself. The Church does so by adopting the self-sufficiency of its particular language and culture. The question is whether this vision has to be *exclusive*.

Exclusivity turns the Church into a "communal enclave," a notion which Rowan Williams strongly opposes. On politically pragmatic grounds such as peaceful co-existence, a radically pluralist society withdraws from judgment. But, in seeking conversions, the Church's task is to help bring contemporary struggles to judgment. The Church does so by helping individuals to appropriate some new dimensions of the transforming summons of Christ in their lives. To speak of judgment in a fragmented culture presupposes the possibility of shared points of reference. Like legal, artistic and moral judgment, it makes no sense if it is not a public affair. "The communal enclave, if it is not to be a ghetto, must make certain claims on the possibility of a global community, and act accordingly." Postliberalism thus engenders a false dichotomy in the either-or of "intensive in-house catechesis" or modernist sacrifice of the distinctiveness of the Gospel. The world of the Scripture, "so far from being a readily defined territory, is an *historical* world in which meanings are discovered and recovered in action and encounter." A more useful pedagogy would immerse the Church in the language of Scripture-in-Tradition and, at the same time, recommend a full exposure "to political and cultural issues that might help to focus doctrinal language in a new way."

For judgment only takes place in a dynamic interaction between Church and world, *inclusive* of both Church and world. The Church hears God's judgment and in turn mediates it to the world. But there is more, in judging the world the Church "also hears God's judgment on itself in the judgment passed upon it by the world."[265]

To be sure, applying the notions of "communal enclaves" and a "sectarian" stance need not be altogether bad. The churches know that Lindbeck is right in calling attention to the need to give a more rigorous formation to believers "so that their attitude will not simply mirror the ideas and values of the dominant culture." In some respects, to assume a sectarian stance precisely to ensure that the Church is able to make a distinctively Christian contribution is a necessary strategy.[266] But to be true to itself, the Church is always expected to walk a fine line between "sectarian withdrawal from the world and secularist absorption." In Dulles' view, Catholic practice aims at providing *a corrective*: depending on which is the greater temptation at a particular time, the Church may have to lean more in the counterbalancing direction.[267]

Is Lindbeck moving against the tide of change in light of Robert Imbelli's suggestion of a transition currently taking place in theology, a transition he elucidates as a shift from a *Word/faith* to a

---

[265] Rowan Williams, "Postmodern Theology and the Judgment of the World," 93, 98-99, 101, 104-07.

[266] ND, 128; Fergusson, *Community, Liberalism and Christian Ethics*, 42.

[267] Avery Dulles, *The Catholicity of the Church* (Oxford: Clarendon, 1985), 66-67. In the same chapter 3, Dulles addresses the problems associated with nature and grace, including the problem of the Church's relationship to culture and politics. Michael Novak urges resistance against the excesses in the sectarian mentality, which is "absolutist, pure, certain, and righteous." It is a mentality contrary to the Catholic spirit: the Church is not a Church of "the saved, the saints, the true believers ... [but] a gathering of the struggling, the voyaging, the weak, those in whom there remains much unbelief, and sinners." See *Confession of a Catholic* (San Francisco: Harper & Row, 1983), 103.

Spirit/transformation paradigm? The latter paradigm seems better
able to get round the primarily vertical conception of encounter
with God in a private and solitary manner. Under the Word/faith
paradigm, the sphere of God's activity is confined to the ecclesiastical context, in which the Word finds expression. The drawback
of this vision lies in the dichotomy which it sets up between
Church and world, characteristically degrading the latter as being
"hostile," needing redemption and as something to be renounced
(hence, the Christ-against-culture model). By contrast, under the
Spirit/transformation paradigm, the world, ambiguous as it is, is
seen as the locus of a saving encounter. There, the Spirit is already
at work, and Christians relate best to the world if they discern the
signs of the times and cooperate with the action of God in the
world. In post-Vatican II statements concerning justice and peace,
for example, the 1971 Synod of Bishops' declaration on "Justice
in the World" asserts categorically: "Action on behalf of justice
and participation in the transformation of the world fully appear to
us as a constitutive dimension of the preaching of the Gospel, or,
in other words, of the Church's mission for the redemption of the
human race and its liberation from every oppressive situation."[268]
However, faithfulness to Jesus, Dulles observes, will "incline the
ecclesiastical authorities to avoid entanglement in economic and
political issues."[269] Beyond "holding aloft the transcendent vision

[268] *Justice in the World: Statement of 1971 Synod of Bishops* (Washington:
U. S. Catholic Conference, 1972), 34. The American Bishops in their 1986 pastoral letter on "Economic Justice for All" sees Christians as being called also as
citizens, thus requiring them to act through the public political process whereby
the whole society takes responsibility for its problems. Robert Bellah agrees,
arguing that "discipleship and citizenship, though often in tension, are both valid
obligations for Christians." See "Christian Faithfulness in a Pluralist World," in
Postmodern Theology, ed. Frederic Burnham (San Francisco: Harper & Row,
1989), 88.

[269] One must, of course not forget that it was in his understanding of
faithfulness to Christ that Pope John Paul II was actively involved in helping

proposed by Jesus," Dulles adds, the Church has a second responsibility "to guide its members, and all who wish to submit to its influence, in behaving according to the Gospel." But, while deploring "the politicization of the Gospel," Dulles also notes the difficulty in making a "neat separation between the religious, moral and political spheres" and, in view of the spheres-overlap, the Church "cannot totally divorce itself from the political sphere."[270]

Whether Imbelli's discernment is accurate, Hodgson is clearly on the mark in suggesting that there are two potentially productive strategies — "renewal" and "transformation" — for confronting the cultural challenges of our time. *Renewal* represents the approach of the more conservative forms of theological postmodernism, epitomized in the postliberal mode by the affirmations of biblical and confessional identity.[271] In terms of Niebhur's typology, Hodgson places this position as being close to "Christ-and-culture in paradox."[272] Chief among the features of this worthy

to dismantle the Eastern European communist bloc, starting with his home country, Poland.

[270] Avery Dulles, "The Gospel, the Church and Politics," *Origins* 16 (1987) 637-46. It is interesting to note that while, in their joint commentary on the Augsburg Confession, Dulles and Lindbeck acknowledge the abuse of ecclesiastical authority in confusing the power of the gospel with that of the temporal sword, they nevertheless note the difficulties we today have with the manner and sharpness with which the Confession distinguished the two regiments. See "Bishops and the Ministry of the Gospel," in *Confessing One Faith*, ed. G. W. Forell and J. F. McCue (Minneapolis: Augsburg, 1982), 151-52.

[271] This is also the position with which many present-day Reformed and Neo-Orthodox theologians align themselves. Their common link is the influence by Karl Barth and his critique of Protestant liberalism. However, we also see some younger scholars schooled in this theology clearly moving in the direction of transformation. See, e.g., Kathryn Tanner, *The Politics of God: Christian Theologies and Social Justice* (Minneapolis: Fortress, 1992).

[272] Peter C. Hodgson, *Winds of the Spirit: A Constructive Christian Theology* (London: SCM, 1994), 60-61.

renewal option are: caution against cultural accommodation; a prophetic critique of the negative features of modernity; a sophisticated hermeneutic that critically appropriates a pre-liberal mode of understanding biblical authority. While the postliberals eschew a return to pre-Enlightenment times, or a pre-critical authority of Scripture-in-Tradition, they are also suspicious of some of the potentially transformative resources of postmodernity, including the liberation movements. In sum, what principally distinguishes renewal from transformation is that the former is more concerned with the inner renewal of communities of faith and the preservation of Christian identity than it is to respond affirmatively to the ambiguous challenges of the wider culture.

Those in favour of *transformation* are convinced that the preservation of the heritage and identity of the Christian tradition entails a critical dialogue with resources and opportunities presently available to us.[273] In Niebuhr's typology, this is "Christ the transformer of culture." In more recent formulations, such as those typically offered by Tracy and Cobb, our task is to be transformed by the best that we derive from mutually critical correlations of Christian Tradition with the experience and learning in contemporary culture, and to share in the transformation of the world. The underlying assumption about the scriptural witness is that it yields, not pure and original expressions of Christianity, but a series of contextualized expressions born of a creative transformation of both the figure of Christ and the forms of culture. Thus, rather than engage in a wholesale critique of modernity, as the

---

[273] Identified by Tracy as the revisionists in *Blessed Rage for Order*, they include process, existentialist, and hermeneutical thinkers as well as many feminist, liberation, and pluralist theologians. They are heirs of a prophetic and critical liberalism that can be traced back to Schleiermacher and Hegel in the 19th century and that has been mediated through Troeltsch, Tillich, Rahner, and H. Richard Niebuhr in the 20th.

deconstructionists and postliberals do, the revisionists construct a
bridge between enlightenment and liberation: "Enlightenment
without liberation loses its emancipatory dynamic; liberation
without enlightenment loses its critical rationality. Together they
have the possibility of moving toward a communicative rationality, justice, and freedom. In this way the saving resources present
in the classical Christian tradition can be reappropriated and reen-
acted."[274]

5.5.2.5 Doctrine and Christian Identity: A Plea for Intratextual Fidelity

Lindbeck's postliberal project suggests that how one conceives
the nature of doctrine, the nature of theology and the nature of the
Church are all closely related. His project presupposes a particular
ecclesiology in which, as we saw, the Church relates best to the
wider culture by being true to itself. This particular ecclesiology
thus places a high premium on the particularity of Christian identity. It calls for the preservation of that identity through a particular conception of the nature of doctrine and the nature of the theological task that tend to be inward-looking and, to its detractors,
fideistic. In essence, this ecclesiological vision pleads for intratextual fidelity.

A central issue confronting postliberalism concerns the truth
question. Lindbeck speaks of truth primarily in terms of faithfulness to the core claims of the Christian tradition and efficacious-
ness in the creation of character and identity. He is convinced that
the ethos, values, and directions of modernity have subsumed
those of the Christian tradition and that, through that subsumption,
Christianity in the modern world is threatened with the loss of its

---

[274] Hodgson, *Winds of the Spirit*, 60-61 provides a helpful synthesis for this
section.

identity. In the face of eroding traditional Christian values in modern society, the Christian Church, which once spoke with authority to the world, has lost its vitality. The "acids of modernity" can be countered within the Church, but the road to recovery is arduous and long. It will take great effort and time before the discontinuity between Western liberal culture and Christianity can become clear to both the Church and the wider society.[275] The postliberal prescription is a mixed bag of bitter pills.

In the first place, theology has itself contributed, Lindbeck claims, to a "pluralistic cacophony" that does anything but promote a clear Christian identity.[276] A narrative understanding of the Christian life, he suggests, will yield an ecclesiology in which participation in the Church is determined by the believer's commitment to its intratextual reality. In sharp contrast to the liberal construals of the place of the Church in the modern world, the postliberal prescription critically challenges us to decide whether ecclesial relevance is not meaningless without an ecclesial identity. The prescription for relevance is judged by no other standard than scriptural priority and particularity. Christian theology ought not stem from the world's terms, but from the particular thought and language learned through living the Scripture-specific Christian faith.

Secondly, in Lindbeck's assessment, Christendom seems to be passing and Christians are becoming a diaspora. How do we handle new encounters that the historical process brings to bear? The postliberal solution is to utilize the communal belief-system to absorb the new world that Christians encounter, and to transform them into ever-evolving sets of symbols set intratextually. Theological education and missionary activity are then primarily aimed

[275] Craig Dykstra, "A 'Post-Liberal' Christian Education?," *ThT* 42 (1985-86) 156.
[276] Lindbeck, "Scripture, Consensus, and Community," 89.

at nurturing a community faithful to its own system.[277] Lindbeck's regulative approach to doctrine is helpful insofar as it demands right performance. Further, flexibility and constancy being two obvious strengths of rules, Lindbeck argues that Church doctrines understood in regulative terms ensure an enduring structure of faith without, at the same time, hampering necessary changes occasioned by a change in the Church's situation and the need to adapt it to new contexts.[278]

In this regard, Frei highlights a subtle reversal of Ernst Troeltsch by Lindbeck. Troeltsch has noted the reality of cultural change to the extent that it is "basic and permanent." He has, according to Frei, "referred the religious meaning of Christianity to the hidden religious significance of each of its many cultural contexts or epochs." In doing so, Troeltsch manifested what Frei calls "cultural-religious fears" that there was no effective religious norms to "authorize restraint and humaneness" in the stream of chaotic changes. The language of the Church, in this view, was anything but stable and basic. Lindbeck, by contrast, appears to Frei to offer Christian hope in place of fears, by pointing us to the sort of Christian religious strength and cultural confidence that we can have. Lindbeck does so by reminding us of the Church's mission in the name of Jesus of Nazareth. The Christian community is the community founded on the reconciliation wrought by Jesus. In turn, the community of believers are to become a reconciling presence wherever bitter enmity exists between human individuals and groups. Lindbeck elaborates:

---

[277] See Max Stackhouse, *Apologia*, 120-22.

[278] However, although Lindbeck and the postliberals' concern about preserving the distinctiveness of the Christian voice is a most important point, David Bryant doubts that their attempt to find an unchanging structure is very well-grounded, thus saddling us with the prior question of where do we discern a Christian identity? See David J. Bryant, "Christian Identity and Historical Change," 40-41.

It need not be the religion that is primarily reinterpreted as world views change, but rather the reverse: Changing world view may be reinterpreted by one and the same religion.... Jesus Christ, for instance, is in one setting affirmed primarily as the Messiah; in another as the incarnate Logos; and in a third, perhaps as Bonhoeffer's 'Man for Others' or Barth's 'Humanity of God.' Yet amid these shifts in Christological affirmations and in the corresponding experiences of Jesus Christ, the story of passion and resurrection and the basic rule for its use remain the same. Theological and religious transformations that lead to relativistic denials of an abiding identity ... can be seen, if one adopts rule theory, as the fusion of a self-identical story with the new worlds within which it is told and retold.[279]

What, then, ought the character of the Church be in times of progressive dechristianization? Unlike the time of missionary expansion, the churches in the present situation are diagnosed by Lindbeck as accommodating themselves to prevailing culture rather than shaping it. When the primary goal of administering the sacrament of baptism is to bolster Church-membership and augment political influence in society, the immediate casualty is the Church's ability to attract "assiduous catechumens" and to provide "effective instruction in distinctively Christian language and practice."[280] Christian doctrine is a cultural-linguistic system of biblical rootage which is ultimately confessional in character. Intratextual fidelity is the only decisive point of reference for promoting Christian identity. The system makes sense only when we are socialized into it. Ultimately, the postliberals perceive the preeminent challenge for the Church to lie in the cultivation of its own language and practice. High on the agenda of a postliberal ecclesiology is thus the question of the proper schooling of today's Christians.

---

[279] ND, 82-83; Hans Frei, "Epilogue: Lindbeck and *The Nature of Doctrine*," 280-81.

[280] ND, 133.

5.5.2.6 Schooling Christians in the Contemporary Age: A Plea for an Ecclesial Pedagogy

In Lindbeck's vision of Church, Christian education takes on a renewed importance. Lindbeck has diagnosed both social and theological factors as contributing negatively to the Church. In sum, he perceives the Church as being "perched precariously on the brink of banality." Having accommodated itself to the prevailing culture, the Church has neither a distinctive voice nor an ability to shape and mold the characters of individual believers. The Church seems to have been "all but silenced by the cacophany of individuals murmuring their personal prayers to a personal God in private relationship."[281] Individualism, Robert Bellah's *Habits of the Heart* reports, underlies people's refusal to submit themselves to a distinctively religious form of life. The structures of modernity press people to pick and choose from multiple suppliers of the same commodity, Lindbeck observes, so that a Church that is too anxious to pander to the prevailing culture of the day, fails to assert itself in its uniqueness and becomes a purveyor of "individual quests for symbols of transcendence" rather than a community that socializes its members into "coherent and comprehensive religious outlooks and forms of life."[282] To redress this, Christian education must be reenvisioned as one of initiation and immersion in the particular culture of Christianity. Catechesis is most successful when it goes together with learning the language of faith and its correlative life of faithfulness. Becoming a Christian is a matter of being socialized and fully assimilated into the communal tradition of religious language and culture, thereby orienting one's life in a

---

[281] Mark L. Horst, "Engendering the Community of Faith in an Age of Individualism," *QR* 8 (1988) 92.

[282] ND, 126.

new and distinctive way. Lindbeck is confident that those who become "steeped " in the authoritative text of the Bible and use this text as their interpretive framework will find that "no world is more real" for them than the world of that text. This involves a process of skills-acquisition through training, practice and the "tutelage of expert practitioners."[283] In this regard, two elements in postliberal theology are particularly significant.

[a] *The Catechumenal Vision of Faith*

Relative to Christian formation, Lindbeck's work yields a clear thesis that any kind of common life and any community wisdom must be *learned* to be understood. Positive faith-formations, he rightly argues, have basic characteristics in common with languages. Chief among these is that languages are cultural in nature and *can* and *must* be learned to be understood and, above all, *practised*, in order to be appreciated.[284] Proficiency in a language through performance is acquired through time and practice. Likewise, competency in the Christian faith demands a lengthy process of learning, both to enable believers to make sense of the language they hear and speak, and to locate their lives in the larger story of Christianity.[285]

And yet, on Lindbeck's assessment, Western culture is now at an intermediate stage, "where socialization is ineffective, catechesis impossible and translation a tempting alternative."[286] The

---

[283] ND, 123.

[284] For observations to similar effect, see van Beeck, *God Encountered*, II/1:61 and 309.

[285] See Gregory C. Higgins, "The Significance of Postliberalism for Religious Education," *RelEd* 84 (1989) 77-89. Cp. Berard L. Marthaler, "Towards a Revisionist Model in Catechetics." *LL* 13 (1976) 458-69; Fayette Breaux Veverka, "Re-Imagining Catholic Identity: Toward an Analogical Paradigm of Religious Education," *RelEd* 88 (1993) 238-54.

[286] ND, 133.

problem of effective catechesis partly stems from the false assumption that knowledge of a few "tag ends" of the Christian language is knowledge of the Christian faith. That said, however, the lasting influence of the religious past offers grounds for hope in that, while the unchurched masses are somehow immunized against catechesis under the present social climate, there are signs to indicate that the biblical heritage continues to be powerfully present, albeit in "detextualized forms."[287] Lindbeck, thus, does not question the existence of a "latent Christianity." People may be immunized against catechesis, but their latent Christian interest may find expressions in existential, depth-psychological, or liberationist language derived from translations of the Gospel. The Church will profit most, in the long run, from a catechetical enterprise that is not chiefly concerned with augmenting its membership and bolstering its influence in society. Rather, the postliberal approach recommends a prolonged catechetical instruction in a language and form of life that is essentially alien to the modern liberal minds, before a candidate is deemed able, intelligently and responsibly, to profess the faith, or, in a word, to be baptised.[288] The catechetical model best suited to this job, in Lindbeck's view, is the ancient catechumenate which forms lives along a pattern of faithfulness.

In preferring an ancient, assiduous catechumenal model of catechesis, Lindbeck's recommendation resonates with what the Catholic Church has been doing for some three decades. Aware of the need to provide effective instruction in distinctively Christian language and practice within a communal context but, in addition, in a programme that is mindful of the new insights into adult pedagogy, the Roman Catholic Church has, since 1972, officially

---

[287] ND, 133.
[288] ND, 132.

commenced the restoration of the ancient catechumenal model of catechesis. Called the Rite of Christian Initiation of Adults, it involves putting catechumens through an assiduous programme of progressive initiation into the Christian faith. It must be pointed out that for the catechumens, the reality of "dechristianisation" may hit home at the end of their initiation harder than it does at the beginning. For, at the end of that journey, the neophytes face the prospect of being disappointed by the reality prevailing in the Church into which they have just been initiated: everywhere they turn, they will encounter veteran Christians unable or unwilling to perform the specific demands of the Christian story. They will also be disappointed by deeply entrenched structures that stifle initiatives and dampen the Spirit. An important key to redressing this malaise is the setting up of support groups which, in the context of the present discussion, resonates well with Lindbeck's idea of *ecclesiolae in ecclesia* – close-knit groups capable of sustaining an alien faith in the face of an increasingly dechristianized culture, and of rampant and aggressive individualism, without having to retreat to sociological ghettoes.[289]

[b] *The Formation of Christian Character*

If the Church is a story-shaped people, this storied community must be *bearer* of the scriptural world, whose members have learned to *embody* the story of Christ.[290] This shaping is preeminently

[289] See ND, 78; Lindbeck, "Ecumenism and World Mission," *Lutheran World* 17 (1970) 72; and Mark L. Horst, who describes Lindbeck's work in this respect as "labor of a compatriot" in "Engendering the Community of Faith," 97.

[290] For the Church as bearer of the scriptural world, see Hauerwas, *A Community of Character*, 57. On embodying the Christ-story, see Stephen E. Fowl and L. Gregory Jones, *Reading in Communion: Scripture and Ethics in Christian Life* (London: SPCK, 1991), 29.

"a matter of virtuous discipline."[291] To be the story's embodiment and bearer, the Church must be first consumed by the "consuming" text. The appropriate ecclesial pedagogy, then, ought to be directed towards guiding the Church in reading and consuming the story, thereby becoming a character within its storied-world and then, once it has interiorised that story, to become teller of that story. "Learning how to consume the scriptural story so that it nourishes and strengthens the body – how to read it in order to tell it aright – is a matter of disciplined practice, of ecclesial (narrative) ethics."[292] This goes to the core of the discipline of discipleship, stretching way beyond the mere use of community-specific words. It goes to the very grammar, the depth-meaning of the Christian language we use, and demands that we be disciplined by the Word incarnate. So the discipline entails letting our lives be patterned, formed and transformed in Christ whose disciples we say we are.[293]

Lindbeck has so far not dealt specifically with character-formation in his allusion to the schooling of Christians. However, Hauerwas, who indicates that the basic perspective of his theological agenda is consonant with Lindbeck's cultural-linguistic model of religion and the latter's postliberal, intratextual theology,[294] provides helpful pointers towards that formation.

The penitential motif in the story of the fall (Genesis 3) — that creation as God's gift was good but became tainted by human sin[295] — coheres well with the Christian story by which we learn

---

[291] Loughlin, *Telling God's Story*, 86.

[292] Loughlin, *Telling God's Story*, 87.

[293] See Fowl and Jones, *Reading in Communion*, 67-80.

[294] Hauerwas, *Against the Nations* (Minneapolis: Winston-Seabury, 1985), 1-22.

[295] The penitential motif in the story of the fall is suggested by Paul Ricoeur in *The Symbolism of Evil*, trs. Emerson Bucanan (New York: Harper & Row, 1967), 232-78.

that we are both the friends of the Crucified and His crucifiers and thus are both the convicted and forgiven sinners. Our fundamental sin, according to Hauerwas, lies in the fact that we act throughout most of our life as if this is not God's world.

The story Christians tell of God exposes the welcome fact that I am a sinner. For without such a narrative the fact and nature of my sin cannot help but remain hidden in self deception. Only a narrative that helps me place myself as a creature of a gracious God can provide the skills to help me locate my sin as fundamentally infidelity and rebellion.[296]

Christian virtue ethics – a discourse made popular by Alasdair MacIntyre who traces its development from Augustine to Aquinas – finds eloquent expression in Hauerwas' presentation which features a few persuasive elements. *First*, the scriptural story of Christ teaches that the problems in our relationship with God and with the world lies in the fact that for the most part we live in stories of our own making instead of living in His. "Sin consists in our allowing our characters to be formed by the story that we must do everything (pride) or nothing (sloth)." *Second*, Christian virtue ethics is not an ethics for the world. We confuse our role in pretending that we can do ethics for anyone outside of our community: "By virtue of the distinctive narrative that forms their community, Christians are distinct from the world. They are required to be nothing less than a sanctified people of peace who can live the life of the forgiven."[297] *Third*, however, the question again arises whether the Church has not thereby become sectarian. Hauerwas' rebuttal to the sectarian charge is to point out an incipient violence inherent in a universal ethical claim: "When Christians assume that their particular moral convictions are independent of narrative, that they are justified by some universal

---

[296] Hauerwas, *The Peaceable Kingdom*, 30.
[297] Hauerwas, *The Peaceable Kingdom*, 34 & 60.

standpoint free from history, they are tempted to imagine that
those who do not share such an ethic must be perverse and should
be coerced to do what we know on universal grounds they really
should want to do."[298] The shape of the Church patterned on
Christ is a "sanctified people of peace" called to a life of "service
and sacrifice." Called to be a sacrament of Christ or, as Schillebeeckx would describe it, as a sacrament of "the human face of
God," or foretaste of the Kingdom of God, the Church lives out its
role best as a holy people, "capable of maintaining the life of
charity, hospitality, and justice."[299] On this postliberal trajectory,
the Church, even as it seems to turn its back on the world, is in
substance strategically positioned towards the world, albeit counterpoised in its stance as "the sign of the world's contradiction,
serving the world by being other than the world."[300]

5.5.2.7 Ministries in the Church: A Plea for Trust in the
Community Language

Lindbeck's provocative vision also yields new categories for
rethinking the nature of ministries in the Church. A rule-theory of
Church doctrine based on an intratextual approach to theology and
a cultural-linguistic vision of religion poses a challenge for ministry in a singular fashion: Will ministers be faithful to the
Church's peculiar vision of what it means to live and act as disciples?

Characteristically, postliberals are fighting what they perceive
to be a banality in modern liberal society which is plagued by a

---

[298] Hauerwas, *The Peaceable Kingdom*, 61.

[299] Hauerwas, *The Peaceable Kingdom*, 60 & 109.

[300] Loughlin, *Telling God's Story*, 89. We again note that Hauerwas' stance
represents an approach rather different from Vatican II's call to embrace the
world.

cacophony of tongues. Postliberal ministers, challenged by a pervasive narrow individualistic reading of experience and of a liberalism which dissipates all norms for articulating a distinctive Christian identity, are to insist upon the primacy of the historical community of faith and its distinctive and distinguishing language. In this post-Constantinian era, when we are living in a diaspora situation which increasingly resembles that of the first centuries, the *fundamental ministerial task* is to bring the Gospel to the world outside the Church. What needs to be stressed is the ultimate supremacy of the Word, rather than detailed problems of sacramentality.[301] The *fundamental stance* of Church ministers, the postliberals urge, is that of *trust* in the community's language – communal stories and doctrines, sacraments and life. "It is not we who measure them, but they who measure and stretch us."[302] To this, a few matters at once cohere, three of which are of particular importance to our discussion.

Firstly, ministers of a postliberal Church do not embark on their ministry with a critical-evaluative attitude towards what the Tradition of the Church has to offer. Before anything else, the initial requirement is one of willingness to *appropriate* the language that is meaningful to the community of faith. In highlighting religion's concern with the practice of *appropriation*, the aim of the postliberals is preeminently that of renewal in,

---

[301] See Lindbeck, "The Lutheran Doctrine of the Ministry: Catholic and Reformed," *TS* 30 (1969) 603 & 612.

[302] Robert Imbelli, "Theology: Trends in Systematic Theology," *Church* 1 (1985) 56. In appreciating Lindbeck's basic call for us to recover the integrity of our own faith and its lived expression, Bellah comments: "If we do not recover the language and practice of Christianity, if we do not discover the kingdom is our only true home, the place that defines our most essential identity, then not only can we not contribute to a genuine pluralism, but we will be lost in the wilderness of decayed traditions and vulnerable to the domination of modernity's suicidal infatuation with power, the exact opposite of the Gospel message." See Bellah, "Christian Faithfulness in a Pluralistic World," 91.

and conformation to, the particularistic faith in Christ, following from which the ministers can better serve the renewal and
conformation of the members of the community. An untrans-
formed self is prey to the danger of premature-evaluation and
rushed-judgment. Imbelli's analysis is instructive: "Logically
prior to specific actions undertaken in the name of religion
stands the foundational activity of self-making: who is the self
we bring to our encounters, involvements, ministries? From
Lindbeck's perspective, this self is formed through incorporation into a community of faith and in a real sense does not pre-
exist this incorporation." [303]

Secondly, recalling the basic inspiration of the Catholic R.C.I.A
programme, this insight must also have a close bearing on the formation programme for ministers. Lindbeck dreads the idea of
leaving an illiterate ministry, especially in regard to competency
in one's own particular religious heritage. Moreover, he scoffs at
pastoral preparations that produce liberal social activists, psychological counsellors, and busy administrators for what is lost in the
process is the task of forming a distinctively Christian community
around Word and sacrament – a community of *consensus fidelium*
where meaningful communication and ministerial transmission of
community-forming traditions are possible. [304] When socialization
into communal traditions is difficult and personally-committed
internalization of the Christian language is weak, Lindbeck suggests as essential for seminarians a programme of spiritual formation.

---

[303] Imbelli, "Theology: Trends in Systematic Theology," 56.

[304] See Lindbeck, *University Divinity Schools* (New York: Rockefeller Foun-
dation, 1976); "Theologians, Theological Faculties, and the ELCA Study of
Ministry," *Dialog* 28 (1989) 202; "Reflections on the New York Forum: From
Academy to Church," *ThEd* 19 (1983) 68.

Looked at non-theologically, spiritual formation may be described as the deep and personally committed appropriation of a comprehensive and coherent outlook on life and the world .... The spiritually mature ... have to a significant degree developed the capacities and dispositions to think, feel, and act in accordance with their world view no matter what the circumstances. They have, in the Aristotelian language, the habits or virtues distinctively emphasized by the encompassing vision which is theirs. In the Christian sense, these are traditionally named faith, hope and love.[305]

In this regard, Vatican II's *Decree on the Training of Priests (Optatam Totius)* emphasizes the object of priestly training as the formation of shepherds of souls in light of the ministry of the Word, the ministry of worship and sanctification, and the ministry of the shepherd. In the same context, it bears mentioning that, despite a healthy proliferation of catechetical approaches all aimed at making good or better Christians, the 1985 Synod of Bishops announced that: "Very many have expressed the desire that a catechism or compendium of all Catholic doctrine regarding both faith and morals be composed, that it might be, as it were, a point of reference for the catechisms or compendiums that are prepared in various regions." This led to the 1992 *Catechism of the Catholic Church.* Offered as a "statement of the Church's faith and of Catholic doctrine, attested to or illuminated by Sacred

---

[305] In relation to biblical scholarship, he suggests that it would be easier to retain the capacity for "spiritually formative reading," if one learned a scholarship different from the historical-critical approach. This different approach would regard "attention to implications for the practise of the faith in past and present [as] methodically part of the interpretive process." Spiritual maturity is identified with "the interiorization of a comprehensive and coherent religious outlook." See Lindbeck, "Spiritual Formation and Theological Education," *ThEd* 24, Suppl. 1 (1988) 12, 16 & 29. D. J. Hall advocates a return to the traditional biblical language of discipleship as the context for theological education to combat the bifurcation of mind and spirit which he judges to be at the core of the malaise of our society. See Hall, "Theological Education as Character Formation?" *ThEd* 24, Suppl. 1 (1988) 69.

Scripture, the Apostolic Tradition, and the Church's Magisterium," it deserves to be received and appropriated by pastors and faithful alike in a "spirit of communion," and to be put to use "assiduously in fulfilling their mission of proclaiming the faith and calling people to the Gospel life."[306]

Thirdly, trust in the particularity of the Christian language leads inevitably to trust in the power of the cross. Ministers are called to be suffering servants of humankind like their Lord. Their primary duty is not to convert large numbers, for the Christian system of values and worldview can, almost by definition within Lindbeck's postliberal project, only be nourished in sectarian enclaves. The question of success ought to be cheerfully left to God whom, we can trust, is using ministerial witness "in apparent defeat as in apparent success." As Mother Teresa of Calcutta was fond of saying, God wants only our faith, not our successes. When faithfulness is the key, one ought to live the parabolic language of Jesus in the narrative of the Good Samaritan whose concern is for every kind of human need and suffering. Lindbeck is acutely aware of this. He even suggests that work for the poor must not be left to the "extratextualists." But, his Lutheran background apparently makes it difficult for him to regard this as our concern. There is evidently an unresolved tension in Lindbeck's postliberal theology at this point. In any case, like the Church that they serve, ministers must stand with the poor and oppressed, for justice, human dignity and reconciling love, even for the rich and the oppressors. Above all, they stand not for hatred, but non-violence. This, in Lindbeck's view, is the most difficult part of ministry, because those who really fight for true humanity "will be met with implacable hostility." For the story of Christ teaches the difficult lesson that

[306] Pope John Paul II, "Apostolic Constitution *Fidei Depositum*," in *The Catechism of the Catholic Church* (Mahwah, NJ: Paulist, 1994), 5.

to refuse counter-force and counter-hostility leads to what he describes as "an inner death," if not an outer one as well.[307]

5.5.2.8 The Church's Sacraments: A Plea for a Performative Sacramentology

In conceiving of religion as a gigantic proposition correlative to a form of life, and making *contextual* and *performative* aspects essential requirements to the *ontological* truth of religious statements, Lindbeck's postliberal project carries implications for sacramentology which [1] differ sharply from those of a liberal approach and [2] challenge the Church to survey its spiritual topography to see if the faith community is not comprised of nominal "Christians."[308]

On the first count, postliberals resist a sacramentology that presents the sacraments of the Church as merely explicitating a reality already implicitly present. Imbelli suggests that instead of

[307] See Lindbeck, "Ecumenism and the Future of Belief," *Una Sancta* 25:3 (1968) 14-15. Giving prominence to the language of community in *Easter in Ordinary*, Nicholas Lash suggests that the way ministers lead the faith community in making a difference in society is to remember the crucified and risen One. "It is, therefore, hardly surprising that the history of God's spirit in the world, the history of his holy people, the sacramental visibility of which we call 'Israel' or 'Church,' should be (in the measure that the people is, in fact, faithful to its mission) a 'counter-history of peace regained through atoning suffering'." See *Easter in Ordinary* (Charlottesville, VA: The University Press of Virginia, 1988), 284. The internal quotation is from John Milbank, "The Second Difference: For a Trinitarianism Without Reserve," *ModTh* 2 (1986) 227.

[308] What the Church needs are men and women who are "intrinsically religious," for whom "faith is often an uncomfortable transforming power." But the mass of Church members are "extrinsically religious" who use religion as "a security blanket, as a legitimation and support for the way they already live." See Lindbeck, "The Crisis in American Catholicism," in *Our Common History as Christians*, ed. John Deschner et al. (New York: Oxford University Press, 1975), 54-55.

naming what is in effect present "anonymously," as symbolists insist, sacraments in a cultural-linguistic model "evoke, provoke, and empower the emergence of a new reality, a new self constituted by new relations."[309] Instead of giving a name to what is already metaphysically there, sacraments concretely bring about a reality that is yet to be.[310]

On the second count, postliberals once again awaken us to the reality that Church membership may well be packed by people who perhaps possess only an academic appreciation of the Christian faith without a personal commitment. There may be some vague perception of transcendence. Beyond that, the inescapable reality is a lack of coherence between perception and actual application in faith-life. Borrowing from the well-known distinction of John Henry Newman, would a survey of what members of the faith community think about the sacraments not reveal that many have lived only in a *notional* assent to the truths of faith without having made this assent something *real* in their lives? An affirmative answer would point to a dismal picture of the Church in which what is held to be important in a sacrament is not the encounter with its risen Lord, but the correct performance of a rite or some inconsequential debate over divine-presence.[311]

---

[309] Imbelli, "Theology: Trends in Systematic Theology," 56.

[310] Lindbeck has proposed the thesis that Rahner's understanding of the sacrament of holy orders was *compatible* with Lutheran doctrine of the ministry on account of a "basically functional understanding of the ministry rather than a static, ontological one." It exists for the Church, not the other way around. See Lindbeck, "Karl Rahner and a Protestant View of the Sacramentality of the Ministry," *CTSAP* 21 (1966) 267-88.

[311] See Terrence Merrigan, *Clear Heads and Holy Hearts: The Religious and Theological Ideal of John Henry Newman* (Louvain: Peeters, 1991), 98: "The object of the Christian idea is Christ himself. He is the ground, the source of coherence, and the continuing dynamic of Christian life and reflection, in and through which He is now known and apprehended." For a study of doctrine

In Lindbeck's framework for understanding ecclesiology, to be baptised essentially means to enter the Church's performance of the Scriptural story. To be baptised is to be inscribed into the biblical world and to take an active part in an unfolding ecclesial drama both informed and transformed by Scriptures. To be received into the Church through baptism is to be "invited to 'create' [oneself] in finding a place within this drama – an improvisation in the theatre workshop, but one that purports to be about a comprehensive truth affecting one's identity and future."[312]

Given that the Bible serves to give life and to reinvigorate, it is perhaps better to speak of absorbing the text rather than of being absorbed by the text. Baptism, then, may be approached as the grafting onto a community of people learning "to live toward a different end than elsewhere, ... to grow in the strength and shape of Christ, ... to live in the world as people who are not of the world, ... to speak a new language: the tongue of Pentecost."[313]

Baptism, however, does not obliterate one's previous identity by substituting the new for the old. The old takes you to where you are, but now it is enfolded within a new story, a story which a different future. Baptism takes one into a Church that is always on the way, provisional,[314] unaccomplished, always struggling to become more Christ-like, suffering for the sake of greater joy for

---

founded on an equation between Newman's "idea" and Lindbeck's "story," see Ronald Burke, "Newman, Lindbeck and Models of Doctrine," in *John Henry Newman: Theology and Reform*, ed. Michael E. Allsopp and Ronald R. Burke (New York: Garland, 1992), 19-43.

[312] Rowan D. Williams, "Postmodern Theology and the Judgment of the World," in *Postmodern Theology: Christian Faith in a Pluralist World*, ed. Frederic B. Burnham (New York: Harper Collins, 1989), 97.

[313] Loughlin, *Telling God's Story*, 217.

[314] See, e.g., Christian Duquoc, *Provisional Churches: An Essay in Ecumenical Ecclesiology* (London: SCM, 1986).

all,[315] living out an adventure where the peace of Christ is something which, though given, remains unachieved, and is constantly
being "learned, negotiated, betrayed, inched forward, discerned
and risked."[316] In this vision of Church, there is a prominent place
for hagiography, for there is no better way to learn to perform the
story of Christ than to be guided by the saints who left their lega-
cies of exemplary lives lived after the manner of Christ's. If the
Church is constituted by the narrative it retells, then it needs to
constantly recall those stories of collective history and exemplary
individuals central to the meaning and tradition of the faith community.

     In a postliberal mode of thought, Christian marriage will not
primarily be seen as a sacrament achieved at the altar. Rather,
marriage is a life-long relationship between a man and a woman
who promise to be committed to each other till death and who, *to
the extent* that they perform that promise in Christ, convert their
marriage into a symbol of the love and presence of Christ. They
become, intrasystematically speaking, truthful performers of their
marital vows; their matrimony, indeed, *becomes* holy and sacramental.[317] If a Christian couple believe that their marriage is a
sacrament, then, "the burden of proof lies on [them as] believers
and the life they lead."[318]

     As for the Eucharist, if we draw from Lindbeck's postliberal
approach, it would seem to require a synthesis, a bringing

---

[315] See, e.g., John Milbank, "The Name of Jesus: Incarnation, Atonement,
Ecclesiology," *ModTh* 7 (1991) 317.

[316] Rowan Williams, "Saving Time: Thoughts on Practice, Patience and
Vision," *NewBf* 73 (1993) 321.

[317] For an attempt at combining Rahner's *Realsymbol* and a performatory
understanding of the sacrament of marriage, see Jeffrey C. K. Goh, "Christian
Marriage as a *Realsymbol*: Towards a Performative Understanding of the Sacrament," *QL* 76 (1995) 254-64.

[318] Dietrich Ritschl, *The Logic of Theology* (London: SCM, 1986), 237.

together, of the two sides of the intratextual hermeneutic – the
Bible as a consuming text and the consumption of the biblical text
in the life of the Church. Again, the emphasis will not primarily be
on the inner substance of the Eucharist. Rather, it will be on the
more provocative challenge to the Church to coherently enact – in
all its preaching, praying and living — the traditional understanding of the Eucharist. To partake of the Eucharist is to "eat the
Word." We legitimately consume the Word only if we embody
the Word and become Word to the rest of humanity. Thus, just as
the Eucharist makes the Church, and the scriptural story shapes
the Church in the truthful telling of the story,[319] we ought also to
revert back to an ancient dictum of the Church Fathers: it is not
only the Eucharist that makes the Church, it is the Church that
makes the Eucharist. In this light, the Christ-story is not truthfully
told without the members of the faith-community living as a
Eucharistic people — as bread broken and shared – outside the
liturgy. In *The Constitution on the Sacred Liturgy*, Vatican II
defined the Eucharist as the fount and summit of Christian life.
This beautiful statement, though theologically justifiable, remains
largely vacuous at the level of praxis where a gap clearly exists
between liturgy and daily life, and where the "inner reality and
dynamism" of the Eucharist does not inspire the self-understanding of Christians. "Do this in memory of me" has become anything but a communally authoritative rule of discourse, attitude,
and action. The central driving force of the Eucharist is lame
where the reciprocity between liturgy and life is neglected. At
every celebration of the Eucharist, we proclaim the death of Christ
who has given his life for us, and who looks to us to be willing to
do the same. In the context of the institution of the Eucharist, John

---

[319] This synthesis of the two sides of the postliberal hermeneutic is gleaned
from Gerard Loughlin's reflection on the Eucharist in chapter 8 — "Eating the
Word" — of *Telling God's Story*, 223-45.

590 J.C.K. GOH

13 narrates the foot-washing pedagogy by which his disciples are asked to *do* what he was doing.[320] Unless we "do it," both at the table and after leaving the table, it makes no sense to claim that Christ is with us.

5.5.2.9 Church and Ecumenism: A Plea for Consensus-Fidelium-Building

The notion of *consensus fidelium* plays a significant role in different areas of Lindbeck's thoughts, not least in the area of Church and ecumenism. Within his overall scheme, *consensus fidelium* is comparable to that universal agreement about language, the common grammar and vocabulary, that makes communication possible. A *consensus fidelium* is the key to fruitful and lasting ecumenism for, without some measure of consensus on what it means to be Christians, or to be Church, there is no meaningful context within which dialogue can be conducted. But a *consensus fidelium* presupposes a well-founded *sensus fidelium*, in regard to which Lindbeck's assessment is unsettling.

We saw, in chapter two, Lindbeck's concern for a critical retrieval of the pre-modern mode of reading Scripture. It yielded the conditions for the promotion of a biblically informed and communally unified *sensus fidelium*. In that mode, Scripture was read as a Christ-centred, typologically unified whole and, in conformity to a Trinitarian *regula fidei*, with figural applications to the whole of reality. The world of Scripture was for believers the most real,

[320] This section on the Eucharist is inspired by Paul Bernier, who suggests two crucial movements: [a] from a devotional (private, individualistic) understanding of the Eucharist to a communal one, and [b] from a passive to an active appreciation of the meaning of the Eucharist and, indeed, every sacrament. See *Eucharist: Celebrating Its Rhythms in Our Lives* (Notre Dame, IN: Ave Maria, 1993). See also his earlier work, *Bread Broken and Shared* (Notre Dame, IN: Ave Maria, 1981).

the one by which their minds, imaginations and behaviour were molded. It was within the scriptural framework that they lived and moved and had their being, both as individuals and as communities. Time and again, Lindbeck suggests, when change and diversification were called for, recourse to Scripture helped shaped the needed consensus with which the community could again move forward. Read in this classical fashion, not only was Scripture a followable and inhabitable text, it actually manifested great consensus-and-community-building power. But, Lindbeck laments the current state of *sensus fidelium* in mainline Christian churches where "there seems to be less and less communal sense of what is or is not Christian." A decline in Bible-knowledge is identified as the general reason for this predicament. Specifically, the problem stems from a shift away from the "once-universal classic hermeneutical framework" as a result of the onset of modernity, and the ushering in of an inordinate historical-critical preoccupation with "fact" over "narrative" and individual over communal consciousness.[321]

Today, Lindbeck is convinced, the Bible again can be profitably read in ways that are typologically applicable to our contemporary settings. The Bible offers great ecumenical potential. A pre-dialogical task for the diverse confessional traditions is to again begin the slow journey of cultivating a biblically-funded *sensus fidelium*, one that is solidly based only if it is intratextually determined and critically pre-modern-orientated.[322] That they do so is, for Lindbeck, ecumenically imperative, for without

[321] Lindbeck, "Scripture, Consensus, and Community," 5-6, 10-12.

[322] Curtis W. Freeman agrees with Lindbeck that modern historical-critical and grammatical-historical methods have failed to enhance the *sensus fidelium*. See idem, "Toward a *Sensus Fidelium* for an Evangelical Church," in *The Nature of Confession*, ed. T. R. Phillips and D. L. Okholm (Downers Grove, IL: InterVarsity, 1996), 162-79.

J.C.K. GOH

a biblically-informed *consensus fidelium*, it is impractical to speak of genuine reconciliation.[323]

While many would agree with Lindbeck that the interrelation of canon, hermeneutics, and the *sensus fidelium* renders the Catholic/Protestant argument on the priority of Church or Scripture redundant, Catholics will continue to press the argument that without an authoritative magisterium, *consensus fidelium* remains unattainable in practice.

5.6 Concluding Remarks

With Lindbeck's exposition of the nature of doctrine, we have come full circle — back to Tradition and authority with which we began. There is, as we saw, an implicit appeal to Tradition amongst Christian theologians. Where they part company, however, has to do with the ways they elevate certain dominant elements within the past as normative. Lindbeck accentuates the radically social and cultural character of Christian life and the historical nature of the Tradition within which we live and find meaning. His theological hermeneutics operates on a particular notion of doctrine as intra-ecclesial grammar. In isolating ecclesial doctrines as authoritative rules for organising and regulating life and nurturing communal identity, Lindbeck's working hypothesis presupposes a doctrinal core as an unchanging given. This central doctrinal core is found primarily in the Scripture and is tied to the three regulative principles of monotheism, the historicity of Jesus,

[323] This has been extensively argued by Lindbeck in "Scripture, Consensus, and Community," and "Ecumenical Theology." If, however, in view of the state of de-christianization, Lindbeck is implying that we need to wait for the formation of pioneering small communities of faith and hope that they will develop a biblically-funded *sensus fidelium*, Donald Bloesch argues this is quite unnecessary. For, through the Holy Spirit, we already have access to God's revealed Word. See idem, *Holy Scriptures*, 218.

and the centrality of Jesus maximally interpreted within a monotheistic framework. Lindbeck ought to be appreciated for his retrieval for Christian theology of "its true ground again in the common confession expanded to the plain sense of the common narratives."[324]

As all good writers do, Lindbeck takes us to a new and higher level of thought, while leaving room for questions and debates. There is a sense in which the level of what has to be criticized cannot be reached by criticism. Even when criticizing Lindbeck, one has much to learn from him. But no theological system is free from criticism and Lindbeck himself expects no moratorium. In particular, his anti-foundationalist and historicist vision of theology leaves unanswered the question of how traditions are to relate to each other. He does not address the relationship of Church and doctrine to the wider society and how they can and should contribute to public discourse in a radically pluralistic society.[325] Critics are not altogether off the mark who find that his position represents "a retreat to fideistic isolation, an arbitrary absolutizing of the past and a concomitant failure to recognize the dynamic and innovative nature of traditions."[326]

[324] Tracy, "On Reading the Scripture," 56. While he acknowledges the utmost seriousness with which we ought to take Lindbeck's call for *resourcement*, by returning to the Bible as source, in order to achieve the *consensus fidelium* that might be able to reconcile the various confessional traditions, Ted Peters also suggests that we cannot do without the thesis of Heinrich Fries and Karl Rahner. On the possibility of attaining church unity in our time, their thesis reads: "The fundamental truths of Christianity, as they are expressed in Holy Scripture, in the Apostles' Creed, and in that of Nicaea and Constantinople are binding on all partner churches of the one Church to be" [Fries and Rahner, *Unity of the Churches* (Philadelphia: Fortress, 1985), 7]. See Ted Peters, *God – the World's Future* (Minneapolis: Fortress, 1992), 70.

[325] See Rowan Williams, "Postmodern Theology and the Judgment of the World," 107.

[326] Davaney and Brown, "Postliberalism," 456. See also Ormond Rush, *The Reception of Doctrine* (Rome: Gregorian University Press, 1997), 286.

As for the thesis on the dialectical revelation of truth[327] with which we began, Lindbeck has contributed much to calling attention to one side of the equation. While he is clearly right in criticising any theology that fails to attend to the powerful impact that linguistic and cultural traditions have on the way we interpret the world, critics are correct in taxing him as to whether this crucial insight has to be advanced at the expense of abandoning "half the dialectic"[328] by maintaining that the meaning and truth of Christianity as a way of life can be apprehended by a process of simple retrieval from Scripture-in-Tradition. Tracy rightly suggests that *"mutually critical* correlations" between an interpretation of the meaning and truth of Scripture and Tradition on the one hand and an interpretation of the contemporary situation on the other are requisite for a judgment that Christianity is true and worthy of belief. If an experiential-expressive model for theology eclipses the former pole of this dialectic, Lindbeck's cultural-linguistic model, which harbours a disturbing totalism, according to which our experience is totally structured by the language of our community, may be seen as unduly curtailing the latter pole.[329] Immensely astute in using the language and skills yielded by contemporary intellectual resources, Lindbeck nevertheless differs very little from Barth insofar as he elevates the objective pole and silences the subjective pole of the human relationship with God.

Besides, he is reticent on the fact that the Christian Tradition has shown that it has both the resources and the resilience to establish and profit from "points of contact" between the Church and other communities, whether scientific, artistic, moral-political, or religious.

---

[327] For recent works that are attentive to the dialectic of openness and concealment in divine revelation, see Louis-Marie Chauvet, *Symbol and Sacrament*, trs. P. Madigan and M. Beaumont (Collegeville: Liturgical, 1995); Bruno Forte, "Thinking of God Beyond the Crisis of Critical Rationality," *Bulletin ET* 9 (1998) 2, 128-43.

[328] Tracy, "Lindbeck's New Program," 464.

[329] Hollenbach, "Fundamental Theology and the Christian Moral Life, "178

ABBREVIATIONS

AmBenR	-	American Benedictine Review
ACPhilQ	-	The American Catholic Philosophical Quarterly
Am	-	America
AJTP	-	American Journal of Theology and Philosophy
AmPhQ	-	American Philosophical Quarterly
AEccR	-	American Ecclesiastical Review
ASCE	-	The Annual of the Society of Christian Ethics
ATR	-	Anglican Theological Review
BibInt	-	Biblical Interpretation
BTB	-	Biblical Theology Bulletin
B&R	-	Books and Religion
Bulletin ET	-	Bulletin ET: Zur Theologie in Europa
Com	-	Commonweal
Ch&Cr	-	Christianity and Crisis
ChCent	-	The Christian Century
ChrT	-	Christianity Today
CrCur	-	Cross Currents
CSR	-	Christian Scholars Review
CTSAP	-	Catholic Theological Society of America Proceedings
CTJ	-	Calvin Theological Journal
D&L	-	Doctrine & Life
EcuRev	-	The Ecumenical Review
ExpT	-	The Expository Times
ETL	-	Ephemerides Theologicae Lovanienses
EuroJT	-	European Journal of Theology
F&Ph	-	Faith and Philosophy
HTR	-	Harvard Theological Review
IDB	-	The Interpreter's Dictionary of the Bible, ed. G. A. Buttrick. New York: Abingdon, 1962.
HeyJ	-	The Heythrop Journal: A Quarterly Review of Philosophy and Theology
IBMR	-	International Bulletin of Missionary Research
Int	-	Interpretation
JAAR	-	Journal of American Academy of Religion

JBL	-	Journal of Biblical Literature
JES	-	Journal of Ecumenical Studies
JETS	-	Journal of the Evangelical Theological Society
JPh	-	The Journal of Philosophy
JR	-	The Journal of Religion
JRE	-	The Journal of Religious Ethics
JTS	-	The Journal of Theological Studies
KuD	-	Kerygma und Dogma
LL	-	The Living Light
LS	-	Louvain Studies
LTP	-	Laval Théologique et Philosophique
ModB	-	Modern Believing
ModSch	-	The Modern Schoolman
ModTh	-	Modern Theology
NCR	-	National Catholic Reporter
NewBf	-	New Blackfriars
NZsTR	-	Neue Zeitschrift für systematische Theologie und Religionsphilosophie
PRS	-	Perspectives in Religious Studies
Ph&Th	-	Philosophy and Theology
PhFor	-	The Philosophical Forum
PhT	-	Philosophy Today
QL	-	Questions Liturgiques
QR	-	Quarterly Review
RelEd	-	Religious Education
RelSt	-	Religious Studies
RSRev	-	Religious Studies Review
RevMet	-	The Review of Metaphysics
Rev&Exp	-	Review and Expositor
SJT	-	Scottish Journal of Theology
SR	-	Studies in Religion
StuMor	-	Studia Moralia
TD	-	Theology Digest
ThEd	-	Theological Education
Th	-	Theology
ThT	-	Theology Today
TJT	-	Toronto Journal of Theology
TR	-	Theologische Revue
TrinJ	-	Trinity Journal
TS	-	Theological Studies

Thomist	-	The Thomist
USQR	-	Union Seminary Quarterly Review
ZfdT	-	Zeitschrift für dialektische Theologie

BIBLIOGRAPHY

I. GEORGE A. LINDBECK'S WORKS (CITED)

a. Books:

The Future of Roman Catholic Theology: Vatican II – Catalyst for Change. Philadelphia: Fortress, 1970.

Infallibility (The Pere Marquette Theology Lecture). Milwaukee: Marquette University Press, 1972.

University Divinity School: A Report on Ecclesiastically Independent Theological Education (in association with Karl Deutsch and Nathan Glazer). New York: The Rockefeller Foundation, 1976.

The Nature of Doctrine: Religion and Theology in a Postliberal Age. Philadelphia: Westminster, 1984.

b. Articles:

"The *A Priori* in St Thomas' Theory of Knowledge." In *The Heritage of Christian Thought* (Essays In Honor of Robert Lowry Calhoun), ed. Robert E. Cushman and Egil Grislis. New York: Harper & Row, 1965, 41-63.

"The Status of the Nicene Creed as Dogma of the Church: Some Questions from Lutherans to Roman Catholics." In *The Status of the Nicene Creed as Dogma of the Church*, ed. Paul C. Empie and William W. Baum. Washington, DC: National Catholic Welfare Conference, 1965, 11-15.

"Karl Rahner and a Protestant View of the Sacramentality of the Ministry." *CTSAP* 21 (1966) 267-88.

"Ecumenism and the Future of Belief." *Una Sancta* 25/3 (1968) 3-17.

"The Lutheran Doctrine of the Ministry: Catholic and Reformed." *TS* 30 (1969) 588-612.

"The Future of the Dialogue: Pluralism or the Eventual Synthesis of Doctrine." In *Christian Action and Openness*, ed. J. Papin. Villanova, PA: Villanova University Press, 1970.

"Ecumenism and World Mission." *Lutheran World* 17 (1970) 69-77.

"The Sectarian Future of the Church." In *The God Experience*, ed. Joseph Whelan. New York: Newman, 1971, 226-43.

"The Infallibility Debate." In *The Infallibility Debate*, ed. John J. Kirvan. New York: Paulist, 1971, 35-65.

"Protestant Problems with Lonergan on Development of Dogma." In *Foundations of Theology: Papers from the International Lonergan Congress 1970*, ed. Philip McShane. Dublin: Gill & Macmillan, 1971, 115-23, 243-44.

"Unbelievers and the 'Sola Christi'." *Dialog* 12 (1973) 182-89.

"*Fides ex auditu* and the Salvation of Non-Christians." In *The Gospel and the Ambiguity of the Church*, ed. Vilmos Vajta. Philadelphia: Fortress, 1974, 91-123.

"Papacy and *ius divinum*: A Lutheran View." In *Papal Primacy and the Universal Church*, ed. Paul Empie and T. A. Murphy. Minneapolis: Augsburg, 1974, 193-207.

"Papal Infallibility: A Protestant Response." *Com* 102 (1975) 145-46.

"The Crisis in American Catholicism." In *Our Common History as Christians*, ed. John Deschner et al. New York: Oxford University Press, 1975.

"Theological Revolutions and the Present Crisis." *TD* 23 (1975) 308-19.

"A Battle for Theology: Hartford in Historical Perspective." In *Against the World for the World: The Hartford Appeal and the Future of American Religion*, ed. Peter L. Berger and Richard J. Neuhaus. New York: Seabury, 1976, 20-43.

"Lutherans and the Papacy." *JES* 13 (1976) 368-78.

"Problems on the Road to Unity: Infallibility." In *Unitatis Redintegratio: 1964-1974: Eine Bilanz der Auswirkungen des Ökumenismusdekrets*, ed. Gerard Békés and Vilmos Vatja (*Studia Anselmiana* 71). Frankfurt: Verlag Otto Lembeck, 1977, 98-109.

"Theologische Methode und Wissenschaftstheorie." *Theologische Revue* 74 (1978) 267-80.

"Review of John Hick, ed. *The Myth of God Incarnate*." *JR* 59 (1979) 248-50.

"The Bible as Realistic Narrative." *JES* 17 (1980) 81-85.

"The Reformation and the Infallibility Debate." In *Teaching Authority and Infallibility in the Church*, ed. Paul C. Empire et al. (*Lutherans and Catholics in Dialogue* 6). Minneapolis: Augsburg, 1980, 101-19.

"Ebeling: Climax of a Great Tradition." *JR* 61 (1981) 309-41.

and Avery Dulles. "Bishops and the Ministry of the Gospel." In *Confessing One Faith: A Joint Commentary on the Augsburg Confession by Lutheran and Catholic Theologians*, ed. George Wolfgang Forell and James F. McCue. Minneapolis: Augsburg, 1982, 147-72.

"An Assessment Reassessed: Paul Tillich on the Reformation." *JR* 63 (1983) 376-93.

"Reflections on the New York Forum: From Academy to Church." *ThEd* 19 (1983) 65-70.

"The Ratzinger File." *Com* 112 (1985) 635-36.

"Barth and Textuality." *ThT* 43 (1986) 361-76.

"The Story-Shaped Church: Critical Exegesis and Theological Interpretation." In *Scriptural Authority and Narrative Interpretation*, ed. Garrett Green. Philadelphia: Fortress, 1987, 161-78.

"The Church." In *Keeping the Faith: Essays to Mark the Centenary of Lux Mundi*, ed. Geoffrey Wainwright. Philadelphia: Fortress, 1988, 179-208.

"The Search for Habitable Texts." *Daedalus* 117 (1988) 153-56.

"Spiritual Formation and Theological Education." *ThEd* 24, Suppl. 1 (1988) 10-32.

"Scripture, Consensus, and Community." In *Biblical Interpretation in Crisis: The Ratzinger Conference on Bible and Church*, ed. Richard John Neuhaus. Grand Rapids: Eerdmans, 1989, 74-101.

"Theologians, Theological Faculties, and the ELCA Study of Ministry." *Dialog* 28 (1989) 198-205.

"Ecumenical Theology." In *The Modern Theologians: An Introduction to Christian Theology in the Twentieth Century*, ed. David F. Ford. Oxford: Blackwell, 1989, II:255-73.

"The Church's Mission to a Postmodern Culture." In *Postmodern Theology: Christian Faith in a Pluralist World*, ed. Frederic B. Burnham. New York: Harper and Row, 1989, 37-55.

"Review of Jeffrey Stout's *Ethics after Babel: The Languages of Moral and Their Discontents*." *ThT* 46 (1989) 59-61.

"Two Kinds of Ecumenism: Unitive and Interdenominational." *Gregorianum* 70 (1989) 647-60.

"Confession and Community: An Israel-like View of the Church." *ChCent* 107 (1990) 492-96.

"Tilting in the Ecumenical Wars." *Lutheran Forum* 26:4 (1992) 19-27.

"Dulles On Method." *ProE* 1 (1992) 53-60.

"Response to Michael Wyschogrod's 'Letter to a Friend'." *ModTh* 11 (1995) 205-10.

"Atonement and the Hermeneutics of Intratextual Social Embodiment." In *The Nature of Confession: Evangelicals and Postliberals in Conversation*, ed. Timothy R. Phillips and Dennis L. Okholm. Downers Grove, IL: InterVarsity, 1996, 221-40.

"The Gospel's Uniqueness: Election and Untranslatability." *ModTh* 13 (1997) 423-50.

II. DOCUMENTS

Documents of the Second Vatican Council, 1962-1965. In *The Documents of Vatican II*, ed. Walter Abbot. New York: America, 1966; *Vatican Council*

II: The Conciliar and Post Conciliar Documents, ed. Austin Flannery. Collegeville, MN: Liturgical, 1975; *Decrees of the Ecumenical Councils, Vol. II (Trent – Vatican II)*, ed. Norman P. Tanner. London: Sheed & Ward, 1990.

COCU: The Reports of the Four Meetings. Cincinnati, OH: Forward Movement Publications, 1965.

Justice in the World: Statement of 1971 Synod of Bishops. Washington: United States Catholic Conference, 1972.

Congregation for the Doctrine of the Faith. "The Instruction on Certain Aspects of the 'Theology of Liberation'." *Origins* 14:13 (1984) 193-204.

Final Report of the Extraordinary Synod of Bishops, December 7, 1985. *Origins* 15 (1985) 444-50.

Congregation for the Doctrine of the Faith. "Instruction on Christian Freedom and Liberation." *Origins* 15:44 (1986) 713-28.

The Evangelical Roman Catholic Dialogue on Mission 1977-1984, ed. B. Meeking and J. Scott. Grand Rapids, MI: Eerdmans, 1986.

United States Conference of Catholic Bishops. "Economic Justice for All: Catholic Social Teaching and the United States Economy." *Origins* 27 (1986) 409-55.

Congregation for the Doctrine of the Faith. "Instruction on the Ecclesial Vocation of the Theologian." *Origins* 20 (1990) 117-26.

John Paul II. "Apostolic Constitution on Publication of Catechism of the Catholic Church '*Fidei Depositum*'." *Origins* 22 (1993) 525-29.

Documentary History of Faith and Order, 1963-1993, ed. Günther Gassmann. Geneva: WCC, 1993.

John Paul II. *As the Third Millennium Draws Near*. Origins 24:25 (1994) 402-16.

The Catechism of the Catholic Church. Mahwah, NJ: Paulist, 1994.

John Paul II. *Fides et Ratio*. Origins 28 (1998) 317-47.

III. WORKS BY OTHER AUTHORS

ACHTEMEIER, P. Mark. "The Truth of Tradition: Critical Realism in the Thought of Alasdair MacIntyre and T. F. Torrance." *SJT* 47 (1994) 355-74.

ALLIK, Tiina. "Karl Rahner on Materiality and Human Knowledge." *Thomist* 49 (1985) 367-86.

"Narrative Approaches to Human Personhood: Agency, Grace, and Innocent Suffering." *Ph&Th* 1 (1987) 305-33.

"Nature and Spirit: Agency and Concupiscence in Hauerwas and Rahner." *JRE* 15 (1987) 14-32.

"Religious Experience, Human Finitude, and the Cultural-Linguistic Model." *Horizons* 20 (1993) 241-59.

"Theory-Making, Transference, and Anthropology: On D. Z. Phillips' Rejection of Nonfoundationalist Theorizing." *Horizons* 22 (1995) 29-48.

ALSTON, William P. "Two Types of Foundationalism." *JPh* 73 (1976) 165-85.

AVIS, Paul. "Theology in the Dogmatic Mode." In *Companion Encyclopedia of Theology*, ed. Peter Byrne and Leslie Houlden. London: Routledge, 1995, 976-1000.

ANDERSON, Gary A. *A Time to Mourn, a Time to Dance: The Expression of Grief and Joy in Israelite Religion*. University Park: Pennsylvania State University Press, 1991.

ALLEN, Charles W. "The Primacy of *Phronesis*: A Proposal for Avoiding Frustrating Tendencies in Our Conceptions of Rationality." *JR* 69 (1989) 359-74.

ARNAL, William. "Major Episodes in the Biography of Jesus: An Assessment of the Historicity of the Narrative Tradition." *TJT* 13 (1997) 201-26.

ARENDT, Hannah. "What Is Authority?" In *Between Past and Future*. New York: Penguin, 1956, 1987 reprint, 91-141.

AUERBACH, Erich. *Mimesis: The Representation of Reality in Western Literature*, trs. Willard R. Trask. Princeton, NJ: Princeton University Press, 1968.

AUSTIN, John A. *How to Do Things with Words*. Oxford: Clarendon, 1962.

"Performative Utterances." In *Philosophical Papers*. Oxford: Clarendon, 1972², 232-52.

BAAR, James. "Story and History in Biblical Theology." *JR* 56 (1976) 1-17.

BAKER, Kenneth. "Rahner: The Transcendental Method." *Continuum* 2 (1964) 51-9.

BARNES, Elizabeth. "Community, Narrative, and an Ecological Doctrine of Creation: Creation and Ecology Beyond Modern Atheism." In *Theology Without Foundations*, ed. Stanley Hauerwas et al. Nashville: Abingdon, 1994.

BARRETT, Lee C. "Theology as Grammar: Regulative Principles or Paradigms and Practices." *ModTh* 4 (1988) 155-72.

BARTH, Karl. *Protestant Theology in the Nineteenth Century*, trs. Brian Cozens and John Bowden. London: SCM, 1972.

Church Dogmatics, Vol. I/1, trs. G. T. Thomson. Edinburgh: T & T Clark, 1978.

Church Dogmatics, Vol. II/1, trs. T. Parker et al. Edinburgh: T & T Clark, 1985.

BAUM, Gregory. "The Bible as Norm." *Ecumenist* 9 (1971) 71-77.

BAYNES, Kenneth. "Rational Reconstruction and Social Criticism: Habermas's Model of Interpretive Social Science." *PhFor* 2 (1989-90) 122-45.

BEAUMONT, Daniel. "The Modality of Narrative: A Critique of Some Recent Views of Narrative in Theology." *JAAR* 65 (1997) 125-39.

BEECK, Frans Jozef Van. *Catholic Identity after Vatican II: Three Types of Faith in the One Church*. Chicago: Loyola University Press, 1985.

God Encountered: A Contemporary Catholic Theology, Vol. 1: Understanding the Christian Faith. San Francisco: Harper & Row, 1989.

"Tradition and Interpretation." *Bijdragen* 51 (1990) 257-71.

God Encountered: A Contemporary Catholic Theology, Vol. II/1:The Revelation of the Glory. Collegeville, MN: Liturgical, 1993.

BEHRENS, Georg. "Schleiermacher *contra* Lindbeck on the Status of Doctrinal Sentences." *RelSt* 30 (1994) 399-417.

BELLAH, Robert N. "Christian Faithfulness in a Pluralistic World." In *Postmodern Theology: Christian Faith in a Pluralist World*, ed. Frederic B. Burnham. New York: Harper & Row, 1989, 74-91.

"Public Philosophy and Public Theology in America Today." In *Civil Religion and Political Theology*, ed. R. Bellah et al. New York: Clarendon, 1989, 79-97.

BELLAH, Robert et al. *Habits of the Heart: Individualism, Commitment in American Life*. New York: Harper and Row, 1985.

BENHABIB, Seyla. Situating the Self: Gender, Community and Postmodernism in Contemporary Ethics. New York: Routledge, 1992.

BENNE, Robert. *The Paradoxical Vision: A Public Theology for the Twenty-first Century*. Minneapolis: Fortress, 1994.

BERGER, Peter. *Rumours of Angels: Modern Society and the Rediscovery of the Supernatural*. New York: Doubleday, 1969.

"Secular Theology and the Rejection of the Supernatural: Reflections on Recent Trends." *TS* 38 (1977) 39-56.

The Heretical Imperative: Contemporary Possibilities of Religious Affirmation. New York: Doubleday, 1980.

BERGER, Peter L. and Richard J. Neuhaus, ed. *Against the World for the World: The Hartford Appeal and the Future of American Religion*. New York: Seabury, 1976.

BERNARDIN, Joseph. "What Can the Church Expect from Catholic University?" *Origins* 4 (1975) 513-19.

BERNIER, Paul. *Bread Broken and Shared*. Notre Dame, IN: Ave Maria, 1981.

Eucharist: Celebrating Its Rhythms in Our Lives. Notre Dame, IN: Ave Maria, 1993.

BERNSTEIN, Richard J. *Beyond Objectivism and Relativism*. Philadelphia: University of Pennsylvania Press, 1983.

"Philosophy and Virtue for Society's Sake." *Com* 115 (1988) 306-07.

BETHGE, Eberhard. "The Challenge of Dietrich Bonhoeffer's Life and Theology." *The Chicago Theological Seminary Register*, February, 1961.

BETZ, Hans D. *Galatians: A Commentary on Paul's Letter to the Churches in Galatia*. Philadelphia: Fortress, 1979.

BIERINGER, Reimund. "The Normativity of the Future: The Authority of the Bible for Theology." *Bulletin ET* 8 (1997) 52-67.

BLEICHER, Josef. *Contemporary Hermeneutics: Hermeneutics as Method, Philosophy and Critique*. London: Routledge and Kegan Paul, 1980.

BLOESCH, Donald G. *A Theology of Word and Spirit: Authority and Method in Theology*. Downers Grove, IL: InterVarsity, 1992.

Holy Scripture: Revelation, Inspiration and Interpretation. Carlisle: Paternoster, 1994.

BLONDEL, Maurice. *History and Dogma*, trs. Illtyd Trethowan. London: Harville, 1964.

BOEVE, Lieven. "Bearing Witness to the Differend: A Model for Theologising in the Postmodern Context." *LS* 20 (1995) 362-79.

"Postmodern Sacramento-Theology: Retelling the Christian Story." *ETL* 74 (1998) 326-43.

BOFF, Clodovis. *Theology and Praxis: Epistemological Foundations*. Maryknoll, NY: Orbis, 1987.

BONHOEFFER, Dietrich. *Letters and Papers from Prison*, ed. Eberhard Bethge. London: SCM, 1971.

BOUILLARD, Henri. "Dialectical Theology." In *Sacramentum Mundi*, ed. Karl Rahner et al. New York: Herder and Herder, 1968, II:75-78.

BRAATEN, Carl E. *Principles of Lutheran Theology*. Philadelphia: Fortress, 1983.

No Other Gospel! Christianity Among the World's Religions. Minneapolis: Fortress, 1992.

"The Problem of Authority in the Church." In *The Catholicity of the Reformation*, ed. C. E. Braaten and Robert W. Jensen. Grand Rapids: Eerdmans, 1996, 53-66.

BRAATEN, Carl E. and Robert W. Jensen (ed.). *Reclaiming the Bible for the Church*. Grand Rapids: Eerdmans, 1995.

BRETT, Mark. *Biblical Criticism in Crisis: The Impact of the Canonical Approach on Old Testament Studies*. Cambridge: Cambridge University Press, 1991.

BROWN, David. *The Divine Trinity*. London: Duckworth, 1985.

"God and Symbolic Action." In *Divine Action*, ed. B. Hebblethwaite and E. Henderson. Edinburgh: T & T Clark, 1990, 103-29.

BROWN, Delwin. "Struggle Till Daybreak: On the Nature of Authority in Theology." *JR* 65 (1985) 15-32.

Boundaries of Our Habitations: Tradition and Theological Construction. Albany, NY: State University of New York Press, 1994.

BROWN, Delwin and Sheila Greeve Davaney. "Liberalism: USA." In the *Encyclopedia of Modern Christian Thought*. Oxford: Blackwell, 1993, 325-30.

BROWN, Raymond E. *The Sensus Plenior of Sacred Scripture: A Dissertation*. Baltimore: Pontifical Theological Faculty of St. Mary's University, 1955.

"Hermeneutics." In *The Jerome Biblical Commentary*, ed. Raymond E. Brown et al. Englewood Cliffs, NJ: Prentice-Hall, 1968, 605-23.

An Introduction to New Testament Christology. Mahwah, NJ: Paulist, 1994.

BROWN, R. MacAfee. "My Story and 'the Story'." *ThT* 32 (1975) 166-73.

BRYANT, David J. *Faith and the Play of Imagination*. Georgia: Mercer University Press, 1989.

"Christian Identity and Historical Change: Postliberals and Historicity." *JR* 73 (1993) 31-41.

BRUEGGEMANN, Walter. *Texts Under Negotiation*. Minneapolis: Fortress, 1993.

Theology of the Old Testament. Minneapolis: Fortress, 1997.

BUCKLEY, James J. "Review of *The Nature of Doctrine*." *Am* 153 (1985) 105.

"Doctrine in the Diaspora." *Thomist* 49 (1985) 443-59.

"The Language of Dogma and Theological Discourse." *CTSAP* 42 (1987) 140-43.

"Revisionists and Liberals." In *The Modern Theologian*, ed. David F. Ford. Oxford: Blackwell, 1989, II: 89-102.

"The Hermeneutical Deadlock between Revelationists, Textualists, and Functionalists." *ModTh* 6 (1990) 325-39.

Seeking the Humanity of God: Practices, Doctrines, and Catholic Theology. Collegeville: Liturgical, 1992.

BULTMANN, Rudolf. *Theology of the New Testament*, Vol. II, trs. Kendrick Grobel. London: SCM, 1955.

"The Problem of Hermeneutics." In *Essays Philosophical and Theological*. London: SCM, 1955, 234-69.

"Is Exegesis Without Presuppositions Possible?" In *Existence and Faith*, ed. Schubert Ogden Cleveland: World Publishing, 1960, 289-06.

BURKE, Ronald R. "Newman, Lindbeck and Models of Doctrine." In *John Henry Newman: Theology and Reform*, ed. M. E. Allsopp and R. R. Burke. New York: Garland, 1992, 19-43.

BURKHARD, John J. "*Sensus Fidei*: Theological Reflection Since Vatican II: 1964-1984, 1985-1989." *HeyJ* 34 (1993) 41-59, 123-36.

BURNHAM, Frederic C. (ed.). *Postmodern Theology: Christian Faith in a Pluralist World*. San Francisco: Harper & Row, 1989.

BURREL, David B. "From Particularity to a Discourse for All." *Com* 108 (1981) 310-11.

"Review of *The Nature of Doctrine*." *USQR* 39 (1984) 322-24.

"Analogy." In *The New Dictionary of Theology*, ed. Joseph Komonchak et al. Collegeville, MN: Liturgical, 1987, 14-16.

CADY, Linell E. "Hermeneutics and Tradition: The Role of the Past in Jurisprudence and Theology." *HTR* 79 (1986) 439-63.

"Resisting the Postmodern Turn: Theology and Contextualization." In *Theology at the End of Modernity*, ed. Sheila G. Davaney. Philadelphia: Trinity, 1991, 81-98.

"Theories of Religion in Feminist Theologies." *AJTP* 13 (1992) 183-93.

CAMUS, Albert. *Resistance, Rebellion and Death*, trs. Justin O'Brien. New York: A. A. Knopf, 1961.

CARR, Anne. "Theology and Experience in the Thought of Karl Rahner." *JR* 53 (1973) 359-76.

CHAPMAN, Mark D. "Why the Enlightenment Project Doesn't Have to Fail." *HeyJ* 39 (1998) 379-93.

CHAUVET, Louis-Marie. *Symbol and Sacrament: A Sacramental Reinterpretation of Christian Existence*, trs. Patrick Madigan and Madeleine Beaumont. Collegeville: Liturgical, 1995.

CHESTERTON, G. K. *Orthodoxy: The Romance of Faith*. New York: Doubleday, 1959.

CHILDS, Brevard S. *Introduction to the Old Testament as Scripture*. Philadelphia: Fortress, 1979.

The New Testament as Canon. London: SCM, 1984.

CHOPP, Rebecca S. *Saving Work: Feminist Practices of Theological Education*. Louisville, KY: Westminster John Knox, 1995.

CHRISTIE, Dolores L. *Adequately Considered: An American Consideration on Louis Janssens' Personalist Morals*. Louvain: Peeters, 1990.

CLADIS, Mark S. "Mild-Mannered Pragmatism and Religious Truth." *JAAR* 60 (1992) 19-33.

CLAPP, Rodney. *A Secular People: The Church as Culture in a Post-Christian Society*. Downers Grove, IL: InterVarsity, 1996.

CLOONEY, Francis X. "Reading the World in Christ: From Comparison to Inclusivism." In *Christian Uniqueness Reconsidered*, ed. Gavin D'Costa. Maryknoll, NY: Orbis, 1992, 63-80.

COLEMAN, John. "A Response to Ellen Leonard." *CTSAP* 43 (1988) 62-64.

COLERIDGE, Mark. "Life in the Crypt or Why Bother with Biblical Studies." *BibInt* 2 (1994) 139-51.

COLLINS, Raymond F. *Introduction to the New Testament*. New York: Doubleday, 1983.

COLOMBO, J. A. "Rahner and His Critics: Lindbeck and Metz." *Thomist* 56 (1992) 71-96.

COMSTOCK, Gary. "Truth or Meaning: Ricoeur Versus Frei on Biblical Narrative." *JR* 66 (1986) 117-40.

CONGAR, Yves. *Dialogues Between Christians*: Catholic Contributions to Ecumenism. Westminster, MD: Newman, 1966.

Tradition and Traditions: An Historical and a Theological Essay, trs. Michael Naseby and Thomas Rainborough. New York: MacMillan, 1967.

"Reception as an Ecclesiological Reality." *Concilium* 72 (1972) 43-86.

"Norms of Allegiance and Identity in the History of the Church." *Concilium* 3:9 (1973) 11-26.

"Towards a Catholic Synthesis." *Concilium* 148 (1981) 68-80.

Diversity and Communion, trs. John Bowden. London: SCM, 1984.

COOK, Michael L. "Revelation as Metaphoric Process." *TS* 47 (1986) 388-411.

Christology as Narrative Quest. Collegeville: Liturgical, 1997.

COOKE, B. "The Experiential 'Word of God'." In *Consensus in Theology?*, ed. Leonard Swidler. Philadelphia: Westminster, 1980.

CORNER, Mark. "Review of *The Nature of Doctrine*." *ModTh* 3 (1986) 110-13.

COULSON, John. *Religion and Imagination*. Oxford: Clarendon, 1981.

COX, Harvey. *Religion in the Secular City: Toward a Postmodern Theology*. New York: Simon & Schuster, 1984.

CRAGHAN, John F. "Kerygma." In *The New Dictionary of Theology*, ed. Joseph Komonchak et al.. Dublin: Gill and Macmillan, 1987, 556-57.

CRITES, Stephen. "The Spatial Dimensions of Narrative Truthtelling." In *Scriptural Authority and Narrative Interpretation*, ed. Garrett Green. Philadelphia: Fortress, 1987.

CROSSON, Frederick J. "Reconsidering Aquinas as Postliberal Theologian." *Thomist* 56 (1992) 481-98.

CROWE, Frederick E. "Dogma Versus the Self-Correcting Process of Learning." In *Foundations of Theology*, ed. Philip McShane. Dublin: Gill & Macmillan, 1971, 22-40.

CROWLEY, Paul G. "The Crisis of Transcendence and the Task of Theology." In *Finding God in All Things*, ed. Michael J. Himes and Stephen J. Pope. New York: Crossroad, 1996, 197-214.

In Ten Thousand Places: Dogma in a Pluralistic Church. New York: Crossroad, 1997.

DALFERTH, Ingolf U. *Theology and Philosophy*. Oxford: Blackwell, 1988.

DALY, Gabriel. "Theological Analysis and Public Policy Debate in a Pluralist Society." *D&L* 45 (1995) 75-91.

DAVANEY, Sheila G. "Problems with Feminist Theory: Historicity and the Search for Sure Foundations." In *Embodied Love: Sensuality and Relationship As Feminist Values*, ed. Paula M. Cooey et al. New York: Harper, 1987, 79-95.

"Options in Post-Modern Theology." *Dialog* 26 (1987) 196-200.

"Between the One and the Many: Response to Delwin Brown's Theory of Tradition." *AJTP* 18 (1997) 135-45.

DAVANEY, Sheila G. and Delwin Brown. "Postliberalism." In *The Blackwell Encyclopedia of Modern Christian Thought*, ed. Alister E. McGrath. Oxford: Blackwell, 1993, 453-56.

DAVIDSON, Donald. "The Very Idea of a Conceptual Scheme." In idem, *Inquiries into Truth and Interpretation*. Oxford: Clarendon, 1985.

DAVIS, Charles. *Religion and the Making of Society: Essays in Social Theology.* Cambridge: Cambridge University Press, 1994.

DE SCHRIJVER, Georges. "Hermeneutics and Tradition." In *Authority in the Church*, ed. Piet F. Fransen. Leuven: Leuven University Press, 1983, 32-47.

"Postmodernity and Theology." *Philippiniana Sacra* 27 (1992) 439-52.

DEAN, William. "Humanistic Historicism and Naturalistic Historicism." In *Theology at the End of Modernity*, ed. Sheila G. Davaney. Philadelphia: Trinity, 1991, 41-59.

DiNOIA, Joseph A. "Implicit Faith, General Revelation and the State of the Non-Christians." *Thomist* 47 (1983) 209-41.

"American Catholic Theology at Century's End: Postconciliar, Post-modern, Post-Thomistic." *Thomist* 54 (1990) 499-518.

The Diversity of Religions: A Christian Perspective. Washington, DC: The Catholic University of America Press, 1992.

DONAHUE, John R. "Scripture: A Roman Catholic Perspective." *Rev&Exp* 79 (1982) 231-44.

DONOHUE, John W. "Dreading to Leave an Illiterate Ministry." *Am* 134 (1976) 258-60.

DOODY, John A. "MacIntyre and Habermas on Practical Reason." *ACPhilQ* 65 (1991) 143-58.

DOYLE, Dennis M. "Lindbeck's Appropriation of Lonergan." *Method* 4:1 (1986) 18-28.

"Communion Ecclesiology and the Silencing of Boff." *Am* 167 (1992) 139-43.

DUQUOC, Christian. *Provisional Churches: An Essay in Ecumenical Ecclesiology.* London: SCM, 1986.

DUFFY, Stephen J. "Justification by Faith: A Post-Conciliar Perspective." In *Church and Theology*, ed. Peter C. Phan. Washington, DC: Catholic University of America Press, 1995, 182-214.

DULLES, Avery. "Method in Fundamental Theology: Reflections on David Tracy's *Blessed Rage for Order*." *TS* 37 (1976) 304-16.

The Resilient Church: The Necessity and Limits of Adaptation. New York: Doubleday, 1977.

"'Latent Heresy' and Orthodoxy." *ChCent* 94 (1977) 1053-54.

"Scripture: Recent Protestant and Catholic Views." *ThT* 13 (1980) 7-26.

Models of Revelation. Garden City, NY: Doubleday, 1983.

"Observations on George Lindbeck, *The Nature of Doctrine.*" (Unpublished paper delivered at the Divinity School, Yale University, September 4, 1984.)

The Catholicity of the Church. Oxford: Clarendon, 1985.

"Paths to Doctrinal Agreement: Ten Theses." *TS* 47 (1986) 32-47.

"The Gospel, the Church and Politics." *Origins* 16 (1987) 637-46.

"Theology for a Post-Critical Age." In *Theology Toward the Third Millennium: Theological Issues for the Twenty-First Century,* ed. David G. Schultenover. Lewiston: Edwin Mellon, 1991, 5-21.

"Faith and Revelation." In *Systematic Theology,* ed. Francis S. Fiorenza and John P. Galvin. Minneapolis: Fortress, 1991, I:89-128.

"Handing on the Faith Through Witness and Symbol." *LL* 27 (1991) 295-302.

"Tradition and Creativity." *First Things* 27 (Nov. 1992) 20-27.

"Rejoinder to George Lindbeck." *ProE* 1 (1992) 61-62.

The Craft of Theology: From Symbol to System. New York: Crossroad, 1996.

"The Cognitive Basis of Faith." *Ph&Th* 10 (1998) 19-31.

DUPUIS, Jacques. *Jesus Christ at the Encounter of World Religions.* Maryknoll, NY: 1991.

DYKSTRA, Craig. "A 'Post-Liberal' Christian Education?" *ThT* 42 (1985-86) 153-57.

EBELING, Gerhard. *Dogmatik des christlichen Glaubens,* vol. 1, *Der Glaube an Gott den Schöpfer der Welt.* Tübingen: J. C. B. Mohr (Paul Siebeck), 1979.

EDWARDS, Tilden H. *Spiritual Friend: Reclaiming the Gift of Spiritual Direction.* New York: Paulist, 1980.

ELSHTHAIN, Jean Bethke. "Theology and Political Life." *ModTh* 12 (1996) 367-76.

EMMANUEL, Steven M. "Kierkegaard on Doctrine: A Postmodern Interpretation." *RelSt* 25 (1989) 363-78.

FACKRE, Gabriel. *The Christian Story: A Pastoral Systematics,* Vol. 2. Grand Rapids: Eerdmans, 1987.

"David Tracy, Evangelically Considered." In *Ecumenical Faith in Evangelical Perspective.* Grand Rapids: Eerdmans, 1993, 199-224.

The Doctrine of Revelation: A Narrative Interpretation. Edinburgh: Edinburgh University Press, 1997.

FAHEY, Michael A. "Church." In *Systematic Theology: Roman Catholic Perspectives,* ed. Francis S. Fiorenza and John P. Galvin. Minneapolis: Fortress, 1991, II:1-74.

FERGUSSON, David. "Meaning, Truth and Realism in Bultmann and Lindbeck." *RelSt* 26 (1990) 183-98.

Community, Liberalism and Christian Ethics. Cambridge: Cambridge University Press, 1998.

FICHTNER, J. A. "Tradition (In Theology)." In *New Catholic Encyclopedia.* New York: McGraw Hill, 1967, 14:225-28.

"Tradition (In Theology)." In ibid., 1989, 18:667-68.

FINGER, Thomas N. *Christian Theology: An Eschatological Approach.* Scottdale, PA: Herald, 1985.

FIORENZA, Francis Schüssler. "Karl Rahner and the Kantian Problematic." In the Introduction to Rahner's *Spirit in the World*, trs. W. Dych (London: Sheed & Ward, 1968), xix-xlv.

Foundational Theology: Jesus and the Church. New York: Crossroad, 1984.

"Systematic Theology: Task and Methods." In *Systematic Theology: Roman Catholic Perspectives*, ed. F. S. Fiorenza and J. P. Galvin. Minneapolis: Fortress, 1991, I:1-88.

FITZMYER, Joseph A. *Scripture, the Soul of Theology.* New York: Paulist, 1994.

The Biblical Commission's Document "The Interpretation of the Bible in the Church" : Text and Commentary. Roma: Editrice Pontificio Istitutio Biblico, 1995.

FOERSTER, Werner. "κύριος." In *Theological Dictionary of the New Testament*, ed. Gerhard Kittel. Grand Rapids, MI: Eerdmans, 1965, III:1039-58.

FOLDER, James. *Christian Hermeneutics: Paul Ricoeur and the Refiguring of Theology.* Oxford: Clarendon, 1995.

FORD, David F. "The Best Apologetics is Good Systematics: A Proposal about the Place of Narrative in Christian Systematic Theology." *ATR* 67 (1985) 232-54.

"Review of *The Nature of Doctrine.*" *JTS* 37 (1986) 277-82.

"On Being Theologically Hospitable to Jesus Christ: Hans Frei's Achievement." *JTS* 46 (1995) 532-46.

FORTE, Bruno. "Thinking of God Beyond the Crisis of Critical Rationality." *Bulletin ET* 9 (1998) 128-43.

FOWL, Stephen. "The Canonical Approach of Brevard Childs." *ExpT* 96 (1985) 173-76.

FOWL, Stephen E. and L. Gregory Jones, *Reading in Communion: Scripture and Ethics in Christian Life.* London: SPCK, 1991.

FOWLER, James W. *Faithful Change.* Nashville: Abingdon, 1996.

FREEMAN, Curtis W. "Toward a *Sensus Fidelium* for an Evangelical Church: Postconservatives and Postliberals on Reading Scripture." In *The Nature of Confession*, ed. T. R. Phillips and D. L. Okholm (Downers Grove, IL: InterVarsity, 1996), 162-79.

FRIES, Heinrich and Karl Rahner. *Unity of the Churches: An Actual Possibility*, trs. Ruth C. L. Gritsch and Eric W. Gritsch. Philadelphia: Fortress, 1985.

FREI, Hans W. *The Eclipse of Biblical Narrative: A Study in Eighteenth and Nineteenth Century Hermeneutics.* New Haven: Yale University Press, 1974.

The Identity of Jesus Christ: The Hermeneutical Bases of Dogmatic Theology. Philadelphia: Fortress, 1975.

"Response to 'Narrative Theology: An Evangelical Appraisal'." *TrinJ* 8 NS (1987) 21-24.

"Epilogue: Lindbeck and *The Nature of Doctrine.*" In *Theology and Dialogue: Essays in Conversation with George Lindbeck,* ed. Bruce D. Marshall. Notre Dame: University of Notre Dame Press, 1990, 275-82.

Types of Christian Theology, ed. George Hunsinger and William C. Placher. New Haven: Yale University Press, 1992.

"The 'Literal Reading' of Biblical Narrative in the Christian Tradition." In *Theology and Narrative: Selected Essays (Hans Frei),* ed. George Hunsinger and William C. Placher. New York: Oxford University Press, 1993, 117-52.

FRYE, Northrop. *The Great Code: The Bible and Literature.* New York: Harcourt Brace Jovanovich, 1982.

FULKERSON, Mary McClintock. "'Is There a (Non-Sexist) Bible in This Church?' A Feminist Case for the Priority of Interpretive Communities." *ModTh* 14 (1998) 225-42.

GADAMER, Hans-Georg. "On the Scope and Function of Hermeneutical Reflection." *Continuum* 8 (1970) 77-95.

Truth and Method, trs. Garret Barden and John Cumming. London: Sheed and Ward, 1975;

"On the Universality of the Hermeneutical Problem." In *Philosophical Hermeneutics,* trs. and ed. David E. Linge. Berkeley: University of California Press, 1976.

Reason in the Age of Science, trs. Frederick G. Lawrence. Cambridge, MA: MIT Press, 1981.

Truth and Method, trs. Joel Weinsheimer and Donald G. Marshall. New York: Continuum, 1994.

GAILLARDETZ, Richard R. *Witnesses to Faith: Community, Infallibility and the Ordinary Magisterium of Bishops.* New York: Paulist, 1992.

GAMWELL, Franklin I. *The Divine Good: Modern Moral Theory and the Necessity of God.* New York: Southern Methodist University Press, 1996.

GANNON, J. F. "MacIntyre's Historicism." *CrCur* 38 (1989) 91-96.

GARRETT, Graeme. "Rule 4? Gender Difference and the Nature of Doctrine." *Pacifica* 10 (1997) 173-86.

GEERTZ, Clifford. *The Interpretation of Cultures.* New York: Basic Books, 1973.

GEISELMANN, Josef Rupert. *The Meaning of Tradition*, trs. W. J. O'Hara. London: Burns and Oates, 1966.

GELLMAN, Jerome J. *Experience of God and the Rationality of Theistic Belief*. Ithaca: Cornell University Press, 1997.

GENNETTE, Gerard. *Figures of Literary Discourse*, trs. A. Sheridan. New York: Columbia University Press, 1982.

GEORGE, Robert P. "Moral Particularism, Thomism, and Tradition." *RevMet* 42 (1986) 593-605.

GERHART, Mary. "Paul Ricoeur's Hermeneutical Theory as Resource for Theological Reflection." *Thomist* 39 (1975) 496-527.

GERRISH, B. A. "The Nature of Doctrine." *JR* 68 (1988) 87-92.

GILKEY, Langdon. "Anathemas and Orthodoxy." *ChCent* 94 (1977) 1026-29.

GILKEY, Langdon et al. "Responses to Peter Berger." *TS* 39 (1978) 486-507.

GILLIS, Chester. *Pluralism: A New Paradigm for Theology*. Louvain: Peeters, 1993.

GIURLANDA, Paul. "Post-liberal Theology." *CrCur* 35 (1985) 321-23.

"The Challenge of Postliberal Theology: Testimony, Community, and Non-violence." *Com* 64 (1987) 40-42.

GOLDBERG, Michael. *Jews and Christians, Getting Our Stories Straight: The Exodus and the Passion —Resurrection*. Nashville: Abingdon, 1985.

"God, Action, and Narrative: *Which* Narrative? *Which* Action? *Which* God?" *JR* 68 (1988) 39-56.

GOH, Jeffrey C. K. "Christian Marriage as a *Realsymbol*: Towards a Performative Understanding of the Sacrament." *QL* 76 (1995) 254-64.

GREEN, Garrett. *Imagining God: Theology and the Religious Imagination*. San Francisco: Harper & Row, 1989.

GRIFFITHS, Paul J. "An Apology for Apologetics." *F&Ph* 5 (1988) 409-11.

"The Uniqueness of Christian Doctrine Defended." In *Christian Uniqueness Reconsidered*, ed. Gavin D'Costa. Maryknoll, NY: Orbis, 1990, 157-73.

An Apology for Apologetics: A Study in the Logic of Interreligious Dialogue. Maryknoll, NY: Orbis, 1991.

GRIFFITHS, Paul and Delmas Lewis. "On Grading Religions, Seeking Truth, and Being Nice to People — A Reply to Professor Hick." *RS* 19 (1983) 75-80.

GRILLMEIER, A. "The Reception of Chalcedon in the Roman Catholic Church." *EcuRev* 22 (1970) 383-411.

GRIMES, Ronald. "Of Words the Speaker, of Deeds the Doer." *JR* 66 (1986) 1-17.

GUARINO, Thomas. "The Truth-Status of Theological Statements: Analogy Re-visited." *ITQ* 54 (1988) 140-55.

"Revelation and Foundationalism: Toward Hermeneutical and Ontological Appropriateness." *ModTh* 6 (1990) 221-35.

Revelation and Truth: Unity and Plurality in Contemporary Theology. Scranton: University of Scranton Press, 1993.

"Philosophy within Theology in Light of the Foundationalism Debate." *Ph&Th* 9 (1995) 57-69.

"Spoils from Egypt: Contemporary Theology and Nonfoundationalist Thought." *LTP* 51 (1995) 573-87.

"Review of John E. Thiel, *Nonfoundationalism.*" *Thomist* 60 (1996) 141-45.

"Postmodernity and Five Fundamental Theological Issues." *TS* 57 (1996) 654-89.

GUNTON, Colin E. *A Brief Theology of Revelation.* Edinburgh: T & T Clark, 1995.

GUSTAFSON, James M. *Treasure in Earthen Vessels: The Church as a Human Community.* New York: Harper and Row, 1961.

"The Sectarian Temptation: Reflections on Theology, the Church and the University." *CTSAP* 40 (1985) 83-94.

GUTIÉRREZ, Gustavo. *A Theology of Liberation: History, Politics and Salvation*, trs. Sr. Caridad Inda and John Eagleson. Maryknoll, NY: Orbis, 1973.

HABERMAS, Jürgen. "The Universality of the Hermeneutical Problem." In *Hermeneutics, Questions and Prospects.* Amherst: University of Massachusetts Press, 1976.

"A Review of Gadamer's *Truth and Method.*" In *Understanding and Social Enquiry*, ed. Fred R. Dallmayr and Thomas McCarthy. Notre Dame: University of Notre Dame Press, 1977.

The Theory of Communicative Action, Vol. 1, trs. Thomas McCarthy. Boston: Beacon, 1979.

"On Hermeneutic's Claim to Universality." In *The Hermeneutics Reader: Texts of the German Tradition from Enlightenment to the Present*, ed. Kurt Mueller-Vollmer. Oxford: Blackwell, 1986.

"The Hermeneutic Approach." In *On the Logic of the Social Sciences*, trs. Shierry Weber Nicholsen. Cambridge, MA: MIT Press, 1988.

HAERS, Jacques. "A Risk Observed." *LS* 21 (1996) 46-60.

HAIGHT, Roger. "Critical Witness: The Question of Method." In *Faithful Witness: Foundations of Theology for Today's Church*, ed. Leo J. O'Donovan and T. Howland Sanks. New York: Crossroad, 1989, 185-204.

Dynamics of Theology. New York: Paulist, 1990.

HALL, Douglas J. "Theological Education as Character Formation?" *ThEd* 24, Suppl. 1 (1988) 53-75.

Professing the Faith: Christian Theology in a North American Context. Minneapolis: Fortress, 1993.

HAMPSON, Daphne. *After Christianity.* London: SCM, 1996.

HARAKAS, Stanley. "Must God Remain Greek?" *EcuRev* 43 (1991) 194-99.

HARDY, Daniel W. "A Magnificent Complexity: Letting God be God in Church, Society and Creation." In *Essentials of Christian Community*, ed. D. F. Ford and D. L. Stamps. Edinburgh: T & T Clark, 1996, 307-56.

HARRINGTON, Daniel. *The Gospel of Matthew*. Collegeville, MN: Liturgical, 1991.

HARRINGTON, Wilfrid. " Senses of Scripture." In *The New Dictionary of Theology*, ed. Joseph A. Komonchak et al. Dublin: Gill & Macmillan, 1987, 945-47.

HART, Ray L. *Unfinished Man and the Imagination: Toward an Ontology and a Rhetoric Revelation*. New York: Seabury, 1979.

HARTT, Julian. *Theological Method and Imagination*. New York: Seabury, 1974.

HARVEY, Barry. "Insanity, Theodicy, and the Public Realm: Public Theology, the Church, and the Politics of Liberal Democracy." *ModTh* 10 (1994) 27-57.

HAUERWAS, Stanley. *Character and the Christian Life: A Study in Theological Ethics*. San Antonio: Trinity University Press, 1975.

A Community of Character. Notre Dame: University of Notre Dame Press, 1981.

The Peaceable Kingdom: A Primer in Christian Ethics. Notre Dame: University of Notre Dame Press, 1983.

Against the Nations: War and Survival in a Liberal Society. Minneapolis: Winston-Seabury, 1985.

"Some Theological Reflections on Gutiérrez's Use of 'Liberation' as a Theological Concept." *ModTh* 3/1 (1986) 67-76.

"The Church as God's New Language." In *Scriptural Authority and Narrative Interpretation*, ed. Garrett Green. Philadelphia: Fortress, 1987, 179-98.

"Will the Real Sectarian Stand Up?" *ThT* 44 (1987) 87-94.

Christian Existence Today: Essays on Church, World and Living in Between. Durham: Labyrinth, 1988.

After Christendom. Nashville: Abingdon, 1991.

Unleashing the Scriptures. Nashville: Abingdon, 1993.

Dispatches from the Front: Theological Engagements with the Secular. Durham: Duke University Press, 1994.

"Communitarians and Medical Ethicists: or 'Why I Am None of the Above'." *CSR* 23 (1994) 293-99.

HAUERWAS, Stanley and L. Gregory Jones. "Seeking a Clear Alternative to Liberalism." *B&R* 13:1 (1985) 9.

(Eds.). *Why Narrative? Readings in Narrative Theology*. Grand Rapids: Eerdmans, 1989.

HAUERWAS, Stanley and William H. Willimon. "Embarrassed by God's Presence." *ChCent* 102/4 (1985) 98-100.
Resident Aliens: Life in the Christian Colony. Nashville: Abingdon, 1989.
HAUGHT, John F. "Revelation." In *The New Dictionary Of Theology*, ed. J. A. Komonchak et al. Dublin: Gill and Macmillan, 1987, 884-99.
Mystery and Promise: A Theology of Revelation. Collegeville, MN: Liturgical, 1993.
HAWKINS, Charles. *Beyond Anarchy and Tyranny in Religious Epistemology: Postliberalism, Poststructuralism, and Critical Theory.* Lanham: University Press of America, 1997.
HAYMES, Brian. *The Concept of the Knowledge of God.* London: Macmillan, 1988.
HEALY, Nicholas M. "Indirect Method in Theology: Karl Rahner as an Ad Hoc Apologist." *Thomist* 56 (1992) 613-33.
HEBBLETHWAITE, Brian L. (ed.). *Divine Action.* Edinburgh: T & T Clark, 1990.
"God and Truth." *KuD* 40 (1994) 2-19.
HEFLING, Charles C. "Turning Liberalism Inside Out." *Method* 3:2 (1985) 51-69.
HEILER, Friedrich. "The History of Religion as a Preparation for the Cooperation of Religions." In *The History of Religions*, ed. M. Eliade and J. Katigawa. Chicago: The University of Chicago Press, 1959, 142-53.
HEIM, S. Mark. "The Nature of Doctrine and the Development of Asian Theology." *Bangalore Theological Forum* 19 (1987) 14-31.
HELLWIG, Monica. *Whose Experience Counts in Theological Reflection?* Milwaukee: Marquette University Press, 1982.
"Foundation for Theology: A Historical Sketch." In *Faithful Witness: Foundations of Theology for Today's Church*, ed. Leo J. O'Donovan and T. Howland Sanks. New York: Crossroad, 1989, 1-13.
HENRY, Carl F. H. "Narrative Theology: An Evangelical Appraisal." *TrinJ* 8 NS (1987) 3-19.
HENSLEY, Jeffrey. "Are Postliberals Necessarily Antirealists? Reexamining the Metaphysics of Lindbeck's Postliberal Theology." In *The Nature of Confession: Evangelicals and Postliberals in Conversations*, ed. T. R. Phillips and D. L. Okholm. Downers Grove, IL: InterVarsity, 1996, 70-80.
HETTEMA, Theo L. *Reading for Good: Narrative Theology and Ethics in the Joseph Story from the Perspective of Ricoeur's Hermeneutics.* Kampen: Kok Pharos, 1996.
HIBBS, Thomas S. "MacIntyre, Tradition and the Christian Philosopher." *ModSch* 68 (1991) 211-23.

"MacIntyre's Postmodern Thomism: Reflections on *Three Rival Versions of Moral Enquiry.*" *Thomist* 57 (1993) 277-97.
HICK, John (ed.). *The Myth of God Incarnate.* Philadelphia: Westminster, 1977.
Problems of Religious Pluralism. London: Macmillan, 1985.
Disputed Questions in Theology and Philosophy of Religion. New Haven: Yale University Press, 1993.
HICK, John and Paul F. Knitter (ed.). *The Myth of Christian Uniqueness: Toward a Pluralistic Theology of Religions.* Maryknoll, NY: Orbis, 1987.
HIGGINS, Gregory C. "The Significance of Postliberalism for Religious Education," *RelEd* 84 (1989) 77-89.
HIGTON, M. A. "'A Carefully Circumscribed Progressive Politics': Hans Frei's Political Theology." *ModTh* 15 (1999) 54-83.
HIGTON, Mike. "Frei's Christology and Lindbeck's Cultural-Linguistic Theory." *SJT* 50 (1997) 83-95.
HILKERT, Mary C. "Experience and Tradition — Can the Center Hold?" In *Freeing Theology: The Essentials of Theology in Feminist Perspective*, ed. Catherine M. LaCugna. New York: HarperSanFrancisco, 1993, 59-82.
HIMES, Michael J. "The Ecclesiological Significance of the Reception of Doctrine." *HeyJ* 33 (1992) 146-60.
HINZE, Bradford E. "Postliberal Theology and Roman Catholic Theology." *RSRev* 21 (1995) 299-304.
HITTINGGER, Russel. *A Critique of the New Natural Law Theory.* Notre Dame: University of Notre Dame Press, 1988.
HODGSON, Peter C. *Winds of the Spirit: A Constructive Christian Theology.* London: SCM, 1994.
HOGAN, John P. *Collingwood and Theological Hermeneutics.* Lanham: University Press of America, 1989.
HOLLAND, Scott. "How Do Stories Save Us? Two Contemporary Theological Responses." *LS* 22 (1997) 328-51.
HOLLENBACH, David. "Fundamental Theology and the Christian Moral Life." In *Faithful Witness: Foundations of Theology for Today's Church*, Leo J. O'Donovan and T. Howland Sanks. New York: Crossroad, 1989, 167-84.
HOLMER, Paul L. "Wittgenstein and Theology." In *New Essays on Religious Language*, ed. Dallas M. High. New York: Oxford University Press, 1969, 25-35.
HORST, Mark L. "Engendering the Community of Faith in an Age of Individualism." *QR* 8 (1988) 89-97.
HUANG, Yong. "Foundation of Religious Beliefs after Foundationalism: Wittgenstein between Nielsen and Phillips." *RelSt* 31 (1995) 251-67.

HUNSINGER, George. "Karl Barth and Liberation Theology." *JR* 63 (1983) 247-63.

"A Response to William Werpehowski." *ThT* 43 (1986) 354-60.

"Beyond Literalism and Expressivism: Karl Barth's Hermeneutical Realism." *ModTh* 3 (1987) 209-23.

How to Read Karl Barth: The Shape of His Theology. New York: Oxford University Press, 1991.

"Afterword: Hans Frei as Theologian." In *Theology and Narrative: Selected Essays (Hans Frei)*, ed. George Hunsinger and William C. Placher. New York: Oxford University Press, 1993, 235-70.

"Truth as Self-Involving: Barth and Lindbeck on the Cognitive and Performative Aspects of Truth in Theological Discourse." *JAAR* 61 (1993) 41-56.

HUNTER, J. F. M. "'Forms of Life' in Wittgenstein's *Philosophical Investigations*." *AmPhQ* 5 (1968) 233-43.

HUYSSTEEN, J. Wentzel Van. "Tradition and the Task of Theology." *ThT* 55 (1998) 213-28.

IMBELLI, Robert. "A New Paradigm for Theology." *The Ecumenist* 14 (1976) 81-85.

"Theology: Trends in Systematic Theology." *Church* 1 (1985) 54-58.

INBODY, Tyron. *The Constructive Theology of Bernard Meland: Postliberal Empirical Realism.* Atlanta: Scholars, 1995.

ISASI-DÍAZ, Ada M. "Experiences." In *Dictionary of Feminist Theology*, ed. Letty M. Russell and J. Shannon Clarkson. London: Mowbray, 1996, 95-96.

JACKSON, Timothy P. "Against Grammar." *RSRev* 11 (1985) 240-45.

"The Theory and Practice of Discomfort: Richard Rorty and Pragmatism." *Thomist* 51 (1987) 270-98.

JAMES, William. *Pragmatism: A New Name for Some Old Ways of Thinking.* New York: Longman, Green, 1970.

JANSSENS, Louis. "Personalist Morals." *LS* 3 (1970) 5-16.

"Artificial Insemination: Ethical Considerations." *LS* 8 (1980) 3-29.

JEANROND, Werner G. "Community and Authority: The Nature and Implications of the Authority of Christian Community." In *On Being the Church: Essays on the Christian Community*, ed. Colin E. Gunton and Daniel W. Hardy. Edinburgh: T & T Clark, 1989, 81-109.

Theological Hermeneutics: Development and Significance. London: Macmillan, 1991.

"Theology in the Context of Pluralism and Postmodernity: David Tracy's Theological Method." In *Postmodernism, Literature and the Future of Theology*, ed. David Jasper. New York: St. Martin's, 1993, 143-63.

"After Hermeneutics: The Relationship between Theology and Biblical Studies." In *The Open Text: New Directions for Biblical Studies*, ed. Francis Watson. London: SCM, 1993, 85-102.

"The Problem of the Starting Point of Theological Thinking." In *The Possibilities of Theology*, ed. John Webster. Edinburgh: T & T Clark, 1994, 70-89.

"Thinking about God Today." *D&L* 47 (1997) 14-21.

JENSON, Robert W. "Karl Barth." In *The Modern Theologians*, ed. David Ford. Oxford: Blackwell, 1989, I:23-49.

JONES, Gareth. *Critical Theology: Questions of Truth and Method*. Cambridge: Polity, 1995.

JONES, Gregory L. "Why There Is No One Debate between 'Communitarians' and 'Liberals': An Essay on the Importance of Community." *PRS* 17 (1990) 53-70.

"Narrative Theology." In *The Blackwell Encyclopedia of Modern Christian Thought*, ed. Alister E. McGrath. Oxford: Blackwell, 1993, 395-98.

JOHNSON, William S. *The Mystery of God: Karl Barth and the Postmodern Foundations of Theology*. Louisville: Westminster John Knox, 1997.

JOHNSTONE, B. V. "Faithful Action: The Catholic Moral Tradition and *Veritatis Splendor*." *StuMor* 31 (1993) 283-305.

JÜNGEL, Eberhard. *Karl Barth: A Theological Legacy*, trs. Garrett E. Paul. Philadelphia: Westminster, 1986.

KALLENBERG, Brad J. "Unstuck from Yale: Theological Method after Lindbeck." *SJT* 50 (1997) 191-218.

KAMITSUKA, David G. "The Justification of Religious Belief in the Pluralistic Public Realm: Another Look at Postliberal Apologetics." *JR* 76 (1996) 588-606.

"Salvation, Liberation and Christian Character Formation: Postliberal and Liberation Theologians in Dialogue." *ModTh* 13 (1997) 171-89.

KATONGOLE, Emmanuel. *Particularity and Moral Rationality: Questioning the Relation between Religion and Ethics with Reference to the Work of Stanley Hauerwas*. Ph.D. Dissertation, Catholic University of Leuven, 1996. [Forthcoming in February, 2000, as *Beyond Universal Reason: The Relation between Religion and Ethics in the Work of Stanley Hauerwas*, University of Notre Dame Press.]

KASPER, Walter. *Jesus the Christ*, trs. V. Green. New York: Paulist, 1976.

"Postmodern Dogmatics: Toward a Renewed Discussion of Foundations in North America." *Communio* 17 (1990) 181-91.

KAUFMAN, Gordon. "Review of *Blessed Rage for Order*." *RSRev* 2 (1976) 7-13.

"Is There Any Way from Athens to Jerusalem?" *JR* 59 (1979) 340-46.

"Theology as Imaginative Construction." *JAAR* 50 (1982) 81-85.

KEIFERT, Patrick. "Labor Room or Morgue: The Power and Limits of Pluralism and Christology." *Word & World* 5 (1985) 78-88.

KELLY, Geffrey B. (ed.). *Karl Rahner.* Edinburgh: T & T Clark, 1992.

KELLY, Joseph E. (ed.). *Perspectives on Scripture and Tradition.* Notre Dame: Fides, 1976.

KELLY, Michael. "MacIntyre, Habermas, and Philosophical Ethics." *PhFor* 2 (1989-90) 70-93.

KENNESON, Philip D. "The Alleged Incorrigibility of Postliberal Theology. Or, What Babe Ruth & George Lindbeck Have in Common?" In *The Nature of Confession: Evangelicals and Postliberals in Conversation*, ed. T. R. Phillips and Dennis L. Okholm. Downers Grove, IL: InterVarsity, 1996, 93-106.

KELSEY, David H. *The Uses of Scripture in Recent Theology.* Philadelphia: Fortress, 1975.

"Biblical Narrative and Theological Anthropology." In *Scriptural Authority and Narrative Interpretation*, ed. Garrett Green. Philadelphia: Fortress, 1987, 121-43.

"Church Discourse and the Public Realm." In *Theology and Dialogue*, ed. Bruce D. Marshall. Notre Dame: University of Notre Dame Press, 1990, 7-33.

KERR, Fergus. "Wittgenstein and Theological Studies." *NewBf* 63 (1982) 500-08.

Theology After Wittgenstein. Oxford: Blackwell, 1986.

KILMARTIN, Edward J. "Reception in History: An Ecclesiological Phenomenon and Its Significance." *JES* 21 (1984) 34-54.

KINGSBURY, J. D. *Matthew as Story.* Philadelphia: Fortress, 1986.

KITCHENER, Michael. "Review of *The Nature of Doctrine*." *Th* 89 (1989) 51-53.

KORT, Wesley A. *Bound to Differ: The Dynamics of Theological Discourses.* University Park: Pennsylvania State University Press, 1992.

KRIEGER, David K. *The New Universalism: Foundations for a Global Theology.* Maryknoll, NY: Orbis, 1991.

KÜNG, Hans. *Infallible? An Inquiry*, trs. Edward Quinn. New York: Doubleday, 1971.

LADRIERE, Jean. "Meaning and Truth in Theology." *CTSAP* 42 (1987) 1-15.

LAKELAND, Paul. "Accommodation to Secularity." *The Month* 239 (1978) 162-66.

Postmodernity: Christian Identity in a Fragmented Age. Minnesota: Fortress, 1997.

LAMMERS, Ann C. "The Complications of Experience." *ATR* 75 (1993) 10-33.

LANE, Dermot A. "Eschatology." In *The New Dictionary of Theology*, ed. Joseph A. Komonchak et al. Dublin: Gill and Macmillan, 1987, 329-42.

The Experience of God. New York: Paulist, 1992.

LASCH, Christopher. "The Communitarian Critique of Liberalism." *Soundings* 69 (1986) 60-76.

LASH, Nicholas. "How Large Is a Language Game?" *Th* 87 (1984) 19-28.

"Review of *The Nature of Doctrine*." *NewBf* 66 (1985) 509-10.

Theology on the Way to Emmaus. London: SCM, 1986.

Easter in Ordinary: Reflections on Human Experience and the Knowledge of God. Charlottesville: The University Press of Virginia, 1988.

LAURITZEN, Paul. "Is 'Narrative' Really a Panacea? The Use of 'Narrative' in the Work of Metz and Hauwerwas." *JR* 67 (1987) 322-39.

LAWRENCE, Fred. "Athens and Jerusalem: The Contemporary Problematic of Faith and Reason." *Gregorianum* 80 (1999) 223-44.

LEONARD, Ellen. "Experience as a Source for Theology." *CTSAP* 43 (1988) 44-61.

LIBERATORE, Albert. "Symbols in Rahner: A Note on Translation." *LS* 18 (1993) 145-58.

LINTS, Richard. "The Positivist Choice: Tracy or Lindbeck?" *JAAR* 61 (1993) 655-77.

The Fabric of Theology. Grand Rapids: Eerdmans, 1993.

LONERGAN, Bernard. *Insights: A Study of Human Understanding*. New York: Philosophical Library, 1957.

Method in Theology. New York: Herder & Herder, 1972.

LOVIN, Robin W. "When the Church Is a Church: Doctrinal Standards in Denominational Contexts." *The Drew Gateway* 57 (1986) 1-15.

LOUGHLIN, Gerard. "See-Saying/Say-Seeing." *Th* 91 (1988) 201-09.

Telling God's Story: Bible, Church and Narrative Theology. Cambridge: Cambridge University Press, 1996.

"The Basis and Authority of Doctrine." In *The Cambridge Companion to Christian Doctrine*, ed. Colin E. Gunton. Cambridge: Cambridge University Press, 1997, 41-63.

LYOTARD, Jean-Francois. *The Postmodern Condition: A Report on Knowledge*, trs. Geoff Bennington and Brian Massumi. Minneapolis: University of Minnesota Press, 1984.

MacAFEE, Brown. "My Story and 'The Story'." *ThT* 32 (1975) 166-73.

MacINTYRE, Alasdair. *The Religious Significance of Atheism*. New York: Columbia University Press, 1966.

"Epistemological Crises. Dramatic Narrative and the Philosophy of Science." *The Monist* 60 (1977) 453-72.

After Virtue: A Study in Moral Theory. Notre Dame: University of Notre Dame Press, 1984.

Whose Justice? Which Rationality? Notre Dame: University of Notre Dame Press, 1988.

Three Rival Versions of Moral Enquiry. Notre Dame: University of Notre Dame Press, 1990.

MACQUARRIE, John. *The Scope of Demythologizing: Bultmann and His Critics.* London: SCM, 1960.

Principles of Christian Theology. New York: Scribner, 1966.

"Usefulness of Doctrines." *ExpT* 96 (1985) 315-16.

Theology, Church and Ministry. London: SCM, 1986.

Twentieth Century Religious Thought. London: SCM, 1988[4].

MARKHAM, Ian. "World Perspectives and Arguments: Disagreements about Disagreements." *HeyJ* 30 (1989) 1-12.

"Faith and Reason: Reflections on MacIntyre's 'Tradition-Constituted Enquiry'." In *Critical Perspectives on Christian Education*, ed. Jeff Astley and Leslie J. Francis. Leominster: Gracewing, 1994, 484-93.

MARSHALL, Bruce D. "Aquinas as Postliberal Theologian." *Thomist* 53 (1989) 353-402

"Truth Claims and the Possibility of Jewish-Christian Dialogue." *ModTh* 8 (1992) 221-40.

"Thomas, Thomisms, and Truth." *Thomist* 56 (1992) 499-524.

"George Lindbeck." In *A New Handbook of Christian Theologians*, ed. Donald W. Musser and Joseph L. Price. Nashville: Abingdon, 1996, 271-77.

MARTHALER, Berard L. "Towards a Revisionist Model in Catechetics." *LL* 13 (1976) 458-69.

MARTIN, James A., Jr. *Beauty and Holiness: The Dialogue between Aesthetics and Religion.* Princeton, NJ: Princeton University Press, 1990.

MARTINSON, Paul Varo. "Speaking the Truth: Contemporary Approaches to Religious Pluralism." In LWF Report No. 23-24 (Jan. 1988) 40-73.

MARTY, Martin E. et al. "We Still Have Some Unresolved Differences." *NCR* 14 (1977) 9-10 & 15-16.

MAXON, Monica J. et al. "A Challenge to Willimon's Postliberalism." *ChCent* 104 (1987) 306-10.

MAY, John D'Arcy. "Integral Ecumenism." 25 (1988) 573-91.

McCARTHY, John P. "David Tracy." In *A New Handbook of Christian Theologians*, ed. D. W. Musser and J. L. Price. Nashville: Abingdon, 1996, 468-78.

McCARTHY, Thomas. *The Critical Theory of Jürgen Habermas.* London: Hutchinson, 1978.

McCOOL, Gerald. "The Tradition of St. Thomas Since Vatican II." *TD* 40 (1993) 324-35.

McCORMACK, Bruce L. "Beyond Nonfoundational and Postmodern Readings of Barth: Critically Realistic Dialectical Theology." *ZdT* 13 (1997) 67-95.

"Revelation and History in Transfoundationalist Perspective: Karl Barth's Theological Epistemology in Conversation with a Schleiermacherian Tradition." *JR* 78 (1998) 18-37.

McFADYEN, Alister. "Truth as Mission: The Christian Claim to Universal Truth in a Pluralistic Public World." *SJT* 46 (1993) 437-56.

McGRATH, Alister E. *The Genesis of Doctrine: A Study in the Foundations of Doctrinal Criticism.* Oxford: Blackwell, 1990.

"The Christian Church's Response to Pluralism." *JETS* 35 (1992) 487-501.

"Theology and Experience." *EuroJT* 2 (1993) 65-74.

"An Evangelical Evaluation of Postliberalism." In *The Nature of Confession: Evangelicals and Postliberals in Conversation,* ed. Timothy R. Phillips and Dennis L. Okholm. Downers Grove, IL: InterVarsity, 1996, 23-44.

MEEKS, Wayne A. *The First Urban Christians: The Social World of the Apostle Paul.* New Haven: Yale University Press, 1983.

"A Hermeneutics of Social Embodiment." *HTR* 79 (1986) 176-86.

MEHL, Peter J. "In the Twilight of Modernity: MacIntyre and Mitchell on Moral Traditions and Their Assessment." *JRE* 19 (1991) 21-54.

MERRIGAN, Terrence. *Clear Heads and Holy Hearts: The Religious and Theological Ideal of John Henry Newman.* Leuven: Peeters, 1991.

"The Craft of Catholic Theology." *LS* 18 (1993) 243-57.

"Religious Knowledge in the Pluralist Theology of Religions." *TS* 58 (1997) 686-707.

"The Anthropology of Conversion: Newman and the Contemporary Theology of Religions." In *Newman and Conversion,* ed. Ian Ker. Edinburgh: T & T Clark, 1997, 117-44.

MERTENS, Hermen-Emiel. *Not the Cross, But the Crucified: An Essay in Soteriology.* Leuven: Peeters, 1992.

METZ, Johann B. *Faith in History and Society,* trs. David Smith. New York: Seabury, 1980.

MICHAELSON, Gordon E. "The Response to Lindbeck." *ModTh* 4 (1988) 107-20.

MILBANK, John. "The Second Difference: For a Trinitarianism Without Reserve." *ModTh* 2 (1986) 213-34.

"An Essay Against Secular Order." *JRE* 15 (1987) 199-224.

Theology and Social Theory: Beyond Secular Reason. London: Blackwell, 1990.

"The Name of Jesus: Incarnation, Atonement, Ecclesiology." *ModTh* 7 (1991) 311-33.

The Word Made Strange: Theology, Language, Culture. Oxford: Blackwell, 1997.

MISCAMBLE, Wilson D. "Sectarian Passivism?" *ThT* 44 (1987) 69-77.

MOINGT, Joseph. "Authority and Ministry." In *Authority in the Church and the Schillebeeckx Case*, ed. Leonard Swidler and Piet F. Fransen. New York: Crossroad, 1982, 202-25.

MOLTMANN, Jürgen. *The Theology of Hope*, trs. James W. Leitch. London: SCM, 1967.

Theology Today, trs. John Bowden. London: SCM, 1988.

MORAN, Gabriel. *Scripture and Tradition: A Survey of the Controversy*. New York: Herder and Herder, 1963.

MORRIS, John. "Chalcedon and Contemporary Christology." *Angelicum* 74 (1998) 3-45.

MORRISBY, Will. "Two Critiques of Nihilism." *Int* 12 (1984) 131-36.

MUELLER, J. J. *What Are They Saying About Theological Method?* New York: Paulist, 1984.

MURPHY, Nancey. "Introduction: With or Without Foundations." In *Theology Without Foundations: Religious Practice and the Future of Theological Truth*, ed. Stanley Hauerwas et al. Nashville: Abingdon, 1994, 9-27.

"Textual Relativism, Philosophy, and the Baptist Vision." In ibid., 245-70.

Anglo-American Postmodernity: Philosophical Perspectives on Science, Religion, and Ethics. Boulder: Westview, 1997.

MURPHY, Nancey and James Wm. McClendon, Jr. "Distinguishing Modern and Postmodern Theologies." *ModTh* 5 (1989) 191-214.

NASH, Jesse. "Tracy's Revisionist Project: Some Fundamental Issues." *AmBenR* 34 (1983) 240-67.

NELSON, Paul. *Narrative and Morality: A Theological Enquiry*. University Park, PA: Pennsylvania State University Press, 1987.

NEUHAUS, Richard J. *The Naked Public Square*. Grand Rapids: Eerdmans, 1984.

The Catholic Moment: The Paradox of the Church in the Postmodern World. San Francisco: Harper & Row, 1987.

(ed.). *Biblical Interpretation in Crisis: The Ratzinger Conference on Bible and Church*. Grand Rapids: Eerdmans, 1989.

NEWLANDS, George. *God in Christian Perspective*. Edinburgh: T & T Clark, 1994.

NEWMAN, John Henry. *University Sermons: Fifteen Sermons Preached before the University of Oxford 1826-1843*. London: SPCK, 1970.

NICHOLSON, Michael W. *A Theological Analysis and Critique of the Postmodern Debate*. Lewiston: Edwin Mellon, 1997.

NIEBUHR, Richard H. *Christ and Culture*. New York: Harper and Row, 1965.

NIELSON, Kai. *Ethics without God*. New York: Prometheus, 1973.

NOTH, Martin. "The Re-presentation of the Old Testament in Proclamation." In *Essays on Old Testament Hermeneutics*, ed. C. Westermann. Richmond: John Knox, 1963.

NOVAK, Michael. *Confession of a Catholic.* San Francisco: Harper & Row, 1983.

OAKES, Edward. "Apologetics and the Pathos of Narrative Theology." *JR* 72 (1992) 37-58.

O'CONNELL, Timothy E. "Vatican II and Moral Theology: Legacy and Agenda." *Chicago Studies* 35 (1996) 96-109.

O'COLLINS, Gerald. *Fundamental Theology.* London: Darton, Longman and Todd, 1981.

Retrieving Fundamental Theology: The Three Styles of Contemporary Theology. London: Chapman, 1993.

OGDEN, Schubert M. *Christ Without Myth.* London: Collins, 1962.

"Problems in the Case for a Pluralistic Theology of Religions." *JR* 68 (1988) 493-508.

OMMEN, Thomas B. "The Preunderstanding of the Theologian." In *Theology and Discovery: Essays in Honor of Karl Rahner*, ed. William Kelly. Milwaukee: Marquette University Press, 1980, 231-61.

"Bultmann and Gadamer: The Role of Faith in Theological Hermeneutics." *Thought* 59 (1984) 348-59.

"Theology and Foundationalism." *SR* 16 (1987) 159-71.

"Theology and the Fusion of Horizons." *Ph&Th* 3 (1988) 57-72.

O'NEILL, Colman E. "The Rule Theory of Doctrine and Propositional Truth." *Thomist* 49 (1985) 417-42.

ORIGEN. "Letter to Gregory." In *The Ante Nicene Fathers.* Grand Rapids: Eerdmans, 1956, 4:393-94.

O'SHEA, Paul. "Theology, Pluralism and Postmodernity." *Miltown Studies* 36 (1995) 32-42.

OUTLER, Albert C. "Toward a Postliberal Hermeneutics." *ThT* 42 (1985-86) 281-91.

PANNENBERG, Wolfhart. *Basic Questions in Theology*, trs. George H. Kehm. London: SCM, 1970.

Theology and the Philosophy of Science, trs. Francis MacDonagh. Philadelphia: Westminster, 1976.

Systematic Theology, Vol. I, trs. Geoffrey Bromiley. Grand Rapids: Eerdmans, 1991.

PAUW, Amy Plantinga. "The Word Is Near You: A Feminist Conversation with Lindbeck." *ThT* 50 (1993) 45-55.

PERKINS, Pheme. "Crisis in Jerusalem? Narrative Criticism in New Testament Studies." *TS* 50 (1989) 296-313.

PERRY, Michael. *Love and Power: The Role of Religion and Morality in American Politics.* New York: Oxford University Press, 1991.

PETER, Carl J. "Justification and the Catholic Principle." *Lutheran Theological Seminary Bulletin* 61 (1981) 16-32.

PETERS, Ted. *God — the World's Future: Systematic Theology for a Postmodern Era*. Minneapolis: Fortress, 1992.

PHILLIPS. D. Z. "Lindbeck's Audience." *ModTh* 4 (1988) 133-54.

Faith After Foundationalism. New York: Routledge, 1988.

PHILLIPS, John A. *Christ for Us in the Theology of Dietrich Bonhoeffer*. New York: Harper & Row, 1967.

PHILLIPS, Timothy R. and Dennis L. Okholm. "The Nature of Confession: Evangelicals and Postliberals." In *The Nature of Confession: Evangelicals and Postliberals in Conversation*. Downers Grove, IL: InterVarsity, 1996, 7-20.

PIERIS, Aloysius. *An Asian Theology of Liberation*. Edinburgh: T & T Clark, 1988.

Love Meets Wisdom. Maryknoll, NY: Orbis, 1988.

PIPER, O. A. "Gospel (Message)." In *IDB* 2:442-48.

PLACHER, William C. "Revisionist and Postliberal Theologies and the Public Character of Theology." *Thomist* 49 (1985) 392-415.

"Paul Ricoeur and Postliberal Theology: A Conflict of Interpretations." *ModTh* 4 (1987) 35-52.

Unapologetic Theology: A Christian Voice in a Pluralistic Conversation. Louisville: Westminster, 1989.

"Postliberal Theology." In *The Modern Theologians*, ed. Daivd F. Ford. Oxford: Blackwell, 1989, II: 115-28.

"Introduction." In *Theology and Narrative: Selected Essays (Hans Frei)*, ed. George Hunsinger and William C. Placher. New York: Oxford University Press, 1993, 3-25.

Narratives of a Vulnerable God: Christ, Theology, and Scripture. Louisville: Westminster, 1994.

PLATTEN, Stephen. "Culture: Speeches to Its Theological Despisers." *ModB* 39 (1998) 4:10-18.

POLAND, Lynn. *Literary Criticism and Biblical Hermeneutics*. Missoula, MO: Scholars, 1985.

POLANYI, Michael. *Personal Knowledge: Towards a Post-Critical Philosophy*. London: Routledge & Kegan Paul, 1969.

PROUDFOOT, Wayne. "*Regulae Fidei* and Regulative Idea: Two Contemporary Theological Strategies." In *Theology at the End of Modernity*, ed. Sheila Greeve Davaney. Philadelphia: Trinity, 1991, 99-113.

QUIRK, Michael J. "Beyond Sectarianism?" *ThT* 44 (1987) 78-86.

RADCLIFFE, Timothy. "Tradition and Creativity: The Paradigm of the New Testament." *NewBf* 70 (1989) 57-66.

RADNER, Ephraim. *The End of the Church: A Pneumatology of Christian Division in the West.* Grand Rapids: Eerdmans, 1998.

RAHNER, Karl. "The Theological Concept of Concupiscentia." In *Theological Investigations*, trs. Cornelius Ernst. Baltimore: Helicon, 1961, I: 347-82.

"Reflections on the Experience of Grace." In *Theological Investigations*, trs. K-H and B. Kruger. London: Darton, Longman and Todd, 1967, III:86-90.

"Virginitas In Partu." In *Theological Investigations*, trs. Kevin Smyth. Baltimore: Helicon, 1966, IV:134-62.

"Christianity and the Non-Christian Religions." In *Theological Investigations*, trs. Karl-H Kruger. London: Darton, Longman and Todd, 1966, V:115-34.

"What Is a Dogmatic Statement?" In *Theological Investigations*, trs. K-H Kruger. Baltimore: Helicon, 1966, V:48-51.

Spirit in the World, trs. William Dych. New York: Herder & Herder, 1968.

Hearers of the Word, trs. Michael Richards. New York: Herder & Herder, 1969.

"Scripture and Tradition." In *Sacramentum Mundi*, ed. Karl Rahner et al. New York: Herder and Herder, 1970, VI:54-57.

"Theology and Anthropology." In *Theological Investigations*, trs. Graham Harrison. London: Darton, Longman and Todd, 1972, IX: 28-45.

"Pluralism in Theology and the Unity of the Creed in the Church." In *Theological Investigations*, trs. David Bourke. London: Darton, Longman and Todd, 1974, XI:3-23

"Reflections on Methodology in Theology." In *Theological Investigations*, trs. David Bourke. London: Darton, Longman and Todd, 1974, XI:68-114.

"Two Basic Types of Christology." In *Theological Investigations*, trs. D. Bourke. New York: Seabury, 1975, XIII:213-23.

Foundations of Christian Faith: An Introduction to the Idea of Christianity, trs. William V. Dych. New York: Seabury, 1978.

RAMSEY, Ian T. *Religious Language.* London: SCM, 1957.

RASMUSSEN, Larry. "Worship in a World-Come-of-Age." In *A Bonhoeffer Legacy: Essays in Understanding.* Grand Rapids: Eerdmans, 1981, 268-80.

RASMUSSON, Arne. *The Church as Polis: From Political Theology to Theological Politics as Exemplified by Jürgen Moltmann and Stanley Hauerwas.* Lund: Lund University Press, 1994.

RATZINGER, Joseph. "Dogmatic Constitution on Divine Revelation, Chapters I, II and VI." In *Commentary on the Documents of Vatican II*, ed. Herbert Vorgrimler. New York: Herder & Herder, 1969, III:170-80, 181-98, and 262-72.

"Pastoral Constitution on the Church in the Modern World, Chapter I, Part I." In *Commentary on the Documents of Vatican II*, ed. Herbert Vorgrimler. New York: Herder & Herder, 1969, V:115-63.

Principles of Catholic Theology: Building Stones for a Fundamental Theology, trs. Mary Frances McCarthy. San Francisco: Ignatius, 1987.

Church, Ecumenism and Politics, trs. Robert Nowell. Slough: St Paul, 1988.

"Relativism: The Central Problem for Faith Today." *Origins* 26 (1996) 310-16.

RAUSH, Thomas P. *The Roots of the Catholic Tradition*. Wilmington: Michael Glazier, 1988.

READER, John. *Beyond All Reason: The Limits of Post-Modern Theology*. Cardiff: Aureus, 1997.

REYNOLDS, Terrence. "Walking Apart, Together: Lindbeck and McFague on Theological Method." *JR* 77 (1997) 44-67.

RHOADS, D. and D. Michie. *Mark as Story*. Philadelphia: Fortress, 1982.

RICHARDS, Jay Wesley. "Truth and Meaning in George Lindbeck's *The Nature of Doctrine*." *RelSt* 33 (1997) 33-53.

RICOEUR, Paul. *The Symbolism of Evil*, trs. Emerson Bucanan. New York: Harper & Row, 1967.

"The Hermeneutical Function of Distanciation." *PhT* 17 (1973) 129-41.

"Ethics and Culture: Habermas and Gadamer in Dialogue." *PhT* 17 (1973) 153-65.

"Biblical Hermeneutics." *Semeia* 4 (1975) 29-148.

Interpretation Theory: Discourse and the Surplus of Meaning. Fortworth, TX: Texas Christian University Press, 1976.

"What Is Dialectical?" In *Freedom and Morality*, ed. John Bricke. Lawrence: University Press of Kansas, 1976, 173-89.

"Toward a Hermeneutic of the Idea of Revelation." *HTR* 70 (1977) 1-37.

"Explanation and Understanding: On Some Remarkable Connections Among the Theory of Text, Theory of Action, and Theory of History." In *The Philosophy of Paul Ricoeur: An Anthology of His Work*, ed. C. E. Reagan and D. Stewart. Boston: Beacon, 1978, 149-66.

"The Hermeneutics of Testimony." *ATR* 61 (1979) 435-61.

Time and Narrative, Vol. 1, trs. K. McLaughlin and D. Pellauer. Chicago: Chicago University Press, 1984.

Figuring the Sacred: Religion, Narrative and Imagination, ed. M. I. Wallace. Minneapolis: Fortress, 1995.

RING, Nancy C. "Deposit of Faith." In *The New Dictionary of Theology*, ed. Joseph A. Komonchak et al. Dublin: Gill and Macmillan, 1987, 277-79.

RITSCHL, Dietrich. *The Logic of Theology: A Brief Account of the Relationship between Basic Concepts in Theology*, trs. John Bowden. London: SCM, 1986.

ROOT, Michael. "Truth, Relativism, and Postliberal Theology." *Dialog* 25 (1986) 175-80.

RORTY, Richard. *Philosophy and the Mirror of Nature*. Oxford: Blackwell, 1980.

ROY, Louis. "Bruce Marshall's Reading of Aquinas." *Thomist* 56 (1992) 473-80.

RUETHER, Rosemary R. "Feminist Interpretation: A Method of Correlation." In *The Liberating Word. A Guide to Nonsexist Interpretation of the Bible*, ed. Letty M. Russel. Philadelphia: Westminster, 1976.

Sexism and God-Talk: Toward a Feminist Theology. Boston: Beacon, 1983.

RUF, Frederick J. "The Consequences of Genre: Narrativity, Lyric, and Dramatic Intelligibility." *JAAR* 62 (1994) II: 799-817.

RUSH, Ormond. "Reception Hermeneutics and the 'Development' of Doctrine: An Alternative Model." *Pacifica* 6 (1993) 125-40.

The Reception of Doctrine: An Appropriation of Hans Robert Jauss' Reception Aesthetics and Literary Hermeneutics. Rome: Gregorian University Press, 1997.

SACHS, John R. "Transcendental Method in Theology and the Normativity of Human Experience." *Ph&Th* 7 (1992) 213-25.

SANDERS, E. P. *Jesus and Judaism*. London: SCM, 1985.

SANKS, Howland T. "David Tracy's Theological Project: An Overview and Some Implications." *TS* 54 (1993) 698-727.

SARTORI, Luigi. "What Is the Criterion for the *Sensus Fidelium*?" *Concilium* 148 (1981) 56-60.

SCALISE, Charles J. *Hermeneutics as Theological Prolegomena: A Canonical Approach*. Macon, GA: Mercer University Press, 1994.

SCHILLEBEECKX, Edward. *Interim Report on the Books Jesus and Christ*, trs. John Bowden. London: SCM, 1980.

"Toward a New Consensus in Catholic (and Ecumenical) Theology." In *Consensus in Theology?*, ed. Leonard Swidler. Philadelphia: Westminster, 1980, 1-17.

Christ: The Christian Experience in the Modern World, trs. John Bowden. London: SCM, 1980.

SCHLEIERMACHER, Friedrich. *The Christian Faith*, trs. H. R. Mackintosh and J. S. Stewart. Edinburgh: T & T Clark, 1928.

SCHNEIDERS, Sandra M. "Feminist Ideology Criticism and Biblical Hermeneutics." *BTB* 19 (1989) 3-10.

The Revelatory Text. San Francisco: HarperSanFrancisco, 1991.

"Living Word or Dead(ly) Letter: The Encounter between the New Testament and Contemporary Experience." *CTSAP* 47 (1992) 45-60.

SCHNER, George P. "The Appeal to Experience." *TS* 53 (1992) 40-59.

"Postliberal Theology and Roman Catholic Theology." *RSRev* 21 (1995) 304-10.

SCHOKEL, Luis A. *The Inspired Word*, trs. Francis Martin. New York: Herder & Herder, 1972.

SCHOLES, Robert and R. Kellogg. *The Nature of Narrative*. New York: Oxford University Press, 1966.

SCHÜSSLER FIORENZA, Elizabeth. *In Memory of Her. A Feminist Theological Reconstruction of Christian Origins*. New York: Crossroad, 1983.

But She Said: Feminist Practices of Biblical Interpretation. Boston: Beacon, 1992.

SCHWARZ, Hans. *Method and Context as Problems for Contemporary Theology: Doing Theology in an Alien World*. Lewiston: Edwin Mellon, 1991.

SEGUNDO, Juan Luis. *Theology and the Church: A Response to Cardinal Ratzinger and a Warning to the Whole Church*, trs. John W. Diercksmeier. Minneapolis: Fortress, 1985.

The Liberation of Dogma, trs. Phillip Berry. Maryknoll, NY: Orbis, 1992.

SELLARS, Wilfrid. *Science, Perception, and Reality*. London: Routledge & Kegan Paul, 1963.

SENIOR, Donald. "Living Word or Dead(ly) Letter: A Response to Sandra Schneiders." *CTSAP* 47 (1992) 61-68.

SHAPIRO, Susan E. "Rhetoric as Ideology Critique: The Gadamer-Habermas Debate Reinvented." *JAAR* 62:1 (1994) 123-50.

SHEA, William et al. "Review Symposium: The Analogical Imagination." *Horizons* 8 (1981) 313-39.

SMITH, Stephen G. "Karl Barth and Fideism: A Reconsideration." *ATR* 66 (1984) 64-78.

SOMMERVILLE, C. John. "Is Religion a Language Game? A Real World Critique of the Cultural-Linguistic Theory." *ThT* 51 (1995) 594-99.

SONG, Robert. *Christianity and Liberal Society*. New York: Oxford University Press, 1997.

SOSKICE, Janet M. "Theological Realism." In *The Rationality of Religious Belief*. Oxford: Oxford University Press, 1987, 105-19.

SPONHEIM, Paul. "The Word in the World Is True." *Dialog* 25 (1986) 167-74.

STACKHOUSE, Max. *Apologia*. Grand Rapids: Eerdmans, 1988.

"Alasdair MacIntyre: An Overview and Evaluation." *RSRev* 18 (1992) 203-8.

STALLSWORTH, Paul T. "The Story of an Encounter." In *Biblical Interpretation in Crisis: The Ratzinger Conference on Bible and Church*, ed. Richard J. Neuhaus. Grand Rapids: Eerdmans, 1989, 102-90.

STEELE, Richard B. "Narrative Theology and the Religious Affections." In *Theology Without Foundations: Religious Practice and the Future of Theological Truth*, ed. Stanley Hauerwas et al. Nashville: Abingdon, 1994, 163-79.

STELL, Stephen L. *Hermeneutics and the Holy Spirit: Trinitarian Insights into a Hermeneutical Impasse*. Dissertation, Princeton Theological Seminary, 1988.

"Hermeneutics in Theology and the Theology of Hermeneutics: Beyond Lindbeck and Tracy." *JAAR* 61 (1993) 679-703.

STENDAHL, Krister. "Biblical Theology, Contemporary." *IDB* 1: 418-32.

STIVER, Dan R. "Much Ado about Athens and Jerusalem: The Implications of Postmodernism for Faith." *Rev&Exp* 91 (1994) 83-102.

The Philosophy of Religious Language: Sign, Symbol and Story. Oxford: Blackwell, 1996.

STOUT, Jeffrey. *The Flight from Authority: Religion, Morality, and the Quest for Autonomy*. Notre Dame, IN: University of Notre Dame Press, 1981.

"Virtue among the Ruins." *NZsTR* 26, no.3 (1984) 256-73.

Ethics after Babel: The Language of Morals and Their Discontents. Boston: Beacon, 1988.

"Homeward Bound: MacIntyre on Liberal Society and the History of Ethics." *JR* 69 (1989) 220-32.

STROUP, George. "Theology of Narrative or Narrative Theology?: A Response to Why Narrative." *ThT* 47 (1991) 424-32.

SULLIVAN, Francis A. *Magisterium: Teaching Authority in the Catholic Church*. New York: Paulist, 1983.

SURIN, Kenneth. "'Many Religions and the One True Faith': An Examination of Lindbeck's Chapter Three." *ModTh* 4 (1988) 187-209.

The Turnings of Darkness and Light: Essays in Philosophical and Systematic Theology. Cambridge: Cambridge University Press, 1989.

SYKES, John. "Narrative Accounts of Biblical Authority: The Need for a Doctrine of Revelation." *ModTh* 5 (1989) 327-42.

TANNEHILL, Robert C. *The Narrative Unity of Luke-Acts*. Philadelphia: Fortress, 1986 (Vol. I), 1990 (Vol. II).

TANNER, Kathryn E. "Theology and the Plain Sense." In *Scriptural Authority and Narrative Interpretation*, ed. Garrett Green. Philadelphia: Fortress, 1987, 59-78.

God and Creation in Christian Theology. Oxford: Blackwell, 1988.

The Politics of God: Christian Theologies and Social Justice. Minneapolis: Fortress, 1992.

Theories of Culture. Minneapolis: Fortress, 1997.

TAVARD, George H. "Tradition." In *The New Dictionary of Theology*, ed. Joseph A. Komonchak et al. Dublin: Gill and Macmillan, 1987, 1037-41.

"The Ecumenical Search for Tradition: Thirty Years After the Montreal Statement." *JES* 30 (1993) 315-30.

TAYLOR, Mark Kline. "In Praise of Shaky Ground: The Liminal Christ and Cultural Pluralism." *ThT* 43 (1986) 36-51.

TE SELLE, Salle Mc Fague. "A Report from the Field." *Am* 134 (1976) 256-57.

TERRIEN, Samuel. *The Elusive Presence: Toward a New Biblical Theology.* New York: Harper & Row, 1978.

THEISSEN, Gerd. *The Social Setting of Pauline Christianity: Essays on Corinth*, trs. John H. Schuetz. Philadelphia: Fortress, 1982.

THIEL, John E. "Review of Lindbeck's *The Nature of Doctrine.*" *HeyJ* 29 (1988) 107-09.

"Theological Authorship: Postmodern Alternatives?" *HeyJ* 30 (1989) 32-50.

Imagination and Authority: Theological Authorship in the Modern Tradition. Minneapolis: Fortress, 1991.

Nonfoundationalism. Minneapolis: Fortress, 1994.

"Schleiermacher as 'Catholic': A Charge in the Rhetoric of Modern Theology." *HeyJ* 37 (1996) 61-82.

THIEMANN, Ronald F. *Revelation and Theology: The Gospel as Narrated Promise.* Notre Dame: University of Notre Dame Press, 1985.

"Response to George Lindbeck." *ThT* 43 (1986) 377-82.

"Radiance and Obscurity in Biblical Narrative." In *Scriptural Authority and Narrative Interpretation*, ed. Garrett Green. Philadelphia: Fortress, 1987, 21-41.

Constructing a Public Theology. Louisville: Westminster, 1991.

THISELTON, Anthony C. *The Two Horizons.* Grand Rapids: Eerdmans, 1980.

New Horizons in Hermeneutics. Grand Rapids: Zondervan, 1992.

THOMAS, Owen C. "Review of *The Nature of Doctrine.*" 67 (1985) 106-08.

"On Stepping Twice into the Same Church: Essence, Development, and Pluralism." *ATR* 70 (1988) 293-306.

THOMPSON, William M. "Sensus Fidelium and Infallibility." *AEccR* 167 (1973) 450-86.

TILLARD, J. M. R. "Was the Holy Spirit at Canberra?" *One in Christ* 29 (1993) 34-64.

TILLEY, Terrence W. *Story Theology.* Wilmington, Del.: Michael Glazier, 1985.

"Incommensurability, Intratextuality, and Fideism." *ModTh* 5 (1989) 87-111.

Postmodern Theology: The Challenge of Religious Diversity. New York: Orbis, 1995.

TOLBERT, Mary A. "Defining the Problem: The Bible and Feminist Hermeneutics." *Semeia* 28 (1983) 113-126.

TORRANCE, Alan. "Christian Experience and Divine Revelation in the Theologies of Friederich Schleiermacher and Karl Barth." In *Christian Experi-*

ence in Theology and Life, ed. I. Howard Marshall. Edinburgh: Rutherford, 1988, 83-113.

TORRANCE, T. F. *Reality and Scientific Theology.* Edinburgh: Scottish Academic, 1985.

TRACY, David. *Blessed Rage for Order: The New Pluralism in Theology.* New York: Harper & Row, 1976.

"The Catholic Analogical Imagination." *CTSAP* 32 (1977) 234-44.

The Analogical Imagination: Christian Theology and the Culture of Pluralism. New York: Crossroad, 1981.

"Defending the Public Character of Theology." *ChCent* 98 (1981) 350-56.

"Lindbeck's New Program for Theology: A Reflection." *Thomist* 49 (1985) 460-72.

Plurality and Ambiguity: Hermeneutics, Religion, Hope. Chicago: The University of Chicago Press, 1987.

"The Uneasy Alliance Reconceived." *TS* 50 (1989) 548-70.

"Hermeneutical Reflections in the New Paradigm." In *Paradigm Change in Theology: A Symposium for the Future*, ed. H. Küng and D. Tracy. New York: Crossroad, 1989, 34-62.

Dialogue with the Other. Louvain: Peeters, 1990.

"On Naming the Present." *Concilium* (1990) 1:66-85.

"On Reading the Scriptures Theologically." In *Theology and Dialogue: Essays in Conversation with George Lindbeck*, ed. Bruce D. Marshall. Notre Dame: University of Notre Dame Press, 1990, 35-68.

"God, Dialogue and Solidarity." *ChCent* 107 (1990) 900-04.

TRACY, David and John B. Cobb. *Talking about God: Doing Theology in the Context of Modern Pluralism.* New York: Seabury, 1983.

TRACY, Thomas F. "Narrative Theology and the Acts of God." In *Divine Action*, ed. B. Hebblethwaite and E. Henderson. Edinburgh: T & T Clark, 1990, 173-96.

TREMBATH, Kern R. *Divine Revelation: Our Moral Reflection with God.* Oxford: Oxford University Press, 1991.

TRIPOLE, Martin R. "Review of *The Nature of Doctrine*." *TS* 46 (1985) 384.

VAN DEN TOREN, Benno. "A New Direction in Christian Apologetics: An Exploration with Reference to Postmodernism." *EuroJT* 2 (1993) 49-64.

VANHOOZER, Kevin J. *Biblical Narrative in the Philosophy of Paul Ricoeur: A Study in Hermeneutics and Theology.* Cambridge: Cambridge University Press, 1990.

VAUX, Roland de. *The Early History of Israel*, trs. David Smith. London: Darton, Longman and Todd, 1978.

VEVERKA, Fayette Breaux. "Re-Imagining Catholic Identity: Toward an Analogical Paradigm of Religious Education." *RelEd* 88 (1993) 238-54.

VIA, Dan O. *The Revelation of God and/as Human Reception in the New Testament.* Harrisburgh, PN: Trinity Press International, 1997.

VILADESAU, Richard. "The Cultural Linguistic Model for Theology: A Critical Evaluation." *Jeevadhara* 21 (1991) 371-79.

VISSERS, John A. "Interpreting the Classic: The Hermeneutical Character of David Tracy's Theology in *The Analogical Imagination.*" *CTJ* 25 (1990) 194-206.

VOLF, Miroslav. "Theology, Meaning, and Power." In *The Future of Theology: Essays in Honor of Jürgen Moltmann*, ed. M. Volf et al. Grand Rapids: Eerdmans, 1996, 98-113.

WAINWRIGHT, Geoffrey. "Ecumenical Dimensions of Lindbeck's 'Nature of Doctrine'." *ModTh* 4 (1988) 121-32.

WALGRAVE, J. H. "Faith as a Fundamental Dimension of Religious Experience." In *Religious Experience, Its Unity and Diversity*, ed. Thomas Mampra. Bangalore: Dharmaram Publications, 1981, 1-13.

WALKER, Andrew. *Telling the Story.* London: SPCK, 1996.

WALKER, Andrew and Anne Davison. "Belief and Faith in a Religiously Plural Society." *ModB* 35 (1994) 22-9.

WALLACE, Mark I. "The New Yale Theology." *CSRev* 17 (1987) 154-70.

"Karl Barth's Hermeneutic: A Way Beyond the Impasse." *JR* 68 (1988) 396-410.

The Second Naiveté: Barth, Ricoeur, and the New Yale Theology. Macon GA: Mercer University Press, 1990.

"Can God be Named Without Being Known? The Problem of Revelation in Thiemann, Ogden, and Ricoeur." *JAAR* 59 (1991) 281-308.

WALLS, Andrew F. "Old Athens and New Jerusalem: Some Signposts for Christian Scholarship in the Early History of Mission Studies." *IBMR* 21 (1997) 146-53.

WARD, Barbara. *Faith and Freedom.* New York: Norton,1954.

WARD, Keith. *Religion and Revelation.* Oxford: Clarendon, 1994.

WATSON, Francis. *Text, Church and World: Biblical Interpretation in Theological Perspective.* Edinburgh: T & T Clark, 1994.

Text and Truth. Edinburgh: T & T Clark, 1997.

WEBB, Stephen H. *The Gifting of God: A Trinitarian Ethics of Excess.* New York: Oxford University Press, 1996.

WEGER, Karl-Heinz. "Tradition." In *Sacramentum Mundi*, ed. Karl Rahner et al. New York: Herder and Herder, 1968, 6:269-74.

WEINSHEIMER, Joel C. *Gadamer's Hermeneutics: A Reading of Truth and Method.* New Haven: Yale University Press, 1985.

WELBORN, L. L. "On Discord in Corinth: 1 Corinthians 1-4 and Ancient Politics." *JBL* 106 (1987) 85-111.

WERPEHOWSKI, William. "Ad Hoc Apologetics." *JR* 66 (1986) 282-301.

WESTERHOFF III, John H. "Will Our Children Have Faith? A Query Revisited." In *The Echo Within: Emerging Issues in Religious Education*. Allen, TX: Thomas Moore, 1997, 177-90.

WHITE, Graham. "Karl Barth's Theological Realism." *NZsTR* 26 (1984) 54-70.

WILES, Maurice. *Working Papers in Doctrine*. London: SCM, 1976.

What Is Theology? Oxford: Oxford University Press, 1976.

"Scriptural Authority and Theological Construction: The Limitations of Narrative Interpretation." In *Scriptural Authority and Narrative Interpretation*, ed. Garrett Green. Philadelphia: Fortress, 1987, 42-58.

WILLIAMS, Rowan D. "Trinity and Revelation." *ModTh* 2 (1986) 197-212.

"Postmodern Theology and the Judgment of the World." In *Postmodern Theology: Christian Faith in a Pluralist World*, ed. Frederic B. Burnham. New York: Harper Collins, 1989, 92-112.

"The Incarnation as the Basis of Dogma." In *The Religion of the Incarnation: Anglican Essays in Commemoration of Lux Mundi*, ed. Robert Morgan. Bristol: Bristol Classical, 1989, 85-98.

"Saving Time: Thoughts on Practice, Patience and Vision." *NewBf* 73 (1992) 219-26.

WILLIAMS, Stephen. "Lindbeck's Regulative Christology." *ModTh* 4 (1988) 173-86.

WILLIAMSON, Joseph C. "Challenging Lindbeck." *Ch&Cr* 50 (1990) 299-301.

WILLIMON, William H. "Answering Pilate: Truth and Postliberal Church." *ChCent* 104 (1987) 82-85.

WITTGENSTEIN, Ludwig. *Philosophical Investigations*, trs. G. E. M. Anscombe. London: Macmillan, 1973.

WOLTERSTORFF, Nicholas. *Reason within the Bounds of Religion*. Grand Rapids: Eerdmans, 1976.

What New Haven and Grand Rapids Can Learn from Each Other. Grand Rapids: Calvin College, 1993.

"Will Narrativity Work as Linchpin? Reflections on the Hermeneutic of Hans Frei." In *Relativism and Religion*, ed. Charles M. Lewis. London: Macmillan, 1995, 71-107.

WOOD, Charles M. *The Formation of Christian Understanding*. Philadelphia: Fortress, 1981.

"Review of *The Nature of Doctrine*." *RSRev* 11 (1985) 235-37 & 240.

"Hermeneutics and the Authority of Scripture." In *Scriptural Authority and Narrative Interpretation*, ed. Garrett Green. Philadelphia: Fortress, 1987, 3-20.

WYSCHOGROD, Michael. *The Body of Faith*. New York: Seabury, 1983.

YEAGO, David. "A New Paradigm for Theology and Church." *Lutheran Forum* 18 (1984) 29-32.

YODER, John H. *The Priestly Kingdom: Social Ethics as Gospel*. Notre Dame: University of Notre Dame Press, 1984.

The Politics of Jesus. Grand Rapids: Eerdmans, 1994⁴.

ZAHRNT, Heinz. *The Question of God*, trs. R. A. Wilson. New York: Harcourt Brace Jovanovich, 1969.

ZORN, Hans. "Grammar, Doctrines, and Practice." *JR* 75 (1995) 509-20.

INDEX

PRINTED ON PERMANENT PAPER • IMPRIME SUR PAPIER PERMANENT • GEDRUKT OP DUURZAAM PAPIER - ISO 9706

ORIENTALISTE, KLEIN DALENSTRAAT 42, B-3020 HERENT